GII00372588

DEPARTMENT OF IMMIGRATION
PERMITTED TO ENTER
AUSTRALIA.
24 APR 1986
on
For stay of 12 Month
SYDNEY AIRPORT 54

IMMIGRATION DIVISION BANGKOK THAILAND
A
72
DEPARTED
-9 FEB 1987
SIGNED

- 4 OCT 19
DEPARTED
(1095)
HONG KONG

30 OCT 1989
DEPARTED
AUSTRALIA
SYDNEY 32
Person
ETHNIC AFFAIRS

T R A V E L E R ' S
CALIFORNIA
C O M P A N I O N

中华人民共和国
广东省公安厅

上陸許可
ADMITTED
15. FEB. 1986
4
Status: 4-1-
Duration: 90 days
NARITA(N)
Immigration Inspector

ADMITTED
OCT. 1988
Status: 4-1-16
Duration 180 days
Port: HANEDA
Signature

U.S. IMMIGRATION
160-LOS C-4125

MAY 23 1999

ADMITTED_____
UNTIL   (CLASS)

HONG KONG
(1038)
-7 JUN 1987
IMMIGRATION
OFFICER

The 1998–1999 Traveler's Companions

ARGENTINA • AUSTRALIA • BALI • CALIFORNIA • CANADA • CHINA • COSTA RICA • CUBA •
EASTERN CANADA • ECUADOR • FLORIDA • HAWAII • HONG KONG • INDIA • INDONESIA • JAPAN •
KENYA • MALAYSIA & SINGAPORE • MEDITERRANEAN FRANCE • MEXICO • NEPAL • NEW ENGLAND •
NEW ZEALAND • PERU • PHILIPPINES • PORTUGAL • RUSSIA • SPAIN • THAILAND • TURKEY •
VENEZUELA • VIETNAM, LAOS AND CAMBODIA • WESTERN CANADA

Traveler's CALIFORNIA Companion

First Published 1999 in the United Kingdom by
Kümmerly+Frey AG,
Alpenstrasse 58, CH 3052 Zollikofen, Switzerland
in association with
World Leisure Marketing Ltd
Unit 11, Newmarket Court, Newmarket Drive, Derby, DE24 8NW, England

Website: http://www.map-world.co.uk

ISBN: 1-8400-6052-2

© 1999 Kümmerly+Frey AG, Switzerland

Created, edited and produced by
Allan Amsel Publishing,
53, rue Beaudouin, 27700 Les Andelys, France.
E-mail: Allan.Amsel@wanadoo.fr
Editor in Chief: Allan Amsel
Editor: Anne Trager
Original design concept: Hon Bing-wah
Picture editor and designer: Maud Vink

Printed by Samhwa Printing Co. Ltd., Seoul, South Korea

TRAVELER'S
CALIFORNIA
COMPANION

by Joe Yogerst and Maribeth Mellin
photographs by Nik Wheeler

Kümmerly+Frey

Contents

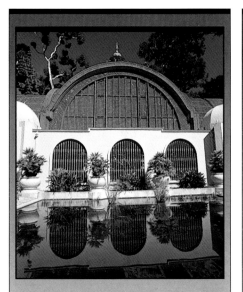

TRAVELER'S
CALIFORNIA
COMPANION

Crescent City
Fort Dick
Yreka Montague
Klamath
National Forest Perez
Klamath
National Forest
Weed
Mount Shasta
Castella
McKinleyville Lamoine
Eureka Arcata Weaverville Burney
Fortuna Shasta Lake
Rio Dell Redding Lassen Volcano
National Forest
Anderson
Weott Trinity
National
Forest Red Bluff Mill Creek
Miranda
Garberville Corning
Rockport Orland Chico Parad
Laytonville Thermalito
Longvale Willows
Fort Bragg Mendocino
National Forest Pale
Mendocino Marysville
Gr
Ukiah Yuba City
Oli
Linda Lin
Clearlake
Woodland
Healdsburg Davis
Windsor Dixon
Santa Rosa
Sonoma Napa
Petaluma Fairfield
Vallejo
San Rafael Richmond Oakland Lathrop
SAN FRANCISCO
San Carlos Freemont
Los Altos San Jose
Saratoga
Gilroy
Santa Cruz
Watsonville
Pacific Grove Sali
Monterey Carmel
PACIFIC Big Sur
King
OCEAN
San Sime

Washington
Montana North
Dakota
Minnisota
Oregon South
Idaho Dakota Michigan
Wyoming Wisconsin Maine
Nebraska Iowa Vermont
New York New Hampshire
Conneticut
Nevada Utah Illinois Indiana Ohio Pennsylvania New Jersey
Colorado Kansas W.Virginia Maryland
California Missouri Kentucky Virginia
Arizona New Oklahoma Tennessee N. Carolina
Mexico Arkansas S. Carolina
Alabama
Texas Mississippi Georgia
Luisiana
Florida

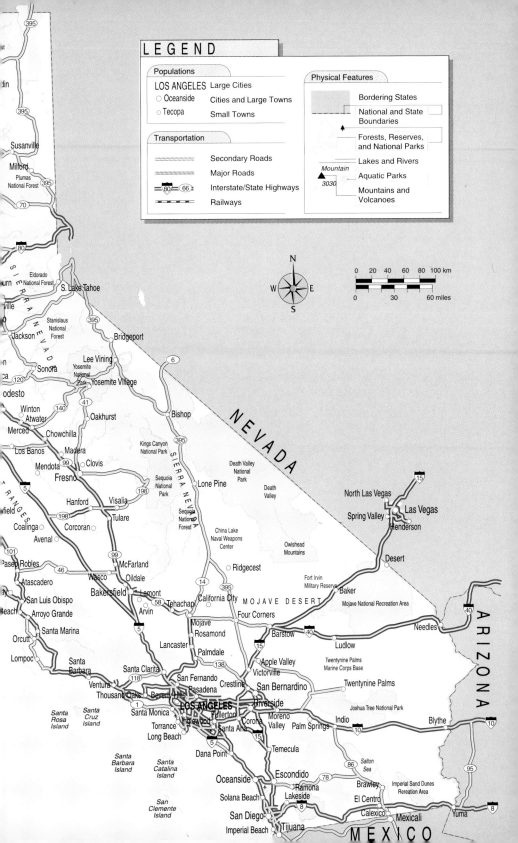

TOP SPOTS

Desert Nights

THE STARS HAVE A SPECIAL TWINKLE ABOVE THE DESERT AT NIGHT, AND THEY SEEM TO GO ON FOREVER. The Milky Way washes across a midnight-blue palette like soft chalk on a blackboard. Shooting stars trailing muted sparks fall slowly from straight above to the flat horizon.

It really doesn't matter which desert you're in; some things are common. Coyotes might wail outside your tent in Joshua Tree National Park; clear scorpions could slither about the sand in Death Valley. Still, the night sky is bound to put on a show. San Diegans drive to the Anza Borrego desert during the Perseid meteor showers every August and watch the natural fireworks from reclining beach chairs. Comets, eclipses and other phenomena bring out the crowds.

Though the best way to enjoy the night sky in the desert is from a remote campsite, you can catch the star show from more comfortable surroundings. You need only walk a few yards from the low-lying buildings at La Casa del Zorro in Borrego Springs (which books weeks in advance when desert wildflowers bloom in spring) to spot the full moon. Drinks on the terrace at Furnace Creek Ranch, settled at sea level in Death Valley, need no accompanying entertainment. You can sit for hours, until your neck refuses to unbend, and stare into utter infinity, or so it seems.

Dedicated desert rats know no season. The rest of us need a few creature comforts. Thus, one needs to be equipped to enjoy the desert any time of year. Winter nights can be bitterly cold, while day temperatures call for T-shirts and shorts. Summer is just plain hot, no doubt about it. Yet nature puts on quite a display in July and August, with lightning bolts shimmering and slashing into the ground. Rain, when it comes, is unrelenting; flash floods are common and all travel warnings should be heeded unwaveringly. It may sound silly when you're cruising to the desert on a day trip from the coast, but always carry more water and film than you could possibly need.

Smell the Jasmine in Bloom

ORANGE BLOSSOMS, HONEYSUCKLE, ROSES AND LAVENDER SCENT THE AIR ALONG CALIFORNIA'S COASTLINE. Flaming red ocotillo petals sway above golden teddy-bear cholla cacti and waxy white agave in the desert. Candy-colored succulents cover highway medians with pink and blue blankets in spring; sunflowers tower above corn, tomatoes and lettuce in summer. Fall is more subtle in the

OPPOSITE: Spring flowers paint the desert near Indian Wells. ABOVE: Zabriskie Point overlooks a sweltering desert depression called Death Valley.

south, where deciduous oaks and red maples make a muted show of autumn colors. Red and white poinsettias flutter on multibranched shrubs in front of mission churches for Christmas.

Nearly anything will grow somewhere, during some season, in California. Birds of Paradise stand sentry by front doors in San Diego; ferns tumble down wet hillsides in Mendocino. Fields of blossoming ranunculus tubers draw crowds to Carlsbad for photos of hillsides striped yellow and red. Fuschias shed pink and purple petals from hanging baskets in Carmel; jacarandas shade neighborhood streets with clouds of lavender blooms in Beverly Hills. Public gardens, botanical parks, nature trails and arboretums are on the list of must-sees in most regions of the state. My personal favorite is the Huntington Gardens in San Marino (see PASADENA, page 233), covering 200 acres (81 hectares) of the railroad tycoon's estate at the Henry E. Huntington Library, Art Gallery and Gardens.

One can spend several days touring groves of bamboo and weeping willows in the Japanese Garden, rows of perfect roses beside terraced lawns, herb patches, cactus-filled canyons, seasonal flower beds shaded by rare palms, and the spread-about collection of garden ornaments, from fountains and gazebos to the white marble mausoleum designed by John Russell Pope in the style of Washington, DC's Jefferson Memorial. Afternoon tea is served in the Huntington's restaurant beside the herb garden; linen dresses and straw bonnets are the preferred attire, though garden lovers are a varied lot. Should it rain, one can always tour the collection of rare books and fine art in the Huntington Library.

Experience Redwood Solitude

DRIVING ALONE THROUGH A TUNNEL OF REDWOODS AT DUSK ON A SEPTEMBER NIGHT IS THE CLOSEST I'VE EVER COME TO UTTER SOLITUDE. The smell of bark and loam, air damp on the forearm, nerves spooked alert. The sense of deer poised at attention just out of view. Imminent utter darkness.

In 1938, John Muir wrote "The clearest way into the universe is through a forest wilderness." Fifty years later, strapped into in an automobile rather than hiking boots, I understood the sentiment as I drove in my compact rental car from the Oregon Coast to San Francisco. My supplies consisted of a hammock, a sleeping bag, a small Coleman cooler and a saucepan and spoon. The tunes, as I recall, were a mix of Pink Floyd, Bonnie Raitt and Joni Mitchell.

Most of the time, nature provided the music — waves crashing against granite cliffs, wind rustling through pines, gulls and hawks screeching in flight. I followed the coastland into Redwood National Park, where I slept above a wild sea on a wooded clifftop. There was absolutely no one in the campground except the retired couple keeping watch. They sold me firewood for warmth and comfort; the flames danced in gusts of sparks and smoke, then dwindled to glowing coals. Similar scenes were repeated as I followed US Highway 101 through a series of state parks, forests and groves. It was just after Labor Day, the official end of summer family vacations, and the road was bereft of other traffic. In seaside villages fishermen with faces toughened by sun and wind stashed their nets sans spectators, and every interesting restaurant or snack shack featured salmon and crab. I drove through Mendocino, where locals had reclaimed the prime seats beside bay windows in restaurants and bookshops, and lingered to sample fresh-squeezed lemonade, sniff roses and run my fingers along the smooth and rough curves of redwood sculptures in rustic galleries.

On the final day of my journey I aimed for Muir Woods National Monument campground, but misjudged the distance and my desire to wander about along the way. I hit the final redwood grove at dusk and felt a sense of awe and fear combined. Trees higher than the skylines of most major cities trapped the asphalt much like a narrow hiking trail, branching to block the purple sky. Stars glittered through pine needles only occasionally, and headlights barely brightened the darkness enveloping my view. I thought of flat tires, crazed killers and self defense, but wasn't actually scared. I could hardly imagine the forest a threat.

The campground was shrouded in utter darkness when I hauled my gear to a campsite I could hardly see. When I awoke the next morning, three white-tailed deer stood at attention before a cluster of pine trees. I boiled water for instant coffee, washed up a bit and prepared to cross the Golden Gate Bridge into San Francisco (with a stop in Sausalito for books and city shoes to replace my muddy hiking boots).

That drive has stayed vivid in my mind for over a decade, though I have no snapshots or

A north coast giant climbs toward the summer sky.

notebooks to remind me of the bracing smells of loamy earth, redwood bark, saltwater and kelp. What I do have are memories of solitude and emotional intensity, and an experience that gave me strength and hope.

Mingle in the Melting Pot

A VISIT TO CALIFORNIA IS LIKE A MINI-TOUR OF POLYNESIA, LATIN AMERICA, THAILAND AND JAPAN, WITH A HEAVY SPRINKLING OF EUROPEAN CUSTOMS. California is a land of transplants and to this day attracts more immigrants than any other state in the nation. All major urban areas have Vietnamese, Cambodian, Japanese, Italian and Mexican communities. Spanish is close to English as the most common language in the barrios of Los Angeles and the fields of the Ojai Valley. Arabian sheiks own vast portions of the state's most valuable real estate. There are Samoan neighborhoods along the coast, Middle Eastern markets and Filipino *lumpia* restaurants in all mid-sized towns, Brazilian music clubs by the beach.

New cities have sprawled over the state's canyons, through forests and atop desert mesas no matter the era. Newcomers arrive through real estate booms and busts, ignoring earthquakes, floods, mudslides, droughts and tired jokes, in search of the California lifestyle. They bring the customs, traditions and languages of home, though many are quick to shed outer accouterments that label them as outsiders. The wide-eyed traveler spots opportunities to mingle with people from throughout the world who continuously import fresh ideas, flavors and styles to the California scene.

California's first immigrants came from Spain and Mexico in the early seventeenth century, settling in uneasy alliances with indigenous groups on the coast and in fertile valleys. They lived around a chain of 21 missions spreading from San Diego to Sonoma, forming multinational communities. Their haciendas, ranches and towns have been preserved in Santa Barbara, San Juan Capistrano, and Sonoma, which was an important center during the *Californio* era. Some travelers follow the Mission Circuit in framing their itineraries. The best novel about the era is *Ramona* by Helen Hunt Jackson, written in 1884.

The 1880s Wild West style of Texas or Oklahoma petered out as it reached the Mojave Desert, the California Sierras and the Pacific Ocean. Pockets of farms and ranches formed in Death Valley and Borrego Springs as wagon trains brought immigrants of European descent to the West. Mormons, Quakers and Methodists gathered in the unlikeliest spots, sometimes forced to create settlements simply from sheer inability to move on. The gold rush brought rough-and-tumble Swedes and Germanic prospectors to the High Sierras' still flourishing gold rush towns like Eureka and Sacramento, now the capital of the state. Fertile fishing grounds brought Portuguese seamen to San Diego. Irish, Italian and German magnates from the East Coast targeted all areas of the coast for development, importing Chinese laborers to build railroads and empires throughout the region.

California didn't become a United States state until 1850, when San Francisco, Los Angeles and San Diego were fully established cities. Mexican architecture, food, customs and music were already firmly entrenched in the California culture, and to this day roads and

famous buildings throughout the state bear Spanish names. Mexican culture is presented for tourist and local consumption in Sonoma Plaza, Olvera Street in Los Angeles, and San Diego's Old Town, though you can find great Mexican cooking and learn a few Spanish phrases in nearly every part of the state. San Francisco's Chinatown is hands-down the best place to play mah jong, eat dim sum and shop for Tiger Balm.

There were large Chinese settlements in Eureka, Weaverville, Los Angeles, San Diego and anywhere a rail track was being laid in the late 1800s; but the residents were either run out of town or moved on to work elsewhere. Today, one of the largest Chinese population centers is in Mexicali, in the capital of the Mexican state of Baja California. Japanese Californians were interred in miserable war camps during World War II, and have now settled in the cities and

agriculture valleys. San Diego and Los Angeles have large communities of Vietnamese, Cambodian and Hmong immigrants driven from their country during and after the Vietnam War.

These waves of immigration flavor the California culture with a mix worth checking out. Jesters and New-Age devotees are convinced California will someday break away and become a nation unto itself — the first true global nation.

Revisit the 1960s

LONDON MAY HAVE BEEN THE FASHION TRENDSETTER, BUT WHEN IT CAME TO OTHER ASPECTS OF 1960S CULTURE, NORTHERN CALIFORNIA

San Francisco's Chinatown is the most renowned of California's ethnic enclaves.

1967. Twenty thousand people clad in paisley shirts, bell-bottom pants, love beads and bandanas (or perhaps naked) gathered to drop acid, light incense and listen to the Jefferson Airplane sing about white rabbits.

The "California sound" bloomed at a cutting-edge music club called the Fillmore West, at the corner of Geary and Fillmore in San Francisco. The brainchild of virtuoso rock promoter Bill Graham, Janis Joplin opened the Fillmore on June 19, 1967. Nearly anyone who was anybody in 1960s music played the Fillmore at one time or another; except the Beatles, who had already taken a hiatus from touring. The Fab Four had played what turned out to be their last-ever concert at San Francisco's Candlestick Park stadium the year before.

WAS THE NAVEL OF THE UNIVERSE. San Francisco gave the world "flower power" — a strange blend of free love, folk music and fantasy-inducing drugs. The anti-Vietnam War crusade first took root in Berkeley, the university town on the eastern shore of San Francisco Bay. The Black Panthers and other militant manifestations of African-American power were born on the mean streets of Oakland. Monterey hosted the world's first rock festival (no it wasn't Woodstock).

The cultural and political forces that were to have the most profound effect on the century's most eccentric decade were already taking shape in the Bay Area as early as 1960. City Lights Bookstore in San Francisco was a magnet of beat poets and pop philosophers from around the nation, led by Allen Ginsberg and Michael McClure. In later years City Lights, which still thrives near the intersection of Broadway and Columbus Avenue, was a hangout for other 1960s icons including Bob Dylan, author Ken Kesey and political agitator Jerry Rubin.

San Francisco's "happening" Haight-Ashbury district came into its own in 1966 as the mecca of flower power. Free love and psychedelic music were the neighborhood's manifesto, LSD and peace signs were its highest status symbols. You can still see the house where Jerry Garcia formed the Grateful Dead (710 Ashbury Street) and Janis Joplin's old crash pad (112 Lyon Street). The Polo Field at nearby Golden Gate Park is where the famous Human Be-In — the world's first and largest "love in" — took place on January 14,

Monterey, the tranquil fishing village made famous by writer John Steinbeck, exploded to the forefront of the world music scene in the summer of 1967 when the Monterey Pop Festival took place at the county fairgrounds. Woodstock (staged in the summer of 1969) may have drawn more people and publicity, but Monterey had more big-name 1960s stars — the Mamas and the Papas, Janis Joplin, Otis Redding, Ravi Shankar, Simon and Garfunkel, The Who and Jimi Hendrix. This was the concert where Hendrix lit his guitar on fire and simulated sex on stage — footage that's still banned from American network television.

Northern California also played host to the less "groovy" aspects of the 1960s revolution. The rolling green hills of Altamont Pass, along Interstate 580 east of San Francisco, hosted the notorious Altamont Rock Festival of 1969, during which Hell's Angel security guards beat a fan to death while The Rolling Stones played "Sympathy for the Devil." Giant high-tech windmills hover above the scene today, like silent tombstones.

You can explore the various 1960s sights on your own or join an guided excursion like the Haight-Ashbury Flower Power Walking Tour ((415) 863-1621 or the Black Power Tour (bus) of Oakland and Berkeley ((510) 986-0660.

Go on a Surfin' Safari

SURFING ISN'T INDIGENOUS TO CALIFORNIA (HAWAIIANS WERE "HANGING TEN" AS FAR BACK AS THE FIFTEENTH CENTURY), but the golden state is where modern surf culture came into full bloom. Around the turn of the century, before surfing had even made its way to the West Coast, California redwood was the favored material for Hawaii's classic longboards. And

ABOVE: Flower Power has been passed down to younger generations. OPPOSITE: California girls come in all shapes and sizes.

Three decades later surf culture is still going strong, not just at Windansea but up and down the entire California coast. Some of the best waves — and bods — can be found at San Onofre near San Diego; Huntington, Manhattan and Malibu beaches in the Los Angeles area; Isla Vista near Santa Barbara; and Steamers Lane in Santa Cruz. During El Niño winters and tropical storms off the Mexican west coast, the wave height can sometimes hit 20 ft (seven meters) or more, some of the world's most spectacular — and dangerous — surf.

Aficionados of the sport should check out the various surf competitions staged during the summer, like the Hotline Longboard Invitational in Santa Cruz (May), the United States Open professional tournament at Huntington Beach (August), the California Beach Festival in Ventura (September) and the International Surf Festival (July) in neighboring Manhattan, Hermosa and Redondo beaches. Serious surf dudes can also browse museums in Santa Cruz and Huntington Beach dedicated to the sport and lifestyle.

among those who introduced the sport to California was legendary Hawaiian surfer Duke Kahanamoka who tested his longboards at Huntington Beach in the 1920s.

Surfing remained a relatively local phenomenon until the late 1950s and early 1960s when three things propelled California surf culture into the world spotlight: the music of The Beach Boys, a group of high school friends from Manhattan Beach who pioneered the quintessential surf sound; a series of popular "Beach Party" movies staring Frankie Avalon and Annette Funicello; and a 1965 book by author Tom Wolfe called *The Pump House Gang*, which dissected the offbeat lifestyles of surfers at San Diego's Windansea Beach in much the same manner as Margaret Mead might have scrutinized a tribe of South Pacific islanders. "It began to dawn on me that surfing was just 25% sport and 75% way of life," Wolfe wrote. "It was a curious thing to build a communal life around."

If you want to hit the waves yourself, a number of outlets in San Diego, Los Angeles, Santa Barbara and Santa Cruz offer surfboard and wetsuit rental. For surfing lessons try the San Diego Surfing Academy ((619) 565-6892 TOLL-FREE (800) 447-SURF; Surf Diva ((619) 454-8273 (women-only lessons) in San Diego; Club Ed Surf School ((408) 459-9283 TOLL-FREE (800) 287-7873 in Santa Cruz; or Davey Smith's Surf Academy ((805) 687-7298 in Santa Barbara.

Pan for Golden Nuggets

MANIFEST DESTINY ASIDE, THERE'S AN ARGUMENT TO BE MADE THAT CALIFORNIA WOULD HAVE BECOME PART OF THE UNITED STATES AT A LATER DATE IF GOLD HADN'T BEEN FOUND IN THE SIERRA NEVADA FOOTHILLS IN THE LATE 1840S. The prospect of vast riches brought a flood of gringos to the West Coast and hastened the end of Mexican rule. After the American "liberation," gold spurred the development of San Francisco, funded construction of the first continental railroad, endowed one of the world's great universities (Stanford), and generally set the tone for California's emergence as a major political, cultural and economic force of the twentieth century.

The gold rush may be long gone, but there's still gold in "them thar hills" — golden memories of prospecting days and golden nuggets that still tumble down from the High

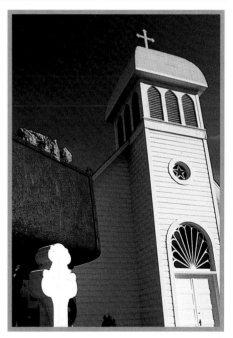

Sierras in the numerous rivers that bisect the Gold Rush Country. Well, maybe not nuggets, but certainly flecks of gold. Enough precious metal to make prospecting a rewarding profession for hundreds of Californians.

Wannabe Forty-Niners should apply for a gold dredging permit through the California Department of Fish and Game ((916) 358-2900 in Sacramento. The cost is $32.25 per person and the permit is good until the end of the calendar year in which the purchase is made. The dredging season varies from county to county and not all rivers are open. Sierra Gold ((916) 289-3515 in Downieville or Jackson's Prospecting & Supplies ((209) 966-4827 in Mariposa can provide just about anything you need in the way of mining equipment and provisions. Less serious prospectors can sign up for a one-day gold-panning tour offered by several dozens companies in the Gold Rush Country. Among outfitters are Gold Prospecting Expeditions ((209) 984-4653 TOLL-FREE (800) 596-0009 in Jamestown, or the aforementioned Jackson's Prospecting in Mariposa.

If you think you're pretty handy with a pan, sign up for the gold panning championship staged in historic gold mining towns like Mariposa (August) and Coloma (October). Coloma hosts another celebration Gold Discovery Days   at the end of January each year to mark the anniversary of John Marshall's historic find in 1848. Other

gold rush related special events include Gold Nugget Days in Paradise (April), the Forty-Niner Festival in Groveland (June), the Gold n' Fiddle Festival in Auburn (June), and the Gold Rush Fair and Grape Stomp in Murphys (October).

A number of historic gold rush towns feature museums where you can "dig" into the region's fascinating history. Among the better collections are the El Dorado County Museum in Placerville, the Angels Camp Museum and the California State Mining and Mineral Museum near Mariposa. Meanwhile, the Miners Foundry Cultural Center in Nevada City stages numerous seasonal events related to gold rush history and culture.

The gold rush heritage is also preserved within half a dozen state and municipal parks. Empire Mine State Historic Park in Grass Valley boasts several mines, as well as historic buildings and mining artifacts. Malakoff Diggins State Historic Park near Nevada City preserves the sight of California's largest hydraulic gold mine. Columbia State Historic Park preserves a dozen blocks of gold rush era buildings including the original Wells Fargo office, fire house and saloons. Gold Bug Park in Placerville is America's only community

OPPOSITE: Modern-day forty-niners reenact history during Coloma's annual Gold Discovery Days. ABOVE: Mariposa's County Courthouse (left) and the Serbian Orthodox Church at Angels Camp (right) are both relics of the Gold Rush.

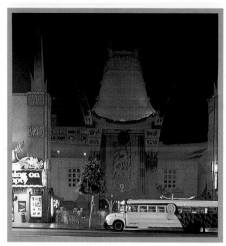

owned and operated gold mine. Self-guided tours help you explore the mine and the heritage of gold mining. (See also THE OPEN ROAD, page 32, and GOLD RUSH COUNTRY, page 154.)

Rub Elbows with Hollywood Stars

YOU'RE NOT LIKELY TO SEE MOVIE STARS DRIVING UP AND DOWN THE SUNSET STRIP OR HANGING OUT AT THE CORNER OF HOLLYWOOD AND VINE STREETS, but if you play your cards right, you can see famous faces in Los Angeles and maybe even garner a couple of autographs.

You could try hanging out where the stars spend their leisure time; trendy restaurants and exclusive clubs where the tab can quickly run as high as your mortgage. Among current "in" eateries are Drai's on La Cienega and The Ivy on North Robertson, as well as the new Spago in Beverly Hills or the ever-popular Citrus on Melrose. The younger showbiz crowd — Brat Packers and Gen-Xers — tend to hang at late-night Sunset Boulevard hot spots like the Viper Room (owned by actor Johnny Depp) and the SkyBar at the Mondrian Hotel, as well as the tacky Lava Lounge on La Brea.

If you haven't got the big bucks, modish haircut or cutting-edge frocks, don't fret. You can always eat or drink at a joint that's owned by a big-name star — although your chances of seeing the celebrity proprietor are like slim and none. Arnold Schwarzenegger has stakes in two restaurants: Planet Hollywood in

Beverly Hills (which he co-owns with Sylvester Stallone, Bruce Willis and Demi Moore) and an Austrian café in Santa Monica called Schatzi. The Thunder Roadhouse in West Hollywood — a shrine to the Harley Davidson and other road bikes — was underwritten by the likes of Dennis Hopper and Peter Fonda of *Easy Rider* fame. Whoopi Goldberg and Steve Seagal are among the owners of Eclipse in West Hollywood. While Dudley Moore and Liza Minnelli are among those who funded 72 Market Street in Venice.

The biggest gathering of stars each year is for the Academy Awards presentation, normally held at the Shrine Auditorium ((213) 749-5123, 665 West Jefferson at Figueroa, in March. Fans line up days in advance to get a spot along the red carpet that leads from curbside to the auditorium front door. If you're not in town for the Oscars, try to catch a glimpse of celebrities arriving for a movie premier. Mann's Chinese Theater on Hollywood Boulevard still hosts many premiers, as do the cinemas in Westwood Village near the University of California at Los Angeles campus.

It may be hard to break into the movies or network television, but it's relatively easy to get onto a studio back lot. Several big Hollywood studios offer regular behind-the-scenes tours including Paramount, Warner Bros., and NBC. Many of the studios also offer free tickets for tapings of television programs including popular "sitcoms" (situation comedies) and talk shows.

Speaking of free, there are a number of other ways to explore Hollywood on the cheap. Buy a star map from one of the curbside vendors along Sunset Boulevard (try the stretch between the University of California at Los Angeles campus and Beverly Hills) and strike out on your own customized tour. But a word of warning: most of these maps are sadly out of date or inaccurate when it comes to the abodes of current stars. However, they are handy for locating houses where the golden greats of Hollywood once lived. Likewise, you can scour the town for movie location shoots. Contact the Entertainment Industry Development Corporation ((213) 957-1000 on Hollywood Boulevard for a "call sheet" of movies being shot on the streets during the time of your visit.

ABOVE: Mann's Chinese Theater is a Hollywood institution. OPPOSITE: You could catch a glimpse of stars at Fair Oaks TOP and Spago Beverly Hills BOTTOM.

The Great Outdoors

From the snow-capped peaks and glacial lakes of the High Sierras to the sun-baked canyons of the Mojave Desert to the redwood forests of the Humboldt Coast, California is blessed with some of America's most spectacular scenery. Although most people opt to explore these scenic wonders by vehicle, the most engaging way to discover the state's wild and rugged regions is on foot.

Indeed, the state is ideal terrain for both casual strollers and long-distance backpackers, an opulence of trails that can take anywhere from an hour to a couple of months to negotiate. Facilities vary greatly from primitive desert campsites where you have to bring in everything yourself (especially water!) to the rustic luxury of the High Sierra camps in **Yosemite National Park**.

California's longest walking route is the **Pacific Crest Trail** which stretches all the way from the Mexican border in the south to the Oregon frontier in the north (it actually runs all the way to Canada if you want to keep walking). The PCT starts out in the uncrowded mountains of Southern California — the Laguna, San Jacinto and San Gabriel ranges — treading a fine line between pine forest and boulder-strewn desert. It continues in the remote southern Sierras, through the little explored back country of Sequoia and Kings Canyon national parks, where the trail skirts Mount Whitney, the highest point in the continental United States. Following the crest of the Sierras, the trail continues northward through pristine Alpine terrain. Yosemite is the next big destination, followed by Lake Tahoe, Lassen Volcano and finally Mount Shasta before reaching the Oregon border in Klamath National Forest. In a pinch, you could probably walk the Pacific Crest Trail in a month; most people take their time, string the journey out across three months as they explore the scenic wonders along the way.

Much shorter in duration, but nearly as spectacular in scenery, is the **Tahoe Rim Trail** which winds 70 miles (112 km) through the heavily wooded mountains around Lake Tahoe. In many respects, the scenery is like a carbon copy of the Alps — jagged granite peaks, glacial lakes and flower-filled highland meadows. Those who don't have the time or endurance for that sort of adventure can choose from more than 50 day hikes in the Tahoe region.

OPPOSITE: Riding through the wilds of Anza Borrego Desert State Park in San Diego County. ABOVE: Pismo Beach is one of countless California strands.

For a completely different type of California wilderness adventure try the **Lost Coast National Recreational Trail** between Eureka and Fort Bragg. This 26-mile (42-km) route is the only way to explore the isolated beaches and coves of the King Range National Conservation Area, the largest stretch of virgin coast in the entire state. There are no roads, no condominiums, no souvenir shops, just unfettered nature — the way California was before the advent of Euro-American civilization. The only vehicle access to the Lost Coast is a narrow road from Garberville (on US Highway 101) to Shelter Cove, where you pick up the trail.

California's most famous long-distance hiking route is the **John Muir Trail** through the heart of the High Sierra. It dips and grooves through 211 miles (340 km) of magnificent back country between Yosemite Valley and Whitney Portal including vast stretches of the pristine John Muir Wilderness Area. Most of the trail is above 7,000 ft (2,100 m), rising as high as 14,000 ft (4,200 m) at several points. Snow covers parts of the route as late as August.

Another alternative is the **Yosemite High Sierra Camps Loop** which links five permanent camps and the Tuolumne Meadows Lodge in the back country of Yosemite National Park. The total length is 50 miles (80 km), but this is considered a "moderate" hike because you don't need to lug a backpack and tent through the high altitude terrain — the camps provide food service and tented accommodation. Depending on the snow cover, the camps are normally open from early July through early September. Reservations are required and should be made at least six months in advance through the Yosemite Concession Services (see WHERE TO STAY, page 167, in YOSEMITE NATIONAL PARK).

California has more federally administered **wilderness areas** than any other state; a grand total of 129 reserves where logging, mining, grazing and other economic activities, as well as resorts, restaurants and private houses, are completely banned. The wilderness areas protect and preserve nearly 5.6 million hectares (14 million acres) and all are accessible by trail. Only "primitive" camping is allowed, which means you must bring in all of your own food, water and other supplies. Some of the more remarkable wilderness areas are John Muir and Ansel Adams in the High Sierra; Desolation and Granite Chief on the western edge of Lake

Zabriskie Point affords spectacular views across Death Valley.

Tahoe; the massive Marble Mountain and Trinity Alps reserves in the far north; and Ventana in the mountains above the Big Sur coast.

The state's urban areas also boast their share of hiking trails. San Francisco's **Golden Gate National Recreation Area** offers several hundred miles of footpaths through an amazing variety of scenery: isolated beaches, rolling green hills, redwood forest, bayside parkland. On the opposite side of the bay, the rambling **East Bay Regional Parks** above Berkeley and Oakland sport numerous mountain and valley trails, many of them offering spectacular views of the bay and its famous bridges. The equivalent down south is the **Santa Monica Mountains National Recreation Area** on the western fringe of the Los Angeles metropolitan area. Several state parks within the federally protected zone offer hiking trails including Topanga Canyon, Malibu Creek and Point Mugu.

All of the big **desert parks** — Anza Borrego, Joshua Tree, Mojave National Preserve and Death Valley — offer day hikes varying in degrees of length, time and difficulty. These trails are best tackled in seasons other than summer, when daytime temperatures surpass 104°F (40°C) on a regular basis.

Sporting Spree

California and sports are almost synonymous. Indeed, the Golden State is one of the world's most sports-oriented places, and one of the most successful in breeding professional athletes and world champions (Tiger Woods, Pete Sampras, Joe DiMaggio, Mark Spitz, O.J. Simpson, Michelle Kwan and Florence Griffith, just to name a few). The fun

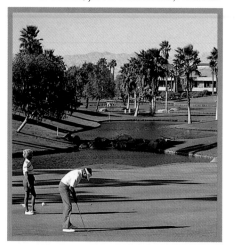

runs year-round — you can snow ski in the middle of summer or scuba dive in the depths of winter. And it covers just about every sport, game and recreational pursuit known to man.

The state offers more than a thousand different **golf** courses ranging from magnificent public links to majestic private country clubs. Thanks to the mild coastal and desert climates, golf is year-round sport in most of California. Many of the courses take full advantage of the glorious scenery, set on the edge of the ocean, in the shadow of snow-capped peaks or the middle of a palm-shaded oasis. Green fees for a round of 18 holes on the better courses generally range from $50 to $150 depending on the day and whether or not the club is public or private.

Pebble Beach Golf Links on the Monterey Peninsula is the state's most famous venues, a picturesque and often difficult course that flirts with the nearby sea. It has hosted numerous championship events over the years and is the home of a famous celebrity tournament each winter. Nearby Spyglass Hill has a similar coastal setting but is considered much more challenging, the kind of course that eats up amateurs. San Francisco's premier course is the Olympic Country Club, the greens and fairways often shrouded in fog. Even more spectacular is the Lincoln Park Golf Course, which sprawls across a wooded ridge near the Golden Gate Bridge. Most of the top courses in Los Angeles are on the west side, clustered around Beverly Hills and Brentwood, including the super luxury Bel Air Country Club, the Riviera Country Club and the Los Angeles Country Club. One of the more picturesque public links in the City of Los Angeles is the Rancho Park Golf Course near Century City. Torrey Pines Golf Course in San Diego offers another splendid setting — perched on windswept cliffs above the sea — and hosts a major professional event in February. The Silverado Country Club offers 18 holes of spectacular play amid the bounty of the Napa Valley wine region, while the Mount Shasta Resort's golf course provides amazing views of California's most famous peak. You can also tee off in the depths of Death Valley Furnace Creek Golf Course and on the edge of Lake Tahoe at the **Resort at Squaw Creek** ✆ (530) 583-6300 TOLL-FREE (800) 327-3353 FAX (916) 581-6632 Squaw Creek and Edgewood.

Tennis is another ideal sport for California's near-perfect climate. Nearly every major hotel and resort has its own all-weather courts, normally with lights. Most of these are offered to non-guests at a nominal fee. There are also plenty of good public courts available free of charge. Some municipal courts work on

a first-come, first-serve basis; others have a telephone reservation service or sign-up sheet. Most of the courts you find in California (and the rest of the United States) are hard-surface cement rather than grass or clay, so expect a much faster pace and bouncier balls. Recommended public tennis facilities include the Moscone Recreation Center in San Francisco's Marina District; the courts in the northeast corner of Balboa Park in San Diego; and the courts adjacent to Cedar Tree Picnic Ground at Griffith Park in Los Angeles. Half a dozen ATP championship events are staged in California each year. Regular stops on the professional circuit include La Costa Spa in San Diego County, La Quinta Resort near Palm Springs, and the Sunset Canyon at the University of California at Los Angeles (where tennis competition took place at the 1984 Summer Olympics).

The quintessential Southern California sport is **surfing**, popularized around the world by The Beach Boys and a 1960s cult film called *The Endless Summer*. On any given day, at almost any given daylight hour, you can see surfers bobbing up and down in the swell off a hundred different beaches. Some of the more renowned surf spots are Windansea, Cardiff and San Onofre in San Diego County; Dana Point, Huntington Beach and Seal Beach in Orange County; Manhattan Beach, Malibu and Zuma in Los Angeles County, as well as Santa Barbara and Steamers Lane in Santa Cruz. Tournaments are staged throughout the

summer, but two of the oldest and largest are the annual professional event at Huntington Beach in August and the Surf Festival in July at Manhattan, Hermosa and Redondo beaches. If you want to learn something about the history of the sport, both Santa Cruz and Huntington Beach have surf museums.

With a coastline that stretches 840 miles (1,352 km) between Mexico and Oregon, as well as hundreds of lakes, lagoons and rivers, California presents water for just about any type of **boating**.

Sailing is a passion for many Californians, with races nearly every weekend in San Francisco Bay, the watery passage between Long Beach and Catalina, or Mission Bay in San Diego. There are several dozen full-service yacht harbors where visiting sailors can tie up including Harbor Island and Shelter Island in San Diego, Newport and Huntington in Orange County, Marina del Rey in Los Angeles (the world's single largest yacht basin), Channel Islands Harbor in Ventura County, Santa Barbara's yacht basin, Monterey Marina as well as Berkeley and San Francisco. In fact, you could easily stage a month-long cruise along the entire California coast, hopping from port to port as the whim takes you.

Reservoirs and rivers provide plenty of open water for **power boating**, **jetskis** and

ABOVE: Championship tennis at the Indian Wells tournament near Palm Springs. OPPOSITE: The Palm Springs area is a golf paradise.

hop in San Diego County. Sea kayaks are available for rent at Richardson Bay in Marin County, Mission Bay in San Diego, Avalon Harbor in Catalina, Channel Islands Harbor in Ventura County, Monterey Bay and Santa Cruz.

Many of the state's rivers are ideal for kayaking and **white-water rafting**, including the Kern River in the Southern Sierra with its hair-raising hydraulics, the rough and tumble Tuolumne River near Yosemite, the moderate Stanislaus and American rivers in the Gold Country, the wild and isolated Klamath River near the Oregon border. California's top river rafting and kayak outfitter is **OARS (** (209) 736-4677, based at Angels Camp in the Gold Country, with trips on all major white-water rivers.

waterskiing. Among popular areas for these three sports are the Delta region between San Francisco and Sacramento, Lake Havasu on the Colorado River near Needles, the below-sea-level waters of the Salton Sea in Imperial County, Lake Tahoe in the High Sierra, the Whiskeytown-Shasta-Trinity National Recreation Area in the Cascade Range, and various reservoirs in the Gold Country including Folsom Lake near Sacramento and Lake Oroville near Chico. Other ideal spots are Lake Mead and Lake Mojave on the Nevada stretch of the Colorado River, just over the border from California.

Paddle sports also highly popular, albeit on much different bodies of water. The ruggedly handsome California coast, with so many beaches, bays and coves, is perfect terrain for **kayaking**. You can float among sea otters off Monterey and Carmel, drift beneath the Golden Gate Bridge, explore the secluded Channel Islands off Santa Barbara or beach

Californians have always been fond of horses, although different breeds of people flock to the state's many riding stables and betting windows. **Horseback riding** is available at various venues ranging from the beaches of Half Moon Bay south of San Francisco to the wilds of Yosemite National Park. In more ways than one, California is still part of the Wild West with working cattle ranches and real-life cowboys. Dude ranches in the northeast counties and the Sierra foothills give visitors a glimpse of the frontier lifestyle. Overnight pack horse trips can be arranged in Yosemite, Sequoia, Kings Canyon and Lassen Volcanic national parks, while the United States Forest Service maintains a network of equestrian trails and campgrounds in the Sierra national forests. Those with more limited time can rent mounts by the hour and explore the equestrian trails near major urban areas: the Carmel and San Dieguito valleys north of San Diego, Griffith Park in Los Angeles, the San Jacinto Mountains east of Riverside, and the East Bay parks above Oakland and Berkeley.

Horse racing is another abiding passion. Santa Anita Park in the San Gabriel Valley east of Los Angeles is the state's premier facility, host of many top races (including the prestigious Oak Tree). Los Angeles' other pony track is Hollywood Park in Inglewood. San Francisco punters flock to Bay Meadows in the East Bay. But the state's most beautiful venue is Del Mar Race Track near San Diego, a wonderful waterfront location with a breeze right off the Pacific. Founded by Bing Crosby and Bob Hope, Del Mar has long attracted a celebrity crowd.

After Colorado's Rocky Mountains, California's Sierra Nevada range is the country's biggest winter **snow sports** region. Dozens of winter resorts offer downhill and

cross-country skiing, as well as trendy new sports like snowboarding and snowshoeing. The biggest cluster of resorts is around Lake Tahoe, world-renowned runs like Heavenly Valley, Alpine Meadows, Northstar and Squaw Valley (host of the 1960 Winter Olympics). Nearby Donner Pass offers the Royal Gorge area and its myriad cross-country ski trails. Yosemite National Park contains a bright little resort called Badger Pass, one of the best places for kids to learn how to ski and a gateway to more than 350 miles (over 550 km) of cross-country ski trails. On the eastern side of the High Sierras is trendy Mammoth Mountain, the number-one choice among Southern California skiers because of its relative proximity to Los Angeles. Even closer to Los Angeles are the Wrightwood and Big Bear ski areas in the San Gabriel Mountains. The Cascade Mountains in the far north offer only limited downhill skiing in the Mount Shasta area, but almost unlimited cross-country trails.

California is also a mecca for **spectator sports**, with more big league professional sports teams (15) than any other state and half

a dozen colleges that field championship caliber athletic teams. National Football League (NFL) franchises include the Oakland Raiders, the San Diego Chargers and the highly successful San Francisco Forty-Niners. Major League baseball teams include the Los Angeles Dodgers, the Anaheim Angels (owned by Disney), the San Diego Padres, the San Francisco Giants and the Oakland Athletics. National Basketball Association (NBA) franchises include the Los Angeles Clippers, the Golden State Warriors (Oakland), the Sacramento Kings and the Los Angeles Lakers, the legendary team of the 1980s with players like Magic Johnson and Kareem Abdul-Jabbar. National Hockey League teams include the San Jose Sharks, the Los Angeles Kings and the Mighty Ducks of Anaheim (also owned by Disney).

OPPOSITE TOP: USC versus UCLA, the annual clash of college football titans in Los Angeles. BOTTOM: Monterey Bay Aquarium displays the state's rich ocean life. ABOVE: Divers and snorkelers flock to Channel Islands National Park.

The atmosphere at American **college sports** events is a marked contrast to a professional game, like a big picnic that just happens to include a match. The University of California at Los Angeles (UCLA) has America's most successful college sports program, with national championships (more than any other university) in everything from football and basketball to volleyball, water polo and soccer. UCLA plays its home football games at the Rose Bowl in Pasadena, its home basketball games at Pauley Pavilion in Westwood. The University of Southern California is a traditional football powerhouse, the school that produced O.J. Simpson and other legendary players. Home games are played at the Los Angeles Coliseum. Stanford is another sports power, especially strong in "country club" sports like tennis, golf and swimming. Among its vaunted alumni are Tiger Woods, John McEnroe and Janet Evans.

The Open Road

California is where modern "car culture" was invented — images of speeding along a sun-drenched highway with the top down, the wind in your hair and music blaring from the radio. Long distance commuting is taken for granted, as are various other manifestations of the automobile age — drive-in movies, drive-in restaurants, drive-in banks and even drive-in churches (although no one has devised a drive-in confessional).

Urban roads are often clogged, veritable "parking lots" where traffic creeps along. But don't get discouraged. With thousands of miles of rural roads and freeways, California has plenty of open roads. The state is ideal for exploring by car, truck, motorcycle or the ubiquitous recreational vehicles you see huddled around campsites. The farther you get from urban areas and major tourist attractions, the more unencumbered the driving conditions. Another distinct advantage of local motoring is the fact that California presents diverse landscapes: snow-capped mountains and barren deserts, palm-fringed beaches and rugged seascapes, vineyards and endless farm fields — more highway variety than any other state.

The following itineraries will give you an idea of some of the drives you can make in California.

BIG SUR JOURNEY

State Highway 1 runs nearly the entire length of California, but the most famous stretch is between San Luis Obispo and Santa Cruz along the ruggedly beautiful Big Sur Coast. The southern terminus of this route is 200 miles (323 km) north of Los Angeles via US Highway 101 through Santa Barbara. After rolling through 13 miles (20 km) of emerald green hillsides studded with majestic oak trees, the highway spills down onto the shore at **Morro Bay**, a popular resort and retirement community that's the unofficial capital of the Central Coast. The panorama is dominated by Morro Rock, a monolith that rises from the bay like a giant sea monster.

Leaving Morro Bay, the highway starts to hug the coast with the Pacific Ocean to the west and the verdant Santa Lucia Mountains to the east. It passes through quaint seaside towns like Cayucos and Cambria before reaching San Simeon, home of the world famous **Hearst Castle**, which perches on a hillside above the hamlet. This amazing private home was built by San Francisco newspaper magnet William Randolph Hearst in the 1920s and 1930s and later transformed into a state historic park. Filled with priceless European art and antiques, the castle's architecture is something of a cross between Hollywood fantasy and the California mission style. Guided walking tours are offered daily (see HEART SAN SIMEON STATE HISTORICAL MONUMENT, page 183).

Civilization fades away to unfettered nature north of San Simeon, as State Highway 1 enters **Los Padres National Forest**. The road twists and turns, climbing higher and higher, often perched on the edge of geological oblivion, hundreds of feet above the pounding waves. The coastal views are sensational and there are plenty of places to pull to the side of the road for a look-see and a few snapshots. Several places offer access to the windswept beaches below including **Julia Pfeiffer Burns State Park** and **Andrew Molera State Park**.

Wedged on clifftops between the two parks is the town of **Big Sur**, a counter-culture hangout since the 1960s when hippies and other alternative lifestyle advocates began taking up residence there. The **Esalen Institute** is a world-famous center of offbeat philosophy and holistic medicine, but it's also got redwood hot tubs and hot springs where you can rejuvenate your road-weary body. The **Ventana Inn** is a great place to grab a good meal and spectacular coast view.

State Highway 1 plunges back to sea level near **Point Lobos State Reserve,** a sanctuary for all sorts of marine birds and the highly endangered California sea otter. **Carmel River Beach** is a handsome little strand that is usually deserted on weekdays. The highway skirts around the highly scenic **Monterey Peninsula** but it's easy to detour into Carmel, Monterey or other local towns. **Carmel** is one of California's most popular seaside retreats with numerous tourist shops and trendy restaurants and one of the state's most charming Spanish missions. The famous **17-Mile Drive** connects Carmel with Pacific Grove and Monterey on the north side of the peninsula, an amazing private road that winds past multimillion-dollar mansions, various stunning seascapes and the Pebble Beach golf course. **Monterey** offers the somewhat seedy **Cannery Row**, a pale and plastic imitation of the tumultuous waterfront district described by John Steinbeck in his landmark novel of the same name. However, **Monterey Bay Aquarium** is an excellent facility, the best of its kind in California.

North of Monterey, State Highway 1 transforms into a four-lane freeway with speeding cars and harried motorists. But relief comes after just 15 miles (24 km). Exit the freeway at **Castroville**, the self-proclaimed "Artichoke Capital of the World" with its giant green artichoke statue and little country restaurants that serve everything from artichoke omelets and burgers to French fried

Lake Shasta is one of the state's favorite "fishing holes" as well as a popular boating spot.

artichokes. State Highway 1 continues due north, passing through an old whaling port called **Moss Landing** that now harbors numerous antique and craft shops. There are half a dozen good **beaches** in this area including Salinas River, Zmudowski, Sunset and Manresa. Finally the highway curves around the north end of Monterey Bay and into **Santa Cruz** with its acclaimed Boardwalk and seaside roller coaster. San Francisco is another 78 miles (125 km) north via State Highway 17 and US Highway 101.

MOJAVE DESERT DRIVE

You see a lot of the California arid landscapes while driving the interstates to Las Vegas or Arizona. But the best of the desert is far beyond the madding crowds, on the obscure roads that link the various desert parks.

From Los Angeles, the quickest way to reach the desert is Interstate 10 via San Bernardino and the San Gorgonio Pass (with its factory outlets, Indian casino and giant plaster dinosaur). Beyond Indio, 164 miles (264 km) east of downtown Los Angeles, is the turnoff to **Joshua Tree National Park**. The narrow road runs north through stark desert scenery, up and over Cottonwood Pass to the "high desert" with its famous Joshua tree cactus. The park boasts two visitor centers (Oasis and Cottonwood) and several campgrounds but not much else in the way of facilities.

At the north end of the park is the town of **Twentynine Palms**, a one-time oasis now famed as the desert training ground for the United States Marines. Another lonely desert road runs the 49 miles (78 km) between Twentynine Palms and Amboy, passing through Sheep Hole Summit and across the white-washed bed of Bristol Dry Lake. **Amboy**

is a secluded railroad junction and the inspiration for the film *Bagdad Café*. West of town is **Amboy Crater** where a meteor once slammed into the earth. Drive east from Amboy along old Route 66, about five miles (eight kilometers) until you reach the turnoff to Kelso. This tiny road bisects a broad desert valley between the Bristol and Marble mountains, eventually reaching Interstate 40.

Cross over the bridge and keep heading north, into the wonderful wilds of the **Mojave National Preserve**. Established in the early 1990s to safeguard rare plants and animals, the reserve embraces thousands of acres of virgin desert. The park is an excellent example of how desert landscapes can vary — Joshua tree forests and mesquite thickets, dry lake beds and rocky peaks, sprawling black lava beds and a huge sandy area called the **Kelso Dunes**. One of the preserve's more unique features is **Mitchell Caverns** with its lovely

stalagmites and stalactites. The National Park Service has established campgrounds at **Mid Hills** and **Hole-in-the Wall**, but otherwise there are very few visitor facilities. The town of **Kelso** lies near the park's geographic center, but there really isn't much there except an old train station.

From Kelso, take the road leading northwest toward **Baker** on Interstate 15. Baker is an elongated collection of gas stations and fast-food joints, but it also boasts the world's biggest thermometer and the **Mojave Desert Information Center (** (760) 733-4040, 72157 Baker Boulevard. Between May and September the temperatures rarely dip below 104°F (40°C), making Baker one of the hottest places in America. State Highway 127 heads north toward Death Valley, through more vacant desert. **Dumont Dunes**, 10 miles (48 km) north of Baker is an off-highway vehicle (OHV) area run by the Bureau of Land

Management. The park features dirt bike and dune buggy trails that lead up and down steep sand dunes.

The tiny desert hamlet of **Shoshone**, 58 miles (93 km) north of Baker, is the southern gateway to Death Valley. State Highway 178 leads into the valley via Salisbury Pass. But a more interesting route is continuing north on State Highway 127 to **Death Valley Junction** and its tiny desert **Opera House**, founded in gold rush days and still the scene of occasional performances. State Highway 190 leads west to **Death Valley National Park**, the state's premier desert reserve. The trail and overlooks at Zabriskie Point, just off the highway, offer a good

ABOVE: Trona Pinnacles tower above the Mojave Desert north of Los Angeles. OPPOSITE: Zabriskie Point stands like a sentinel at the entrance to Death Valley.

introduction to the area's super stark landscapes before you plummet to the valley floor. The first thing you see at the bottom of the hill is a remarkable Spanish-style building which houses a plush desert resort called **The Furnace Creek Inn**. Even if you don't stay overnight, pop into the inn for a meal or drink or maybe just a wander through the palm-shaded gardens. **The Furnace Creek Ranch**, just down the road, offers horseback riding, golf and souvenir shopping, as well as the park's **visitor center** and a small **desert mining museum**.

Detour south from Furnace Creek to **Badwater**, the lowest elevation in the western hemisphere (282 ft/86 m below sea level). Double back to Furnace Creek and continue north along State Highway 190 to the **Harmony Borax Works** (now an open-air museum) and **Stovepipe Wells**, where food and accommodation are available. Several side trips are possible from Stovepipe: due east through Daylight Pass to **Rhyolite** ghost town in Nevada; north to **Scottys Castle** and **Ubehebe Crater**. Either way, you want to double back through Stovepipe and exit the park on State Highway 190 by way of Emigrant Junction. The road forks at this point: the right fork heads west to US Highway 395 in the Owens Valley, within easy reach of Yosemite National Park and Lake Tahoe; the left fork heads south through the Panamint Valley to Los Angeles.

GOLD RUSH ROUTE

Whoever designed California's state highway system had a deep appreciation for history, because a single road — State Highway 49 — runs the entire length of the Mother Lode from Nevada City to Oakhurst. Along the way are dozens of historic towns that preserve

their gold-rush heritage in museums, state parks, Victorian architecture and quaint bed and breakfast inns. The scenery is also spectacular, rolling hills covered in wild flowers and oak trees, snow-capped peaks in the distance and the giant Central Valley spreading out before you.

To reach the northern terminus of the Gold Rush Route, leave Sacramento and drive 42 miles (67 km) on State Highway 99 until you reach Marysville. Follow State Highway 20 east into the Sierra Nevada foothills 39 miles (62 km) to a restored mining town called **Nevada City**, once called the "Queen City of the Northern Mines." The **Miners Foundry Cultural Center** ((530) 265-5040, 325 Spring Street in Nevada City stages numerous seasonal events related to California history and culture. Twenty-nine miles (47 km) north of town is the **Malakoff Diggins** ((530) 265-2740, 23579 North Bloomfield Road, California's largest hydraulic gold mine and now an open-air museum. Nearby **Grass Valley** boasts the **Empire Mine State Historic Park** ((530) 273-8522, 10791 East Empire Sreet, with its numerous mine sites, historic buildings and mining artifacts.

State Highway 49 runs due south from Grass Valley, crosses the Bear River and then converges with Interstate 80 which leads to Sacramento (west) and Reno (east). Just beyond this junction is the **Auburn State Recreation Area** which protects the watershed of the Middle Fork of the American River, popular for **white-water rafting**. The river empties into Folsom Lake, a paradise for fishing, boating and waterskiing. Farther south is a tiny town called Coloma, where the gold rush started in 1849. The **Marshall Gold Discovery State Historic Park** comprises most of the town including the spot where carpenter George Marshall found the first nugget.

Placerville is the next town along the Gold Rush Route, at the junction of US Highway 50, which cuts east, through the heart of the Sierra Nevada range, to the south shore of Lake Tahoe. **Gold Bug Park** in Placerville is America's only municipal gold mine, and the town's **El Dorado County Museum** is another good place to "dig" into the region's golden heritage. Another half hour down the road is **Amador County** with its myriad mining towns including Plymouth, Sutter Creek, Jackson and Volcano. This is also wine country with several local grape crushers including **Montevina Winery** near Plymouth.

State Highway 49 leaps the Mokelumne River on a sturdy bridge, rolling into **Calaveras County**, perhaps the

most famous of the Gold Country's counties because of its association with authors Bret Harte and Mark Twain. The latter wrote about the Jumping Frog Contest that still takes place in **Angels Camp** each summer, now part of the Calaveras County Fair. The Angels Camp Museum is another excellent gold-era collection and there are several wineries in the area if you're in the mood for some libation. Other nearby distractions include the giant sequoias of the **Calaveras Big Trees State Park** and the underground enchantments of the **Mercer Caverns**.

The Stanislaus River, once the scene of an epic environmental battle to halt construction of the New Melones Dam, divides Calaveras from **Tuolumne County**. South of the river are a cluster of old mining towns on either side of State Highway 49 — Sonora, Columbia and Jamestown. **Columbia State Historic Park** is perhaps the best of all the Gold Country's heritage areas with

numerous restored buildings and mining exhibits. State Highway 49 crosses over an arm of **Don Pedro Lake** in the southern part of Tuolumne County. At Moccasin, you can veer left onto State Highway 120, which leads 47 miles (75 km) to **Yosemite National Park**. Even though the number of old mining towns dwindles to few and far between, the Gold Rush Route continues another 60 miles (96 km) through Coulterville, Mariposa and Oakhurst where it intersects with State

OPPOSITE: Hangman's Tree in Placerville reflects the vigilante justice of gold rush days. ABOVE LEFT: St. James Episcopal Church crowns the town of Sonora. ABOVE RIGHT: The historic Jeffery Hotel in Coulterville. RIGHT: Whistling Billy no longer carries gold nuggets through Coulterville.

Highway 41 to Fresno and southern Yosemite.

Other recommended open road journeys include the Redwood Empire Route (US Highway 101) between San Francisco and the Oregon border; the State Highway 1 between Marin County and Fort Bragg; State Highway 89 between Lake Tahoe and Mount Shasta (including Lassen Volcanic National Park); State Highway 78 from Escondido (near San Diego) through the Anza-Borrego Desert and Imperial Valley to the Colorado River; the Sierra Vista Scenic Byway through the central High Sierras (south of Yosemite National Park); and the new which stretches from Fort Bragg on the Mendocino Coast to the western shore of Lake Tahoe.

Backpacking

Cost-conscious travelers, especially those from overseas, will find that California presents some unique challenges when it comes to keeping expenses down. Like much of the rest of the United States, the biggest challenge is space — the fact that so many of the travel highlights are scattered so far apart. You can certainly explore places like Yosemite, the Redwood Empire, the Big Sur coast and the Mojave Desert by public transportation; but it will take weeks rather than days, you will have limited access to many of the more interesting sights, and you may end up spending more money than if you had your own vehicle. This means that renting a car is probably the most cost-effective means to tout California.

Rental car rates vary widely according to where you rent, the time of year and the type of vehicle you desire. Generally, the cheapest rates are offered by rental agency offices at or near the Los Angeles and San Francisco international airports because there is so much competition in the immediate area. A small "compact" or "economy" car should run about $30 per day including unlimited mileage, but not including insurance. There are also special weekly and monthly rates if you want a long-term rental. If you're traveling in a group of, say, four people, that works out to $7.50 a day for unlimited transportation. Some of the small, independent rental agencies — like Bargain Rent-A-Car in San Diego and Stopless Rent-A-Car in Los Angeles — offer even better deals. Many of the established companies will not rent to people under age 25 or anyone who doesn't possess a major credit card. But there are ways to get around these restrictions: independent firms like All International Rent-A-Car and Fox Rent-A-Car in Los Angeles readily rent to young people and accept cash deposits. Filling up your gas tank in California runs about a third of the cost of Europe, Japan or Australia ($1 to $1.50 per gallon).

If you have enough people — four or more in your travel group — it might be cost effective to rent a motor home or other recreational vehicle. Two reputable outfits are El Monte RV Center, with six California locations, and Cruise America Motorhome Rental in Buena Park, near Disneyland (see MOTOR HOME RENTALS, page 344, in TRAVELERS' TIPS). Other transportation options include buses, trains, planes and hitching. Greyhound Lines offers quite reasonable bus fares between most California cities, but the journey usually includes frequent stops and can take two to three times as long as a private car to travel the same distance. Amtrak, the national rail company, also offers "thruway" bus service along select tourist routes — Merced to Yosemite Valley, Bakersfield to Las Vegas, Napa Valley to Eureka just to name a few. Amtrak offers economical train service along short, heavily-used routes like San Diego–Los Angeles, San Francisco–Sacramento and Los Angeles–Santa Barbara. But longer train journeys tend to be more expensive than flying the same route.

The best deals on airfares are flights between major airports in Southern California (Los Angeles, San Diego, Burbank, Orange County) and major airports in Northern California (San Francisco, Oakland, San Jose, Sacramento). Otherwise, flying is the most expensive way to travel from one city to

another. Top discount airlines are Southwest and Reno Air which often publish special inter-city fares in local newspapers.

Back in the 1960s and 1970s, thousands of young people took to the highways and byways of California each summer in search of a free ride. Hitchhiking is no longer a viable alternative… unless you are prepared to wait hours for a ride. The basic problem is personal safety: too much publicity about serial killers and random rapists — most of it unfounded — has dampened the joy of "thumbing" for both the hitchers and motorists. The only real alternative is checking the "ride boards" at the student unions at college and university campuses, where students who want to drive to other destinations look for people share the cost of gas.

Once you've got your wheels, the next challenge is finding a place to stay. California has some notoriously expensive hotels, especially in the big cities. And unlike Europe, there is not an extensive network of youth hostels. But there are plenty of economical alternatives. A number of nationwide motel chains — groups like Days Inn, Comfort Inn,

Vagabond Inn and Motel 6 — stake their reputations on cheap accommodation. Rates for double and single rooms can vary from $25 per night in rural areas to as much as $80 in big cities. Use their toll-free reservation numbers to book a room in the next place on your itinerary (see ACCOMMODATION, page 344, in TRAVELERS' TIPS). Another way to seek out budget accommodation is consulting the latest *Traveler Discount Guide* available at airport and roadside tourist information counters. Updated every four months, this green-covered magazine lists hotel and motel bargains throughout the state.

Camping is another cost-conscious alternative. California has more than 1,500 public and private campgrounds from which to choose, ranging from beach and bayside retreats to desert oases and high mountain sanctuaries. Rates per night range from $2 to $10 per campsite or vehicle depending on the

OPPOSITE: Recreation vehicles (RVs) gather in the parking lot of Circus Circus Hotel in Las Vegas. ABOVE: A Jeep tackles a back country road in Anza-Borrego Desert State Park.

location and facilities. All national parks and national forests, and nearly all state parks, have campgrounds. Some areas also offer county and BLM (Bureau of Land Management) campsites. Campground reservations for about 150 California state parks can be made up to seven months in advance by calling a private state-wide booking service called **Mistix** TOLL-FREE (800) 444-7275. For information about campground reservations for national parks in California, see NATIONAL PARKS, page 341, in TRAVELERS' TIPS. Information is also available from the **American Camping Association (** (818) 223-9232 (in Southern California) TOLL-FREE (800) 362-2236 (in Northern California). One of the best guides on this subject is *California Camping* by Tom Stienstra which includes information on nearly 1,200 campgrounds.

The final challenge is finding reasonably priced food, and here again California offers many alternatives. If you are camping, chances are you'll be rustling up your own grub. But when you're out on the road or exploring big cities, stoking a campfire is more likely to get you arrested than satiated (the brush and forest fire hazard is extreme is most parts of California, especially in the summer and autumn months). The concept of drive-in restaurants originated in the Golden State and there are plenty of chains where you can eat your fill for less than five dollars — McDonalds, Burger King, Taco Bell and Dairy Queen among them. Dennys, the ubiquitous roadside diner chain, offers vast meals at amazingly cheap prices. Another good bargain is Soup Plantation (locations around the state), which offers all-you-can-eat salad bar, soup, pizza, pasta and desert for under $10 per person. Mexican eateries are also pervasive, offering tacos, enchiladas, burritos and other

south-of-the-border delights at a fraction of what you would pay in a proper sit-down restaurant.

Living It Up

EXCEPTIONAL HOTELS
Every major city in California has landmark, world-renowned hotels that capture the essence of their locales. In San Francisco, **Sherman House** in Pacific Heights offers impeccable service in an 1876 Italianate mansion and carriage house, while the **Mandarin Oriental** echoes the city's Asian influences in an opulent setting high above the skyline. All the grandeur and haughty casualness of Los Angeles is captured in the **Beverly Hills Hotel**. This icon on the Los Angeles scene is a real-life stage-set for celebrities who hang about in the sporting togs of the era amid a backdrop of sparkling pools, pink California-Spanish buildings and the legendary Polo Lounge. Owned in the late 1990s by the Sultan of Brunei, the hotel has undergone renovations costing enough to bail out several third-world countries. **Château Marmont**, above the Sunset Strip, is a rare survivor from Hollywood's glamorous 1920s. Stylized as a California version of a French

château, the main hotel and cottages have ensconced famed recluses including Greta Garbo and Howard Hughes. **The Argyle** is listed in the National Registry of Historic Places for its Art Deco style and the role it has played in the social scene between Beverly Hills and Hollywood. **Shutters on the Beach** in Santa Monica is quintessentially hip. Deliberately modernistic and quaint, all blue and white shutters and clapboard by the sand, the hotel is an idyllic base for exploring the sun and sand scene, and offers endless scenarios in easy walking distance—or just a chance to survey the monied beach set.

San Diego's most famous façade may well be the **Hotel del Coronado**, a castle-like confection of red-tiled turrets and towers set against the village and beach of Coronado. Nearby, the **Loews Coronado Bay Resort** is the ultimate self-contained resort for those seeking solitude, pampering, and relaxation. La Jolla's **La Valencia Hotel**, just minutes from downtown San Diego, blends classic California and Mediterranean design in a village landmark which first opened in 1926. Featured in Raymond Chandler detective novels, the "La V" has one of the most beautiful settings in Southern California, above Ellen Browning Scripps Park and La Jolla Cove. Brides-to-be find it irresistible.

There are several luxurious accommodations managed under brand names scattered about the state. **Four Seasons** puts on a classy, comfortable spread in San Diego, Orange County, Palm Springs, Los Angeles and San Francisco. The **Four Seasons Aviara** in Carlsbad, in North San Diego County, is one of the newest in the group, and provides a 1990s view of the Southern California coast. An Arnold Palmer golf course rises and falls toward Batiquitos Lagoon, a bird preserve and the ocean in front of the hotel's low-rise Mediterranean-style buildings, rose gardens, 20-ft (six-meter)-high palms and oasis of pools. In Santa Barbara, the chain manages the stately **Biltmore**, which sprawls like a small village of cottages over 20 acres (eight hectares) of lawns beside the sea. The **Ritz-Carlton Laguna Niguel** is consistently rated one of the top hotels in the United States, due in part to its idyllic location on an amazingly uncrowded Southern California beach.

Natural settings enhance the beauty of certain mountain and country lodges,

OPPOSITE: La Valencia Hotel affords rooms with a view in chic La Jolla. ABOVE: Marriott's Desert Springs Resort is among the most lavish of California's desert inns.

YOUR CHOICE

especially in Northern California. The **Ahwahnee Hotel** in Yosemite is one of the best hotels in the state. Constructed of heavy timbers, stone and glass in 1927, the hotel is a must-see even if you're not staying there; if you're a guest, be sure to take advantage of the lounge's vast fireplace and the excellent dining room. **Drakesbad Guest Ranch** in Lassen Volcanic National Park was built in the late 1800s and offers the only accommodations in the park. **The Resort at Squaw Creek** by Lake Tahoe is a skier's delight in the High Sierras. In the Napa Valley wine region, the **Auberge du Soleil** in Rutherford has all the charm of a French country inn nestled amid vineyards, while the **Benbow Inn** on the banks of the Eel River in Garberville by the Redwood Highway allows guests to experience the essence of the forests.

Coastal California's scenery encourages hoteliers to create one-of-a-kind hotels and bed and breakfast inns that take advantage of the ocean's mists and spray. The **Stanford Inn by the Sea** on State Highway 1 in Mendocino is the perfect coastal retreat, as is **La Ventana** in Big Sur. **El Encanto** in Santa Barbara takes advantage of a hillside panorama of the sea with canopied lawn swings amid jasmine, wisteria and geraniums fed by the coastal fog.

Desert inns surrounded by oases of palms and golf courses pamper sunloving guests in Palm Springs, Las Vegas, Death Valley and Borrego Springs. Naturally, the finest choices are spread throughout the Coachella Valley towns around Palm Springs, the center of well-heeled vacationers. The **Marriott's Desert Springs Resort** is among the most lavish mega-resorts, with plush, airy suites overlooking pools, ponds, fountains, streams and the inevitable golf greens. **The Willows** has all the beauty and refined taste of a

historic Palm Springs home, while the **La Quinta Resort** in ritzy Rancho Mirage is more like a desert estate. Indian Wells, one of the wealthiest communities in the United States, is home to the recently restored Mediterranean-style **Miramonte**.

The desert is obliterated by bright lights in Las Vegas, home to mega-hotels with 1,000 to 5,000 rooms. Though it's hard to imagine such a behemoth having character, some pull size off quite well. The aptly named **Caesars Palace** has suites and swimming pools fit for Roman royalty; the **Desert Inn** is understated in contrast to nearly everything on the Vegas Strip, and offers a welcome sense of elegant decorum. Baja's hotels tend to cater to a rowdy Southern California crowd, though the **Camino Real** in Tijuana is up to luxury standards and the **Rosarito Beach Hotel** evokes a faded sense of glamour.

EXCEPTIONAL RESTAURANTS

California's fine-dining experiences run the gamut from star-studded celebrity cafés in Los Angeles to fish houses by the beach. In San Francisco, chef Alice Water's **Chez Panisse** is considered to be one of the best restaurants in America. Waters inspired the movement toward healthy, fresh cooking in California; it only stands to reason that her kitchen would be in the cutting-edge community of Berkeley. **Masa's**, near Union Square, may well be the best French restaurant in the state, while the **Plumpjack**

Café on Fillmore Street is a long-time favorite for American bistro food and its selection of California wines. Yosemite's **Ahwahnee Dining Room** offers the ultimate in mountain lodge dining with both a staggering view and creative California cuisine; wineries in Northern California hold vintner's dinners here. Napa Valley's hottest new restaurant is the **Wine Spectator at Greystone** in Saint Helena, run by the prestigious Wine Spectator magazine and affiliated with the Culinary Institute of America (which trains future chefs at the same location). **Château Souverain** is the heralded restaurant at the winery of the same name which serves French and California cuisine. The **Mono Inn** presents spectacular views of Mono Lake and good California cuisine.

Exceptional dining experiences seem to coincide with outstanding scenery along the Central Coast between San Francisco and Los Angeles. The **Ventana Inn** and the **River Inn** are both worth a stop when driving through Big Sur. Santa Barbara, which sits between the ocean and the fertile Ojai Valley, is blessed with a wealth of fresh ingredients and great chefs. **Citronelle**, located in the Santa Barbara Inn across from the beach, is the workshop for Los Angeles chef Michael Richards, big on the California cuisine scene. The **Wine Cask** features the best local wines (and rivals from the north) and cheeses, olives and produce from nearby gardens, as does the dining room at **El Encanto**.

Los Angeles, hotbed of all that is trendy and hip, has certain traditions that can not be surpassed. **Yamashiro**, an Asian mansion with a stunning view of old Hollywood, has been courting the famous since 1960. **Musso & Frank Grill**, which first opened in 1919, is Hollywood's oldest restaurant, and **Barney's Beanery** in Santa Monica is classic neighborhood hangout with pool tables and solid, moderately priced meals. **Gladstone's 4 Fish** in Pacific Palisades is the best beach-side seafood restaurants with tanks of live lobster and crab. On a trendier note, Wolfgang Puck continues to woo the hip set with **Spago**, his Beverly Hills headquarters. Puck's line of cafés and Asian-themed Chinois restaurants are popping up all over California and Las Vegas, which is home to an endless series of offshoots and one-of-a-kind restaurants from interior designers and chefs. There are plenty of places to blow your winnings in this town of excess. **Monte Carlo** and **Andre's French Restaurant** are among the most elegant spots for fine dining; **Hyakumi** offers Japanese cuisine and decor at its best. Steaks and prime rib, which seem to go well with the general Las Vegas inclination toward hard liquor, cigarettes, and unhealthy pursuits are served with decorum at the **Palm** and **Morton's**.

OPPOSITE: TOP: Rosti potato with golden caviar at Fenix Restaurant in Los Angeles. BOTTOM: The Ahwahnee Hotel is an oasis of fine dining in Yosemite National Park. ABOVE: Pernille is one of Carmel's more savory restaurants.

San Diego has yet to distinguish itself in the state's culinary limelight, though there are many excellent chefs. The best lean heavily on fresh seafood for their signature dishes, such as the seared ahi at **Café Pacifica** and the imported oysters at **Top of the Market** overlooking the harbor downtown. La Jolla is filled with excellent dining rooms, many facing the lawns and palms at La Jolla Cove. **George's at the Cove** and **Top of the Cove** both have elegant enclosed dining rooms and outdoor roof terraces serving state-of-the-art California cuisine. Nothing beats **Point Loma Seafoods** for casual crab sandwiches, fish and chips, and shrimp cocktails at patio tables by the sport fishing docks.

Southern Californians have the good fortune to live close to the Mexican border, and frequently cross into Tijuana and Ensenada for fine regional Mexican cuisine and authentic tacos, enchiladas and tamales. **Cien Años** is Tijuana's best upscale restaurant; **El Rey Sol** features French cooking and fine wines from vintners in the nearby Guadalupe and Santo Tomás valleys.

Family Fun

It would be difficult, anywhere on the planet, to find a place with more family-oriented activities than California. In many respects, the Golden State is a children's paradise: half a dozen major theme parks, endless beaches and other water sports activities, myriad national parks and nature areas, numerous kid-friendly museums, shops and restaurants that cater to families.

MICKEY & FRIENDS

California is the place where the modern theme park was invented, when Walt Disney unveiled an amazing place called **Disneyland** in 1956. Surrounded by orange groves in a sleepy little town called Anaheim south of Los Angeles, Disneyland was revolutionary for its time. Five imaginary lands — Main Street USA, Adventureland, Frontierland, Fantasyland, and Tomorrowland — transport visitors on time trips to the past and future. From the very start, Disneyland bore heavy-duty Hollywood overtones, and that's still true of many of the park's top attractions; rides based on *Indiana Jones, Star Wars, Roger Rabbit* and various Disney classics.

OPPOSITE TOP: Santa Monica's Third Street Promenade is a pedestrian paradise. BOTTOM: Family fun takes many forms at San Francisco's raucous Pier 39.

One of the best ways for families to enjoy Disneyland is a special two-day package that includes park admission and accommodation at one of the adjacent Disney hotels (including a wake-up call from Mickey Mouse himself). Depending on the time of year, the packages also let you into the park an hour earlier than general admission, which means quick and easy access to the more popular rides.

Knott's Berry Farm, in nearby Buena Park, started life as a berry farm and roadside fried chicken stall in the 1930s. By the 1960s it had evolved into a Wild West theme park with mine train, log flume rides and cowboy stunt shows. Before Halloween each year, the entire complex is transformed into a haunted ghost town.

Universal Studios offers the ultimate Hollywood theme park experience. The original tram tour of the studio back lot is still the park's anchor attraction, but it has evolved into an adventure ride that includes a simulated earthquake and an attack by King Kong.

Many other attractions have been added over the years, spinoffs from various Universal films: the Waterworld movie stunt extravaganza, the Flintstones song and dance show, the E.T. fantasy ride and a boat cruise through dinosaur-infested Jurassic Park. You need two days to see everything that Universal Studio offers.

About an hour's drive north of Los Angeles is **Six Flags Magic Mountain**, which tends to cater more to a teenage audience (many rides have a minimum height restriction, which eliminates most younger children). With five massive roller coasters — like the new Superman Escape, which bills itself as the tallest, fastest thrill ride on the planet — this is the place to come if you really want to get your adrenaline pumping. Next door is a large water park called **Hurricane Harbor** with numerous pools and slides. The best way for families to tour both parks is a combined two-day ticket; a dozen motels and motor lodges in the area offer overnight accommodation.

America's best marine-based theme park is **Sea World** in San Diego, home of the original Shamu the killer whale. Among the popular attractions are Wild Arctic (polar bears, beluga whales and other cold-weather creatures), Rocky Point Reserve (a huge free-form dolphin habitat), a massive shark tank with an underwater walkway, and a sprawling adventure playground for pre-teens. Set on the shores of beautiful Mission Bay, Sea World features acrobatic and comedic performances laced with an

environmental message that many of the animals you are seeing are highly endangered in the wild. The park doubles as an oceanographic research institute and a rescue mission for sea lions, whales and other animals that wash up on Southern California beaches.

The **San Diego Wild Animal Park**, about a 45-minute drive north of downtown San Diego, is another world leader in terms of family fun and scientific research. A monorail takes visitors on an hour-long journey through rolling hills and grasslands that team with African and Asian animals — lions and tigers, rhinos and hippos, elephants, giraffes, zebras and antelope. The park is so vast and the herds so big that you could almost swear that you're travelling by train through Kenya or northern India rather than the foothills of Southern California. The park also features educational animals shows, nature trails, aviaries where you can feed colorful tropical birds, and a baby animal nursery and petting kraal. During summer months, the park is open at night and offers special "camp outs" in tents adjacent to the African plains.

Not to be left out, the San Francisco Bay Area also has its theme parks, although they aren't as unique as those in Southern California. **Paramount's Great America** in San Jose offers an array of roller coasters and other thrill rides. **Marine World Africa USA** in Vallejo is a cross between a zoological garden and a water-based theme park with a killer whale and dolphin show, elephant encounter, shark aquarium and wildlife theater.

ENDLESS SUMMER: CALIFORNIA'S BEACHES

California offers hundreds of beaches of all shapes and sizes from the wild and rugged strands of Point Reyes National Seashore north of San Francisco to perpetual human motion of Venice Beach in Los Angeles.

As a general rule, Northern California beaches are too cold for swimming except during the summer months — and even then a wetsuit isn't a bad idea. Southern California's beach season runs year-round, although even in summer the water is chilly compared to the Caribbean or South Pacific.

Choosing the right beach is largely a function of your children's ages and interests. Toddlers really only need a bucket, spade and stretch of open sand, which means that just about any beach will do. But it also helps to have a shady **picnic area** and a **playground** nearby in case they get bored building sand castles. Strands that fit the bill include Del Mar and Mission Bay Park in San Diego,

Cabrillo Beach in Santa Barbara, and the Manhattan–Hermosa–Redondo strip in Los Angeles.

Several popular beaches feature adjacent amusement parks with thrill rides, arcade games and fast food. **Belmont Park**, on Mission Beach in San Diego, boasts a pink and turquoise roller coaster and a huge indoor saltwater swimming pool called The Plunge. Santa Cruz offers the historic **Beach Boardwalk** with the Giant Dipper roller coaster and numerous other nausea-inducing rides, as well as Neptune's Kingdom indoor family fun center. Los Angeles's version is of the permanent beachside carnival is **Santa Monica Pier** with its small roller coaster, bumper cars and carousel.

Active teenagers have several waterfront choices. Venice and Santa Monica beaches in Los Angeles, Mission Beach in San Diego and Santa Cruz beach in Northern California offer long boardwalks where **rollerblades** and **bicycles** can be rented by the day or hour. Manhattan Beach near Los Angeles is the undisputed capital of **beach volleyball** in California. **Board surfing** is possible at numerous beaches including Huntington, Hermosa, Malibu, San Onofre, Santa Cruz, Cardiff and Windansea.

Although the ocean may look placid, many California beaches have a strong riptide or undertow. Never let your children go into the water alone and always swim at a lifeguard-tended beach.

GREEN SPACES: URBAN AND OTHERWISE

California boasts some of America's oldest, largest and most varied parks and nature areas. Many of them are ideal for family outings, whether it's an afternoon picnic or a week-long camping trip.

San Francisco's **Golden Gate Park** is an endless and ageless wonder, a West Coast equivalent of London's Hyde Park or New York's Central Park. It features the country's oldest public playground (down in the southwest corner by Kezar Stadium) as well as the California Academy of Science with its planetarium and aquarium, a Japanese Garden in which children love to gambol, a small lake where you can rent rowboats, a model boat pond, and a paddock where a herd of bison roams. One of the park's main roads is closed off to traffic on Sundays for rollerblading, skating and biking beneath the leafy trees. Grassy meadows and wooded picnic areas abound.

Down south, the sprawling mesas and canyons of San Diego's **Balboa Park** blanket the site of an ancient Spanish hacienda. The park's foremost attraction is the world-famous San Diego Zoo. But this is no "one hit wonder" like so many parks. Balboa features at least a dozen museums including collections devoted to natural history, airplanes and outer space, sports and recreation, vintage cars, fine art and local history. There's a puppet theater, a model railroad hall, historic carousel, arts and crafts village and numerous picnic grounds.

Yosemite National Park in the Sierra Nevada mountains has been a family mecca for years. Summer activities include camping, hiking, rock climbing, horseback riding, cycling the bike paths of Yosemite Valley, swimming in Lake Tenaya and inner-tubing down the Merced River. Winter endeavors include downhill and cross-country skiing, snowboarding, snowshoeing and ice skating. Yosemite is the best park in California to spot bears and other wildlife. Badger Pass Ski School offers an excellent children's program.

If your kids are interested in volcanoes, California offers several "hot spots" — **Lassen Volcanic National Park** and **Lava Beds National Monument**. Lassen provides the opportunity to clamber over an active volcano which last blew its top in 1917. Hiking trails lead across lava fields, bubbling mud pots and stinky sulfur pools. Lava Beds features more than 300 "lava tubes" — underground caves that can be explored by foot.

The **Lake Tahoe** area, while not a protected area per se, certainly has the feel of a big American national park with snow-capped mountains, lush evergreen forests, cozy lodges and waterfront cottages. This is one of California's top year-round recreation spots with something for just about every member of the family. Summer fun includes swimming, fishing, boating and waterskiing on the lake; hiking, camping, horseback riding and mountain climbing in the surrounding mountains, and hot-air ballooning and bungee jumping in the lakeside villages. A thick cloak of snow covers the region in winter, as Tahoe transforms itself into California's premier snow sports area with more than a dozen separate ski resorts.

California has several hundred state parks that protect areas of outstanding natural, historical or recreational interest. The largest state preserve is **Anza-Borrego Desert State Park** about two hour's drive east of San Diego, an ideal spot for desert camping and recreation. You can walk among giant redwood trees at more than a dozen state preserves including **Calaveras Big Trees** near

Yosemite, **Prairie Creek** near Eureka, and **Big Basin** in the mountains between San Jose and Santa Cruz.

Relics of the gold rush era are preserved at several locations including **Marshall State Park** in Coloma, the **Empire Mine State Park** near Grass Valley and **Columbia State Park** in Tuolumne County.

MUSEUMS, ZOOS, AND AQUARIUMS

Many museums are not children-friendly, but the people who have put together California's collections seem to have gone out of their way to make them accessible to people of all ages.

Anyone who's into trains will relish the **California State Railroad Museum** in Sacramento, one of the largest collections of its kind, with 21 restored locomotives and carriages and other exhibits related to the building of the trans-continental railroad and the Age of Steam.

The Exploratorium at the Palace of Fine Arts in San Francisco's Marina District is a superb children's museum with more than six hundred "hands on" exhibits related to science, technology and nature. The cavernous venue adds a mystical dimension, like you've

Anza-Borrego Desert State Park is ideal for camping and off-road frolics.

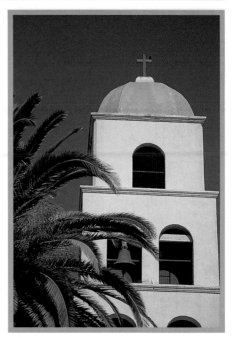

stumbled into some giant cave filled with whirling, whizzing, flashing machines.

Wannabe cowboys and cowgirls will enjoy the **Gene Autry Museum of Western Heritage** in Los Angeles's Griffith Park. Autry was a famous Western film star of bygone days and much of the collection reflects Hollywood's fascination with the Wild West. There's a great exhibit on gunslingers, train robbers and general bad guys. Another room dedicated to silver-studded saddles and other glittering cowboy accessories.

Los Angeles's other great kid's collection is the **George C. Page Museum** on Wilshire Boulevard, which displays real-life bones and

fossils dredged from the adjacent **La Brea Tar Pits**. The pits are post-dinosaur, which means woolly mammoths, giant sloths and cave bears rather than Tyrannosaurus Rex.

San Diego County boasts two different kid's collections with hands-on exhibits: the **Children's Museum** in downtown San Diego, opposite the Convention Center and Seaport Village; and the **Carlsbad Children's Museum** in north county. San Diego's Balboa Park has a number of collections that might interest youngsters including the excellent **Aerospace Museum** with historic planes and space vehicles (the huge jet in front is an authentic United States Air Force Blackbird spy plane) and the **Reuben H. Fleet Space Theater and Science Center** which includes a planetarium, OMNIMAX theater with nature or science films, and many hands-on exhibits related to astronomy, physics and other disciplines.

Sea World aside, the state has two excellent ocean museums. The **Monterey Bay Aquarium** showcases the various creatures that inhabit the coves, bays and beaches of Northern California. The aquarium's centerpiece is a giant glass-fronted tank that replicates one of the underwater kelp forests found off Monterey. The touch pools are a great way to get a close encounter of the creature kind. **Stephen Birch Aquarium** at Scripps Institute of Oceanography in San Diego offers a similar take on Southern California's offshore waters. The jellyfish exhibit is especially intriguing.

The **San Diego Zoo** is arguably the world's single best animal collection. The facility scores points for size (4,000 animals) and assortment (more than 1,000 different species) as well as the artistic methods in which they are presented. San Diego was one of the first zoos to relinquish steel cages in favor spacious, open-air enclosures that reflect the creatures' natural habitats. Hippo Beach and Polar Bear Plunge are two of the newer attractions and the whole primate mesa — gorillas, chimps, orangutans and gibbons — is a marvel of modern zoo architecture. You can explore the zoo by foot, double-decker bus or aerial skyway. The adjacent Children's Zoo features a petting area and baby animals. And don't miss the entertaining and educational sea lion and endangered species shows at the zoo's two outdoor amphitheaters.

Cultural Kicks

California's often ephemeral nature has prompted some critics to scorn its indigenous society as a "fast-food" or "drive-by" culture. Without doubt, there is a fleeting, frivolous quality to much of the "art" produced in the Golden State over the last 50 years, especially the mindless pulp that often pours forth from Hollywood. But those who know California well perceive a much different situation. Behind the billboards and neon signs lies a treasure chest of enduring culture —
YOUR CHOICE

architecture, painting, sculpture, music, theater and dance.

ARCHITECTURE LEGACY
Unlike Arizona and New Mexico where the Native Americans left a wealth of pre-Columbian architecture and artifacts, there isn't much left from the days before the Spanish settled in California. Here and there are a few Indian sights — **Grinding Rock State Park** in Amador County and the petroglyphs of **Chumash Painted Cave** near Santa Barbara. But California's original inhabitants didn't build adobe cities like the Southwest tribes or serpentine mounds like America's Midwestern Indians.

However, the Spanish and their Mexican successors left quite a mark on the state's architectural legacy. The Hispanic period lasted less than 80 years, from 1769 when the first Spanish mission was founded until 1848 when California became part of the Yankee realm. Yet many vestiges of that era remain. The most obvious are the **California missions**, 21 chapels in total, stretching from San Diego in the south to Sonoma in the north. Each of the missions bears a distinctive

OPPOSITE TOP: California's Spanish heritage includes Mission San Antonio de Padua LEFT the Church of the Immaculate Conception in San Diego RIGHT and Carmel Mission ABOVE. OPPOSITE BOTTOM: The brand new Getty Center is Los Angeles' latest architectural landmark.

architectural personality. **Mission San Diego de Alcala** is the oldest and in many respects its simple, sinuous design is still the most eye catching. **Mission Santa Barbara** is often called the "Queen of the Missions" because of its stately brick façade with twin bell towers. Much of **Mission San Juan Capistrano** in Orange County remains in ruins, the victim of several earthquakes, but that seems to add rather than distract from its charm. **La Purisima Mission** in the Santa Ynez Valley seems more like an old Spanish ranch than a place of spiritual refuge. **Mission San Miguel Arcangel** in the Salinas Valley doesn't look like much from the outside. But the interior, especially the sumptuous altar, is one of the great gems of California's Spanish colonial design.

Given the church's dominance of early California, secular architecture was nearly always muted and modest. Several old

Mexican adobes can be found in San Diego's **Old Town** district. Perched on the hillside above is the **Junipero Serra Museum**, housed in a fine reproduction Spanish-style building. Directly in front of the museum, an archeological dig has been underway for many years, uncovering the remains of the eighteenth-century Spanish presidio that once occupied this strategic sight. Although sometimes it's hard to tell through all the tourist kitsch, **Olvera Street** near downtown Los Angeles is all that remains of the tiny pueblo that gave birth to one of the world's largest cities. The oldest building here (indeed the most elderly in Los Angeles) is **Avila Adobe**, constructed in 1818. Founded in 1770, Monterey was the political capital of both Spanish and Mexican California. Many of its most historic buildings — including the **Custom House** and **Cooper-Molera Adobe**, which both date from the 1820s — are

assimilated into the **Monterey State Historic Park**.

Even though Spanish and Mexican rule gave way to American hegemony, and much of the hacienda culture faded away, Mediterranean architecture themes lingered in California well into the twentieth century. Many of the state's most exquisite public buildings were inspired by the adobe designs of the Franciscan friars. **Santa Barbara County Courthouse** (1929) with its horseshoe arches and flamboyant plaster accents is like a Spanish castle dominating the city center. Many of the museums in San Diego's **Balboa Park** are pseudo-Iberian masterpieces built for world exhibition in 1915. Many have been rebuilt or restored including the exquisite Museum of Man with its ornate bell tower and domed roof. The **University of California at Los Angeles** (UCLA) boasts a cluster of wonderful Romanesque-style buildings that

date from the 1920s. But the ultimate expression of the California-Mediterranean style is **Hearst Castle** at San Simeon, a magnificent private home constructed in the 1920s and 1930s by newspaper tycoon William Randolph Hearst. It was later bequeathed to the state and is now open to the public as a museum.

Despite the enduring Spanish influence, the dominant theme of the late nineteenth and early twentieth centuries was Victorian. The original gold rush and other natural resource exploitation fueled a state-wide building frenzy as California's wealthy competed to see who could build the largest and most lavish wooden homes. Despite the 1906 earthquake and fire that destroyed so much of its architecture, **San Francisco** retains more than 14,000 Victorian structures. The most impressive collection is around **Alamo Square**, but neighborhoods like **Haight-Ashbury** and **Pacific Heights** are also well endowed with wooden masterpieces. The coastal towns north of San Francisco, which thrived on timber, are also chock-full of Victoriana. **Eureka** boasts numerous nineteenth-century gems including the ornate Carson House and the outrageous Pink Lady. Although the prize for the largest Victorian house goes to **San Jose** and its massive **Winchester Mystery House** (160 rooms), built over a 38-year span by a woman who thought she would never die if she kept adding rooms to her mansion. Given its relatively late start in the urbanization game, Southern California doesn't have nearly as many Victorian baubles. But there is one superb example: San Diego's **Hotel del Coronado**, one of the state's largest wooden structures and as impressive today as when the first guests arrived in 1888. Other Victoriana hubs include **Sacramento**, **Santa Rosa**, **Ferndale**, **Mendocino** and **Pasadena**.

Neo-classical and Beaux-Arts architecture — big, bold buildings that exuded the might of Western Civilization — also had their impact on late nineteenth-century California. The most stunning example of the former is the **State Capitol Building** (1869) in Sacramento with its soaring rotunda dome and glittering white façade. A great example of the latter is San Francisco's **City Hall** (1881) with its towering green dome and ornate wrought-iron features.

The handsome Botanical Building in San Diego's Balboa Park is the vestige of the city's 1915 world's fair.

The dearth of Victoriana and other nineteenth-century structures in Los Angeles (except for the impressive **Bradbury Building**) shows just how unimportant that city was during the first 70 years of California statehood. It wasn't until the 1920s — and the art deco period — that Los Angeles really came into its own as an architectural showcase. The 27-story **City Hall** (1927) and the nearby **Central Library**, which blend Egyptian and Babylonian motifs, are two of America's best art deco government buildings. **Union Station**, built in the early 1930s, was supposed to reflect the Spanish Mission style. But with its sharp edges and sensuous curves — and the strategically-placed palm trees out front — it expresses much more of an art deco exuberance. **Griffith Park Observatory** (1935), a squat building with multiple green domes, is another art deco gem. A drive down **Wilshire Boulevard** between downtown Los Angeles and Beverly Hills reveals dozens of other classy art deco structures.

California has been at the cutting edge of the post modern and retro movements that have dominated architecture since the 1960s. Los Angeles-based architects like Richard Neutra and Frank Geary are among the modern masters, as celebrated today as Frank Lloyd Wright was a half century ago. Among the state's modern landmarks are the **Transamerica Pyramid Building** in San Francisco, the space-age **LAX Theme Building** and the **Getty Center** in Los Angeles, the **Salk Institute** in La Jolla, and that wonderful arc of blue steel called the **San Diego–Coronado Bridge**.

FINE ART FULCRUM

California isn't considered a museum mecca in the tradition of New York or Paris because its museums aren't huddled together in a single city. But taken as a whole, the combined collections of Los Angeles, San Francisco and San Diego are as impressive — and priceless — as anything you will find elsewhere on the globe. For instance, Los Angeles has more resident Rembrandts (14) than any other city in the world.

The state's premier museum, indeed one of the world's most stunning collections, is the new **Getty Center** in Los Angeles, a glimmering depository of Renaissance skill and Impressionist genius. Funded by the financial legacy of oil tycoon J. Paul Getty, the $1 billion structure perches on a commanding hilltop above the posh homes of Brentwood

and the leafy University of California at Los Angeles campus. It debuted in December 1997 to rave reviews for both its architecture and art. The permanent collections include European masters (Rembrandt, Rubens, Van Gogh, Monet, Mantegna), medieval illuminated manuscripts, decorative arts and twentieth-century photography. The old Getty Museum out in Malibu, situated in a mock Roman villa, is being transformed into one of the world's foremost centers for ancient Greek and Roman studies.

If you can't find works by your favorite artists at the Getty, try the **Norton Simon Museum** in Pasadena. Funded by another California tycoon with a passion for amassing inestimable art, the collection runs the gamut from Old Masters like Rembrandt and Goya to twentieth century stars like Pablo Picasso and Auguste Rodin. Two of the latter's greatest works — *The Thinker* and *The Burghers of Calais* — are on view here. The Simon also boasts the world's single largest hoard of Degas sculpture. Another important collection in the Pasadena area is the **Huntington Library**, which harbors Gainsborough's *Blue Boy* and Lawrence's *Pinkie*, as well as first edition Shakespeare, an original Gutenberg Bible and other priceless books and maps.

The **Los Angeles County Museum of Art** (LACMA) is adjacent to the La Brea Tar Pits, but there's nothing the least bit sticky about the collection: an eclectic ensemble that spans the Asia-Pacific region and then leaps over to Europe. This could be the best assembly of Japanese art outside of Japan. The pre-Columbian ceramics are also remarkable. And let's not forget the Impressionists and Surrealists on display here. California's best post-modern collection is the MOCA — the **Museum of Contemporary Art** in downtown Los Angeles — which features paintings, sculptures, installations and mixed media works by many of the top artists of the last fifty years including Jasper Johns and Mark Rothko. Music industry mogul David Geffen is responsible for a large part of the collection. Yet another Los Angeles collection with strong tycoon connection is the **UCLA Armand Hammer Museum** ((310) 443-7000, 10899 Wilshire Boulevard in Westwood, noted for its riveting and often controversial shows and temporary exhibits.

San Francisco's foremost art collection, and one of the oldest on the West Coast, is the **M.H. de Young Museum** in Golden Gate Park. This expansive building harbors 22 galleries of American art from the seventeenth through the twentieth centuries and is especially strong on American masters like Winslow

The Getty Center is already one of the world's premier art museums.

Homer and John Singer Sargent. Next door is the renowned **Avery Brundage Collection/ Asian Art Museum**, the largest collection in the Western world dedicated exclusively to Asian art. More than 1,000 objects are on display at any one time in changing exhibits from the permanent collections.

The **California Palace of the Legion of Honor** in Lincoln Park was originally a showcase of French art amassed by the Spreckels family. Since its debut in 1915, the museum has grown into a comprehensive array of European art including one of the world's best collections of Rodin sculpture. The **San Francisco Museum of Modern Art** moved into an exciting new space in the city's trendy South of Market district several years ago. The permanent collection includes works by Matisse, Braque, Picasso, de Kooning, Kandinsky, O'Keefe and Ansel Adams.

The **San Diego Museum of Art** in Balboa Park is a surprisingly thorough anthology of global art, housed in a splendid California Spanish building with an intricate stucco façade and adjacent modern wing. The collection is especially strong on Impressionist masters (Van Gogh, Renoir, Degas, Monet), but you'll also find everything from El Greco and Picasso to Indian Mogul miniatures and

priceless Chinese buddhas. San Diego's **Museum of Contemporary Art** (with branches downtown and in La Jolla) is another well-respected institution.

PERFORMING ARTS MECCA

Los Angeles may be leagues ahead when it comes to world-class painting and sculpture, but San Francisco is still the grand dame of California's performing arts scene. San Francisco boasts the state's only functioning opera house and is the only city in California with world-class opera and ballet companies and a major symphony orchestra. The **San Francisco Opera** and the **San Francisco Ballet** perform in the War Memorial Opera House at the Civic Center, a wonderful Beaux-Arts building adjacent to City Hall. The **San Francisco Symphony** performs at the ultra-modern Davies Symphony Hall. For a change of pace, the **American Conservatory Theater** (ACT) stages major dramas and musicals at the Geary Theater.

Los Angeles doesn't lag far behind. The Dorothy Chandler Pavilion at the downtown Music Center is home to the acclaimed **Los Angeles Philharmonic** under the direction of Finnish maestro Esa-Pekka Salonen, as well as the **Los Angeles Opera** and the **Los Angeles Master Chorale**. In summer, the Philharmonic moves up US Highway 101 to a sumptuous outdoor venue called the **Hollywood Bowl**. But Los Angeles' real forte is contemporary American theater — Broadway musicals,

Shopping choices in Los Angeles include the lively Third Street Promenade in Santa Monica OPPOSITE and the ever-glitzy Rodeo Drive in Beverly Hills ABOVE.

comedies and drama. Two of the top venues for big-name mainstream productions are the **Ahmanson Theater** at the Music Center and the **Shubert Theater** at the ABC Entertainment Center in Century City. Other leading drama locals are the Mark Taper Forum at the Music Center, the Doolittle Theater in Hollywood and the Geffen Playhouse in Westwood.

San Diego's specialty is drama. The **Old Globe Theater** in Balboa Park, an exact replica of the wooden playhouse that once stood on the banks of the River Thames in London, is the nation's foremost showcase for Shakespeare. Half a dozen productions are presented each year and many are sold out well in advance. The **La Jolla Playhouse** has a much more contemporary bent, a testing ground for new cutting-edge plays and avant-garde revivals. Many of the productions advance to Broadway fame and fortune, like the mega-hit musical *Rent*, first staged at La Jolla.

Some of California's smaller cities have gained nationwide attention in recent years for the richness of their local arts and culture scene. Eureka, the old timber town and fishing port north of San Francisco, is a good example. The **North Coast Repertory Theater** presents six new productions each year including a Summer Showcase, while the **Eureka Symphony Orchestra** offers a wide range of orchestral music at a variety of local venues. Another splendid regional showcase

is the **Warehouse Repertory Theater** in Fort Bragg which stages everything from Shakespeare to avant-garde contemporary plays. Culture vultures should also be on the lookout for annual events that feature performing arts: the **Bach Festival** in sleepy, seaside Carmel; the **American Musical Summer Festival** in San Francisco; the **Ramona Pageant** at Hemet in Riverside County; and the **Pageant of the Masters** in Laguna Beach.

Shop Till You Drop

Strip malls, souvenir villages, art galleries and crafts exhibits keep dollars flowing in California's consumer-oriented society. Paintings, weavings, sculpture and photography by regional artists can be found in abundance in Laguna, Mendocino, Carmel, La Jolla, Santa Barbara and the Napa Valley. San Francisco's Union Square is known for its excellent department and specialty stores; Fisherman's Wharf, the Embarcadero, Pier 39 and Ghirardelli Square are packed with everything from souvenirs to fine art. Neighborhoods including Castro Street and Haight-Ashbury have an eclectic selection befitting their characters. Los Angeles is home to Rodeo Drive, which rivals Manhattan's Fifth Avenue for the most exclusive boutiques per block. Santa Monica's Promenade and side streets are home to wonderful clothing stores, as is Melrose Avenue. The denizens of Orange County seem to live just to shop, and make frequent jaunts to Southcoast Plaza and Fashion Island, the most elaborate of California malls.

One of the more unique shopping venues is the Public Market in Sacramento, which puts most grocery stores to shame. Farmer's markets are held weekly throughout the state, and offer visitors a chance to mingle with locals, check out the latest produce, and select a bouquet of fresh flowers for their hotel rooms.

Short Breaks

California is ideal for long weekend trips and short holidays. Pick your poison — gastronomy, festivals, cultural kicks, beach trips, sporting sprees, the great outdoors, or simply relaxing in exquisitely restful surroundings — and California is likely to have what it takes to give you a memorable and extraordinary escape from the routine of everyday life.

The most obvious choices are the state's big cities, which offer a wide variety of inducements at every price range. You could literally eat your way across **San Francisco**, sampling the city's numerous gourmet restaurants — Chinese, Japanese, seafood and cutting edge California haute cuisine. Alternatively, you could easily spend two or three days exploring the ever-changing personality of the San Francisco waterfront: pleasure piers and shoreline parks, historic bridges and gun batteries, ferry rides and fresh fish. **Los Angeles** offers a whole different menu. You could go the Hollywood route: Hollywood Boulevard, Mann's Chinese Theater, movie studio tour and shopping Rodeo Drive in Beverly Hills. Or you could get a little bit more funky: a short break that takes in the trendy shops and restaurants of Melrose Avenue and the offbeat lifestyles of Venice Beach. **San Diego** offers both creature comforts (luxury spas, dive golf courses and sublime beaches) and comfortable creatures (Sea World, the Wild Animal Park and the San Diego Zoo).

Speaking of beaches, half a dozen California destinations dish up sun and sand in ample quantities. At the posh end of the seaside spectrum are Orange County enclaves like **Newport Beach** and **Laguna Beach** that sport luxury hotels and gourmet restaurants. The beach towns of Central California — **Santa Cruz**, **Pismo Beach** and **Morro Bay** — are leagues cheaper but no less spectacular.

But the ultimate beach break is **Santa Barbara**, which offers food and accommodation to fit just about any budget.

Wine tasting offers one of the savory choices for a short holiday, especially when combined with gourmet food and comfortable accommodation. The **Napa Valley** is the most obvious choice with its broad range of vineyards and varieties — as well as its Wine Train that chugs the length of the valley. But it's by no means the state's only libation zone. The adjacent **Sonoma Valley** offers a carbon copy of Napa's food and beverage attractions with far fewer people. The **Russian River** region, also in Sonoma County, has its own fine wineries — and water sports too! South of San Francisco, the hills of **Santa Clara County** offer more than a dozen reputable wineries within a short drive of one another. Northern California doesn't have a monopoly on grape cultivation. In recent years several sub-regions of Southern California have come into their own as important wine producers including **Temecula** (about an hour's drive west of downtown Los Angeles) and the **Santa Ynez Valley** north of Santa Barbara.

Nature lovers will be hard pressed to choose between California's many natural and scenic getaways. **Yosemite National Park** is just four hours by car from San Francisco, which makes it perfect for a short trip. However, it's best avoided on summer weekends (between late May and early September) when campgrounds are full and heavy traffic creeps through the valley. The state's other national parks are also ideal for short breaks: **Kings Canyon** and **Sequoia** in the southern Sierras (six hours drive from San Francisco; five hours drive from Los Angeles); **Death Valley** and **Joshua Tree** in the Mojave Desert (five and three hours from downtown

Los Angeles, respectively); **Lassen Volcanic** and **Redwood** in northern California (five and six hours from San Francisco, respectively).

Winter ski weekends have been big in California since the 1960s, when the sport really took off among young people and suburbanites. The state's hottest ski area at the moment is **Mammoth Mountain**, on the eastern flank of the Sierras near Bishop — "hot" in the sense that it's popular with the young and trendy, and also because the volcano that lies beneath Mammoth is starting to show signs of activity. The **Lake Tahoe** region offers more than a dozen ski areas — including world-class resorts like Squaw Valley and Heavenly — which can be combined with the gambling and glitzy entertainment offered by casino hotels on the lake's Nevada side. The slopes are only an hour out of Los Angeles during the winter months, at nearby mountain resorts like **Big Bear** and **Wrightwood**.

You can also construct short breaks around other types of sports. Several areas lend themselves to golf weekends: the **Monterey/ Carmel** area with its famous Pebble Beach course, **San Diego** with its challenging Torrey Pines links, and the palm-fringed fairways of **Palm Springs** and other Coachella Valley resort cities. The desert city of **Indian Wells** and a quaint foothill town called **Ojai** (about halfway between Los Angeles and Santa Barbara) are tennis meccas with famous tournaments and numerous courts.

Those with romantic inclinations (honeymoon or otherwise) have lots of amorous nooks and crannies from which to choose. **Santa Catalina Island**, about an hour by boat south of Long Beach, is like a stretch of the Italian Riviera that's been sliced off and somehow floated onto the cape to California — waterfront cafés, whimsical shops, sub-tropical gardens and hotels that perch precariously on hillsides above the harbor. The **Russian River** region north of San Francisco offers a much different ambiance: dark woods, dashing water, country lodges with stone fireplaces and wood-beamed ceilings. Or you can go the romantic oasis route — the palm-shaded gardens and natural steam-heated pool of Furnace Creek Inn in **Death Valley** or the a Casa del Zorro resort at **Borrego Springs** in San Diego County.

Two of California's most popular weekend getaways are actually across the state line. **Las**

Vegas is just five hours by car and one hour by plane from Los Angeles. You don't have to be a gambler to appreciate this neon-studded metropolis. There's more live entertainment here on any given night — concerts, comedy, circus, musical theater, dance revues, strip shows — than any other city in America. **Baja California** doesn't have much neon, but it's got plenty of other attractions: great seafood, pretty good beaches, bargain shopping, bull fighting and the place where *Titanic* was filmed.

Festive Flings

Californians celebrate an odd assortment of events, many based on agriculture, sports and the sea. The New Year's Day **Tournament of Roses Parade** in Pasadena features floats decorated in riotous displays of flowers depicting cartoon characters, nature scenes

OPPOSITE: Dressed up at the Indio Date Festival. ABOVE and RIGHT: The annual Renaissance Faire in Palm Springs is one of California's many festivals.

Summer Solstice Celebration in Santa Barbara. One of the more unusual events to grace the state annually is the **Festival of Arts and Pageant of the Masters** in Laguna Beach, in July and August. The pageant incorporates local talent in human reproductions of classical and contemporary artwork with music and narration. Laguna's **Sawdust Festival**, held in July and August, is one of the largest arts and crafts shows in the state featuring the work of more than 200 artists. In September, artists congregate at the **Sausalito Art Festival**, featuring more than 225 juried artists and 14,000 works of art.

Californians are naturally interested in films and film making, and several worthwhile film festivals are held annually throughout the state. Among the best known of these festivals is the **Nortel International Film Festival**, held in Palm Springs in January to honor international films and their creators. Santa Barbara hosts the **International Film Festival** each March, with screenings and premiers of American and international films, in addition to workshops and seminars. Also in March is the **Laguna Beach Film Festival**, which showcases more than 15 unreleased and independent films each year. Aficionados of silent films cross the ocean to Avalon on Santa Catalina Island each summer to attend the **Silent Film Benefit**, in which classic silent films are screened at the world-famous Catalina Island Casino. Western film stars gather in late September to promote Western films and art shows at the **Tuolumne County Western Film Festival** in Sonora.

California's varied ethnic communities hold lavish events celebrating traditional holidays. Among the largest are the February **Chinese New Year Festival** in San Francisco, the largest Chinese celebration in the United States. In Los Angeles, the **Golden Dragon Parade** marks the Chinese New Year with a vivid and noisy parade punctuated with fireworks. Santa Barbara celebrates its beginnings with the August **Old Spanish Days Fiesta**, featuring a parade, horse-drawn carriages, Spanish markets and arts and crafts displays. San Francisco's Mexican populace celebrates Mexico's Independence Day beginning September 11 with ¡*Viva Mexico!*, a two-day celebration with traditional music, folk dancing and food. A Mexican Christmas celebration called **Las Posadas and Luminarias** is held in San Diego's Old Town in early December, and features a candlelit procession and Spanish Christmas carols.

and entire cities, followed by the annual Rose Bowl football game. February brings the **National Date Festival** during the Riverside County Fair in Indio. Dates, which grow in abundance here, are blended in milk shakes, coated with sugar for candies and honored with date queens and the like; the fair is a harbinger of all the county fairs to come in spring and summer. March marks the return of the swallows to Capistrano, following the legend that the swallows return to the mission every year on March 19, Saint Joseph's day. **Earth Day** on April 18, is celebrated throughout the state with particular fervor, beginning a series of festivals centered around local agricultural products, including the **Orange Blossom Festivals** in Riverside and Stockton, the **Avocado Festival** in north San Diego County, the **Asparagus Festival** in Stockton, and the **Garlic Festival** in Gilroy, and the September **Artichoke Festival** in Castroville.

County fairs featuring livestock, rodeos, amusement rides and crafts displays hit their peak in May, June and July beginning with the **Calaveras County Fair and Frog Jumping Jubilee** at Angels Camp in May, through the **Sonoma Marin Fair** in Petaluma, the **Marin County Fair** in San Rafael and the **Del Mar Fair** in San Diego. The **California State Fair** held in August in Sacramento tops off the county fair season with a huge event.

Artists, musicians and actors celebrate the longest day of the year on June 20 with the

Several wine regions celebrate their harvests with festivals, the largest of which is the annual June **Napa Valley Wine Auction**, a

lavish three-day event featuring wine tastings, vintners' gala parties, openhouses at local wineries and a live and silent auction of the season's harvest. Smaller celebrations are held throughout the spring in Paso Robles, Lodi, Monterey and Santa Barbara. The **Vintner's Holidays** held in Yosemite National Park in December is one of the finest wine and culinary events in the United States.

All the United States national holidays are celebrated with special fervor as well. Independence Day, July 4, is especially riotous, with parades, fireworks, street fairs and concerts all over the state. For a list of California celebrations contact the **California Division of Tourism** ((916) 322-2881 TOLLFREE (800) 862-2543 FAX (916) 322-3402 WEB SITE gocalif.ca.gov, 801 K Street, Suite 1600, Sacramento, CA 95814.

Galloping Gourmet

California cooks have an abundance of fresh ingredients from agricultural valleys and the sea. They adopt Asian and Latin American herbs and recipes. Some build upon European and East-Coast training, though most can't resist throwing in a new attitude. Pastas are tossed with mussels fresh from the sea or with basil from an organic garden. Whole grain breads are topped with olive oil from the Ojai Valley and sunflower seeds from backyard gourmet gardens. Crisp baby asparagus arrive

in crates from Stockton, yellow tomatoes from the Imperial Valley. California's avocados are shipped world wide, and grow in many a San Diego yard.

Travelers are happy to find an enormous choice of ethnic cuisines in the big cities, including Thai, Japanese, Creole, French, and an abundance of Italian cafés. Mexican cooking predominates, however. Californians buy far more salsa than catsup, and revere the tortilla. Cilantro grows in flowerpots on kitchen windowsills, and beans and rice are the staples in many homes. Any visitor on a budget is sure to eat Mexican food on a regular basis.

Ingredients vary with each region of the state. Catch-of-the-day seafood is available everywhere; ostrich appears on menus around the Ojai Valley. Southern California growers specialize in citrus, avocados and strawberries. In the north, vast acres of irrigated land produce truckloads of tomatoes and grapes. California's wineries and vineyards seem to duplicate their numbers annually, and every part of the state offers winery tours and tastings.

Gourmet California cuisine is fresh, healthy and innovative. Slivered, blanched vegetables accompany fish and meat entrees,

OPPOSITE: Mexican dancers enliven the Cinco de Mayo celebrations in Los Angeles. ABOVE: Lunch in the Cask Room at the Merryvale Winery in Napa Valley.

many prepared with fresh fruit and herb sauces. Sodium, fat and cholesterol are shunned in the trendiest spots, though there has been an upsurge in steakhouses in the 1990s. Chefs like Alice Waters, Wolfgang Puck and Michael Richards inspire popular trends by creating gourmet pizzas with goat cheese and salmon, salads displayed in artful palettes of greens, fish filets seared and coated with wasabi crusts.

There is also a California style of cooking that seems to mainstream distinct flavors into a blend that pleases everyone. Theme restaurants turn into chains with alarming speed; even Stephen Spielberg has several versions of his Dive! concept in Los Angeles and Las Vegas. Planet Hollywood and Hard Rock rely on local celebrities to keep them current. Restaurants designed to evoke the spirits of mystical islands and rainforests were popping up everywhere in the late 1990s. After all, this is the state that produced McDonald's and Jack in the Box.

SNACKS
They may be called *tapas* in Spain or hors d'oeuvres in France. In California, they're called snacks and they're trendy. Wine bars have caught on to serving plump, flavorful olives from Santa Barbara and cheeses from Sonoma. Beer bars have become gourmet breweries serving bratwurst and burgers to soak up the suds. Coffeehouses or espresso huts on seemingly every corner display

croissants, palmiers, biscotti and scones. And there's always frozen yogurt or Haagen Dazs ice cream by the beach.

Tortilla chips, salsa and guacamole are essential accompaniment to parties, sporting events, after-work drinks and most social gatherings. Nachos, a concoction of tortilla chips with melted cheese, are ubiquitous and diverse: they masquerade at ballparks and concerts as cookie-cutter corn chips draped in a plastic-looking layer of processed cheese, or delight as an elegant appetizer of fresh fried blue-corn tortilla chips topped with black beans, crumbled Mexican cotija cheese, slivers of avocado and alfalfa sprouts. Instead of candy bars, health-conscious Californians munch on candied papaya and pineapple, dried figs and dates, walnuts, almonds and trail mix.

FRUITS AND VEGETABLES
Nearly anything that will grow in a tropical climate will also grow somewhere in California. Growers are always experimenting with kiwis, pineapples, bananas, papayas, and macadamia nuts. Citrus fruits, dates and avocados flourish in the state's more arid regions, fed by massive irrigation projects. Orange and lemon trees grow in backyards all over Southern California, feeding the air with the sweet scent of their blossoms. Juicy, thick-skinned navel oranges are among the best, and nothing tops a fresh pink grapefruit from the Coachella Valley. Avocados, which are

piled high in grocery stores and produce marts when in season, should be kept in a brown bag to ripen; when ready, their meat slips away from the skin, soft as butter. Strawberries cover fields and hillocks from San Diego to the Oregon border; those sold at farmer's markets have the sweetest flavor.

Since much of California's produce is grown in the equivalent of agricultural factories, tomatoes, cucumbers and broccoli suffer from too much pumped in water and not enough rich soil. Lettuce, sprouts and spinach, however, have reached gourmet status, and salads made with produce from the best growers are sublime. Artichokes were first planted by Italian immigrants, and today they are the domain of Central California growers. Castroville has the distinction of being the "artichoke capital of the world," and has a festival in honor of the spiny thistle each year. Garlic is king in Gilroy. Dates thrive in the inland deserts, and growers specialize in medjool, deglet, noor and zahidi dates, most of which are exported. The date is celebrated in Indio; date shakes made with milk, yogurt or ice cream are served in towns around Palm Springs.

Vegetarian restaurants, which had their heyday in the 1970s, have flourished and dwindled in popularity, though most towns and cities have at least a few stalwarts. Juice bars are becoming more common, and salad bars will never disappear. Nearly every restaurant worth visiting has at least a few vegetarian selections on the menu, and the finest restaurants offer irresistible non-meat dishes.

SEAFOOD

The Pacific Ocean provides Californians with a wealth of fresh seafood, from lobster and Dungeness crab to fresh swordfish, tuna, halibut, dorado (also called mahi mahi or dolphinfish) and yellowtail. Every coastal town has its commercial and sports anglers, and the rivers of Northern California attract fly fishermen for trout and salmon. This abundance keeps California chefs busy creating new preparations. *Cioppino*, a fish stew enjoyed throughout the world, was actually created during California gold rush days by Italian and Portuguese immigrants. It is a medley of seafood, including crab, shrimp, fish, and mussels, in a base of tomatoes, bell pepper, garlic and herbs, with a splash of wine. North Beach, the Italian district in San Francisco, is the home of this California native. Mexican-style *ceviche*, made with flaked white fish, lime juice, onions, tomatoes, cilantro and jalapeño chilis, is found on many a menu. Fish tacos were imported from Baja California in the 1970s, and now

OPPOSITE LEFT: Nobu Matsuhisa, owner and master chef of Matsuhisa Restaurant in Beverly Hills. RIGHT. Wolfgang Puck's culinary artistry at Spago. ABOVE: Fat City is one of Sacramento's premier eateries.

constitute a favorite among California's ubiquitous Mexican cuisine. Batter fried or grilled fish or shark, along with cabbage, salsa, and a squeeze of lime are traditionally tucked in one or more warm corn tortillas. Superb sashimi, sliced the day the ahi (yellowfin tuna) are caught, is served in Japanese and seafood restaurants.

MEAT

Californians as a rule are not big consumers of red meat, though there has been an upsurge in expensive steak houses featuring prime cuts. Tri Tip Steak is a regional specialty in the Central Coast, where residents grill this triangular cut usually reserved for stew. Chicken is ubiquitous, barbecued, baked, roasted, fried, and grilled. Chicken tops new-wave Caesar salads, is shredded and rolled in tortillas for burritos, and coated with sesame seeds for sesame chicken. Ostrich, billed as the new red meat, is served in some spa and gourmet restaurants. Pork and beef ribs coated in spicy barbecue sauce are still a staple at summer picnics.

SAUCES

Salsas are sauces based on Mexican recipes and are used for flavoring food or eating as a dip. Salsas come in endless variety, from fresh chopped tomatoes, chiles, onion and cilantro to those made of smoked chiles and cooked tomatoes (green or red). They range from fiery hot to surprisingly mild, and all but the most timid of palates should try them.

Olive trees were planted along with grapes around many of California's missions in the 1700s; California olive oil has reached boutique status in the 1990s. Manzanillo, sevillano, mission, picholine and frantoio olives are grown throughout the state and in Baja; the best oils are sold in gourmet groceries and wine shops.

CHEESES

Cheesemaking was introduced in mission days by Father Junipero Serra, and diversified by European immigrants who came with their own favorite cheeses and recipes. The first successful commercial venture was in 1857, when California transplant Clarissa Steele made Cheddar-style cheese from her native New England. Today, more than 70 varieties of cheese are produced in the state — everything from soft (ricotta, cream cheese, and Mexican requesón) and ripe cheeses (brie, camembert, and teleme) to semi-hards (such as cheddar, Edam, Monterey Jack and feta) and hard and very hard cheeses (parmesan and romano, for example). California is the nation's leading dairy state, and in addition to the large, industrial-size ventures, family-run businesses contribute to the wide variety and high quality of California cheeses.

BREADS AND GRAINS

Sourdough bread has been associated with San Francisco since Isadore Boudin opened his bakery in the Italian district of North

Beach during gold rush days. Although most credit its special flavor to a specific yeast, others insist it is a phenomenon specific to San Francisco alone. Whole grain breads are common everywhere. California chefs use rice and pasta as a staple accompaniment to entrees; polenta, risotto, couscous and tabbouleh are common.

DESSERTS AND SWEETS
Ice cream is probably the number-one dessert throughout the state; each region has its favorite gourmet brands and small Mom-and-Pop ice cream makers. Frozen yogurt runs a close second, and gelato is often served in coffeehouses. Strawberry shortcake and strawberry pie topped with whipped cream is irresistible in the spring.

WINE, BEER, AND LIQUOR
Over 400 wineries dot the hillsides in the Sonoma and Napa valleys, the leading wine-producing areas in the state. Vineyards and wineries also thrive around Mendocino, Santa Barbara and San Diego. California's best Chardonnay, Pinot Noir, Merlot and Cabernet Sauvignon vintages rival their French competitors. Chardonnay is the most widely planted grape in the state; the resulting wines are known for their apple and pear flavors. Sauvignon Blanc grapes were introduced to California in the 1800s, and grow by the northern coast. The trendy craving for Merlot has created a passion among growers for this fruity, spicy grape, and Merlots run second only to Cabernet Sauvignons as the most popular California reds. Zinfandel is the only California grape varietal grown exclusively in the United States; pink Zinfandels are best savored when young and are rather sweet. Grapes more common in Italy are appearing on California hillsides, and vintners are even producing interesting Pinot Noirs from grapes grown in the north valleys. Winery tours are available in all the vineyard regions. Some of the best labels to try are Kenwood, Sebastiani, Mondavi, Beringer and Rutherford. Domain Chandon is the leading producer of *méthode champenoise* sparkling wine.

Imported beers are all the rage in shops and restaurants. Mexico has some excellent beers, both dark (try Negra Modelo, Bohemia, or Dos Equis Oscuro) and light (Corona, Pacifica, Sol). Tecate, which is brewed just across the inland California border at the small town of Tecate, is considered the workingman's beer (the Budweiser of Mexican beers), and was the first beer to be served with lime wedges, possibly to offset the metallic taste to which canned beer is prone.
YOUR CHOICE

Microbreweries hit their peak in the early 1990s; every city has a few local brews, though most of the favorites come from Oregon.

Hard liquors are not very popular here, except when mixed in tropical concoctions. The Margarita, a mix of tequila, lime and cointreau or triple sec served blended into a slush or shaken and poured over the rocks, is the most popular mixed drink. Fruit-flavored Margaritas, blended with strawberries, mangoes, or bananas are served in most tourist-oriented Mexican restaurants and can be ordered "virgin" (without the liquor). Fruit and rum drinks — piña coladas, daiquiris, and other concoctions — are all the rage by swimming pools.

DRINKS
Imported bottled water has replaced liquor among the health-conscious set; instead of stacking up beer cans in their dens, Californians line blue and green water bottles on their windowsills. Fresh lemonade is sold at stands at parks and beaches, and fresh juices are common everywhere. Flavored teas are sold by the bottle and rival soda as the most refreshing drink. Hot tea is often made from herbal blends — those accustomed to strong black tea should request it by name. Coffee is all the rage in coffeehouses and cafés; you can feel somewhat out of the loop if

OPPOSITE: Domaine Carneros is one of hundreds of California vintners. ABOVE: Cask room at Napa's Cakebread Winery.

you order a simple cup of black coffee sans foamed milk, flavorings or cream. Most coffee drinks — lattes, cappuccinos and the like — can be ordered low-calorie and decaffeinated. Brewed decaffeinated coffee is available in most restaurants.

ETHNIC FOOD

Mexican tacos, enchiladas and burritos are as common as hamburgers and hot dogs throughout the state. Until recently, most Mexican restaurants served toned-down versions of Mexican recipes tempered to suit American palates. Californians created their own pseudo-Mexican dishes, often elaborating on simple recipes in their quest to make everything "bigger and better." But there has been a recent upsurge in gourmet Mexican restaurants serving excellent renditions of regional favorites, and bars now feature "sipping" tequilas as smooth as any brandy. There are too many Mexican favorites to mention: most are built around fresh tomatoes, onions, lemon, cilantro, chiles and meat or fish. Most meals are served with corn or flour tortillas, rice, beans, and of course, salsa.

Chinese, Japanese, Thai, Vietnamese and Korean districts are found in all major California cities, not to mention smaller populations of other Asian ethnic groups. All have brought a diversity of flavors and traditions to the eclectic cuisine of California. Although even the tiniest of towns has its Chinese (usually Cantonese) restaurant, larger cities such as Los Angeles and San Francisco have ethnic neighborhoods where Korean, Japanese, Vietnamese and Chinese immigrants have congregated, and these offer some of the most intense and interesting dining experiences. Thai restaurants are also popular, serving some delicious, often fiery hot, dishes flavored with cilantro, lime, ginger, and red peppers.

Special Interests

ARCHITECTURE

California's architecture spans the gamut from the early adobe missions in Southern California to the newest attraction, the Richard Meier designed Getty Museum in Los Angeles. Those interested in early California architecture find a wealth of Spanish-Mexican-Californian buildings from the late eighteenth and early nineteenth centuries in San Diego's Balboa Park, Old Town and missions, as well as in Santa Barbara's State Street area. The city of

Pasadena is one of the best places to study the California Craftsman style; the Pasadena Showcase House of Design is open through much of May and typically features one of the classic Pasadena homes. Los Angeles' neighborhoods are studies in several genres, from the Spanish-style domes and tiled roofs of Union Station to the modernistic mansions in Brentwood, West Hollywood and Malibu.

GARDENS

Though much of California consists of deserts, arid canyons and mountains, flowers accustomed to tropical and temperate climets bloom in abundance. Southern California gardens benefit from plenty of sunshine with enough rain to encourage growth; palms, birds of paradise, cactus and succulents flourish side by side. Some of the best gardens open for touring include the Botanical Gardens and lily pond in San Diego's Balboa Park, the Living Desert exhibit of cacti and wildflowers in Palm Springs, and the Huntington Gardens in Pasadena, the Wrigley Memorial and Botanical Garden on Catalina Island.

San Francisco celebrates spring with a Tulipmania Festival in March on Pier 39, featuring the largest display of tulips in the United States. Rhododendrons and fuschias flourish in the cool mists in northern California, especially in Mendocino, Ferndale and Fort Bragg.

Taking a Tour

Guided tours of California tend to specialize in certain themes or regions, though some large companies span the state with general interest tours. Some of the airlines, such as United and Southwest, and hotel chains, such as Sheraton, offer tours through their travel services departments. Below are some further resources for tours throughout the state.

ADVENTURE

American Wilderness Experience, Inc. ((303) 444-2622 TOLL-FREE (800) 444-0099, 2820-A Wilderness Place, Boulder, CO 80301-5454, offers Sierra pack trips of 3 to 12 days; walking and biking inn-to-inn trips in Redwood country and Central California; and, in Baja California Norte, horseback and fishing trips to Sierra San Pedro Martir, and cattle drives at the Meling Ranch.

Mariah Wilderness Expeditions ((510) 233-2303 TOLL-FREE (800) 462-7424 FAX (510) 233-0956, E-MAIL rafting@mariahwe.com

WEB SITE www.mariahwe.com, PO Box 70248, Point Richmond, CA 94807, offers whitewater rafting trips on the American and Merced rivers between April and September.

Mountain Travel Sobek ((510) 527-8100 TOLL-FREE (888) 687-6235 FAX (510) 525-7710 E-MAIL info@mtsobek.com WEB SITE www.mtsobek.com, 6420 Fairmount Avenue, El Cerrito, CA 94530, offers seven-day kayak tours to Baja California to see the gray whales.

REI TOLL-FREE (800) 622-2236 FAX (206) 395-4744 E-MAIL travel@rei.com WEB SITE www.rei.com/travel, 6750 South 228th Street, Kent, WA 98032, organizes biking in Death Valley, backpacking the John Muir trail, or climbing Mount Shasta.

COACH TOURS

The following companies organize coach tours: **Australian Pacific Tours** TOLL-FREE (800) 290-8687 FAX (818) 755-6396 WEB SITE www.atie.com.au/tours/auspac.html, 4605 Lankershim Boulevard, Suite 620, North Hollywood, CA 91602; for 18- to 35-year-olds, **Contiki Holidays** TOLL-FREE (800) CONTIKI FAX (714) 740-0818 WEB SITE www.contiki.com, 300 Plaza Alicante, Suite 900, Garden Grove, CA 92840; **Collette Tours** TOLL-FREE (800) 832-4656 FAX (401) 727-1000 WEB SITE www.collettetours.com, 162 Middle Street, Pawtucket, RI 02860; and **Mayflower Tours** TOLL-FREE (800) 323-7604 FAX (630) 960-3575 WEB SITE www.travelfile.com/

get?mayflowertrs, 1225 Warren Avenue, Box 490, Downers Grove, IL 60515.

BOAT TOURS

For an inland cruise of California's central waterways, contact **Clipper Cruises** TOLL-FREE (800) 325-0010 WEB SITE www.clippercruise.com, 7711 Bonhomme Avenue, Saint Louis, MO 63105.

ALTERNATIVE

Green Tortoise Adventure Travel ((415) 956-7500 TOLL-FREE (800) TORTOISE WEB SITE www.greentortoise.com, 494 Broadway, San Francisco, CA 94133, offers low-budget, camping-oriented tours. Riders pay a group grocery charge and assist in cooking meals and cleaning up. One tour travels from San Francisco to Bahia Concepcion, in Baja California; others explore Northern California or Yosemite.

Heritage Park in San Diego's historic Old Town flaunts a wealth of Victorian homes.

California:
Myths
and
Realities

FANTASIES FULFILLED

Once upon a time, people dreamed of finding a fabulous island called California. It was "on the right hand of the Indies" and "very near to the Terrestrial Paradise." This fabulous island was ruled by black Amazons "and their arms were full of gold."

A fictional account of such a place was published in Spain in 1510 as *The Exploits of Esplandiandon* (Sergas de Esplandian). It was the kind of heroic adventure Cervantes would later satirize with his *Don Quixote*. But the real adventurers Spain sent to explore the New World obviously believed there was such a place. In the 1530s, an expedition sent by Cortez thought they'd found it in the long gnarled peninsula of Baja California. They found no warrior queens and they found no gold, but for more than 200 years, the Spaniards continued to believe they'd found the mythical island. Then in 1746, an exploring padre discovered the mouth of the Colorado River, and proved that California was attached to the mainland.

But the name, California, stuck, not just for the peninsula but for 800 miles (1,290 km) of Spanish territory north of what is now the Mexican border. It is fitting that California began as a fantasy island, because in many ways that is what it has remained. And, maybe, it is also important that the myth cut across the racial and sexual barriers of the time. But — most important — was the promise of gold — more than 300 years before any real gold was discovered in California.

Cortez made his first expedition to Baja in 1533. Several attempts to establish a settlement on the peninsula failed until Jesuits founded a mission at Loreto in 1697. The native population presented a unique challenge to the missionaries. They were the most primitive people ever encountered by European explorers in the Americas. They had only the crudest of weapons, built no kind of shelter, wore no clothes except for a tiny apron on the women, and would eat anything including the boots of their conquerors. Their only sense of time was the annual fruiting season of the *pitahaya* cactus when they would gorge themselves on the refreshing red-fleshed fruit. Having no words for shame, love, vice or virtue, they could make no sense of the missionaries' talk of morality.

The Jesuits responded in kind. One wrote back to Spain that the natives were "stupid, awkward, rude, unclean, insolent, ungrateful, mendacious, thievish… They are an unreflecting people… who possess no self-control but follow, like animals in every respect, their natural instincts."

The Jesuits would found 20 missions in Baja in 70 years, but their attempts to convert the Indians to Christianity did not succeed. The Indians were brutally put down in uprisings in 1734 and

1736; most of those who survived later died of diseases brought by the Spanish. By the time the Franciscans arrived in 1768, to take up the mission vacated by the Jesuits (who were earlier expelled), the native population had dropped from 40,000 to 7,000. The Franciscans would establish only one more mission in Baja, before moving on to more fertile territories in upper California. (In 1804, the Spanish divided California into Baja and Alta, lower and upper, with the boundary near present-day Rosarito Beach, 20 miles (32 km) south of the current international boundary, which was set at the end of the Mexican War in 1849.

FATHER SERRA

His name adorns everything from streets, museums, and libraries, to taco shops, car washes, and real estate companies. In the United States Capitol he is one of the two most honored men from California, standing in Statuary Hall.

In September of 1988, Father Serra moved a step closer to sainthood when he was beatified in an elaborate three-hour ceremony in Rome. To mark the event, vandals in San Diego splashed blood-red paint on Serra's statue and scrawled "Genocidal Maniac" on the walls of the Serra Museum. Some 200-odd years after the little padre's death, his "good works" are still a subject of controversy — and he still lacks the two miracles needed to be canonized.

Pope John Paul II was expected to announce Serra's beatification during his 1987 visit to California, but he chose to avoid the controversy. He merely visited Serra's grave, and said nothing about sainthood. The reasons are perhaps as personal as they are political. For in the life of Junipero Serra, there was much that in the harsh light of modern psychiatry would be regarded as bizarre. Born on the island of Mallorca, Serra could barely see over the lectern when he began studying for the priesthood. Taking the name of Saint Francis' best pal and traveling companion, Junipero (pronounced: hoo-NEE-perro), he followed the example of another missionary who became a saint by converting the heathen Indians in South America.

His was a classic case of one who enjoyed poor health; a few days after he landed in Mexico, he refused to treat an infected insect bite on his foot and was lame for the rest of his life. He would insist on walking when he could ride. Serra's own best friend and biographer, Francisco Palou, described "the severe pains he experienced in his chest, which doubtless were occasioned by striking it with a stone during the acts of contrition he

OPPOSITE: The Mammoth Lakes area in the High Sierras has become one of California's most popular winter and summer resorts.

made at the end of his sermons, also by putting against his bare chest a lighted torch, in imitation of Saint John Capistrano, because in putting it out he used to tear out a piece of skin… ." Palou also tells of Serra inspiring others to similar self-abuse: "During one of his sermons—in imitation of Saint Francis Solanus, to whom he was devoted — he took out a chain, and after lowering his habit so as to uncover his back, having exhorted his hearers to penance, he began to scourge himself so violently that the entire congregation broke into tears. Thereupon, a man from the congregation arose and hurriedly went to the pulpit, took the chain from the penitential Father, descended from the pulpit and went and stood in the highest part of

While many of the Jesuits regarded the Indians as animals without souls, the Franciscans, at least, saw them as human beings, who could be saved from the devil by accepting Christianity.

A more recent Franciscan biographer of Serra, Omer Englebert, praised Serra's missions in California as a uniquely successful "Christian republic of the communal type." In the peak year of 1828, the California missions had 252,000 head of cattle, 268,000 sheep, 3,500 mules, 34,000 horses, 8,300 goats, and 3,400 pigs—all in an area where horses and livestock had never been seen before the Spanish arrived. The missions also introduced the experimental agriculture that would eventually bring more money into the state than the gold

the sanctuary. Imitating the venerable preacher, he uncovered himself to the waist and began to perform public penance, saying amid tears and sobs: 'I AM the sinner who is ungrateful to God, who ought to do penance for my many sins — and not the father who is a saint.' So violent and merciless were the strokes, that, before the whole congregation, he fell to the floor, they judging him dead. After he received the Last Sacraments where he fell, he died. Concerning this soul we may piously believe that he is enjoying God."

These were among the stories Palou put forward in his 100,000-word biography of Serra published just two years after his death. No mere biography, it was Palou's case for declaring Serra a saint. When the Pope finally responded 204 years later, he, of course, made no mention of Serra's bizarre life-style, focusing instead (as Californians always have) on his work among the Indians.

discoveries. One impressed visitor was moved to say he'd finally discovered a country without poor people. Another said, "You would never imagine what orange trees, olive trees, vines and fruit trees of all kinds are growing… Looking at these mills, these workshops, these machines, these roads, these bridges, these canals, and all these well-constructed buildings, how can one believe that it is the natives… who have done it."

But the title Englebert chose for his Serra biography is perhaps more telling than the text: Last of the Conquistadors. In fact, the lame padre was the omnipotent ruler of his own little Indian kingdom. There seems to have been no precise plan for what he did. But in California, there were no existing towns or cities as there had been in Mexico. So, Serra was able to build his little nation at will. There was no private property and the missionary rule was absolute. Until they were converted, the Indians were regarded as savages possessed by the devil, "the enemy." After conversion, they were subjected to near-slave conditions as forced laborers in the mission shops and fields. If they tried to escape, they were chased down and brutally punished. Although Serra claimed to be holding the land in trust for the Indians, no such legal provisions were ever put in writing. At his death, at the headquarters mission in Carmel in 1784, there were nine missions in operation; 12 more would be built by friars carrying on essentially what Serra started.

THE END OF THE MISSIONS

When an independent Mexican government seized the mission lands and ordered the padres back to Europe in 1833, the Indians were left with no religion and no title to the land. As Englebert observed: "they vanished, to rejoin other savages and become savage once more with them." Without the Indians, however, the Mexican dons were never able to succeed as the missionaries had in utilizing the vast tracts of land for agriculture and raising livestock. This period of Mexican California was later romanticized, but it was, in fact, a short-lived failure, not helped by the continuing political turmoil back in Mexico itself.

At the time of its independence in 1821, Mexican territory extended into what is now the United States from Louisiana to Oregon. Settlers from the United States and Europe soon began moving into Texas and California. The Donner Party of 87 settlers from Illinois were on their way to Mexican California in 1846, when they took a wrong — and late — turn and got stranded in the deep snows of the High Sierras. Only 47 survived the brutal winter, some of them by resorting to cannibalism and murder.

The Donners were on their way to a settlement founded by a Swiss immigrant named John Sutter. He wanted the area where Sacramento is now located to be called New Helvetia, but everybody called it "Sutter's Fort" and the name stuck. After failing in business in Germany, Sutter had made his way to California, became a Mexican citizen, and was given the largest land grant allowed, 11 leagues or 48,400 acres (19,600 hectares).

Sutter was but one of the "Yankee dons" who helped the Mexicans divvy up the huge acreage left vacant by the padres. Their names have endured even if they were not all that successful. A decidedly non-Catholic — if not outright irreligious — population would thus find its major towns and bays named for the saints and the sacraments. The pragmatic Americans simply adopted these existing names as geographical names — San Francisco was thus named for the bay, Sacramento for the river.

The Yankees were quick to adopt the lifestyle of the Mexican dons even as they were writing

home disdaining it. Horse racing and gambling became major preoccupations and endured as the chief pastimes of the Californians. Mexico found, as Spain had previously, that her reach exceeded her grasp; she had more territory than she could possibly defend. In fact, the Americans marched into Monterey and what is now San Francisco and took over without firing a shot. The design of the state flag still in use was taken from that of the "Bear Flag Revolt," a confused month in history when a handful of Americans announced the creation of the Republic of California. An actual declaration of war with Mexico rendered the republic null and void, and most of its "officials" joined the fight. In truth, there weren't that many people

in California to wage much of a war, and there were no battles comparable to the Alamo and San Jacinto in Texas.

STATEHOOD AND THE GOLD RUSH

In the little Mexican town of Guadalupe Hidalgo, the treaty ending the war was signed on February 2, 1848. The United States agreed to pay $15 million to Mexico, and was granted almost half of that country's territory — comprising the current states of California, Nevada, Utah, New Mexico, Arizona, and parts of Wyoming and Colorado.

OPPOSITE: California's impressive State Capitol in Sacramento. ABOVE: The Mission at Carmel was the mother church of all California missions and remains an important Catholic shrine as the burial place of Father Serra.

The date of that treaty reflects a bitter irony in history. The Spanish and then the Mexicans had surely come for gold, or they wouldn't have called the place California. But at the time of occupation, no gold was found — until nine days before the treaty turned over the land to the United States.

On January 24, 1848, James Marshall was working at a new saw mill for John Sutter when he found what he thought was a gold nugget. It proved to be real gold, and the rush was on. Everybody stopped working and began panning for gold. It was a "gold mine" in another sense. Those worried about getting people to make the hazardous trek to California soon found thousands pouring in from throughout the world. Califor-

got there. The overland journey was technically possible in three months, but it would often take two and three times that long. "If there is a California," one man wrote back, "I don't think we will ever see it." There were scorching deserts and impossible mountain walls they hadn't planned for.

And, as if the trip itself weren't bad enough, life in the gold rush country in the rolling hills around Sacramento was often rougher. Conditions were unsanitary, at best, and people died every day from dysentery, cholera, and "the fevers" yet unnamed. "Little did I think that the first digging I did would be digging a grave," one would-be miner wrote.

nia had a non-Indian population of 6,000 in 1840; more than 100,000 in 1850; and 379,994 by 1860. Most of the new territories went through a probationary period, but California was admitted with full privileges as a state in 1850.

The first promoters of California had written back East that the gold was just lying there for the taking — with no mention of the incredible hardships people went through to get there. Those who could afford it went by ship from New York or Charleston down the Atlantic to the Isthmus of Panama, across land to another ship, and up the Pacific coast to San Francisco, the newly-created village that was an overnight boom town.

For every one that made it, there were hundreds who didn't. One who made it described a boat taking settlers from Saint Louis upriver to Independence for the trek west; all but one of the 101 passengers died of cholera before they

In fact, a great deal of gold was mined. According to historian James D. Hart, about $245,301 worth of gold was mined in 1848; $10,151,360 in 1849. The figure would rise to $81,294,700 in the peak year of 1852 then taper off to $17 million in 1865.

Oddly, the major fortunes made at the time were not the miners' but those of the various businessmen who sold — at ridiculously inflated prices — to the miners. San Francisco's "Big Four" all started out as merchants in Sacramento. They were soon functioning as banks, and in possession of much of the gold themselves. That led to their interests in dozens of other businesses, most notably, the first transcontinental railroads.

As for James Marshall and John Sutter, they both ended up badly. Not long after he died, Marshall was memorialized by a statue that had cost $10,000, a sum that surely represented more than what he had ever made in a lifetime. For a brief time, he went about making speeches and was on a pension from the state. But, when he showed up drunk at the state Capitol to beg for more, he lost even the pitiful sum he had been getting. He died a pauper; ironically, even the little nugget he found that started the gold rush has come down in history as the "Wimmer nugget," from one of Marshall's co-workers. Sutter started out richer, but fared no better. For decades, he fought to retain his title to the lands the Mexican government had granted him. He had to deal with squatters on the one hand, and the Unites States government legally seizing his property on the other. Late in life, he moved back East to be near

Washington to press his cause with Congress for restitution of his land, and payment for his contribution to the great gold rush. He never got his gold or his reward and in 1880, at age 77, John Sutter, too, died impoverished.

THE RAILROAD BOOM

With the gathering clouds of civil war in the East, California was just about the best place to be during a war: 3,000 miles (5,000 km) away from it. However, the gold from California played a vital role in the Union cause, and there was a ready market for any and all of its products. The speeded-up war productions also hastened the advances in railroad technology that would allow construction to begin on a transcontinental railroad. Incorporated by the Big Four former hardware store owners in 1869, the Central Pacific Railroad began construction in Sac-

ramento in 1863; the last spike was driven on May 10, 1869 at Promontory, Utah. The same owners (of what was by then called The Octopus) acquired the Southern Pacific Railroad in 1868 and a virtual monopoly on rail traffic to California.

The railroads opened up California to settlers from the East as never before. They also made the great markets of the East accessible to California produce and livestock. Southern California had been a virtual wasteland before this; Los Angeles had a population of only 4,385 in 1860 and only 5,728 in 1870. But with the coming of the Southern Pacific, southern California drew the attention of speculators and developers of all kinds.

The arrival of a competing railroad, the Santa Fe, in 1887, assured Los Angeles's future. In spite of a recent period of boom and bust, when the population went from 10,000 to 50,000 and quickly back to 25,000, the wealthy railroad owners now had a vested interest in promoting the city. Hollywood, Pasadena, and a number of new developments were laid out in the vast open spaces surrounding the original Pueblo de los Angeles. The shift in population would begin slowly, but Southern California would set out on a period of growth that has continued to this day.

Once city officials had mastered the water problem—by diverting the Owens River from the Owens Valley in the High Sierras to Los Angeles — the developers would take off full speed and never stop. After the railroads made it easier for people to get to California, and for Californians to ship their products out, other developments speeded life along.

Oil was discovered in Los Angeles and created a big new industry. Then automobiles arrived and not long after, the motion picture.

Los Angeles has been called the first city of the automobile. It really never was a city in the usual sense, with a central core and everything spreading outward. Parts of the city were separated by distances of 40 and 50 miles (65 and 80 km). But the automobile made such a city possible. It also made much more of California accessible to its citizens. A whole culture centered on the automobile grew out of California and spread. The first use of the word "motel" for what had been a "motor court" took place in California. "Drive-in everything" became a way of life in California and the rest of America. It included Maurice and Richard McDonald's original hamburger drive-ins in San Bernardino — and reached a climax with the construction of the 12-story-tall Crystal Cathedral, an enormous glass-and-steel church which opens out to a huge parking lot where people can worship in their cars.

OPPOSITE: The restored buildings in Sacramento's Old Town recall the wild days when the city was at the heart of Gold Rush Country. You won't find these grand old Santa Fe Railway engines anywhere but in the museums, such as this one ABOVE in Old Town, Sacramento.

THE MOVIES

If the railroads made California easier to get to, and the automobile made it easier to get around it, it was the movies that put Hollywood — and California in general — at the center of popular culture in the world. On screen were fantasy flights to every place in the world and beyond, but people knew that the real settings were in California. Not just the sets, but also the people. In movies, and later, television, California's history became everybody's history. The world knew about the Mexican period through *Zorro* and *Ramona*, the 1870s near Stockton through *The Big Valley*, and the 1880s and 1890s in Death Valley through *Death Valley Days*. Would people ever believe that actor Ronald Reagan was anything but the honest, trusting fellow he'd played in the *Death Valley* series? Would he ever have been elected president without that trust?

In 1988 there arose a typically irrelevant controversy in Los Angeles over construction of a "Gateway to the West," some kind of monument that would match New York's Statue of Liberty. The competition that ensued among architects ignored the fact that an impressive gateway to the West already exists. It's called The Golden Gate Bridge and it's in San Francisco. And who in the world can ignore the magnificent symbol of Los Angeles — the Hollywood sign, high up on the mountains overlooking Hollywood and the city. Erected in 1923, the full sign read "Hollywoodland" (for a new development of that name) until 1949. The letters, made of white sheet metal are 50 ft (15 m) high and 30 ft (9 m) wide. For many years the letters peeled and sagged in ruin; but the sign was restored in 1978, and refurbished again in time for the 1984 Olympics.

While depicting the history and culture of the rest of the world, Hollywood was also creating legends of its own. And not surprisingly, it soon depicted those, too, in film. *Sunset Boulevard* and *A Star Is Born* are just two in that genre. Several famous authors began writing for the movies and some, like F. Scott Fitzgerald in *The Last Tycoon*, wrote about what they saw in movietown. Budd Schulberg's *What Makes Sammy Run?* drew on his first-hand knowledge of Hollywood. His father came out with the first wave of moviemakers and Schulberg grew to become one of the best screenwriters in the business. His book, *Moving Pictures: Memories of a Hollywood Prince*, combines his father's memoirs with his own for one of the best insider histories of the movie business.

Aside from providing new material for the movies, World War I also speeded up the development of a new industry in California. The air-

plane was still being tested before the war — and where better to experiment than in an area where it's usually warm and never rains. Douglas, Lockheed, and Northrop are just three of the giant aerospace corporations that grew out of small experimental airplane factories in the Los Angeles area.

The government turned out to be another client. It needed space to train its new legions of military recruits, and California had deserts, mountains, seashore; just about any terrain they might ever fight on. Huge areas of the state were transformed into military camps and training grounds. Edwards Air Force Base grew out of one of the most adventurous military training programs in the Mojave Desert, and that is where the latest space shuttle flights land today.

During the period between the wars, California suffered, along with the rest of the world, in the Great Depression. But the state also prospered as did few other places in America. It was still where everybody wanted to live; if you couldn't be rich, you could at least be warm. Some extraordinary public works projects, including the Golden Gate and Bay Bridges in San Francisco, highways, bridges, tunnels and dams throughout the state, were completed during this period. And there were expositions in San Francisco and San Diego to celebrate the recovery.

As had happened many times in the past, there was also a nasty selfish turn to this prosperity. When thousands had sought refuge in California, especially the "Okies" from the dustbowl of Oklahoma, the state tried to legally block them at the state line as if they were from another country. The "agricultural checkpoints" that still exist on the California borders are a carry-over from that effort to stem emigration in the 1930s. Woody Guthrie, the great balladeer of that period in America, was among those looking for a new life in California. And he sang bitterly of this "Garden of Eden...but believe it or not, you won't find it so hot, if you ain't got the do re mi..."

If California was considered important in World War I, it was vital to the Americans fighting in the Pacific during World War II. The fledgling airplane industry passed from the experimental stage and become one of the state's major industries. From the first basic developments in flight to the most far-reaching plans for "Star Wars," California scientists have been involved, and California corporations have reaped the rewards. It was Edward Teller who first suggested Star Wars to fellow Californian Ronald Reagan, and it was, naturally, the University of California's Lawrence Livermore Laboratory, run by Teller, which got the first major multi-billion-dollar contracts to build this science-fiction shield against nuclear weapons. At stores in the town of Livermore, once the center of vast vineyards and orchards, you can now buy T-shirts with the slogan, "Better a Shield than a Sword," which is also the title of Teller's last book.

The tumultuous decade of the 1960s actually began in the 1950s in California. The beatnik poets and writers found it an open and tolerant place for their free expression and easy lifestyles. There was long hair and free love in San Francisco long before they became the norm in the rest of America.

During the 1960s, California became a center for radical changes taking place in American society. Starting with the free speech movement at Berkeley, the later movement for "Peace and love and pass it on" sprang naturally from the sunshine and good times the young people knew best in California. And, typically American, for every progressive change, there was a reactionary step backward. If many of the liberal changes of the 1960s had their start in California, so did the reaction that later took over the country.

There is no understanding or even explaining California politics any more than there is an easy explanation of its people. California's governor, Earl Warren, was named as a conservative Chief Justice of the United States Supreme Court only to become the court's most noted liberal. Liberal Governor Edmund G. ("Pat") Brown was succeeded by the conservative Ronald Reagan who, in turn, was succeeded by Brown's liberal son, Jerry.

When Reagan was governor, he and his wife Nancy moved out of the old Victorian house in Sacramento that had traditionally been the governor's mansion, calling it a "firetrap." At their insistence, an elaborate modern mansion was built for the governor, but it was not completed until Reagan's term expired. The Reagans had been fashion-conscious society people, who loved the good life. Succeeding him was Jerry Brown, an ascetic bachelor who had once studied for the Catholic priesthood and followed Zen Buddhism. He chose to live in a simple rented room while the new mansion sat vacant until it was eventually sold.

As always, Californians have proved amazingly adaptable to political changes — even managing to be at the center of these changes. Jerry Brown had been at the center of 1960s activism, rekindled in his 1992 presidential candidacy; Ronald Reagan emerged on a national level, as the symbol of the return to conservatism. As president, Richard Nixon tried to establish a "western White House" at San Clemente but scandal soon clouded everything he did. Nixon never seemed that attached to California; he vacationed in various other places during his term as President. The Reagans, on the other hand, always came home to California, spending more than one entire year of his eight-year presidency in the state. As his term came to an end, he would smile and say: "California, here I come."

FROM FRONTIER TO HIGH-TECH STATE

In a relatively short period California has gone from the frontier state of miners and ranchers to the high-tech capital of the world, from an inaccessible desert island to the most populous state in America. But, as a recent author warned, it would be wrong to read too much into these outward and visible changes. In fact, there is much to suggest that the pioneer spirit lives on, that when Americans exhaust one frontier, they simply move on to another one. In a book entitled, *The Legacy of Conquest* (W.W. Norton, 1987), Patricia Nelson Limerick observed that "there is, in fact, nothing mythic" about California and the American West. "It has a history grounded in primary economic reality — in hard-headed questions of profit, loss, competition, and consolidation. Behind every trapper lay a trader; before every Indian lay a homeland lost to an encroaching farmer or avid oil man; with every cowboy and every sheriff rode a rancher, eager to add to his herd and the land and water to sustain it. They, and hundreds of thousands like them, meant business. In dozens of ways, their descendants mean business today."

Of course, the real gold ran out a long time ago. But that hasn't stopped the emigration to California. With a population of 33,252,000 in 1998, it's the country's most populous state, and more people are coming every day. In the century following 1860, California's population doubled five times. From 1975 to 1998, more than 12 million new people moved to California. In spite of that, the unemployment rate dropped to a 30-year low of 5.9% in 1998. Personal income of California residents in 1997 was $857 billion, by far the highest in the United States. California also boasts the country's largest manufacturing complex including 23% of America's aerospace industry ($29 billion per year) and 19% of the computer software business ($21 billion per annum). The state also leads the nation in agricultural production with farmers receiving more than $25 billion per year for their produce.

Big and getting bigger; rich and getting richer. That is the story of California as it moves into the twenty-first century. Statistics read more like those of a country than those of a state. In fact, Californians like to brag that their trillion-dollar annual economy is the seventh largest in the world — and still growing.

Four hundred years after the Spaniards went looking for the sunshine and gold of a mythical California, the lure of the real place endures. Call it high-tech, kiwi fruit or avocados, the gold is still there for those who want to work for it.

Whether it's an overnight fad, a serious new trend or a major scientific development, you can bet there's a Californian somewhere back there making a buck off of it. That, after all, was what brought most people here. The others will be content to lie back and enjoy the sunshine, content to live in a place where it's almost always warm.

NATURAL HISTORY

NOT WITHOUT FAULTS

If you want a quick education in geology, bring along your textbooks to California. Here, you will find vivid illustrations of every period and era of the geologic past. Just as California is thought of as a young state in terms of its people, the very land they live on is also "young" in geological terms. Whereas the Blue Ridge Mountains in the East, for example, are so old they've been weathered down, silted over, and covered with vegetation, much of the geologic activity in California is so recent that you can still see where and how the earth cracked and moved. Seismologists explain that the earth is still moving in California almost every day. "California is still an uneasy land," was how an official state report phrased it in 1966.

It has the most varied landscape in America, containing the highest and lowest points found in the contiguous 48 states. California's rich earth contains at least 602 different minerals; 74 of them first discovered in California.

While it may not have been a true island surrounded by water, as mythology would have us believe, California was an island in more ways than one. Until the breakthroughs in transportation in this century, the state was accessible only by sea or overland travel of more than three months. While its entire western border of more than 800 miles (1,300 km) lies along the Pacific Ocean, its eastern border is protected by formidable deserts and the sheer impenetrable walls of the High Sierra mountains.

Geologists have identified 12 "geomorphic provinces" in California. What separates and defines each province are the types of rocks, geologic structure, and history of the major landforms in the area. By far, the most impressive of these is the grand Sierra Nevada range of mountains that extends for 400 miles (640 km) from northeast of Lake Tahoe south to near Bakersfield. Sierra means

"saw" in Spanish; Americans call the mountains "sawtooth" ranges because their jagged edges resemble the edge or teeth of a saw. Nevada is the word for snowfall or snow-covered. The "High Sierras" as Californians call them were formed by a fault block, giving rise to a severe eastern wall that reaches a peak of 14,495 ft (4,418 m) at Mount Whitney. The gentler western slopes are more congenial to man.

About two million years ago, the entire area was covered by ice up to half a mile (800 m) thick. These glaciers shaped Lake Tahoe and some of the more spectacular valleys and basins in Yosemite National Park. The deep snow that still covers the high peaks in wintertime used to be

regarded with fear and dread by the first settlers. But now, it offers months of fun to skiers and has added yet another revenue-earner to California's tourism industry.

Near the Oregon border are two other mountain ranges that form separate geomorphic provinces. These are the Klamath and Cascade mountains. The Klamath mountains extend 130 miles (210 km) into California, taking up much of the northwest corner of the state. They include the Siskiyou, Salmon, and Trinity mountains. This is one of the last heavily logged areas in the state, but much is protected as federal and state forest preserves with only a few small roadways penetrating the mountain wilderness. The adjoining Cascade mountains extend 525 miles (845 km) north through Oregon and Washington into Canada. In California, the Cascades consist of more than 120 volcanoes, the most famous being Mount

Shasta and Mount Lassen. Both are at the center of national parks. Shasta, rising to a height of 14,163 ft (4,317 m), is visible from Interstate 5. It is a magnificent snow-covered natural monument. Mount Lassen, lying in a more remote area to the southeast, is 10,466 ft (3,190 m) high. Until Mount Saint Helens erupted in Washington in 1980, Mount Lassen was the only volcano in the contiguous 48 states that had been active in historic times (1914–1917).

The Great Valley is another of the geomorphic provinces, extending 400 miles (645 km) from Redding in the north to Bakersfield in the south. An alluvial plane between the High Sierras and the coastal mountains, it is one of the richest ag-

California's landscape, however, is best known for being unstable. The fears about devastation in California are often exaggerated. It is not the only place in the United States where earthquakes have occurred. The town of New Madrid, Missouri was leveled by an earthquake in 1811; Charleston, South Carolina was heavily damaged in a quake in 1886; and a massive temblor shook Alaska in 1964. But few earthquakes have captured the world's attention as did the San Francisco quake of 1906. People now laughingly say that if it had been Cleveland, nobody would have noticed — they might even have looked on it as urban renewal. But San Francisco had been a lively pleasure-loving place, long known for the beauty of its setting and the exuber-

ricultural areas on earth. The Coast Ranges are parallel mountains extending along much of the coast from just north of Eureka to just south of San Luis Obispo. Here, the north-south ranges run into the Transverse ranges that form the north wall of the Los Angeles basin. Formed by uplifted faults, these east-west ranges include the Santa Monica Mountains on the east, and the San Gabriel and San Bernardino mountains on the west.

The great deserts of eastern California are often separated in two, and sometimes three, different geomorphic provinces. In general, these areas have north-south mountain ranges separated by huge valleys or basins or troughs; they are part of a "basin and ranges" province that includes much of Utah and Nevada. In the great Mojave Desert, all the streams, except the Colorado River, end in dry lakes; more than 50 of these closed basins have one or more dry lakes in them.

California: Myths and Realities

ance of its residents. Although 80% of the resulting damage came from the fires that followed the quake, when the dust had settled more than 3,000 people had been killed, 490 blocks in the heart of the prosperous city destroyed, and 250,000 people left homeless. Losses were estimated at $400 million. If it happened once, it could happen again. The legend of "The Big One" grows with every year that passes that no major quake is recorded. The thinking is that California is due for another shock even greater than the one that hit San Francisco in 1906, and there are dozens of theories as to when it will occur and how bad it will be.

OPPOSITE: Peaceful scenes await those who visit Yosemite in winter, when mountain trails are virtually empty and blazing fires warm hikers in lodges at night. ABOVE: Skateboarding at the Youth Festival in front of San Francisco's elaborate City Hall, as fine as many state and national capitols.

In fact, California is part of a seismic belt around the Pacific, running from Japan across the Aleutian Islands down to Mexico. This belt accounts for 80% of the world's earthquakes. Thousands of quakes are recorded in California every year, some 500 of them strong enough for people to feel.

Since the 1906 earthquake and several smaller but damaging quakes in the intervening years, many buildings in California have been built with earthquakes in mind. But others remain unprotected. The worst danger is from falling beams and plaster — which is why you are warned to quickly get under a table or in a doorway so that the door frame or the table can protect you. You can prepare for the aftershocks, but the truth is, there is very little preparation you can make for the initial shock. It comes unannounced and is over in seconds.

The San Francisco earthquake was the result of movement along the San Andreas Fault, the longest lateral moving fault in the world. From well south of the Baja Peninsula in Mexico, the San Andreas Fault extends more than 500 miles (800 km) across California, cutting across the city of San Francisco. The most dramatic illustration of the fault's movement is the Baja Peninsula itself. Once part of the Mexican mainland, it broke off during one of the massive shifts along this great crack in the earth. The San Francisco quake was said to have involved a shift of 28 ft (8.5 m) in places and affected an area of 100 miles (161 km) on either side of the city. While the San Andreas is the biggest and most feared, there are a number of lesser faults along which minor quakes occur.

"The Big One" has become so much a part of California mythology that it has become a joke. From car salesmen to bar owners, you'll hear commercials warning you to take advantage of their deals "before the Big One comes." In 1988, Big One fever seemed to have reached its peak. In May of that year, followers of Nostradamus proclaimed that Los Angeles would be destroyed in the worst earthquake ever. A film was based on the writings of this sixteenth-century astrologer called, *The Man Who Saw Tomorrow*, and the Los Angeles prediction set off a minor panic — well, as near to panic as Californians can get. More than 2,000 copies of the film video were sold the week before the prophesied catastrophe. Observatories were so swamped with anxious callers that some, like the Griffith Observatory in Los Angeles, prepared an information kit explaining that earthquakes were not caused by extraterrestrial events and, by the way, "there will be no planetary alignment or conjunction in May."

The video was actually a timely re-release of a 1981 film produced by David Wolper and narrated by the late Orson Welles. Asked about the impending doom of his home city, Wolper said he planned to be out of town that week in May. But he had the typical Californian's response to the prospects: "If the quake does happen, we'll sell a lot more copies, maybe enough to rebuild my house." The *New York Times* pointed out that the filmmakers were confused about the Nostradamus texts, and had the wrong year and the wrong natural disaster (destruction by hail storm instead of earthquake). But that didn't prevent the panicky phone calls — or the run to video stores.

Nor did it prevent the cynical reaction from some quarters. A group calling itself the Skeptics banded together to combat such non-scientific nonsense. Claiming more than 2,000 members in California, its founder said the group was formed by "people who found themselves going crazy living next door to someone trying to fix their cars with crystals."

The final word on the Nostradamus scare and the perpetual earthquake paranoia was spoken by a devout Californian who told *People* magazine: "In spite of its many faults, California is still the best place in the world to live."

In Mount Lassen Volcanic National Park, California's majestic pines rise once again in the area once covered with molten lava and ash.

California: Myths and Realities

San Francisco and the Bay Area

SAN FRANCISCO WAS LONG KNOWN IN California as "the City," simply because there was nothing to compare with it in terms of population — and sophistication. San Franciscans, of course, still call it *the* City. And perhaps no other American city is loved so passionately by its residents. At the time of the great earthquake and fire in 1906, a crusty old boxing manager said: "I'd rather be a busted lamppost on Battery Street in San Francisco than the Waldorf-Astoria in New York."

The city has two official songs, both all-time national favorites: *San Francisco*, sung by Jeanette MacDonald as the title song of the 1936 movie, and the more recent *I Left My Heart in San Francisco*, popularized by crooner Tony Bennett. So many songs, poems, and books have been written about the place that the name alone has come to signify beautiful people, fabulous restaurants and hotels, magnificent views of mountains and bay — and, above all, a sense of fun. There is the usual American respect for wealth and success, but in San Francisco it is tempered with a delightful irreverence.

In 1970, French president Georges Pompidou said San Francisco "is remarkable not only for its beauty. It is also, of all the cities in the United States, the one whose name, the world over, conjures up the most visions and more than any other incites one to dream." British author and television personality Alistair Cooke called it "the most individual and engaging of American cities." Adlai Stevenson said the United Nations would have worked much better if it had stayed in San Francisco rather than moving to New York. And Robert Kennedy said, "I love this city. If I am elected, I'll move the White House to San Francisco."

BACKGROUND

THE BAY AREA

San Francisco is the urban core of Northern California's "Bay Area" — a nine-county metropolitan region with 6.5 million people and more than a hundred separate towns and cities. You can see much of the Bay Area through the huge open arches of the 500-ft (152-m)-high **Coit Tower** on Telegraph Hill. The beauty of the setting is striking, and it's easy to understand why so many people consider themselves lucky to live here. Directly west is the famous **Golden Gate Bridge**. Few man-made structures inspire the kind of awe and affection that San Franciscans continue to feel for this spectacular engineering masterpiece, and nearly every citizen is an authority on the subject. You can see **Sausalito** hugging the waterfront north of the bridge and **Angel Island** (a state park) in the bay. Also unmistakable is the rock-solid **Alcatraz**. Although the name is Spanish for the amiable pelican, Alcatraz once had a feared reputation as the world's most escape-proof prison; the currents around it are so fierce that only one man ever successfully swam away from it. Farther east is the sprawling university town of **Berkeley**, the city of **Oakland**, and the handsome **Bay Bridge**, which would be a major landmark in any city that didn't have a Golden Gate.

THE SPIRIT OF SAN FRANCISCO

The reason San Francisco ranks third among Californian cities in population (only 724,000) is its limited size — 46.38 sq miles (120 sq km); by comparison, Los Angeles covers 463.7 sq miles (1,200 sq km) and harbors 3.5 million people. San Francisco's density results in a real spirit of neighborhood.

But the special appeal of San Francisco lies in its people, both past and present. At Coit Tower

you begin to understand why. A sign at the base advises that the tower was *not* built in the shape of an upturned fire hose nozzle; the shape was simply judged the best design for the setting. But the fire hose legend has a basis in fact. Lillie Hitchcock Coit (1843–1929) specified in her will that $125,000 of her fortune would go to "adding beauty to the city which I have always loved." Lillie Coit loved to ride on fire trucks — she was even dubbed the mascot of one hook and ladder company. She also dressed as a man, gambled in the North Beach saloons, smoked cigars, and generally entertained San Francisco with her antics while outraging her relatives, one of whom took a shot at her in a San Francisco hotel, causing her to move to Europe where she became the darling of royalty in several countries.

From Coit Tower, at the foot of the hill, down some old wooden steps, is a beautiful flower gar-

den known as **Grace's Garden**. Grace Marchant, one of Mac Sennett's bathing beauties in the days of silent films, moved into a little house on the hillside in the 1940s and started cleaning up the garbage dump that people had made of the unused hillside. It became a garden spot so loved by local residents that they took up a collection and bought the property when Grace died a few years ago to ensure that it would always remain a lovely retreat.

It is a city where civic pride goes hand in hand with civic generosity. Of the two huge windmills at the ocean end of **Golden Gate Park**, designed as part of the park's irrigation system but deteriorated

PREVIOUS PAGES: The Yerba Buena Gardens bloom in front of San Francisco's dazzling city skyline and downtown tram-like flower stall.
ABOVE: The Transamerica pyramid, left, is an identifier of San Francisco amid the lighted grids of buildings soaring into the evening sky.

from disuse, one is now working again thanks to funds raised by a private citizen. In 1988, when the police department announced that the mounted patrols in the park would have to be discontinued due to a shortage of funds, soon another private subscription assured that they would always be there as they had always been there. A more famous gesture was the public subscription of $10 million which returned San Francisco's famed **cable cars** to use after they were closed down in 1982 due to safety hazards in the old equipment. This gesture, combined with federal and city grants of more than $60 million, enabled the complicated cable system to be restored to its original working condition.

SAN FRANCISCO HISTORY

Despite its Spanish name, San Francisco was an American invention from the very beginning. The Spanish and Mexicans had their capital in Monterey, with only a small mission and garrison fort in what is now San Francisco. United States Navy Captain John B. Montgomery sailed into the bay and took possession without ever firing a shot, raising the Stars and Stripes on July 9, 1846. He renamed the town square in honor of his ship, the *Portsmouth*, and the then waterfront street after himself. The tiny settlement had been called Yerba Buena, for the "good herb" or sweet grass that grew on the dunes there; but the American invaders soon rechristened it San Francisco.

With the end of the Mexican War in 1848 and the discovery of gold, San Francisco was suddenly a boom town. The miners struck gold in the Sierra foothills to the east, but they came down to San Francisco to resupply and spend their profits. Twice during those raucous years the city was taken over and run by vigilante committees. The very rich built elaborate mansions on Nob Hill, where they could be safe from the boisterous city below.

Sailors from around the world called it the "Barbary Coast" because navigating in and out of San Francisco's red-light district could be as treacherous as sailing the Mediterranean with its pirates. The city became a pleasure capital and, in spite of rampant political corruption, gained an international reputation for its love of the arts and culture.

At 5:13 AM on April 18, 1906 San Francisco woke to a devastating earthquake and fire. One Los Angeles newspaper headlined its report on the earthquake: "San Francisco Punished." To which San Franciscans responded with a rhyme:

If, as they say, God spanked the town
For being over-frisky,
Why did He burn all the churches down
and spare Hotaling's Whiskey?

(Hotaling's, a popular saloon, survived both the earthquake and the fire.)

The public spirit of San Franciscans was never more in evidence than in the days following the earthquake and fire. It remains the worst natural disaster ever to befall an American city. More than 3,000 people were killed, 28,000 buildings destroyed, and 250,000 people left homeless. The earthquake caused extensive damage for a hundred miles along the San Andreas fault line, from Eureka to Salinas; in San Francisco alone, the damage was estimated at more than $400 million.

With amazing determination, the city cleared the ruins (at a cost of more than $20 million) and rebuilt on the spot. Within three years, more than 20,000 structures had been replaced and the city was making plans for a world's fair.

However, the earthquake had exposed more than a fault in the earth's crust. The magnificent Beaux-Arts City Hall stood in ruins, exposing a flimsy steel superstructure where the dome was supposed to be. Corrupt city officials and builders had swindled the city out of millions of dollars during construction. But City Hall was only the most obvious place where the public had been shortchanged. "They was all a-grafting," said one old-timer about the city's widespread corruption.

By the time the great Panama-Pacific International Exposition was held in 1915, the city had been reconstructed from the rubble and ashes of the earthquake and fire. The **Palace of Fine Arts** in the Marina District is a permanent reminder of what the exposition meant in restoring the city's pride.

In the 1930s, during the Great Depression, San Francisco again faced disaster, along with the rest of the world. But the city pulled itself out of the economic crisis with two extraordinary construction projects: the Golden Gate Bridge and the San Francisco-Oakland Bay Bridge. An international exposition staged on **Treasure Island** in 1939 proclaimed the successful completion of these projects, indicating to the world that San Francisco was a survivor with strength and style. World War II brought even greater prosperity to the city, when it served as one of the major ports for the war in the Pacific.

In the 1950s, while the rest of America was lulled by the do-nothing spirit of the Eisenhower years, San Francisco was home to the "Beat Generation." Local newspaper columnist Herb Caen was the first to call the bohemian poets and artists "beatniks," a name which eventually became a badge of honor. Poet Lawrence Ferlinghetti's **City Lights Bookstore** in North Beach became the cultural center of the movement, with Allen Ginsberg, Gregory Corso, and Jack Kerouac frequently in residence.

The area was fertile ground for the free speech movement, born at the University of California

Children learn about ships and sailing lore at Hyde Street Pier.

in Berkeley in the fall of 1964, setting the stage for the social and political activism that would spread throughout America in the coming decade. San Francisco gave its own special stamp to this political action, a gentle persuasion that emphasized peace and love — "flower power." Taking a line from Scott McKenzie's 1967 hit song, "If you're going to San Francisco, be sure to wear some flowers in your hair." The original "human be-ins" and "love-ins" were staged in Golden Gate Park, near the **Haight-Ashbury** district, a neglected slum when the "flower children" and hippies laid claim to it as their national capital.

With the bitter divisions over the Vietnam War, the movement that had begun with flowers in San Francisco ended with bloodshed and tear gas in places like Chicago, Kent State and Washington, DC. But the city had made its mark on the decade, not least of all through its folk and rock 'n' roll music. Joan Baez was the Joan of Arc of free speech, civil rights, and peace and love — she would always call San Francisco and Carmel home. The late Bill Graham's Fillmore Auditorium (a converted roller-skating rink in Haight-Ashbury) became La Scala of rock 'n' roll and launched any number of careers, including Graham's own.

During the "me" decade of the 1970s, old-time San Franciscans became concerned that the place was turning into another Manhattan. The once low and gentle skyline was fast becoming a wall of skyscrapers; developers were "New Yorking" it to death, some said. At the center of this new conglomeration of buildings was a pyramid rising 48 stories to a point. Designed by William Pereia as the headquarters of a huge insurance company, the **Transamerica Pyramid** was at first greeted with derision. But, with time, this too became another distinctive piece of San Francisco's fabric, a dramatic reminder that the city is not only a cultural center but also the banking and insurance capital of the American West.

Also in the 1970s, a number of serious social issues confronted the populace. The city was stunned when it learned that Jim Jones, a local cult leader, had led his followers (most of them San Franciscans) in a mass murder-suicide — more than 900 men, women, and children lost their lives in the remote commune of Jonestown in Guyana. And when a bright, energetic mayor, George Moscone, and the city's first gay supervisor, Harvey Milk, were assassinated by an embittered ex-fireman and supervisor, the people of San Francisco were united in their outrage. The mayor's name lives on in the huge **Moscone Center** for conventions and special events, south of Market Street.

In the 1980s, the city was the first to discover the dreaded virus that would become known as Acquired Immune Deficiency Syndrome, or AIDS.

San Francisco has been especially hard hit because of its large homosexual population. But the city's program for helping AIDS victims is superior to that of any other American metropolis. One doctor said, "If I had AIDS, I would crawl to San Francisco to get help."

On October 17, 1989 at 5:04 PM, Northern California was again hit by a major earthquake, measuring 6.9 on the Richter scale (the 1906 earthquake measured 8.25). Much of San Francisco was devastated by the tremors, particularly the Marina District, which also suffered from fires caused by ruptured gas mains. Part of the Bay Bridge and a 1.5-mile (2-km) section of the Nimitz Freeway in Oakland collapsed during rush-hour traffic, killing more than a hundred commuters. The resort towns of Santa Cruz and Carmel, near the earthquake's epicenter, were hit even worse.

Despite various natural disasters and an economic slump during much of the previous 20 years, San Francisco experienced another renaissance during the 1990s. Spurred by Silicon Valley's worldwide leadership of the computer industry, the Bay Area developed a thriving economy. With it came a fresh campaign for urban renewal. The once depressed South of Market area in San Francisco was transformed into an area of trendy restaurants, bars and boutiques, and the new **Yerba Buena Center for the Arts** and **San Francisco Museum of Modern Art** were built. The vast **Presidio** military base, sprawling on hills near the Golden Gate, was decommissioned in 1994 and transformed into one of the country's largest urban recreation areas.

Though leveled by fire, destroyed by earthquakes, and hit by violence and disease, the spirit of the place endures. It isn't so much that you leave your heart in San Francisco, but that it gives its heart to you. As author and one-time San Francisco resident William Saroyan opined: "If you're alive, you can't be bored in San Francisco. If you're not alive, San Francisco will bring you to life."

GENERAL INFORMATION

The **San Francisco Convention & Visitors Bureau (SFCVB)** ((415) 391-2000 WEB SITE www.sfvisitor.org, 201 Third Street, Suite 900, San Francisco, CA 94103, offers a wealth of information on the city and the surrounding area. The SFCVB maintains a 24-hour recorded events information hotline in several languages: ((415) 391-2001 (English), ((415) 391-2003 (French), ((415) 391-2004 (German), ((415) 391-2122 (Spanish), ((415) 391-2101 (Chinese). The bureau's walk-up **visitor information center** is located in the Benjamin Swig Pavilion on the lower level of the Hallidie Plaza at Market and Powell Streets in the Financial District. It is open Monday to Friday from 9 AM to 5 PM, and Saturday and from Sunday 9 AM to 3 PM.

Other tourist information outlets in the Bay Area include the **Berkeley Convention & Visitors Bureau** ((510) 549-8710 TOLL-FREE (800) 847-4823, 2015 Center Street, Berkeley, CA 94704; the **Marin County Convention & Visitors Bureau** ((415) 472-7470 FAX (415) 499-3700 WEB SITE www.visitmarin.org, Avenue of the Flags, San Rafael, CA 94903; and the **San Jose Convention & Visitors Bureau** ((408) 295-9600 FAX (408) 295-3937 WEB SITE www.sanjose.org, 333 West San Carlos Street, Suite 1000, San Jose, CA 95110.

tory of California should have its "Chrysopylae," or Golden Gate. Never mind that the area still belonged to Mexico; by the time it became part of the United States three years later, the gold rush was on and the name became known around the world.

Although the opening into the bay is relatively narrow, it was still a treacherous sea passage, 318 ft (97 m) deep with fierce ocean currents proving a formidable obstacle to any serious plans for a bridge. In 1917, international bridge builder Joseph B. Strauss arrived in San Francisco with a grand plan for connecting Northern California with the San Francisco peninsula by means of the most magnificent bridge the world had ever seen.

CHRYSOPYLAE: THE GOLDEN GATE

GOLDEN GATE BRIDGE

Just as Winston Churchill claimed to have created the nation of Jordan "with the stroke of a pencil," so the famed Golden Gate was born with the pen-stroke of a brash young United States Army explorer and mapmaker named James C. Fremont. Considering the area was a virtual wasteland which the Spanish had never seen any use for, it was somewhat pretentious of Fremont to label the narrow entrance to the huge San Francisco Bay "The Golden Gate."

In 1846, before gold was discovered in the hills beyond, Fremont explained that ancient Byzantium had its "Golden Horn," so the terri-

Construction didn't begin until 1933, and Strauss would later say: "It took two decades and 200 million words to convince the people that the bridge was feasible; then only four years and $35 million to put the concrete and steel together."

It was an awesome project and 11 workers were killed despite elaborate safety precautions; another 19 workers were saved from certain death by safety nets. The bridge was suspended between two enormous towers the height of a 65-story building; only the Empire State Building was taller at that time. Other bridge statistics are equally impressive: enough steel wire in the cables to circle the earth three times, and enough concrete to pave a five-foot (one-and-a-half-meter)-wide sidewalk

Fog drifts through pilings and cables at the Golden Gate Bridge. OVERLEAF: The Yuerba Buena Gardens is a good place to relax and admire impressive modern architecture.

from San Francisco to New York. The central span of the 9,022-ft (2,750-m) bridge is 4,200 ft (1,280 m), the world's longest at that time.

There are few manmade structures one can describe as breathtaking — the Golden Gate Bridge is one. When President Franklin Roosevelt pushed the button that opened the bridge on May 27, 1937, some 200,000 people walked across the amazing structure. Fifty years later, more than 800,000 people showed up when the city celebrated the anniversary of the bridge, still its most famous landmark, and more than 41 million vehicles cross it each year. When Pope John Paul II visited San Francisco in 1987, his only sightseeing request was to see the Golden Gate Bridge.

Tolls are charged for southbound traffic only. There is no charge to pedestrians, and the bridge offers one of the city's most picturesque and popular walking and jogging courses.

GOLDEN GATE NATIONAL RECREATION AREA

Stretching north and south on either side of its namesake bridge is Golden Gate National Recreation Area (GGNRA). With more than 116 square miles, this is one of the world's largest urban parks and the single most popular unit of the United States national park system, with 20 million visitors each year.

Golden Gate was established in 1972 with several goals in mind: preserving a beautiful 30-mile (45-km) stretch of coast that might otherwise be gobbled up by developers; saving and

displaying an area that has witnessed more than 200 years of California history; taking pressure off increasingly crowded wilderness parks like Yosemite and Yellowstone; and giving urban dwellers especially those with limited mobility and time — a giant green space close to home. "I don't know of any other city in America with this kind of green space," says one Park Service official.

Thousands of acres were purchased from private sources or turned over by the United States military, the state of California, the city of San Francisco and Marin County to create Golden Gate National Recreation Area. Today the park includes the entire waterfront between Fisherman's Wharf and the Golden Gate Bridge, the sprawling Presidio, all of San Francisco's open-ocean beaches, the Marin Headlands and Muir Woods on the north side of the bridge, as well as Angel and Alcatraz islands in the bay.

The variety of landscapes is astounding: beaches, marshes, redwood forest, farmland, windswept cliffs, rolling green grasslands, celebrated wharfs and docks, athletic fields, and more than 400 historic buildings including Alcatraz Prison, the Cliff House and Fort Winfield Scott beneath the Golden Gate Bridge. Golden Gate National Recreation Area also lends itself to numerous recreational pursuits including hiking, jogging, mountain biking, kayaking, swimming, surfing, fishing, picnics and camping.

For general information on this enormous park, contact the **Golden Gate National Recreation Area Headquarters** ((415) 556-0560, Building 201, Fort Mason, San Francisco, CA 94123.

Fort Point

Perhaps because they'd been able to seize the place without ever firing a shot, the United States government set about building a huge and sturdy fort on the south side of the narrow Golden Gate opening to the suddenly busy and valuable San Francisco Bay. Constructed between 1853 and 1861, **Fort Point National Historic Site** ((415) 556-1693 is a classic Civil War bastion whose thick walls were built to house 500 soldiers and 126 cannons. "None were ever fired in anger," the National Park Service guides — dressed in authentic Union uniforms — will tell you. Even if no fort were there, you would want to visit the site because it's located right under the Golden Gate Bridge. The fort is open Wednesday through Sunday from 10 AM to 5 PM. Admission is free. Take Lincoln Boulevard to Long Avenue, which ends at the fort.

The Presidio

Until it was turned over to the National Park Service in 1994, the Presidio was one of the most beautiful military reservations in America. The **Presidio Army Museum** ((415) 561-4331 is located in one of its oldest buildings, the Old Station Hospital, part of which dates back to 1857. The Army played an important role in keeping order and getting the city back on its feet after the 1906 earthquake, and a couple of restored "earthquake cottages" are included in the collection. The museum is at Lincoln Boulevard and Funston Avenue. It is open Wednesday through Sunday from 10 AM to 4 PM. Admission is free.

Angel Island

The 750-acre (300-hectare) Angel Island, the largest island in San Francisco Bay, is now a nature preserve, inhabited only by park rangers, wild birds, and deer. Dubbed the "Ellis Island of the

part of the federal prison system — the last resort prison, where the most notorious inmates were jailed and from which there was no escape. The most unruly and infamous prisoners were brought here from all over America, kept in line by rigid discipline and the latest in "electric eye" surveillance. A total of 1,576 convicts were incarcerated on the island in its 30 years as a penitentiary. Abandoned as a prison in 1963, the island was occupied from 1969 to 1971 by Native Americans wishing to draw attention to their plight. In 1972, it became part of the National Park Service.

Today, you can wander about the grim gray cell blocks while listening to cassette tapes of former inmates and guards describing conditions

West," from 1910 to 1940 the island was a station to process new immigrants arriving in America, including 175,000 Chinese arrivals. During World War II, the buildings were used to house Italian and Japanese prisoners of war. Today, Angel Island is a favorite weekend retreat for San Franciscans with its biking and hiking trails, beaches and picnic areas, historic buildings and tram tour. Blue & Gold Fleet ((415) 773-1188 has regular ferry service from Pier 41 at Fisherman's Wharf ($10 round trip).

Alcatraz

"The Rock," as it's so often called, is a barren 12-acre (five-hectare) island in the middle of San Francisco Bay that evolved into the most formidable prison in America. Originally a Spanish fortress, it became an American military prison and "disciplinary barracks" in the 1850s. In 1933, it became

as they were on Alcatraz. Blue & Gold Fleet ((415) 773-1188 or (415) 705-5555 (advanced booking) has frequent ferry departures each day starting at 9:30 AM from Pier 41 at Fisherman's Wharf; the $11 round trip includes audiocassette rental for the 90-minute tour. Advanced booking is highly recommended.

Marin County

From the northern end of the bridge, Golden Gate National Recreation Area extends another 23 miles

---

The botanical Conservatory in Golden Gate Park ABOVE was shipped from England and reconstructed after the conservatory in London's Kew Gardens was demolished. The Japanese Tea Garden OPPOSITE in Golden Gate Park is an authentic reproduction complete with magnificent carved gates constructed by master craftsmen from Japan.

(37 km), to the town of Olema. This area includes much of picturesque Marin County, in particular, Mount Tamalpais and the Muir Woods.

At 2,560 ft (790 m), **Mount Tamalpais** or Mount Tam ((415) 388-2070 is the highest point on the western shores of San Francisco Bay. The peak is one of those breathtaking places that is hard to describe in words. Like Corcovado in Rio de Janeiro or Stanley Peak in Hong Kong, you gaze down from the summit on a bustling city and busy harbor. On a clear day, you can see more than 100 miles (160 km) from the top of Mount Tam. San Francisco author Harold Gilliam once wrote that "Tamalpais not only tempers the weather of the region; it tempers the psychic climate as well.... In sun or clouds, rain or shrouded by fog, the mountain offers visions of splendor, intimations of unlimited possibilities." Located 15 miles (24 km) north of San Francisco by way of US Highway 101, Tamalpais has three camping areas and numerous hiking trails and viewing points.

Muir Woods ((415) 388-2595, located 17 miles (27 km) north of San Francisco by way of US Highway 101 and State Highway 1, is a true shrine to environmentalists. It preserves the memory of John Muir, the Scottish-born naturalist who was instrumental in getting Yosemite designated a national park and also in establishing a commission in 1896 which created 13 national forest preserves. Muir called his namesake woods "the best tree-lovers' monument that would be found in all the forests of the world." Muir Woods is the closest place to San Francisco where you can walk among the ancient redwood trees. Some of the 250-ft (76-m)-high giants are more than a thousand years old. The 550-acre (200-hectare) grove of redwoods was dedicated in 1908 under the Act for the Preservation of Antiquities and was incorporated into Golden Gate National Recreation Area in 1972.

GOLDEN GATE PARK

Golden Gate Park is truly one of the great city parks of the world, and unique in its appreciation of beauty and fun. Even the city's own brochure describes it as a "space for both the silly and the solemn." With more than 1,000 acres (400 hectares) of woods and meadows, the park cuts a green swath from the ocean front through the city's residential areas.

Originally a wasteland of sand dunes and scrub oak, the park began to take shape in 1870 through the creative use of manure from the city streets. Plantings from all over the world eventually made it one of the greatest botanical gardens in America. The beautiful Victorian greenhouse, or Conservatory of Flowers, was shipped from England around Cape Horn and reassembled in the park in 1879. The **Strybing Arboretum and Botanical Gardens**, in another area of the park, have more than 6,000 plants on display including the California redwood.

But Golden Gate Park is not a pristine nature preserve; it's used by thousands of people every day for outdoor sports and recreation. The soccer fields are at the ocean end of the park, Kezar Stadium at the other (east) end; in between is a golf course, tennis courts, baseball fields, a polo stadium, a fly-casting pond, and a delightful miniature yacht racing pool with its own elegant little clubhouse. There is also a bison paddock, the five-acre (two-hectare) **Japanese Tea Garden**, the 1912 carousel in the children's playground, and two Dutch-style windmills that were once part of the park's own irrigation system. The city's major science and art museums are also located in the park (See ART MUSEUMS, page 102). The Golden Gate Park Explorer Pass includes admission to four of the park's major museums and attractions at 25% savings over regular adult admission prices. For park information call ((415) 666-2700. Free guided walking tours of the park are also available ((415) 263-0991.

SAN FRANCISCO'S LOCALITIES

NOB HILL

The name Nob Hill comes from a British corruption of the Hindu word "nabob" or "nawab," a person of wealth and power. San Francisco's nabobs, who got rich off Nevada mines and the transcontinental railroad, claimed this hilltop as their own in the 1870s. It was 376 ft (115 m) above the rabble of San Francisco, with a steep grade that discouraged the uninvited and prompted the hill's residents to build their own railroad, which is still in service as part of the city's cable car system.

Robert Louis Stevenson dubbed it the "hill of palaces" in 1882. Some of the homes were so grandiose — Mrs. Mark Hopkins' mansion in particular — they drew scorn from the rest of the city. But their lofty perch and wealth couldn't save them from the 1906 earthquake and fire. All but one of the mansions on Nob Hill were destroyed; James G. Flood's sturdy brownstone has endured as the Pacific Union Club, where successive generations of capitalist barons still hold forth. Some of the names of the mansions have survived in the hotels and parks. The **Mark Hopkins Hotel** is on the site of the Hopkins mansion; Huntington Park is where that family's house once stood; and the **Fairmont Hotel** is on the former estate of James G. Fair. Here you will find the ultimate in San Francisco accommodation: the Fairmont's penthouse suite (described as a "rooftop manor") rents for $6,000 a day, complete with butler, maid and limousine service.

Grace Cathedral, at 1051 Taylor Street, sits on land donated by the Crocker family after their two

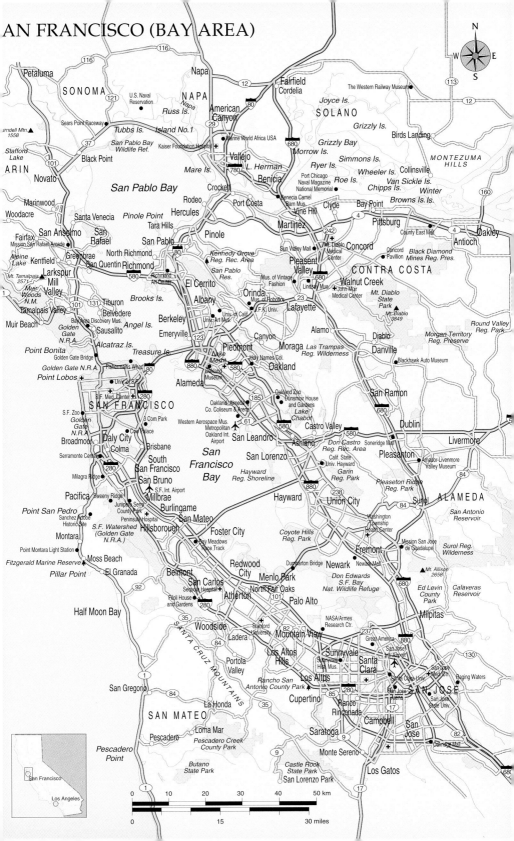

mansions were destroyed by the 1906 fire. Erected in 1910, the cathedral is the largest Gothic structure in the American West; its huge gilded brass doors are copies of a fifteenth-century work by the Italian Florentine master Lorenzo Ghiberti for the Baptistery in Florence.

UNION SQUARE

Not only famous as a hotel and shopping center, Union Square is also a thing of beauty in and of itself. The banks of flowers at every corner are arranged so tastefully you forget they are there to be sold. The two-and-a-half-acre (one-hectare) square was set aside as a public park in 1850, the

same year the city was incorporated. It got its name from a series of violent pro-Union demonstrations staged there just prior to the Civil War. In 1902, the 97-ft (29-m) Corinthian column at the center of the square was erected, commemorating an episode in the Spanish-American War — Commodore George Dewey's victory at Manila in the Philippines in 1898.

The most historic of the hotels around the square is the **St. Francis**, which dates from the time when "hotels" were nothing more than tents, with cots for beds. The St. Francis prided itself on being the first hotel in San Francisco to provide sheets. Rousted out of his bed in the St. Francis by the 1906 earthquake, the actor John Barrymore was one of thousands who took refuge in Union Square, where he was promptly pressed into service by the United States Army. His actor-uncle, John Drew, said, "It took an act of God to get Jack out

of bed and the United States government to get him to work." A grand new St. Francis had opened in 1904, only to be gutted by fire two years later. An elegant banquet was staged in the embers of the old ballroom to celebrate the hotel's reconstruction within the same walls.

Underneath Union Square is a four-level parking garage built in 1941, with enough space for 1,000 cars. Don't count on finding a space, though; parking is a problem throughout the city, but especially in the more popular tourist areas.

The **Financial District** with its towering skyscrapers is wedged between Union Square, Market Street and the Embarcadero. The **Wells Fargo History Museum** ((415) 396-2619 takes up two floors of the bank's 43-story headquarters at 420 Montgomery Street. Founded in New York and San Francisco in 1852 by Henry Wells and William G. Fargo, Wells Fargo became the bank and the overland stagecoach line of the American West. The banking and shipping operations were separated in 1906 and Wells Fargo continued to grow as one of the region's major banks. The centerpiece of this collection is a real Wells Fargo overland Concord stagecoach and a display dedicated to the notorious hijacker, Black Bart, who alone ambushed 28 coaches from 1877 to 1885. The museum is open Monday through Friday from 9 AM to 5 PM. There is no charge for admission.

CHINATOWN

The old Chinatown was truly a closed city within the larger city of San Francisco. Founded in the 1850s, in the past it was a place of mystery and intrigue, not to mention danger. The old Chinatown, with its opium dens, brothels, and gambling parlors, was destroyed by the 1906 earthquake and fire. But the new Chinatown that replaced it is still an exotic and foreign place. Police are warned not to chase a suspect underground, because it's believed a labyrinth of escape tunnels still exists there; and the most recent Asian gang war took place not in the 1800s, but in the 1970s.

Until the 1950s, the Chinese had their own telephone system that depended on the remarkable ability of operators to remember 30,000 names instead of numbers.

Few other immigrant groups have met with the intense hostility the Chinese faced in California in the early days. They were willing to work hard for much lower wages, and were the victims not just of vigilante actions but of legal discrimination as well. Asians could not testify against whites in the courts, and Chinese immigration was prohibited by state laws passed as late as 1902. In the face of all this, the Chinese developed their own Chinese Benevolent Association—also called the "Six Companies" because it was comprised of six *tongs* — that looked after the community and represented the Chinese in all disputes with state and federal officials.

Today's 24-block Chinatown is a relatively peaceful place. A huge stone "Gateway to Chinatown" was erected in 1970 as a bridge of understanding with the rest of the city. Even the modern banks and telephone booths are built in pagoda style. For a glimpse of authentic Buddhism, you can visit the **Kong Chow Temple** at 855 Stockton Street near Clay, the **Tin Hou Temple** at 125 Waverly Place (dedicated to the Queen of Heaven in 1852), and a more recent symbol of cultural assimilation and endurance, **Buddha's Universal Church** ((415) 982-6116, 720 Washing-

corner of Grant Avenue and California Street. Old **Saint Mary's Church** was originally built as a cathedral in 1845 and was twice destroyed, by the 1906 quake and again 60 years later by fire. From Saint Mary's Church there is a lovely view of Rafael Bufano's statue of Dr. Sun Yat-Sen in the middle of Saint Mary's Square. Dr. Sun, the first president of the Republic of China, albeit briefly, spent several years of political asylum in San Francisco.

From Saint Mary's Square, a walk along Grant Avenue away from the Civic Center will bring you to several sights of interest. A plaque on the wall of **Dick Young House**, 823 Grant Avenue, commemorates the first human habitation of Yerba Buena, as San Francisco was originally called, on

ton Street, reputedly the largest Buddhist temple in the United States. On the roof is a Bodhi tree, said to be a shoot from the tree under which Buddha himself became enlightened more than 2,500 years ago. Advanced notification is required to visit the temple.

Three museums in Chinatown offer exhibits and performances on the role of the Chinese and other immigrants from Asia: the **Chinese Historical Society** ((415) 391-1188, 650 Commercial Street, open Tuesday through Friday from 10 AM to 4 PM and Saturday from 11 AM to 3 PM; the **Chinese Culture Center** ((415) 986-1822, 750 Kearny Street, open Tuesday through Saturday from 10 AM to 4 PM; and the **Pacific Heritage Museum** ((415) 399-1124, 608 Commercial Street.

The oldest Catholic church in San Francisco can be found in the middle of Chinatown, at the

June 25th, 1835. Nearby are two beautiful examples of Sino-American architecture — the **Bank of America** (1971), 701 Grant, covered in ornate gilded tiles, and the pagoda-like **Bank of Canton** (1909), 743 Washington Street, originally the Chinatown telephone office and built on the site where the first newspaper in California was published. Near the intersection of Jackson and Grant are several Chinese theaters. The performances are particularly interesting because of the simple staging, elaborate costuming and the dissonance of the traditional music played.

OPPOSITE: Young Japanese girls in San Francisco reflect a happier time in a state where Orientals suffered a history of legal oppression. ABOVE: San Francisco's Chinatown is an exotic city within a city and one of its big attractions, especially the extensive oriental dining options.

Walking is the best way to see Chinatown, and you may want to make an adventure out of discovering a little dim sum place or an elegant restaurant on your own. If you prefer a guided tour, one of the best is offered by cooking instructor Shirley Fong-Torres. For information on her **"Chinatown Adventure Tours with the Wok Wiz"** ((415) 981-8989 TOLL-FREE (800) 281-9255 E-MAIL wokwiz@aol.com, 654 Commercial Street, San Francisco, CA 94111.

NORTH BEACH

North Beach better expresses both the city's raucous and sophisticated past than any other part of San Francisco. Here, great writers such as Mark Twain, Bret Harte, Robert Louis Stevenson, and Rudyard Kipling once walked, and might still walk if they were to come back. The literary whimsy even extends to the name: "North Beach where there is no beach; with Washington Square where the statue is not of Washington but of Franklin." In fact, it was once much closer to the waterfront and there was a "north beach" before a huge landfill was created.

The area was once famous for its unruly brothels and bars, and was where most of the Italian immigrants settled. A legacy of the past endures at the intersection of Columbus and Broadway. The area's mainstays are now strip-tease joints, jazz clubs and cabarets, flanked by Italian restaurants and the ubiquitous cafés, among the best of which is **Enrico's** ((415) 982-6223, 504 Broadway, where you can sit and watch the crowds outside **Finocchio's** ((415) 982-9388, famous for its drag shows for the past 50 years.

In addition to Enrico's (which features live jazz at night), several nice old coffee houses carry on North Beach's Italian tradition. **Tosca Café** ((415) 986-9651, 242 Columbus Avenue features a jukebox filled with all the classic favorites of Italian opera. **Mario's Bohemian Cigar Store Café** ((415) 362-0536, 566 Columbus Avenue, also has a wonderful old Italian ambiance, but its main attraction is the grilled eggplant sandwich, which draws customers from throughout the city.

The **Church of Saint Peter and Saint Paul** stands in the middle of Washington Square, at 666 Filbert Street, in the heart of North Beach. Off the square you'll find any number of comfortable old bars and restaurants. This area is the traditional gathering place for San Francisco's journalists, mainly at the **Washington Square Bar & Grill** ((415) 982-8123, 1707 Powell Street. Across the square is **Mama's** ((415) 362-6421, 1701 Stockton Street, one of the city's most popular breakfast places. Although the restaurant has now expanded to a branch on Union Square, this is the original, where "Mama" Fran Sanchez often does the cooking, as she has for 40 odd years. There's nothing dainty about Mama's

breakfasts — the omelets, waffles, and pancake plates are so huge it's a meal that can last all day.

Little Joe's and Baby Joe's ((415) 433-4343, 523 Broadway, is one of the area's best known eateries, where huge portions of incredibly hearty and authentic Italian food are served. The restaurant, unfortunately, generally lives up to its motto: "Rain or shine, there's always a line." It's a wonderful place to go for a late lunch when business slows down a bit. Little Joe's has also expanded to include a Union Square branch, which is quite a bit more upscale than the Broadway location, but which also, as a result, lacks much of its predecessor's charm.

San Francisco's best-known bookstore is **City Lights** ((415) 362-8193 at 261 Columbus Avenue. Run by beat poet Lawrence Ferlinghetti for more than 30 years, City Lights is a wonderfully relaxed literary institution, where a love of books, rather

than a love of business (which it incidentally sees quite a bit of) seems to have been established as the store's raison d'être.

THE EMBARCADERO

Being a peninsula, San Francisco has a waterfront on three sides. The ocean front is taken up by the Golden Gate National Recreation Area, but most of the rest is still a busy working port area, or embarcadero.

The earthquake in 1989 caused gas leaks from burst mains that ignited and damaged parts of the shoreline. But the most significant change as a result of the earthquake was the dismantling of the infamous Embarcadero Freeway that had for years obstructed views of the bay. Rather than repair extensive damage to the freeway, the city chose to demolish it.

Embarcadero Center, between Battery Street and the Ferry Building, is an enormous shopping, office and residential complex comprised of five skyscrapers and the 20-story Hyatt Regency Hotel. The buildings are connected by plazas and footbridges designed by famed Atlanta architect John Portman and filled with all sorts of shops, vendors and artistic exhibits. The buildings themselves are not of much interest, except for the Hyatt Regency with its amazing atrium lobby and four-story sculpture by Charles Perry. The rooftop **SkyDeck** TOLL-FREE (888) 737-5933, at Embarcadero Center, offers incredible views of downtown San Francisco and the waterfront.

A short stroll north along the Embarcadero brings you to the **Northeast Waterfront Historic**

San Francisco's quirky characters are drawn to the promenade and salt-scented air at North Beach.

SAN FRANCISCO (DOWNTOWN)

District, bounded by Union Street and Broadway. In the shadow of Telegraph Hill and Coit Tower, the area harbors many nineteenth-century commercial and industrial buildings, spared the destruction of the 1906 quake and subsequent natural disasters.

FISHERMAN'S WHARF

The Embarcadero, Columbus Avenue and the Hyde Street cable car lines all terminate at

Fishermen's Wharf, a San Francisco icon and one of the city's premier tourist attractions. A widely diverse area, the Wharf literally has something for everyone — although you're more likely to find visitors than locals browsing the shops, bars and restaurants. Once an authentic haven for colorful Italian-American fishermen, the Wharf has become almost the exclusive domain of tourists, a somewhat tawdry parody of what it once was. However, the area still supports a small resident fishing

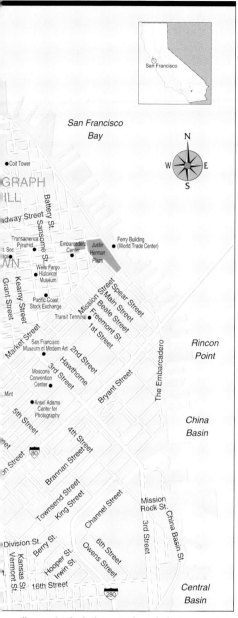

San Francisco
Bay

N
W E
S

● Coit Tower

GRAPH
ILL

Battery St.
idway Street
Transamerica
Pyramid
t. Soc
ice●
WN
Sansome St.
Embarcadero
Center
Justin
Herman
Plaza
Ferry Building
(World Trade Center)
● Wells Fargo
● Historical
Museum
Keamy Street
Grant Street
● Pacific Coast
Stock Exchange
Transit Terminal
Mission Street
Spear Street
Main Street
Beale Street
Freemont St.
1st Street
San Francisco
Museum of Modern Art
Market Street
2nd Street
Moscone
Convention
Center ●
3rd Street
Hawthorne
Street
Bryant Street
The Embarcadero
● Mint
● Ansel Adams
Center for
Photography
5th Street
4th Street
Brannan Street
Townsend Street
King Street
Channel Street
Mission
Rock St.
3rd Street
China Basin St.
Division St.
Berry St.
Kansas St.
Vermont St.
t.
16th Street
Hooper St.
Irwin St.
6th Street
Owens Street
280

San Francisco

Rincon
Point

China
Basin

Central
Basin

fleet, which shelters each night between piers 45 and 47.

Jefferson Street is the Wharf's main thoroughfare and perhaps the most garish street in America with its myriad T-shirt shops, souvenir outlets and carnival-like attractions. Ripley's Believe It or Not Museum ((415) 771-6188, 175 Jefferson Street, displays two thousand oddities from around the world. It is open daily from 10 AM to 10 PM. The nearby Wax Museum TOLL-FREE (800) 439-4305, 145 Jefferson Street, has over 270 wax replicas of

famous personages, plus a Chamber of Horrors and a recreation of King Tut's treasure-laden tomb. It is open daily from 9 AM to 10 PM.

The kitsch spills over into **Pier 39** ((415) 981-PIER WEB SITE www.pier39.com, at the foot of Jefferson Street. With more than a hundred specialty shops and a dozen food outlets, plus various carnival-like attractions and buskers, the pier is something of a permanent circus on the San Francisco waterfront. Some of the shops are downright strange, like one that sells nothing but refrigerator magnets, another dedicated solely to boxes of all shapes and sizes, and another that hawks Alcatraz souvenirs (handcuffs, cell keys, zebra-striped prison outfits, etc). There are also shops peddling hammocks, puppets, kites, needlework, crystal, coffees and teas, seashells, cable car memorabilia, and a year-round Christmas decorations outlet. Among other Pier 39 stalwarts are a high-tech adventure simulator called the **Turbo Ride** and a "diver's-eye view" aquarium called **Underwater World**. If you get tired of all the glitz, stroll over to K-dock, where as many of the wharf area's 600 resident sea lions sun themselves each day.

Eclectic attractions also anchor the western end of Fisherman's Wharf. **Ghirardelli Square** ((414) 775-5500 WEB SITE www.ghirardellisq.com, at the corner of Beach and Larkin, includes more than 70 shops and restaurants set around a bustling cobblestone piazza. Unveiled in 1964, this was the country's first example of a seemingly useless old warehouse or factory building being renovated into an elegant shopping and eating complex. The success of Ghirardelli spawned hundreds of imitators, from the restored Cannery Row in Monterey to Covent Garden in London to the Rocks in Sydney. The red-brick belfry (1916) was modeled after the Château de Blois in France. The square's oldest building dates back to 1864, when it was used as a woolen mill. The Ghirardelli family chocolate factory occupied the site from 1893 until its modern conversion and the **Ghirardelli Chocolate Shop** is still the square's main attraction with a wonderful assortment of sundaes, shakes, banana splits and other taste treats.

Within easy walking distance of Ghirardelli Square is another factory-to-retail conversion called **The Cannery** ((415) 771-3112 WEB SITE www.thecannery.com, at the corner of Beach and Leavenworth. The structure dates from 1893 and was used as a fruit cannery by the Del Monte Company for many years. Restored in 1968, it now boasts 50 shops and restaurants, some with a lovely view of the bay and others fronting a colorful courtyard filled with hundred-year-old olive trees and busy with jugglers and mimes.

Directly opposite the Cannery is **Aquatic Park** with its cable car turnabout and fishing pier. There's also a small sandy beach where local residents can be seen swimming laps at the crack of dawn (rain or shine). The park is also home to the superb **National Maritime Museum** ((415) 556-3002. Originally a prosperous casino, the museum opened in 1939 and features two floors of exhibits on San Francisco's long and lively association with the sailing trade. Included in the collection are handcrafted model ships, scrimshaw carvings, painted figureheads, and rare waterfront photographs. It is open from 10 AM to 5 PM daily. Admission is free.

Several historic ships in the museum collection are docked at nearby **Hyde Street Pier** including the *C.A. Thayer*, a three-masted lumber schooner built in 1895; the *Eureka*, a wonderfully restored 1890 steam ferry that once plied the bay; and the *Balclutha*, a steel-hulled square-rigger built in Scotland in 1886. Open from 10 AM to 5 PM daily, admission is $3 for adults.

SOUTH OF MARKET

Following the lead of New York's Soho area, San Francisco has created what some are calling "SoMa" (South of Market), a huge urban renewal area wedged between the Financial District, Union Square and the Mission District. For many years, this area of dilapidated warehouses and slum housing was called "south of the slot." But after the $126-million, six-acre (two-and-a-half-hectare) **Moscone Convention Center** ((415) 267-6400 was built, the whole area revitalized. SoMa is now home to dozens of very popular restaurants and discotheques, experimental theaters and art galleries, and a design center called Showplace Square.

The cultural heart of SoMa is the brand new **Yerba Buena Center for the Arts** ((415) 978-ARTS, on Third Street between Mission and Howard. The complex features a broad menu of exhibits and events that showcase San Francisco's cultural diversity including films, music, dance and drama. Next door is the **Esplanade**, a downtown park with outdoor cafés, a walk-through waterfall fountain and an outdoor performance area with lawn seating for 5,000 people.

The South of Market area boasts several fine museums including the excellent **San Francisco Museum of Modern Art** ((415) 357-4000 at Third and Howard (see ART MUSEUMS, page 102). The **Cartoon Art Museum** ((415) 227-8666, 814 Mission Street, is the world's foremost collection of comic strips, caricatures and funnies. It is open Wednesday through Saturday from 11 AM to 5 PM and Sunday from 1 PM to 5 PM. The **Ansel Adams Center for Photography** ((415) 495-7000, 240 Fourth Street, displays the work of landscape master Ansel Adams and other eminent shooters. The **California Historical Society Museum** ((415) 357-1848, 678 Mission Street,

casts a spotlight on the Golden State's rich heritage. It is open Tuesday through Saturday from 11 AM to 5 PM.

THE MISSION DISTRICT

Often overlooked amidst all of the glitter of San Francisco is the Mission District, cultural heart of San Francisco's large Hispanic population. Unlike neighborhoods that cater to the thriving tourist industry, the Mission exists only for itself and its multi-faceted population, whose culture is emblazoned even on the colorful murals found on nearly every street.

The neighborhood takes its name from **Mission Dolores** ((415) 621-8203, on Dolores Avenue near 16th Street, open from 9 AM to 4 PM daily. Established in 1776 as the sixth of the California missions, it was originally called San Francisco de Assisi. It was later rechristened Laguna de Nuestra Senora de los Dolores (Lake of Our Lady of Sorrows), shortened to Mission Dolores. The current building, erected between 1782 and 1791, survived the 1906 earthquake and is the oldest structure in San Francisco. There is a lovely Baroque altar inside, but a basilica has replaced the original inner courtyard. In the mission cemetery lie the remains of some of San Francisco's earliest inhabitants, including Costonoan Indians. The building is now maintained as a museum, its religious functions superseded by a much larger church constructed nearby in 1916.

La Cumbre ((415) 863-8205, 515 Valencia Street, and **La Taqueria** ((415) 285-7117, 2889 Mission Street, are widely recognized as among the best *taquerias* (taco bars) in the city. While rather rustic in their simplicity (burritos are served in plastic baskets), the food is practically sublime, and the variety to be found in Mexican fare is truly revelatory.

While in the Mission, try **Café Picaro** ((415) 431-4089, 3120 16th Street, for a cappuccino, a glass of wine or a pastry. Across the street is the **Roxie Theater** ((415) 863-1087, an alternative cinema where you can see movies that most probably will never hit your neighborhood or even your local video store. Offbeat films, foreign movies and revivals of Hollywood classics are the cinema's forte.

Modern Times Bookstore ((415) 282-9246, 888 Valencia Street, is a collectively-run operation with a decidedly left-wing bent. At 3284 23rd Street is **Pathfinder Bookstore** ((415) 282-6255, the place to go in search of revolutionary or seditious literature that has, at one time or another, been banned by governments here or abroad. For further information about the Mission District, contact the **Mission Cultural Center** ((415) 826-1401, 2899 24th Street.

THE CASTRO

Largely recognized as the heart of San Francisco's "gay culture," the Castro Street area has a large number of shops, restaurants, cafés and the like. In the neighborhood, you can find anything from quality leather goods (of all varieties) to kitsch souvenirs. A local landmark is the **Castro Theater** ((415) 621-6120, 429 Castro Street, built in 1922 and one of the last "grand dame" movie palaces in San Francisco. The cinema specializes in foreign films and classic Hollywood revivals.

Café Flore ((415) 621-8579, 2298 Market Street, is an often crowded, trendy, but invariably fasci-

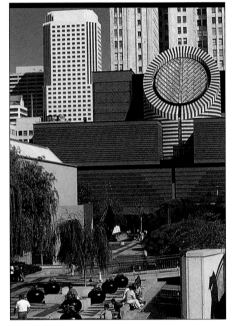

nating café, for decor, quality of food and clientele. The *San Francisco Chronicle* has written it up as being the place to go to see offbeat hair-styles. Fantastic Mexican dishes can be had at **Pozole** ((415) 626-2666, 2337 Market Street. Pozole blends Latin-American authenticity with California cuisine. Burritos are made with traditional cactus fillings and their ingredients are delightfully fresh.

A Different Light ((415) 431-0891, 489 Castro Street, is a bookstore carrying predominantly gay and feminist literature. **Gauntlet** ((415) 431-3133, 2377 Market Street, carries leather paraphernalia, from jackets to whips, and offers an undiluted view of the possibilities of cowhide. **Rolo** ((415) 626-7171 at 450 Castro and ((415) 864-0505 at 535 Castro, caters to a more mainstream fashion sense, with trendy Californian styles.

San Francisco and the Bay Area

HAIGHT–ASHBURY

Undoubtedly the Haight is one of the most overburdened neighborhoods in the city. On weekends and holidays it teems with masses looking for some last gasp of its hippie past. Just blocks from Golden Gate Park, the corner of Haight and Ashbury, once the epicenter of the American flower-child movement of the 1960s, was the spot to which young people once flocked, claiming this corner and the neighborhood surrounding it as their own.

Though it went through a long period of decline, the mid-1980s produced a period of gentrification, during which the neighborhood once again flowered. Shops cropped up between the liquor stores, and eventually the area became one of the main shopping strips of the city. During the day, the Haight is a bustling, laid-back neighborhood, full of energy. At night, unfortunately, street-people tend to give it a rather ominous and somewhat vitriolic air. It has evolved, however, into a trendy mecca for teens and young adults. A few 1960s landmarks remain. Deepthroated singer **Janis Joplin** once lived at 112 Lyon Street while the **Grateful Dead** got their start at 710 Ashbury Street.

There are a number of very good restaurants along Haight Street. **Dish** ((415) 431-3534 at the corner of Haight and Masonic is undoubtedly one of the oldest and best known of the lot. Similar heaping plates can be found at the rather small **Pork Store Café** ((415) 864-6981, 1451 Haight Street, a wonderful place to have breakfast or brunch at reasonable prices. **Cha-Cha-Cha** ((415) 386-5758, at 1801 Haight Street, is a crowded Cuban bistro, well-frequented for its comfortable atmosphere, moderate prices, bountiful sangria and exotic fare. Neighboring **Chabela** ((415) 751-6204 is one of the city's great values, with enormous burritos for less than $5. **Zona Rosa** ((415) 668-7717, 1797 Haight Street, serves similar fare, but in a somewhat more upscale environment — there's actually plenty of space to sit down and enjoy your meal. **Crescent City Café** ((415) 863-1374, 1418 Haight Street, specializes in New Orleans-style Cajun food. Try their blackened catfish.

As a clothing experience, **Villains** ((415) 626-5939, 1672 Haight Street, will either attract or repulse. Its fashions tend to cater to many of the neighborhood's more eccentric and youthful frequenters — patent leather and studs seem to be de rigueur. **Ambiance** ((415) 552-5095, 1458 Haight Street, features clothing made by local designers stressing moderate prices and up-to-

The city's Latin, Asian, and Italian influences are showcased in the Yerba Buena Center for the Arts.

the-minute styling. Their fashion sense leans toward the slightly eccentric and anachronistically cool. **Forever After Books** ℓ (415) 431-8299, 1475 Haight Street, is a very pleasant spot to browse through piles of used books. Haight Street's main shopping attraction seems to be the numerous trinket and thrift shops that line either side of the street, where one can discover anything from a rare find to over-priced garbage.

CULTURAL LIFE

San Francisco is the only city in California — and one of the few in America — that has world-class opera and ballet companies and a major symphony orchestra. Opening nights for all three are major dress-up events for the city's high society. But, in the true spirit of San Francisco, the day after opening night at the San Francisco Opera in September, the public is invited to a free performance of Opera in the Park at the band shell in Golden Gate Park.

The San Francisco Opera and San Francisco Ballet perform in the 3,535-seat **War Memorial Opera House** ℓ (415) 864-3330, on Van Ness between McAllister and Grove, a wonderful Beaux-Arts building in the complex surrounding City Hall. You get some idea of the city's place in the cultural life of California when you realize that this is the only functioning opera house in the state. Built in 1932 by Arthur Brown Jr., also responsible for the Veteran's Building opposite City Hall, the Opera House has had a large share in the civil and cultural history of San Francisco. The United Nations was inaugurated here June 26, 1945, and until 1980, the San Francisco Opera, Ballet and Symphony shared the space. The San Francisco Symphony now performs in the new **Davies Symphony Hall** ℓ (415) 846-6000, 201 Van Ness, a modern 2,958-seat addition to the center.

Bass Ticket Agency ℓ (510) 762-2277 handles tickets to most local performing arts events and has outlets throughout the city including Union Square, Four Embarcadero Center, and the Tower Records store at Bay and Columbus. **Mr. Ticket** ℓ (415) 775-3031 sells premium seats for Bay Area concerts, theater and sporting events.

While cultural events of every description are often sold out long in advance, **TIX Bay Area** ℓ (415) 433-7827 provides reduced-rate tickets on the day of a performance through an outlet on the Stockton Street side of Union Square. It is open Tuesday through Thursday from 11 AM to 6 PM, and Friday and Saturday from 11 AM to 7 PM; all sales are cash and there are no reservations.

ART MUSEUMS

When one looks around at all the beautiful private houses and public parks, it would seem that San

Franciscans look on their city itself as a work of art. With this generous attitude toward the place, it's not surprising that many of the city's wealthiest families have helped to establish here some of the greatest art museums in America. The main collection is the **M.H. de Young Museum** ℓ (415) 750-3600 or (415) 863-3330, in Golden Gate Park. This is the city's most expansive museum with 22 galleries of American art from the seventeenth through the twentieth century.

Adjoining the older museum is a new wing built to house the **Avery Brundage Collection/Asian Art Museum** ℓ (415) 379-8800 WEB SITE www.asianart.org. Opened in 1966, the museum is the largest collection in the Western world dedicated exclusively to Asian art. More than 1,000 objects are on display at any one time in changing exhibits from the permanent collections.

One of the most unusual art museums in San Francisco is the **California Palace of the Legion of Honor** ((415) 750-3600 or (415) 863-3330. Situated on a plateau near Land's End in Lincoln Park, the structure itself is worth a visit. Modeled after the Legion of Honor building in Paris, it was built in 1915 to house an all-French collection from the Spreckels family. Alma de Bretteville Spreckels was an early patron of Rodin, among other French artists of the time, and the familiar Rodin sculptures (such as the *Thinker*) shown here were among the first cast by the sculptor. The Achenbach Foundation for Graphic Arts, the largest of its kind, is also located in the Legion of Honor museum.

Admission to the above museums varies from $7 for adults to free for children under 12. One admission, however, admits you to both the de Young and the Brundage on the same day. You can also purchase a **Golden Gate Park Explorer**

Pass which renders a 25% saving on regular adult admission to the de Young and Brundage, as well as the Japanese Tea Garden and the California Academy of Sciences.

The **San Francisco Museum of Modern Art** (SFMMA) ((415) 357-4000, 151 Third Street, was the first museum dedicated solely to modern art in California. SFMMA features lively exhibits that are frequently changed; it places a special emphasis on abstract expressionism and photography. Its permanent collection includes works by Henri Matisse, Georges Braque, Pablo Picasso, William de Kooning, Karl Hofer, Wassily Kandinsky, Geor-

---

The Palace of Fine Arts, the only surviving structure from the 1915 Panama-Pacific International Exhibition. Originally built of plaster, it was strengthened in 1967 and in one wing houses the Exploratorium, considered by many to be the best science museum in the world.

gia O'Keefe and Ansel Adams. Admission is $7 for adults, $3.50 for seniors and students with identification; children under age 13 are free.

VICTORIANA

In most American cities you'll find that a little jewel box of a house built in the late 1800s has somehow escaped the wrecking ball and is now preserved as a public treasure. In San Francisco, you'll find row upon row of beautiful old Victorian houses spread out over the city's 43 hills, houses preserved not by government edict but through the concern of its citizens. Even though 514 blocks of the old city were destroyed in the fire following the 1906

Several Victorian houses are maintained as museums. The Foundation for San Francisco's Architectural Heritage has its headquarters in the **Haas-Lilienthal House** ((415) 441-3004, 2007 Franklin Street. The house is open for tours and information.

You can see fine examples of all of these if you wander through any of the older parts of the city. However, if you want to be sure you're seeing the best examples, you should join a **Victorian tour**. Several groups offer walking tours of the more interesting areas. The best of these are: **City Guides** (Friends of the Library) ((415) 557-4266 at the Civic Center; **Victorian Home Walk** ((415) 252-9485, 2226 15th Street; and **San Francisco Then and Now** ((415) 931-4021, 925 Sutter, Suite 101.

earthquake, there are still more than 14,000 examples of this elaborate architecture dating from 1850 to 1900, particularly in the Bernal Heights, Eureka, Haight-Ashbury, Mission District and Potrero Hill areas. So treasured are these houses that municipal law prohibits any change in existing structures and new residential buildings must incorporate bay windows into the design.

There are three basic schools of Victorian architecture found in San Francisco. The Queen Anne school was copied from a style popular in England in the 1860s and features rounded corners, hooded domes, high gables and redwood shingle siding; the Italianate style was popular from 1850 to 1875 and is seen in doorways framed by narrow columns; the Stick, or Eastlake, style took Italianate to delightful vertical extremes and into the twentieth century with horseshoe arches and corners perched on columns.

SPORTS

No one in San Francisco would ever admit it, but it's surely because of the frequently damp weather that **golf** is not the major sport here that it is further south in drier, sunnier parts of California. Still, there are several courses in and near the city, two of the most picturesque being public courses operated by the city.

Some of the greens on the 18-hole **Lincoln Park Golf Course** ((415) 221-9911 offer a stunning a view of the Golden Gate Bridge. The start of the course is located at 34th Avenue and Clement Street. Green fees are $23 weekdays, $27 weekends. There is a nine-hole course in beautiful Golden Gate Park and an 18-hole course in the Presidio, both with reasonable green fees.

One of the most difficult courses in Northern California is located at Half Moon Bay, just

25 miles (40 km) south of San Francisco off State Highway 1. **Half Moon Bay Golf Links** ((650) 726-4438, which sprawls along the Pacific coast, is at 2000 Fairway Drive. Situated in Napa Valley, about 45 minutes north of San Francisco, is the **Chardonnay Golf Club** ((707) 257-1900, 2555 Jamieson Canyon Road, near the intersection of Highways 29 and 12. Chardonnay features two 18-hole courses framed in oak trees and vineyards.

Despite their sophisticated façade, Bay Area residents are just as fanatic about their home **professional sports** teams as fans in Los Angeles and elsewhere in America. You may have trouble getting tickets to National Football League (NFL) games hosted by the **San Francisco Forty-Niners** at 3-Com Park ((415) 468-2249, or the **Oakland Raiders** at Oakland Coliseum ((510) 762-BASS across the bay. However, there are nearly always tickets at the gate for Major League baseball games hosted by the **San Francisco Giants** ((415) 467-8000 and the **Oakland Athletics** ((510) 568-5600 or (510) 638-0500, at the same venues.

American football season runs from September to January, with games kicking off at 1 PM. Baseball season runs from April to October, with either 1 PM afternoon or 7:30 PM evenings starts. Windy, 70,000-seat 3Com Park is located eight miles (12.8 km) south of downtown San Francisco off US Highway 101. Oakland Coliseum is situated just off the Bayshore Freeway, near Oakland Airport.

The only National Basketball Association (NBA) team in the Bay Area is the **Golden State Warriors**, which play at Oakland Coliseum Arena ((510) 762-BASS. The National Hockey League (NHL) is represented by the **San Jose Sharks** ((510) 762-BASS, who play at the San Jose Arena in the south bay.

GETTING AROUND

In San Francisco, you may find that getting around is half the fun. There is no city anywhere that can offer as many different — and fun — ways of getting around on public transportation.

CABLE CARS

It's not unusual to visit a national historic landmark, but in San Francisco you can actually ride on one when you climb aboard one of the city's famous cable cars. This is the only system of its kind in the world, as well as one of the globe's oldest public transportation systems, established in 1873.

By the early 1980s, it seemed as if the cars might have had their day, as the peculiar underground cable system was beyond repair. However, a vig-

orous local campaign raised $10 million which, with $60 million in state and federal funding, enabled the entire system to be dug up and restored. You can study the mechanism that powers the cable cars firsthand at the **Cable Car Museum, Powerhouse, and Car Barn** ((415) 474-1887 on the side of Nob Hill, at Washington and Mason Streets. The Car Barn is a three-story, red-brick structure dating from 1907 which now houses the original prototype cable car, models of other cars, and the cable mechanism itself.

The cable cars were the brainchild of Andrew Hallidie, who was appalled by the sight of horses and mules trying to negotiate San Francisco's steep hills. The current system involves a circular, or

"endless," steel cable 1⅜ inches (3.5 cm) thick and 8.8 miles (12 km) long that is let out at a speed of nine miles per hour (15 kph). The cable cars move by grasping onto the moving cable and stop by letting go. There are now 39 cable cars in operation (28 on the two Powell Street lines and 11 on the California Street route) and they convey 9.6 million passengers each year. It's a unique and historic way to see the city, and 14 million people ride the cars each year.

There are three cable car routes in all: the **Powell-Hyde Line** originates at Powell and Market Streets and ends at Victorian Park, not far from the Maritime Museum and Aquatic Park; the

---

OPPOSITE: Some of the greens at the Lincoln Park Golf Course in San Francisco offer spectacular views of the ocean and the Golden Gate Bridge. ABOVE: Locals claim the streets around Fisherman's Wharf in early morning, before the crowds arrive.

Powell-Mason Line also starts at Powell and Market, but terminates at Bay Street near Fisherman's Wharf; while the **California Street Line** goes from the foot of Market Street up and over Nob Hill to Van Ness Avenue. The fare on the cable cars is $2. Tickets must be purchased before boarding and can be bought from automatic machines at the major stops.

THE MUNI

"Muni" is the pet name for the San Francisco Municipal Railway, which operates all the municipal transportation facilities including buses, trams and cable cars. The Muni Metro is a streamlined electric version of the cable cars, operating underground downtown and aboveground in the outer city. Fares on the Muni, both buses and trams, are only $1, and exact change is required. Muni Passports are available for one day ($6), three days ($10) or seven days ($15); the passes are also good on cable cars. For information on routes and schedules call ((415) 673-6864. A free pamphlet called *Tours of Discovery* describes nine tours of the city using Muni trains and is available by writing to the San Francisco Municipal Railway, 949 Presidio Avenue, San Francisco, CA 94115.

THE BART

"BART" is an acronym for the city's modern mass transportation system, Bay Area Rapid Transit, a $5-billion space-age underground and underwater system that links Daly City and San Francisco with Oakland, Berkeley, and other spots on the East Bay. The 95-mile (140-km) system is described as "the tourist attraction that gets people to other tourist attractions." The three-mile (five-and-a-half-kilometer) stretch that runs under the bay was the longest of its kind in the world until the completion of the English Channel tunnel. The fares on BART depend on your destination and all tickets must be bought from machines at any of the 36 stations. A free brochure, *Fun Goes Farther on BART*, is also available at the stations. For other information, contact: BART ((415) 788-BART, 800 Madison Street, Oakland 94607.

BUSES

Bus services operate throughout the Bay Area. In addition to the regular electric buses you see on the city streets, there is also a regular service to the outlying areas. **AC Transit** ((415) 817-1717 operates buses to Oakland, Berkeley and other East Bay areas from the Transbay Terminal at First and Mission Streets. **Golden Gate Transit** ((415) 923-2000 operates out of the same terminal, with service

across the Golden Gate Bridge to Marin and Sonoma counties. Also operating from Transbay Terminal is **Samtrans** TOLL-FREE (800) 660-4BUS, which offers service to San Francisco International Airport and other peninsula destinations as far south as Palo Alto.

FERRY SERVICES

Once a vital link between San Francisco and other parts of the Bay Area, more than 50 ferry boats were in service when the Golden Gate and Bay bridges put them out of service. In recent years, the ferries have come back as a popular way of crossing or seeing the bay.

Golden Gate Ferries ((415) 923-2000 depart from the south end of the Ferry Building at the foot of Market Street, making regular runs back and forth to Sausalito and Larkspur. Sausalito passage is $4.25; Larkspur passage is $4.25 on weekends, $2.50 on weekdays; there are discounts for senior citizens, children and disabled persons.

The **Blue & Gold Fleet** ((415) 773-1188 or (415) 705-5555 operates from Fisherman's Wharf. Boats leave from Pier 41 on a regular daily schedule to Sausalito, Tiburon and Alcatraz, as well as Angel Island (summer, weekends and holidays only). Blue & Gold also offers daily round trip service to Oakland's Jack London Square, Alameda Main Street and Vallejo in the north bay (from Pier 39 and the Ferry Terminal). Fares range from $4 for a one-way ticket to Oakland to $11 for a round trip to Alcatraz, with discounts for seniors and children.

WHERE TO STAY

Almost from the days when the first gold miners came back with money to spend on a lavish night on the town, San Francisco has boasted America's most luxurious hotels. Nob Hill was where the first of the gold and silver millionaires built their fabulous private mansions and that is where the city's better hotels are located, some on the site of the old mansions and preserving the pioneer family names.

Union Square is the other center of luxury hotels in San Francisco. There are more than 40 hotels in and around the beautiful old square, convenient to the city's premier shopping district. Of course, there are many newer luxury-class hotels in other parts of the city, but the most interesting development in recent years has been the popularity of smaller hotels, many of them restored to a turn-of-the-century elegance befitting the Victorian residential areas. Not least among the places to stay are the many bed and breakfast places available in San Francisco. This is a way to stay in one of the old homes, but "bed and breakfast" does not necessarily mean inexpensive lodging, as it does in Europe; this has become one of the most elegant and expensive American means of lodging.

NOB HILL

Very Expensive

The impeccable **Renaissance Stanford Court** ((415) 989-3500 TOLL-FREE (800) HOTEL-1 FAX 989-3500, 905 California Street, stands on the site of the Leland Stanford Mansion, the home of California's first Republican Governor and famous railroad magnate. The mansion was destroyed in the 1906 earthquake, but the land was purchased

and the foundations of the hotel laid in 1912. The Stanford Court has 400 rooms, an award-winning restaurant, and two bars. Room rates include complimentary amenities including admission to the Nob Hill Health Club across the street.

If flagrant opulence is your cup of team, head for the **Fairmont Hotel** ((415) 772-5000 TOLL-FREE (800) 527-4727, 950 Mason Street. The lobby is an instant trip back to the turn of the century when velvet chairs and marble columns were all the rage. The Fairmont boasts 596 rooms, seven restaurants, ten lounges, and a supper club with world-class entertainment.

Celebrities visiting the City by the Bay seem to prefer the smaller and cozier **Huntington Hotel** ((415) 474-5400 TOLL-FREE (800) 227-4683, 1075 California Street. The 140 rooms are more extravagant than the Fairmont or Stanford Court, and privacy reigns supreme.

San Francisco and the Bay Area

The 390 rooms of the **Mark Hopkins Inter-Continental** ((415) 392-3434 TOLL-FREE (800) 327-0200, 1 Nob Hill, offer some of the best views in San Francisco, as does the Top of the Mark penthouse restaurant and bar.

Inexpensive

Stepping down from the luxury class, but still on Nob Hill, there are several small hotels that give you the classy address at a fraction of the cost. One of the best of these is the **San Francisco Residence Club** ((415) 421-2220, 851 California Street, a European-style pension which charges $235 to $600 per week for rooms with bay views.

UNION SQUARE

Some of the city's grandest old hotels are located in this beautiful old shopping and hotel district. Most are now owned and operated by the major chains, but much of their local charm lives on. The most historic is the St. Francis.

Very Expensive

The **Westin St. Francis** ((415) 397-7000 TOLL-FREE (800) WESTIN-1, 335 Powell, right on Union Square, is one of the city's preeminent hotels and its reputation has been well earned. Since its opening in 1904, many prominent guests have stayed there including Princess Grace, Bing Crosby, Mother Teresa, Al Jolson, and Bill

The elegant, yet cozy atmosphere of Washington Square Inn in North Beach.

Clinton. The five glass elevators that run up the outside of the 32-story tower offer tremendous views of downtown San Francisco. Its great "Magnata" clock in the lobby has been a famous rendezvous since its installation in 1907. Another odd indication of the uniqueness of the St. Francis is the fact that it's the only hotel in the world that washes its money. Arnold Batliner, who was the hotel's coin-washer for 31 years, retired in 1993 after scrubbing $17 million in coins. The St. Francis boasts 1,200 rooms, a fitness center, four restaurants (including the award-winning Victor's on the 32nd floor), five bars and a nightclub.

Another luxury hotel in the Union Square area is **The Clift** ((415) 775-4700 TOLL-FREE (800) 652-5438, 495 Geary Street. With 326 large and gracious rooms, this has long been one of San Francisco's top luxury hotels, situated right in the heart of the Theater District.

Asia's reputation for impeccable service and fervid hospitality comes to Union Square in the form of two hotels. The **Pan Pacific** ((415) 771-8600 TOLL-FREE (800) 327-8585, 500 Post Street, has 330 rooms equipped with marble baths and cable television, a restaurant and bar, conference facilities and a ballroom. **Hotel Nikko** ((415) 394-1111 TOLL-FREE (800) NIKKO-US, 222 Mason Street at O'Farrell, offers 522 rooms including Japanese *tatami* suites.

Expensive

Campton Place ((415) 781-5555 TOLL-FREE (800) 235-4300, 340 Stockton Street, has 117 rooms, a fine restaurant and rooftop garden, as well as facilities for small business meetings. The **Grand Hyatt** ((415) 398-1234 TOLL-FREE (800) 233-1234, 345 Stockton Street on Union Square, has 693 rooms, two restaurants, and three lounges. Also in this category is the 1,914-room **San Francisco Hilton** ((415) 771-1400 TOLL-FREE (800) 445-8667, 333 O'Farrell Street, and the **Sir Francis Drake** ((415) 392-7755 TOLL-FREE (800) 227-5480, 450 Powell Street, which has 417 rooms.

Moderate

There are also dozens of less-expensive and cozy hotels in the Union Square area.

The **Beresford** ((415) 673-9900 TOLL-FREE (800) 533-6533 WEB SITE www.beresford.com, 635 Sutter Street, and its younger sister the **Beresford Arms** ((415) 673-2600, 701 Post Street, are family-owned hotels with comfortable, friendly Victorian accommodation. The Beresford offers more traditional fare, while the Beresford Arms is the more luxurious of the two, with 38 suites equipped with kitchens and Jacuzzi tubs. Both have several complimentary amenities, such as continental breakfasts, tea socials and computer equipped with modems.

One of the best bargains in the Union Square area is the **King George Hotel** ((415) 781-5050 TOLL-FREE (800) 288-6005, 334 Mason Street. The 143 rooms are recently refurbished. English afternoon tea is served in the lounge accompanied by chamber music. Another good bet for cost-conscious travelers is the **Galleria Park** ((415) 781-3060 TOLL-FREE (800) 792-9639, 191 Sutter Street.

Inexpensive

The **Golden Gate Hotel** ((415) 392-3702 TOLL-FREE (800) 835-1118, 775 Bush Street, is a small turn-of-the-century bed and breakfast inn with antique furnishings and a homey ambiance. There's a cable car stop right outside. And after all that walking up and down the city's famous hills, you can soak your weary feet in a clawfoot tub.

NORTH BEACH/WATERFRONT

Very Expensive

What a view! The **Mandarin Oriental** ((415) 885-0999 TOLL-FREE (800) 622-0404, 222 Sansome Street, occupies the top 11 floors of the third highest building in San Francisco. Dramatic vistas of the bay and skyline from every guest room. But this hotel is more than just a panorama: Asian elegance permeates both decor and service. Silks restaurant offers one of the city's best East-West fusions.

Expensive

A landmark of post-modern architecture, the John Portman-designed **Hyatt Regency** ((415) 788-1234 TOLL-FREE (800) 233-1234, 5 Embarcadero Center, features a stunning atrium lobby and a convenient bayside location at the foot of Market Street. Cable car station right outside.

Moderate

Pensione d'Assisi ((800) 553-1900, 610 Vallejo Street, is a European-style inn built in 1908 as the rectory for the church next door. It has only ten rooms, each of them immaculate and comfortable. Breakfast on the rooftop garden includes pastry, coffee and a killer view of the San Francisco skyline.

Just steps from Fisherman's Wharf and Pier 39, the **Ramada Plaza** ((415) 885-4700 TOLL-FREE (800) 228-8408, 590 Bay Street, offers 232 comfortable, clean and quiet rooms. **Washington Square Inn** ((415) 981-4220 TOLL-FREE (800) 388-0220, 1660 Stockton Street, is another excellent base for exploring North Beach, Chinatown and Fisherman's Wharf.

Inexpensive

European ambiance also permeates the **San Remo Hotel** ((415) 776-8688 TOLL-FREE (800) 352-7366 2237 Mason Street, a small North Beach abode built in 1906 and impeccably restored.

OTHER AREAS

Moderate

Mr. and Mrs. Claude Lambert have run the **Cornell Hotel de France (** (415) 421-3154 TOLL-FREE (800) 232-9698 WEB SITE www.sirius.com/hotelweb/ cornell, 715 Bush Street, with flair for more than 30 years. Situated between Union Square and Nob Hill, the Cornell offers a special weekly rate of $665 for a double room including seven breakfasts and five dinners at the Jeanne D'Arc Restaurant.

If you want to stay in the oldest building in the Bay Area currently being used as lodging, check into the **Inn San Francisco (** (415) 641-0188 TOLL-

Inexpensive

One of the great bargains in downtown accommodation is the **Atherton Hotel (** (415) 474-5720 TOLL-FREE (800) 474-5720, 685 Ellis Street. Rates include breakfast and a free newspaper. Near the Civic Center and Tenderloin District, the Atherton is a wonderfully restored 1927 relic with a British-style pub off the lobby.

The **Marina Motel (** (415) 921-3430 TOLL-FREE (800) 346-6118, 2576 Lombard Street, is a touch of old California in the Marina District. This 38-unit motor lodge began life in 1939 as Spanish-style apartment complex. Murals and flowers abound in the central courtyard and each room has its own small garage.

FREE (800) 359-0913, 943 South Van Ness. This hotel is situated in an 1872 Victorian mansion tucked away in the Mission District. Among quaint features are a roof deck with amazing views of the skyline and flower garden with hot tub.

The **Majestic (** (415) 441-1100 TOLL-FREE (800) 869-8966, 1500 Sutter Street, is a five-story Edwardian gem with 57 rooms, first opened in 1902 as a "grand hotel."

There is nothing especially luxurious about the **Seal Rock Inn (** (415) 752-8000, 545 Point Lobos Avenue, but what a remarkable location — a clifftop perched above Seal Rock on the Pacific Ocean side of San Francisco. Walking distance to both Lincoln and Golden Gate parks.

Queen Anne ((415) 441-2828 TOLL-FREE (800) 227-3970, 1590 Sutter Street, offers 49 rooms in a building that survived the 1906 quake. It is located near the Japanese Cultural Center.

San Francisco and the Bay Area

BED AND BREAKFAST

Expensive

Sherman House ((415) 563-1882, 2160 Green Street in Pacific Heights, makes a game attempt to replicate tycoon life for ordinary citizens, if only for a weekend. Situated in an 1876 Italianate mansion and carriage house, the Sherman offers marble bathrooms and antique furnishings. But the real luxury here is personal service: butlers who will unpack your suitcases, chauffeurs who will whisk you around town, maids who tidy up your room twice a day, and even someone who will do your shopping if you just can't get up the energy.

The lobby of the Fairmont Hotel reflects the generations' old elegance of Nob Hill.

Moderate

Albion House ((415) 621-0896 TOLL-FREE (800) 6-ALBION, 135 Gough Street, is a snug inn only three blocks from the Civic Center. Seven of the nine rooms have a private bath.

Tucked amid San Francisco's largest surviving Victorian district is the **Archbishops' Mansion Inn (** (415) 563-7872 TOLL-FREE (800) 543-5820, 1000 Fulton Street, which overlooks Alamo Square. This fabulous belle époque house was home to local archbishops for many years. It's now one of the city's most elegant little inns.

The Mansions ((415) 929-9444, 2220 Sacramento Street, is an elegant 1887 Queen Anne-style structure with 21 rooms. The Pacific Heights location is near Lafayette Park and the Webster Street Historic District.

Take a trip back to the Summer of Love at the **Red Victorian (** (415) 864-1978, 1665 Haight Street, a classic Haight-Ashbury crash pad turned bed and breakfast. There's even a guest meditation room. **Victorian Inn on the Park (** (415) 931-1830 TOLL-FREE (800) 435-1967, 301 Lyon Street, a three-story Queen Anne house built in 1897, overlooks the "panhandle" of Golden Gate Park in the Haight-Ashbury area.

Inexpensive

For a little touch of England in the Marina District try the **Edward II Inn (** (415) 922-3000 TOLL-FREE (800) GREAT-IN, 3155 Scott Street. Amenities include afternoon tea, coffee and cookies, evening sherry, English country furnishings, and a pub next door. Twenty of the 31 rooms have private baths. The building dates from 1915.

Another cozy bed and breakfast overlooking Alamo Square is the **Grove Inn (** (415) 929-0780 TOLL-FREE (800) 829-0780, 890 Grove Street. This Italianate Victorian structure dates from the 1870s.

WHERE TO EAT

According to local San Francisco lore, there are so many restaurants (4,200) in the city, every resident could be seated at one time. This is a slight exaggeration, but the number of restaurants for the population is still much higher than in New York or any other American city. San Franciscans love good food, and they love to eat out three meals a day. You will find almost as many locally famous breakfast places as you will dinner places. The following are some of the best restaurants in the city.

UNION SQUARE/NOB HILL

Very Expensive

Many of the habitués think **Masa's (** (415) 989-7154, 648 Bush Street near Union Square, is the best French restaurant on the entire West Coast. The kitchen,

under the direction of Julian Serrano, is nothing short of brilliant; the desserts are to die for.

Expensive

Top of the Mark ((415) 392-3434, is just what it says, at the top of the Mark Hopkins Hotel on Nob Hill. Even if you don't eat or drink here, it's worth the trip up for the best panoramic view of the city short of Coit Tower. Prices are fairly moderate by luxury hotel standards and the Sunday brunch is lavish at any price. High tea is served Monday through Friday from 3 PM TO 5 PM.

Moderate

Scala's Bistro ((415) 395-8555, 450 Powell Street

near Union Square, serves regional Italian cuisine including fresh pasta and seafood dishes.

Inexpensive

Irish Bank ((415) 788-7152, 10 Mark Lane near the intersection of Bush and Kearny, a traditional Irish bar and restaurant, has everything from corn beef and cabbage to Guinness Stout. There's even an old confessional booth if you start to feel guilty about imbibing too much.

Lori's Diner ((415) 392-8646, 336 Mason Street, offers a delightful trip back to the 1950s, with thick burgers and shakes and decor to match. It is open 24 hours a day.

OPPOSITE: Outdoor dining is an enduring lure at Fisherman's Wharf's cafés. ABOVE: Traditional recipes and exotic settings bring locals and visitors to Chinatown's restaurants.

White Horse Restaurant ((415) 673-9900, 635 Sutter Street, is an English-style pub with hearty chops-and-potatoes fare to match the decor.

CHINATOWN

Following are some of the older, more established, restaurants in Chinatown. All are inexpensive to moderately priced depending on your appetite.
Brandy Ho's On Broadway ((415) 362-6268, 450 Broadway Street.
Empress of China ((415) 434-1345, 838 Grant Avenue.
Golden Phoenix ((415) 989-4400, 728 Washington Street.

standby, popular for years with local writers and journalists.

Inexpensive
O'Reilly's Irish Pub ((415) 989-6222, 622 Green Street. This North Beach stalwart is like a piece of the Emerald Isle sliced off and somehow relocated to San Francisco. Even the Irish accents are authentic.

FISHERMAN'S WHARF/EMBARCADERO

Very Expensive
Chez Michel ((415) 775-7036, 804 North Point Street, is situated in a cozy setting near Ghirardelli

Hang Ah Tea Room ((415) 982-5686, 1 Hang Ah Street, near the Chinese Playground (great *dim sum*).
Imperial Palace ((415) 982-8889, 919 Grant Avenue.
The Pot Sticker ((415) 397-9985, 150 Waverly Place.

NORTH BEACH

Moderate
Ristorante Firenze ((415) 392-8585, 1429 Stockton Street, offers up sumptuous Italian cuisine in an intimate setting.
   New on the North Beach scene but already popular is **Rose Pistola** ((415) 399-0499, 532 Columbus, with its open-plan kitchen and tasty Italian cuisine.
   Washington Square Bar & Grill ((415) 982-8123, 1707 Powell Street, is an old North Beach

Square. This café proves there's more to Fisherman's Wharf than mass-produced seafood.
   Perched on Pier 7 is the popular **Upstairs at the Waterfront** ((415) 391-2696, Embarcadero at Broadway, which features "Asian fusion" food with a less cluttered view of the bay.

Expensive
One of the most popular restaurants in the city is **Pier 23 Café** ((415) 362-5125, a favorite with the local celebrities. What is special about Pier 23 is not the ambiance created by the clientele, but the waterfront vistas, with freighters docking and unloading at the next pier.

Moderate
Two of the Wharf's oldest seafood establishments are **A. Sabella's** ((415) 771-6775, 2766 Taylor Street, and **Alioto's** ((415) 673-0183, 8 Fisherman's Wharf,

which claims to be the oldest restaurant on the pier.

Buena Vista ((415) 474-5044, 2765 Hyde Street on Fisherman's Wharf, is the bar and restaurant that allegedly invented Irish coffee. A great place for people watching, it is also one of the best spots in San Francisco for breakfast.

Across the street from Pier 23 is **Fog City Diner** ((415) 982-2000, 1300 Battery, with a variety of dishes served *dim sum*-style. An overwhelming success among locals and tourists alike, Doug Biederbeck opened this place after his success with Prego's in Los Angeles.

FINANCIAL DISTRICT (DOWNTOWN)

Very Expensive
Rubicon ((415) 434-4100, 558 Sacramento Street in the Financial District, is one of the city's more intriguing restaurants, offering a fusion of French and California culinary traditions in an intimate loft-like setting.

Expensive
Bix ((415) 433-6300, 56 Gold Street near Montgomery, serves superb American cuisine in a raucous setting.

Jack's ((415) 421-7355, 615 Sacramento Street, has been in the same building since 1864 and remains a landmark for its fine cuisine.

The huge bistro **One Market** ((415) 777-5577, 1 Market Street, is popular with the lunchtime crowd from the nearby banks and office blocks for its panoramic views through huge windows and its modern American cuisine from chefs George Morrone and Bradley Ogden.

Shanghai 1930 ((415) 896-5600, 133 Steuart Street near Mission, evokes the ambiance of pre-war Shanghai including live jazz, cigar divan and Chinese haute cuisine.

Tommy Toy's Haute Cuisine Chinoise ((415) 397-4888, 655 Montgomery Street, has received many awards for Toy's elaborate menu of French and Chinese cooking.

An urbane restaurant in the base of the Transamerica Pyramid, **Vertigo** ((415) 433-7250, 600 Montgomery Street, serves a mix of contemporary American and Continental cuisine.

SOUTH OF MARKET (SOMA)

Expensive
Boulevard ((415) 543-6084, 1 Mission Street, is an offbeat SoMa restaurant with unusual "New American" cuisine served in a warehouse setting.

One of the area's best new restaurants is **LuLu** ((415) 495-5775, 816 Folsom Street, which offers southern French cuisine in a rowdy warehouse setting.

For Italian country cuisine in a modern urban setting, **Ristorante Ecco** ((415) 495-3291, 101 South Park Street, is located not far from the Moscone Center.

Moderate
Elroys ((415) 882-7989, 300 Beale Street, is a gargantuan restaurant with hearty American food. **Le Charm** ((415) 546-6128, 315 Fifth Street, near the Museum of Modern Art, has a bistro-style menu and a casual setting. **South Park Café** ((415) 495-7275, 108 South Park Street, is among the oldest and best of the SoMa hangouts.

Inexpensive
Off Fourth between Mission and Howard, **Cadillac Bar** ((415) 543-8226, 1 Holland Court, cooks up some of the city's best Mexican cuisine. It can be a bit loud with guitars and mariachis playing at full blast, but it can also be fun if you're in the mood for it.

Natoma Café ((415) 495-3289, 145 Natoma Street, is typical of the eating places you found South of Market before the area got trendy. It's still a favorite spot for breakfast and lunch. Closed Saturdays and Sundays, it doesn't serve alcoholic beverages and it accepts no credit cards.

Thirsty Bear ((415) 974-0905, 661 Howard Street, is a traditional West Coast brewpub with tasty Spanish *tapas*.

THE MISSION/CASTRO

Moderate
The Mission District hot spot **Slanted Door** ((415) 861-8032, 584 Valencia Street, offers sublime Vietnamese food at reasonable prices.

Inexpensive
By all accounts, the most authentic and oldest Mexican restaurant in San Francisco is the **Roosevelt Tamale Parlor** ((415) 550-9213, 2817 24th Street at York. It was named for Teddy, not Franklin.

Thep Phanom ((415) 431-2526, 400 Waller Street at Fillmore, in the upper Castro District serves tasty Thai food in an intimate setting. It offers good value for your money.

MARINA DISTRICT

Expensive
A friendly neighborhood café in the Cow Hollow neighborhood, **Plumpjack Café** ((415) 563-4755, 3127 Fillmore Street, has been around longer than most people can remember. It serves American bistro food and an excellent California wine selection.

Moderate

Baker Street Bistro ((415) 931-1475, 2953 Baker at Lombard, is a re-creation of a Parisian boulevard bistro churning out good food at great prices. The Zagat guide calls BSB a "neighborhood delight with très friendly service."

At **Café Marimba** ((415) 776-1506, 2317 Chestnut Street, margaritas, music and a savory menu mark this popular south-of-the-border hangout in the Marina District.

Inexpensive

Ace Wasabi ((415) 567-4903, 3339 Steiner Street, serves mouth-watering Japanese cuisine at reasonable prices.

Moderate

Cha-Cha-Cha ((415) 386-5758, 1801 Haight Street, is a crowded Cuban bistro in the Haight-Ashbury district known for its bountiful sangria and Hispanic cuisine.

Kabuto Sushi (415) 752-5652, 5116 Geary Boulevard is one of the city's better sushi bars, including traditional *tatami* rooms.

Max's Opera Café ((415) 771-7300, 601 Van Ness Avenue, features big New York-style delicatessen sandwiches served up by opera-singing waiters.

Upstairs at the Cliff House ((415) 386-3330, 1090 Point Lobos, overlooks Ocean Beach. A light fare of omelets and salads is

OTHER AREAS

Very Expensive

If you're in the mood for "surf and turf," **Harris'** ((415) 673-1888, 2100 Van Ness at Pacific, is the place to come for its fresh lobster flown in daily from Maine and the best steaks in San Francisco.

Flamboyant chef/owner Jeremiah Towers has turned the oyster bar/pizza joint **Stars** ((415) 861-7827, 150 Redwood Alley near the Civic Center, into a local institution. Stars features the longest bar in San Francisco and some of the city's best desserts.

Expensive

Vivande Ristorante ((415) 673-9245, 670 Golden Gate Avenue, is a bustling Italian café near the Opera and Davies Hall popular with culture vultures heading for an evening performance.

featured in the daytime. It is a favorite (and rare) spot from which to watch the sun set over the Pacific.

Inexpensive

Dish ((415) 431-3534, at the corner of Haight and Masonic in the Haight-Ashbury district specializes in hearty and health-oriented meals, and takes its name from the vast collection of plates that line the walls and adorn the tables as decor. The omelets are immense and many of the fresh seafood specials are delicious.

It's not the raucous "Barbary Coast" it once was, but Columbus Avenue still offers some spicy entertainment.

NIGHTLIFE

Although the nightlife in San Francisco has calmed considerably since the raucous days when sailors regarded it with fear and longing as the Barbary Coast, it is still a pleasure-loving city where having a good time is high on the list of life's priorities.

If you accept that San Francisco is the gay capital of America, you will understand that there is a congenial mixture of lifestyles here that you don't often find even in the most cosmopolitan cities. In other words, none of the really popular dance clubs are exclusively gay or straight—you'll find cross-over crowds at all the bars. And if two

men or two women dancing together—or someone dancing alone, for that matter—offends you, then you'd do best to stick to Fisherman's Wharf and the Top of the Mark.

DANCE AND MUSIC CLUBS

If you're out for a wild night, you can't beat the clubs of San Francisco. The most popular clubs, predominantly straight, feature live music and/or DJs. Worth trying are the **Club Oz** ((415) 774-0166 on the top floor of the Westin St. Francis on Union Square; the **Holy Cow** ((415) 621-6087, 1531 Folsom Street, with its mix of 1970s, 1980s and 1990s tunes; **Lou's Pier 47 Club** ((415) 771-0377, 300 Jefferson Street in Fisherman's Wharf, which features as many as two dozen bands each week; and **The Paladium** ((415) 434-1308 WEB SITE www.citysearch7.com, 1031 Kearny Street in North Beach.

Paradise Lounge ((415) 861-6906, 1501 Folsom, offers an alternative music scene; **Rawhide II** ((415) 621-1197, 280 Seventh Street, a local country and western music showcase; while **The Stud** ((415) 863-6623, 399 Ninth Street, South of Market, is the city's oldest gay leather bar, but the disk jockeys and the music they play here are so popular you'll find a happy mix of all the city's lifestyles, with men and women in evening dress dancing alongside the leather aficionados.

STAGE PERFORMANCES

Several performance groups express San Francisco's special blend of politics and humor, rare in other American cities. The most famous of these is the **San Francisco Mime Troupe** ((415) 285-1717, a non-profit collective of actors formed in 1961 to perform free in the city parks. Performances are held in July, August and September. The season opener and finale are usually in Dolores Park in the Mission District. The group now has a national reputation, no longer as a silent mime troupe, but as outspoken political theater at its best.

You can see the San Francisco drag tradition on outlandish display five nights a week at the famous **Finocchio's** ((415) 982-9388, 506 Broadway in North Beach. For 50 years, Finnochio's has featured the best female impersonators found anywhere in America. The lavish, Las Vegas-style revues are staged every night except Monday and Wednesday, starting at 9 PM.

San Francisco also has several traditional theaters where you can see the latest in American drama and musical productions. The highly esteemed **American Conservatory Theater** (ACT) ((415) 749-2228 WEB SITE www.act-sfbay.org, performs at the 1300-seat Geary Theater, 415 Geary Street, with a regular schedule from October through May. The same theater houses the **American Musical Summer Festival** in the summer months.

Two other theaters regularly stage popular plays on the way to Broadway or on tour from New York: the 1,768-seat **Curran Theater** ((415) 776-1999 WEB SITE www.bestofbroadway-sf.com, 445 Geary Street; and the 800-seat **Theater on the Square** ((415) 433-9500, WEB SITE www.showgate.com, 450 Post Street.

HIGH LIFE

The many new high-rise hotels and office buildings have extended San Francisco's elegant supper club high life from the Top of the Mark at the Mark Hopkins Hotel on Nob Hill to several other new high spots throughout the city.

Although it's only on the 19th floor, the **Top of the Mark** ((415) 392-3434 at the Mark Hopkins

Hotel still reigns supreme on Nob Hill, where generations of San Franciscans have memories of special evenings spent looking over the city spread out below. The Top of the Mark has a Sunday brunch from 10 AM to 2 PM and serves cocktails until 12:30 AM nightly.

Here are some other vantage points from the upper stories of modern San Francisco: **Carnellian Room** ((415) 433-7500, 555 California Street, is on the 52nd floor of the Bank of America Building; **Cityscape** ((415) 771-1400, 333 O'Farrell Street, is on the 46th floor of the San Francisco Hilton; **Club 36** ((415) 398-1234 is on the 36th floor of the Grand Hyatt on Union Square; **Compass Rose** ((415) 774-0167 is on the 32nd floor of the Westin St. Francis

Columbus Day is celebrated during the first week of October honoring America's Italian roots. In addition to a parade, the week-long festival features a procession of Madonna del Lume and a blessing of the fishing fleet at Fisherman's Wharf.

The local Chinese offer one of the most raucous (with fireworks galore) of the city's ethnic celebrations. **Chinese New Year** is celebrated with a parade through Chinatown in late January or February according to the lunar calendar. The parade is be preceded by a week of special events in the Chinese and Asian communities.

The Irish take to the streets for **Saint Patrick's Day** on March 17. For information, call the United Irish Cultural Center ((415) 661-2700.

Hotel on Union Square; the **Crown Room** ((415) 772-5131, 950 Mason Street, is on the 24th floor of the Fairmont Hotel on Nob Hill; and the **Starlite Room** ((415) 395-8595 is on the 21st floor of the Sir Francis Drake Hotel on Union Square.

FESTIVALS

The frantic rush for gold in the 1850s brought people from nearly every country in the world to the then-tiny port city of San Francisco. This cosmopolitan atmosphere has endured through the several ethnic neighborhoods in the city, but also in its major parades and festivals. In most cases, parades and festivals are held on different dates each year, so for specific dates you should check with the **San Francisco Convention & Visitors Bureau** ((415) 974-6900 or (415) 391-2000, 201 Third Street, Suite 900, San Francisco 94103.

In recent years, the Japanese have presented one of the city's most beautiful events, with the annual **Cherry Blossom Festival** in early April. For information call the Japan Center Information Line ((415) 922-6776.

The city's Spanish and Mexican past and present are honored in the annual **Cinco de Mayo** parade and festival, although they are not always held on May 5, but usually the weekend before. For information call the Mission Economic and Cultural Association ((415) 826-1401.

Finally, San Francisco's **Gay Pride Parade** is held in June each year with as many as half a million people (gays, lesbians and straights) taking to the streets of the Castro District. Although the spirit

ABOVE: A child gazes at the action of a Chinese New Year parade. OPPOSITE: A float queen at Mission Street Carnival.

of carnival prevails, there is also an underlying tone of earnestness since the advent of the AIDS crisis. For information call San Francisco Pride ((415) 864-3733.

SHOPPING

Beverly Hills has Rodeo Drive, New York has Fifth Avenue — San Francisco has all this and more in the fabulous shopping area in and around old **Union Square**. It's not just the premier shopping district in the Bay Area, but one of the heaviest concentrations of retail outlets anywhere in the country. The most famous fashion houses in the world — Saks Fifth Avenue, Burberry's of

London, Bally of Switzerland, Macy's, Neiman-Marcus of Texas — are right on the square, and hundreds of others are located in the blocks nearby. The latter include Gucci, Tiffany, Jaeger, Brooks Brothers, Louis Vuitton, Gump's, and Hermes.

The Neiman-Marcus building is a striking Philip Johnson design that would be a treasured piece of modern architecture in most cities, however, it was the subject of a bitter controversy here because it involved the destruction of a beautiful old Beaux-Arts building, the City of Paris, which featured a delightful neon Eiffel Tower on top. The rotunda of the older building was

ABOVE: Produce and flowers from Northern California's farms tempt city dwellers at the Farmer's Market. OPPOSITE: Union Square, a premier shopping district.

preserved and incorporated into the new design, providing the very elegant setting for Neiman-Marcus' restaurant.

The **Crocker Galleria** is one of several new enclosed malls that have enlivened and expanded the city's shopping possibilities. Not far from Union Square, the Crocker Galleria features a magnificent glass-fronted atrium and covers the block bounded by Post, Kearny, Sutter, and Montgomery Streets. More than 50 shops and restaurants are located under the glass-domed structure modeled after the Galleria Vittorio Emmanuelle in Milan.

Embarcadero Center is yet another huge shopping area with a plus in San Francisco, where parking is always difficult — there is plenty of parking, which is free on Sundays, and at a discount other days with validation from any of the 175 shops and restaurants in the area. First planned in 1959 by the Atlanta-based architect John Portman, construction of the center began in 1966 on the site of the city's old produce market. Work was completed in 1982 on the five towers and the Hyatt Regency Hotel which are linked by several footbridges and plazas. The center complex is located on the Embarcadero between Sacramento, Clay, and Battery streets.

Japan Center is surely the city's most exotic shopping area. Covering three square blocks, it was designed by renowned architect Minoru Yamasaki and completed in 1968. In addition to the best of Japanese restaurants and sushi bars in the city, the five-acre (two-hectare) complex includes an array of Japanese art galleries, bookstores, theaters, a temple shrine, the 14-story Miyako Hotel and numerous other shops offering Asian specialties. You will also find the Japanese General Consulate there.

HOW TO GET THERE

San Francisco International, the world's seventh busiest airport, is located just 14 miles (23 km) south of San Francisco and is served by daily or weekly flights from major cities in Europe, Asia and Latin America, as well as nearly every major American city. A new international terminal and an airport BART station are currently under construction.

At least a dozen companies offer airport transfers to downtown San Francisco and other parts of the Bay Area. **SFO Airporter** ((415) 495-8404 offers frequent (every 10 to 20 minutes) motor coach service to and from Union Square and the Financial District. No reservations are required. **Supershuttle San Francisco** ((415) 558-8500 offers reliable door-to-door transfer in comfortable vans to anywhere in San Francisco and the peninsula area. **Taxi** fare from the airport to downtown San Francisco is roughly $30. For information on

ground transportation to and from the airport call TOLL-FREE (800) SFO-2008.

Depending on where you want to go in the Bay Area, it might be more convenient to use one **Oakland International Airport** in the East Bay or **San Jose Airport** in the South Bay, which also serve as gateways from other parts of the United States.

Amtrak TOLL-FREE (800) 872-7245 offers convenient rail service to the Bay Area from a number of cities including Seattle, Portland, Reno, Salt Lake City, Chicago, Sacramento, Los Angeles and San Diego. Cross-country road connections are also abundant. Interstate 5 and US Highway 101 connect San Francisco with Los Angeles and other parts of Southern California, as well as Oregon and Washington states in the Pacific Northwest. Interstate 80 runs east across the Bay Bridge, eventually making its way to Sacramento, Reno, Salt Lake City and points in the Midwest.

EAST BAY

BERKELEY

Across the bay, only 12 miles (19 km) from San Francisco, lies Berkeley. Founded as a ranch in 1866, the city's claim to fame is its university, often cited as one of the best in the country. With over 31,000 students, the **University of California at Berkeley** is the second largest in the prestigious University of California system, after the University of California at Los Angeles.

Berkeley has an intensely tranquil and tolerant atmosphere, and the city exudes a sybaritic feel unlike any other in California. A love of good weather, fine food, and nice cafés is ever-present and Berkeley indulges its citizens handsomely in these endeavors. Most of the city, it seems, is an extension of the university. It has a carefree campus atmosphere somewhat at odds with its volatile history. The university was home not only to numerous Nobel Prize winners, but also to the student movement genesis of the 1960s. Though much of the city's political ardor has died down in recent years, a strong spirit of individualism remains to this day.

Berkeley's most predominant landmark is the **Campanile**, an impressive clock tower that affords wonderful views of the campus and all the way across the bay to the Golden Gate Bridge and San Francisco. The best times to visit it are at 8 AM, noon, and 6 PM, when the tower bells ring out in concert. The university's **Lawrence Hall of Science** features numerous hands-on displays and science exhibits for children. It's also possible to take a guided walking tour of the vast campus; call the university's **Visitor Services** ((510) 642-5215.

While in Berkeley, stroll down the city's commercial center, **Telegraph Avenue**, a quirky street lined with jewelry and tie-dye vendors, casual pizza joints, huge record stores and hip cafés. It's not really a street that one can be guided along, but it, and all of its eccentricities, should be discovered at your own pace.

Cody's Bookstore and **Moe's Books** are among the largest and most impressively stocked bookstores in Berkeley. Cody's stocks over 250,000 titles and has an enormous children's selection, as well as fiction, art, history, philosophy, and on and on. Moe's specializes in new, used and sale items, and has four floors of great book bargains in a fabulously literate environment.

OAKLAND

"There's no *there* there," Gertrude Stein once griped about Oakland. Long berated by outsiders, this East Bay metropolis is completely different from its more sophisticated cousin, yet only eight miles (12 km) across the bay. It is a large, ethnically diverse city that lives on its own terms. While San Francisco was captivated by flower power and Berkeley by the free speech movement, Oakland was the cradle of the Black Panther organization and the Black Power crusade.

Though there is little to draw crowds away from San Francisco, Oakland is not without its own

OPPOSITE: It's hard to resist buying a few bars of chocolate at the former candy factory in Ghiradelli Square. ABOVE: Couples of all genders feel free to walk hand-in-hand in San Francisco's streets.

charm of opportunities. The city centers around tranquil **Lake Merritt**, a 155-acre (63-hectare) lagoon filled with salt water and migrating birds that provides a recreation area and picnic spot in the middle of an otherwise bustling city. The boat house on the north shore rents out water craft (small sailboats and rowboats), while the leafy park around the lake includes a **Natural Science Center** and a children's "fairyland" playground.

Nearby is the superb **Oakland Museum** ((510) 238-2200, at Oak and 10th streets, one of the best city museums in America. The collection, housed in stark post-modern buildings designed by Kevin Roche, sprawls across four city blocks including comprehensive displays on California history, natural science, culture and fine art. It is open Wednesday through Saturday from 10 AM to 5 PM and Sunday from noon to 7 PM. Admission is $5 for adults, $3 for students and seniors, and free from 4 PM to 7 PM on Sundays.

Much like San Francisco, Oakland is endowed with a wealth of splendid Victorian structures. **Preservation Park**, at 14th Street and Martin Luther King Jr. Way, flaunts a number of nineteenth-century structures, most of them moved to the site from elsewhere in Oakland. But the city's real forte is art deco. The department store **I. Magnum** ((510) 444-7722, at 20th and Broadway in downtown Oakland, is situated in a beautifully restored art deco theater. For the price conscious, it stocks reams of remainders by fashionable designers at great sale prices. Another beautiful old art deco theater is the **Paramount Theater** ((510) 465-6400, at 2025 Broadway, built in 1931. It now hosts films, concerts and special events.

The **Black Panthers** have also become a tourist attraction. On the last Saturday of each month, the **Dr. Huey P. Newton Foundation** ((510) 986-0660 conducts guided bus tours of local Panther sights including the boyhood homes of movement founders Newton and Bobby Seale, as well as the intersection where a policeman was killed during a confrontation with Panthers in 1967.

Perhaps the city's most picturesque area is **Jack London Square**, a ten-block waterfront area that preserves many of Oakland's oldest structures. The name derives from the fact that author Jack London spent much of his youth here. The area harbors a small-craft marina and numerous restaurants that overlook an estuary of San Francisco Bay. The Presidential yacht *Potomac* anchors at the end of Water Street. This national historic landmark was once the "Floating White House" of Franklin D. Roosevelt. It is open Sunday from 10 AM to 4 PM from November to March, and Wednesday through Sunday from 10 AM to 4 PM the rest of year.

WHERE TO STAY

Very Expensive

If Berkeley strikes your fancy and you want to make more than a day trip of it, by far the classiest place to stay is the famed **Claremont Resort** ((510) 843-3000 TOLL-FREE (800) 551-7266, 41 Tunnel Road in Berkeley. The grande dame of East Bay accommodation, this huge Victorian-era holiday retreat features swimming pool, spa, sauna, Jacuzzi, fitness center, ten tennis courts, three restaurants and 239 incredibly posh rooms.

Moderate

Days Inn ((510) 547-7888 TOLL-FREE (800) 325-2525, 1603 Powell Street, Emeryville, is a 150-room motel featuring a restaurant, swimming pool, and lounge; and easy access to Berkeley, Oakland and the Bay Bridge.

Inexpensive

Berkeley Budget Inn ((510) 524-8778, 1720 San Pablo Avenue, is a recently renovated motel featuring cable television, movie channels and non-smoking rooms.

WHERE TO EAT

Very Expensive

Chez Panisse ((510) 548-5525, 1517 Shattuck Avenue, Berkeley, is regarded as one of the best restaurants in America. Owner Alice Waters is one of the leading exponents of the American food renaissance, which relies heavily on freshness and quality of ingredients without the loss of taste commonly associated with healthiness in cooking. Upstairs from the main dining area is the café with more casual food and ambiance. Reservations for the café are only taken for the same day, while reservations for the main restaurant are essential.

Expensive

Oliveto ((510) 547-5356, 5655 College Avenue, Oakland, offers exceptional Northern Italian food. Reservations, though not essential, are recommended.

Moderate

Hong Kong East Ocean ((510) 655-3388, 3199 Powell Street, Emeryville, offers Dim sum and other Chinese taste treats, but the big attraction here is the expansive view of the bay and San Francisco across the water.

Yoshi's ((510) 238-9200, 510 Embarcadero West, Oakland, offers a welcome break from the burgers and brew that dominate Jack London Square, this cozy restaurant features Japanese-style *tatami* rooms and great sushi, sashimi and tempura.

For the most part, restaurants at Oakland's Jack London Square offer similar dining options, concentrating on American fare consisting of steaks, burgers and seafood. Two of the nicest are **Jack's Waterfront Restaurant and Bar** ((510) 444-7171, 1 Broadway in the Waterfront Plaza Hotel; and **Shenanigan's** ((510) 839-5853, 30 Jack London Square.

Inexpensive

Bette's Oceanview Diner ((510) 644-3230, 1807 4th Street, Berkeley, is one of the best breakfast deals in the East Bay, wrapped in art deco charm.

Great brunches, intrinsically Californian, can be had at **Café Fanny** ((510) 524-5447, 1603 San Pablo Avenue in Berkeley, owned and operated by the same person (Alice Waters) who pilots the ultra expensive Chez Panisse. The setting is casual, with food served at a stand-up counter.

Pizzeria Uno Chicago Bar and Grill ((510) 251-8667, Jack London Square, Oakland, serves Chicago-style deep dish pizza, pasta and huge salads. For a delicious slice of Berkeley, try **Blondie's Pizza** ((510) 548-1129, 2340 Telegraph Avenue, the most popular of the city's pizza places.

Cafés are abundant in Berkeley. One of the best because of the consistently high quality of its coffee and pastries is **Caffe Strada** ((510) 843-5282, 2300 College Avenue. All of its coffee drinks are made from espresso rather than American "family-style" coffee. Strada offers outdoor seating under the pleasant shade of trees.

Mexicali Rose ((510) 451-2450, 701 Clay Street in Oakland is reputedly the oldest Mexican restaurant in the Bay Area (opened 1927). It offers much more elegant surroundings than most Mexican restaurants and has equally delicious food.

THE PENINSULA

San Francisco sits at the tip of a huge peninsula that stretches up from the Santa Clara Valley and the Santa Cruz Mountains. The area is home to several dozen suburban towns ranging from opulent enclaves like Hillsborough and Atherton to blue-collar communities like San Bruno, San Mateo and Daly City.

The Peninsula is connected to the city by two busy highways: the Bayshore Freeway on the flatlands and the Junipero Serra Freeway which snakes its way through the hills, much of its route tracing the infamous **San Andreas Fault**. San Andreas Lake and the two Crystal Springs reservoirs literally sit in the bottom of the world's most acclaimed earthquake fissure.

Farther south is leafy **Palo Alto**, home of the state's most prestigious educational institution, **Stanford University**. From President Herbert Hoover to golfer Tiger Woods and First Kid Chelsea Clinton, a long line of distinguished Americans are connected with the school.

Stanford sits at the northern end of **Silicon Valley**, where the world's computer revolution largely took shape in the 1970s and 1980s. The area is not a valley per se, rather a collection of adjacent high-tech communities — Mountain View, Los Altos, Sunnyvale, Cupertino — where capital, know-how and marketing wizardry have concentrated over the past 20 years. Among the information technology companies that started in Silicon Valley garages and bedrooms were Apple, Intel, Seagate, Quantum, Pacific Telesis and Sun Microsystems.

The vast Santa Clara Valley, once home to orange groves, is filled with seemingly endless suburbs, the largest of which is San Jose. Despite the vast blandness, the area does boast several worthwhile sights.

Fans of the *X Files* and other sci-fi capers will enjoy the **Winchester Mystery House** ((408) 247-2101, 525 South Winchester Boulevard in San Jose. This huge Victorian mansion (160 rooms) was built by heiress Sarah Winchester, who believed that she would live forever — as long as she kept adding rooms to her house. Needless to say, it didn't work. But the result was California's weirdest home. There are frequent guided tours starting at 9:30 AM. Admission is $12.95 for adults, $9.95 for seniors and $6.95 for children age 6 to 12.

Paramount's Great America ((408) 988-1776, off US Highway 101 in Santa Clara, is a typical American theme park with loads of thrill rides, souvenir shops and fast-food outlets. Given the ownership (Paramount Studios) many of the attractions have film or television themes: the Top Gun roller coaster, the Drop Zone stunt tower and Nickelodeon's Splat City. The season lasts from March 15 to October 15. Admission is $28.99 for adults, $18.99 for seniors, and $15.99 for children age three to six.

Northern
California
and the
Sierras

THE WINE COUNTRY

Nearly all roads north from San Francisco lead to the gently rolling hills and valleys that have become famous as the Wine Country. In fact, vineyards and wineries are found throughout California; there is even a winery located right beside the Los Angeles International Airport. Until the late 1800s, the Los Angeles area was the state's major wine producer.

The wine industry dates back to mission days. The Spanish padres planted grapes and made a syrupy sweet concoction for sacramental and personal use, although this wine had little in common with the more refined products that would follow in later years. As the gold rush created a market for livestock and other products, it also gave a boost to the wine industry.

California wine production received an impetus from a Hungarian wine maker, Agoston Haraszthy, who, around 1851, went to Europe and brought back hundreds of new varieties of grapes to see if they would prosper in California. Word spread of his experiments, and soon French, Italian, and German wine specialists were moving to the new fields of California.

There is myth in the story that the American vines saved the French vineyards when they were virtually wiped out in the 1870s by a plague of phylloxera, a plant lice that attacks the roots of the vines. The prized vinifera grapes in the United States were also killed off by phylloxera. What saved them all was the discovery — in the 1880s — that the native American Labrusca grapes were immune to the lice. These were the plants that grew in such profusion, they prompted Leif Eriksson to call North America "Vineland." By grafting the finer European vinifera onto the hardier Labrusca roots, the wine industry was saved in France — and in California.

The French and other Europeans were involved in California wine-making from the beginning. But in the 1970s, the French government became alarmed at the growing involvement of California in French wine making and placed heavy restrictions on the percentage of Californian wine that could be sold as French in France. The snob appeal of French superiority in wine making was all but destroyed "one crisp May morning in 1976," according to Robert Finnigan in his book, *Essentials of Wine*, when nine of the top French wine experts agreed to a blind test of Californian wines against French wines. The American wines won hands down, much to the consternation of the judges. The incident was soon being called, "The wine-tasting heard around the world."

Something else happened around that same time: American tastes changed and wine became a favored drink among the middle class. Prohibition had dealt a brutal blow to the vintners of California; some were able to endure the Noble Experiment of 13 years by converting to table grapes, but many went under. In the late 1960s and early 1970s, there was an extraordinary surge in wine consumption in America. And the American palate moved up from ordinary jug wine to the fine Chardonnay and Cabernet Sauvignon popular in Europe. More than 75% of the wine consumed in America is home-grown; more than 90% of that is produced in California. In May 1984, Baron Philippe de Rothschild of France and Robert Mondavi of California held a press conference in San Francisco to announce that the two great wine makers had joined forces to produce a new

red wine. Vineland and California had truly come of age.

While vineyards and wineries are found throughout California, the heaviest concentration is found in a region of three counties 45 to 90 miles (70 to 150 km) north of San Francisco, making this area perfect for a day or overnight trip from the city. The Wine Country is also one of the state's foremost tourist regions, so most of the wineries are visitor-oriented, offering tours, tastings, shops and occasional concerts, art exhibits and other events. The Wine Country consists of the **Napa**, **Sonoma** and **Russian River** valleys.

PREVIOUS PAGES: Lush Napa Valley grapes on the vine and RIGHT Carmel Mission. OPPOSITE: The vineyards in the Napa Valley north of San Francisco offer a picturesque industry suited to the gently rolling landscape. Paul Draper ABOVE samples the product in the Ridge Winery in Napa Valley.

NAPA VALLEY

Napa Valley is the best known of the three, both for its wine and its beautiful surroundings. Napa is an Indian word of unknown origin, but it has stood for pastoral retreat among Californians for many years. The narrow valley is one to five miles (one and a half to eight kilometers) wide, and stretches for 30 miles (65 km) along the Saint Helena Highway (State Highway 29) and a parallel route called the Silverado Trail. The Napa Valley comprises some 35,000 acres (14,000 hectares) of planted vineyards in five major areas — Napa, Yountville, Oakville/Rutherford, Saint Helena and Calistoga.

The town of **Napa** is the largest and most historic in the area, as well as an important supply center for the valley. Founded in 1848, many of California's newly-wealthy built beautiful old Victorian mansions in Napa, many of which have since been converted to lovely bed and breakfast inns. The numerous shops and restaurants, recreational facilities and parks make this a perfect base from which to explore the valley.

Many of the wineries in the valley are more than a century old; their castle-like buildings and landscaped grounds are an inviting attraction even if you don't get to taste the wine.

GENERAL INFORMATION

Several organizations disseminate tourist information on the Napa region including the **Napa Valley Conference & Visitors Bureau** ((707) 226-7459 FAX (707) 255-2066 WEB SITE www .napavalley.com, 1310 Napa Town Center Mall, Napa, 94559.

The **Napa Valley Vintners Association** 24-hour hotline ((707) 942-9783 offers harvest news, vintage insights and information on winery events.

Bookings for accommodation, restaurants, guided wine tours, glider rides and hot-air balloons can be made through **Napa Valley Reservations Unlimited** ((707) 252-1985 TOLL-FREE (800) 251-6272, 1819 Tanen Street, Suite B, Napa, 94559.

WINERIES

Beaulieu Vineyard ((707) 967-5230 or (707) 963-2411, 1960 South Saint Helena Highway in Rutherford, is one of the best known of the large wineries in the valley, with 1,500 acres (600 hectares) of estate vineyards. Its ivy-covered brick winery building dates from 1885, though the winery wasn't founded until 1900 by the Frenchman Georges de Latour. Beaulieu is renowned for its Cabernet Sauvignon, which became the "Queen of Californian wines" thanks to Andre Tshelistcheff. The 400,000-case producing winery

was bought by the Heublein Corporation in 1969. Tours, tasting and sales are available from 10 AM to 5 PM daily.

Beringer Vineyards ((707) 963-4812 WEB SITE www.beringer.com, 2000 Main Street in Saint Helena, founded in 1876 by Jacob and Frederich Beringer, is the oldest continuously operating winery in the Napa Valley. Like Beaulieu Vineyards, it didn't even close during Prohibition when it sold its goods to the Catholic Church. The nineteenth-century Rhine House, now the visitor center, was once the Beringer mansion. You can explore caves and tunnels dug into the hillside in the 1880s to store the aging wine. The 1,400-acre (560-hectares) vineyard is now owned by Swiss multinational Nestle. From May to September, it is open daily from 9:30 AM to 6 PM; the rest of year it is open daily from 9:30 AM to 5 PM. The last tour is at 5 PM in summer and 4 PM in winter.

The modern buildings of **Clos Pegase** ((707) 942-4981, 1060 Dunaweal Lane in Calistoga, were awarded the San Francisco Museum of Modern Art's top design award for their Greco-Roman-influenced tribute to wine-making history. Outside, there's a formal garden that invites strolling. This winery specializes in Chardonnay, Merlot, Cabernet Sauvignon and its "Hommage" Reserve Cabernet. The tasting room is open daily from 10:30 AM to 5 PM (a nominal fee is charged). Tours start at 11 AM and 2 PM, with private visits to the cellars by appointment only.

The first wholly French-owned winery in America, **Domaine Chandon** ((707) 944-2280 WEB SITE www.dchandon.com, 1 California Drive in Yountville, was established in 1973 by Moët-Hennessy, makers of the Champagne Moët & Chandon, Hennessy Cognac and Dior perfumes. They are without question the best producers of *méthode champenoise* sparkling wine. Like the valleys of France, the grounds of the winery are delicately sculptured with ponds, gardens, and a small French restaurant (reservations recommended). Domaine's Napa Valley Brut and Blanc de Noirs are well known, but you may want to try their sweet wine, Panache. Tours, tasting (for a fee) and sales are available daily from 11 AM to 6 PM from May to October; from 11 AM to 6 PM Wednesday to Sunday, November to April.

Franciscan Oakville Estate Vineyards ((707) 963-7112, extension 33 TOLL-FREE (800) 529-6463, 1178 Galleron Road/State Highway 29 in Saint Helena, is housed in a large redwood structure. Franciscan Winery produces over 100,000 cases of wine a year, mostly estate-bottled varietals. Although it was only established in 1972, the winery has an antique collection of corkscrews and an eighteenth-century German grape press on display. Currently owned by the German Peter Eckes Company, its Cabernet Sauvignon,

Merlot, Zinfandel and Sauvignon Blanc retain the flavor and spirit of its monastery founders. Tours (by appointment), tasting (for a fee) and sales are available daily from 10 AM to 5 PM.

Charles Krug Winery ((707) 967-2201 TOLL-FREE (888) ASKKRUG, 2800 Main Street in Saint Helena, was founded in 1861 by pioneer wine-maker Charles Krug; the winery is a California historical landmark and is the oldest operating winery in Napa Valley. Krug was the first in California to use grape-presses rather than the more traditional foot-stomping method. The Mondavi family acquired the winery in the 1940s. It is open daily from 10:30 AM to 5:30 PM with tours available at 11:30 AM, 1:30 PM and 3:30 PM.

Monticello Vineyards ((707) 253-2802, 4242 Big Ranch Road in Napa, was founded in 1980. This winery's main attraction is a replica of its namesake, Monticello—Thomas Jefferson's home in Virginia — which houses the visitor center. Monticello periodically offers certain wine-related cooking classes, seminars and tastings. Its estate-grown Chardonnay and Gewurztraminer, as well as its vintage Cabernet Sauvignon and Zinfandel, are produced from its 200 acres (80 hectares) of vineyards. The estate is open daily for tasting (for a fee) and sales from 10 AM to 4:30 PM; tours begin at 10:30 AM, 12:30 PM and 2:30 PM.

Niebaum-Coppola Estate ((707) 963-9099, 1991 Saint Helena Highway in Rutherford, was

Robert Mondavi Winery ((707) 226-1395 extension 4312 TOLL-FREE (800) MONDAVI, 7801 Saint Helena Highway in Oakville, was established in 1966 by Robert Mondavi, who left the Charles Krug operation to make his own vintage varietals like Cabernet Sauvignon, Chardonnay, Johannisberg Riesling, Pinot Noir, Napa Gamy and Zinfandel. Its Bordeaux-style "Opus One" was produced in collaboration with the late Baron Phillipe de Rothschild. The Italian-Mediterranean-style winery is surrounded by 1,000 acres (400 hectares) of estate vineyards and includes an art gallery and gift shop. Several music concerts and cooking seminars are held at the winery every year. It is open daily for tasting and sales from 9 AM to 5:30 PM, May to October; from 10 AM to 4:30 PM, November to April. Daily tours are held from 9:30 AM to 4:30 PM November through April, and from 9 AM to 5 PM May through October.

formerly called Inglenook and was founded in 1879 by Gustave Niebaum. It is one of the premier producers of California varietals and table wines, with an annual output of more than one million cases. The estate is dominated by a century-old mock gothic château draped in ivy. Film director Francis Ford Coppola and his wife Eleanor acquired the property several years ago. Open daily for tasting ($7.50 fee) and sales from 11 AM to 5 PM.

Pine Ridge Winery ((707) 252-9777 TOLL-FREE (800) 575-9777 E-MAIL prw@community.net, 5901 Silverado Trail in Yountville, is one of the smaller wineries producing fine Chardonnay, Cabernet Sauvignon, Merlot and Chenin Blanc. Owner-operated since 1978, this property was formerly

A mechanical grape picker moves through a vineyard in the Napa Valley in the heart of California's wine country.

the Luigi Domenicioni Winery. Perfect for the outdoor enthusiast who enjoys a good glass of wine, Pine Ridge has a lovely picnic area and hiking trail. Tours are by appointment; the winery is open daily for tasting and sales from 11 AM to 5 PM.

Rutherford Hill Winery ((707) 963-7194 TOLL-FREE (800) 726-5226 E-MAIL rhw@nbn.com WEB SITE rutherfordhill.com, 200 Rutherford Hill Road in Rutherford, was established in 1976 and is one of the larger wineries in the area. Rutherford Hill uses some of the most up-to-date wine-making equipment and technology to produce its 100,000 cases of estate grown varietals. Its large facility, with picnic area, is located at the foot of the eastern hills of the Napa Valley which contain some 30,000 ft (9,000 m) of cellars where Cabernet Sauvignon, Merlot, Pinot Noir, Chardonnay and Gewurztraminer are aged in enormous French oak barrels. Open daily for tasting (for a fee) and sales from 10:30 AM to 4:30 PM (to 5 PM on Saturday and Sunday), tours begin at 11:30 AM, 1:30 PM and 3:30 PM.

Sutter Home Winery ((707) 963-3104 WEB SITE www.sutterhome.com, 277 Saint Helena Highway in Saint Helena, is Napa Valley's oldest winery built entirely from wood. Sold to the land-baron John Sutter and then bought by its present owners, the Trinchero family, in 1946, Sutter is the largest Zinfandel producer in America. The winery is open for tastings and sales from 9:30 AM to 5 PM; private group tours and tastings by appointment.

WHAT TO SEE AND DO

The **Napa Valley Wine Train** ((707) 253-2111 TOLL-FREE (800) 427-4124 FAX (707) 253-9264 WEB SITE www.napavalley.com/winetrain.html, provides a 36-mile (54-km) ride between the towns of Napa and Calistoga aboard restored 1915 Pullman lounge cars. The three-hour ride takes you through marvelous scenery and affords unspoiled views of a large part of the Wine Country. The only stops along the way are Yountville and Grgich Hills Cellars winery in Rutherford, although a station at Saint Helena is currently in the works. The original Napa Valley train line was established in 1868 and then abandoned in 1929 when the California wine business collapsed in the wake of Prohibition. The Wine Train came to life in 1989 when Rice-A-Roni tycoon Vincent DeDomenico and partners purchased the right-of-way from Southern Pacific for $2 million. Gourmet meals are served in the train's antique dining cars. Fares range from $35 for ordinary passage to $100 for special events like the Murder Mystery Dinner Theater on the train.

The new **Napa Valley Museum** ((707) 944-0500, 55 Presidents Circle, opened in Yountville in 1998. The collection celebrates the unique historical, artistic and environmental heritage of the Napa region. It is open Wednesday to Monday from 10 AM to 5 PM (to 8 PM the first Thursday of every month).

Old Faithful Geyser ((707) 942-6463, 1299 Tubbs Lane, is the oldest and most famous of Calistoga's water spouts. Taking its name from Yellowstone's Old Faithful, this geyser erupts approximately every 40 minutes and is one of only three regularly erupting geysers in the world. It spits boiling water and steam up to 60 ft (18 m) in the air. Visiting hours in summer are from 9 AM to 6 PM and in winter from 9 AM to 5 PM.

The **Petrified Forest**, roughly six miles (10 km) from Calistoga, is a redwood forest that was uprooted over one million years ago by volcanic eruptions and turned to stone. The most impressive of these stone trees is 80 ft (24 m) in length and 8 ft (2.4 m) in diameter. The forest is open from 10 AM to 5 PM daily. Admission is $4 for adults and $2.50 for children.

Hot air balloons and gliders are some of the other ways to explore the valley. Several companies offer balloon adventures including sunrise flights and champagne brunch: **Above the West** ((707) 944-8638 TOLL-FREE (800) 627-2759, PO Box 2290, Yountville 94599; **Balloon Aviation of Napa Valley** ((707) 944-4400 TOLL-FREE (800) 367-6272, 6525 Washington Street in Yountville; and **Bonaventure Balloon Company** ((707) 944-2822 TOLL-FREE (800) 359-6272, 133 Wall Road in Napa. For glider flights with FAA-licensed pilots try **Calistoga Gliders** ((707) 942-5000, 1546 Lincoln Avenue, Calistoga.

Napa County contains many picturesque areas for camping, hiking and fishing including **Robert Louis Stevenson State Park** and **Lake Berryessa**. Stevenson and his bride Fannie Osbourne lived in this part of the Napa Valley in the spring and summer of 1880 as the author researched and began writing *The Silverado Squatters*. For information on these and other activities, contact the **Napa Valley Conference and Visitors Bureau** ((707) 226-7459.

WHERE TO STAY

The accommodations in Napa Valley vary as much as the wines. There are the usual motel and hotel chains, but for the same $100 a night you could spend on a standard four-walled cubicle, in Napa Valley you can stay in an antique furnished bedroom with garden views, homemade-bread breakfasts, a private bath and fireplace at one of the numerous bed and breakfasts in the valley. For $70 a night, you can lounge in a hot spring mineral bath after a Swedish massage at one of the many spa resorts in the area. The following is a sample of some Napa Valley accommodations, but there are as many beautiful accommodations as you have time to find.

Very Expensive

The most prestigious luxury hotel in the Napa Valley region is the **Auberge du Soleil** ((707) 963-1211 TOLL-FREE (800) 348-5406 FAX (707) 963-8764, 180 Rutherford Hill Road in Rutherford. Nestled in an olive grove, this lovely French country inn offers swimming pool, Jacuzzi, tennis court and continental breakfast. The Auberge has 50 suites and 11 hillside cottages complete with fireplaces and terraces, along with a restaurant and 24-hour room service.

Expensive

La Residence ((707) 253-0337, 4066 Saint Helena Highway in Napa, is a wonderfully restored French barn and 1870 home set amid two acres of parkland with swimming pool and spa. The 20 rooms feature private baths and fireplaces. A full breakfast as well as wine and hors d'œuvres at sunset are included in the room rate.

Silverado Country Club ((707) 257-0200 TOLL-FREE (800) 532-0500 FAX (707) 257-5400, 1600 Atlas Peak Road in Napa, is a luxury 280-unit resort complete with two Robert Trent Jones-designed golf courses, 23 tennis courts, eight swimming pools and three gourmet restaurants. Accommodation ranges from studios to three-room cottages with fireplaces.

Villa Saint Helena ((707) 963-2514, 2727 Sulphur Springs Road in Saint Helena, is a Mediterranean villa with three exclusive rooms of period decor on a private 20-acre (8-hectare) mountain estate. Continental breakfasts are served in the solarium. The courtyard pool, picnic area and walking trails offer splendid views of the valley.

Moderate

Ambrose Bierce House ((707) 963-3003 FAX (707) 963-5100 WEBSITE innformation.com/CA/bartels, 1515 Main Street in Saint Helena, was formerly the home of the author Ambrose Bierce. Its two luxurious, air conditioned suites are named after nineteenth-century personages and furnished with brass beds, armoires, and clawfoot tubs. The house has bicycles for the guests and country breakfasts of homemade pastries and fresh fruit plus complimentary beverages and snacks.

Brannan Cottage Inn ((707) 942-4200, 109 Wapoo Avenue in Calistoga, is a historic, award-winning inn built by Sam Brannan in 1860. There are six alluring rooms in this gingerbread Victorian, set in a delightful garden.

Calistoga Spa Hot Springs ((707) 942-6269, 1006 Washington Street in Calistoga, has 57 motel-style, air-conditioned units with kitchenettes designed for family resort vacations. The resort features two outdoor hot mineral pools, covered jet pool, outdoor wading pool, weight and work-out rooms, aerobics classes, mud baths and massages.

Chestelson House ((707) 963-2238, 1417 Kearney Street in the heart of Saint Helena, is a 1900 Victorian mansion with a wide verandah looking out toward the mountains. It offers complimentary wine and gourmet breakfast.

Hennessy House ((707) 226-3774 FAX (707) 226-2975 WEB SITE www.napavalley.com/hennessey, 1727 Main Street in Napa, offers 10 rooms in a charming antique-furnished 1889 Queen Anne Victorian house with featherbeds and private baths, as well as four beautiful rooms in an ad-

joining carriage house with whirlpool baths and fireplaces. Full breakfasts, sauna and wine tastings available.

Maison Fleurie ((707) 944-2056, 6529 Yount Street in Yountville, is reminiscent of a Provençal farmhouse with its thick brick walls, terracotta tiles and paned windows. It has 13 antique-filled rooms with private baths, a swimming pool and Jacuzzi, and serves country-style breakfasts. Mountain bikes are available for guest use.

The Pink Mansion ((707) 942-0558 TOLL-FREE (800) 238-7465 FAX (707) 942-0558 WEB SITE www.pinkmansion.com, 1415 Foothill Boulevard in Calistoga, is a delectable turn-of-the-century Victorian mansion surrounded by three acres (a little more than a hectare) of woods and

ABOVE: One of the thousands of Mexican migrant workers who pick the grapes that make the world-famous wines of California.

Northern California and the Sierras

gardens. It offers six cozy rooms, a heated indoor pool, Jacuzzi, game room and gourmet breakfasts.

Roman Spa Hot Springs Resort ((707) 942-4441 TOLL-FREE (800) 820-4463, 1300 Washington Street in Calistoga, and its sibling, the Oasis Spa, offer a perfectly balanced package. The Roman Spa provides 60 modern, air-conditioned rooms with television and kitchenettes, as well as some cottages. Outdoor and indoor mineral pools, Jacuzzi, Swedish sauna and a large swimming pool supply hours of enjoyment. Meanwhile, Oasis Spa furnishes all varieties of treatments from Japanese enzyme baths to simple mud baths and massages.

Wine Country Inn ((707) 963-7077 FAX (707) 963-9018, 1152 Lodi Lane in Saint Helena, sits atop a hill overlooking vineyards. Each of the 24 rooms is individually decorated with handmade quilts and antiques. Some have fireplaces and balconies. There is a pool and spa.

Inexpensive

Golden Haven Hot Springs ((707) 942-6793, 1713 Lake Street in Calistoga, has a covered pool, hot mineral pools, exercise room, sun deck, mud baths and massage. There are 28 air-conditioned units, some with kitchenettes, others with private sauna and Jacuzzi.

Napa Valley Railway Inn ((707) 944-2000, 6503 Washington Street in Yountville, looks like an antique gold rush train. In fact, the nine elegant rooms with private baths, sitting rooms and bay windows overlooking the vineyards are in the restored railway cars and cabooses of a vintage train.

WHERE TO EAT

Vintners Court ((707) 257-0200 at the Silverado Country Club in Napa, serves innovative East-meets-West dishes in an elegant dining room with a view of the golf course. Copious brunches are served on Sunday. Prices are somewhat high, and reservations are recommended. It is open for dinner Wednesday to Saturday from 6:30 PM to 9:30 PM and for Sunday brunch from 10 AM to 2:30 PM.

Napa Valley's hottest new restaurant is the **Wine Spectator at Greystone** ((707) 967-1010, 2555 Main Street in Saint Helena. Run by the prestigious *Wine Spectator* magazine and affiliated with the Culinary Institute of America (which trains future chefs at the same location), it's hard to go wrong with the food or drink at this upscale establishment. Greystone is situated in a splendid stone mansion that once housed the Christian Brothers Winery. The Mediterranean-style cuisine features pastas, salads and main courses like fennel-crusted ahi tuna, ricotta and garlic gnocchi, sirloin of lamb and grilled hanger steak. Tours of the cooking school are available. It is open daily for lunch from 11:30 AM to 2:45 PM and for dinner from 5:30 PM to 9 PM (to 10 PM on weekends).

Moderate

Mustard's Grill ((707) 944-2424, 7399 Saint Helena Highway in Yountville, is a popular Napa Valley restaurant that serves mesquite-grilled seafood prepared in a wood-burning oven. It attracts clientele from throughout Northern California. Reservations are recommended.

Napa Valley Grille ((707) 944-8686, 6795 Washington Street, State Highway 29 in Yountville features four private rooms for gracious dining with an umbrella-shaded patio and an exhibition kitchen to enhance this casual but elegant restaurant. It offers an innovative seasonal menu of country cuisine for lunch and dinner Monday through Thursday from

11:30 AM to 9:30 PM, Friday and Saturday from 11:30 AM to 10 PM, and Sunday from 10 AM to 2:30 PM for brunch and from 4:30 PM to 9:30 PM for dinner.

Inexpensive

Bosko's ((707) 942-9088, 1364 Lincoln Avenue, Calistoga, has been a long-time favorite with locals. This Italian restaurant serves up all the usual favorites from pasta to pizza to home-baked focaccia sandwiches. Housed in a beautiful sandstone building which dates to the late 1800s, it is open daily from 11 AM to 10 PM for lunch and dinner.

HOW TO GET THERE

The Napa Valley starts at the north end of San Francisco Bay and the Napa River actually flows into the bay at Vallejo, but the bulk of the wineries are in the middle and upper reaches of the valley, 60 to 90 minutes drive from downtown San Francisco.

The quickest way to reach the Wine Country is to take Interstate 80 across the Bay Bridge and then north across the Carquinez Bridge into Vallejo. Five miles (eight kilometers) north of the bridge, exit the freeway and take State Highway 37 east for two miles (three kilometers). Turn right (north) onto State Highway 29 which runs the length of the Napa Valley via Napa, Yountville, Oakville, Rutherford, Saint Helena and Calistoga. State Highway 29 continues to Clear Lake in the Coastal Range mountains.

Here, General Mariano Vallejo built a town plaza and his own adobe Casa Grande, the finest house in northern California. It is also where the "Bear Flag" was raised over the short-lived California Republic. Vallejo's adobe mansion didn't survive, but **Lachryma Montis** (Spanish for "mountain tears"), the Victorian house he built after the American takeover, is now open to the public in a state historic park.

Sonoma Plaza is the largest and most vivid of California's Spanish-style plazas. It contains a park, a pond, and an outdoor theater. Surrounding the plaza are several historic buildings from the 1830s and 1850s that have been restored magnificently. Of these the **El Dorado**, **Sonoma**, **Swiss**

An alternative route is to take US Highway 101 across the Golden Gate Bridge and through Marin County to the town of Novato. Exit the freeway and take State Highway 37 around the north end of San Francisco Bay (via Sears Point and Mare Island) until you reach State Highway 29.

SONOMA VALLEY

Sonoma Valley takes its name from an early Indian tribe but it was popularized by novelist Jack London as the "Valley of the Moon." It is second in California wine production only to the adjoining Napa Valley. This is where Count Agoston Haraszthy founded his historic Buena Vista estate vineyards, becoming the "father of Californian viticulture."

The town of **Sonoma** at the southern end of the valley was an important Mexican rancho seat.

and **Toscano** hotels are particularly grand, as is the **Sonoma Mission**, the last and northernmost of the 21 Spanish missions.

The Sonoma Valley encompasses several other towns including (south to north) **Boyes Hot Springs**, **Glen Ellen**, **Kenwood** and **Oakmont**. Most of the wineries mentioned here are located in the town of Sonoma itself or a short jaunt away, but there are several charming and rather historic wineries further north into the valley along State Highway 12.

GENERAL INFORMATION

The **Sonoma Valley Visitors Bureau** ((707) 996-1090, 453 East First Street, maintains an informa-

The extensive vineyards in Sonoma Valley.

tion desk on Sonoma's main plaza. It is open daily from 9 AM to 5 PM. As an alternative you can get in touch with the excellent **Sonoma County Convention & Visitors Bureau (** (707) 586-8100 TOLL-FREE (800) 326-7666 FAX (707) 586 8111 WEB SITE visitsonoma.com, 5000 Roberts Lake Road, Rohnert Park 94928.

WINERIES

Buena Vista Carneros Winery ((707) 938-1266 TOLL-FREE (800) 926-1266, 18000 Old Winery Road in Sonoma was founded in 1857 by Agoston Haraszthy. This is California's oldest winery. Chinese coolies dug its caves in 1862 and its original cellar is now a state historic landmark. Featured at the winery are a museum, an art gallery, a visitor center, a tasting room and a picnic area. The winery is open from 10:30 AM to 5 PM in the summer and 10:30 AM to 4:30 PM the rest of the year.

Glen Ellen Winery ((707) 939-6277, 14301 Arnold Drive, Glen Ellen, is housed in an old barn dating from 1860 when the property was part of the 122-acre (49-hectare) Rancho Petaluma land grant. The vineyard, once neglected, was bought and revived in 1980 by the Benziger family and now produces a fine Cabernet Sauvignon, Chardonnay and Sauvignon Blanc. The winery is adjacent to the Jack London State Historic Park and has a delightfully shaded picnic area. It is open daily for tours (by appointment), tasting and sales from 10 AM to 4:30 PM.

Gloria Ferrer Champagne Caves ((707) 996-7256, 23555 State Highway 121 in Sonoma, is one of the newest wineries in the valley. Opened in 1986 by Freixenet of Spain, the largest *méthode champenoise* wine producer in the world, the $12-million investment has beautifully spacious facilities created in the Spanish style. A trip to the limestone aging caves on the hillside overlooking the vineyards is truly exciting. The winery is named after the wife of Freixenet's president, Jose Ferrer. It is open daily for tours, tasting and sales from 10:30 AM to 5:30 PM.

Kenwood Vineyards ((707) 833-5891 FAX (707) 833-1146 WEB SITE www.kenwoodvineyards.com, 9592 Sonoma Highway in Kenwood. Founded in 1970 at the site of a historic Sonoma winery, this family-owned establishment produces several premium wines including Cabernet Sauvignon, Chardonnay, Sauvignon Blanc, Zinfandel, Pinot Noir and Merlot. The tasting room is open 10 AM to 4:30 PM daily.

Landmark Vineyards ((707) 833-0053 FAX (707) 833-1164, 101 Adobe Canyon Road in Sonoma, is owned by Damaris Deere Wiman Ethridge, great great granddaughter of John Deere, inventor of the steel plow. This winery's focus turned exclusively to Chardonnay in the early 1980s. The hos-

pitality center, which features a tasting bar, is open daily 10 AM to 4:30 PM. There is also a gift shop and pondside picnic area.

Sebastiani Sonoma Cask Cellars ((707) 938-5532 TOLL-FREE (800) 888-5532, 389 Forth Street East in Sonoma, was founded by the mission padres in 1825. This huge vineyard was bought by Samuele Sebastiani in 1904 and has been owned by his family ever since. Sebastiani has what is believed to be the largest collection of hand-carved redwood casks in North America and an Indian artifact museum. Daily tours, rich in Italian heritage, are given from 10:30 AM to 4 PM. The gift shop and winery are open daily from 10 AM to 5 PM.

Smothers Tasting Room ((707) 833-1010, 9575 State Highway 12 in Kenwood, is where Tom and Dick Smothers went into exile when their *Comedy Hour* got too controversial for American television. Their "Mom's Favorite" red and white wines were an overnight success. The Tasting Room was opened in 1985 to show wines produced from the vineyards on Tom Smothers' ranch in Kenwood. It is open daily from 10 AM to 4:30 PM.

Valley of the Moon Winery ((707) 996-6940, 777 Madrone Road in Glen Ellen, has been owned since its founding in 1857 by a variety of infamous people including General "Fighting Joe" Hooker, Eli Shepard, George Hearst and William Randolph Hearst. It is currently owned by the well-known wine producing Parducci family which took over in 1941. The historic winery offers jug wines and estate-bottled varietals such as French Columbard, Semillon, Zinfandel Rose and Pinot Noir Blanc. The winery is open daily for tasting and sales from 10 AM to 5 PM.

WHAT TO SEE AND DO

Jack London State Historic Park ((707) 938-5216 WEB SITE parks.sonoma.net/, 2400 London Ranch Road, is in Glen Ellen. Located in this 800-acre (320-hectare) park is the legendary "Beauty Ranch" where the American novelist Jack London lived and worked until his death in 1916, writing *Call of the Wild* (1903) and *White Fang* (1906), among other works. There are also the ruins of London's "Wolf House" and a boulder marking his grave. A 1919 stone mansion ("The House of Happy Walls"), built by his wife, is now a museum displaying artifacts from the author's life and his impressive collection of South Pacific art. The museum is open daily April to October from 10:30 AM to 5 PM and November to March from 10:30 AM to 5 PM.

Sonoma Mission ((707) 938-1519, on the corner of Spain and East First Streets in Sonoma, was the last mission founded by the Franciscan fathers. Established in 1823 it has historical displays and a magnificent collection of paintings of the 21 Californian Spanish missions. Open daily from 10 AM to 5 PM, admission includes entrance to the

Sonoma Barracks, an 1840s adobe edifice that housed Mexican troops, and the Vallejo Home.

Vallejo Home (Lachryma Montis), built in the early 1850s, sits on beautifully landscaped grounds and was once the home of General Mariano Vallejo, Mexican governor of California. The house contains Vallejo's original furniture as well as an extensive collection of historical photographs, and is open daily from 10 AM to 5 PM.

What's a wine tasting tour without cheese? The **Sonoma Cheese Factory** ((707) 996-1931 TOLL-FREE (800) 535-2855 E-MAIL scheese@napanet.net WEB SITE www.sonomajack.com, 2 Spain Street in Sonoma, offers some of the best in the region. Visitors can watch cheese being made and view a short slide show on the process. There's also a deli and wine shop on the premises. The Cheese Factory is open Monday to Friday from 8:30 AM to 5:30 PM and Saturday and Sunday from 8:30 AM to 6 PM.

WHERE TO STAY

Expensive

The charming **Madrona Manor** ((707) 433-4231 TOLL-FREE (800) 258-4003 FAX (707) 433-0703, 1001 Westside Road, in Healdsburg, offers 18 rooms and three suites with private bathrooms and air conditioning. Built in 1881, this three-story manor is surrounded by beautifully landscaped gardens with a swimming pool. An expansive breakfast buffet is prepared by the manor's internationally acclaimed chef.

Moderate

One of the more delightful places to stay in the Wine Country is **Gaige House Inn** ((707) 935-0237 TOLL-FREE (800) 935-0237 FAX (707) 935-6411 E-MAIL gaige@sprynet.com WEB SITE www.gaige.com, 13540 Arnold Drive in Glen Ellen. It features 11 spacious rooms (six in the original house) with queen or king size beds, private bathrooms and direct dial phones. It offers a premium wine hour and 24-hour cookie supply. The resident gourmet chef provides imaginative breakfasts. The swimming pool is set in leafy garden. Only children over 14 are allowed.

Sonoma Mission Inn & Spa ((707) 938-9000 TOLL-FREE (800) 862-4945 FAX (707) 996-5358, 18140 Sonoma Highway in Boyes Hot Springs, offers resort accommodations in 200 rooms. Facilities include restaurants, swimming pools and a fully equipped spa.

Vintners Inn ((707) 575-7350 TOLL-FREE (800) 421-2584 FAX (707) 575-1426, 4350 Barnes Road in Santa Rosa, has a heavy Spanish touch. The inn's atmosphere is buttressed by its fountains and plaza, surrounded by a 50-acre (20-hectare) vineyard. Many of the 44 rooms have fireplaces and balconies. Rates include a complimentary continental breakfast.

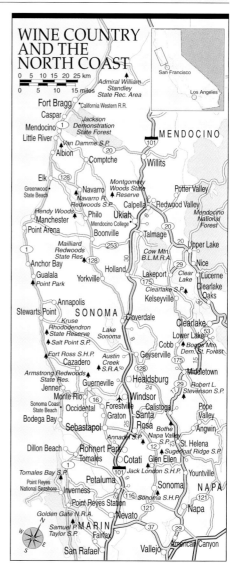

WHERE TO EAT

Expensive

With just eight tables, the **Glen Ellen Inn Restaurant** ((707) 996-6409, 13670 Arnold Drive in Glen Ellen, is a very cozy establishment. The menu, heavily into Californian cuisine, changes frequently. Garden and patio dining are available in summer. The restaurant serves nightly in summer from 5:30 PM, and in winter Thursday to Tuesday from 5:30 PM.

For excellent French dishes at very affordable prices try **Babette's** ((707) 939-8921, 464 First Street East in Sonoma. The ambiance is homey and casual. It is open from 6 PM to 10 PM Thursday to Sunday.

Moderate

Della Santina's ((707) 935-0576, 133 East Napa Street in Sonoma, is a relaxed and friendly trattoria-style Italian restaurant with a menu that includes a good selection of pasta. It is open daily from 11:30 AM to 9:30 PM.

HOW TO GET THERE

Like the neighboring Napa Valley, the Sonoma Valley spills down to the northern shore of San Francisco Bay and is easy to reach from the city. The drive takes about one hour depending on traffic.

The fastest way to reach Sonoma is US Highway 101 across the Golden Gate Bridge and through Marin County to the town of Novato. Exit the freeway and take State Highway 37 around the north end of San Francisco Bay. At Sears Point, turn left onto State Highway 121 which runs due north to the town of Sonoma. From Sonoma, State Highway 12 runs the entire length of the valley via Boyes Hot Springs, Kenwood and Oakmont, eventually intersecting with US Highway 101 at Santa Rosa.

RUSSIAN RIVER REGION

The third among the major wine-producing counties, the Russian River region, is first in many people's minds for scenery. It combines a rugged coastline, the redwood forests, and the valley vineyards in a mix you don't find elsewhere. There are two major rivers cutting through the region: the Eel River that goes through the north, creating the fertile dairy valley by Ferndale; and the Russian River.

The **Russian River** is where San Franciscans go to the beach. Since the ocean beach is often clouded over by fog, many in San Francisco have adopted the sandy banks along the Russian River as their place to get away into the sunshine. The river runs south out of Mendocino county into Sonoma County where it angles west to the ocean. **Guerneville** functions as a kind of inland beach town, and its small restaurants and bars are especially popular with gay men and women from San Francisco and elsewhere. The coastal town of **Jenner**, another popular beauty spot, is where the Russian River empties into the Pacific.

GENERAL INFORMATION

The **Russian River Region Visitors Bureau** TOLL-FREE (800) 253-8800 WEB SITE www.sonoma.com/rusriver, PO Box 255, Guerneville, 95446, maintains two tourist information offices: the first ((707) 253-8800, 13250 River Road in Guerneville in the railroad station at Korbel Champagne Cellars; the second ((707) 875-2868 at 850 Coast Highway in Bodega Bay.

WINERIES

Château Souverain ((707) 433-3141, 400 Souverain Road at Independence Lane and US Highway 101 in Geyserville, is a 500,000 case winery as famous for its award-winning restaurant as for its prized Chardonnay and Cabernet Sauvignon. The winery is situated in a château with two identical stone towers and a beautifully landscaped courtyard with a central fountain. Art shows, concerts, theater performances and fairs are held here throughout the year. The winery is open daily from 10 AM to 5 PM.

Clos du Bois ((707) 857-3100 TOLL-FREE (800) 222-3189, 5 Fitch Street in Healdsburg, has 650 acres (260 hectares) of vineyards. Established in 1974, the winery offers a wide range of Sauvignons, Chardonnays and other estate-grown varietals. Of particular interest is the Merlot, impressively smooth and supple, with a delicate balance of tannins. Also worth imbibing is the proprietary red, Marlstone, a mellow blend of Cabernet Sauvignon and Merlot. Open daily for tours (by appointment), tasting and sales from 10 AM to 4:30 PM.

The **Korbel Champagne Cellars** ((707) 887-2294 FAX (707) 869-2981 WEB SITE www.korbel.com, 13250 River Road in Guerneville, are located in one of the region's most beautiful spots — an ivy-covered brick building set among lush flower gardens and redwoods on the banks of the Russian River. Korbel produces 400,000 cases of brandy and 500,000 cases of sparkling wine annually. Historical tours are offered daily from 10 AM to 3:45 PM May to September, from 10 AM to 3 PM October to April. A micro-brewery and gourmet deli are open daily. Wine tastings are held daily from 9 AM to 4:30 PM.

Mark West Estate Vineyard & Winery ((707) 544-4813 FAX (707) 836-0147, 7010 Trenton-Healdsburg Road in Forestville, is a pioneer vineyard and winery celebrating more than two decades of excellent Russian River Chardonnay, Pinot Noir and Gewurztraminer. It has a lovely picnic area with expansive views of the Russian River valley and bordering Mayacamas Mountains. Tasting is available daily November to May from 11 AM to 4 PM, and June to October from 10 AM to 4:30 PM.

Martini & Prati Winery ((707) 823-2404 or (707) 829-6150 FAX (707) 829-6151, 2191 Laguna Road in Santa Rosa, is one of the oldest wineries in continuous operation in Sonoma County. It has been managed by the Martini family since 1902. One of the few "redwood wineries" still operating, some 1.5 million gallons of wine are stored in 100-year-old redwood casks. Visitors can purchase an empty jug and fill it with a rustic, Italian-style red wine directly from a tank. Daily tastings are available November to May from 11 AM to 4 PM and June to October from 10 AM to 5 PM. There is a daily tour at 11 AM or by appointment.

Simi Winery ((707) 433-1907 or (707) 6981, 16275 Healdsburg Avenue in Healdsburg, has an ancient stone cellar dating from the days when the Italian immigrants Pietro and Guiseppe Simi founded the winery in 1876. The property is now owned by the prestigious French Moët-Hennessey company. The results of an extensive 1979 renovation include a nice picnic area, gift shops and some of the most modern, high-tech wine-making equipment in the region. Tasting and sales available daily from 10 AM to 4:30 PM, with tours at 11 AM, 1 PM and 3 PM.

Windsor Vineyards TOLL-FREE (800) 204-9463, 239A Center Street in Healdsburg, is one of America's most award-winning wineries and has sold premium wines since 1959. Its numerous varietals including Petite Sirah, Cabernet Sauvignon and Pinot Noir under several labels, are available. You can have a personal message or your company logo printed on bottle labels. Tasting and sales are available from 10 AM to 5 PM on weekdays, and until 6 PM on weekends.

WHAT TO SEE AND DO

Armstrong Redwoods State Reserve is a 752-acre (301-hectare) park off State Highway 116 in Guerneville. There are extensive hiking trails through the park, which is home to the last of the Sonoma County virgin redwoods.

Regional history comes into sharper focus at the superb little **Healdsburg Museum** ((707) 431-3325, 221 Matheson Street. The exhibits include vivid portrayals of the Indian, Mexican and American influences on Healdsburg's diverse cultural formation, including thousands of interesting photographs. It is open Wednesday to Sunday from noon to 5 PM. Admission is free.

The **Sonoma County Wine Library** ((707) 433-3772, Center and Piper Streets in Healdsburg, features an outstanding collection of 3,000 wine-related volumes.

WHERE TO STAY

Healdsburg Inn on the Plaza ((707) 433-6991 TOLL-FREE (800) 431-8663, 110 Matheson Street in Healdsburg, has 10 guest rooms in a splendid Victorian setting. Some of the qualities that set it apart are the art gallery on the first floor and breakfast in the rooftop solarium.

Down on the rugged Sonoma County coast is **The Inn at the Tides** ((707) 875-2751 TOLL-FREE (800) 541-7788 E-MAIL iatt@monitor.net WEB SITE www.innatthetides.com, 800 Coast Highway in Bodega Bay. The Inn features 86 guest rooms in 12 lodges scattered across six hillside acres

(roughly two and a half hectares) with bay and harbor views. Each room has a stocked mini bar, a coffee maker and a 24-hour video entertainment system. There is a heated pool, spa and Finnish sauna (massages available), and two restaurants. Rates include complimentary continental breakfast.

Moderate

Belle de Jour Inn ((707) 431-9777, Healdsburg Avenue, Healdsburg, has four fresh, white cottages nestled amid six acres of parkland. All units are air-conditioned and have fireplace or wood burning stove, refrigerator, and hot tub or Jacuzzi. Full country breakfast is included in the rate and is served on the deck of the main house.

At the confluence of the Russian River, Alexander Valley and Dry Creek you'll find the cozy little **Grape Leaf Inn** ((707) 433-8140 FAX (707) 433-3140 E-MAIL sweet@sonic.net WEB SITE www.grapeleafinn.com, 539 Johnson Street, Healdsburg. This bed and breakfast is situated in a magnificently restored turn-of-the-century Queen Anne Victorian home within a 15-minute drive of over 60 Sonoma County wineries. The seven air-conditioned bedrooms all have private baths, most with whirlpool. A full country breakfast and afternoon wine and cheeses are included in the rate.

Rustic sophistication makes the **Ridenhour Ranch House Inn** ((707) 887-1033, 12850 River Road, one of the more interesting places to sleep in Guerneville. This eccentric redwood ranch house has eight rooms decorated with antiques and quilts. Amenities include hot tub, croquet on the lawn and gourmet breakfast spreads. The minimum stay is two nights.

WHERE TO EAT

Expensive

Healdsburg's town square is the setting for **Bistro Ralph** ((707) 433-1380, 109 Plaza Street East, an upscale eatery housed in an intimate storefront. It serves good food with an emphasis on local ingredients and is open for dinner daily and lunch Monday to Friday from 11:30 AM.

Château Souverain ((707) 433-3141, 400 Souverain Road in Geyserville, is the heralded restaurant at the winery of the same name which serves French and California cuisine. It offers a choice between the dining room or the outdoor patio overlooking the vineyards and reservations are recommended. The restaurant is open for lunch and dinner Friday to Sunday.

Inexpensive

Bear Republic Brewing Co. ((707) 433-2337, 345 Healdsburg Avenue, Healdsburg, serves much more than their award-winning ales. Hearty food and drink are available for the whole family in a relaxed and friendly atmosphere for lunch and dinner daily.

HOW TO GET THERE

The Russian River region is about 90 minutes north of San Francisco by car. The best way to reach the area is US Highway 101 across the Golden Gate Bridge and then through Marin County and the lower part of Sonoma County. At Santa Rosa, exit the freeway and drive west along State Highway 12 until you reach Sebastopol. Turn right (north) onto State Highway 116, which winds along the Russian River through Forestville, Guerneville and Monte Rio, eventually terminating at State Highway 1 and the Pacific Ocean.

HIGHWAY ONE

The segment of California State Highway 1 between Big Sur and San Simeon is probably the most dramatic drive in California. But the continuation of State Highway 1 north of San Francisco is nearly as stunning and perhaps even more engaging because of its fishing villages, historic attractions and redwood groves.

To reach this fabulous stretch of coast, drive across the Golden Gate Bridge into Marin County and exit the freeway at Shoreline Highway in Marin City. The twisting highway hits the coast at **Muir Beach**, a lovely cove with bluffs at either end, reminiscent of windswept English coast. Right behind the strand is another little slice of the British Isles: a Tudor-style restaurant and pub called the **Pelican Inn** ((415) 383-6000 FAX (415) 383-3424 that serves up roast beef, Yorkshire pudding, cottage pie and British beer in draft. The Pelican also rents out seven bed and breakfast rooms, each with canopy bed, Oriental carpet and a hearty English breakfast.

State Highway 1 continues through the northern reaches of Marin County to **Stinson Beach** and **Bolinas** before heading inland again through rolling pastures and woodland. At **Olema** you can continue straight along State Highway 1 or turn west and venture into **Point Reyes National Seashore** with its breezy landscapes, flower-filled meadows and long stretches of white-sand beach (including the spot where Sir Francis Drake came ashore in 1579). Created in 1962 by President Kennedy, the park protects one of California's largest stretches of undeveloped coast (70,000 acres, or over 28,000 hectares). **Point Reyes Lighthouse** at the park's southwest tip is a great place for whale watching and **Limantour Beach** presents seven miles (11 km) of virgin sand. More than 45% of North American bird species have been sighted at Point Reyes and more than one-

fifth of all plant species found in California can be found on the Point Reyes Peninsula. Popular activities in the park include hiking, sea kayaking, mountain biking, horseback riding, bird-watching and beachcombing. **Bear Valley Visitor Center** ((415) 663-1092 offers trail maps, campground reservations and environmental education programs.

Beyond Olema, State Highway 1 follows the eastern shore of Tomales Bay — a sunken branch of the San Andreas earthquake fault. The tiny town of **Marshall** on the bay is famous for its fresh oysters and other shellfish. **Hog Island Oyster Company** ((415) 663-9218 sells oysters, clams and farm-raised live abalone in the shell.

Crossing over into Sonoma County, State Highway 1 runs through **Bodega Bay**, one of the most picturesque fishing villages on the entire California coast and the place where Alfred Hitchcock filmed his classic horror movie *The Birds* in the early 1960s. **Sonoma Coast State Beach** presents another chance to take a dip in the sea. The Russian River empties into the Pacific at **Jenner**, another charming coastal town, after which the highway snakes north to Fort Ross, Mendocino and Fort Bragg.

FORT ROSS

Fort Ross was not named for Betsy or anyone else with that English-sounding name. It comes rather from "Rossiya," the last reminder (along with the Russian River) of the Czar's attempt to claim Northern California. In fact, the practical reason for sending Father Serra's sacred mission-founding expedition to California in 1770 was because the Russians were known to be hunting and fishing further and further south from their Aleutian Islands base, and were taking a serious interest in California's northern coast.

Located about 10 miles (16 km) north of present-day Jenner and the mouth of the Russian River (which they called "Slavianka" or Slav Woman), Fort Ross was not established until 1811. The original founding party included 95 Russians and 80 natives from the Aleutians who helped in the hunting (and destruction) of the vast sea otter herds that then roamed the area. The Russian presence further inspired the young United States Congress to enact the Monroe Doctrine against foreign incursion into this hemisphere. But with the otter hunted to near extinction, the Russians sold their property and left of their own free will in 1839. At one time, the fort consisted of more than 50 buildings inside a high palisade, including a wooden onion-domed church with bells cast in Saint Petersburg. The remaining ruins of the fort were leveled during the 1906 earthquake. The palisade, the church and several other buildings have been carefully rebuilt on the site. The fort's centerpiece, the Russian Orthodox Church, was rebuilt and restored twice after the earthquake of 1906, only to burn down in 1970 and get rebuilt yet again in 1974. **Fort Ross State Historic Park** ((707) 865-2391 is open daily from 10 AM to 4:30 PM; there is a $2 parking fee.

MENDOCINO

The town is located on the verge of two of California's most beautiful regions — the Wine Country and the Redwood Empire. If you arrive for the first time in the beautiful old town with its turn-of-the-century store fronts and rambling wooden country houses, and think you've seen it all before, you probably have. The town has long been favored as a movie location. *The Summer of '42* is just one of many filmed on location here — and nearly all of them are supposedly set on Cape Cod or some coastal village in Maine.

While the name apparently is an Anglicized version of Mendoza, the Spanish viceroy in Mexico for whom Cape Mendocino was named, there is nothing else in Mendocino to recall the Spanish and Mexican presence in California. With so much wood handy, the first settlers built big houses with wide porches and surrounded their flower-filled yards with picket fences, a real oddity in California. The distinctive old water towers that once provided gravity flow into each house have also been preserved. A number of successful artists and writers, such as Alice Walker (author of *The Color Purple*), now call Mendocino home.

While the architecture may evoke New England, the mood in Mendocino is very much like the laid-back, casual style of a Southern California beach town. The waters off the rocky coast are popular with surfers. The several fine restaurants are popular with San Franciscans who often drive up for lunch. Most of the old houses have been converted into bed and breakfast inns.

If you start to feel overwhelmed by all this quaintness, duck into the **Fetzer Vineyards Tasting Room** ((707) 937-6190, 45070 Main Street, for a sip of the local vintage. The place also sells a large array of organically grown, earth-friendly merchandise, much of it made along the Mendocino Coast.

GENERAL INFORMATION

Tourist information on towns along the Mendocino Coast can be obtained from the **Fort Bragg-Mendocino Coast Chamber of Commerce** ((707) 961-6300 TOLL-FREE (800) 726-2780 FAX (707) 964-2056 WEB SITE www.mendocinocoast.com, 332 North Main Street, PO Box 1141 Fort Bragg, 95437.

Information on local wineries is available from the **Mendocino Winegrowers Alliance**

((707) 744-1363 FAX (707) 744-1364 WEB SITE www.mendowine.com.

WHERE TO STAY

Expensive

You don't have to be a honeymoon couple to appreciate the abiding romance of the **Stanford Inn by the Sea** ((707) 937-5615 TOLL-FREE (800) 331-8884 FAX (707) 937-0305 E-MAIL stanford@ stanfordinn.com, State Highway 1 at Comptche-Ukiah Road. With expansive views of the village and coast, fireplaces in nearly every room, and a greenhouse with pool and spa, the Stanford has just about everything you need for a serene retreat.

Albion River Inn ((707) 937-1919, at 3790 North Harbor Drive, has 20 rooms with private bathrooms, fireplaces and ocean views.

Reed Manor Bed & Breakfast Inn ((707) 937-5446, Palette Drive, offers five rooms with private bathrooms, fireplaces, television and telephone.

Moderate

MacCallum House Inn ((707) 937-0289 TOLL-FREE (800) 609-0492, 45020 Albion Street, was built in 1882 and is one of the most homey lodgings along the Mendocino Coast. It has a popular bar called the **Grey Whale** and a restaurant in the main house.

While Mendocino may pass for a New England town, it's still in California, which means that hot tubs, sauna, and massage are popular. For a taste, try **Sweetwater Spa & Inn** ((707) 937-4076 TOLL-FREE (800) 300-4140, 44840 Main Street.

Mendocino Coast Accommodations ((707) 937-5033 TOLL-FREE (800) 262-7801 can provide information and reservations for bed and breakfasts and rental homes in the Mendocino area.

HOW TO GET THERE

Mendocino is 160 miles (256 km) north of San Francisco via Highway 1, a journey that takes about six and a half hours under normal driving conditions. A quicker but less scenic alternative (about four hours) is US Highway 101 north to Willits and then State Highway 20 west across the coastal mountains (via Jackson State Forest) to Noyo, where you turn south onto State Highway 1 and drive about nine miles (14 km) to Mendocino.

Mendocino Transit Authority TOLL-FREE (800) 696-4MTA offers daily coach service to the Mendocino from San Francisco and Oakland airports and Santa Rosa.

FORT BRAGG

Fort Bragg was founded in 1854, and by 1857 was the site of an Army post designed to put down Indian insurrection. Abandoned by the military only ten years later, it became a busy logging and lumber center. This lumbering past and present is celebrated every year on Labor Day, with the annual **Paul Bunyan Days** festival.

You don't have to be in the area long to understand you're in a company town and the company is Georgia Pacific. Only the government owns more redwoods than this huge paper and lumber conglomerate. Along any of the roads from here northward, you'll see the firm's big logging trucks zooming downhill or chugging slowly upwards. At Fort Bragg, it is possible to see a positive side of Georgia Pacific: at State Highway 1 and Walnut Street is the **Georgia Pacific Nursery**, open to the public free of charge from 8 AM to 5 PM,

months, cut to one daily trip from mid-September through mid-June. The entire route is 40 miles (65 km) through rugged redwood country, with two tunnels and some of the crookedest railroad you'll ever ride on. Most of the cars are the self-powered gas engine skunks; but two diesel-powered locomotives from the old logging days have been restored. Willits is at the eastern end of the full route; there is a halfway stop at Northspur, where some of the summer trips end for those wanting a shorter ride. The shortest ride takes three hours round-trip; the longest lasts eight and a half hours, all the way from Fort Bragg to Willits and back. For information and reservations call ((707) 964-6371 TOLL-FREE (800) 77-SKUNK. The longer

Monday through Friday, May through October. More than three million redwood and Douglas fir seedlings are grown here to be used in the reforestation of the ancient forests cut by Georgia Pacific. There is a visitor center, an arboretum and tables for picnics.

Georgia Pacific also operates a **Logging Museum** at 339 North Main Street in Fort Bragg, which is open from 8:30 AM to 4:30 PM, Wednesday through Sunday.

The town's most famous attraction is the California Western Railroad — better known as the "**Skunk Train**." The train got its name from the first gas engines that powered trains. People used to say that like a skunk, you could smell the train before you could see it. The train was originally a logging railroad, but passenger service started in 1904. A busy schedule offering ten different trips is available during the summer

trip is $26 for adults and $12 for children; the trip to Northspur is $21 for adults and $10 for children.

Just south of Fort Bragg on State Highway 1 is the **Mendocino Coast Botanical Garden** ((707) 964-4352, which houses 47 acres (19 hectares) of native flowers and trees. It is open from 9 AM to 5 PM March to October and from 9 AM to 4 PM November to February. **Ricochet Ridge Ranch** ((707) 964-7669 on the northern outskirts of town offers horseback riding on the beach (you can often spot seals and whales) and week-long horse-back trips into the redwoods forest and Coast Range.

HOW TO GET THERE

Fort Bragg is 172 miles (275 km) north of San Francisco via Highway 1, a journey that takes about seven hours. A faster but less scenic alternative (about four hours) is US Highway 101 north to Willits and then State Highway 20 west across the coastal mountains (via Jackson State Forest).

Mendocino Transit Authority ((800) 696-4MTA offers daily coach service to Mendocino from the San Francisco and Oakland airports and from Santa Rosa, along with public bus service between Fort Bragg and Mendocino, Santa Rosa and San Francisco.

THE REDWOOD EMPIRE

The redwood is no mere plant, you will quickly learn from Californians. It is the world's tallest tree, and one of the oldest living things on earth. The coastal redwoods (Sequoia sempervirens) are found from Big Sur into Oregon; the inland redwoods (Sequoia gigantea) are in the Sierra Nevada. The Sierra redwoods live to be 3,200 years old, the coastal trees up to 2,200 years old. The bristle-cone pine lives longer, up to 4,500 years, but you can only find them in the White Mountains near Death Valley in eastern California.

The Spaniards, the Russians, and everybody else who beheld the mighty redwoods quickly transformed the forests into board feet of lumber. In 1984, redwood logging was a $138-million industry in California. In addition, a fierce conservation effort dates back into the mid-1800s. The Sierra Club has been a leader in creating parks and nature preserves; the Save-the-Redwoods League was founded in 1918 and has created more than 135,000 acres (55,000 hectares) of state parks where redwoods are fully protected.

Nearly all the coastal roads north of San Francisco take you in among the redwoods. The main routes are California State Highway 1 along the coast and US Highway 101 inland. The town of **Leggett**, where these two roads come together, is a good place to begin a trip into the redwoods. Just north of Leggett is **Richardson's Grove State Park** ((707) 247-3318, 1,500 acres (more than 600 hectares) of old-growth redwoods along the South Fork of the Eel River, where you can camp among the giants. From here north, you will find any number of parks and groves. Often the highway grows almost dark as it meanders among the giant trees.

A 33-mile (53-km) stretch of old US Highway 101 between Jordan Creek and Phillipsville has been christened "**Avenue of the Giants**," a sometimes garish attempt to profit from the presence of the redwoods. The best-known attraction along this route is the **Shrine Drive-Thru Tree** at Myers Flat. This is no state park, but rather a purely commercial enterprise. Its main draw is a huge redwood that has been hollowed out enough to drive a car through; there's also a single log so wide you can pilot a car across the top of it. If you're interested in souvenirs, there is a redwood fac-

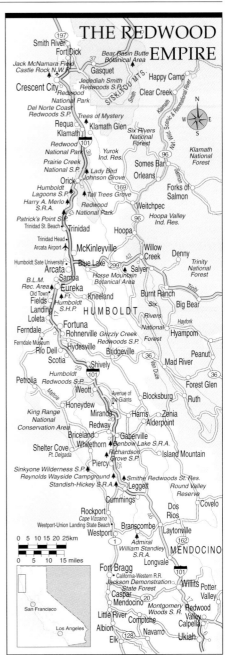

tory where you can buy redwood burl clocks, wall plaques and jewelry.

If redwood coffee tables and ash trays leave you cold, you may want to avoid this route, though

OPPOSITE: An engineer on one of the main lines in northern California, now devoted exclusively to hauling timber and other freight; fortunately the old "Skunk Train" preserves one old line for passenger excursions.

it does take you to some of the more beautiful state preserves, like **Humboldt Redwoods State Park**. With more than 17,000 acres of old-growth forest, this is the world's largest stand of redwoods. The park boasts a Visitor Center Museum ((707) 946-2409, along with numerous nature walks and hiking trails through the groves.

WHERE TO STAY

Moderate

Set on the banks of the Eel River, the **Benbow Inn** ((707) 923-2124 TOLL-FREE (800) 355-3301 FAX (707) 923-2897, E-MAIL benbowInc@aol.com, 445 Lake Benbow Drive, Garberville, has been around since 1926 when the Redwood Highway was first completed. The neo-Tudor design looks more like something from the Sherwood Forest than the Northern California woods, but there is nothing "mock" about the elegance and impeccable service of this cozy abode.

FERNDALE

If anyone has a complaint about this amazingly well-preserved Victorian village it is that it's too pretty to be real. No mere restoration, you get the feeling that this place never went through a period of decay, that the owners of these fabulous old gingerbread houses and stores valued them from the start and always took care of them.

Ferndale is set in a fertile valley thick with dairy cattle — and the rich odors that come with livestock. Founded in 1852, Ferndale was known as the "Cream City" for its dairy industry, which was passed on by an odd mixture of Portuguese, Swiss, Italian, Danish, and German immigrants. These hardy Europeans held on to the farms and saved the area from the new developments that overwhelmed every other American city. And there was Viola McBride, now the town's leading landlady, who started a campaign in the 1940s to buy up and preserve the old stores and houses as they faced destruction.

Ferndale is hardly the sterile restoration it appears from a quick ride-through. Behind the colorful façades are some interesting characters, who give life to the old buildings and color to the town's cultural agenda. Carlos Benneman won his bookstore in a card game at Becker's, a bar next door. **Becker's** is called "the investment club" by others in town because of the games that go on there. Along with games of chance, it offers delicious polenta, a stew made with cornmeal mush. Many of the old family homes that Viola McBride saved have now been converted into popular guest houses or bed and breakfast inns. Nearly all of the houses are surrounded by lavish gardens of dahlias,

fuchsias and zinnias to match the "butterfat" (as the dairymen call them) houses.

WHERE TO STAY

Expensive

Gingerbread Mansion ((707) 786-4000 TOLL-FREE (800) 952-4136, 400 Berding Street, is one of Ferndale's most photogenic Victorian relics. All rooms have bathrooms, some have fireplaces. The Mansion offers special rates mid-week and in winter.

Moderate

Shaw House Inn ((707) 786-9958, 703 Main Street, is another showcase Victorian inn, built in 1854 and now on the national register of historic places. Decorated with antiques and surrounded by lush garden, all rooms have private baths, clawfoot tubs and balconies.

The classic **Victorian Village Inn** ((707) 786-4949 TOLL-FREE (800) 576-5949, 400 Ocean Avenue at Main, was once named the most beautiful building in Humboldt County. All rooms have private baths; some feature fireplaces and clawfoot bath tubs. There is a restaurant and tavern with entertainment.

HOW TO GET THERE

Ferndale is about 260 miles (419 km) north of San Francisco and 16 miles (25 km) south of Eureka via US Highway 101. Exit the freeway at Fernbridge and drive southwest along the coast road.

EUREKA

Eureka is a refreshing and robust change from the prettiness of Mendocino and Ferndale. If you're driving there, you'll sense the difference long before you reach the old logging and sailing town — country music plays on the radio, logging trucks run the highways.

Like Fort Bragg, Eureka is a company town and that company is the same Georgia Pacific of Fort Bragg. Logging is still the major industry here, and you can see the smokestacks rising from the lumber mills south of town.

GENERAL INFORMATION

Tourist queries for the entire region are handled by the **Eureka and Humboldt County Convention & Visitors Bureau** ((707) 443-5097 TOLL-FREE (800) 346-3482 FAX (707) 443-5115 WEB SITE www .redwoodvisitor.org, 1034 Second Street, Eureka, CA 95501. Information bureaus are located at 850 G Street, Suite D in Arcata ((707) 826-9043; and 123 F Street, Suite 6 in Eureka ((707) 442-9054.

WHAT TO SEE AND DO

Founded in 1850, during the gold rush in the nearby mountains, Eureka was a violent frontier town in the midst of Wiyot Indian territory. A young Captain, Ulysses S. Grant, was among those stationed at the military garrison in 1854. In 1860, a young newspaperman in nearby Arcata, Bret Harte, condemned the white men of Eureka for massacring a village of Indian women and children while the men were away hunting and fishing. Similar racism broke out in 1885, when the Chinese were run out of Eureka. Much of the region's history is documented at the **Fort Humboldt State**

more than a hundred Victorian structures in and around the city.

Further along Second Street is the **Humboldt Bay Maritime Museum** ((707) 444-9440, which features exhibits on the maritime history of the northwest California coast. The collection includes ship models, artifacts and old photos and is open 11 AM to 4 PM daily. For a closer look at the area's maritime history hop aboard the **SS** *Madaket* ((707) 445-1910, a vintage ferry that offers 75-minute tours of Humboldt Bay. It's the oldest passenger vessel still operating in American waters.

Eureka has gained nationwide attention in recent years for the richness of its local arts and

Historic Park ((707) 445-6567, Highland Avenue off Broadway. The old infirmary inside the fort has been converted into a museum with military, pioneer and Native American exhibits. It is open Tuesday through Saturday from 9 AM to 5 PM. Admission is free.

Modern Eureka (population 27,800) recalls its past in a ten-block **Old Town** along the waterfront. The crown jewel on the city's old section is **Carson Mansion**, one of the most beautiful Victorian mansions ever built in America, built in 1885 for lumber baron William Carson. The green-and-gold mansion commands a high hill at the end of Second Street. Although it is now a private club, you can see from the sidewalk how the Victorian architect outdid himself in piling one gingerbread on top of another. The **Eureka Chamber of Commerce** ((707) 442-3738, 2112 Broadway, offers a free brochure describing a self-guided, drive-by tour of

culture scene. The **North Coast Repertory Theater** ((707) 442-6278, 300 Fifth Street, presents six new productions each year including a Summer Showcase. Despite its tiny size, Eureka also has its own **Symphony Orchestra** ((707) 444-2889, which offers a wide range of orchestral music at a variety of local venues. The **Redwood Coast Dixieland Jazz Festival** ((707) 445-3378 comes to town each March for three days of toe-tapping fun. **Blues on the Bay** is staged each August, with live bands from around the world playing on an outdoor stage adjacent to the water.

In Ferndale, you'll find a whole town of Victorian homes and shops; the local dairy farmers called the gingerbread decorations "butterfat," because that's what gave them the money to build these fancy houses.

WHERE TO STAY

Expensive

Eureka Inn ((707) 442-6441 TOLL-FREE (800) 862-4906, 518 Seventh Street, first opened in 1922 and soon became Northern California's finest hotel. Its celebrity guests included President Hoover, actor John Barrymore, and industrialists John D. Rockefeller Jr. and Cornelius Vanderbilt Jr. The Inn went through a period of decline and decay in the 1950s, but was bought by its present owners in 1960. They have carried out a thorough and ongoing restoration of the mock Tudor building and its two restaurants — the Rib Room & Wine Cellar and the Bristol Rose Café.

Moderate

Abigail's ((707) 444-3144 FAX (707) 442-5594, 1406 C Street, is a meticulously restored Victorian masterpiece (1888) with opulent gingerbread exterior and antique furnishings. It was voted the best bed and breakfast in California by several travel publications, and it serves a French gourmet breakfast.

Doubletree ((707) 445-0844 TOLL-FREE (800) 222-8733, 1929 Fourth Street, is Eureka's largest (178 rooms) hotel and one of the most modern. The swimming pool makes it ideal for families.

Inexpensive

Comfort Inn ((707) 444-0401 TOLL-FREE (800) 228-5150, 2014 Fourth Street, offers inexpensive, comfortable and clean motel lodging.

Eagle House ((707) 444-3344, 139 Second Street, is a smaller, cozier and older Victorian inn which dates from 1880.

WHERE TO EAT

Expensive

One of the most elegant restaurants on the northwest coast, **Eureka Inn Rib Room** ((707) 442-6441, 518 Seventh Street, an upmarket "meat and potatoes" place, serves barbecued ribs, steaks, seafood and other American trademarks.

Moderate

Café Marina ((707) 443-2233, Woodley Island Marina, offers a fantastic view of Humboldt Bay and great seafood (including oyster shooters).

Samoa Cookhouse ((707) 442-1659, Cookhouse Road, just across the Samoa Bridge from downtown Eureka, is the last surviving cookhouse from the old lumber camps in the area. It serves food that the real loggers might have lived on. There's even a small museum with (heavy) artifacts from the sawmills and lumber camps. The restaurant uses old chairs, long tables, and big food

platters passed around family style. The menu includes meat and potatoes, fried chicken and ham.

Inexpensive

Los Bagels ((707) 442-8525, 402 Second Street, is a tiny place which describes itself as a "multicultural bakery café" serving Jewish-Mexican food. Try a bagel sandwich and espresso on the sidewalk terrace.

Lost Coast Brewery ((707) 445-4480, 617 Fourth Street is a popular California brewpub with its own brand of homegrown beer and a menu that features burgers, salads and seafood.

HOW TO GET THERE

Eureka is 278 miles (444 km) north of San Francisco via US Highway 101. If driving has begun to seem a high price to pay for the scenery, you might consider traveling to Eureka on the **North Coast Daylight train**, ((707) 444-8055 TOLL-FREE (800) 305-RAIL, Box 3666, Eureka, CA 95502. From Willits, the ride takes ten hours, affording wonderful views of the coast and redwoods.

United Express and Horizon Airlines offer regularly scheduled flights from the San Francisco Bay Area to Eureka / Arcata Airport. Amtrak offers daily coach service from Martinez (in the East Bay) to Eureka, a journey which takes six hours.

REDWOOD NATIONAL PARK

Forty miles (64 km) north of Eureka is **Redwood National Park**, home to more than half of the world's old-growth coast redwoods and the planet's single tallest tree — 367 ft (110 m). Located in the extreme northwestern corner of the state, the park covers more than 110,000 acres (44,500 hectares) of virgin (not logged) forest in Del Norte and Humboldt counties and includes three state parks — Prairie Creek, Jedediah Smith and Del Norte Coast — as well as federal lands. Only about half a million people a year visit the park, and most of them linger for only a few hours, making this one of the least visited units in the entire National Park system, a wonderful place to get away from it all.

Redwood National Park offers numerous hiking trails, including a self-guided loop trail through the Lady Bird Johnson Grove, the Holter Ridge Bike Trail, and a 28-mile (45-km) Coast Trail which runs the entire north-south length of the park. Secluded dirt roads are also abundant, including Davison Road, which leads to the lush vegetation of **Fern Canyon** and the wonderfully secluded **Gold Bluffs Beach**. Wildlife in the area includes black bear and Roosevelt elk. The **Redwood Information Center** ((707) 464-6101, near the town of Orick, offers maps, trail guides, camping permits and other information on the park.

Trinidad, a charming fishing village with a population of 360, is the southern gateway to the national park. Footpaths wind around and over **Trinidad Head**, a mighty bluff that protects the bay from the open Pacific. The wharf area supports a small commercial fishing fleet and sports fishing boats. **Trinidad Bay Charters (** (707) 839-4743 TOLL-FREE (800) 839-4744, at the harbor, offers half-day trips for salmon and rock cod including all gear.

Just north of town is **Patrick Point State Park (** (707) 677-3570, a heavily forested preserve that perches on cliffs above the sea. The park sports numerous hiking trails and long stretches of un-fettered beach. You can sometimes see migrating whales from the bluffs. In addition, there is a re-

Moderate

A romantic hideaway on the bluffs north of town, **Lost Whale Bed & Breakfast (** (707) 677-3425 TOLL-FREE (800) 677-7859, 3452 Patrick's Point Drive, features amazing ocean vistas, a hot tub and its own little beach.

Shadow Lodge ((707) 677-0532, 687 Patrick's Point Drive has a dozen cottages in a redwood grove, each with antique furnishings and kitchens.

HOW TO GET THERE

Redwood National Park is 318 miles (508 km) north of San Francisco and 40 miles (64 km) north of Eureka via US Highway 101.

constructed Yurok Indian village that shows how the coastal tribes once lived. An interesting foot-note: Patrick Point doubled as the Costa Rican rain forest in the Steven Spielberg film *Lost World*.

The logging town of **Crescent City**, astride US Highway 101, lies close to the Oregon border. It's a long, jagged and tortuous trip up the coast from San Francisco — which leaves the place well off the beaten path and a favored spot to those who want to commune with nature and the mighty redwoods.

WHERE TO STAY

Expensive

Trinidad Bay Bed & Breakfast ((707) 677-0840, 560 Edward Street provides cozy accommoda-tion in a Cape Cod-style house overlooking Trinidad Bay.

MOUNT SHASTA REGION

One of the most dramatic peaks on the American West Coast dominates the upper reaches of North-ern California. **Mount Shasta**, the crown jewel of the Southern Cascade range, is visible for a hundred miles around, a magnificent natural wonder, rising to 14,162 ft (4,317 m) and snow-capped well into summer.

The town of Mount Shasta is located at the southern base of the volcanic mountain, right on Interstate 5, a convenient jumping off spot for exploring the surrounding **Shasta Trinity Na-tional Forest**. There is a road (county route A-10) up to the 8,000-ft (2,500-m) level of Mount Shasta, offering a spectacular view of the surrounding

Snow smothers Mount Shasta well into summer, gradually melting into raging rivers.

mountains and valleys. The area offers myriad opportunities for hiking, fishing and camping in summer; cross-country skiing, snowmobiling and snowshoeing in winter. An 18-hole golf course, **Lake Shastina Golf Resort (** (530) 938-3201, is located to the north of Mount Shasta, beside Lake Shastina.

Farther south along Interstate 5 is the sprawling **Whiskeytown-Shasta-Trinity National Recreation Area**, which embraces three giant lakes in the Cascade foothills. Houseboats can be rented by the day, week or month. Just beyond the lakes is a completely roadless region called the **Trinity Alps Wilderness**, ideal for hiking and camping among rugged coastal forest.

GENERAL INFORMATION

For information on activities and attractions and just about anything you want to know about accommodation, food and recreation in the Shasta region contact the **Mount Shasta Visitors Bureau (** (530) 926-4865 TOLL-FREE (800) 926-4865 FAX (530) 926-0976 WEB SITE www.mtshasta.com, 300 Pine Street, Mount Shasta, 96067. Walk-up information is available Monday to Saturday from 9 AM to 5 PM and Sunday from 10 AM to 4 PM.

WHERE TO STAY

Moderate

Summer or winter, **Mount Shasta Resort (** (916) 926-3030 E-MAIL msresort@macshasta.com WEB SITE www.mountshastaresort.com, 1000 Siskiyou Lake Boulevard, Mount Shasta, is one of the more popular places in the region. The fifty chalets with one and two bedrooms on the forested shores of Lake Siskiyou have phones, cable television, full kitchens, fireplaces and hot tubs. The clubhouse restaurant serves good California cuisine.

For a total contrast in style try **Tiffany House Bed & Breakfast (** (530) 244-3225 E-MAIL tiffanyhe @aol.com WEB SITE www.sylvia.com/tiffany.htm, 1510 Barbara Road, Redding. This beautifully refurbished Cape Cod-style house has three guest rooms with private bath plus a cottage with an indoor spa.

Inexpensive

Abrams Lake RV Park ((916) 926-2312, 2601 North Old Stage Road, Mount Shasta, has twenty pull-through recreational vehicle sites and tent camping in a quiet setting beside the lake.

One of the cheaper places to put a roof over your head is **Alpenrose Cottage Hostel (** (916) 926-

Horses graze in a meadow beside the steep forested peaks near Mount Lassen at the northern end of the Sierra Nevada mountains.

6724, 204 East Hinckley Street, Mount Shasta. This is a dorm-style guest house for singles with one private room for couples. It provides kitchen, laundry facilities and television.

Alpine Lodge ((916) 926-3145 TOLL-FREE (800) 500-3145 FAX (916) 926-5897, 908 South Mount Shasta Boulevard, Mount Shasta, is another inexpensive option with phones, cable television and a coffee maker in each room. A family suite and kitchen units are available, as is an outdoor hot tub and a heated pool.

Tall pine trees surround a log-cabin inn called **Joanie's Bed & Breakfast** ((916) 964-3106, 417 Lawndale Court, McCloud.

History comes alive at the old **McCloud Hotel** ((916) 964-2822, 408 Main Street, McCloud. This beautifully restored building dates from 1916. The 18 rooms are decorated with antiques, many with four-post beds. The large suites have whirlpool tubs and sitting area.

Mount Shasta Cabins and Cottages ((916) 926-5396, 500 South Mount Shasta Boulevard, Mount Shasta, operates 12 cabins and cottages of various sizes throughout Mount Shasta area. Pets are allowed.

Mount Shasta Ranch Bed & Breakfast ((916) 926-3870 E-MAIL alpine@macshasta.com, 1008 West A. Barr Road, Mount Shasta. Four spacious bedrooms with private bathrooms are available in the historical, two-story main house, along with five rooms sharing two bathrooms in the adjacent Carriage House. There is also a two-bedroom cottage.

Train buffs flock to the **Railroad Park Resort** ((916) 235-4440, 100 Railroad Park Road in Dunsmuir, which features 27 rooms in funky cabooses once used on the Southern Pacific, Santa Fe and Great Northern railroads. Tnere are phones, television, in-room coffee, spa, and pool. Some pets are allowed.

Shasta Lodge Motel ((916) 926-2815 TOLL-FREE (800) SHASTA 1, 724 North Mount Shasta Boulevard, Mount Shasta, near the center of town, has twenty rooms with queen-size beds, cable television, in-room coffee, and Jacuzzi access.

One of the larger resorts in the Mount Shasta region is **Stewart Mineral Springs** ((530) 938-2222, 4617 Stewart Springs Road. The resort has a variety of accommodation options from campsites and teepees (bring your own bedding) to basic cabins with kitchens and modest motel rooms. Located in a forested canyon, the resort offers lots of wet adventure including mineral baths, sauna, creek and large pond.

Families and small groups are welcome at **Stoney Brook Inn Bed & Breakfast** ((916) 964-2300 TOLL-FREE (800) 369-6118, 309 West Colombero Drive, McCloud. Sixteen private rooms, with kitchen suites are available. It has

outdoor hot tub, Finnish sauna, massage, conference facilities in an alpine setting.

WHERE TO EAT

Café Maddalena ((916) 235-2725, 5801 Sacramento Avenue, Dunsmuir, serves Mediterranean country cooking including pasta, seafood and vegetarian dishes. It is open Thursday to Sunday from 5:30 PM to 10 PM during the spring and summer; from 5:30 PM to 9:30 PM during the fall and early winter. It is closed from January to March.

Steaks of all shapes and sizes are offered at **Jack's Grill** ((530) 241-9705, 1743 California Street. Located in a tavern dating back to the 1930s, Jack's also lays on salad, garlic bread and potatoes with every meal. You may have to wait a couple hours to get a table on weekends. It is open for dinner Monday to Saturday from 5 PM.

Lily's ((916) 926-3372, 1013 South Mount Shasta Boulevard, Mount Shasta, serves California cuisine with vegetarian, pasta, seafood, steaks, and Mexican dishes. Lily's is open daily in the summer from 7 AM to 10 PM and in the winter from 8 AM to 9 PM. Brunch is served on weekends from 7 AM to 2 PM.

Lalo's ((916) 926-5123, 520 North Mount Shasta Boulevard, Mount Shasta, serves Mexican and American dishes in a large banquet room from Monday to Friday from 11 AM to 11 PM and on Saturday and Sunday from 8 AM to 10 PM.

Michael's ((916) 926-5288, 313 North Mount Shasta Boulevard, Mount Shasta. House specials include pasta, seafood, beef, chicken and vegetarian dishes. Micheal's serves Tuesday to Friday from 11 AM to 2:30 PM and from 5 PM to 9 PM; and Saturday from noon to 9 PM.

A local favorite for more than 50 years, **Mike & Tony's Restaurant** ((916) 926-4792, 501 South Mount Shasta Boulevard, Mount Shasta, features home-made ravioli, minestrone soup and steaks. Vegetarian dishes are available. It is open Monday, Tuesday and Thursday from 4 PM to 9 PM; Friday and Saturday from 4 PM to 10 PM; and Sunday from 1 PM to 9 PM.

For casual dining with fine French cuisine and low-fat entrees, **Serge's** ((916) 926-1276, 531 Chestnut Street, Mount Shasta, offers a large wine selection and delicious deserts. They have a great view of Mount Shasta from the deck. It is open Wednesday to Sunday from 5 PM; and for Sunday brunch from 10 AM to 2 PM.

HOW TO GET THERE

The town of Mount Shasta is 290 miles (464 km) north of San Francisco and 60 miles (96 km) north of Redding via Interstate 5. Coming over from the coast, the town is 210 miles (336 km) from Eureka via State Highway 299 (through Weaverville) and Interstate 5.

WEAVERVILLE

A gold-rush town, Weaverville sits astride State Highway 299, and calls itself the gateway to the rugged wilderness of northwestern California. From the coastal roads, take State Highway 299 through these mountains and get a taste of what the land looked like when the first prospectors came here. In fact, if you look out at some of the cabins along the way, you'll see what present-day prospectors look like. While timber is the major industry in the area, there are still those odd ones looking to get rich finding gold in those hills.

Actually, gold was discovered in the area not long after it was first found at Sutter's mill further south. This led to the area's own gold rush and the quick development of a town called Weaverville. The wooden buildings in the town were prone to fire and finally, more sturdy brick structures were built.

At one time, there was a large Chinese community in Weaverville. In the 1850s, an influx of more than 2,000 Chinese who worked in the gold mines boosted the town's population to 5,000, almost double its present population. However, in the Tong War of 1854, a conflict between local Chinese communities, a large portion of the Chinese neighborhood was burned to the ground, resulting in the relocation of many of its residents. A survivor of this period in the town's history is the **Taoist Temple**, built in 1874, and California's oldest, which managed to survive the hostility and vigilante raids by the area's resident xenophobes. The temple is maintained as a state park and, like everything else, is located on State Highway 299, the town's main street.

A quaint little **Jake Jackson Museum** ((530) 623-5211, 508 Main Street, is maintained in memory of a local boy who started collecting guns and other historical artifacts before World War I. The exhibits here include an 1849 hand pump fire engine which the town bought from San Francisco in 1906.

GENERAL INFORMATION

The present-day residents are proud of their little town, and they maintain what is surely the friendliest visitors center located anywhere at the **Trinity County Chamber of Commerce** ((530) 623-6101 TOLL-FREE (800) 487-4648 WEB SITE www .trinitycounty.com, 210 Main Street, PO Box 517, Weaverville, 96093. Here, you can get information on the national parks in the area, hunting and fishing, and of course, "recreational gold panning." There are also some very educational leaflets that explain the flora and fauna of the area and help identify the many different pines and pine cones you see.

WHERE TO STAY

Inexpensive

Willie and Patty Holder run a rustic little place called **Red Hill Motel and Cabins** ((916) 623-4331 FAX (916) 623-4341, situated at the west end of town across the street from the new library. Accommodation here includes simple cabins with queen-size beds, one- and two-room cottages, and housekeeping units with kitchens. Amenities include a fish-cleaning station with hot/cold wash-up sink. The Holders can arrange fishing guides and white-water rafting in the area.

Motel Trinity ((916) 623-2129 on Main Street is another quiet and relaxed abode, with a swimming pool, kitchen units and coffee makers in every rooms.

The town's largest property is **Hodges Weaverville Victorian Inn** ((916) 623-4432 FAX (916) 623-4264, 1709 Main Street. The 65 air-conditioned units include 17 suites with hot tubs. Cribs and roll-away beds are available for families. Amenities include a swimming pool and in-room phones.

HOW TO GET THERE

Coming up from the coast, Weaverville is 104 miles (166 km) from Eureka via State Highway 299. Coming from the Central Valley and Mount Shasta, the town is 48 miles (76 km) from Redding via State Highway 299.

The nearest **Amtrak** TOLL-FREE ((800) 872-7245 train stations are Redding and Dunsmuir, both served by the daily *Coast Starlight* from the Bay Area, Sacramento, Portland and Seattle. The train's glass-enclosed lounge car affords magnificent views of Mount Shasta and the Cascade Range.

The denizens of Weaverville welcome travelers to the Gold Rush Country.

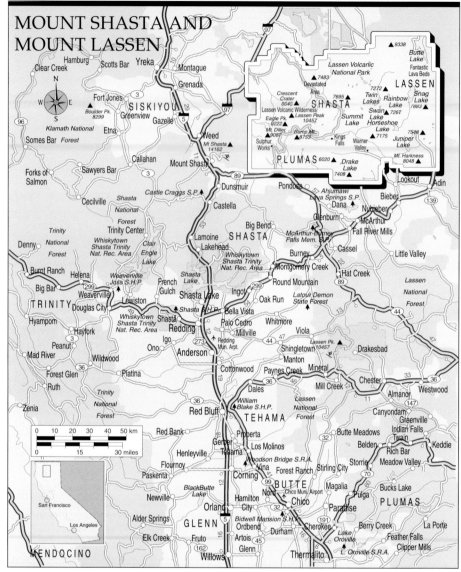

MOUNT SHASTA AND MOUNT LASSEN

LASSEN VOLCANIC NATIONAL PARK

There is some evidence that Mount Shasta has been active in the last 300 years. But until Mount Saint Helen's in Washington exploded in 1980, the only volcanic eruption in historic times within the contiguous 48 states was that of Mount Lassen, about 75 miles (120 km) southeast of Shasta. The 10,457-ft (3,187-m) peak is now the centerpiece of **Lassen Volcanic National Park** ((530) 595-4444, PO Box 100, Mineral, 96063.

In 1907 President Theodore Roosevelt declared Lassen Peak and nearby Cinder Cone national monuments. When the eruptions began in 1914, the entire 165 sq mile (427 sq km) area was set aside as a national park. There are seven campgrounds within the park. At the southwest campground is a ski chalet where ski equipment can be rented or bought. There is also a small lunch counter at the Lassen Chalet. Otherwise, there is no commercial development.

State Highway 89 is a scenic route right across the park. An excellent road guide to the park is available at the northern entrance, right off State Highway 44. There are small numbered markers along the roadway, so you can match the color pictures in the guide and the text with what you're seeing. There are stops before all the major spots of geologic interest, but you'll also learn about the wildflowers and trees growing in the park. The small **Loomis Museum** overlooks Reflection Lake near the north end of State Highway 89.

The most interesting short hike from the main road is a two-and-a-quarter-mile (three-and-a-half-kilometer) walk to the hot springs basin called **Bumpass Hell**. The park has other hot springs and bubbling mudpots, but this is the most spectacular of the active hydrothermal areas, steaming escape valves from the molten lava beds deep beneath the earth's crust. Bumpass Hell was given its name in recognition of the tribulations of Kendall Bumpass, the "discoverer" of the area. Bumpass fell into one of the hot springs and burned his leg so severely he had to have it amputated. Another good bet is **Cinder Cone Nature Trail** in the northeast corner of the park, which leads through rugged volcanic scenery to an overlook with a sweeping view of the entire park.

The main "devastated area" gives an awesome demonstration of the power of nature. More than 70 years after the last eruption in 1917, there is nothing but ash and lava beds as far as you can see. The mud-flow from the eruptions covered the meadows with 20 ft (6 m) of mud and debris. (A local property dispute involving the route of a creek was hopelessly confused when the volcanic eruption covered over everything in question.) The steam you see rising from the various mudpots and hot springs is not the only surface evidence of the unstable ground beneath. An earlier visitors' center had to be relocated because of the shifting grounds above and below it. State Highway 89 is constantly being rebuilt in places because of slides.

The park has four campgrounds with nearly 400 total sites on a first-come, first-serve basis. There is a general store and gas station at **Manzanita Lake** inside the park.

WHERE TO STAY

Drakesbad Guest Ranch ((530) 529-9820, WEB SITE calguest@mci.com, is the only accommodation inside the park. This century-old lodge offers room and board in a rustic setting. Swimming and horseback riding are available. Its season runs from mid-June to mid-October depending on the snow cover. Rooms are $199 to $299 per night for doubles (two people) including all meals. Reservations should be made well in advance. To reach the Drakesbad, take State Highway 36 to Chester and drive 17 miles (10.5 km) north along the Chester Warner Valley Road.

The **Weston House Bed and Breakfast** ((530) 474-3738 is situated in Shingletown, 19 miles (30 km) west of the park's north entrance. It is owned and operated by the grandson of re-nowned nature and art photographer Edward Weston.

HOW TO GET THERE

If you're coming down from Shasta, the park's north entrance is 48 miles (77 km) east of Redding via State Highway 44. If you're coming up from San Francisco or Sacramento, the park is about 40 miles (64 km) from Red Bluff via State Highways 36 and 89. Red Bluff is 200 miles (320 km) from San Francisco (three hours) and 130 miles (208 km) from Sacramento (two hours) via Interstate 5.

SACRAMENTO

Sacramento became the state capital of California in 1854. Looking at the state from the heavily populated southland of today, one wonders how the capital could ever have been located so far north. However, until water was brought in the early twentieth century, Southern California was a sparsely populated desert wasteland, with only a few thousand people living in the pueblos of Los Angeles and San Diego.

Sacramento, moreover, was at the heartland of early California. Gold was first discovered near Sacramento, and this led to the rush on all of "them thar hills" in the surrounding area. The city took its name from the county which, in turn, got its name from the river; presumably there was a religious Spaniard back there somewhere who did intend for something to be named for the Holy Sacrament, or Sacramento. It lies at the confluence of the American and Sacramento rivers, and the rich delta farmlands spreading out around them.

Nearly all of the land on which the central city now sits was originally owned by John Sutter, a German-born Swiss who came to California in 1839, became a Mexican citizen, and was given the largest land grant allowed, 11 square leagues or 48,400 acres (19,595 hectares). Sutter set himself up as baron of what he called "Nueva Helvetia" (New Switzerland), forcing Indians to work as serfs on his farms, orchards and vineyards. Nearly everyone else called his property "Sutter's Fort" because of a massive bulwark built by Sutter with walls three feet (one meter) thick and 15 ft (4.5 m) high. It was to this fort that the ill-fated pioneering Donner party was heading and, in fact, where the survivors settled.

While you hear little about the miners, their gold quickly enriched the area and brought in thousands of new immigrants, the result being that California never went through the probational period as a territory before becoming a state. Among those who profited immensely were the "Big Four" — four storekeepers in Sacramento who would become the richest and most powerful men in the country at that time: Charles Crocker,

Mark Hopkins, Collis P. Huntington, and Leland Stanford. No ordinary storekeepers, they also functioned as bankers—making loans and taking gold as repayment. Starting out with a short-line railroad from Sacramento to Folsom, they went on to build the first transcontinental railroad. Eventually, their company monopolized rail traffic into California and earned the sobriquet "Octopus" because of its strangle hold on the state's commerce and politics.

GENERAL INFORMATION

The best source of information on the state capital is the **Sacramento Convention & Visitors Bureau** ((916) 264-7777 FAX (916) 264-7788 WEB SITE www .sacto.org/cvb, 1303 J Street, Suite 600, Sacramento 95814. The **Sacramento Visitor Information Center** ((916) 442-7644 is situated at 1101 Second Street in Old Sacramento and is open daily from 9 AM to 5 PM.

A number of other tourist related services are based in Sacramento including the **California Division of Tourism** ((916) 322-2881 TOLL-FREE (800) 862-2543 FAX (916) 322-3402 WEB SITE gocalif .ca.gov, 801 K Street, Suite 1600, Sacramento 95814. The **California Department of Parks and Recreation** ((916) 653-6995 WEB SITE ceres.ca.gov/ceres/ calweb/state-parks.html, PO Box 942896 Sacramento, 94296, also makes its home in the state capital. For state park campground reservations, call TOLL-FREE (800) 444-PARK.

WHAT TO SEE AND DO

You get some idea of the wealth of Sacramento and early California compared to the rest of the United States when you consider that Sacramento's magnificent neo-classical **Capitol** with its 237-ft (72-m) dome was constructed in 1861. At that time, the United States Congress could not find the money to complete the dome on its own capitol building or to finish the Washington Monument — both of them weathering away as unfinished nubs as the country faced civil war. The Capitol is located on 10th Street and Capitol Mall, set in a 40-acre (16-hectare) park. Free guided tours of the building are offered from 9 AM to 5 PM daily, starting from the **State Capitol Museum** ((916) 324-0333 at 10th and L Streets.

A reproduction of **Sutter's Fort** ((916) 445-4422 is located at 27th and L Streets. The exhibits include important artifacts and displays on the early history of the area, as well as facsimiles of gold rush era shops — blacksmith, cooper, bakery, etc. Self-guided audio tape tours are available. Next door is the excellent **California State Indian Museum** ((916) 324-7405, with displays on the diverse culture of the Golden State's native peoples. Both the fort and museum are open from 10 AM to 5 PM daily. Both attractions charge an admission of $3 for adults and $1.50 for children ages 6 to 12.

Although Sacramento is a true city of nearly 400,000 inhabitants, much of it still recalls a quiet old river port town. There are many elaborate Victorian houses along the tree-lined streets. Most of the older houses are located in the area from Seventh to 16th and E to I Streets. Two of the more elaborate structures are the **Stanford House** at 800 N Street and the **Heilbron House** at 740 O Street.

Also worth a visit is the fabulous 15-room **Governor's Mansion** ((916) 324-7405, 1526 H Street (at 16th). Built in 1877 as a private home, the Victorian masterpiece hosted 13 California governors from 1903 to 1967, when Ronald and Nancy Reagan refused to move in, calling it a "firetrap." (Later revelations about Nancy's White House astrologer came as no surprise to old hands in the state capital — Reagan insisted on being sworn in as governor at some odd minutes after midnight on the advice of an astrologer.) Now a museum, the Governor's Mansion is open from 10 AM to 5 PM daily. Admission is $3 for adults and $1.50 for children ages 6 to 12.

The **Crocker Art Museum** ((916) 264-5423, in a restored Victorian mansion at 216 O Street, houses the oldest art museum in the West. Started in 1873, the original collection of European masters has been expanded to include nineteenth-century and twentieth-century California artists. It is open Tuesday to Sunday from 10 AM to 5 PM (to 9 PM on Thursday). Admission is $4.50 adults and $2 for those under 18.

The movement to restore **Old Sacramento** ((916) 442-7644 WEB SITE www.oldsacramento.com, kicked off about 30 years ago a huge revitalizing the city's waterfront and downtown areas. Since then more than a hundred historic buildings have been refurbished or reconstructed in a ten-block area wedged between the Sacramento River and Interstate 5. "Old Sac" offers a wide variety of shops, restaurants and other attractions including four museums.

The **Public Market** sprawls across three historic buildings on the waterfront, with 17 shops offering wares that might have been sold on this same site a hundred years ago: meat, poultry, fish, wine, bread, dairy products and flowers just to name a few. The **B.F. Hastings Building** ((916) 445-4655, at the corner of Second and J Streets, was once the western terminus of the Pony Express and later the first home of the California State Supreme Court. Across the street is the **Pony Ex-**

OPPOSITE TOP: Revived and restored, Old Sacramento has become the centerpiece of the city's waterfront. BOTTOM: Interpretive exhibits and polished antique trains fascinate rail buffs at the California State Railroad Museum.

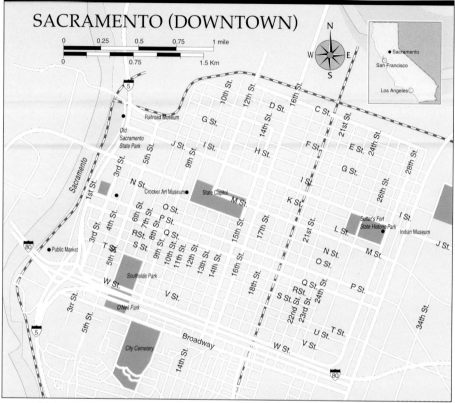

SACRAMENTO (DOWNTOWN)

press, which commemorates the 80 riders who delivered the mail by horseback in 1860 an 1861, a 2,000-mile (over 3,000-km) marathon from Saint Joseph, Missouri to Sacramento.

Old Sac's most popular attraction is the **California State Historic Railroad Museum (** (916) 448-4466, 125 I street, which claims to be the largest interpretive railroad museum in the world. With more than 100,000 sq ft (9,000 sq m) of space housing 21 restored locomotives and cars, and 46 exhibits, it's hard to argue with that boast. Admission is $3 for adults, $1 for children, and includes entrance to the Pacific Railway Station — Sacramento's oldest, dating from the nineteenth century. It is open from 10 AM to 5 PM daily.

The **Discovery Museum (** (916) 264-7057, 101 I Street, includes more than a million dollars in gold nuggets, other historical exhibits and hands-on science and technology displays for kids. The **California State Military Museum (** (916) 442-2883, 1119 Second Street, contains more than 30,000 documents and artifacts related to the various military forces (Spanish, Mexican, American) that have been posted in the Golden State since the late eighteenth century.

Old Sac is also a jumping off point for Sacramento River trips. The reproduction paddle-wheel steamers *Matthew McKinley* and *Spirit of Sac-*

ramento **(** (916) 552-2933 TOLL-FREE (800) 433-0263 WEB SITE www.oldsacriverboat.com, ply the river on a frequent basis. The third riverboat you find moored along the waterfront is the *Delta King* **(** (916) 444-5464, which once conveyed passengers between San Francisco and Sacramento. It no longer makes the run or any other journey, being permanently anchored in Old Sac as a floating hotel.

Just south of Old Sac and also perched on the banks of the Sacramento River is the **Towe Ford Museum of Automotive History (** (916) 442-6802, 2200 Front Street. Although far from Detroit, this fine little museum houses a collection of over 150 Ford automobiles. From the Model-T to the T-Bird and beyond, at least one model from every year of Ford's production history is on display from 10 AM to 6 PM daily. Admission is $4.50 adults, $2.50 for teenagers, and $1 children.

Keep in mind that Sacramento is a delta town and there is still a great deal of life on the river — most of it recreational in recent years. For information on houseboat rentals in the region contact **Forever Resorts (** (602) 998-1981 TOLL-FREE (800) 255-5561 FAX (602) 998-7399 WEB SITE www.foreverresorts.com, 11540 West Eight Mile Road, Stockton 95208. **Sacramento Boat Rentals (** (916) 321-0007 or (916) 455-8615 offers powerboat rentals in the heart of downtown for fishing, skiing or sightseeing on the river. **River Otter Taxi Company** ((916) 448-4333 offers water taxi service on the Sacramento River at $7 per round trip.

WHERE TO STAY

The state capital has a wealth of convenient hotels, as well as tasteful bed and breakfast accommodation in the central city.

Expensive
Visiting politicians and businessmen flock to the **Hyatt Regency Sacramento** ((916) 443-1234 TOLL-FREE (800) 233-1234 FAX (916) 497-0132, 1209 L Street, which claims the largest number of rooms (500) and best facilities in the state capital. It's also hard to beat the location: opposite the Capitol building and adjacent to the Sacramento Convention Center. The Hyatt pool is an oasis of tranquillity in the middle of the busy city and the hotel's rooftop nightclub is one of the few places where you can catch a bird's eye view of Sacramento after dark.

Moderate
For a trip into the past try the **Amber House Bed & Breakfast Inn** ((916) 444-8085 TOLL-FREE (800) 755-6526 FAX (916) 552-6529, 1315 22nd Street. The property comprises three elegant Victorian mansions on a leafy property near the Capitol building. Antique furnishings abound but not at the expense of modern conveniences like marble spas in the bathrooms.

    Abigail's Bed & Breakfast Inn ((916) 441-5007 TOLL-FREE (800) 858-1568 FAX (916) 441-0621, 2120 G Street, is a smaller, more intimate bed and breakfast set in a single mansion near the Capitol.

    Clarion ((916) 444-8000 TOLL-FREE (800) 443-0880 FAX (916) 442-8129, 700 16th Street is located downtown, close to Capitol and Convention Center, and has a pool, restaurant, and free parking.

    A good bet outside the downtown area is the **DoubleTree Sacramento** ((916) 929-8855 TOLL-FREE (800) 222-TREE FAX (916) 924-0719, 2001 Point West Way. This full service hotel with 448 rooms, situated off Capital City Freeway near Arden Fair Mall, has in-room movies, spa, pool, fitness room, and restaurants.

    Holiday Inn Capitol Plaza ((916) 446-0100 TOLL-FREE (800) HOLIDAY FAX (916) 446-0117, 300 J Street, is close to Old Sacramento and Downtown Plaza Mall. It is a full service hotel with 364 rooms, meeting space, a pool, and a restaurant.

Inexpensive
A great bargain in downtown Sac is the **Capitol Center Travelodge** ((916) 444-8880 TOLL-FREE (800) 578-7878 FAX (916) 447-7540, 1111 H Street.

Situated just four blocks from the Capitol, it has 71 rooms, cable television, complimentary coffee and newspapers, and free parking.

WHERE TO EAT

There are many new and old restaurants to match the charm and sophistication of the revitalized state capital.

Expensive
The government gang tends to frequent **Biba's** ((916) 455-2422, 2801 Capitol Avenue, popular with legislators, lobbyists and other politicos. Their authentic Italian cuisine changes seasonally. It is

open for lunch Monday to Friday and for dinner Monday to Saturday.

    One of the more romantic places in Sacramento is **Chanterelle** ((916) 448-1300, 1300 H Street. Situated in the historic Sterling Hotel, this gourmet restaurant offers California-French cuisine. Outdoor patio dining is available.

    Morton's of Chicago ((916) 442-5091, Downtown Plaza, 521 L Street is a steakhouse serving USDA prime aged steaks as well as seafood. It has an extensive wine list and private dining rooms are available.

Moderate
Fat City Bar & Café ((916) 446-6768, 1001 Front Street, is a century-old café which offers up all American food from light appetizers to full meals.

The Crocker Art Museum.

Open for lunch weekdays and dinner nightly, it also serves brunch on Saturday and Sunday.

It's not quite 1930s Hollywood, but **Harlow's** ((916) 441-4693, 2714 J Street, makes a game effort to rekindle the romance of that era. This casual restaurant with a great art deco setting indoors and on the patio offers a varied menu, full bar, and live music.

Paragary's Bar & Oven ((916) 457-5737, 1401 28th Street, is one of Sacramento's best known restaurants and serves up hardy American cuisine. It is located in the heart of midtown's restaurant row.

Rio City Café ((916) 442-8226 1110 Front Street, serves up creative California cuisine with a beautiful view of the river and Old Sacramento. Indoor and outdoor dining are available. It is open Monday to Thursday from 11 AM to 10 PM, Friday and Saturday from 11 AM to 11 PM, and Sunday from 10 AM to 10 PM.

Scott's Seafood Grill ((916) 489-1822, 545 Munroe Street, serves fresh seafood (delivered daily from around the world) as well as steak, Monday to Saturday from 11:30 AM to 10 PM, and Sunday from 4 PM to 10 PM.

33rd Street Bistro ((916) 455-2282, 3301 Folsom Boulevard, features Pacific Northwest cuisine like grilled panini and hardwood-roasted poultry, along with great deserts.

Inexpensive

Chico's Tacos ((916) 649-8226, 807 Howe Avenue, offers imaginative Mexican dishes featuring carne asada, fish and charbroiled chicken. Chico's is open Monday to Saturday from 11 AM to 9 PM.

Tower Café ((916) 441-0222, 1518 Broadway, serves international dishes in a historic setting next to the Tower Theater.

HOW TO GET THERE

Sacramento is 97 miles (155 km) northeast of San Francisco via Interstate 80, and 386 miles (617 km) north of Los Angeles via Interstate 5.

Sacramento International Airport ((916) 929-5411 is served by frequent flights from San Francisco, Los Angeles, San Diego and other Western United States cities.

The city is also well-served by **Amtrak** ((800) 872-7245 passenger trains including the *Capitol Line* to and from Oakland and San Jose (with bus connections to San Francisco); the *Coast Starlight* to and from Los Angeles, Portland and Seattle; and the *California Zephyr* to and from Chicago, Denver and Salt Lake City.

It is also possible to reach Sacramento by **Greyhound bus** ((916) 444-7270 from other major cities in California.

State Highway 49 meanders through the Gold Rush Country, traveling along the shores of Lake McClury.

GOLD RUSH COUNTRY

Gold rushes actually took place throughout California — from the hills west of San Diego to Catalina Island, Death Valley, and up into the northwestern redwood forests. But the original rush, the one that captured the imagination of thousands of people throughout the world, was in the area east and south of Sacramento.

GENERAL INFORMATION

There is no central information bureau for the California Gold Country, but each county in the region maintains its own chamber of commerce or visitor bureau. These include the **Calaveras Visitors Bureau** ((209) 736-0049 TOLL-FREE (800) 225-3764 FAX (209) 736-9124, PO Box 637, Angels Camp 95222; the **El Dorado Chamber of Commerce** ((916) 621-5885 TOLL-FREE (800) 457-6279 FAX (916) 642-1624, 542 Main Street, Placerville 95667; the **Placer County Visitor Information Center** ((916) 887-2111 FAX (916) 887-2134 WEB SITE www.placer.ca .gov; and the **Toulumne County Visitors Bureau** ((209) 533-4420 TOLL-FREE (800) 446-1333 FAX (209) 533-0956, PO Box 4020, 55 West Stockton Road, Sonora 95370.

These information bureaus and others in the region stock two useful free brochures: *California's Gold Country Visitors Map* by JB Publishing and the *California Gold Country Guide* by Robert Bellezza. The WEB SITE www.calgoldcountry.com has general information on the region.

WHAT TO SEE AND DO

To get to the heart of the old gold country, take US Highway 50 east from Sacramento to the town of **Placerville**. With a population of 7,000, Placerville is located just south of the spot where the first gold was found at Sutter's Mill. It was earlier called "Dry Diggins" and "Hangtown," the latter a morbid reference to the area's preferred method of maintaining law and order. Where the gallows once stood is a full-sized sculpture of a lynched man — a memorial, of sorts. Now surrounded by apple and cherry orchards, Placerville was an important stop on the stage and, later, the rail lines.

Three major industrialists worked in Placerville as young men: railroad man Mark Hopkins; meatpacker Philip Armour, and John Studebaker, who worked as a wheelwright in Placerville in preparation for his later career as auto-maker. You can learn more local history at the **El Dorado County Historical Museum** ((530) 621-5865, 104 Placerville Drive. Among the exhibits are gold rush, Native American, and Pony Express artifacts, as well as an original Studebaker wheelbarrow. **Gold Bug Park** ((530) 642-5238 is

America's only municipal-owned and operated gold mine. Self-guided tours help you explore the mine and the heritage of gold mining in this part of the world.

Eight miles (12 km) north of Placerville is the place where it all began: **Sutter's Mill** in the quiet little town of **Coloma**. Carpenter James W. Marshall found gold on the banks of the river that runs beside the mill on January 24, 1848, setting off the largest gold rush in North American history. The **Marshall Gold Discovery State Historic Park** ((530) 622-3470, which takes up more than two-thirds of the town, includes a gold mining museum, a replica of Sutter's Mill, pleasant walks along the American River, and leafy picnic grounds. James Marshall's grave is also inside the park, a pleasant spot adjacent to the river. Park admission is $5 per vehicle.

California State Highway 49 — once called Mother Lode Street — runs south from Placerville into Calaveras (Spanish for "skulls") County and the heart of the **Mother Lode**, the 120-mile (194-km) stretch where the first major gold mines were found and incorrectly believed to be part of the same vein or lode.

Mark Twain lived and wrote in the area; in fact, one of his most popular early stories was entitled *The Celebrated Jumping Frog of Calaveras*. It was set in **Angels Camp**, just one of the many picturesque towns you'll find in gold rush country today. Thousands of people flock to the hamlet in May for the **Jumping Frog Jubilee**, the world's premier frog jumping contest. Those who don't bring their own frogs can actually rent one and participate in this amphibian olympiad. The jubilee is part of the **Calaveras County Fair** ((209) 736-2561, which also includes carnival rides, country western music, rodeo events and lots of down-home American food.

If you tire of gold rush stories, head up into the Sierra foothills to see the giant sequoias of **Calaveras Big Trees State Park** ((209) 795-2334. Besides an intimate glimpse of the world's largest living things, the park also provides opportunities for camping, hiking, fishing, white-water rafting and kayaking. Admission is $5 per vehicle. Nearby are the **Mercer Caverns** ((209) 728-2101 WEB SITE www.caverntours.com, a series of limestone caves buried deep beneath the foothills.

On the zigzag upper road between Angels Camp and Sonora you pass signs to the **Columbia State Historic Park** ((209) 532-4301. Any questions you may have about the gold rush will be answered in this unusually fine attraction. Columbia was considered "the gem" of the Mother Lode. From the first strike in 1850 through three decades later, more than $87 million in gold was taken from the Columbia mine. The town matched its new found wealth with blocks of tree-lined streets, and fine brick and stone stores and houses. Twelve full

blocks — the entire town — are now preserved in the historic park. The Wells Fargo office, the dry goods store, the Masonic temple, the churches, the private houses, and, of course, the saloons, have all been carefully restored. For a more authentic atmosphere, there are mule-drawn wagons moving about, and a human-powered water pump with its own uniformed Columbia Fire Department force. There are also exhibits on Lola Montez and Lotta Crabtree who once entertained here before going on to fame and notoriety in the big cities. Other exhibits describe the life and deeds of the notorious Black Bart, and Joaquin Murietta, the Mexican hero-bandit whose head was pickled and displayed in a jar for many years after his death.

Farther south in Tuolumne County (a Native American tribal name pronounced "twallomee") is **Jamestown**, another important gold rush town.

Of special interest here is **Railtown 1897 State Historic Park** ((209) 984-3953. The old depot is carefully preserved, as are the Sierra steam locomotives, passenger and freight cars. These are often used in movies — like *High Noon* with Gary Cooper and *My Little Chickadee* with W.C. Fields. But the depot's real moment of fame came when it was used as the setting for the popular television series *Petticoat Junction*.

WHERE TO STAY

Moderate

Chichester-McKee House ((530) 626-1882 TOLL-FREE (800) 831-4008 E-MAIL inn@innercite.com WEB SITE www.el-dorado.ca.us/-inn/, 800 Spring Street, Placerville, has four guest rooms in a Victorian mansion built in 1892. Antiques, fireplaces and stained glass abound.

Coloma Country Inn ((530) 622-6919, 345 High Street, Coloma, is an intimate seven-room hotel on five landscaped acres in Marshall Gold Discovery State Historic Park. Owners Alan and Cindi Ehrgott offer white-water rafting trips and hot-air balloon rides on weekends.

Columbia City Hotel ((800) 532-1479 WEB SITE www.cityhotel.com, Main Street, Columbia State Historic Park, has ten rooms, each with private toilet, restored to original 1870s splendor. They serve good food and have the historic What Cheer Salon.

Cooper House Bed & Breakfast Inn ((209) 736-2145 TOLL-FREE (800) 225-3764, 1184 Church Street, Angels Camp, has three guests rooms, each with private bath, and is the only bed and breakfast in Angel Camp, a peaceful setting for this arty house.

Gold rush fortunes helped create civic monuments replete with rotundas and domes in Auburn and other small mining towns.

Three guest rooms and one suite are offered at **Dunbar House** ((209) 728-2897 TOLL-FREE (800) 692-6006, 271 Jones Street, Murphys, an attractive home built in 1880. Don't let the wood-burning stoves and lace-trimmed bed linens fool you — the rooms are stocked with all modern conveniences from mini bars to hairdryers.

Jamestown Hotel ((209) 984-3902 TOLL-FREE (800) 205-4901 E-MAIL jthotel@sonnet.com WEB SITE www.sonnet.com/jhotel, PO Box 539, Main Street, Jamestown, is a colorful country inn with eleven charming rooms and restaurant in a building that predates the American Civil War.

Inexpensive

Although originally opened in 1857, **Fallon Hotel** ((209) 532-1470, Washington Street, Columbia State Park, has been renovated to reflect the later part of the Wild West era. This attractive two-story structure has 14 guest rooms each with private toilet, but only one with private bath.

National Hotel ((209) 984-3446 TOLL-FREE (800) 894-3446 FAX (209) 984-5620, PO Box 502, Main Street, Jamestown. This combination hotel, restaurant and saloon reflects old-fashioned Gold Country style. It first opened its doors in 1859.

Saint George Hotel ((209) 296-4458, 16104 Main Street, Volcano, has 14 guest rooms sharing four bathrooms in the main building, and six rooms with private bathrooms in the modern annex. There is no heating or air conditioning.

WHERE TO EAT

Expensive

Zachary Jacques ((530) 626-8045, 1821 Pleasant Valley Road, Placerville, offers French country cuisine at its best with a menu that changes with the seasons. Wednesday night features the house specialty of cassoulet, the classic country stew of duck, sausage, lamb and white beans. There is a deck for al fresco dining when the weather allows. It is open for dinner Wednesday to Sunday.

Moderate

Converted from an old Bank of America building, **B of A Café** ((209) 736-0765, 1262 South Main Street, Angels Camp, has lots of artifacts to prove it — from teller windows on the walls to the vault which is now used as a wine tasting room. The bistro-style menu offers fresh fish, pasta, salads and a quiche of the day plus sandwiches and other hot dishes. B of A is open for lunch Wednesday to Sunday, and for dinner Thursday to Sunday.

Camps ((209) 736-8181, 676 McCauley Ranch Road, Angels Camp, serves a fusion menu featuring Asian, European and Caribbean cooking methods used to prepare local ingredients for surprising, but mouth-watering results. This restaurant is situated by a golf course, so a table on the verandah offers a peaceful backdrop to your meal. It is open for breakfast Friday and Saturday, for brunch on Sunday, for lunch Monday to Saturday and for dinner Wednesday to Sunday.

At **Grounds** ((209) 728-8663, 402 Main Street, Murphys, the menu here changes twice a week but it usually includes delicious omelets and sandwiches for lunch with pasta, seafood plus other hearty meat dishes. On Monday the menu turns Mexican. Grounds is very popular with locals, offers outdoor dining offered on the back patio, and is open Wednesday to Monday from 11 AM to 3 PM and from 5:30 PM to 9 PM.

Situated in the western-styled Jamestown Hotel, **Jenny Lind Room** ((209) 984-3902 TOLL-FREE (800) 205-4901, 18153 Main Street Jamestown, serves country-style cuisine with a few modern twists. Indoor and deck dining are available Monday to Saturday from 11 AM to 3 PM and daily from 4:30 PM to 9 PM. They also serve a champagne Sunday brunch from 10 AM to 3 PM.

Unassuming **Lil' Mama D. Carlo's** ((530) 626-1612, 482 Main Street, Placerville, is situated across from the courthouse and has been serving up reasonably priced, home-made-from-scratch Italian food for nearly twenty years. All entrees come with salad or soup as well as garlic bread. It is open Sunday to Thursday from 3 PM to 9 PM and Friday and Saturday from 3 PM to 10 PM.

The **North Beach Café** ((209) 536-1852, 14317 Mono Way, in Sonora, started life as an auto parts store but now serves up simple lunches of soups, salads, sandwiches and burgers and predominantly Italian dinner menu of pastas and fish as well as chicken, pork and steak dishes. The owner/chef is quite a character and can bombard customers with questions—so if you're not in the mood to socialize, stay away from the counter area. The café is open daily from 11 AM to 9 PM (to 10 PM on weekends).

Inexpensive

Good Heavens ((209) 532-3663, 49 North Washington Street, Sonora, offers a good choice of good old home-made American food, including soups, salads, unusual but delicious crepes and sandwiches, as well as tempting deserts. It serves daily specials and memorable jams. Good Heavens is open for lunch Tuesday to Sunday from 11 AM to 2:30 PM.

HOW TO GET THERE

The sprawling Gold Country is accessible via dozens of different routes. But perhaps the easiest way is US Highway 50, from Sacramento to Placerville, a distance of just 40 miles (64 km). From Placerville you can hook into State Highway 49, which runs the length of the Mother Lode from Nevada City to Oakhurst. State Highway 49 hits most of the major gold-rush towns including Coloma, Sutter Creek, Jackson, Angels Camp, Sonora, Jamestown and Mariposa.

LAKE TAHOE

Your mind runs out of superlatives when you come around a curve in one of the roads over the High Sierras and behold for the first time Lake Tahoe spread out before you. It is the crown jewel of the Sierras, a glistening emerald so breathtakingly beautiful it must be experienced. It is the largest alpine lake in America, 6,228 ft (1,898 m) above sea level, 22 miles (35 km) long, and 12 miles (19 km) wide. There is no water in North America as clear and pure — so clear you can see 120 ft (37 m) beneath the surface.

The lake went through several political names before the state finally settled on Tahoe, which was believed to be the Washo Indian word for "lake." Development along the lake is mainly divided up into South Shore and North Shore, although there are an east and west shore as well. The South Shore is more crowded, but it is also the oldest, and many beautiful old turn-of-the-century mansions are located here.

Tahoe's North Shore isn't so crowded; life is slower here, and the mood is decidedly more cultured than that of the busy casinos to the south. There is a North Tahoe Fine Arts Council which sponsors an annual art fair and regular musical and dramatic presentations.

GENERAL INFORMATION

Visitor information on the Lake Tahoe region is divided between "North Shore" and "South Shore" organization. The best source of information on the North Shore (Truckee, Tahoe City, Incline Village) is the **North Lake Tahoe Resort Association (** (530) 583-3494 TOLL-FREE (800) 824-6348, 950 North Lake Boulevard, Suite 3, Tahoe City 96145, which links up with a handy WEB SITE www.tahoefun.com. The North Shore **Visitor Information Center** TOLL-FREE (800) 824-6348 is located at 245 North Lake Boulevard in Tahoe City. It is open Monday to

Friday from 9 AM to 5 PM, Saturday and Sunday from 9 AM to 4 PM.

For information on the South Shore try the **Lake Tahoe Visitor Authority (** (530) 544-5050 TOLL-FREE (800) AT-TAHOE FAX (530) 544-2386 WEB SITE www.virtualtahoe.com, 1156 Ski Run Boulevard, South Lake Tahoe 96150.

The latest information on ski conditions at all Tahoe area resorts can be obtained from **Snow Web** WEB SITE www.snoweb.com. This excellent online service also provides data on lift ticket rates, weather and road conditions.

OPPOSITE: The Fallon Hotel flaunts its William Morris-like decor. ABOVE: Skiers ride one of the many chair lifts up to the snow covered slopes that have made Lake Tahoe one of the most popular winter resorts in California.

WHAT TO SEE AND DO

Like nearby Squaw Valley, Tahoe is famous as a winter sports resort. But in recent years, it has also gained popularity as a summer resort for hiking, boating, and — on the Nevada side — casino gambling. Anyone interested in the lake's spotted history should visit the **Lake Tahoe Historical Society** in South Lake Tahoe, 3058 US Highway 50.

Lake Tahoe's summer activities run the gamut from boating, hiking and camping to golf, horseback riding and hot-air ballooning. The best hiking and backpacking can be found in the ominously named **Desolation Wilderness**, near the lake's southwestern banks. Required wilderness permits for all of the aforementioned activities are issued at the **El Dorado National Forest Visitor Center**.

Just east of Desolation Wilderness is **Emerald Bay**, whose pristine waters reflect images of the lush conifers that line its shores. **Emerald Bay State Park (** (530) 988-0205 offers a hundred lakeshore campsites. South Lake Tahoe is home port of the *Tahoe Queen* TOLL-FREE (800) 238-2463, a genuine steam paddleboat that offers both daytime and evening cruises across the lake.

TAHOE SKI AREAS

Squaw Valley ((530) 583-6985 TOLL-FREE (800) 545-4350, where the 1960 Winter Olympics were held, offers 8,300 acres (3,360 hectares) of skiing. Twenty-seven lifts serve the six peaks. Facilities are located at 6,200 ft (1,890 m) and at 8,200 ft (2,500 m), with excellent lodging and restaurant facilities at the lower elevation. There is a regular shuttle bus service between Squaw Valley and the North Shore of Lake Tahoe. Squaw Valley is located on State Highway 89 between Truckee and Tahoe City. For more information, write to Squaw Valley USA, Squaw Valley 96146.

At **Alpine Meadows (** (530) 583-4232 TOLL-FREE (800) 441-4423, Box 5279, Tahoe City 96145, there are 13 lifts up two mountains. It offers an excellent ski instruction program and is popular with families. Facilities include several restaurants, a lodge, and free shuttle bus service to the North Shore.

Northstar-at-Tahoe ((530) 562-1010 TOLL-FREE (800) GO-NORTH, Box 129, Truckee 96160, is located on State Route 267 between Truckee and the North Shore. This ski area is popular for its long gentle runs through beautiful fir forests.

Heavenly Ski Resort ((702) 586-7000 TOLL-FREE (800) 2-HEAVEN, Box 2180, Stateline, NV 89449, located right on the South Shore of Lake Tahoe, is the largest ski resort in America, with 20 sq miles (52 sq km) of skiable terrain on nine mountains in California and Nevada. There are 25 lifts. An aerial tram goes up to the **Top of the Tram Restaurant**, which has excellent food and awesome views of two states.

WHERE TO STAY

Very Expensive
The 405-room, $130-million **Resort at Squaw Creek (** (530) 583-6300 TOLL-FREE (800) 327-3353 FAX (916) 581-6632 E-MAIL rr-rsc@worldnet.att.net WEBSITE www.squawcreek.com, 400 Squaw Creek Road, Olympic Valley, opened in 1990 and offers visitors all the amenities you could wish for including quick access to Squaw Valley downhill ski slopes, cross country ski trails, an ice-skating rink, three pools, tennis courts, a fitness center, a spa, an equestrian center, a shopping promenade, an 18-hole golf course, plus numerous food and beverage outlets. Children's and teen's activity programs exist. Guest rooms are situated in a dramatic black glass-and-steel building and come well equipped.

Expensive
Caesar's Tahoe ((702) 588-3515 TOLL-FREE (800) 648-3353, 55 US Highway 50, Lake Tahoe, was built in the early 1980s and recently renovated to all its faux Roman glory. This 16-story, 448-room hotel is smaller than its Las Vegas counterpart but just as garish. The theme suites are particularly amusing. Besides the 24-hour casino, the hotel offers six restaurants (including **Planet Hollywood**), an indoor swimming pool, tennis courts, a fitness room, plus major entertainment acts.

Harrah's Lake Tahoe ((702) 588-6611 TOLL-FREE (800) 427-7247 FAX (702) 586-6607, US Highway 50 at Stateline Avenue, Lake Tahoe, is located on the Nevada side of the South Shore. It's the most luxurious of South Tahoe's many hotels and casinos. Each of the 540 rooms comes with two full baths, three telephones, and three television sets. The **Summit Restaurant** on the 18th floor offers a panoramic view and the best food of any of the casino restaurants. Harrah's Family Fun Center is sure to keep the kids happy, while other amenities include pool, health club and arcade.

Harvey's Casino Resort ((702) 588-2411 TOLL-FREE (800) HARVEYS FAX (702) 588-6643, US Highway 50 at Stateline Avenue, Lake Tahoe, is connected to Harrah's by a pedestrian tunnel. The largest hotel in Tahoe, this 19-story property boasts an 88,000 square-foot casino, eight restaurants, a swimming pool, shopping arcade, health club, spa and even its own wedding chapel. Children's activities program, family fun center and big cabaret acts ensure that the whole family is kept entertained.

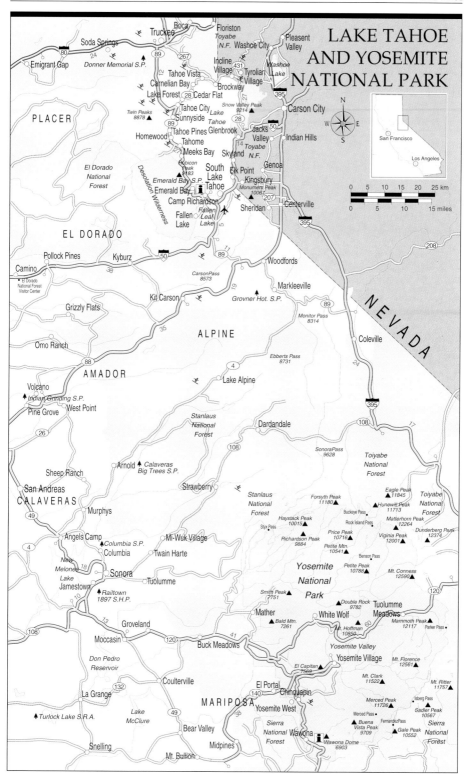

Although a casino hotel, you won't find any Vegas glitz at the **Hyatt Regency Lake Tahoe** ((702) 832-1234 TOLL-FREE (800) 233-1234 FAX (702) 831-7508, Country Club at Lakeshore, Incline Village. Waterside cottages offer unobstructed views of the Hyatt's private beach and the lake. A variety of watersports are available as well as the ever popular Camp Hyatt kids' club. Swimming pool, health club, spa, tennis courts and numerous food and beverage outlets round out the facilities.

Moderate

Lakeland Village Beach & Ski Resort ((530) 544-1685 TOLL-FREE (800) 822-5969 FAX (530) 541-6278 E-MAIL lakeland@sierra.net WEB SITE www .lakeland-village.com, 3535 Lake Tahoe Boulevard, South Lake Tahoe, is set on 19 acres (seven and a half hectares) with more than 1,000 ft (305 m) of beachfront. Units range from studios to five-bedroom lakeside townhouses with kitchens, fireplaces and daily maid service. There is no restaurant at the resort but there's a grocery store and a restaurant within walking distance. There are pools, tennis, volleyball and a sauna.

Sunnyside Lodge ((530) 583-7200 TOLL-FREE (800) 822-2754, 1850 West Lake Boulevard, Tahoe City, was originally built as a private home. This 23-room lodge offers rustic elegance. All rooms have a private deck and almost all offer a unobstructed view of the lake. Continental breakfast is included and Californian cuisine is offered at other meals in the very popular restaurant.

Tahoma Meadows Bed & Breakfast ((530) 525-1553 TOLL-FREE (800) 355-1596 E-MAIL sandytahoe @telis.org WEB SITE www.tahoecountry.com/ wslodging/tmeadows.html, 6821 West Lake Boulevard, Homewood, offers eleven private cabins on a forested slope, each with private bath and television. Some have fireplaces. A full breakfast is served at the main lodge and there is also a restaurant on-site.

Inexpensive

In excellent proximity to ski resorts, **River Ranch Lodge** ((530) 583-4264 TOLL-FREE (800) 535-9900, State Highway 89 at Alpine Meadows Road, Alpine Meadows, is an historic, wood-shingled lodge situated on the banks of the Truckee River. All rooms have private baths, telephones and televisions. Some have private balconies overlooking the river. Continental breakfast is included in the room rate. There is a lounge and restaurant.

WHERE TO EAT

Expensive

Le Petit Pier ((916) 546-4322 or (916) 546-4464, 7252 North Lake Boulevard, Tahoe Vista, offers a spectacular lakeside view and fabulous cuisine. Founded in 1972 by chef Jean Dufau, it offers an extensive menu of classic French dishes.

Sister restaurant to its famous namesake in San Francisco, **Plumpjack Café** ((530) 583-1576 TOLL-FREE (800) 323-7666, 1920 Squaw Valley Road, Squaw Valley, serves the same tempting modern American treats and impeccable service but at slightly reduced prices. In summer, it is open Thursday to Monday from 6 PM to 9:30 PM; in winter, it is open daily for breakfast from 7 AM to 10:30 AM, for lunch from 11 AM to 3 PM, and for dinner from 5:30 PM to 10 PM.

Wolfdale's ((530) 583-5700, 640 North Lake Boulevard, Tahoe City, serves California-Japanese fusion cuisine with an ever-changing menu. The emphasis is on food rather than decor, which is decidedly laid-back but elegant. Outdoor dining, with a lake view, is offered in the summer. Wolfdale's is open daily in July and August, and during other months from Wednesday to Monday, 6 PM to 10 PM.

Moderate

Don't let the gaudy exterior or simple interior put you off, **Scusa!** ((530) 542-0100, 1142 Ski Run Boulevard, South Lake Tahoe, serves good Italian food. It is open daily from 5 PM to 10 PM.

Sunsets on the Lake ((530) 546-3640, 7320 North Lake Boulevard, Tahoe Vista, offers an extensive Californian-Italian menu with lots of duck, lamb and other meats, but dishes for vegetarians too. The heated outdoor deck provides another dining option when its not too cold. It is open daily June 15 to October 10 from 11:30 AM to 2:30 PM and from 5 PM to 10 PM; in winter, it is open daily from 5 PM to 10 PM.

Inexpensive

Bridgetender Tavern & Grill ((530) 583-3342, 30 West Lake Boulevard, Tahoe City, offers reasonably priced pub grub and is very popular with locals. It is open daily from 11 AM to 2 AM, and has outdoor dining in summer.

Fire Sign Café ((530) 583-0871, 1785 Lake Boulevard, is one of the most popular places for breakfast since nearly everything is homemade and delicious. Lunches offer burgers, salads, sandwiches and the like. Fire Sign is open daily from 7 AM to 3 PM.

For healthy, wholesome food at its best — from soups to sandwiches and smoothies — try **Sprouts Natural Foods Café** ((530) 541-6969, 3125 Harrison Street, South Lake Tahoe, which is open daily from 8 AM to 10 PM.

Za's (530) 583-1812, 395 North Lake Boulevard, Tahoe City, serves excellent Italian food at bargain basement prices. Pastas, pizzas, calzones — it's all on this menu. Za's is open daily from 4:30 PM to 9:30 PM.

How to Get There

The South Shore of Lake Tahoe is 100 miles (160 km) east of Sacramento via US Highway 50 through El Dorado National Forest. The North Shore is 116 miles (185 km) via Interstate 80 and State Highway 89. From Reno, the North Shore is 34 miles (54 km) via US Highway 395 and Nevada State Highway 431; the South Shore is 44 miles (70 km) via US Highway 395 and US Highway 50 (through Carson City).

YOSEMITE NATIONAL PARK

Yosemite Valley is one of most dramatically beautiful landscapes on earth and it has held an awesome mystique over Californians from the very first to behold it. A young militiaman, among those sent in by the state to remove the Indians from the valley in 1851, thought the tribal name was "yosemity." Apparently, he had heard "Yo-Semite," the word for grizzly bear, which is what the valley has been called since. The Miwok Indians actually called the place *ahwahnee* — "valley that looks like a gaping mouth" — a name which persists in the park's most famous hotel. Artists and adventurers took to the place from the start, as did tourists. The first party of sightseers entered the valley in 1855 and three years later the first hotel was built. Since then, entrepreneurs have worked overtime to make the park into one of the most overdeveloped in the nation. The state government declared Yosemite Valley and the Mariposa Grove protected areas in 1864; a national park covering the surrounding area was created in 1890. The park now includes 1,189 sq miles (3,080 sq km) and attracts four million visitors each year.

The park lies at the heart of the High Sierras and contains spectacular landforms and waterfalls created by the earthquakes and glaciers over millions of years. **Yosemite Valley**, which gave the park its name, is seven miles (11 km) long and approached from the western entrance to the park. Lush and green, the valley floor is a stark contrast to the bare stone walls that surround it. Here, wrote the great Scottish-American naturalist John Muir, "God himself seems to be always doing his best."

The valley's eastern extreme is anchored by **Half Dome**, one mighty piece of rock, a sheer granite wall that rises 3,000 ft (900 m) straight up. Carved by glacial action over 50 million years, visitors can reach the summit of Half Dome by hiking up the Merced River Canyon and then scaling a rope ladder on the mountain's back side. The view from the top nothing short of breath taking, a sweeping panorama of the valley and its other granite monuments — **Glacier Point, Sentinel Rock** and **El Capitan**. At the base of Half

Dome, easily reached by foot from Curry Village or the Ahwahnee Hotel, is famed **Mirror Lake**. This is all that's left of the glacial lake that once filled the valley to a depth of 2,000 ft (609 m). For years this was one of the park's top tourist attractions, a place to swim and fish in summer, a spot to ice skate in winter. But in recent years the Park Service has let nature take its course and now Mirror Lake is gradually silting up. By the middle of the next century it should be totally transformed into a meadow.

Yosemite Falls, North America's highest cascade at over 2,400 ft (720 m), plunges down the valley's north face in two magnificent leaps. In the early morning you can often see a rainbow

arched over the lower falls and on full-moon nights a faint "moon bow" or lunar rainbow takes shape across the upper falls. At the base of the falls, marked by a bronze monument, is the place where Muir's sugar pine cabin once stood. **Bridalveil Fall** near the valley's western extreme — one of the first things you see when you enter the park — lives up to its reputation for nuptial beauty. Indians called the fall *pohono* or "powerful wind" which is exactly what you feel when you stand at its base. Hiking up the **Mist Trail** through Merced River Canyon from the valley floor brings you into contact with two other great gushers — a mighty cataract called **Nevada Fall** and the broad cascade called **Vernal Fall** — part of a granite formation called the Giant's Stairway.

PRECEDING PAGES: Emerald Bay, Lake Tahoe.
ABOVE: The Gates of the Yosemite Valley.

The park harbors two stands of giant sequoia trees: the **Mariposa Grove** near the south entrance and the smaller **Tuolumne Grove** near Crane Flat. Both can be reached via short hikes from their respective parking lots. The single largest tree among the two groves is the Grizzly Giant which shoots 209 ft (62 m) into the Sierra sky.

Yosemite's **back country** — the vast wilderness area that lies beyond the valley — contains hundreds of miles of footpaths and the majority of the park's wildlife. Grizzly bears no longer roam the region (the last one spotted inside the park was shot in 1895) but there are plenty of black bears and they can be a real pest around campsites and picnic areas. Other denizens include the mountain lion, coyote, bighorn sheep, bobcat, mule deer, badger, raccoon and yellow-bellied marmot. **Tioga Road** (closed in winter) traverses the back country from east to west, a spectacular highway that affords views of **Tenaya Lake** (boating, swimming, fishing) and the crest of the High Sierra. **Tuolumne Meadows** with its ranger station, campground and lodge is the hub of the back country, the best place to start your exploration. From here you can pick up the **John Muir Trail** (which links Yosemite, Kings Canyon and Sequoia national parks), the **Pacific Crest Trail** (which stretches all the way from Mexico to Canada) and the popular **High Sierra Camps Loop** with its cozy tented accommodation in summer. Anyone who intends to camp overnight in the back country must obtain a wilderness permit from a Park Service ranger station.

The **Yosemite Valley Visitor Center**, as well as the park's main hotels, lodges and campgrounds, are situated at the eastern end of Yosemite Valley. The Visitor Center offers an information counter where rangers answer questions on all aspects of Yosemite, as well as a bookstore and small museum. Behind the museum is reproduction **Miwok Indian village** with a self-guided trail that explains various aspects of Native American life in the valley in the era prior to the appearance of the first white men. West of the village is the **Pioneer Cemetery**, where many of the parks original Euro-American inhabitants are buried. Also laid to rest here are early tourists who fell victim to accidents in the park. A booklet available at the Visitor Center explains the significance of various graves.

The entrance fee to Yosemite National Park is $20 per vehicle or $10 per individual (arriving by foot, bus, bike or horse); your admission ticket will be valid for seven days. For general information about the park call ((209) 372-1000; for recorded weather and road conditions updates and park permits call ((209) 372-0200. For information via the internet log onto the Yosemite

home page of the National Park Service WEB SITE www.nps.gov/yose.

YOSEMITE IN WINTER

Yosemite is a much different park in winter. The summer mobs have faded to a trickle of visitors, there's no bumper-to-bumper traffic in the valley, and you can actually make hotel or dinner reservations without booking decades in advance. But the biggest change, of course, is the scenery. Like something from a classic Ansel Adams photograph, Yosemite is a winter wonderland of snow. Fresh white powder covers Half Dome and El Capitan. Even the giant sequoias have their mantel of snow.

Badger Pass is California's oldest downhill run and one of the best ski schools on the West Coast. The park sports 350 miles (563 km) of cross-coun-

try ski trails including 23 miles (37 km) of machine groomed track between Badger Pass and Glacier Point (with its fabulous views of the valley). Guided cross-country ski and snowshoe tours are available at Badger Pass. **Curry Village** in the valley offers one of the few outdoor ice-skating rinks in the Western United States — with Half Dome as its mighty backdrop.

Good deals on accommodation are available in winter. For instance, midweek overnight guests at any lodging inside the park get free lift tickets to Badger Pass. A midweek ski lesson package (only $25 per person) includes two consecutive downhill or cross-country lessons, child care (or child ski lessons) and ice-skating passes.

Travelers willing to shiver through winter's snowy chill find solitude and beauty at Yosemite National Park.

WHERE TO STAY

All indoor accommodation in the park, including the Ahwahnee Hotel, Yosemite Lodge, Curry Village, Wawona Hotel and High Sierra Camps, is managed by a private firm called **Yosemite Concession Services** (YCS), 5410 East Home, Fresno, CA 93727. The **central reservations line** for all these abodes is ℂ (209) 252-4848. You can also request reservations from November to March on the YCS WEBSITE www.yosemitepark.com. For the summer months and holiday periods you need to make reservations several months in advance.

Expensive

The most exclusive place to stay in Yosemite is the **Ahwahnee Hotel**, a beautiful lodge built of heavy timbers, stone and glass built in 1927. It's spacious and elegant — to match the splendor of nature all around it. The hotel's 123 rooms are recently renovated and all include private bath, cable television and splendid views. The JFK Suite is where President Kennedy once stayed (allegedly on a secret rendezvous with actress Marilyn Monroe), while the entire sixth-floor once played host to Queen Elizabeth II during a royal visit to the park. Even if you don't stay at the Ahwahnee, the hotel warrants a look-see: breakfast in the vast, wood-beamed dining room or cuddling up with a book in front of the stone fireplace of the Great Lounge. Free guided tours of the hotel's magnificent public rooms are offered several times each week.

Moderate
Yosemite Lodge is far less elegant but offers better views of Yosemite Falls. Accommodations are motel-style rooms. Amenities include restaurant, cafeteria, bar, gift shop and swimming pool.

The historic **Wawona Hotel** overlooks a rolling meadow down in the southwest corner of the park. A registered National Historic Landmark, the hotel underwent major renovation in the winter of 1997–1998 and is now up to scratch with similar accommodation in the Yosemite area.

Just outside the national park's southern boundary is a gorgeous new place called **Tenaya Lodge** ((209) 683-6555 TOLL-FREE (800) 635-5807 FAX (209) 683-8684, 1122 State Highway 41, Fish Camp, CA 93623. A modern take on the wilderness lodge concept, the hotel perches on a high wooded ridge with views of Bass Lake in the distance. A huge stone fireplace and wrought-iron chandeliers dominate the magnificent lobby. The 242 guest rooms are spacious and comfortable, with sweeping views of the mountains and forest outside. Facilities include swimming pool, health spa, massage, playground and business center. Tenaya's "guest experience center" can arrange **Tenaya Lodge** ((209) 683-6555 TOLL-FREE (800) 635-5807 FAX (209) 683-8684 myriad outdoor activities including hiking, horseback riding, waterskiing, fishing, mountain biking, golfing and numerous snow sports in winter.

Inexpensive
Curry Village offers rustic rooms and "tent cabins" with canvas walls and wooden plank floors in an atmosphere reminiscent of a mining camp or military outpost. Nothing fancy here: most units don't have their own toilets or showers; heating and air conditioning are scarce commodities. But it's a great place to get into the spirit of camping in the wilderness without hauling your own gear up the mountain.

White Wolf Lodge and **Tuolumne Meadows Lodge** off Tioga Road in the back country offers modest cabins with bath, open in the summer only (early July to early September).

Campgrounds
Fifteen campgrounds are available inside the national park including four in the valley and 11 in the back country. There used to be more than 900 campsites in the valley, but the great flood of January 1997 wiped out nearly half of those. Sites are still available at Lower Pines, North Pines and Upper Pines campgrounds at $15 per night. Facilities include fire pits, toilet blocks and drinking water. Sunnyside walk-in campground, a favorite with young backpackers, is just $3 per night. Advanced reservations for the most popular campgrounds can be made up to three months in advance by calling TOLL-FREE (800) 436-7275.

Beyond the valley, campgrounds are located at Wawona and Bridalveil Creek in the south; Crane Flat, Tamarack Flat, Hodgdon Meadow and Hetch Hetchy (walk-in only) in the northwest; White Wolf, Yosemite Creek, Porcupine Flat, Tenaya Lake (walk-in only) and Tuolumne Meadows along Tioga Road. Rates range from $3 per night for walk-in camps to $12 per night for the better drive-in sites.

High Sierra Camps includes five permanent tented camps arranged along a 50-mile (80 km) loop in the Yosemite back country. Within a day's (easy) walk of one another, the camps offer food service and indoor sleeping in a part of the world where you normally have to fend for yourself. Normally open from early July to early September depending on the weather and snow cover. The route is highly popular and is booked by lottery only.

WHERE TO EAT

Expensive
Wilderness dining has never been finer than at the **Ahwahnee Dining Room** ((209) 372-1489 in the historic hotel of the same name. From thick steaks to fresh salmon to creative California cuisine, the food here is simply divine. But you'll need to wear a jacket and tie. Simpler meals (with no dress code) are available at the **Ahwahnee Bar** off the lobby.

The Ahwahnee stages numerous special events during the year including the Vintners' Holiday dinner series in November and early December and the Chefs' Holiday dinner series in January and February. But the hotel's most famous event is the annual Bracebridge Dinner during Christmas Week. This lavish feast was started by renowned photographer Ansel Adams and his friends right after the hotel first opened. It's a four-hour-long pageant of song and feasting based on Washington Irving's description of Christmas dinner at Squire

Bracebridge's in Yorkshire. The dinner proved so popular that a lottery to pick the participants had to be devised. To be considered, get your name in by January 15, a year before the event. Only 1,750 guests are chosen. For information, contact the Reservations Department, Bracebridge Dinner, Yosemite Concession Services ((209) 252-4848, 5410 East Home Avenue, Fresno 93727.

Moderate

After years of being chided for both its ambiance and cuisine, the **Mountain Room** at Yosemite Lodge has undergone a recent revamp of both decor and kitchen. The food is mighty good these days, second only to the Ahwahnee when it comes to eateries in the valley. The big new picture windows on the north side afford marvelous views of the falls.

Inexpensive

Half a dozen outlets provide cheap eats at Yosemite including **Degnan's Deli** in Yosemite Village, the **Garden Terrace** at Yosemite Lodge, the **Curry Village Cafeteria**, and the fast-food restaurant at Badger Pass ski area. Groceries can be purchased at the Yosemite Village Store, El Portal Market, the Wawona Store and the Tuolumne Meadows Store. For the best burgers in the High Sierra, try the bar at **Tenaya Lodge** in Fish Camp.

HOW TO GET THERE

Yosemite is on the eastern edge of the state and roughly at its geographical center. It's about 200 miles (323 km) and a four-hour drive from San Francisco; about 300 miles (480 km) and a seven-and-a-half hour drive from Los Angeles. From San Francisco, take Interstate 580 east and State Highway 99 south to Merced, then State Highway 140 east through El Portal and the main entrance to the park. From Los Angeles, take Interstate 5 north toward Bakersfield, State Highway 99 to Merced and State Highway 140 on into the park. From the eastern side of the Sierra, you can reach Tuolumne Meadows from US Highway 395 via Tioga Pass (summer only).

SEQUOIA AND KINGS CANYON

These twin parks in the southern Sierra are another showcase of nature. Most people come to see the big trees, the world's largest collection of giant sequoias, gathered at **Grant Grove** in Kings Canyon and **Giant Forest** in Sequoia. The General Sherman Tree, the world's largest living thing, and other resident redwoods tower more than 200 ft (60 m) and are as thick as a railroad car at their base. Many of the trees are more than

2,700 years old, which means they were saplings around the time that the Greek city states were first emerging.

You can easily view sequoias while driving along the Generals Highway (State Highway 198), the two-lane road that connects the parks. But the best way to explore them is on foot. **Congress Trail** offers a quick two-mile (a little over three-km) jaunt through Grant Grove, although you'll have to go a bit farther to see the Fallen Monarch, a toppled-over tree that you can walk through. A slightly more strenuous hike is the **Trail of the Sequoias** which winds through Giant Forest, much of the path cast in perpetual shade because the sunlight never reaches the ground.

The big trees are limited to moderate elevations on the western edge of both parks. The vast majority of Kings Canyon and Sequoia national parks is High Sierra back country — thousands of square miles of granite peaks, alpine lakes and evergreen wilderness — a paradise for hikers, campers, climbers and kayakers. **Cedar Grove** is the gateway to the wonders of Kings Canyon, one of the least crowded national parks in the lower 48 states. Among the main attracts is **Kings Canyon** itself, the deepest gorge in the United States, carved by glacial action and the rushing waters of the Kings River. Granite walls tower 5,000 ft (over 1500 m) above the valley floor.

Sequoia's back country is dominated by **Mount Whitney**, the tallest peak in the lower 48 states at 14,492 ft (4,347 m). The summit can be reached in a single (very long) day, but the most direct route — the **Whitney Portal Trail** — is only accessible from the eastern side of the Sierra Nevada near the town of Lone Pine. Sequoia's other treasure is **Kern Canyon**, another massive glacial valley, which can be reached on foot from **Mineral King**. The National Park Service maintains **visitor centers** with information desks and small museums at Grant Grove in Kings Canyon, and at Lodgepole and Foothills in Sequoia. For general information on the park call ((209) 565-3341.

WHERE TO STAY

All indoor accommodation in both parks is managed by a private company called **Kings Canyon National Park Services Co**. ((209) 335-5500, PO Box 909, Kings Canyon National Park 93633. Properties range from upmarket motels like the **Cedar Grove Lodge** and **Giant Forest Lodge** to the rustic cabins or the **Grant Grove Lodge**.

Thirteen **campgrounds** are accessible by car, although only Lodgepole and Dorst in Sequoia accept advance bookings TOLL-FREE (800) 365-2267 which can be made up to three months in advance. The others sites are handed out on a first-come, first-serve basis and fill up quickly in summer.

If everything is booked up inside the park, the nearby city of Visalia in the San Joaquin Valley has a wide variety of hotels and motels from which to choose. One of the best bets is the moderately priced **Radisson Hotel**, ((209) 636-1111 TOLL-FREE (800) 333-3333, 300 South Court Street, which offers a swimming pool, restaurant, bar and room service.

WHERE TO EAT

The Kings Canyon National Park Services Co. runs a number of food and beverage outlets in the two parks including a snack bar at Cedar Grove, a pizza and ice cream outlet at Lodgepole, the Fireside and Village restaurants at Giant Forest, and the Grant Grove village café.

HOW TO GET THERE

Sequoia and Kings Canyon national parks are roughly five hours from Los Angeles and five and a half hours from San Francisco by car. From Los Angeles, head north on Interstate 5 into the Central Valley, veering off on State Highway 99 to Bakersfield and Visalia. State Highway 198 runs from Visalia to via Three Rivers to the south entrance of Sequoia National Park. Total distance equals 233 miles (375 km). From the Bay Area, take Interstate 580 into the Central Valley, turning south at Manteca onto State Highway 99. Follow State Highway 99 south to Fresno, where you pick up State Highway 180 leading east to the Grant Grove section of Kings Canyon National Park. Total distance is 277 miles (445 km).

EASTERN SIERRA

The rainshadow side of the mighty Sierra Nevada isn't as heralded as the great national parks, but the scenery is stunning in its own right. A more muted sort of wilderness beauty punctuated by high mountain peaks and deep valleys—the start of the basin and range country that extends all the way across Nevada and Utah to the Rocky Mountains. The landscapes and lifestyles are stark contrasts to the Sierra's western slopes. It's much drier on this flank, with spartan pine forest and scrubland rather than giant sequoias. White-water rivers are few and far between — although the region does have one of California's largest and most unusual lakes. For the most part, this is a land of ranches and ghost towns rather than wineries and gold rush attractions. And there are far fewer people, no bumper-to-bumper traffic like Yosemite Valley and trails where you can go for days without seeing another soul.

Mammoth Lakes lies at the heart of the region, one of California's great recreation grounds in both summer and winter. This is one of the state's highest towns, perched at 7,860 ft (2,358 m) in the

Inyo National Forest. As such, it's a gateway into the John Muir and Ansel Adams wilderness areas in the High Sierra, with connections to the John Muir and Pacific Crest Trails. Even if you're not interested in trekking into the back country, there are plenty of opportunities for recreation within an hour's drive of Mammoth town center: hiking, camping, trout fishing, kayaking, rock climbing and mountain climbing. Mammoth rests inside the caldera of a giant volcano and is one of California's most active geothermal regions. Small earthquakes are an almost daily occurrence and some volcanologists predict that Mammoth will blow its top again one day.

But Mammoth really comes into its own in winter when the village transforms into one of America's top ski resorts. With more than 30 lifts and 150 pistes, there's plenty of choice for every level of skier. The nearly perpetual sunshine and the 3,000 ft (900 m) incline make for pretty ideal downhill conditions. But Mammoth is also perfect for cross-country skiing and snowboarding, as well as snowshoe adventures. In fact, Mammoth seems to cater to the youthful snowboard crowd more than any other California resort.

A few miles west of Mammoth Lakes is a peculiar natural attraction called **Devils Postpile National Monument**. The "postpiles" are 60-ft (18-m) columns of jagged lava, thus named because early pioneers thought they resembled stacks of mail. The columns were originally formed underground and later revealed by glacial erosion. Despite its small size, the park offers great hiking including short stretches of the John Muir/Pacific Crest trails. Devils Postpile is only open in summer and fall (until the first heavy snowfall). Motor vehicles are banned during summer; the best way to reach the park is the shuttle bus from the Mammoth Mountain Inn Parking lot.

Twenty miles (32 km) north of Mammoth is a smaller resort area called **June Lake** which functions as both a summer and winter recreation zone. There are actually four lakes (June, Gull, Silver and Grant) strung around the highly scenic June Lake Loop Highway. Another ten miles (16 km) along US Highway 395 brings you to **Lee Vining**, where you turn off for Tioga Pass and the eastern entrance to Yosemite National Park. Lee Vining has a small **museum** and the **Mono Lake Visitors Center** which tells you all you need to know about California's strangest body of water. The lake itself is just east of town, a major refuge for migratory birds and a scenic wonder with its bizarre salt formations and volcanic islands. Mono Lake was the object of a fierce environmental crusade in the 1970s and 1980s to keep it from drying up. Luckily, common sense prevailed and the lake has been preserved for the benefit of future generations. **Bodie**, one of California's more authentic ghost towns, is about 20 miles (32 km) northeast of Lee Vining via US Highway 395 and State Highway 270.

GENERAL INFORMATION

For more information on Mammoth Lakes and the Eastern Sierra contact the **Mammoth Lakes Visitors Bureau** ((760) 934-2712 TOLL-FREE (888) GO-MAMMOTH FAX (760) 934-7066 WEB SITE WWW .visitmammoth.com.

WHERE TO STAY

If you've got an urge to be close to the slopes, try the moderately priced **Mammoth Mountain Inn** ((760) 934-2581 TOLL-FREE (800) 228-4947 FAX (760) 934-0701, Minaret Road, Mammoth Lake. The 173 rooms are comfortable and well equipped. The inn offers a variety of outdoor activities besides skiing, including fishing, horseback riding, and hiking, along with daycare facilities, playground, a games room and spa.

    Sierra Lodge ((760) 934-8881 TOLL-FREE (800) 356-5711 FAX (760) 934-7231, 3540 Main Street, Mammoth Lake, offers 35 surprisingly contemporary, spacious non-smoking rooms with cable television, kitchenettes. Amenities include outdoor Jacuzzi, free parking and continental breakfast.

    Rustic seclusion is the trademark of **Tamarack Lodge** ((760) 934-2442 TOLL-FREE (800) 237-6879 FAX (760) 934-2281 E-MAIL info@tamaracklodge .com WEB SITE www.tamaracklodge.com, Twin Lakes Road, Mammoth Lakes. This lakeside lodge has 11 guest rooms with shared or private bathrooms and 25 cabins with private bathrooms and kitchens that can accommodate up to nine people. American and Continental food is served in the dining room.

WHERE TO EAT

Despite its name, **Mono Inn** ((760) 647-6581 FAX (760) 647-6181 WEB SITE www.theierraweb .com, 55620 US Highway 395, Lee Vining, offers no lodging at the present time. But you can get great food and spectacular views of Mono Lake. The menu is California cuisine from steaks to seafood to vegetarian. Don't miss the Ansel Adams Gallery upstairs which features original Ansel Adams photographs as well as work of emerging and well-known artists and their interpretations of nature. Open for dinner mid April to October on Wednesday to Monday; December to mid-March on Thursday to Sunday.

    Nevados ((760) 934-4466, Main Street, Mammoth Lakes, serves innovative European/California cuisine at reasonable prices in a cozy French country ambiance, and a good wine selection. It is open daily from 5:30 PM to 9:30 PM.

    The Restaurant at Convict Lake ((760) 934-3803, Convict Lake Road, serves continental fare in a very romantic setting. Located in a lakeside wooden cabin, the tables surround a copper-hooded, free-standing fireplace. It is open daily in summer from 11 AM to 3 PM and from 5:30 PM to 9:30 PM; and daily in winter from 5:30 PM to 9:30 PM.

HOW TO GET THERE

Mammoth Lakes is 307 miles (494 km) north of Los Angeles via State Highway 14 and US Highway 395, a trip that takes you through the heart of the Mojave Desert before the road ascends

into the eastern Sierra foothills. Reaching the area from San Francisco takes a bit more time: you can proceed via Yosemite National Park and Tioga Road over the High Sierra; or drive Interstate 80 and US Highway 50 to Lake Tahoe and then Carson City, Nevada, where you intersect with US Highway 395.

    If you're short on time, try flying. **Mountain Air Express** ((562) 595-1011 offers flights from San Jose, Fresno and Long Beach airports to Mammoth.

Convict Lake, near Mammoth Lakes, is in the heart of the Sierra Nevadas, one of California's top recreation areas.

Central
California
Coast

ONE OF THE MOST BEAUTIFUL HIGHWAYS in the world is the Pacific Coast Highway, California State Highway 1. It snakes along the rugged coast south of San Francisco all the way to Santa Barbara, and on into the vast megalopolis of southern California. In remarkable contrast to the southern routes, you will find almost no development along much of Highway 1 on the central coast. But State Highway 1 is very narrow by modern standards and often crooked; it is no highway for those in a hurry. In other words, it is best to relax, take your time and enjoy the scenery. If you should happen to get behind a slow truck, or any of a million campers and vans on the roads, you will have to slow down anyhow because there just aren't many places where the road is wide enough for passing. It is possible to drive from San Francisco to Los Angeles on the coastal road in one day, but that is rushing it through some of the state's most beautiful scenery. Slow down, stop along the way, and enjoy the views.

SANTA CRUZ

Santa Cruz is called the "new Berkeley" by some in San Francisco because it is the site of a very liberal branch of the University of California, where the activist students seem a throwback to earlier days at Berkeley. The 2,000-acre (800-hectare) campus sits atop gently sloping hills overlooking the town, and is surrounded by giant redwoods. Santa Cruz is a lovely old town of tree-lined streets with Victorian houses comparable to San Francisco's but, here, many of them are surrounded by beautiful yards and gardens. The approach roads to Santa Cruz appear like a massive study in deep, nearly black, green—miles and miles of artichokes and brussels sprouts in fields that reach to the very edge of oceanfront cliffs.

GENERAL INFORMATION

The Santa Cruz County Conference and Visitors Council's **Information Center** ((831) 425-1234 TOLL-FREE (800) 833-3494, 701 Front Street, provides maps and dispenses other information useful for visitors.

WHAT TO SEE AND DO

The town was named for Mission Santa Cruz, the twelfth — and one of the least successful — of the 21 California missions. Heavily damaged by earthquakes in the early 1800s, the mission buildings were abandoned in the face of a feared pirate attack in 1818 and left to ruin after 1833. In 1931, a smaller replica of the mission church was built; it is now maintained as a museum. **The Mission** ((831) 426-5686, 126 High Street,

is open from 10 AM to 4 PM Tuesday through Saturday and from 10 AM to 2 PM on Sunday.

The town's main attraction is a fabulous old **boardwalk** which runs along Beach Street in downtown Santa Cruz. It is California's oldest, and one of the few with an amusement park located right on the beach. Situated at the northern tip of Monterey Bay, it stretches along a mile and a half (two and a half kilometers) of beachfront, lined with shops, galleries, rides, and games. The **Giant Dipper** is a wooden roller-coaster built in 1924; the carousel dates to 1911.

The cool damp climate in Santa Cruz is ideal for raising begonias, and the colorful **National Begonia Festival** is held at the **Antonelli Begonia Gardens** ((831) 475-5222, 2545 Capitola Road, every year, the weekend after Labor Day. The Gardens are located nearly three miles (five kilometers) south of Santa Cruz. Another event that celebrates nature is the annual **Welcome Back Monarch Butterfly Festival** ((831) 423-4609 at the **Natural Bridges State Beach**, at the western edge of Santa Cruz. The beach is famous for the bridges and arches constantly being carved into the soft sandstone. In mid-October, the festival welcomes back the monarch butterflies which arrive by the thousands every year and stay to the end of February.

If you're looking for strange sensations, visit the **Mystery Spot** ((831) 423-8897, 1953 Branciforte Drive, just over two miles (three kilometers) north of Santa Cruz. It is a 150-ft (46-m)-wide clearing in a grove of redwoods where normal gravity doesn't seem to apply. Walking uphill, you seem to be on a flat surface; two people standing on a level block appear to be at a great distance from each other; and you can roll a ball uphill as easily as down. The Mystery Spot is open from 9:30 AM to 5 PM daily; admission is $2.50 for adults and $1.25 for children five to 11 years old; children under five are admitted free.

About five miles (eight kilometers) north of Santa Cruz on California State Highway 9 is the **Henry Cowell Redwood State Park** ((831) 335-4598, a 1750-acre (700-hectare) redwood forest, with 15 miles (24 km) of hiking and riding trails. Camp sites can also be found in the park. In the park, near Felton, is the starting point for the 100-year-old **Roaring Camp and Big Trees Narrow Gauge Railroad** ((831) 335-4484. The trains take a stunning route through parts of the Redwood Forest.

One of the great surfing spots, **Steamer Lane**, is located in Santa Cruz. Host to some of the largest waves in the area, the Lane can sport waves of 15 ft (four and a half meters) and up. Still, for sheer size and power, **Mavericks**, up the coast near Half Moon Bay, is known world wide as one of the

PREVIOUS PAGES: Stalwart pines stand firm atop windswept cliffs along the Carmel coast while flower gardens thrive in sunlit valleys.

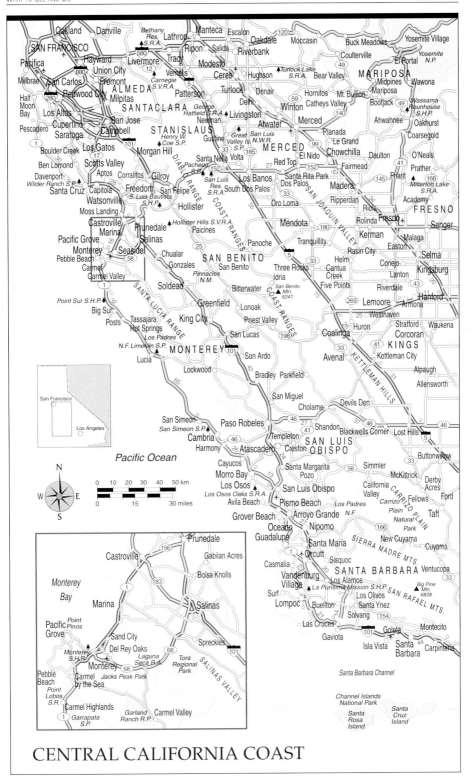

CENTRAL CALIFORNIA COAST

heaviest breaks in the world, with waves approaching 30 ft (nine meters).

Though spread out over a hilltop, and with 10 campuses, the University of California Santa Cruz is a lovely place to spend an afternoon. The arboretum on campus has thousands of exotics as well as a New Zealand garden. The campus itself is nestled among towering redwoods, with many of the buildings connected only by small meandering paths that take you through the trees. It is a great place for self-guided tours, but if you want a general campus tour call University Information ((813) 459-4008. There is also a gift shop and library available.

Since Santa Cruz is a college town, it is loaded with interesting bookstores, shops, cafés and restaurants; the best streets for strolling are Pacific Avenue and Soquel Avenue. For nightlife, live bands can be seen at The Catalyst ((831) 423-1338, 1101 Pacific Avenue. You can listen to blues and swing seven nights a week at Moe's Alley ((831) 479-1854, 1535 Commercial Way.

WHERE TO STAY

Expensive
In this category, try either the Seascape Resort ((831) 688-6800 TOLL-FREE (800) 929-7727 FAX (831) 685-2753, which is located nine miles (14.5 km) south of Santa Cruz in Aptos, on Monterey Bay; or Ocean Pacific Lodge ((831) 457-1234 TOLL-FREE (800) 995-0289 FAX (831) 457-0861, 120 Washington Street in Santa Cruz.

Moderate
The Seacliff Inn ((831) 688-7300 TOLL-FREE (800) 367-2003 FAX (831) 685-3603 WEB SITE www.seacliffinn.com, 7500 Old Dominion Court, Aptos, features 140 rooms and suites with Jacuzzis amid lush grounds and a convenient location within walking distance of the beach, shopping, and golf. Another moderately priced stay can be found at Davenport Bed and Breakfast Inn ((831) 426-4122 TOLL-FREE (800) 870-1817 FAX (831) 423-1160, located nine miles (14.5 km) north of Santa Cruz on State Highway 1.

Inexpensive
Those on a tight budget can try Harbor Inn ((831) 479-9731, 645 Seventh Avenue in Santa Cruz by the harbor.

WHERE TO EAT

Try the Ostrich Grill ((831) 477-9181, 820 Bay Avenue in Capitola, or the Hindquarter Bar and Grill ((831) 426-7770 located at 303 Soquel Avenue, for an expensive meal. More moderately-priced fare can be had at Black's Beach Café ((831) 475-2233, located at 15th and East Cliff

Drive, and at Jeffrey's Restaurant ((831) 425-1485, 2050 Soquel Avenue. An inexpensive meal can be had at Carpo's Restaurant ((831) 476-6260, 2400 Porter Street in Soquel, four miles (a little over six kilometers) south of Santa Cruz.

HOW TO GET THERE

If you are driving, State Highway 17 takes you west through the mountains and into Santa Cruz. If you are making the trip south from San Francisco, a longer yet more scenic route is directly down the coast on State Highway 1 from Daly City. As Daly City is the last stop on San Francisco's BART subway system, it is worth the time to rent a car and make the trip from there. The drive takes you through Half Moon Bay, Pacifica and the state reserve at Año Nuevo, home to a large population of elephant seals. From Monterey, you take State Highway 1 north to Santa Cruz. This is also a lovely drive as the highway takes you around the eastern perimeter of Monterey Bay.

MONTEREY

Formerly the Spanish and Mexican capital of California, Monterey is known to many as the somewhat decadent setting of John Steinbeck's *Cannery Row*. In recent years, everything—including the huge sardine and tuna cannery buildings—has been restored to an elegance the place never knew as a working port town. In fact the only criticism you'll hear about present-day Monterey is that it's too pretty.

BACKGROUND

Discovered by the Spanish explorer Vizcaíno in 1602, Monterey was named for the viceroy of Mexico, the Conde de Monte Rey. Vizcaíno had described the bay in such elaborate terms that later explorers went right by it without recognizing it. However, the sacred mission of Father Serra found it and planned it as their capital and headquarters. All too soon, Serra saw that he had to put some distance between his Indian "neophytes" and the bawdy Spanish soldiers if he was ever going to train the Indians in the straight and narrow path. So, he moved on to Carmel; Monterey remained the civilian and military capital.

Several United States citizens and even a military contingent were already living peaceably in the Mexican capital in 1846, when United States forces took over the presidio without firing a shot. The state government was formed in meetings in Monterey and it remained the seat of government until Sacramento was made the capital in 1854.

Bypassed by government (for Sacramento) and business (for San Francisco), Monterey became a beautiful old relic of California's Spanish and

Mexican years. Robert Louis Stevenson described it well in *The Old Pacific Capital* in 1879. The whaling and fishing industries and the canneries, with some very wealthy citizens at the top of the social scale and a very colorful working class made up largely of Mexicans below, kept the city prosperous. These people were celebrated in one of John Steinbeck's early novels, *Tortilla Flats*, the author's first major success. A native of nearby Salinas, Steinbeck moved to Monterey as a young man, and most of his major works drew on the life he knew in the agricultural valley and in the old port town of Monterey. His later work, *Cannery Row*, was based on the adventures of a contingent of genial bums and a marine biologist friend, with

WHAT TO SEE AND DO

Along the old waterfront, you'll find a small-scale **Fisherman's Wharf** ((831) 373-0600, its creaking old docks still jammed with working fishing boats. There are small shops where you can buy cups of chowder and all kinds of fresh seafood to go. The oldest and best restaurant is at the very end of the wharf — **Rappa's** ((831) 372-7562, a busy comfortable place which has been there since 1951 — you can buy fresh fish not only for yourself, but also for the hundreds of sea lions you'll hear honking from their habitat under and around the old wharf. The citizens

whom he had earlier written *The Sea of Cortez*, a non-fiction account of life in what is also called the Gulf of California. The lovable bums in Steinbeck's book would be astounded to see the present-day transformation of Cannery Row. Gone are the smelly fish factories and canneries; on the same spot are elegant restaurants and hotels, boutiques, and all manner of fancy shops.

Don't despair of such gentrification, it has saved the old buildings from ruin. And Monterey — it has carried on the old flavor of the city in the "new" shops and restaurants.

GENERAL INFORMATION

The **Monterey Peninsula Visitor and Convention Bureau** ((831) 649-1770 WEB SITE WWW .Monterey.com, is located at 380 Alvarado Street, Monterey 93942.

of Monterey are ferociously protective of these sea creatures that live under the old docks. Jet skis and speed boats are prohibited in the areas where the sea lions live. If some of the restoration work seems too pretty, the sea lions — with their rude honking through the night — are a great leveler.

The beautiful old stucco and tile-roofed houses from the Spanish and Mexican period are found throughout the city. The more important ones come with plaques and signs explaining their role in history. For a self-guided tour of the downtown area, the Visitor and Convention Bureau provides an excellent map. Many historic buildings are clustered in a park. **Colton**

These buildings started life as huge canneries for sardines and tuna, the setting immortalized in John Steinbeck's *Cannery Row.*

Hall, where the state constitution was drawn up, and the **Maritime Museum** ((831) 375-2553, at Custom Plaza, are also worth visiting. Monterey's biggest attraction is the **Monterey Bay Aquarium** ((831) 648-4888 WEB SITE www .mbayaq.org, 886 Cannery Row. First opened in 1984, it was built at a cost of $40 million and is the largest in the United States. With over 6,000 living things, its exhibits are considered the most innovative anywhere; along with the huge kelp forest and shark tanks are smaller "touch pools" where youngsters (and oldsters) can reach in and touch a bat ray, or stroke a starfish or a decorator crab. Located in one of the old sardine factories on Cannery Row, the Monterey

Monterey reopened in 1986 after a total restoration. It is a cozy, friendly place, and a free breakfast comes with the room. For a more lavish and elegant setting, go to the **Spindrift Inn** ((831) 646-8900 TOLL-FREE (800) 841-1879 at 652 Cannery Row Monterey, CA 93940. The inn is right on the beach and is close to the aquarium and everything else in Cannery Row. Rates are moderate to very expensive. For $45 an hour, you can rent the hotel's chauffeured Rolls Royce for a minimum of three hours and a maximum four people. **Cibo Ristorante Italiano** ((831) 649-8151 is a moderately priced Sicilian restaurant featuring locally grown produce.

Bay Aquarium is open from 10 AM to 6 PM everyday; it is closed on Christmas Day. Once you turn off State Highway 1 into Monterey, there are signs marking the way to the Aquarium. Salinas, 20 miles (32 km) east of Monterey, is home to the **National Steinbeck Center** ((831) 753-6411 FAX (831) 753-0574, 1 Main Street, Salinas. The center highlights the life and writings of John Steinbeck.

WHERE TO STAY AND EAT

Of the many fine old and new hotels in Monterey, one of the most comfortable is the recently restored **Monterey Hotel** ((831) 375-3184, 406 Alvarado Street, Monterey 93940. Rooms are in the moderate range. It is within walking distance of Fisherman's Wharf and the historic district. First opened in 1904, the

HOW TO GET THERE

Monterey is located at the southern end of the Monterey Bay. Traveling south from Santa Cruz on State Highway 1, it's 44 miles (71 km) to Monterey. State Highway 68 connects to Monterey by way of Salinas and US Highway 101 just a short drive to the east. Connecting flights to Monterey Municipal Airport can be arranged from San Jose, San Francisco, and Los Angeles airports.

PEBBLE BEACH

This beautiful 17-mile (27-km) stretch of beach, nestled among the windswept pines along the rocky coast between Monterey and Carmel, is famous for its golf courses and annual tournaments. The 17-Mile Drive is so famous it bears signs all along the route pointing the way past small parks with twisted cypress tress and a lineup of palatial private homes.

WHAT TO SEE AND DO

The **Pebble Beach Golf Links** is one of the greatest courses ever built, with an extraordinary view of the beach and ocean from many of the links. Golf enthusiast Bing Crosby started an annual tournament at Pebble Beach in 1946 and it has since become one of golf's biggest tournaments. Now known as the Nabisco Golf Championships, it carries an annual pot of $2 million and contributes an additional $2 million to charities of PGA tour events.

Two less expensive golf courses are **Spyglass Hill** and the **Del Monte Course** both 18-hole and 72-par. For information and reservations, call ((831) 624-6611.

Golf is Pebble Beach's main claim to fame, but there is also an **Equestrian Center** ((408) 624-2756 where numerous events for serious horse enthusiasts are held. Watch out for the annual California Challenge Polo Match and the Annual Dressage Championship.

WHERE TO STAY AND EAT

The **Lodge at Pebble Beach** ((831) 624-3811 TOLL-FREE (800) 654-9300, 17-Mile Drive, with its well-

The present structure of **Golf Links** (at the Lodge at Pebble Beach Hotel) has remained one of the world's premier golfing resorts since it first opened in February 1919. The green fees are expensive. For more information, contact the **Lodge at Pebble Beach** ((831) 624-3811, 17-Mile Drive, Pebble Beach 93953.

Another traditional event at The Lodge is the **Pebble Beach Concours d'Elegance** ((831) 659-0663 FAX (831) 659-1822, an automobile show held on the lawn between the Golf Links' 18th hole and the Lodge's Club XIX restaurant. Started in 1950, it has become a major charity event and a premier competition among the world's great automobiles. The Concours d'Elegance is held in August.

The **Spanish Bay Golf Links** ((831) 624-6611 is a newer championship golf course designed by Robert Trent Jones, Tom Watson, and Frank Tatum. It is located at 17-Mile Drive and Congress Road.

known Golf Links is a very expensive luxury resort. Originally named the Del Monte Hotel, the first hotel was, in fact, a log lodge, which was built in 1908 and burned in 1917. Just north of Pebble Beach is a resort built by architect Henrik Bull — the **Inn at Spanish Bay** ((831) 647-7500 TOLL-FREE (800) 654-9300, 2700 17-Mile Drive. Before building the 270-room resort, Bull restored 176 acres (71 hectares) of sand dunes in the area, hauling in 675,000 cu yd (516,000 cu m) of sand. The low stucco and tile-roofed buildings were designed to blend in with the dunes, "to look as if they'd always been there," and were landscaped with local plants. Rates are very expensive.

ABOVE AND OPPOSITE: Displays in and out of water at Monterey Bay Aquarium, the most spectacular conversions of the old cannery buildings that once supported the city.

CARMEL

Father Serra retreated to Carmel when he could no longer put up with the "liaisons" between the Spanish soldiers and his Indian "neophytes" at Monterey. Since then, lovely "Carmel-by-the-Sea" has become home to a wide diversity of artists, writers, and celebrities such as folk singer Joan Baez and Clint Eastwood, "Dirty Harry" of the movies. Eastwood owns a popular bar here and served a term as mayor of Carmel. The writers' colony in Carmel dates to 1904, and has included such American authors as Lincoln Steffens, Upton Sinclair, Sinclair Lewis, Jack London, and the poet Robinson Jeffers who used the area as a setting for many of his later poems.

GENERAL INFORMATION

The **Carmel Business Association** ((831) 624-2522 WEB SITE www.carmelfun.com/frames.htm provides information regarding Carmel. You can also contact **Monterey Peninsula Visitors and Convention Bureau** (see above).

WHAT TO SEE AND DO

At the south edge of town is the **Mission San Carlos Borromeo del Río Carmelo**. Although it has always been called the Carmel Mission, the name Carmel actually antedates the mission. It came from the Carmelite friars who accompanied the explorer Vizcaíno and named the river for their order in 1602. The mission, named for a sixteenth-century Italian cardinal, served as Serra's headquarters for all the missions; he died here. Serra's remains are buried at the foot of the altar in the church built in 1794. That structure is still intact, although it stood in ruins from 1840 until a major restoration in 1936. Pope John XXIII elevated the church to the status of a basilica in 1960, and in 1987, Pope John Paul II visited the site. The old mission has been a functioning parish church since 1933 and the mood inside the garden walls here is decidedly, refreshingly, religious. No tourists are allowed in during services, and the only request for contributions is a tiny sign in the museum and gift shop which suggests a $1 donation.

The town center is loaded with galleries, specialty shops and small cafés. **Point Lobos State Reserve** ((831) 624-4909 is four miles (a little over six kilometers) south of Carmel on State Highway 1.

The beautifully restored Mission San Carlos Borromeo del Rio Carmelo was headquarters for all the missions and it was here that Father Serra died and was buried. A museum is open to the public and a refreshingly religious air is maintained throughout the compound.

The 13,000-acre reserve (5,200-hectare), half of which is underwater, has hiking trails on bluffs above the rough sea; sea lions congregate on the beach near the picnic grounds.

WHERE TO STAY

The mood is casual and comfortable in Carmel. The streets are lined with beautiful old twisted sea pines. Nothing is over two or three stories high; even the tract houses seem tucked into their own cluster of pines. The chain motels are built in low village-inn-style, and flowers are found everywhere. Most of the more popular bars and restaurants have open fireplaces to counteract the chilly fog.

Very Expensive

The **Quail Lodge and Golf Club** ((831) 624-1581 TOLL-FREE (800) 538-9516 FAX (831) 624-3726 E-MAIL info@quail-lodge-resort.com, is set amid 614 acres (248 hectares) in Quail meadows. With 86 guest rooms and 14 suites, the lodge is considered one of the finest on the coast and has a championship golf course. The **Highlands Inn** ((831) 624-3801 TOLL-FREE (800) 682-4811 FAX (831) 626-1574, PO Box 1700, Carmel 93921, is an elegant, exclusive resort on a 12-acre (5-hectare) cliff top setting south of Carmel at Point Lobos.

Moderate

There are several modest motels and hotels in Carmel, including the **Dolphin Inn** ((831) 624-5356 located at San Carlos Street and Fourth Avenue; **Horizon Inn** ((831) 624-5327 on Junipero and Third Avenue; the **Sandpiper Inn** ((831) 624-6433, 2408 Bayview, at Martin Street; and the **Wayfarer Inn** ((831) 624-2711 at Fourth Avenue and Mission Street.

WHERE TO EAT

Clint Eastwood's place is called the **Hog's Breath Inn** ((831) 625-1044, at Fifth and San Carlos Streets, and serves moderately priced steaks, chicken and seafood. Across the street, at the same intersection is a popular restaurant, the **Casanova** ((831) 625-0501, serving expensive country French and Italian meals. The charming **Porta Bella** ((831) 624-4395 on Ocean Avenue between Lincoln and Monte Verde, offers seafood, pasta, chicken and a nice wine selection in a beautiful setting. The **Mediterranean Market** ((831) 624-2022 is the best place to shop for picnic lunches.

HOW TO GET THERE

Carmel is just two miles (a little over three kilometers) south of Monterey on State Highway 1 and 26 miles (42 km) north of Big Sur.

BIG SUR

Located 25 miles (40 km) south of Carmel, the Big Sur area is the southernmost point where the redwoods grow and the giant trees literally heighten the dramatic landscape, where the sheer cliffs rise straight up from the pounding surf, and where the steep rugged mountains of Los Padres National Forest loom behind. The name is an English corruption of the Spanish name for the river, El Río Grande del Sur, Big River of the South. Even today, there is almost no development along the narrow State Highway 1 that meanders through the wilderness around Big Sur.

One of the most lovely stretches of coast in California, the Big Sur area stretches from Carmel to San Simeon. It is home to several state parks, including **Andrew Molera State Park** and **Julia Pfeiffer Burns State Park**, and some of the most spectacular coastal scenery in the country. The narrow, twisting highway twists between the Santa Lucia Mountains and the ocean, often edging steep cliffs. Mountain bikers are fond of this ride, though it requires energy and strength for some steep climbs. Auto drivers are torn between the scenery and the road, and miss some of the best scenery unless they pull off at every lookout point along the way. The road is often closed in winter due to heavy rains and mudslides.

Big Sur is one of those wild places that are dear to the hearts of Californians — a special blend of Nature's eccentric artwork and that of man's. Beatnik author, Jack Kerouac, born in the factory town of Lawrence, Massachusetts, wrote *Big Sur*, the story of an early counter-culture hero who settled there; Henry Miller, born in New York and a resident of Paris most of his life, wrote several books here and died in a secluded house in Big Sur.

GENERAL INFORMATION

There is no tourist information office on the road. You can write ahead or call the **Big Sur Chamber of Commerce** ((831) 667-2100, PO Box 87, Big Sur 93428.

WHAT TO SEE AND DO

The few commercial places along the road still look and feel like the 1950s; and here writers and artists are still regarded with special respect. The house where Henry Miller lived is not open to the public, but signs announce the **Henry Miller Memorial Library** ((831) 667-2574 WEB SITE WWW .henrymiller.org at a sharp bend in the road (no street address). The library is closed on Mondays. Miller wrote *The Rosy Crucifixion* and *Big Sur and the Oranges of Hieronymus Bosch* here. The library includes first editions of Miller's books, his type-

writer and other memorabilia. Big Sur ends at Morro Bay and San Luis Obispo, known for its mission church.

WHERE TO STAY AND EAT

Big Sur's restaurants and motels are built like mountain lodges, nearly all have nice old paneled bars, high ceilings with broad exposed beams, and big stone fireplaces. Everything in Big Sur is right on State Highway 1. One of the more expensive and captivating lodges is the **Ventana Inn** ((831) 667-2331. Moderate and inexpensive rooms are available at the **River Inn** ((831) 667-2700, which has a very good restaurant with seating in an outdoor porch overlooking the river. The **Lucia Lodge** ((831) 667-2391 is located at the southern edge of Big Sur and has 10 cottages and a restaurant; rates are expensive.

There are numerous camp grounds, the best at the **Pfeiffer Big Sur State Park** ((831) 667-2315 TOLL-FREE (800) 444-7275, 26 miles (42 km) south of Carmel, which is set in a thick grove of redwoods. It includes the **Big Sur Lodge** ((831) 667-3100 TOLL-FREE (800) 424-4787 with 61 units in rustic cottages, a restaurant, camping sites and hiking trails. **Andrew Molera State Park** and **Julia Pfeiffer Burns State Park** TOLL-FREE (800) 444-7275 also have campgrounds.

HEARST SAN SIMEON STATE HISTORICAL MONUMENT

Ninety-four miles (151 km) south of Monterey on State Highway 1, signs lead to what is now called "Hearst Castle," although William Randolph Hearst himself liked to call it "The Ranch." This was just another quirk of the controversial newspaper tycoon who built this grandiose monument for his mother and led one of the most extravagant lifestyles ever seen in America.

The name San Simeon was borrowed from a local ranch; Hearst's mother liked to called it "La Cuesta Encantada" (the Enchanted Hill), a more fitting name any visitor can appreciate. As far as the eye can see, north and south, there is the rocky shore and the gentle hills rising up behind. It was an actual ranch when Hearst's father owned it (and still is), almost 244,000 acres (97,600 hectares) with 50 miles (80 km) of beachfront; a small tract compared to the many millions of acres the mining magnate owned in the United States and Mexico.

BACKGROUND

William Randolph Hearst grew up spoiled, the only child of a refined and doting mother and a

The rugged coastline at Big Sur has long been a haven for artists and writers and much of that earlier spirit lives on in its lodges and campgrounds.

barely literate millionaire father. He ran a nation-wide chain of newspapers that had the potential to wield extraordinary power in America, but Hearst's own muddled thinking and writing usually canceled that out. He was a man of contradictions. He helped get the United States into war with Spain, only to become a bitter isolationist during World War I and World War II. Starting out as an enlightened Democrat and friend of the common man, he later became a violent anti-union leader; he helped elect Franklin Roosevelt and then turned on his administration with a vengeance. He wrote piously about fidelity and the sanctity of marriage while living openly with a mistress.

But through these 60 turbulent years in American politics, Hearst remained constant to San Simeon, this enchanting landscape on the then nearly inaccessible coast of California and the castle he was building for himself there. The family had built several ranch houses on the property since Hearst was a child, but he began work on the castle in 1919. After 30 years and millions of dollar spent, he had still not finished with it, and today you can see an enormous wing that was never completed.

Hearst's newspapers are credited — or, more accurately discredited — with having originated "yellow journalism," and are now considered part of journalism's sordid past. What endures is "Hearst Castle." Although Hearst died in 1951, the state did not take over the 127 acres (50 hectares) at San Simeon until 1957 — and then only reluctantly. Much to everyone's amazement, the public was standing in line to get a glimpse inside.

WHAT TO SEE AND DO

Hearst Castle is a rare state park that has been in the black from the start. In 1985, a modern **visitor's center** TOLL-FREE (800) 444-4445 was constructed just off State Highway 1. It cost $7.5 million, almost as much as Hearst spent on his fabulous castle in the sky. Nearly a million people now visit the site every year.

There is an excellent interpretive exhibit in the visitor's center which does an accurate job of describing Hearst's strange career and his life at San Simeon. The Hearst Corporation still owns all the surrounding property and, in the early days, it was feared that his family's frequent visits would affect any objective presentation of the man's life. The new exhibits, however, explain in detail how, for the last half of his life, he lived openly with his mistress Marian Davies, a B-grade actress and a lightweight intellectual (with girlish schemes to shake hands with Hitler and Mussolini), but a shrewd businesswoman. She was the real mistress of San Simeon.

San Simeon is an enduring monument to Hearst's unbelievable extravagance. From his first

visit to Europe as a boy with his mother, Hearst set about buying up its greatest art treasures. In her memoirs, Miss Davies tells about his shipping an entire medieval monastery to San Simeon, and leaving it boxed up along the road for years because he couldn't decide where to put it. Even now, guides tell you, there are four floors of a huge warehouse filled with Hearst's art treasures. When he came close to bankrupting the family corporation, many of his pieces were put on sale at Gimbel's and Saks Fifth Avenue. The sale lasted two years, and more than 700 pieces were sold each day.

The winding road up to the castle goes through the old ranchlands; a herd of zebras now graze where Hearst once had the world's largest pri-

vate zoo. (The animals were put in regular zoos during World War II.) Arriving at the base of the steps leading up to the castle, you behold not a castle but a cathedral. The stonework in the façade was taken from a fifteenth-century Spanish convent, and much of the woodwork tapestries, and silk banners inside were likewise taken from religious places in Europe.

Today's visitor will see it all as a clutter of styles, Greco-Roman, Italian and Spanish, much of it uncomfortable and impractical. One of the purest and most beautiful sites is the Neptune Pool, an outdoor re-creation of a Greek temple pool, where you can gaze into the distance, taking in the magnificently beautiful coastline, and the Piedras Blancas, white rock formations that jut up like ancient monuments from the sea.

W.A. Swanberg's 1961 book, *Citizen Hearst*, remains the best biography of William Randolph

Hearst. For a more personal view of Hearst and San Simeon, Marion Davies' *The Times We Had* is recommended. Both of these are available in paperback in the motels and shops located just south of San Simeon. The best contemporary biography of Hearst is *Hearst: Lord of San Simeon,* by Oliver Carlson and Ernest Sutherland Bates. First published in 1936, this book is now out of print, but available in all California libraries.

Visitors to San Simeon are warned that you must walk a minimum of 150 steps on any of the four tours of the castle. Tours cost $14 for adults and $8 for children age 6 to 11; younger children are free. Advance reservations are recommended year-round. The tours last about two hours, but

Although there are no lodging or restaurant facilities right at the castle, a fairly tasteful cluster of commercial buildings is located five miles (eight kilometers) south of San Simeon. The motels on the oceanside of the road have the better view, direct beach access, and are more expensive. Two of the better moderate choices for accommodation are **The Best Western Cavalier** ((805) 927-4688, with wood-burning fireplaces and a spa, and the **El Rey Inn** ((805) 927-3998.

Ten miles (16 km) south of San Simeon lies **Cambria**, billed as a "picturesque" village of art galleries and quaint shops. Overdeveloped and packed with touristy shops and restaurants, Cambria does make one appreciate the effort to

you should allow an extra hour to go through the exhibits in the visitors center.

WHERE TO STAY AND EAT

Aside from the snackbar in the state-run visitors center, the only commercial enterprise at San Simeon itself is a wonderful old country store across the road from the entrance to San Simeon. Everything else is either owned by the state or the Hearst Corporation. **Sebastian's Store** ((805) 927-4217, 442 San Simeon Road, has been there since 1852. Located just up the road from the state beach and across from the original private docks and warehouses used by Hearst's father, it is crammed with an amazing variety of stuff, complete with a gas pump on the side and a United States Post Office at the back. There is also a nice little patio restaurant, serving fresh-caught seafood.

preserve the beautiful coastline north of here. And Cambria does have the best restaurants in area, including **Bistro Sole** ((805) 927-0887, 1980 Main Street, an expensive but excellent seafood house. **Cambria Village Bakery** ((805) 927-0887, 2214 Main Street, is the best place for inexpensive to moderate quiches, pastries and breads. The moderately priced **FogCatcher Inn** ((805) 927-1400 TOLL-FREE (800) 425-4121 FAX (805) 927-0204 has 60 rooms in a Tudor-style building above the beach.

Once the exclusive preserve of the eccentric William Randolph Hearst and his invited guests, San Simeon or "Hearst's Castle" is now open to anyone for the price of admission. One of the purest and most beautiful designs on the cluttered mountain top is the Neptune Pool OPPOSITE designed after a Greek temple pool. Indoors ABOVE there is an equally extravagant heated pool featuring classic statuary and good mosaic tiles.

SANTA BARBARA

The wealthy city of Santa Barbara is known as the Queen of the Missions, having grown up in this century around the old mission. It is also the queen of California's coastal cities. The Santa Ynez Mountains back hillsides covered with red-tiled roofed mansions and estates overlooking miles of beach and the town harbor. Many of the area's residents are descendants of families who settled around the mission; others have moved here to escape the crowds and smog of Los Angeles. The city relies heavily on tourism for its local economy, and all go out of their way to make guests feel comfortable. There is enough to do to keep interested sightseers busy for a week.

GENERAL INFORMATION

There are several visitor information centers in Santa Barbara. These include the **Santa Barbara Chamber of Commerce Visitor Information Center** ((805) 965-3021, 504 State Street; and the **Beachfront Visitor Information Center**, 1 Santa Barbara Street (at Cabrillo Boulevard, near Stearns Wharf). To receive information regarding this area before you travel, contact the **Santa Barbara Conference and Visitors Bureau** ((805) 966-9222 or (805) 965-3021 TOLL-FREE (800) 927-4688 FAX (805) 966-1728 WEB SITE www.santabarbaraca.com, PO Box 299, Santa Barbara 93102. The bureau, located at 1330 State Street, also offers free guided tours of the downtown area.

WHAT TO SEE AND DO

Mission Santa Barbara ((805) 682-4149 was named in honor of a Roman girl who was beheaded by her father because she had embraced Christianity. At a perilous point in their voyage to Mexico, Father Serra and his Franciscan brothers felt they'd been saved by appealing to Saint Barbara. And she was so honored by the tenth of the 21 missions. An earlier mission building was destroyed by the earthquake of 1812, but the present stone structure has endured since its construction in 1815 and 1833. With its impressive twin-towered façade, the church became known for its architecture; it was also built on a rise and used as a landmark and beacon by ships at sea for many years. Located at East Los Olivos and Upper Laguna Streets, the mission now includes a large monastery and seminary. Although it is a parish church, the mission is open to the public from 9 AM to 5 PM Monday through Saturday, and from 1 PM to 5 PM on Sundays. The rose gardens in front of the mission are gorgeous in spring.

Municipal buildings aren't usually on anybody's list of places to see. But the **Santa Barbara County Courthouse** ((805) 962-6464, 1100 Anacapa Street, is an exception. It is open weekdays from 8 AM to 5 PM, Saturday and Sunday from 9 AM to 5 PM with free guided tours on Wednesday and Friday at 10:30 AM and again on Monday through Saturday at 2 PM. Part of a vast reconstruction effort after a 1925 earthquake that reduced much of the city to rubble, it looks for all the world like a Spanish castle — with carved doors and elaborate tilework throughout. At the top of the 70-ft (21-m) clock tower, there is an observation deck with a splendid 360-degree view of the seaside city and the mountains beyond. Another part of the post-1925 reconstruction is De la Guerra Plaza and El Paseo, an area of shops and restaurants built around the de la Guerra home, part of which dates to 1827.

The **Presidio** ((805) 965-0093, 122 East Canon Perdido Street, was a Spanish fortress constructed in the late eighteenth century. It was badly damaged by earthquakes in 1806 and 1812, and only the soldiers' quarters and the Canedo Adobe are still standing, though the rectory and chapel have been restored. The Presidio is open from 10:30 AM to 4:30 PM Monday through Friday, and from noon to 4 PM on weekends. Admission is free.

The oldest and most popular festival in Santa Barbara is the annual **Old Spanish Days Fiesta**, in early August. The festival involves four days of equestrian parades, costume parties, and nightly shows in the sunken gardens at the courthouse.

The tranquility of Santa Barbara was disturbed by the construction of offshore oil drilling rigs in the Santa Barbara Channel. Started in 1958, the oil drilling now produces nearly 90% of the 435 million barrels of oil produced annually in Califor-

nia. During the latter part of the drilling operation a massive spill from one of the rigs killed wildlife throughout the area and fouled beaches for miles. This led to one of the state's first major battles over the environment — and Santa Barbara becoming a center for environmentalist action. Many of the wells have been landscaped to look like small islands; they're visible from the highway and from **Stearn's Wharf**, at the foot of State Street. The wharf is a great place for a stroll. The Channel Islands are visible from here, and local anglers fish from the end of the pier. There are a few shops and several restaurants serving fresh fish meals. The **Nature Conservancy** ((805) 962-9111, 213 Stearns Wharf, is one of the country's

The Mission Santa Barbara is often called the Queen of California Missions, offering an excellent example of Spanish-Californian architecture set amid rose gardens.

most active environmental groups. At its headquarters on Stearns Wharf, and on the group's nature preserve on Santa Cruz Island, you can see exhibits on the environment. Next door to the Nature Conservancy is the **Santa Barbara Museum of Natural History's Sea Center** ((805) 682-4711, with aquarium exhibits and a huge model of a gray whale. **State Street** is the heart of the shopping and dining district, and is loaded with shops and cafés. **Paseo Nuevo**, a shopping center at State and De la Guerra streets, was constructed to blend with the architecture and the pedestrian-friendly style of Santa Barbara. **De la Guerra Plaza** and **El Paseo** are both older shopping arcades. The **Red-Tile Tour** through the historic area around

the loveliest seaside resorts in California. Its red tile roofed buildings are spread over 20 acres of lawns and gardens across the street from the beach. The restaurants, shops and architecture are all worth experiencing, even if you can't afford the very expensive room rates. Stop by for a look. **El Encanto** ((805) 687-5000 TOLL-FREE (800) 346-7039 FAX (805) 687-3903 is an enchanting historic inn set on a hillside high above the town and sea. Cottages, some dating back to 1915, are surrounded by flowers, vines and fountains, and terrace and restaurant are perfect for sunset drinks and excellent meals. The room rates are moderate, but the restaurant a bit pricey. There are several good hotels located directly across from Santa

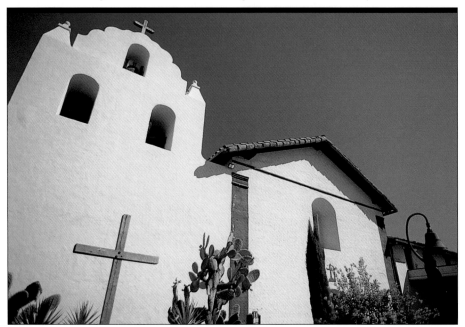

State Street includes stops at the oldest streets and buildings in downtown. A self-guided map of the tour is available at visitor information offices. The **Santa Barbara Museum of Art** ((805) 963-4364, 1130 State Street, is a fine regional museum with a wonderful art and sculpture collection and shows by local artists. In the mountains above the city, the **Santa Barbara Botanic Garden** ((805) 682-4726, 12212 Mission Canyon Road is a wonderful country escape with fields of poppies and wildflowers and a redwood grove by a stream. The **Santa Barbara Zoological Gardens** ((805) 962-5336, 500 Niños Drive, is as captivating for its lawns and gardens as for its collection of wild animals.

WHERE TO STAY

The **Four Seasons Biltmore** ((805) 969-2261 TOLL-FREE (800) 332-3442 FAX (805) 969-4682 is one of

Barbara's long lawns and beaches. Among the best are the **Santa Barbara Inn** ((805) 966-2285 TOLL-FREE (800) 231-0431, 901 Cabrillo Boulevard (expensive); **Fess Parker's Double Tree Resort** ((805) 564-4333 TOLL-FREE (800) 879-2929 FAX (805) 962-8198, 633 East Cabrillo Boulevard (expensive); the **Harbor View Inn** ((805) 963-0780 TOLL-FREE (800) 755-0222 FAX (805) 963-7967, 28 West Cabrillo Boulevard across from the harbor (moderate to expensive); and the **Cabrillo Inn at the Beach** ((805) 966-1641 TOLL-FREE (800) 648-6708, 931 East Cabrillo Boulevard, an inexpensive motel-like hotel beside far more expensive places across from the beach. The **Motel 6** ((805) 564-1392 TOLL-FREE (800) 466-8356 FAX (805) 963-4687, 443 Corona del Mar, is immensely popular for its low rates and location near the beach; call far in advance for reservations. There are dozens of charming bed and breakfasts in old Victorian homes; for information contact **Bed and Breakfast of Santa Barbara** TOLL-FREE (800) 557-7898.

WHERE TO EAT

Santa Barbara's restaurants make full use of the excellent produce from area farms and the local wineries. One of the finest to showcase the region is the **Wine Cask** ((805) 966-9463, 813 Anacapa Street. Located behind downtown's best wine shop (also called the Wine Cask), the serene dining room is housed in a historic building with a massive fireplace; the menu features imaginative presentations of fresh seafood and meats. The dining room at **El Encanto** (see above) is equally impres-

sive. Both are expensive and reservations are strongly advised. **Citronelle** in the Santa Barbara Inn (see above) is the trendiest place in town featuring the California cuisine of Los Angeles chef Michael Richards. **Downey's** ((805) 966-5006, 1305 State Street, features expensive nouvelle Californian cooking.

Moderately priced restaurants fill the area around State Street. Try **Blue Agave** ((805) 899-4694, 20 East Cota Street, for southwest cuisine; **Andria's Harborside** ((805) 966-3000, 336 West Cabrillo Boulevard, for fresh seafood; **Bistro Med** ((805) 965-1500, 1129 State Street, for Mediterranean dishes; and **El Paseo** ((805) 962-6050, in El Paseo Center on Anacapa Street between de la Guerra and Cañon Perdido, for Mexican food in a cavernous historic building. **Enterprise Fish Company** ((805) 962-3313, 225 State Street, is known for its catch of the day. Several inexpen-

sive restaurants are located on Stearn's Wharf. The best views and burgers are at **Longboard's** ((805) 963-3311, 210 Stearns Wharf, a surfer's hangout. **The Bakery** ((805) 962-2089, 129 East Anapamu Street, is one of the best breakfast spots. The **Paradise Café** ((805) 962-4416, 702 Anacapa Street, has a great patio area and good pastas and burgers. **Café Orleans** ((805) 899-9111, in the center courtyard area of the Paseo Nuevo shopping center on State Street, serves good gumbo and crawfish.

HOW TO GET THERE

Santa Barbara is located on State Highway 1, 92 miles (148 km) north of Los Angeles. Amtrak TOLL-FREE (800) 872-7245 has daily service between Los Angeles and San Francisco with stops in Santa Barbara; the station is at 209 State Street.

THE NORTH COUNTY

A drive through the back country around Santa Barbara takes you through the Santa Ynez, Santa Maria, and Los Alamos valleys, where long stretches of uninhabited countryside are interspersed with wineries, ranches, farms, and charming small towns. **Solvang**, 35 miles (56 km) north of Santa Barbara, is known for its bakeries and restaurants with a charming Danish flavor. For Information contact the **Solvang Visitors Bureau** ((805) 688-6144, 1571 Mission Drive. The best accommodations in the region are at the **Alisal Guest Ranch and Resort** ((805) 688-6411 TOLL-FREE (800) 4-ALISAL FAX (805) 688-2510, 1054 Alisal Road outside Solvang. A working ranch and secluded hideaway, Alisal offers golf, horseback riding, tennis, a 90-acre (36 hectare) spring-fed lake for boating and fishing, and 73 country-style cottages with fireplaces.

Over two dozen wineries dot the countryside; for a driving map contact Santa Barbara Conference & Visitors Bureau (see Santa Barbara GENERAL INFORMATION, above) or call the **Vintner's Association** ((805) 688-0881. **Ojai**, south of Santa Barbara in Ventura County, is one of the largest agricultural areas along the central coast. From US Highway 101, go east on State Highway 33 to reach the Ojai Valley. The **Ojai Valley Inn & Spa** ((805) 646-5511 TOLL-FREE (800) 422-OJAI was renovated in 1997 and attracts crowds of Los Angeles weekend escapists seeking mud baths, aromatherapy massages, and the setting amid 220 acres (89 hectares) of oak groves. Non hotel guests can use the spa facilities for a fee. The rooms are expensive.

OPPOSITE: The agricultural valleys around Santa Barbara serve as a backdrop for Spanish missions and the windmills ABOVE of Solvang.

VENTURA

A shortened version of San Buenaventura, Ventura was the name given to the ninth of the Franciscan missions, the last founded by Father Serra himself. Some say the original name was too long for the railroad schedules; others that the mail was getting sent to San Bernardino. Whatever the origins of the name, Ventura became an important port city for the nearby agricultural areas. In more recent times, the food-processing plants have given way to oil refineries. Now it is known as a charming, historic destination.

The **Ventura Visitors & Convention Bureau** TOLL-FREE (800) 333-2989, is located at 89-C South California Street, Ventura 93001

CHANNEL ISLANDS NATIONAL PARK

Offshore from Ventura, the **Channel Islands National Park Headquarters and Visitors' Center** ((805) 658-5700, 1901 Spinnaker Drive, Ventura Harbor, has films, exhibits, and lectures explaining the life and history of the Channel Islands. The visitors' center is open from 8 AM to 5:30 PM, Sunday through Thursday, and from 8 AM to 7 PM, Friday and Saturday.

The five islands that make up the national park are now almost entirely dedicated to nature preserves. All are open to the public. There are also regular boat trips to all of the islands from and Santa Barbara. **Santa Cruz** is the largest of the islands, a two- or two-and-one-half-hour boat ride from Ventura, depending on which part of the island you land at. Until the Nature Conservancy acquired an interest in the island in 1978, most of it was in a private cattle ranch. The Conservancy now tends its part of the island as a nature preserve within the National Park; the **Scorpion Ranch** at the east end of the island has been acquired by the national park, but visitors are welcome to explore the old ranch buildings and the surrounding countryside on guided tours.

At the other end of Santa is **Christy Ranch**, a renovated 1864 adobe house, where meals are served to visitors on airplane tours from Camarillo airport. The 96 sq miles (249 sq km) island has a varied landscape of two rugged mountain ranges with a fertile valley in between, and a coastline of high cliffs, broad beaches, and secluded coves. The wildlife here has taken some interesting turns; eight plant species grow here and nowhere else, the scrub jay bird is much larger than its counterpart on the mainland, the fox on the island much smaller.

There are campgrounds on the other islands: San Miguel, Anacapa, Santa Rosa, and Santa Barbara. However, visitors should check well in advance with park rangers at the Channel Islands headquarters in Ventura to be sure space is available and to make reservations. In addition to the special Nature Conservancy tours, the Island Packers has regular boats to all of the islands. For information on any of the tours, contact Island Packers.

CATALINA: THE ISLAND OF ROMANCE

Catalina Island has long been a romantic escape for Southern Californians who want to get away from it all. From Al Jolson to the Beach Boys to Roxy Music, singers have kept the romance of Avalon and Catalina alive. Located southeast of the Santa Barbara or Channel Islands, the Catalinas consist of four separate islands. Santa Barbara is the smallest and northernmost of these and is part of the Channel Islands National Monument. San Nicolas Island, the farthest from shore, is famous as a nature preserve. It is also known for the legendary Indian woman who lived alone on the island for 28 years after her people were relocated to the mainland in 1835. The southernmost of the Catalinas is 22-mile (35-km) long San Clemente Island. It is used by the United States Navy for bombing practice and other kinds of training. All three of these islands are uninhabited. Santa Catalina, on the other hand, is very much inhabited and grows downright crowded in the summer. The tourist season is from May through October; room rates are at their highest and the island is bustling. Rates drop in the off season (also called the quiet season), December to May, and though some businesses are closed, the island is delightfully free of crowds.

GENERAL INFORMATION

Since hotel and restaurant accommodation is limited, it is wise to make reservations well in advance. The **Catalina Island Chamber of Commerce** ((310) 510-1520 WEB SITE www.catalina.com, PO Box 217, Avalon 90704, provides information and reservations for all facilities on the island. The **Santa Catalina Island Company** TOLL-FREE (800) 428-2566 provides information about specific camp sites, hotels, and other island attractions. They also run **Discovery Tours**. You can also stop by the Island Company's Office and the **Catalina Island Visitor's Bureau** ((310) 410-1520, located on the Green Pier in Avalon.

WHAT TO SEE AND DO

When most people speak of Catalina, they are referring to Santa Catalina, second-largest of the four islands and the only one developed as a tourist resort. Some 22 miles (35 km) long and eight miles (13 km) across at its widest point, Santa Catalina is 26 miles (42 km) from Los Angeles' San Pedro harbor. It was only in 1919, when the Chicago chewing gum magnate William Wrigley Jr. bought the island, that it began to take on an international reputation as a vacation spot. Wrigley developed the pebble beaches, hidden coves, and canyons in the style they deserved. The Mediterranean-style village of Avalon rose at the heart of the beautiful crescent-shaped Avalon Bay. And, at the heart of Avalon sat a fabulous $2 million casino, a huge round white building with a red tile roof that stands as a prominent reminder of grander days on Santa Catalina.

The **Casino Building**, built from 1928 to 1929 in Mediterranean style with Moorish influences, Via Casino Way along the waterfront promenade, has housed a museum for several years now, its raucous past described and illustrated in guides and various exhibits. The **museum** ((310) 510-2414 is open daily 10:30 AM to 4 PM. Much of the magnificent art deco interior has been preserved. You can still see the murals in the casino's **Avalon Ballroom**, where the best of the big bands once played and glamorous world celebrities danced. Mrs. Wrigley made sure the sea motif was carried out in the specially-designed furniture — the couches shaped like waves, the chairs like sea shells. Completed in 1929, the casino was a success in spite of the Depression. Wrigley also built the first movie theater equipped for sound pictures in this building. It became not only a favorite place for tourists to preview the latest movies, but also for film moguls and stars from Hollywood to see their latest works in such elegant surroundings. For the weekly movie schedule, call ((310) 510-1922 or look for kiosks along Crescent Avenue. The Santa Catalina Company offers daily walking tours of the building; contact Discovery Tours for more information (see GENERAL INFORMATION, above).

Crescent Avenue, Avalon's bayfront pedestrian promenade, was originally built between 1932 and 1935. It has recently undergone a facelift: one designed to retain the original, whimsical look of designer Otis Shepard. Wrigley Fountain has been restored, as has Serpentine Wall. The pedestrian walkway has been extended to incorporate one-block portions of Catalina and Sumner Avenues.

Catalina has remained pretty much unspoiled to this day. Wrigley understood and appreciated the natural beauty of the island and set aside more than 85% of the land in a nature conservancy that is off limits to developers. You can visit **Wrigley Memorial and Botanical Garden** ((310) 510-2288, 1400 Avalon Canyon Road, which covers over 37 acres (15 hectares) and has maintains plants that are native only to Catalina. Trams take visitors to the memorial from the Island Plaza, otherwise it is a 1.7-mile (2.7-km) walk up a gentle slope from

downtown Avalon. The center is open daily 8 AM to 5 PM. There is a small admission fee. Free one-and-a-half-hour nature walks are conducted Tuesday and Saturday at 10:15 AM. Call ((310) 510-2595 to confirm times.

Since the majority of Catalina is protected land, to really see the island you must enter this undeveloped area. The **Two Harbors** area, near the northern end of at the island's isthmus, is the center for outdoor recreational activities of all kinds, including hiking, snorkeling and scuba diving, ocean kayaking, boating and mountain biking. For more information contact **Two Harbors Visitor Services** ((310) 510-1550 FAX (310) 510-0244 WEB SITE www.catalina.com/twoharbors/, PO Box 5044 Two Harbors, 90704.

Permits are needed for biking or hiking; these can be obtained from the **Island Conservancy** ((310) 510-2595, 125 Claressa Avenue. The hiking permit is free, however the biking permit is $50 per year for individuals, $75 per family. You can get to Two Harbors from either San Pedro or Long Beach aboard Catalina Express and Catalina Cruises. From Avalon, year-round bus service and high-season coastal shuttles are available.

Tours

Two companies offer a variety of tours around the islands. For nature lovers, the Catalina Islands are a kind of "American Galapagos," with huge areas of the natural environment preserved. **Catalina Safari Tours** ((310) 510-0303, 1 Banning House Lodge Road, Two Harbors, has regular field trips into the most exotic parts of the islands and can provide lodging at the **Banning House Lodge**, a Catalina landmark built in 1910 at Two Harbors.

A busier and more varied schedule of tours — both on land and out to sea — is offered by **Santa Catalina Island Company** ((310) 510-2000 TOLL-FREE (800) 428-2566. Guided Jeep eco-tours are available from the **Catalina Island Conservancy** ((310) 510-2595 extension 0, with all proceeds going to conservation and education projects.

WHERE TO STAY

Resort prices prevail in Catalina. Two of the most spectacular views of Avalon Bay are available from two private mansions that have been converted into hotels. The Wrigley mansion is now the **Inn on Mount Ada** ((310) 510-2030, 398 Wrigley Road, built in 1921. Overlooking Avalon Bay, the Georgian-style bed and breakfast is listed in the National Register of Historic Places; elegant rooms are in the very expensive category. The most popular author of the Old West, Zane Grey, lived and wrote for many years from another beautiful perch overlooking Avalon Bay. In contrast to the Chippendale elegance of the Wrigley mansion, Grey's spacious quarters reflected his rustic subject matter. The **Zane Grey Pueblo Hotel** ((310) 510-0966 TOLL-FREE (800) 378-3256, offers a high-beamed lodge setting decorated with memorabilia from the Old West and a view to match the Wrigley's. Rooms run from moderate to expensive. **Villa Portofino** ((310) 510-0555 TOLL-FREE (888) 510-0555 FAX (310) 510-0839, at 111 Crescent Avenue, is great for those who want to be across from the beach and in downtown. There are 34 rooms and suites; some offer ocean views, others have fireplaces. Rates are moderate to very expensive.

Some of the rooms at the moderately priced **Hotel Metropole** ((310) 510-1884 TOLL-FREE (800) 300-8528 (in California: TOLL-FREE (800) 541-8528) offers private balconies, fireplace, ocean views and spa tubs. The spa and sundeck have panoramic ocean views.

In the more inexpensive range is the **La Paloma Cottages** ((310) 510-0737 FAX (310) 510-2424. Campsites are available at the **Hermit Gulch Campground** ((310) 510-8368 or (310) 510-0342, one mile (1.6 km) from downtown Avalon; equipment packages and tent cabins available. Shuttles are available from boat landing; otherwise, it is a one-and-a-half-mile (2.4-km) hike. There is another inland campground at **Blackjack**; the island's two beachfront campsites are found at **Parson's Landing**, on the northern shore, and at **Two Harbors**, at the isthmus. The latter also has tent cabins, available only during the off season (October through May). Tent cabins are basic cabins with bunk beds, electrical outlets, and refrigerators; there are communal kitchens and bathrooms. Guests must supply their own bedding. All campgrounds have picnic tables, fire pits, barbecue grills and chemical toilets. Except for Parson's Landing, all campsites have sunshades, fresh water, and rinse-off showers, and firewood, propane, butane and charcoal are available for purchase.

WHERE TO EAT

Recommended in the expensive category is **Villa Portofino** (see above), which serves Italian cuisine highlighting pastas, seafood and veal. Overlooking the harbor is **The Channel House** ((310) 510-1617, 205 Crescent, which has a weekend piano bar and patio dining. Dinner only is served during low season (October through May). Less expensive yet with an Italian emphasis is **Antonio's Pizzeria** ((310) 510-0060 at 114 Sumner; they serve pizza, rotisserie chicken, antipasto and Caesar salads daily for lunch and dinner. A second location is **Antonio's Pizzeria & Cabaret** ((310) 510-0008, 230 Crescent, which serves breakfast in addition to lunch and dinner, and offers a full bar as well as evening entertainment. **Café Prego** ((310) 510-1218, 603 Crescent, on the Bay, is recommended for moderate lunches and candlelight

dinners. There are many inexpensive, quaint cafés and coffee shops to choose from. Check out **Sally's Waffle Shop** ((310) 510-0355, right on the beach near the Green Pleasure Pier; right next door is **Joe's Place** ((310) 510-0491, at the foot of Green Pleasure Pier, which serves basic Americana: burgers, flapjacks, and chicken dinners.

HOW TO GET THERE

Catalina Express ((310) 519-1212 TOLL-FREE (800) 343-4491 WEB SITE www.catalinaexpress.com, San Pedro Offices, Berth 95, San Pedro 90731, books passage from both the Long Beach and San Pedro piers. They offer daily crossings (between 4 and 24 daily, depending on the season) from early morning to late at night. Boats leave from Berth 95 at San Pedro: from Los Angeles, take the Harbor Freeway (Highway 110 south) to the Terminal Island exit. Signs will then lead you to the Catalina Express parking areas. To reach the Long Beach pier from Los Angeles, take Interstate 405 south to State Highway 710 south and on to the Port of Queen Mary exit; follow the signs and park in the Queen Mary lot. Reservations are advised; check in 45 minutes before sailing time.

United States Coast Guard regulations apply to passengers on all boats to Catalina. Those wishing to take camping gear should check in advance to be sure it is allowed. In general, take only light luggage since you will have to carry everything yourself. Special rates for groups of 20 or more are available; individual fares are $18 (one way) for adults; $16.25 for seniors; $13.50 for children.

OPPOSITE: Luxury yachts and ferries sway in the calm waters in Catalina's Avalon Harbor.

Los Angeles

IT TOOK A VERY TALENTED FOREIGNER TO EXPLAIN the role of Los Angeles in the cultural life of America. In accepting the 1988 Academy Award for best picture, Italian film director Bernardo Bertolucci said: "Los Angeles is the nipple of America."

This odd remark did not take long to draw the usual howls of derision from the East Coast. NBC broadcaster Willard Scott said Los Angeles was a nipple all right "because that's where all the boobs are." What Bertolucci meant, of course, was that the city provided nourishment to creative artists, not only in films but also in other areas.

It is easy enough to criticize Los Angeles. The city has the worst air pollution of any place in America. In fact, the word "smog" has become as closely identified with its name as fog once was with London. Hollywood, which brought it glamour and good times, also caused Los Angeles to become known as "Tinseltown," a place where nothing is permanent, where everything is cheap, tacky and temporary, and where dreams are more often of the broken kind.

To many East Coast opinion makers, "La La Land" or "El-Lay" is nothing more than the Los Angeles of Nathanael West's classic Hollywood novel, Day of the Locust, a surrealistic gathering of hordes of people desperately and hopelessly seeking their dream in Lotus-land.

This attitude fails to reckon with several facts. For one, the movies have not been the major industry in Los Angeles since World War II. The aerospace industry was king of the hill between the 1950s and the late 1980s. Now the economy is fueled by the ever-expanding service sector including corporate management, advertising, computer programming, legal services, health services and engineering. Meanwhile, Los Angeles is now America's primary import/export gateway with international trade in excess of $150 billion per year. With a metropolitan area population of more than 14.5 million, the city is now second only to New York (19.3 million) in population. While the image endures of Los Angeles as the rainbow's end for all those small-town mid-westerners seeking an earthly paradise, the facts are radically different, and the population now reflects an incredible diversity. People from 140 different countries call Los Angeles home, including the country's largest enclaves of Hispanics, Asians and Pacific Islanders. In fact, less than half the people living in the five-county Los Angeles metropolitan area are white.

In 1991, the streets of inner Los Angeles became a set for fire and vandalism in the aftermath of the Rodney King trials. These Los Angeles riots reawakened America to the potential for rampant destruction caused by racial tension and stress, factors unfortunately all too common in crowded inner city areas. The long-term ramifications of the riots have yet to be realized, yet it seems that little of the hostility and tension is likely to lessen in the near future. Although the factors of race and economic discrepancy figure into the daily lives of millions in Los Angeles and elsewhere, the physical and spiritual evidence of Los Angeles becoming a great American boom town is often apparent, and an air of vivacity and growth is omnipresent. It is just possible that the place will finally become a real city, and not merely a mass of suburbs in search of one.

BACKGROUND

FROM PUEBLO TO MEGALOPOLIS

However grand the skyline of Los Angeles has become today, it all began around a humble village of mud-adobe huts. The city's name dates to 1769 when a religious expedition of Spaniards, led by Gaspar de Portola, camped by the river on a spot in the heart of present-day downtown Los Angeles. They named the river for the **Río** Porciuncula, which flowed past Saint Francis' favorite chapel, the Nuestra Señora la Reina de los Angeles, the mother church of the Franciscan order. But by the time Governor Felipe de Neve led a band of 44 black, Native American and Spanish settlers to the spot, the name had been shortened to "Pueblo de la Reina de los Angeles." That, in turn, was shortened to "Los Angeles," which was the name adopted for the town and the county when California became part of the United States in 1850.

For most of its first hundred years, Los Angeles was little more than a village of a few hundred farmers and ranchers. After Mexican independence, the land was divided up into enormous ranchos. Among the new lords of these domains were dozens of "Yankee dons" who took Spanish first names, embraced Catholicism, married into the old families, and gained title to their own fiefdoms of hundreds of square miles. Incredibly, some of these families (like the Dominguez-Carson family on Rancho San Pedro, south of Los Angeles) held on to these lands until very recent years. Pio Pico, the last Mexican governor, was a Los Angeles resident who owned 531,263 acres (215,000 hectares) of Southern California; his neighbors included the Alvarados, Castros, Peraltas, and Vallejos. The names of these original dons are preserved in local street names. In the treaty ending the Mexican War, the United

PREVIOUS PAGES: Griffith Park Observatory and RIGHT Hollywood living. OPPOSITE: The downtown skyline TOP has served as a backdrop for countless movies filmed in Los Angeles. Mastering the maze of freeway exchanges BOTTOM is a challenge for Angelinos and their guests.

Los Angeles

States government agreed to respect Mexican ownership, but an act of Congress in 1851 allowed the vast ranches to be broken up.

The world's attention at that time was on the gold rush in Northern California, which indirectly benefited local residents when the overnight surge of immigrants to San Francisco and Sacramento created an insatiable market for Los Angeles livestock. But for the next two decades, Los Angeles continued as a dusty little speck on the map. It had such a bad reputation for violence that some said its name should be changed to El Diablo ("The Devil"). One contemporary observer noted: "Criminals, murderers, bandits and thieves were hung in accordance with the law or without the law, whichever was most convenient or expedient to the good of the town."

The violence reached its peak in 1871 when a vigilante mob went on a rampage and killed 19 Chinese after a Chinese man had accidentally killed a white man. This shocked the more responsible town fathers into action — especially after the incident made headlines in newspapers and magazines throughout the country. In a very short time, the local sponsors would be vitally concerned about outside opinion as they began the first of many boom periods to sell and develop real estate in the Los Angeles area.

In 1876, the city was connected to San Francisco by means of the Southern Pacific Railroad. This seemed to open up unlimited opportunities. Even greater markets were visualized in 1885 when the town's own transcontinental railroad, the Santa Fe line, was completed. For a while, competition was so fierce between the two railroads that the passenger fare from Kansas City to Los Angeles was only a dollar. The town of 12,000 exploded into a city of 50,000 in less than two years. Downtown property went for $1,000 a storefront. Seventy miles (113 km) of new developments were laid out from Santa Monica on the oceanfront all the way inland to San Bernardino. But the bubble burst in 1887. People were fleeing at the rate of 3,000 a month when railroad owners and local businessmen founded the Los Angeles Chamber of Commerce to restore confidence in local investments. The new slogans and publicity campaigns worked, and soon the city's population had doubled again, back to 50,000.

It didn't hurt that oil was discovered in an ordinary front yard by E.L. Doheny and C.A. Canfield. More than 1,400 oil derricks sprang up almost overnight in the area between downtown Los Angeles and Beverly Hills. Until very recent times, you could still see derricks at work in this area. These fields were eventually depleted, but

A stroll in Universal City Walk, Universal City, an oasis of shops, restaurants and cinemas, is one of Los Angeles' most visually exiting experiences.

THE NATURE COMPANY

in 1921, huge new oil fields were discovered south-west of the city, in and around Long Beach.

Some competition had existed between Los Angeles and San Diego, but with the arrival of the Santa Fe Railway, the discovery of oil, and the development of an artificial harbor at San Pedro, the former's commercial supremacy was assured. Water was a serious problem though, since the Los Angeles Basin gets less than 10 inches (255 mm) of rainfall a year, and is technically a desert. But that, too, was solved by a $22.5-million bond issue to build a viaduct that would transport the entire contents of the Owens River 238 miles (148 km) from the Eastern Sierras to Los Angeles.

The millions of dollars allotted for the early water projects gave rise to massive corruption involving some of the town's leading citizens. (Some of the corruption surrounding these projects was a backdrop to Roman Polanski's 1974 movie *Chinatown*.) For a start, the bond issue had only stipulated that the water be brought to the city limits, which meant the pipeline petered out in the arid San Fernando Valley north of Los Angeles. But that didn't prove to be a problem either. The city fathers simply took the city to the water by annexing what was then 108,000 acres (43,725 hect-ares) of desert wasteland, enriching themselves as well as the valley's landowners and property speculators.

It was the coincident development of the au-tomobile and moving pictures that really put Los Angeles on the map and helped it come into its own as a big city. New York and the cities of the East had developed long before the automobile and functioned quite well without it. But Los Angeles was too vast. It was dependent on the automobile: it was the world's first commuter city.

In the early days, people spoke with admira-tion of Los Angeles' grand boulevards that stretched from downtown 18 to 40 miles (30 to 65 km) in every direction. The celebrated freeway system did not begin until 1940, with construc-tion of the Arroyo Seco Parkway, now part of the Pasadena Freeway. But what was then a blessing has now become a curse. It's a shocking bit of déjà vu to experience the freeways now, with their gridlock and bumper-to-bumper traffic, and then to look at a picture of the original highways right after they were first opened. The word "freeway" was coined by a city planner in 1930 to connote "freedom from grade intersections, and from pri-vate entranceways, stores and factories." In Los Angeles, as one author noted, it also meant "the freedom of mobility and personal expression — that captured the hearts and imagination of An-gelenos." In one of his hit songs, Burt Bacharach says, "Los Angeles is a great big freeway," and Randy Newman, in his anthem to Los Angeles, sings: "We were born to ride."

THE MOVIES

Look for origins wherever you will, but it was the movies that put Los Angeles on the map and made it a place nearly everyone in the world wants to visit before dying. The 1939 *W.P.A. Guide to Cali-fornia* says Los Angeles "is known to the ends of the earth as the mother of Hollywood, that daz-zling daughter still sheltered under the family roof."

But, as mystery writer Raymond Chandler observed in *The Little Sister*, that relationship was never one of a happy family: "Real cities have something else, some individual bony structure under the muck. Los Angeles has Hollywood —

and hates it. It ought to consider itself damn lucky. Without Hollywood it would be a mail-order city. Everything in the catalogue you could get better somewhere else."

Originally planned as a temperance colony during the 1880s boom, Hollywood was just an-other suburb until 1911, when the first movie stu-dio opened there. Word spread like wildfire, and the town was soon overrun by actors and movie men. More important, the movies themselves became popular and sold. By the end of the 1920s, the movies were becoming Los Angeles' leading industry. With the development of sound film, they became even more important. Escapist entertain-ment was one of the few businesses making money, and during the height of the Depression, Louis B. Mayer was the highest-paid American executive.

With the coming of World War II, the movies took second place to the area's booming aerospace industry. Some of America's largest airplane manufacturers had grown up in the Los Angeles area because of the dry, warm climate. As fate would have it, they turned out to be convenient to the air bases backing up the massive air war in the Pacific. Allan Loughead (a name he changed to Lockheed) was a native California aviator who established what would become a major aerospace corporation, first in Santa Barbara, and later in Burbank. John K. Northrop was an engineer at Lockheed who founded his own corporation in 1928. Northrop later became part of the Douglas Aircraft Corporation, founded by Donald Douglas in an old movie studio in 1920. These are just three of the corporations that have remained at

trict, southeast of downtown Los Angeles. During five days of rioting in August 1965, 34 people were killed and more than 1,000 injured. More than $40 million worth of property was damaged. If violence in the ghetto didn't sink into the real estate-conscious city, the damage to property did. A state commission investigated and recommended more jobs, better housing and schools. The most enduring result of the riots was the election of a former policeman, Tom Bradley, as the city's first black mayor in 1973. While Bradley served as an symbol to his own people in the ghettos, he was often a rather lackluster leader. He failed in two attempts to become governor of the state, and he was eventually succeeded as mayor by a conservative white republican.

the top of the expanding aeronautics and space industry in America.

Like most of the rest of America, Los Angeles coasted through the 1950s, liking Ike and loving Lucy. Having a neat car and being able to go to the beach every day seemed like heaven to every kid in America. Dozens of movies and songs reflected that "California Dreamin'" was a national pastime. Even the social upheaval of the 1960s didn't rock the city as it did other places; the University of California at Los Angeles (UCLA) and the University of Southern California (USC) campuses were relatively calm compared to Berkeley. But in 1964, the *Los Angeles Free Press* became the first of the New Left counterculture publications. "The Freep" had a tremendous impact on young people nationwide and had many imitators.

Los Angeles was also the scene of the first big race riot of the 1960s. It took place in the Watts dis-

There was a time in the 1960s and 1970s when Hollywood seemed on the verge of becoming a hideous new Skid Row. Drug addicts and hustlers of every description had taken over the streets and many, if not most, of the grand old shops and stores along Hollywood and Sunset Boulevards had either closed down or were just barely making it. The movie industry started to disperse. There were new studios in Northern California and even as far away as North Carolina. But Hollywood merchants began a cleanup of their own streets. For every movie studio that left town, another exciting new one took its place. Once again, Los Angeles and Hollywood managed to endure, nay prevail. The Academy Awards didn't move to a

OPPOSITE: Foreign settings are common when filming occurs at Paramount Studios. ABOVE: Universal Studios has long presided over Los Angeles' most famous industry.

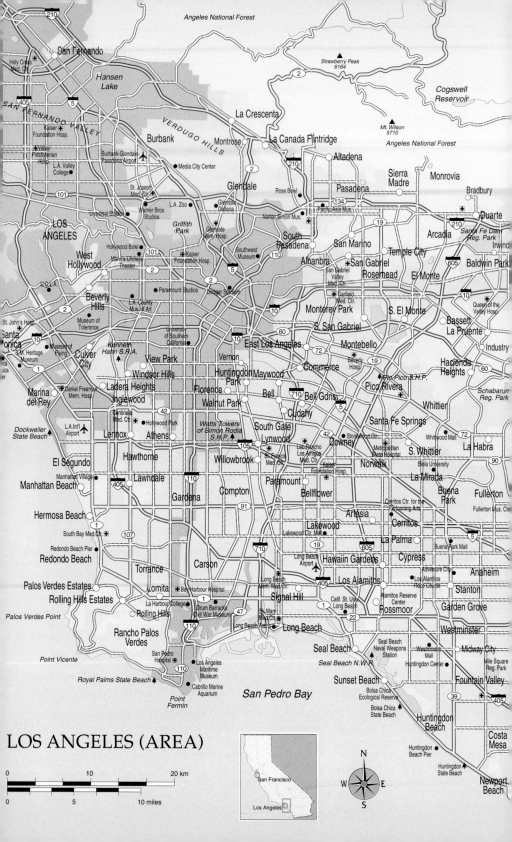

LOS ANGELES (AREA)

non-union town and, every year, millions of people around the world tune in to see a fabulous show and find out just who and what "The Academy" has deemed worthy of its highest awards.

A SOCIAL FOUNDRY

If Chicago suffers from a "Second City" inferiority complex to New York, Los Angeles has had to live with something much worse — being regarded as not quite worthy of serious consideration: in a word, tacky. *Spy* magazine once said that Los Angeles is where people go "to do everything they're too embarrassed to do in New York." Ronald Brownstein observed in the *Los*

backlash against the 1960s drew its first blood with the election of Ronald Reagan as governor in 1965. Environmentalism emerged as a powerful political force after the Santa Barbara oil spill in 1969. In the mid-1970s, Governor Edmund G. (Jerry) Brown sketched the first outlines of a liberalism with limits. And in 1978, crusty Howard Jarvis' Proposition 13 heralded the dawning of the antigovernment rebellion that swept Ronald Reagan into the Oval Office two years later. In the 1980s, California has pioneered the impersonal media- and money-based negative politics that now dominates national elections. All of these trends influenced the nation's life in meaningful ways, but they didn't really challenge the stereotypical view

Angeles Times Magazine: "In the national mythology, California, particularly Southern California, has always been on the front line of social trends. If California didn't initiate the postwar move to suburbia, it perfected it. In the early 1960s, the campus and inner-city unrest that eventually engulfed the nation crystallized in Berkeley and Watts. The singles scene that defined the anomie of the 1970s found its purest expression in the beach-front towns of Los Angeles; it was morning again in America here first, with Los Angeles, and then the nation, awaking to a solipsistic vision of sunshine, greed and the perfect biceps.

Along the way, Southern California also came to be seen as the spawning ground for political trends. The professionalization of politics — the creation of a priesthood of political consultants — began here in the mid-1960s. The conservative

of Los Angeles. Southern California's reputation as the nation's social foundry only reinforced its reputation for obsessively trendy quirkiness...."

But, as Brownstein went on to explain, many of the changes inspired by Los Angeles were not quirks. Suddenly, new and more serious attention was being paid to Los Angeles. He mentioned several authors who point out that immigration into Southern California — at a rate of 110,000 a year during the 1980s — may have exceeded the "historic rush of the huddled masses from Europe at the turn of the century." These new immigrants, largely from Asia and Latin America, have established a new mold for American culture: not the mythical "melting pot," but rather a "collage" of disparate cultures living peacefully side by side.

The faces of Los Angeles reveal its multicultural heritage.

On a less academic scale, Los Angeles has also arrived in that eastern bastion of trends and culture, New York City. The editor of New York's *Metropolitan Home* magazine said: "There are so many cultural signals coming from Los Angeles that are changing ways of socializing, of living at home." But if life in Los Angeles and Southern California is now being seriously scrutinized from the ivory towers of Manhattan, can cultural decline be far behind? Not likely. After all, "doing your own thing" was what made life in "La La Land" fun and different, and that's what brought on all the attention from the East. While the others figure out what it all means, Angelenos are likely to go on being themselves.

GENERAL INFORMATION

The **Los Angeles Convention & Visitors Bureau (LACVB)** ((213) 624-7300 FAX (213) 624-9746 or (213) 624-1992 has a head office located at 633 West Fifth Street, Suite 6000, Los Angeles 90071. LACVB maintains several visitor information centers including one in downtown Los Angeles ((213) 689-8822, 685 South Figueroa Street; and one in Hollywood ((213) 236-2331, 6541 Hollywood Boulevard. Both centers are open Monday to Saturday from 8:30 AM to 5 PM. The bureau also maintains a tourist information hotline TOLL-FREE (800) CATCH-LA.

Other tourist information outlets in the Los Angeles metropolitan region include:

Long Beach Area Convention & Visitors Bureau ((562) 436-3645 or (562) 436-6975, Suite 300, One World Trade Center, Long Beach 90821, whose walk-in tourist office is open Monday to Saturday from 8:30 AM to 5 PM.

Pasadena Convention & Visitors Bureau ((626) 795-9311 WEBSITE www.pasadenavisitor.org, 171 South Los Angeles Avenue, Pasadena 91101.

Redondo Beach Visitors Bureau ((310) 374-2171 TOLL-FREE (800) 282-0333 WEB SITE www.geninc.com, 200 North Pacific Coast Highway,

Redondo Beach 90277, with walk-in information available Monday to Friday from 8:30 AM to 5 PM.

Santa Monica Convention & Visitors Bureau (SMCVB) ((310) 393-7593 FAX (310) 319-6273 WEB SITE www.santamonica.com, 1400 Ocean Avenue, Santa Monica 90401. SMCVB has a visitor information kiosk on the Third Street Promenade.

San Fernando Valley Convention & Visitors Bureau ((818) 766-7572, PO Box 8549 Universal City 91608.

Santa Clarita Valley Tourism Bureau ((805) 259-4787 TOLL-FREE (800) 718-TOUR, Suite 129, 23920 Valencia Boulevard, Santa Clarita 91355.

WHAT TO SEE AND DO

HOLLYWOOD

When you hear someone say "I'm off to Hollywood" they don't necessarily mean the Los Angeles district that goes by that name. That's because "Hollywood" is both a geographical entity and a somewhat hazy state of mind that sprawls across the Los Angeles region.

Cheerleaders strut in a Los Angeles parade.

Hollywood (the neighborhood) lies a few miles northwest of downtown Los Angeles via the Hollywood Freeway (US Highway 101) with the busy intersection of Highland Avenue and Hollywood Boulevard as its major focus. It was born in the early 1920s as a real estate development. Although once the center of the movie industry, there are now very few studios (or cinemas) left in this part of town. You can still find the **Paramount** lot down on Melrose and Gower, but all of the other big silver screen factories are situated in other parts of town. **West Hollywood** is a small city unto itself, one of America's premier gay enclaves and a thriving center for alternative arts and lifestyles. Meanwhile, the **Sunset Strip**—the section of Sunset Boulevard between Crescent Heights and Doheny—remains the foremost focus of the American rock/pop music industry with numerous clubs and recording studios.

Hollywood (the industry) is most evident in the southeast corner of the San Fernando Valley and Los Angeles' west side where most of the major studios make their homes today. Burbank plays host to **Disney**, **Warner Bros.**, and **NBC**. **Universal** has its own "city" on the south side of Burbank. **Twentieth Century Fox** perches on Pico Boulevard between Beverly Hills and Rancho Park. **Sony Pictures** has taken over the old MGM lot in Culver City (where classics like *The Wizard of Oz* and *Gone With the Wind* were filmed). Mega director Steven Spielberg keeps his Amblin Entertainment office on the Universal back lot, but his new **DreamWorks** studio is down in the Westchester area near Marina Del Rey. Most of the independent production companies that actually make today's movies are located in Westwood, Santa Monica and adjacent areas. And most of the big premiers are held in Westwood Village, which is now the world's single largest concentration of movie theaters.

So what's left in Hollywood? Plenty if you take the time to research and explore. Hollywood Boulevard is currently in the midst of a major renaissance brought about by new development and increased police vigilance that has forced most of the hookers and pushers down to Sunset. It's still a bit strange after dark, but tourists flood the boulevard by daylight to see the street that once personified Hollywood glitz and glamour.

The stretch of Hollywood Boulevard between La Brea and Gower, and the blocks of Vine Street between Yucca and Sunset, feature the **Hollywood Walk of Fame** ((213) 922-2712 or (213) 922-2700. More than 2,500 granite stars bearing bronze medallions are set into the sidewalks to honor movie, television, radio, theater or recording personalities, with more being added all the time. In 1994, 222 celebrity star panels between Vine and Gower streets were removed to facilitate the construction of the new subway, but they are now being reinstalled. Some of the more popular sites include Elvis Presley (6777 Hollywood Boulevard), John Lennon (1750 Vine Street), James Dean (1719 Vine Street) and Marilyn Monroe (6744 Hollywood Boulevard). The sidewalk stars eventually lead to **Mann's Chinese Theater** ((213) 464-8111, 6925 Hollywood Boulevard, a bizarre pseudo-Oriental concoction that harbors both a movie theater where many film premiers are staged and a famous courtyard where numerous stars have left their shoe and hand prints in the concrete over the years. Silent film star Norma Talmadge kicked off the trend in 1927 and every major star has followed suit.

The latest addition to Hollywood Boulevard is the **Hollywood Entertainment Museum** ((213) 465-7900, 7021 Hollywood Boulevard, which takes you behind the scenes of your favorite movies, television programs and radio shows including restored sets (*Star Trek* and *Cheers*) and a replica backlot with prop shops and wardrobe. There are also interactive stations and multimedia exhibits, as well as an education wing which allows visitors hands-on involvement in film production. It is open daily from 10 AM to 6 PM. Nearby is another stimulating experience, the **Frederick's of Hollywood Museum** ((213) 466-8506, 6608 Hollywood Boulevard, with an exhibition of lingerie dating back to 1946. The **Celebrity Lingerie Hall of Fame** pays tribute to the stars that donned some of these glamorous undergarments, from old-timers like Joan Crawford and Doris Day to modern-day sirens like Cher and Madonna. It is open Monday to Saturday from 10 AM to 6 PM; Sunday from noon to 5 PM, and admission is free.

The famous **Hollywood sign** that lingers in the background of so many photos perches on a mountainside above the neighborhood. Erected in 1923, the 50-ft (15-m)-high monument can be found at the top of Beachwood Canyon. Anyone who ventures to climb it will likely get arrested.

With so many ghosts from the past and skeletons in the closet, Hollywood has its fair share of cemeteries. Charlie Chaplin, Rudolph Valentino, Cecil B. De Mille and Douglas Fairbanks are pushing up daisies at **Hollywood Memorial Park** next to the Paramount Studios. Glendale's **Forest Lawn** features the graves of Clark Gable, Jean Harlow, Walt Disney, George Burns and Errol Flynn. **Holy Cross Cemetery** in Culver City is the last resting place of Bing Crosby, Gary Cooper, Bela Lugosi, Rita Hayworth and John Candy. While **Westwood Village Memorial Park** near the UCLA campus harbors the plots of Marilyn Monroe, Natalie Wood, Truman Capote, Dean Martin, Roy Orbison and Frank Zappa.

Down in the Fairfax neighborhood just south of Hollywood is **Farmers Market** ((213) 933-9211 WEB SITE www.farmersmarketla.com, 6333 West Third Street. This is a good place to have breakfast before your Hollywood tour or break for lunch around midday. It's also one of the best places in Los Angeles to hunt for tacky souvenirs. The market features more than 100 stalls for fruit, vegetables, meat, cheeses, bread, ice cream, flowers, arts and crafts, and tourist kitsch. You can also choose from an array of restaurants and food stalls. There is communal seating, which means you can choose your entree from one stall, your dessert from another and then eat anywhere that feels right. The market is open Monday to Saturday from 9 AM to 7 PM and Sunday from 10 AM to 6 PM.

Studio Tours
Universal Studios ((818) 622-3801 WEBSITE www
.universalstudios.com, PO Box 8620, Universal City 91608, in the San Fernando Valley (follow the Lankershim or Universal Center exits from the Hollywood Freeway), bills itself as the world's biggest and busiest television and motion picture studio theme park. Visitors can fill their day experiencing rides and watching shows featuring state-of-the-art special effects and explosive stunts or just wander around interacting with the kids' favorite movie and television characters.

The new Jurassic Park ride features some of the most advanced animatronics ever designed. The six-acre (two-and-a-half-hectare) attraction puts you face to face with 65-million-year-old reptiles including an eight-story high Tyrannosaurus Rex. And if that's not enough, before the ride ends you'll go head first down an 82-foot, heart-stopping water plunge.

Another new addition is Totally Nickelodeon which features interactive games and stunts from the popular children's television network as well as the trademark green slime that is dispensed on volunteer guests. Other popular rides and attractions include Back to the Future, E.T. (The Extraterrestrial), Waterworld, Backdraft, Beetlejuice and the Wild Wild West, as well as the Backlot Tram Tour with its simulated earthquake and King Kong attack. It is open in summer from 8 AM to 10 PM and during other months from 9 AM to 7 PM. Admission is $38 for adults and $28 for children.

For a more authentic slice of Hollywood try the **Paramount Studios Guided Tour (** (213) 956-1777, 5555 Melrose Avenue. This two-hour tour, packed with historical information, takes a close look at the daily operations of a working film and television production facility. No two tours are exactly alike due to ongoing production activities. Tours depart hourly Monday to Friday from 9 AM to 2 PM. No children under 10 years old are allowed. Admission is $15 per person. Tickets to **television shows** taped on the Paramount lot must

Hollywood's famous row of stars recall their portrayals on the big screen.

Los Angeles

be booked at least a week in advance. Most network shows film between September and April.

Serious film buffs will also appreciate the **Warner Bros. VIP Studio Tour (** (818) 954-6534 or (818) 972-TOUR, Olive Avenue, Burbank. This two-hour drive and walk "behind the scenes" includes a stop at the new **Warner Bros. Museum** which features artifacts spanning 75 years of the film and television production. The museum is open Monday to Friday from 9 AM to 4 PM and Saturday from 10 AM to 2 PM (summer only). Admission is $29 per person.

The only television network that offers a regular tour is **NBC Studio (** (818) 840-3537, 3000 West Alameda Avenue, Burbank. This 70-minute walk through NBC broadcasting complex includes a visit to the special effects (FX) set. Frequent tours are given on weekdays between 9 AM and 3 PM with extended hours during summer and holiday seasons. Admission is $7 for adults, $3.75 for children age 5 to 12, and children under five are free. Tickets for Jay Leno's *Tonight Show* are given out at 8 AM on the day of taping at the NCB Studio ticket booth, with a limit of two tickets per person. To find out who will be appearing on the next show call **(** (818) 840-3537.

BEVERLY HILLS

While Hollywood itself has gone through a rough cycle to match the broken dreams of one of its stars, the city of Beverly Hills has remained what it was and always has been: an elegant enclave of the super rich. It's probably the cleanest, most well kept city in America, well-known for the efficiency of its firemen, police, garbage collectors, lawyers, restaurants, doctors, and banks, and its tennis courts and swimming pools.

Bought by property developers from Beverly Farms, Massachusetts in 1906, Beverly Hills was planned from the beginning as a place of large public gardens and huge private estates along curving palm-lined boulevards. The lavish Beverly Hills Hotel, built in 1912, set the tone. And, as can be said of few places in America, that very high tone has somehow endured. By 1920, Beverly Hills had only 674 residents; and a more recent count (1990) showed only 31,971. This city within a city is famous mainly for its beautiful estates. It's not only the favored home of movie stars, but also where a number of Texas and Arab oil barons choose to live, alongside Greek shipping tycoons. Even millionaire televangelist Oral Roberts has a home here.

Pickfair, 1143 Summit Drive, the home built by Douglas Fairbanks and Mary Pickford, was the social focal point of Beverly Hills from 1920 to 1935. When they separated in 1935, Mary Pickford continued to live there in seclusion until her death in 1980. Another fashionable house, **Greystone**

Mansion, was built by E. L. Doheny and housed the America Film Institute for a time. For the more curious, maps of the stars' homes can be bought on street corners along Sunset Boulevard.

To fashionable women around the world, Beverly Hills is the home of Rodeo Drive, between Wilshire and Santa Monica Boulevards, one of planet's the most famous and expensive shopping streets. You won't come here looking for bargains. Nearly all of the shops are in old two- and three-story buildings and you'll find the mood here surprisingly low-key. Many of the restaurants are expensive, but there are just as many with reasonably priced food, affordable to those who also work in the area.

A note about the peculiarities of Beverly Hills: it's not the best-kept city without a reason. Beverly Hills has its own set of laws. Beware of overnight car parking, as there are all sorts of special regulations, and one must read the signs carefully. You will also notice that signs are particularly small and that publicity posters are prohibited. A walk through the streets is a bit difficult. For one thing, you may be stopped by the police for loitering, so make sure you have proof of identity. If you really want to see the houses of the stars, it may be best to take a bus tour.

DOWNTOWN LOS ANGELES

Not many years ago, people would have laughed at you if you had talked about going downtown for anything. It was, of course, here that the original pueblo and then the city of Los Angeles began. But the city quickly spread out and forgot about its place of origin. The marvelous art-deco **City Hall,** erected during the boom years of the 1920s, loomed for years as the city's tallest building — although it surely gained more fame in the

Rodeo Drive ABOVE, is Beverly Hills' trendiest shopping street, while the Civic Center OPPOSITE is one of Los Angeles' many modern architectural gems.

movies as the "Daily Planet" building where Superman worked as newspaper reporter Clark Kent.

The real estate and stock market bust of 1929 was especially hard on downtown Los Angeles which owed its very existence to wild speculators. In the 1950s and 1960s, the downtown area seemed destined for decay and total abandonment as grand new business districts sprang up in the outlying areas. However, in the early 1970s, a spectacular downtown renaissance began, creating a real city where none had previously existed. The round glass towers of the **Westin Bonaventure Hotel** were soon dwarfed by other skyscrapers housing offices, condominiums and other hotels, as well as some of the city's best shopping galler-

ies and malls. New theaters sprang up in the downtown area and construction of the **Museum of Contemporary Art** enhanced the area's cultural fare. As for older structures, the **Regal Biltmore Hotel** has been restored to its former elegance when it was the toast of Hollywood.

Just as Walt Disney constantly reminded his people that "it all began with a mouse," Angelenos should remember that their grand modern city began with a tiny pueblo of mud-adobe huts. Remarkably, some of that original pueblo has survived and is preserved a few blocks from all the steel-and-glass skyscrapers.

The historic district is centered around the old plaza bounded by Main, Los Angeles and Marchessault streets, near the beginning of Sunset

Boulevard, in the area known as **El Pueblo de Los Angeles State Historic Park**. The plaza dates to 1800, when it replaced an earlier town square wiped out in a flood. Adjacent to the plaza is the **Old Plaza Firehouse**, a museum with photographs and fire-fighting equipment from the nineteenth century. Its brick building dates from 1884 when it was an inn, boarding-house and shop.

The restoration of **Olvera Street**, just off the plaza, began in 1929. Today it's a colorful Mexican market street full of stalls and shops set among the historic old adobe and brick buildings, many of them either museums or restaurants. **Avila Adobe** at 14 Olvera Street is the oldest existing house in Los Angeles. Built in 1818 by the Spanish mayor, it was only one wing of an 18-room adobe mansion that remained in his family for the next 40 years. After an earthquake of 1971, it was fully restored into an excellent example of a prosperous 1840s Spanish residence. It is open Monday to Friday from 10 AM to 3 PM and weekends from 10 AM to 4:30 PM.

La Golondrina building at 35 Olvera Street is a two-story brick house built before 1865 as a winery. The **Plaza Church**, also called Our Lady Queen of Angels, is a historic structure that still functions as a parish church. To walk into the enormous dark chapel is to step back into old Mexico. It was built between 1818 and 1822 by "Jose" Chapman, one of the Yankee dons. It now belongs to the archbishopric of Los Angeles.

A few other buildings near the plaza are of special interest. **Masonic Hall (** (213) 628-1274, 416 North Main Street, is one of the oldest temples of freemasonry in the city. The building, with its wrought iron balcony, is reminiscent of the Italian Renaissance style. Admission is free. It is open Tuesday through Friday from 10 AM to 3 PM. **Pico House**, 430 Main Street, was built in 1869 in the style of an Italian palazzo. Originally belonging to Pio Pico, the last Mexican governor of California, it was for many years the primary hotel in Los Angeles and is now a private house. **Pelanconi House**, 17 West Olvera Street, another private dwelling, was the city's first brick home. It was named after its second owner, the Italian Antonio Pelanconi.

The **Visitor Center (** (213) 628-1274 for El Pueblo de Los Angeles State Historic Park is located in the Sepulveda Building on North Main Street and is open Monday to Friday from 10 AM to 3 PM, Saturday from 10 AM to 4:30 PM. It offers films and pamphlets on the early history of the pueblo and general information on many of the attractions.

LITTLE TOKYO

Japanese immigrants have arriving in Southern California since the turn of the century and now

Downtown's highrises and promenades are packed during office hours and virtually empty on quiet weekends.

210

Los Angeles

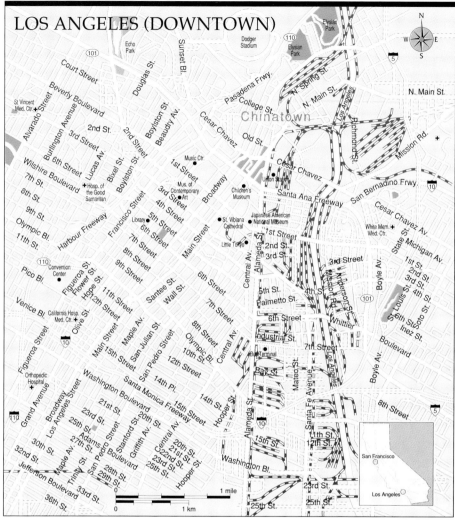

LOS ANGELES (DOWNTOWN)

number around 200,000. But Little Tokyo is a fairly recent phenomenon, largely developed since the 1960s. The neighborhood is a fun and exotic place to wander about, especially good for sampling sushi and sashimi in the various little restaurants. Two local favorites are **Sushi Gen** ((213) 617-0552, 422 East Second Street, and **Hama Sushi** ((213) 680-3454, 347 East Second Street.

The **Japanese American Cultural and Community Center** ((213) 628-2725, 244 South San Pedro Street, has a theater, gallery and library devoted to the Japanese arts. Kabuki and noh groups often appear here, and there are regular performances of bunraku and puppet theater. The gallery has several exhibitions each year on Japanese art, and the library has many current periodicals and books in Japanese and English, including works on Japanese-American relations. The

gallery is open Tuesday to Sunday from noon to 5 PM. The library is open Tuesday to Friday from noon to 5 PM, Saturday from 10 AM to 4 PM, and Sunday from noon to 4 PM.

The **plaza** in front of the cultural center was designed by the Japanese-American sculptor Isamu Noguchi and dedicated to the *issei*, first-generation Japanese immigrants to America. Through the basement of the center you can enter the symbolic garden, half Japanese and half American. Just around the corner is the fascinating **Japanese American National Museum** ((213) 625-0414, 369 East First Street, the world's largest collection of Japanese-American artifacts and documents.

Japanese Village Plaza ((213) 620-8861, 335 East Second Street, is an open square surrounded by all kinds of Japanese shops and restaurants. Each August, the Little Tokyo neighborhood hosts a **Nisei Week Festival** ((213) 687-7193 that highlights various forms of Japanese culture.

CHINATOWN

Los Angeles's Chinatown may not compare in size or splendor with the San Francisco version, but it's amazing that such a large and historic quarter has survived at all given the phenomenal growth of Los Angeles over the last 50 years. Chinese coolies provided much of the labor on the Southern Pacific Railroad and when the tracks reached the end of the line at Los Angeles, many of them settled nearby. Their descendants have managed to hold on to the shops and restaurants in the area — largely because nobody else wanted them.

The heart of Chinatown is the 900 block of North Broadway. These are authentic Chinese places so don't expect too much in the way of decorations and furnishings. One of the better restaurants is **Mon Kee Seafood** ((213) 628-6717, 679 North Spring Street.

MUSEUMS

For a long time, East Coast snobs looked down their noses on Los Angeles as a cultural wasteland — or worse, as a garbage heap of tacky stuff nobody would describe as art. But Southern California now boasts some of the world's finest collections, the likes of which you will find no place else.

Getty Center

The amazing **Getty Center** ((310) 440-7300, 1200 Getty Center Drive, is the most important art museum built in America during the last 30 years and truly one of the world's great collections. Unveiled in December of 1997, permanent exhibits run a gamut from pre-twentieth-century European masters to twentieth-century American photography with important works by Mantegna (*Adoration of the Magi*) and Van Gogh (*Irises*) as well as Rembrandt, Rubens, Cezanne, Renoir and Monet.

Perched on a commanding hilltop above Brentwood, the building itself (designed by Richard Meier) is a work of art. Built at a cost of $1 billion, the complex also includes the offices for the various art institutes and grant programs endowed by the Getty Trust, as well as an advanced art study center, library, theater, bookstore and gardens. It is already considered one of the world's very best facilities for art students and scholars.

The Getty Center is open Tuesday and Wednesday from 11 AM to 7 PM, Thursday and Friday from 11 AM to 9 PM, and Saturday and Sunday from 10 AM to 6 PM. There is no charge for admission, however, the rich neighbors don't allow parking

on nearby streets, and thus parking is very limited, costing $5 and requiring reservations made well in advance. A tram takes visitors from the parking lot to the entrance. Taxis and public buses (MTA 561 and Santa Monica Blue Bus 14) can also take you to the front entrance.

The original **J. Paul Getty Museum** is situated at 17985 Pacific Coast Highway in Malibu, between Sunset Boulevard and Topanga Canyon Boulevard, roughly 25 miles (40 km) west of downtown Los Angeles. Currently undergoing a four-year renovation, the museum is due to open again in 2001 when the collection will focus on ancient Roman and Greek art.

Tycoon philanthropist J. Paul Getty, whose trust funded both museums, was not only the world's richest man, but also one of the most cantankerous and selfish who ever lived. Selfish is hardly the word one would use to describe a man who

left $2.2 billion, the bulk of his estate, to a public art museum. But even in this final act of seeming generosity to the public, Getty was being spiteful toward his own children. A curse on the family was how one biographer described it.

Getty's family members were provided for through various trusts, but the billionaire in a late codicil to his will decided to leave nearly all his estate to the original J. Paul Getty Museum in Malibu. In a sensational kidnapping case played up by the press, he had refused to even consider paying ransom after his grandson and namesake was abducted in Italy — until the boy's severed ear was sent to him. (J. Paul Getty III never recovered from the trauma.)

The Getty Museum started in the tycoon's former home in Malibu, a magnificent ranch with a sweeping view of the Pacific. It first opened to the public in 1953. A new wing was added to the

house for his burgeoning art collection, but even this became too small. At first, Getty wanted to build a copy of his huge English country house to display his collection. An architect talked him out of it, but could not change his mind about reconstructing a fabulous Roman villa covered by lava when Mount Vesuvius erupted in AD 79. In the study of his English house, Getty pored over plans and spent whole days going over the scale model for the Los Angeles museum. Oddly, however, he never visited it during construction or after it was opened in 1974.

With the multi-billion dollar bequest on Getty's death in 1976, the museum became the richest art museum in the world. As his biographer Russell

---

Striking architecture and an overwhelming art collection make the Getty Center one of the world's premier art museums.

Miller wrote in *The House of Getty*, even this last act of philanthropy was tainted: The Getty Museum became feared for its wealth and ability to pillage the global art market.

The original Getty collection comprised Greek and Roman antiquities, French decorative art, and European paintings from the early fourteenth to the late nineteenth century. Needless to say, the museum's collections have greatly expanded. But fears that this California upstart was going to vanquish the world art market turned out to be unfounded. It just didn't happen. More important, the museum directors wisely decided to spend more of their multimillion dollar annual budget on education and research. In 1985, the Getty Museum purchased a 105-acre (42.5-hectare) tract in the Santa Monica Mountains near the University of California at Los Angeles campus and began construction of the 450,000 sq ft (41,800 sq m) Getty Center.

In 1989, the museum went even further in its public service outreach when it launched a huge cooperative program to assist the government of China in preserving many of its antiquities. At the rate it's going, the museum may well outlive the man's reputation and the Getty name may come to stand for something besides greed and selfishness.

Los Angeles County Museum of Art

Another local collection that has grown in stature in recent years is the **Los Angeles County Museum of Art** ((213) 857-6111 WEB SITE www.lacma.org, 9505 Wilshire Boulevard. LACMA (as locals call it) is well worth a visit. The Anderson Building houses twentieth-century painting and sculptures like Matisse, Degas, Gauguin and Magritte. The Ahmanon Building houses the permanent collection and includes the country's largest assortment of textiles and costumes. The Japanese Pavilion is the newest wing and houses a extensive collection of Edo paintings. The Hammer Building is used mainly for visiting exhibitions. Open Tuesday to Thursday from 10 AM to 5 PM, Friday from 10 AM to 9 PM, and Saturday and Sunday from 11 AM to 6 PM, admission is $6 for adults, $1 for children age 6 to 17.

George C. Page Museum

Visitors to Los Angeles will find all kinds of unusual sights to behold, but some of the most extraordinary are those very carefully preserved at the George C. Page Museum ((213) 936-2230, right next to LACMA. One is amazed to come across anything in Los Angeles that has survived the last hundred years, but here you will find a whole museum devoted to Ice Age relics unearthed from

the adjacent **La Brea Tar Pits**. The original Indian inhabitants of this area, as well as early Spanish and Mexican residents, used the tar (*la brea*) to waterproof their baskets, among other things. The first fossils were discovered in 1906, leading to the extraordinary discoveries that are still going on. The big earthquake in 1971 opened new pockets of tar that bubbled up through the surface, and museum construction in the mid-1970s revealed another treasure of prehistoric animal skeletons.

A tour of the museum begins with a film that explains the prehistory of the area, and how and why thousands of animals were trapped in the tar pits (some had come for water and got stuck, others came to eat them and then got stuck themselves). Whatever the cause, the tar preserved the bones and literally thousands of complete skeletons of dozens of extinct animals. Most notable are the huge mastodons and mammoths, but the remains of ancient camels, saber-tooth tigers and other extinct North American species have also been found. In one part of the museum, you can observe the meticulous preservation work going on — tiny insects being pieced together in one section, 30-ft (nine-meter)-high mastodons in another.

The Page Museum is open Tuesday to Sunday from 10 AM to 5 PM. Admission is $6 for adults, $2 for children, and $3.50 for seniors.

Museum of Contemporary Art (MOCA)

Another world-class showcase is the **Museum of Contemporary Art** ((213) 626-6222 WEB SITE www .moca-la.org, 250 South Grand. *Los Angeles Times* columnist Jack Smith describes this downtown landmark as an "architectural bonbon: red terracotta boxes under glass pyramids with a great glass drum on top. It looks like a tiny carved jewel box against the bunch of skyscrapers on Bunker Hill." Others describe the museum building, designed by Japanese architect Arata Isozaki, as a "toy box." Aside from the permanent collection, MOCA also features an outstanding schedule of changing exhibits.

The $6 ticket (children under 11 are free) to MOCA also gets you into the **Geffen Temporary Contemporary**, located in an enormous warehouse at 152 North Central Street (at First Street) in Little Tokyo. Designed as a short-term home for the MOCA collection, the Temporary proved so popular that it became a permanent fixture and the building was renovated by renowned architect Frank Gehry. Later endowed by music industry mogul David Geffen, the collection's official name is the Geffen Contemporary at MOCA.

Autry Museum of Western Heritage

Dedicated to the "real and fictional" heroes of the Wild West, the **Autry Museum** ((213) 667-

---

The main courtyard in the J. Paul Getty Museum OPPOSITE is a copy of a Roman country villa destroyed by the eruption of Mount Vesuvius.

2000 WEB SITE www.questorsys.com/autry-museum/, 4700 Western Heritage Way, sits on the eastern edge of Griffith Park. This $5-million facility opened in late 1988 to widespread approval and is one of the country's best cowboy collections. The exhibits consist of historic documents, costumes, firearms, paintings and art objects like Frederic Remington sculptures. Included, of course, are those giants of the silver screen, the great (if imagined) American cowboy, of which Gene Autry was one the greatest. Open Tuesday to Sunday from 10 AM to 5 PM and on some Monday holidays, admission is $7.50 for adults, $5 for seniors and students, and $3 for children ages 2 to 12.

Museum of Tolerance

One of newest collections on the Los Angeles scene is the **Museum of Tolerance** ((310) 553-8403 WEB SITE www.wiesenthal.com, 9786 West Pico Boulevard. This high-tech, experimental museum near Century City is designed to expose prejudices in America and the history of the Holocaust, as well as to teach tolerance.

In the Holocaust section, visitors are given photo passports with the stories of a child's experience during the Holocaust, updated during the tour. At the end you learn the fate of the child. The "Tolerancenter" includes an interactive exhibit designed to help visitors identify their own prejudices, while the Multimedia Learning Center uses touch screen technology to provide information about World War II and the Holocaust. The museum also features an arts and lectures program.

Open Monday to Thursday from 10 AM to 4 PM, Friday from 10 AM to 1 PM (November to March) or 10 AM to 3 PM (April to October), and Sunday from 11 AM to 5 PM, the museum is closed on Saturdays and Jewish holidays. Admission is $8 for adults and $3 for children age 3 to 10.

California Science Center

Formally the California Museum of Science and Industry, the **California Science Center** ((213) 744-7400, 700 State Drive in Exposition Park, recently reopened after major renovation into a top-flight science education facility. It now offers interactive exhibits, live programming and a multitude of opportunities to explore science through tour themes: World of Life, Creative World, World of the Pacific and Worlds Beyond. There's also an IMAX theater with a seven-story high screen. Open daily from 10 AM to 5 PM, admission is free except for IMAX, which costs $6 for adults, $4.75 for those age 18 to 21, and $4 for children.

Dodger Stadium OPPOSITE, TOP located just off the freeways near the downtown and football BELOW at Rose Bowl Pasadena.

Museum of Neon Art (MONA)

Formerly housed in a warehouse in Little Tokyo, the **Museum of Neon Art** ((213) 626-3187 now has its main exhibition space on the ground floor of the Renaissance Tower in downtown Los Angeles This delightful museum features the latest in modern neon design and technology in exhibits such as "Eclectic Electric." Also on exhibit are older forms of neon from theater marquees and signs. The museum is open Tuesday to Saturday form 11 AM to 5 PM. Admission is $2.50 for adults; children are free. In addition to the exhibits, MONA sponsors bus tours of neon highlights in the Los Angeles area, as well as classes on neon design and technique.

SPECIAL WAYS TO SEE LOS ANGELES

Perhaps Los Angeles was built on four tires, but you can also explore it on two feet. **Hiking in L.A.** ((818) 501-1005 TOLL-FREE (800) 501-1006 FAX (818) 501-2005, JRT International, 14755 Ventura Boulevard, Sherman Oaks, offers walking and hiking tours on scenic trails in the Santa Monica Mountains. Alternatively you can explore urban trails to get a perspective on history, view landmarks and discover the many attractions downtown Los Angeles has to offer. Prices start at $25 per person.

See Hollywood through the tinted windows of a mortuary hearse on a **Graveline Tour** ((213) 469-4149 of places where celebrities took their last breaths and are now buried.

Another unusual way to explore the Southland is from the air. **Group 3 Aviation Inc** ((818) 994-9376 FAX (818) 994-9384 WEB SITE www.group3aviation .com, 16425 Hart Street, offers personal helicopter tours of the Los Angeles area. Prices range from $90 per person for a "Movie Tour" to $170 per person for "The Grand Tour."

Bravo Wing ((310) 325-9565 TOLL-FREE (800) 77 FLYING, 3401 Airport Drive in Torrance, offers a variety of packages from nostalgic flights above Los Angeles in an authentic North American T-6 Fighter to a thrill-seeker's flight in the newest high-tech aerobatics plane. You can also organize customized aerial sightseeing tours at $88 per hour.

SPORTS

Maybe it's because there's so much else to do, or because there are a number of world-class **golf courses** only an hour or two away, but whatever the explanation, golf has never developed as a major pastime in Los Angeles. Many of the golf courses in the area are affiliated with private clubs and closed to the public except to reciprocal members of other clubs.

There are several municipal golf courses in Los Angeles and the adjacent towns and cities. The most popular city-run facility is **Rancho Park Golf Course** ((310) 838-7373, 10460 West Pico Boule-

vard, allegedly the world's busiest golf links. Griffith Park ((213) 663-2555, features two 18-hole courses, named Harding and Wilson after two early twentieth-century American presidents.

If you happen to catch a winning season with any of the **professional sports** teams located in the Los Angeles area, you'll think you're back in small-town America as a wacky mix of celebrities and plain folk shout their heads off for the home team. Movie star Jack Nicholson, for example, never misses a Lakers basketball game. Indeed, the sports and movie industries often overlap. Disney owns the Angels baseball and Mighty Ducks ice hockey teams. Fox recently purchased the Los Angeles Dodgers baseball franchise.

Angeles, one of the most attractive facilities in the major leagues. The **Anaheim Angels** ((714) 940-2159 take to the field at brand-new Edison Field near Disneyland. The **Mighty Ducks** ((714) 704-2701 or (714) 740-2000 face off against NHL opponents at the nearby Anaheim Pond while the **Los Angeles Galaxy** ((213) 817-KICK professional soccer team kicks off at the Rose Bowl in Pasadena.

College sports is also big in the Southland including the arch-rivalry between UCLA and Southern Cal (USC). UCLA is a traditional basketball power, USC one of the country's most vaunted football programs, but the universities field good teams in just about every imaginable

Home games of the National Basketball Association's **Lakers** ((310) 419-3100 take place in the Great Western Forum, located at Manchester Boulevard and Prairie Avenue in Inglewood. The Forum is also where the **Los Angeles Kings** ((310) 673-6003 of the National Hockey League (NHL) play their home games. Note: The Lakers and the Kings are scheduled to host their home games at the new state-of-the-art Staples Center in downtown Los Angelos beginning in October 1999, when it is slated to open. In addition to major sporting events, the Forum also stages a wide variety of musical and other stage performances. The city's other NBA franchise is the **Clippers** ((213) 748-8000 who make their home at the downtown Sports Arena.

The metropolitan area supports two major-league baseball teams. The **Dodgers** ((213) 224-1491 play at Dodger Stadium in downtown Los

sport. For information on athletic events at University of Southern California ((213) 740-GOSC WEB SITE www.usctrojans.com; for information on University of California at Los Angeles athletics ((310) 542-8525 WEB SITE www.uclabruins.com.

SHOPPING

Beverly Hills is the premiere shopping place in Los Angeles. Along **Rodeo Drive** and its cross streets, you will find nearly all of the world's most famous fashion designers — Giorgio Armani, Louis Vuitton, Christian Dior and Valentino just to name a few — as well as Tiffany, Cartier and Fred Hayman. In spite of its great wealth, Beverly Hills has managed to keep its shopping district on a low-key village scale — although quite an expensive one.

Another shopping area that has "just growed" in recent years is **Melrose Avenue**. While it hasn't replaced Rodeo Drive, it does offer a more casual and picturesque alternative. For many years, it was an ordinary run-down street, running parallel to and in-between Santa Monica Boulevard and Beverly Boulevard near West Hollywood's beloved "blue whale" **Design Center**. The area started as a middle-class neighborhood of cottages with well-tended yards and gardens. In recent years, the "cottages" have become high-priced homes and the once run-down shops have become quite fashionable. Here you will find an abundance of antique stores, some of the city's finest restaurants, and dozens of unique designer

se, but a long stretch of asphalt where street vendors and novelty shops rule the roost, making it a great place to buy T-shirts, sunglasses and other warm weather paraphernalia.

But Los Angeles being one vast suburb, the most popular shopping places are the shopping centers, malls, and galleries. Here is a list of some of the city's most intriguing indoor shopping centers:

Beverly Center ((213) 854-0070, 8500 Beverly Boulevard (at La Cienaga), offers world-class shopping including Macy's and Bloomingdale's department stores, and luxury boutiques like Chanel, Gucci, Versace, Armani, Shauna Stein and Dona Karan, not to mention cinema and restaurants.

shops that have given "California style" a new and respectable name even in New York.

Westwood Village is more or less a teenage version of Rodeo Drive, packed with youthful shops that cater to the 35,000 students who attend nearby University of California at Lost Angeles. Coffee shops, cafés and movie theaters are also abundant in the village, although parking is sometimes a problem. Down by the ocean is Santa Monica's popular **Third Street Promenade,** a former skid row area that was transformed into a faddish pedestrian street with shops, restaurants, cinemas — and topiary sculptures of dinosaurs. Third Street is great for people watching and one of the Southland's more pleasant spots to while away a sunny summer afternoon because you can always pop down to the beach if the weather gets too hot. Even closer to the waves is the **Venice Beach Boardwalk**, not a wooden boardwalk per

Bonaventure Shopping Gallery ((213) 687-0680, 404 South Figueroa Street, is perhaps the best of the downtown malls, the gallery features six levels of shops in the Westin Bonaventure Hotel.

Century City Shopping Center and Marketplace ((310) 277-3898, 10250 Santa Monica Boulevard at Avenue of the Stars, is one of the region's best malls and comprises 140 stores including Bloomingdale's, Joan & David, Talbots, Crate & Barrel and Rand McNally (maps and guidebooks), as well as Steven Spielberg's submarine theme restaurant (Dive!) and a cinema complex.

Citadel Factory Stores ((213) 888-1220, Interstate 5 (Washington Boulevard or Atlantic Boule-

OPPOSITE: Shopping is a major preoccupation for the fashionable set. ABOVE: The Venice Beach Boardwalk attracts a more eclectic gathering of vendors and sightseers.

vard exits), City of Commerce, offers forty two factory outlet stores housed within the confines of an old tire factory that's been declared a historic landmark because of its dazzling art deco Babylonian architecture. Outlets include Eddie Bauer, Bennetton, Ann Taylor and Old Navy. Ten minutes south of downtown Los Angeles (on the way to and from Disneyland), it is open Monday to Saturday from 10 AM to 8 PM, and Sunday from 10 AM to 6 PM.

Del Amo Fashion Center ((310) 542-8525 in Torrance is the largest mall in Southern California, even larger than the Mall of the America's in Minnesota (reputed to be the nation's largest) if you count retail space as the criteria. This place is so large that some chains — including Victoria's Secret — have two outlets.

Farmers Market and Shopping Village ((213) 933-9211, 6333 West Third Street, in the Fairfax District, is wedged between CBS Studios and the Writer's Guild of America building. This quaint little "village" features 110 fruit and vegetable stands, outdoor restaurants and retail outlets, most of the latter hawking souvenirs and other novelty items.

Universal City Walk ((818) 622-4455, 1000 Universal Center Drive in the San Fernando Valley, is a colorful pedestrian promenade with shops, restaurants and bars largely based on movie and other show biz themes. The University of California at Los Angeles Extension here offers classes in directing, producing, screenwriting and other entertainment skills.

WHERE TO STAY

The Los Angeles metropolitan offers one of the world's largest accommodation pools, everything from posh Hollywood retreats to typical American motor inns and motels. Tourist abodes tend to cluster in four major areas: Downtown Los Angeles, Hollywood and Beverly Hills, Santa Monica and the West Side, and the Anaheim/Disneyland area. For information on Anaheim accommodation see ORANGE COUNTY, page 242.

DOWNTOWN

Very Expensive
The **Four Seasons Biltmore** ((213) 624-1011 TOLL-FREE (800) 245-8673 FAX (213) 612-1545, 506 South Grand Avenue in the heart of downtown Los Angeles, was given a new lease on life in 1987 with a $40-million restoration that preserved the baronial country house ambiance. Another multimillion dollar renovation program is currently underway. Facilities include a 1923 tile-and brass-inlaid swimming pool, health club, Jacuzzi and business center. It is located within walking distance of various downtown landmarks

including the Museum of Contemporary Art, the Music Center and Pershing Square.

Another grand old dame that's been given another breath of life is the **Wyndham Checkers** ((213) 624-0000 TOLL-FREE (800) 996-3426 FAX (213) 624-9906, 535 South Grand Avenue. This 188-room, high-rise hotel built in the 1920s is listed as a historic and cultural landmark by the Los Angeles Cultural Heritage Commission. Facilities include rooftop spa, heated lap pool and Jacuzzi.

Expensive
For a touch of the Orient in downtown Los Angeles try the **New Otani** ((213) 629-1200 TOLL-FREE (800) 421-8795 FAX (213) 622-0980, 120 South Los Angles Street, in Little Tokyo. This hotel offers guests a choice of Western or Japanese-style suites with futons, *tatami* floors and *ofuro* baths. Another special feature is the Thousand Cranes restaurant which serves traditional Japanese delights in private *tatami* rooms overlooking a huge rooftop Japanese garden. It has a Japanese-style health club too.

The flashy **Westin Bonaventure** ((213) 624-1000 TOLL-FREE (800) 228-3000 FAX (213) 612-4800, at 404 South Figueroa, set the tone for the city's downtown renaissance when it was completed back in the early 1970s. With its round blue-glass towers, the building is a Los Angeles landmark rising above the always jam-packed Harbor Freeway. Unfortunately, with 1,354 rooms and 20 restaurants, the city's largest hotel is so huge and self-contained it can often seem a bit overwhelming and you soon forget you're in sunny California.

Moderate
The faded elegance of the 1920s is readily apparent at the **Wilshire Royale** ((213) 387-5311, 2619 Wilshire Boulevard, Los Angeles. The historic property was recently purchased by the Howard Johnson chain and has undergone extensive renovation. Located 10 minutes from downtown, this 1920s-style hotel has 200 rooms. MacArthur and Lafayette Parks are within walking distance.

Inexpensive
Right across the street from the Convention Center is the **Holiday Inn City Center** ((213) 748-1291, 1020 South Figueroa Street, which offers a full-service restaurant and room service as well as an outdoor heated pool, sauna and sundeck and fitness center. It is five blocks from the Garment District and most downtown sights.

A funky little abode in the downtown area is the **Royal Pagoda Motel** ((213) 223-3381, 995 North Broadway in the middle of Chinatown, one of the few places within walking distance of Dodger Stadium.

HOLLYWOOD AND BEVERLY HILLS

Very Expensive

The Argyle ((213) 654-7100 TOLL-FREE (800) 225-2637 FAX (213) 654-9287, 8358 Sunset Boulevard, West Hollywood, is listed in the National Registry of Historic Places for its art deco architecture and the role it has played in Hollywood history. Stars such as Marilyn Monroe, Errol Flynn, Jean Harlow and Clark Gable have stayed here. Major renovations have recently been completed. The rooms are a little small but are beautifully furnished and offer all amenities from CD players to fax machines. Great location at the base of the Hollywood Hills, between Beverly Hills and Hollywood.

The most romantic hideaway in Los Angeles is the elegant **Hotel Bel Air** ((310) 472-1211 TOLL-FREE (800) 648-4097 FAX (310) 476-5890, 701 Stone Canyon Road (off Sunset Boulevard). Set in beautiful gardens, guest villas are scattered throughout the property, decorated in California Mediterranean style. Near the University of California at Los Angeles and Westwood Village, facilities include a heated pool, health club and nature trails.

The dreamy "Hotel California" of the Eagles' rock anthem, and the setting of Neil Simon's *California Suite*, the **Beverly Hills Hotel** ((310) 276-2251 TOLL-FREE (800) 283-8885, 9641 West Sunset Boulevard, is without doubt the most renowned hotel in Los Angeles, both for its stunning California-Spanish architecture and the long list of celebrities who have bedded down here. With spacious grounds like the surrounding estates, the celebrated pink stucco façade houses 194 rooms with 21 bungalows and garden suites. The Beverly Hills recently underwent a two-year, multimillion dollar renovation under the direction of its latest owner, the Sultan of Brunei, the world's richest man. Facilities include the famous Polo Lounge, meeting place of the stars for more than half a century.

Visions of Julia Roberts and Eddie Murphy are bound to come to mind when you step into the lobby of the **Regent Beverly Wilshire** ((310) 275-5200 TOLL-FREE (800) 421-4354 FAX (310) 274-2851, 9500 Wilshire Boulevard, Beverly Hills. Situated at the south end of Rodeo Drive, this super luxury hotel has been the location for several big budget Hollywood movies including *Pretty Woman* and *Beverly Hills Cop*. The property underwent a $40 million renovation in 1998 which endowed guest rooms with all the latest high-tech amenities. Facilities include a small outdoor heated pool, a health club, and a business center.

Sheraton Universal ((818) 980-1212 TOLL-FREE (800) 325-3535 FAX (818) 985-4980, 333 Universal Terrace Parkway in Universal City, is a 21-story luxury hotel especially convenient to the movie studios and other attractions of the Universal City/Burbank area. New to the hotel is a high-tech executive boardroom with modem and fax jacks at each seat. But the place is still great for families, offering a big game room and baby-sitting services.

Expensive

One of the first modern high-rise hotels in Los Angeles was the acclaimed **Century Plaza** ((310) 277-2000 TOLL-FREE (800) 228-3000 FAX (310) 551-3355, 2025 Avenue of the Stars, in Century City. Ronald Reagan often stayed here during his presi-

dency and many other celebrities have slept here over the last three decades. Within walking distance of the ABC Entertainment Center and Century City shopping mall, rooms overlook posh westside homes and Twentieth Century Fox movie studios.

A rare survivor from Hollywood's golden age is the **Château Marmont** ((213) 656-1010 TOLL-FREE (800) 242-8328 FAX (213) 655-5311, 8221 West Sunset Boulevard. Built in 1927, the elegant main château-like hotel and surrounding cottages sprawl across a steep hillside above the old Sunset Strip. It has been a favorite for those who valued personal service and privacy, most notably Greta Garbo, Howard Hughes and Robert de Niro. This

Beverly Hills Hotel, the grand old lady of Los Angeles glitteratti, has recently undergone extensive rejuvenation.

is also where comedic actor John Belushi died from an overdose of drugs.

Traveling with a dog or cat? Try **Le Montrose Suite Hotel** ((310) 855-1115 TOLL-FREE (800) 776-0666 FAX (310) 657-9192 WEB SITE www.travel2000 .com, 900 Hammond Street, West Hollywood. Both animals and their owners are spoiled in this 130-suite hotel which boasts separate living rooms, private balconies and fireplaces.

L'Ermitage Beverly Hills ((310) 278-3344 TOLL-FREE (800) 800-2113 WEB SITE www .lermitagehotel .com, 9291 Burton Way, recently re-opened under new ownership. This 124-room luxury hotel offers a living room, library, roof-top deck with 360 degree view of the surrounding city, swimming pool with cabanas for added privacy, and state-of-the art fitness center. Guest room amenities include 40-inch (100-cm) televisions, plain paper/color copier faxes, five multi-line telephones including a cellular phone, and audio/visual CD players.

More rock stars have bivouacked at the **Hyatt West Hollywood** ((213) 656-1234 TOLL-FREE (800) 228-9000 FAX (213) 650-7024, 8401 Sunset Boulevard, than probably any other hotel in the world. Led Zeppelin and John Lennon practically lived here back in the 1970s. It overlooks Sunset Strip and Hollywood from a choice spot near many of the best restaurants in the city and offers a super view from the rooftop pool which has featured in many music videos.

Just across the street from the Hyatt is the modish **Mondrian Hotel** ((213) 650-8999 TOLL-FREE (800) 525-8029 FAX (213) 650-5215, 8440 Sunset Boulevard. The structure was transformed from a ordinary apartment building into a super chic hotel under the guidance of innovative owner Ian Schrager and post-modern design doyen Philippe Starck. With overt pomposity, the Mondrian bills itself as an "urban resort" based on the concept of "Hotel as Theater" — a place where Hollywood wannabes come to see and be seen, especially the haughty Sky Bar lounge. Each of the hotel's 245 rooms offers a super view of the Sunset Strip and Hollywood.

Moderate

Situated right in the heart of the city's entertainment district is the **Hollywood Metropolitan** ((213) 962-5800, 5825 Sunset Boulevard. All rooms offer floor-to-ceiling windows with a panoramic view of Hollywood. The 90 units include two VIP floors for corporate club members.

Inexpensive

One of the best bargains in the Hollywood area is the **Ramada Hollywood** ((213) 660-1788 TOLL-FREE (800) 272-6232, 1160 North Vermont Avenue. Winner of the 1997 Ramada Renovation of the Year Award, the room rate includes continental break-

fast and cable television. Children under 17 stay free. Some rooms have refrigerators and microwaves. Facilities include video arcade, heated pool, and sauna.

Travelodge ((213) 665-5735, 1401 North Vermont Avenue, tenders air-conditioned rooms with coffee-maker, free cable television, and a swimming pool.

Comfort Inn ((213) 665-0344, 321 North Vermont Avenue, offers free coffee and continental breakfast. Non-smoking and handicap rooms are available, as is shuttle service to and from Los Angeles Airport. It is located just off the Hollywood Freeway (101) about halfway between Hollywood and downtown Los Angeles. A

couple of blocks away is the **Econo Lodge** ((213) 385-0061 TOLL-FREE (800) 266-0061, 3400 West Third Street. Rates include continental breakfast and newspaper.

One of the few independents in the bargain category is the **Hollywood Celebrity Hotel** ((800) 222-7017 TOLL-FREE (800) 222-7090, 1775 Orchid Avenue. Although somewhat rundown, it's one of the few hotels within walking distance of Mann's Chinese Theater, Hollywood Bowl and Bookseller's Row. Free parking and continental breakfast are offered, and pets are allowed by prior arrangement.

SANTA MONICA AND WEST SIDE

Very Expensive

One of the more stylish hotels along the Southern California coast is the superb **Loews Santa Monica**

Beach Hotel ((310) 458-6700 TOLL-FREE (800) 223-0888 FAX (310) 458-6761, 1700 Ocean Avenue. Located less than a block from the beach and close to Santa Monica Pier, this 346-room property wouldn't look out of place in Hawaii or the Caribbean. There's also a taste treat: Lavande restaurant with its Provence cuisine and sumptuous ocean views. Convenient to major freeways and Los Angeles International Airport, Loews offers children's programs throughout the summer.

Shutters on the Beach ((310) 458-0030 TOLL-FREE (800) 334-9000 FAX (310) 458-4589, 1 Pico Boulevard in Santa Monica, looks more like a giant beach house than a 200-room luxury hotel. Situated directly on the sand, a block south of Santa Monica Pier, rooms offer stunning views of the coastline and Pacific Ocean through floor to ceiling windows. Some rooms have fireplaces and Jacuzzis. Facilities include outdoor heated pool, health club, sauna, beach equipment and bicycle rental.

Overlooking the University of California at Los Angeles campus and bustling Westwood Village is the **Westwood Marquis Hotel and Gardens** ((310) 208-8765 TOLL-FREE (800) 421-2317 FAX (310) 824-0355, 930 Hilgard Avenue. It's expensive but loaded with amenities. Located within walking distance of dozens of shops and restaurants, facilities include two outdoor heated pools, Jacuzzi and a small fitness center.

Expensive
Lush tropical gardens surround the **Miramar Sheraton** ((310) 576-7777, 101 Wilshire Boulevard in downtown Santa Monica. A recently completed $33 million renovation project has included upgrades to its 302 rooms and pool as well as a new state-of-the-art fitness center and indoor-outdoor restaurant. Within walking distance of the beach, pier and Third Street Promenade.

Another wonderful waterfront property is the **Portofino Hotel and Yacht Club** ((310) 379-8481 TOLL-FREE (800) 468-4292, 260 Portofino Way, in Redondo Beach. Understated elegance marks the decor. Comfortable rooms offer a host of amenities including fully stocked mini bars. It is located on a private peninsula, just six miles (nine kilometers) from Los Angeles Airport.

Moderate
Now berthed at the south end of the Interstate 710 freeway in Long Beach, the *Queen Mary* ((562) 432-6964 offers one of the Southland's more unusual accommodation options. The former luxury cruise ship offers 365 hotel rooms and 17 suites including many of the original state rooms from its historic trans-Atlantic days.

The **Venice Beach House** ((310) 823-1966 FAX (310) 823-1842, 15 Thirtieth Avenue, is a fabulous 1911 gray shingled house with nine guest rooms, just a half-block from the beach and all the craziness that is present-day Venice. It's an elegant restoration, a calm and cozy place after the busy boardwalk. Expanded continental breakfast is served in the sunroom and there is also lemonade or tea with cookies served each afternoon.

Inexpensive
Just minutes from the beach and Third Street Promenade is the charming **Hotel Carmel by the Sea** ((310) 451-2469 TOLL-FREE (800) 445-8695, 201 Broadway, Santa Monica. Some rooms have ocean views. Children under 17 stay free. Non-smoking and handicap rooms are available.

The **Santa Monica Travelodge** ((310) 450-5766 TOLL-FREE (800) 231-7679, 3102 Pico Boulevard, is conveniently located just minutes from the beach and other local attractions. Air conditioned rooms feature full kitchens. Continental breakfast and morning paper are included in the rates.

Hi View Motel ((310) 374-4608, 100 South Sepulveda Boulevard, Manhattan Beach, offers rooms with cable television, refrigerators and microwaves. Non-smoking rooms are available. Morning coffee is free.

Nestled in a replica Victorian structure near the San Pedro docks is the charming little **Holiday Inn Los Angeles Harbor** ((310) 514-1414 TOLL-

OPPOSITE: The former H.M.S. *Queen Mary* now serves as a floating hotel at Long Beach. ABOVE: Shutters on the Beach rises like a New England cottage above the sands of Santa Monica.

FREE (800) 248-3188, 111 South Gaffey Street, which offers antique decor with a European ambiance. Amenities include swimming pool and Jacuzzi, in-room coffeemaker, refrigerators, hairdryer and cable television. Rate includes buffet breakfast. Live entertainment is featured on Friday and Saturday nights.

Another bargain in the South Bay area, three blocks from the beach, is the **Inn of Long Beach** ((562) 435-3791 TOLL-FREE (800) 230-7500, 185 Atlantic Avenue. Newly renovated, the rooms have cable television. There is a heated pool and Jacuzzi. Continental breakfast and newspapers are included in the rate. The hotel offers free shuttle to downtown Long Beach and local sights.

WHERE TO EAT

Because Los Angeles is the sometime home of many of the world's most talented people — a vast clientele of people with the flair to appreciate exciting cuisine and with the money to pay for it — it's also home to some truly extraordinary restaurants. Knowing where to see and be seen while dining out is part of the art and fun of living in Los Angeles.

DOWNTOWN

Expensive

Since 1921, businessmen and other downtown denizens have been digging their teeth into the steaks at **Pacific Dining Car** ((213) 483-6000, 1310 West Sixth Street. The house specialty is prime beef cut, aged in the PDC's own cooler and cooked over mesquite charcoal. The menu also includes fresh seafood, veal and lamb dishes. PDC is open 24 hours a day, seven days a week. A second PDC ((310) 453-4000 can be found at 2700 Wilshire Boulevard.

After a quarter century, fine dining returns to historic Union Station in the form of **TRAXX** ((213) 625-1999, 800 North Alameda Street. This new restaurant, whose ambiance evokes the

golden age of train travel, features a sophisticated contemporary menu created by chef/owner Tara Thomas with new interpretations of classic West Coast cuisine like ahi tuna with crispy wontons, pork chops stuffed with prosciutto and figs, wasabi caviar, and New York strip loin sandwich with daikon sprouts and horseradish mayonnaise. TRAXX offers a real taste treat.

Moderate

If you're a traditionalist, don't go anywhere near **California Pizza Kitchen** ((213) 626-2616, Wells Fargo Center, 330 South Hope Street, which offers a distinctive West Coast take on Italian cooking — imaginative pizza, pasta, garlic

bread and the like. Take out and delivery are available.

Several theme restaurants in the downtown area include **Engine Company No. 28** ((213) 624-6996, 644 South Figueroa Street, which serves American food in a historic firehouse setting, and **Epicentre** ((213) 621-4455, 200 South Hill Street, which offers up a light-hearted earthquake decor with its tasty continental cuisine.

Inexpensive

Another night owl hangout is **Fred 62** ((213) 667-0062, 1850 North Vermont Avenue, in the Los Feliz neighborhood between downtown and Griffith Park. This modern version of the classic American diner serves up Asian noodle dishes, burgers and sandwiches. It is open 24 hours, seven days a week.

Los Angeles' oldest Italian eatery is **Little Joe's** ((213) 489-4900, 900 North Broadway. Founded in 1927, the restaurant features Northern Italian delicacies including handmade ravioli, veal piccata and butterflied halibut.

The decor at **Mon Kee Seafood Restaurant** ((213) 628-6717, 679 North Spring Street in Chinatown, is hardly elegant, but this place is one of the best for authentic Chinese food.

You probably won't get invited to dine at the mayor's mansion, but you can at least eat at a place that's owned by Los Angeles mayor Richard Riordan — the **Original Pantry Café** ((213) 972-9279, 877 South Figueroa Street. Its traditional American menu offers huge portions in a relaxed setting; no gourmet food here, but it's the place to go if you' re really hungry. Open 24

hours, it claims to have been closed only once in 74 years.

Philippe, The Original ((213) 628-3781, 1001 North Alameda Street, is the home of the "French dip" sandwich. Philippe's has been serving sandwiches to Hollywood celebrities and neighborhood folks for more than 80 years. In addition to the famous roast beef on French roll, the menu also includes fresh pork, cured ham and lamb sandwiches.

HOLLYWOOD AND BEVERLY HILLS

Very Expensive

Many eaters feel that **Citrus** ((213) 857-0034, 6703 Melrose Avenue, is not just the best Franco-California restaurant but the best restaurant of *any kind* in Southern California. Chef/owner Michel Richard has become a star in his own right. The

place provides a spacious, elegant setting where diners can observe the meals being prepared in the glass-walled kitchen. State-of-the-art *nouvelle cuisine* and a constantly changing menu are Citrus trademarks.

Another Franco-California bastion is **Jimmy's** ((310) 552-2394, 201 Moreno Drive in Beverly Hills. This quietly elegant place has a number of house specialties including rack of veal.

One of Tinseltown's top "see and be seen" dining spots is **The Ivy** ((213) 274-8303, 113 North Robertson Boulevard. Popular with Los Angeles celebrities for many years, the salads and ice cream sundaes are great — too bad about the rest of the menu. But people don't really come here for the

food. It's the ambiance — and attendance — that counts. **Drai's** ((310) 358-8585, 730 North La Cienega Boulevard, West Hollywood is also very hot with movie stars. The decor features leopard-print sofas and an outdoor garden complete with Astroturf. It's another place for people watching, rather than great food.

One of the truly elegant restaurants of Southern California is **L'Orangerie** ((310) 652-9770, 903 North La Cienega, with high prices for quite good food served in a setting reminiscent of eighteenth-century France, including a glass roof that opens up on starlit summer nights. It is open for dinner seven days a week from 6:30 PM to 11 PM.

The Palm ((310) 550-8811, 9001 Santa Monica Boulevard in West Hollywood, is the West Coast branch of New York's famous restaurant of the same name and features predictably heavy East Coast fare: live lobsters flown in from Nova Scotia, thick steaks, and cheesecakes imported from the Bronx. Unfortunately there can be some New York rudeness on the part of the staff as well.

The latest and perhaps most precious jewel in Wolfgang Puck's ever expanding crown of gourmet restaurants is **Spago Beverly Hills** ((310) 385-0880, 176 North Canon Drive, Beverly Hills.

Fine restaurants of every culinary tradition abound in Los Angeles.

Puck's restaurants are largely famous because of their imaginative owner and chef. Successful as a caterer to the rich and famous at a very young age, Puck has become a rare celebrity in his own right. This is partly because of his ever-changing "California nouvelle cuisine" at Spago, but also because of the man himself, one of seemingly unlimited energy who is incredibly generous with his time and talents for any number of charities. The original Puck creation — now called **Spago Hollywood** ((310) 652-4025— is at 1114 Horn Avenue (at Sunset) in West Hollywood.

Yamashiro ((213) 466-5125, 1999 North Sycamore Avenue, is the "hilltop Japanese palace above the magic castle in Hollywood Hills." Located on

top of a steep hill overlooking old Hollywood, this is the most spectacular place to eat in Los Angeles. The Oriental palace with 12 acres (nearly five hectares) of terraced gardens has a colorful history that includes serving as the home of the rich and powerful "400 Club." It became a public restaurant in 1960. Always famous for the view and the setting, the food is also now highly regarded.

Expensive

One of the city's best Italian restaurants is the highly regarded **Alto Palato** ((310) 657-9271, 755 North La Cienega Boulevard. The menu features Roman-style pizzas, calzone and other Italian favorites including very good antipasto and pasta. Wednesday nights here are extra special with a three-course menu from a specific Italian region, a chance for the kitchen to try out new and exciting dishes.

Morton's ((310) 276-5205, 8764 Melrose Avenue in West Hollywood, is also popular with the celebrity set, this time because of its simple but predictably superb food. California grill cuisine used to be Morton's forte, but this has given way in recent years to heartier chophouse dishes.

Hollywood's oldest eatery is the historic **Musso & Frank Grill** ((213) 467-7788, 6667 Hollywood Boulevard, first opened in 1919. It retains

the style and class synonymous with the old Hollywood Boulevard. And the food is still good, too. Try the flannel cakes for breakfast or the barbecued ribs at night. And the martinis are to die for. It is open Monday to Saturday from 11 AM to 11 PM.

Another enticing Wolfgang Puck creation is **ObaChine** ((310) 274-4440, 242 North Beverly Drive in Beverly Hills. Billed as a Pan-Asian bistro and satay bar, the menu is a highly innovative and unusual blend of Thai, Indonesian, Chinese and Japanese cuisine.

Patina ((213) 467-1108, 5955 Melrose Avenue, is a small French-California bistro where the excellent menu changes with the seasons. Service is

good and the atmosphere sophisticated. Patina is open Sunday, Monday, Wednesday, and Thursday from 6 PM to 9:30 PM; Tuesday from noon to 2 PM and from 6 PM to 9:30 PM; Friday from 6 PM to 10:30 PM; and Saturday from 5:30 PM to 10:30 PM.

Recently renovated with big bucks from the Sultan of Brunei, **The Polo Lounge** ((213) 276-2251 at the Beverly Hills Hotel, 9641 Sunset Boulevard, has endured since 1912 as one of the most popular celebrity hangouts in Los Angeles. Lunch is the big meal here, featuring a changing menu of crepes and salads, and a regular menu of delicious sandwiches.

Moderate

Chianti Cucina ((213) 653-8333, 7383 Melrose Avenue — not to be mistaken with the next-door Ristorante Chianti — offers good Italian food, with home-made pasta, at reasonable prices. It features an interesting menu which changes often and is open Thursdays to Sundays from 11:30 AM to 11:30 PM, Fridays and Saturdays from 11:30 AM to midnight.

All of your Arabian Nights fantasies come alive at **Dar Maghreb** ("House of Morocco") ((213) 876-7651, 7651 Sunset Boulevard. You open the door in a plain white building and enter another world, lavishly furnished with bright carpets, cushions, and tiles around a beautiful courtyard fountain. The authentic Moroccan ambiance is carried to the table where no silverware is provided, but the fresh bread helps, and wash cloths are provided after feasts of couscous, chicken, lamb, seafood, rabbit, and quail. Open Monday to Friday from

6 PM to 11 PM, Saturday from 6:30 to 11 PM, and Sunday from 5:30 PM to 10:30 PM.

Harry's Bar and American Grill ((310) 277-2333, Plaza Level, ABC Entertainment Center, 2020 Avenue of the Stars, Plaza Level, in Century City, is a replica of the famous Harry's Bar in Florence, Italy. It's a sophisticated, comfortable place in which to enjoy good northern Italian cuisine. Also offered are grilled prime beef, fresh fish and veal.

A hot new eatery along the La Cienaga restaurant row is the **Shark Bar** ((310) 652-1520, 826 North La Cienega Boulevard. Southern cooking — including scrumptious fried chicken and barbecued ribs — draws the top echelon of the music and entertainment industry.

Siamese Princess ((213) 653-2643, 8048 West Third Street (near Farmer's Market) has a casual neighborhood ambiance, but the fine Thai cuisine attracts a clientele from throughout the city.

Inexpensive

Barney's Beanery ((213) 654-2287, 8447 Santa Monica Boulevard, is one of the last of the old neighborhood bars and beaneries. Nearly every table here is poolside — pool meaning billiards in this case — because almost all of the space in Barney's is taken up by pool tables. There is also a long, narrow bar that has been a cozy neighborhood spot for many years. In addition to chili-beans, Barney's has the usual assortment of sandwiches and daily plate specials. It's a far cry from haute cuisine, but it offers good solid food at low prices and a true neighborly atmosphere that is rare in the sprawling city of Los Angeles.

The man who brought you *E.T.* and *Jaws* now brings you burgers and fries at **Dive!** ((310) 788-DIVE WEB SITE www.dive-subs.com, 10250 Santa Monica Boulevard in the Century City Shopping Center. Pizzas, burgers, gourmet subs, salads and pasta are among the dishes served at this heavily themed restaurant, created by Steven Spielberg and Jeffrey Katzenberg. This great place to entertain the kids is open Sunday to Thursday from 11:30 AM to 10 PM, Friday and Saturday from 11:30 AM to 11 PM.

Across the street from Paramount Studio's famous gateway is the popular **El Adobe Café** ((213) 462-9421, 5536 Melrose Avenue. It was the favorite eating place of Jerry Brown (and his girlfriend Linda Ronstadt) when he was California's governor. The food here is standard Mexican burritos, enchiladas, rice, and beans, but there's plenty of it, and the price is reasonable.

A more endearing Hollywood landmark is **Jerry's Famous Deli** ((818) 980-4245, 12655 Ventura Avenue, in Studio City. The place is open 24 hours and thus a favorite with Los Angeles celebrities who need to eat at odd hours. The

---

Asian restaurants are patronized by local ethnic communities making them both authentic and hugely popular with Angelinos and visitors alike.

huge menu takes nearly half a hour to pore over and touches on almost every known kind of cooking.

SANTA MONICA AND WEST SIDE

Very Expensive

Wolfgang Puck's West Side bastion is the famous **Chinois on Main** ((310) 392-9025, 2709 Main Street. This is where the concept of East-West fusion food was basically created, and it offers an exciting menu of Puck's own interpretations of French, American and Chinese cuisine.

Nearly everyone in town is talking about the brand new **Lavande** restaurant at the Loews Santa Monica Beach Hotel ((310) 576-3181 or (310) 458-6700, 1700 Ocean Avenue, which serves up sumptuous Provençal dishes with its stunning waterfront views.

Expensive

Los Angeles journalist turned epicure Patrick Healy has literally moved West from Pasadena with the recent opening of the **Buffalo Club** ((310) 450-8600, 1520 Olympic Boulevard, in Santa Monica. It has a pretty outdoor garden and serves good American food, but with a little too much attitude from the staff.

Having lived and worked in Hong Kong for several years, chef Serge Burckel has a good understanding of Asian cooking and applies it well to the fusion menu served at **Splash** ((310) 798-5348, 350 North Harbor Drive, Redondo Beach.

Vincenti ((310) 207-0127, 11930 San Vincente Boulevard in Brentwood, offers great modern Italian food with lots of opportunity for people watching.

Moderate

One of the more delightful beachfront eateries is the almost legendary **Alice's Restaurant** ((310) 456-6646, 23000 Pacific Coast Highway. Perched on Malibu Pier, the menu features a typical California mix of salads and seafood, pasta, and some special Mexican dishes. Open Monday to Friday from 11:30 AM to 10 PM, Saturday and Sunday from 11 AM to 11 PM.

Gladstone's 4 Fish ((310) 459-9356, 17300 Pacific Coast Highway in Pacific Palisades, is owned and operated by Bob Morris, one of California's most successful restaurateurs. Located right on the beach, with a magnificent view of the Pacific, it has indoor and outdoor dining areas and a true laid-back beach mood. There are four huge tanks where you can look at the live lobsters and rock crabs. Then you can watch through the glass-walled kitchen as they are tossed into

boiling water. In addition to its famous lunches and dinners, Gladstone's also offers a huge fisherman's breakfast of eggs and a half-pound of swordfish or ham.

Anyone who thinks that gourmet Mexican food doesn't exist should pop into **Guelaguetza** ((310) 837-8600, 11127 Palms Boulevard in West Los Angeles. The food is straight out of Oaxaca — enchiladas, masa turnovers, tacos, mole negro. Breakfasts feature the best huevos rancheros this side of Tijuana.

Joe's ((213) 399-5811, 1023 Abbot Kinney, is a great neighborhood restaurant in a funky little part of Venice with imaginative French-Italian cuisine at reasonable prices. Try for a table in the back patio. Joe's is open Tuesday to Friday from 11:30 AM to 2:30 PM and from 6 PM to 11 PM, Saturday and Sunday from 11 AM to 3 PM and from 6 PM to 11 PM.

Champagne picnics accompany summer concerts at the Hollywood Bowl.

Inexpensive

Aficionados of Thai cuisine flock to **Chan Dara** ((310) 479-4461, 11940 West Pico Boulevard in West Los Angeles. Two other locations include 1511 Cahuenga Boulevard ((213) 464-8585 in Hollywood, and 310 North Larchmont Boulevard ((213) 467-1052 in the Fairfax District.

According to the London *Times*, **Ye Olde King's Head** ((310) 451-1402, 116 Santa Monica Boulevard, is the "only proper pub in Los Angeles." Famous for its fish and chips, it has three dining rooms, two bars and darts.

ENTERTAINMENT AND NIGHTLIFE

Los Angeles is a paradise for night owls with a budding nightlife scene that includes everything from dive bars and trendy music clubs to Broadway plays and world-class symphony.

PERFORMING ARTS

The primary venue for classic performing arts in Southern California is the **Los Angeles County Music Center** ((213) 972-7211, 135 North Grand, downtown. The sprawling sight is the Los Angeles equivalent of New York's Lincoln Center or London's South Bank with several venues that specialize in different formats. **Dorothy Chandler Pavilion** ((213) 972-7211 FAX (213) 972-7474 is home to the acclaimed Los Angeles Philharmonic under the direction of Finnish maestro Esa-Pekka Salonen, as well as the Los Angeles Opera and the Los Angeles Master Chorale. Contemporary drama is the forte of the **Mark Taper Forum** ((213) 972-0700 FAX (213) 972-0746, while the **Ahmanson Theater** ((213) 972-7200 FAX (213) 972-7431 specializes in big-name Broadway musicals.

In summer, the Philharmonic moves up US Highway 101 to a sumptuous outdoor venue called the **Hollywood Bowl** ((213) 850-2000 FAX (213) 617-3065, 2301 North Highland Avenue, which is also a major al fresco rock, jazz and pop venue between May and October. The Bowl's annual **Mariachi Festival** ((213) 848-7717 in June is the world's largest showcase for traditional Mexican song.

The **Pasadena Civic Auditorium** ((626) 793-8014, 300 East Green Street, has been a showcase for ballet, symphony, musical comedy and popular music since 1932 when it was first erected.

Other drama venues include the **Shubert Theater** TOLL-FREE ((800) 447-7400, 2040 Avenue of the Stars, Suite 212, Century City at the ABC Entertainment Center; the **Doolittle Theater** ((213) 462-6666, 1615 North Vine Street in Hollywood; the historic **Pasadena Playhouse** ((626) 356-PLAY FAX (626) 792-7343 WEB SITE WWW .pasadenaplayhouse.com, 35 South El Molino Avenue, where Dustin Hoffman, William Holden and Gene Hackman got theirs starts as young actors; and the **UCLA Geffen Playhouse** ((310) 208-6500 WEB SITE www.geffenucla.edu, 10886 Le Conte Avenue in Westwood.

Theater L.A. ((213) 688-ARTS, 644 South Figueroa Street is an association of more than 150 theater companies in Southern California that runs a 24-hour information hotline on local theater productions and art events.

MUSIC AND DANCE CLUBS

Hollywood's legendary music clubs — where the likes of The Doors, Led Zeppelin and Guns N Roses earned their early kudos — are still belting out tunes on a nightly basis as venues for cutting edge rock. The **Whisky** ((310) 535-0579 or (310) 652-4202, 8901 Sunset Boulevard, first raised the curtain in 1964. The **Troubadour** ((310) 276-6168, 9081 Santa Monica Boulevard, has been around even longer, since 1957. The **Roxy** ((310) 276-2222, 9009 Sunset Boulevard, is a relative newcomer, presenting top acts since 1973. Vying for attention along Sunset Strip is a much newer club called the **Viper Room** ((310) 358-1880, 8852 Sunset Boulevard, owned by Brat Pack actor Johnny Depp and famed as the place where River Phoenix danced his last steps.

The recently renovated and relaunched **Hollywood Palace** ((213) 462-3000 or (213) 467-4571, 1735 North Vine Street, can hold 1,200 people and has again take its place as one of Hollywood's most revered hot spots, with dance club action Thursday to Saturday night, as well as big-name concerts. Flashy new music clubs include the huge **Keyboard Club** ((310) 786-1712, 9039 Sunset Boulevard, the "Godzilla" of the Hollywood music scene with its vast interior and enormous television sets perched on the exterior.

In recent years other forms of American music have also taken root in Hollywood. Despite its name, **House of Blues** ((213) 848-5100 or (213) 650-0476 WEB SITE www.liveconcerts.com, 8430 Sunset Boulevard, is an eclectic showcase for everything from blues, soul and rap to rock, country and cajun tunes. Its Sunday Gospel Brunch is a local institution. **B.B. King's Blues Club** ((818) 622-5464 FAX (818) 622-0440, City Walk, Universal Studios, offers just what the name suggests — unadulterated Chicago, Memphis and New Orleans blues with the occasional appearance by B.B. King himself. Jazz and swing are the "in" thing at **The Derby** ((213) 663-8979, 4500 Los Feliz Boulevard, in the Los Feliz district near Griffith Park, which originally opened in 1927.

Meanwhile, former talk show host and game show doyen Merv Griffen has unveiled the **Coconut Club** at the Beverly Hilton ((310) 274-7777, 9876 Wilshire Boulevard in Beverly Hills. Based on the glamorous supper clubs of 1950s New York, it features big-band music and Latin jazz against a backdrop of over-the-top decor including gold palm trees, faux neon monkeys and midnight blue ceilings. Embraced within the greater "event" is **Chimps Cigar Club**, a trendy smoking divan owned by actors Chuck Norris and Jim Belushi. The Coconut runs Friday and Saturday nights only from 7:30 PM to 2 AM. The $20 cover includes swing/jazz dance lessons, stage entertainment and entry to Chimps.

World music is also pervasive. The ultra-trendy **Luna Park** ((310) 652-0611 FAX (310) 652-7121, 655 North Robertson Boulevard, features alternative rock as well as cutting edge music from around the globe including African, Latin and European artists. The **Mayan Nightclub** ((213) 746-4287 FAX (213) 746-4225, 1038 South Hill Street, in downtown Los Angeles is a hot-blooded showcase for salsa, tango and other Latin beats.

Down by the sea, Santa Monica also swings after dark. **McCabe's Guitar Shop** ((310) 828-4497, 3101 Pico Boulevard, is a legendary folk-rock venue where the likes of Elvis Costello, Jackson Browne, Ry Cooder and Bonnie Raitt have played "unplugged." **Rusty's Surf Ranch** ((310) 393-7437 on Santa Monica Pier hosts a wide variety of music acts from rockabilly and surf punk to Irish folk music and classic rock.

BARS

Los Angeles has a watering hole for just about any taste. The notorious **Sky Bar** at the Mondrian Hotel ((800) 525-8029, 8440 Sunset Boulevard, is packed with music and movie industry types each night, including many wannabe actors and rock stars. The futuristic décor comes courtesy of Philippe Starck. Killer views, too. Just down the road is the equally pretentious **Château Marmont Bar**

((213) 656-1010, 8221 Sunset Boulevard, in the très trendy hotel of the same name.

Quirky little bars abound, especially in the Hollywood and beach areas. **Lava Lounge** ((213) 876-6612, 1533 La Brea Avenue, in Hollywood, is about as tacky as they come — on purpose! The pseudo South Pacific tiki decor attracts a hip crowd including many young actors and musicians. For a touch of 1920s elegance try the **Gallery Bar** ((213) 624-1011, 506 South Grand Avenue, in the Regal Biltmore Hotel downtown. Presidents, prime ministers and even royalty have been known to knock one back at the Biltmore over the years. Another bygone drinking spot is the **Observation Bar** ((562) 435-3511 on the historic ocean liner *Queen Mary* in Long Beach.

For a good old pint it's hard to beat **Ye Olde King's Head** ((310) 451-1402, 116 Santa Monica Boulevard, in Santa Monica. This is the "only proper pub in L.A." according to one London paper. There's even classic British pub grub including fish and chips. Another Santa Monica hangout is **Gotham Hall** ((310) 394-8865, 1431 Third Street Promenade, a flamboyant pool hall where you can test your skill on purple-felt billiard tables.

COMEDY CLUBS

Hollywood was the springboard to fame for many of America's top stand-up comedians. There's no shortage of laughs at any of the following clubs: **Comedy Store** ((213) 656-6225, 8433 Sunset Boulevard; **The Improvisation** ((213) 651-2583, 8162 Melrose Avenue; **Laugh Factory** ((213) 656-1336, 8001 Sunset Boulevard.

Ticket Agencies and Tours

Tickets to various plays, concerts and shows in the Los Angeles area can be purchased from the following ticket agencies: **A Musical Chair** ((310) 207-7070 FAX (310) 826-8002, Suite 309, 11677 San Vincente Boulevard; **Al Brooks Theater Ticket Agency** ((213) 626-5863, Suite 104, Omni Hotel Los Angeles, 900 Wilshire Boulevard; **Ticketmaster** ((213) 381-2000, Suite 700, 3701 Wilshire Boulevard.

L.A. Night-Hawks' Night-on-the-Town ((310) 392-1500, organizes after-dark tours to hot, historic and quirky clubs and bars.

HOW TO GET THERE

Los Angeles World Airport (LAX), the world's third busiest, handles 50 million passengers a year and is served by more than 100 different international and domestic airlines, including flights from nearly every major city around the world and across the United States. The once difficult passage to and from the eight terminals was cleared up in a huge construction project completed in

time for the 1984 Olympics in Los Angeles. Fitting for Los Angeles, the new airport complex is wonderfully convenient to parking garages and car rental places.

Rental car agencies are conveniently located just outside the airport boundaries, with shuttle buses to ferry people to and from the various terminals. If you're not renting your own vehicle, numerous companies offer door-to-door van and coach transport to hotels, residences and other locations in the Los Angeles region. Among the more established airport shuttle operators are **L.A. XPress** ((310) 641-8000; **Prime Time Shuttle** ((818) 504-3600; and **SuperShuttle** ((310) 782-6600. A cheaper but more time-consuming alternative is the **AirportBus** TOLL-FREE (800) 772-5299 with frequent departures to and from downtown and Pasadena area hotels. If you really want to make a splash, have a stretch limo to fetch you from the airport: **Shalimar Limousines** ((310) 674-4000 TOLL-FREE (800) 515-1517.

Travelers to Los Angeles may find that one of the smaller domestic airports is more convenient, depending on their destination. **Burbank Airport**, for example, is more convenient to Burbank, Universal City, Studio City and other places in the San Fernando Valley; **John Wayne/Orange Airport** is more convenient to Disneyland and points south of Los Angeles; **Ontario Airport** is the quickest way to reach eastern suburbs like Riverside and San Bernardino.

Los Angeles can also be reached by train and bus from other major American cities. Major highways leading to the Los Angeles area include Interstate 5 from San Francisco, Sacramento, San Diego and the western Sierra Nevada mountains; US Highway 395 and State Highway 14 from the eastern Sierras; Interstate 10 from Phoenix and southern Arizona; Interstate 15 from Las Vegas and southern Utah; Interstate 40 from the Grand Canyon and northern Arizona; US Highway 101 from Santa Barbara and the Central Coast.

AROUND LOS ANGELES

PASADENA

Pasadena has become so identified with the annual Rose Bowl and the extravagant Tournament of Roses Parade that precedes the college football game, that it's difficult to think of one without the other. Located just seven and a half miles (12 km) north of downtown Los Angeles by way of the Pasadena Freeway (State Highway 110), Pasadena is set in a valley at the foot of the San Gabriel Mountains. Originally called "Indiana Colony" because its first residents came from the Hoosier state, it came to be called "Pasadena" via a peculiar route. The folk from Indiana couldn't understand enough Spanish to pick a suitable local place name, so one of them wrote a missionary friend among the Chippewa Indians in Mississippi. The clergyman suggested a long phrase that meant "crown of the valley" in the Chippewa language. "Pa Sa De Na" was only the last part of that phrase, but it sounded good enough.

Pasadena was a turn-of-the-century equivalent of present-day Palm Springs, although its wealthy residents included an unusual number of artists and writers attracted by the scenery, and the year-round balmy climate. The **Pasadena Playhouse**, a dramatic arts school and theater, was founded there in 1916.

The famous **Rose Parade** was first held on January 1, 1889, when the city was 14 years old. It

fresh flowers — cost millions of dollars and have become another means of advertising for the major corporations. It's a great honor for high school bands to take part in the band competition, and hundreds of high school and college musicians keep the music going throughout the three-hour parade.

In 1978, a local group started the annual **Doo Dah Parade** to make fun of the extravagant Rose Parade. The parody features floats decorated in the poorest of taste, marching "drool" teams such as surfers hoisting their boards up and down and, everybody's favorite, businessmen in suits and ties performing a precision drill with their briefcases. Like so many other popular spoofs, the Doo

was a fund-raising event for the local hunt club and involved a competition for the best decorated horses and carriages — all decked with fresh roses and other flowers. In 1902, the parade was followed by a football game for the first time. Since 1946, the **Rose Bowl** game has pitted the champions of the Pac Ten and Big Ten conferences. The huge stadium with 105,000 seats and no obstructed views was built in 1923. Besides the annual New Year's Day match, it's also the home field of the University of California at Los Angeles Bruins football team, one of the nation's top-rated college programs.

The Rose Parade has become an annual tradition in America. Some people camp out for 48 hours along the route to get the best views. More than a million people come to Pasadena to see it in person and millions more watch the parade on network television. The floats — covered with nothing but

Dah Parade caught on so well that the city had to persuade its organizers to please not stage it on New Year's Day. And, you guessed it, the Doo Dah Parade can now be seen on network television every Thanksgiving.

Parades aside, Pasadena is also an enclave of fine art and culture. New Yorkers and others in the East Coast art world raised a howl in the early 1970s when Norton Simon announced that his world-famous collection of sculptures, paintings and other art objects would be placed in a museum in such an out-of-the-way place as Pasadena. The **Norton Simon Museum** ((626) 449-6840, 411 West Colorado Boulevard, opened in 1975 and has proved a popular Pasadena attraction and a highly successful venture. Casual art lovers and serious students of art can come and appreciate the collection without the hassles of the major inner city museums. Eventually destined to become part of the University of California, the Norton Simon is open Thursday to Sunday from noon to 6 PM. Admission is $4 for adults and free for children 12 and under.

Another Pasadena landmark is the **Henry E. Huntington Library**, **Art Gallery and Gardens** ((626) 405-2275 or (818) 405-2125, 1151 Oxford Road, in San Marino. Henry E. Huntington consolidated two of the state's biggest fortunes and kept the money in the family when he married the widow of his uncle, Collis P. Huntington, one of San Francisco's "Big Four" tycoons. With proceeds from "The Octopus" — as the Southern Pacific Railroad was known — Huntington built a huge mansion on an estate in San Marino, adja-

cent to Pasadena. He spent his later years building up his library of rare books and his art collection, and overseeing the elaborate botanical gardens that surrounded the mansion. In 1919, he set up a trust with a $10.5 million endowment and deeded his estate and all of his collections for public use. Among the rare books are 12 folios and 37 quartos of Shakespeare, and the manuscript of Benjamin Franklin's autobiography. The most famous of the paintings in his art collection is Gainsborough's *Blue Boy*, which Huntington bought in 1922 for $620,000. With its own distinguished research staff, the Huntington Library has continued to add to the original collections which attract scholars from throughout the world. Likewise, the 200 acres (81 hectares) of botanical gardens have become widely known for their collections of camellias, cacti and other plants, as well as the Japanese-style landscaping.

SANTA MONICA AND MALIBU

If you hop onto Wilshire Boulevard in downtown Los Angeles and stay on it for roughly 25 miles (40 km), you eventually reach a dead-end at the oceanfront in **Santa Monica** — the sultry, sordid "Bay City" of Raymond Chandler's novels and the place where English author Christopher Isherwood chose to spend the last half of his life. The Santa Monica Freeway (Interstate 10) is a lot quicker and the way local people would go. But that won't take you through Beverly Hills.

In spite of its recent affluence, Santa Monica still has much of that lazy beach town spirit Chandler described. The mood here is friendly and slow. The famous **Santa Monica Pier** was brutally battered by winter storms in the early 1980s and 300 ft (91 m) of fishing pier with restaurants and shops toppled like matchsticks and floated out to sea. The remaining pier, heavily renovated in recent years, is still popular with fishermen and young lovers.

For family fun on the pier visit **Pacific Park** ((310) 260-8744, where you can thrill to ocean views while riding the giant ferris wheel or surf a roller coaster over the waves. For the less adventurous there are bumper cars and carnival games. You can rent bicycles and skateboards nearby for a ride along the "boardwalk" and its grand parade of California beach life. Keep heading south and you'll come to Venice Beach.

Malibu, just up the coast from Santa Monica, is an Indian name of unknown origin. The 22-mile (35-km) stretch of beachfront was part of a huge ranch for many years. It was subdivided in the 1920s into lots for movie stars and other wealthy people. Many houses are built on cliffs so that there are no neighbors back and front and no view of those on either side. Up there on the mountaintops above the Pacific Highway are the homes of Barbra Streisand, Bob Dylan and other world-famous performers.

VENICE BEACH

Venice Beach shows the extreme side of beach life in California. It's like some sort of throwback to Greenwich Village in the 1960s or San Francisco of the 1950s. Here you will find all the bizarre characters for which Los Angeles is justly famous. The sidewalks and the wide beaches are often body-to-body, a kind of massive outdoor disco with sounds blaring from a thousand different directions. Along the sidewalks, vendors set up food stands and shops selling everything from bad art to good sunglasses. It's no problem here if you

The Malibu Pier offers prime fishing positions and a quiet escape from the bustle of nearby Los Angeles.

don't think you fit in — in Venice, nobody fits and everybody fits. **"Muscle Beach"** is a small outdoor gymnasium for the hard-core bodybuilder. There's even a small bleacher where you can sit and watch; but the bodybuilding is tame entertainment here and there is seldom much of an audience.

The best shows are the spontaneous ones along the sidewalk itself. Many of the performers are regulars, and they come with their own billboards, full of clippings and reviews of their shows. One regular is a sword-swallower. Every sort of juggler and magician can be found here, too. The ones who draw the most crowds are the young gymnasts on skateboards. It's absolutely amaz-

was to create a cultural center patterned on the Chatauqua forums of the East Coast. Sarah Bernhardt appeared in a production of *Camille* at his Venice pier, but that was the area's grandest moment. The little city of the arts never quite lived up to Kinney's grand plan. Some say that decadence is part of Venice's current charm because some of that original spirit of the arts has endured.

REDONDO BEACH

Redondo Beach has the distinction of being the first place in California where the great sport of surfing was seen. The year was 1907. Railroad

ing the kinds of stunts some of them can do on a skateboard.

A small warning should be sufficient for anyone moving about in these crowds. The city now has frequent police patrols to curb the criminal element among the beach crowd. However, that element is still present and it's a foolish tourist who wanders about with large amounts of cash or with loose wallets or pocketbooks.

There is little evidence of it today, but here and there, you do see the arched windows or colonnade of an old building that has survived from the original grand plan of a new Venice beside the Pacific. This was part of a scheme by a developer named Abbot Kinney, a wealthy cigarette heir who bought 160 acres (65 hectares) of oceanfront tidelands in 1904. Abbot dredged canals and constructed a little city in the Venetian style, complete with gondolas and gondoliers. His idea

tycoon Henry E. Huntington had brought George Freeth from Hawaii to stage exhibitions with his long, heavy wooden surfboard, riding the waves into the beachfront property Huntington was trying to develop and sell. Perhaps because of the bulky boards, the sport didn't catch on for many years. When a Californian named Bob Simmons developed a "board" made of lightweight synthetic material in the early 1950s, it was an overnight sensation. Surfing became the sport of young Californians, with theme songs provided by The Beach Boys, starting with "Surfin' USA" in 1961.

Needless to say, the development succeeded and the area between Los Angeles airport and the Palos Verdes Peninsula — Redondo, Hermosa and Manhattan beaches — is now one of the most intensively-developed coastal areas in the world. If the busy crowds are too much for you, however, you can always drive a few miles and still find a secluded spot.

The City of Redondo Beach offers numerous attractions besides surf and sand. The municipal **Visitors' Center** ((310) 372-1171 extension 2329, 164 International Boardwalk, hosts exhibitions of local history, beach and marine life, as well as providing maps, brochures and information about the area. It is open Thursday to Sunday from noon to 6 PM.

The bustling **Redondo Beach Pier** ((310) 318-0648, at the foot of Torrance Boulevard, has recently undergone a multimillion dollar renovation and expansion program and is a popular place for sports fishing, dining, shopping and arcade-type

for youths under 18. Reservations are required through the Redondo Beach Recreation and Community Services Department ((310) 318-0670, Alta Vista Tennis Complex, 715 Julia Avenue.

PALOS VERDES PENINSULA

Spectacular views and isolated coves, where sunbathers feel free enough to dispense with bathing suits, are offered here. Once part of a Sepulveda family rancho, much of the peninsula was developed into large estates in the 1920s. Although privately owned, the areas around the public beaches are protected as nature preserves by the residents. Signs warn you not to disturb any of

entertainment. **Redondo Beach Marina** ((310) 374-3481, 181 North Harbor Drive, offers a wide array of water sports activities including harbor cruises, sport fishing, whale-watching excursions, parasailing, kayaking and glass bottom boats. Restaurants and nightclubs round off the waterfront entertainment experience.

The **Redondo Beach Performing Arts Center** ((310) 318-0610, 1935 Manhattan Beach Boulevard, hosts a variety of shows year round, including performances by the Civic Light Opera of the South Bay Cities ((310) 372-4477. For a little pocket of oceanfront nature visit **Hopkins Wilderness Park** ((310) 318-0668, 1102 Camino Real. Located at the south end of the El Segundo Sand Hills, this microwilderness area and wildlife reserve provides year-round nature study. Overnight camping is allowed. It is open Thursday to Tuesday from 10 AM to 4 PM. Camping fees are $4 for adults, $1

the wildlife you find in the tidal pools or along the beaches. The most interesting architectural site on the peninsula is the **Wayfarer's Chapel**, a modern design of redwood beams and glass by Lloyd Wright, son of Frank Lloyd Wright.

SAN PEDRO

This man-made harbor literally put Los Angeles on the map. Although 25 miles (40 km) away from downtown Los Angeles, it's still within the city limits. The harbor was part of the deal to make

Venice Beach — Muscle men OPPOSITE work out in the open air gymnasium that has given this part of Venice the name "Muscle Beach"; ABOVE, LEFT here is a great place for bikers or walkers taking in one of California's liveliest and most bizarre scenes and RIGHT some of the best shows in Los Angeles are staged by amateurs on the boardwalk.

Los Angeles the western terminus of the Santa Fe Railroad. With the nearby shipbuilding and military installations at Wilmington, Terminal Island and Long Beach, it has become one of the largest and busiest deep water ports in the world.

Two museums explain the area's marine and maritime history. The **Cabrillo Marine Aquarium** ((310) 548-7562, 3720 Stephen M. White Drive, has aquarium exhibits and ship model displays; it also sponsors whale watching cruises in the winter months. It is open Tuesday to Friday from noon to 5 PM and Saturday and Sunday from 10 AM to 5 PM. The **Los Angeles Maritime Museum** ((310) 548-7618 is located at Berth 84 at the end of Sixth Street. The exhibits focus on the history of San Pedro harbor, but there's also a 16-ft (five-meter) scale model of the RMS *Titanic*. The museum is open Tuesday to Sunday from 10 AM to 5 PM. At the south end of the Harbor Freeway, you'll find the **Port O' Call Village** ((310) 548-9970, a replica nineteenth-century fishing port with 65 shops and restaurants.

San Pedro is also a departure point for trips to **Santa Catalina Island**. Cruises to Catalina depart from the Catalina Terminal under the Vincent Thomas Bridge. For schedule information and fares, call ((310) 519-7971 (see also CATALINA, page 190).

LONG BEACH

Just as the name suggests, Long Beach is nearly five and a half miles (nine kilometers) of sand, 500 ft (150 m) wide. Founded as a seaside resort in 1897, it's now the second largest incorporated area in Los Angeles County. It has also become an important military port, and a commercial center for oil refineries and food-processing plants. The city was virtually leveled by an earthquake in 1933. This quake was thought to be just as severe as the big one that hit San Francisco in 1906, but it occurred on a much smaller fault line. It killed 120 people and damaged $50 million worth of property. As in San Francisco, the people rallied to rebuild on the same ground and Long Beach is now one of Southern California's most prosperous communities. In recent years, it has become a major convention center with many attractions to keep visitors busy including the annual **Long Beach Grand Prix** ((562) 981-2600 WEB SITE www .longbeachgp.com, which runs through the downtown streets, the only Formula One race currently staged in the United States.

The **Municipal Beach** that gave the city its name remains the main draw. At the west end of the beach, at Pier J, is a more recent attraction, the famous ocean liner *Queen Mary* ((562) 432-6964. When it was launched in 1934, the ship was one of the most luxurious steamers ever built, flagship of Cunard's White Star Fleet. In a major municipal investment, the city bought the ship and transformed it into a hotel, restaurant, convention center and museum in the 1960s. The investment has paid off handsomely; the *Queen Mary* is now a very popular hotel and tourist attraction. There are regular tours from 10 AM to 6 PM everyday and admission is $10 for adults, $6 for children 4 to 11 years old.

Two historic sites in Long Beach — **Rancho Los Alamitos** ((562) 431-3541, 6400 Bixby Hill Road, and **Rancho Los Cerritos** ((562) 570-1755, 4600 North Virginia Road — preserve the memory of California's rancho period. Both were once owned by the Bixby family — brothers and cousins who came from Maine, and succeeded as sheep

and cattle ranchers in various parts of California. The family became even richer when vast oil reserves at Signal Hill were discovered on Bixby ranch property. There is no admission fee for Rancho Los Alamitos, and a guided tour will take you to the main adobe house, the blacksmith shop, the barns, and the extensive gardens. Rancho Los Cerritos is a 10-room adobe and redwood ranch house with Italian-style gardens. It's open to the public free of charge. Both historic sites are open Wednesday to Sunday from 1 PM to 5 PM.

SIX FLAGS MAGIC MOUNTAIN

The "Rambo of Theme Parks" is situated about a 30-minute drive north of Los Angeles via Interstate 5 in a drowsy foothill town called Valencia. But there's nothing the least bit sleepy about **Six Flags Magic Mountain** ((805) 255-4100 WEB SITE www

.sixflags.com, is famous for its thrill rides, many of them not for the faint-hearted. One of the latest and most publicized rides (hence a wait of over an hour) is Superman the Escape—during which you accelerate from zero to 100 mph (160 kph) in seven seconds while racing down a 41-story tower. Another new ride, The Riddler's Revenge, is said to be the world's tallest and fastest stand-up roller coaster.

Meanwhile, you'll find that the park's older roller coasters are still the meanest in the business. The Great American Revolution involves a 360-degree loop. The rightly named Shock Wave propels its standing riders along an awesome steel track, then up and around that same loop. And then there's Colossus, the world's largest dual-track wooden roller coaster — which starts with a 110-ft (34-m) drop. There are other thrill rides that twist and spin and hurl you about. Good

advice from an experienced thrill rider: never get on a ride until you have watched it go for a full cycle and know what you're in for.

Admission is $34 for adults and $17 for children under 48 inches (1.2 m) in height. It is open daily March through October, weekends and holidays only November to February, from 10 AM to varying closing times between 6 PM and midnight.

The annual Kite Festival OPPOSITE is just one of many events that give Venice Beach the liveliest reputation of all California beaches. Volleyball ABOVE is an endless game on California's beaches, seen here at Hermosa Beach south of Los Angeles.

Orange County

ONE OF THE FASTEST GROWING AREAS IN SOUTHERN CALIFORNIA, Orange County encompasses a series of beautiful beaches and several upscale towns between Los Angeles and San Diego. Largely the province of upscale homeowners, the county has some of the most expensive real estate in the area, several exclusive, gated communities and miles of new housing tracts. The acres and acres of citrus groves that once filled the air with the scent of orange blossoms have mostly been razed for roads and homes, and boundaries between the county's towns have become blurred by shoulder-to-shoulder developments. The main attraction in this area for travelers is Disneyland in the city of Anaheim, one of the most congested areas of the county. Knott's Berry Farm, though not as large as Disneyland, is another popular amusement park. Dana Point, Huntington Beach, Newport Beach, and Laguna Beaches are all worth exploring, as are the upscale shopping and entertainment centers in Costa Mesa and Irvine. San Juan Capistrano is home to one of California's earliest and best restored missions. Travelers to this area are best off having cars, since the nicest accommodations, beaches and attractions are separated by a maze of freeways.

GENERAL INFORMATION

Contact the **Anaheim Orange County Visitor and Convention Bureau** ((714) 765-8888 FAX (714) 991-8963 WEB SITE www.anaheimoc.org, 800 West Katella Avenue, Anaheim, for information about Orange County hotels and attractions. It is open Monday through Friday from 8:30 AM to 5 PM. Some of the towns have visitor information centers, listed below. For up-to-date transportation information call ((714) 724-2077.

HOW TO GET THERE

Orange County's regional **John Wayne Orange County Airport** ((949) 252-5200, 18601 Airport Way, is used by savvy locals to avoid the enormous hassle that Los Angeles International Airport can be. Located in the middle of the county, in Santa Ana, the airport is served by Alaska, American West, American, Continental, Delta, Northwest, Reno Air, TWA and United Airlines, in addition to local commuter planes. Many upscale hotels offer free shuttle service; alternatively, **Super Shuttle** ((714) 517-6600 has 24-hour service.

Amtrak TOLL-FREE (800) 872-7245 provides daily train service from San Diego in the south to Los Angeles and beyond; the Orange County stops (north to south) are Fullerton, Anaheim, Santa Ana, Irvine, San Juan Capistrano, and San Clemente.

PRECEDING PAGES LEFT Expensive, casual hotels and cafes face the sand and sea in the artistic colony of Laguna Beach. RIGHT: Padres in traditional hats and robes reenact history at nearby San Juan Capistrano.

Greyhound buses TOLL-FREE (800) 231-2222 WEB SITE www.greyhound.com, serve the county's cities; the main station ((714) 542-2215 is at 1000 East Santa Ana Boulevard in Santa Ana.

Local bus service is far from convenient; for local city bus schedules, call ((714) 636-7433, extension 10. Most visitors choose to rent a car. The main north-south freeways are Interstate 5 (also known as Santa Ana Freeway or I-5, but called "the 5" by locals) and Interstate 405, also known as the San Diego Freeway. As you head north, Interstate 405 splits off Interstate 5 just southeast of Irvine and parallels the coast, while Interstate 5 continues north on an inland route, passing Disneyland and Knott's Berry Farm. State Highway 91 crosses the top of the county from east to west. There are many other freeways as well. Coast State Highway 1 connects many of the beach towns.

DISNEYLAND

The main attraction in Orange County, Disneyland was the highlight of Soviet Premier Nikita S. Khrushchev's 1959 tour of the United States. So, it came as no surprise that when a member of the Russian gymnastics team was asked what her "favorite city" was in a visit to the United States, she fired back without a moment's hesitation: "Disneyland."

In a series of commercials, the Disney theme ("When you wish upon a star") plays softly in the background as the screen focuses on America's athletic champions. "Pitcher Orel Hershiser, you and the Los Angeles Dodgers have just won baseball's World Series. What are you doing to do now?" A big grin comes over Hershiser's face: "I'm going to Disneyland." Likewise, Joe Montana after he and the San Francisco Forty-Niners won the Super Bowl: "I'm going to Disneyland."

Disneyland is no mere fun park at work, it is a powerful American institution that transcends competition in the business and social world.

Disneyland is not the oldest American theme park, but it has become the most famous. It is a unique American idea created by the great Walt Disney. "And never forget it all began with a mouse," he would tell his colleagues in his own phenomenally successful movie studios. That mouse was, of course, Mickey, who celebrated his 60th anniversary in 1988 with a year-long celebration at Disneyland.

Disney came to Hollywood from Chicago in 1923, but it was his animated talkie starring Mickey Mouse in 1928 that assured his success. His own studios opened in 1940. Many people have enjoyed similar successes in California, but few have given as much back as Disney. Much of his estate was left to the California Institute of the Arts. In 1989, construction began on a huge new music center

240   *Orange County*

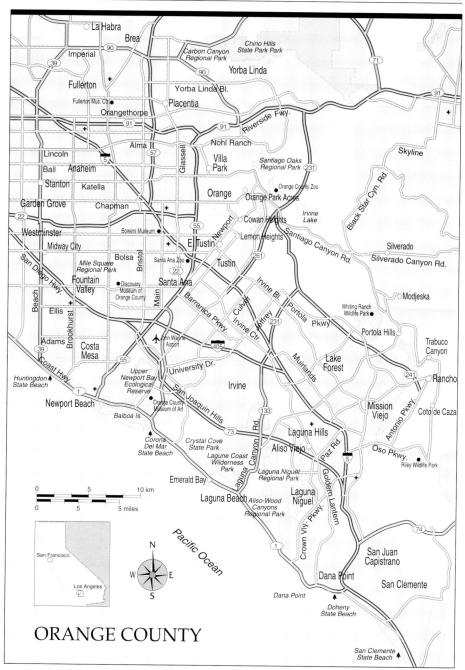

ORANGE COUNTY

in downtown Los Angeles, thanks to a $50 million gift from Disney's widow.

GENERAL INFORMATION

For general information on Disneyland, contact ℂ (714) 781-4565 (recorded information) or ℂ (714) 781-4560. One-day admission (good for all rides)

is $38 for adults, $36 for seniors, and $28 for children from three to 11 years; two- and three-day passes are also available.

WHAT TO SEE AND DO

Disneyland first opened in 1955 on a 76-acre (31-hectare) plot in Anaheim, with 18 major attractions (there are more than 60 attractions today). The park featured four areas: Fantasyland, Adventureland, Frontierland, and Tomorrowland. In this great park, Disney created an America that never was. He has a Main Street that is safe, clean, and fun, unlike many main streets of today. And that is a key to the success of Disneyland. It's not any place as it really is, but as we'd all like it to be. And, after 60 years, who can really separate the original American institutions from those that originated with Walt Disney.

The park now occupies 85 acres (34 hectares) of land and has eight theme lands, including Tomorrowland, where renovations were completed in May of 1998. The new Tomorrowland, with the theme "Imagination and Beyond," presents "the future through the world of the past." New attractions include the Astro Orbitor, where riders drive their own spaceships using interactive controls, and Rocket Rods, where guests whiz along in open-air rockets on the park's fastest, longest ride. Other rides, such as Space Mountain roller coaster and Star Tours, designed by filmmaker George Lucas, have been refurbished. Also popular is the new Honey I Shrank the Audience show, which combines the latest 3-D film techniques with ingenious theatrical effects. A new interactive fountain, based on the Elizabethan hedge mazes, lets guest play in mazes of water that shoot up from the ground in synchronized patterns.

One of the oldest and most popular rides remains the bobsleds off the Matterhorn and the Pirates of the Caribbean, which features some extraordinarily life-like automated and animated swashbucklers. In early 1989, the Magic Kingdom opened a new "Splash Mountain" in the Bear Country area, with a setting based on Disney's classic *Song of the South.*

Due to open in 2001 is the California Adventure, a $1.4 billion, 55-acre (22-hectare) theme park being built in the parking lot of the original park, which will have a separate admission. The theme areas will include one dedicated to Hollywood and the movie industry, with a simulated tour of ABC Studios; another dedicated to beach culture, with rides and attractions from California of the early 1900s; outdoor California, where rides simulate such adventures as whitewater rafting down California rivers, spelunking, and hang gliding over national parks.

WHERE TO STAY AND EAT

The neighborhood around Disneyland is filled with industrial parks, and is one of the least attractive places to stay in Orange County, although the resort area is currently undergoing a beautification project. Those who are limiting their visits in the region to the amusement park are best off

staying here; others might consider using one of the beach towns as their base. The **Disneyland Hotel** (714) 956-6400 or (714) 778-6600 FAX (714) 956-6561, 1150 West Cerritos Avenue in Anaheim, CA 92802, is one of two official Disneyland hotels. It is a 65-acre (26-hectare), 1,136-room resort adjoining the Magic Kingdom with three high-rise towers, rooms from $140 to $240 (including continental breakfast), and a marina playground covering three acres (more than a hectare). The resort complex includes restaurants, entertainment, and shopping facilities. Kids can goof off and meet Disney characters in Goofy's Kitchen, a buffet restaurant open daily for breakfast and dinner (weekends and holidays for lunch). There is a Sports Bar and Grill and a Japanese restaurant with sushi bar. Between the two properties there are four pools, tennis courts, fitness centers and spas. Connected to original hotel, and offering the same facilities and restaurants is the new 500-room **Disneyland Pacific Hotel** ((714) 999-0990 or (714) 956-6400 FAX (714) 956-6582, 1717 South West Street, Anaheim, 92802. Both hotels are in the moderate to expensive range. A moderate choice just across the street from the park is the 172-room **Candy Cane Inn** ((714) 774-5284 TOLL-FREE (800) 345-7057 FAX (714) 772-5462, 1747 South Harbor Boulevard, which has a nice heated swimming pool, children's pool and spa. **Castle Inn and Suites** ((714) 774-8111 TOLL-FREE (800) 227-8530 FAX (714) 956-4736, 1734 South Harbor Boulevard, has the same amenities in the same price range as the Candy Cane Inn, plus a refrigerator in each of the 200 rooms. **Anaheim Vacation Park** ((714) 774-2267, 311 North Beach Boulevard, has 222 full recreational vehicle hookups ($32 to $38) and six tent camping sites ($25). It is located three blocks south of Knott's Berry Farm, in Anaheim. There are a pool and recreation room; the two comfort stations provide toilets, showers and laundry facilities.

HOW TO GET THERE

Disneyland is located at 1313 South Harbor Boulevard, just off Interstate 5, in Anaheim. Exit the Santa Ana Freeway (Interstate 5) at either Harbor or Katella Avenue and follow the signs. Amtrak has a stop in Anaheim, at 2150 East Katella, in the Anaheim Stadium parking lot. From here you can purchase a round-trip bus ticket with one-day pass to Disneyland; transportation cost is about $7.

KNOTT'S BERRY FARM

Though not as famous as the Magic Kingdom, this theme park is located near by and gives kids even more rides and amusements for squandering their parents vacation dollars. Accommodations in the area consist of small chain hotels; there are better options by Disneyland or at the beaches.

GENERAL INFORMATION

Knott's Berry Farm ((714) 220-5200 is located at 8039 Beach Boulevard in Buena Park (just north of Disneyland in Anaheim); admission is good for all rides and costs $35 for adults and $25 for seniors and children age 3 to 11. Kids under two are free. Parking is also charged.

WHAT TO SEE AND DO

Knott's Berry Farm is California's oldest theme park. It started in 1920, when Walter Knott opened a little roadside stand to sell berries from

with a maximum height of 118 ft (36 m), will open in the spring of 1999. Other attractions are found at Wild Water Wilderness, three and a half acres (nearly one and a half hectares) of water rides. Voices and signs warn you before getting into the Bigfoot Rapids Ride that "You will get wet; you may get drenched." Six people at a time board the rafts, and are then spun in and out of the rough waters, over falls and rapids. Two of the more popular older rides are the Log Ride, a fast 15-minute trip along a 2,100-ft (640-m) water course; and the slower Calico Mine, in which you ride an ore car through a (re-created) mine. The park includes several restaurants and take-out food stands.

the farm and jams made from them. Like all good American businessmen, Knott saw opportunities to expand. First, he added a Chicken Dinner restaurant that was so popular he built a little Ghost Town to amuse people while they were waiting. By 1946, more than a million dinners a year were being served and sold. The expansion continued with a narrow gauge railroad, a Chapel by the Lake, and a "Freedom Center," which features a full-scale replica of Independence Hall in Philadelphia.

Now, of course, Knott's Berry Farm has expanded to the point that most people forget it ever was a berry farm. It offers 165 different rides to the more than four million people who visit the park every year. The newest ride is Supreme Scream, opened July 4, 1998: riders drop from one of three towers — 30 stories in three seconds! Ghost Rider, a 4,530-ft (1,381-m) roller coaster,

HOW TO GET THERE

Twenty miles (32 km) southeast of Los Angeles in Buena Park, Knott's Berry Farm can be reached from either Interstate 5 or State Highway 91. Take the Beach Boulevard exit heading south, and then follow the signs.

INLAND TOWNS

Santa Ana, **Orange**, **Irvine** and **Costa Mesa** are all located a bit inland from the beaches off Interstate 5 and Interstate 405. Though not tourist destinations per se, they do include some interesting

Knott's Berry Farm just south of Los Angeles is the state's oldest all-American theme park. The log ride LEFT at is just one of the thrill rides and youngsters RIGHT join in the frivolity at the Grand Snoopy Parade.

attractions for those visiting the area. The **Bowers Museum of Cultural Art** ((714) 567-3600, 2002 North Main Street in Santa Ana, is housed in a mission-style building in downtown Santa Ana. The largest museum in Orange County, the Bowers is devoted to the art and artifacts of indigenous peoples, and holds special shows highlighting cultures from around the world. Permanent exhibits cover Native American art, artifacts from pre-Columbian Mexico, and the Kidseum, an interactive children's space. The city of Orange has one of the loveliest downtown areas in the county in the **Historical District**, with a central green surrounded by historical buildings. Antique and interior design shops line the side streets.

style gambling, virtual reality and bars. In addition there are restaurants (including the Wolfgang Puck Café), food courts, and of course, retail shops. The Center is located at the juncture of the Santa Ana (Interstate 5) and San Diego (Interstate 405) Freeways, in Irvine.

Costa Mesa is located adjacent to Orange County's airport and Newport Beach, and is the region's center for commerce and industry. Mirrored office towers and corporate headquarters rise beside the freeways, while several small middle-class neighborhoods are clustered along side streets. The biggest attractions here are two classic, upscale Southern California shopping malls. **South Coast Plaza** ((714) 435-2000, 3333 Bristol

Irvine consists of mile after mile of housing tracts, all part of a planned community which began development in the 1970s. The **Irvine Meadows Ampitheatre** ((949) 855-8096, off Interstate 405 on Irvine Center Drive, is the best venue in the county for open-air concerts. **Irvine Spectrum Center** ((949) 789-9180 FAX (949) 789-9184, 8001 Irvine Center Drive, Suite 1130, Irvine, is a 250,000 sq-ft (23,226 sq m) entertainment and retail center billed as "the largest master planned business and technology center in the United States." The architecture is styled after that of the Alhambra, built by the Moors in southern Spain in the thirteenth century: there are arched gateways, reflecting pools, and outdoor pavilions with fountains. The center is built around an Edward's 21-Screen Cinema with IMAX 3-D, and Dave & Buster's, which integrates under one roof dining, billiards, golf, shuffle board, Monte Carlo-

Street off Interstate 405, is one of the most profitable malls in the country thanks in part to the high income of Orange County residents and in part to the shoppers who trek here from Los Angeles and San Diego. The plaza's main entrance leads to a soaring glass atrium filled with plants, flowers and fountains; it is gorgeously decorated at Christmas. Every major department store and designer boutique has a branch here, along with nearly every theme restaurant imaginable. Children's shops are clustered around the Carousel Court's turn-of-the-century carousel; high-end shops including Tiffany & Co. and Armani are located in the Jewel Court.

Fashion Island ((949) 721-2000, 401 Newport Center Drive, is in Newport Beach. An imaginatively designed shopping and dining center, the complex includes several excellent restaurants (including a Wolfgang Puck Café), a food court with inexpensive ethnic food counters and patio seating, and several movie theaters. Families stop by just so the children can play in a sidewalk fountain that spurts jets of water skyward from the ground. Outdoor paths lead past department stores, shops and boutiques. The Farmer's Market, located in the Atrium, is a massive open space bordered by a series of ethnic takeout food stands, coffee and wine bars, and produce markets.

WHERE TO STAY AND EAT

Costa Mesa is a good overnight option for those visiting several destinations in Orange County.

FAX (714) 662-0828, 325 South Bristol Street include full breakfast and the morning papers. Rooms have refrigerators and television; video cassette recorders can be requested. There are two pools, each with an adjacent hot tub, and a small fitness room. Discounts are available for longer stays.

The best restaurants are in the shopping centers and hotels.

THE BEACH TOWNS

State Highway 1 runs south into Orange County from Los Angeles, and passes by several beach towns and parks, starting with **Bolsa Chica State**

There is easy access to both interstates and most highways, and the hotels, which typically cater to business travelers, are very reasonably priced. Connected to South Coast Plaza by a pedestrian bridge, the **Westin South Coast Plaza** ((714) 540-2500 TOLL-FREE (800) 937-8461 FAX (714) 662-6695, 686 Anton Boulevard, Costa Mesa has 390 plush rooms and suites. Facilities include restaurants, fitness center, outdoor pool and two lighted tennis courts. There is a complimentary shuttle from John Wayne Airport. Room rates are in the moderate range. **Costa Mesa Marriott Suites** ((714) 957-1100 TOLL-FREE (800) 228-9290 FAX (714) 966-8495, 500 Anton Boulevard, Costa Mesa, has 253 moderately priced suites; the living rooms have wet bar, coffeemaker and refrigerator. There is a complimentary airport shuttle. The moderate room rates at the modern **Country Side Inn and Suites** ((714) 549-0300 TOLL-FREE (800) 322-9992

Beach and Ecological Preserve ((714) 848-1566, which has parking lots, fire rings, showers, restrooms and a campground. The main reason to go to **Huntington Beach**, next in line, is to surf, body surf, or to watch the surfers—or to get a tan. Some of the most challenging surf happens around the pier, at the base of Main Street. This pier is the latest of many, which have been beaten by the Pacific Ocean and jostled by earthquakes since the first was built in 1914. The pier, which was totally rebuilt and inaugurated in 1992, is almost 2,000 ft (600 m) long. It's a good place to fish, or watch the surfers. The main city beach starts just north of the pier and continues south until the start of Huntington State Beach ((714) 848-1566, south of

OPPOSITE: Artists display their work in galleries, parks, and festivals in Laguna Beach. ABOVE: The sun casts an enchanting light over the Newport Pier.

Main Street. The state beach continues south for several miles until it abuts Newport Beach just south of the Santa Ana River. There state beach has plenty of facilities, including restrooms, paid parking ($6 for both city and state beaches), picnic tables, snack stands and fire rings. Camping is not permitted and the beach closes at 11 PM. Blade skates, bikes and beach equipment can be rented at **Dwight's Snack Bar** ((714) 536-8083, on the beach one block south of the pier. The **International Surfing Museum** ((714) 960-3483, 411 Olive Street, is installed in a building with its own history as the former site of Safari Sam's club, an institution with locals until the mid-1980s. Inside are the requisite old surfboards as well as memo-

rabilia from the surf culture of the 1950s and 1960s. The museum is open daily during the summer months, from noon to 5 PM; and Wednesday to Sunday during winter months. If you want to see the professionals in action, check out the **OP Pro Surfing Championships** are usually held in July, or the **US Open of Surfing**, most often held in August.

Newport Beach, located 50 miles (80 km) south of downtown Los Angeles by way of Interstates 405 and 5, and California State Highway 55, and State Highway 1, is a self-styled "American Riviera." It has some of the world's most expensive residential real estate and is the preferred home of California's wealthiest people for at least part of the year. It boasts a six-mile (10-km)-long beach and a harbor that is considered the premier dock for private yachts and pleasure boats in Southern California. Balboa

Island, Lido Isle, and Corona del Mar are all small bayside communities within Newport Beach.

Heading into Newport Beach from the State Highway 1 you pass Lido Island, an area of exclusive homes reached by a causeway, on your left. Newport Boulevard runs through the center of this beach town, which is actually located on a small peninsula between the Pacific Ocean and Newport Bay. **Newport Pier**, at the end of McFadden Place about a half a mile (800 m) into town, is a reconstruction of an older pier destroyed by a hurricane in the 1930s. On one side of the pier is an open-air market selling fish caught by the "dory fishing fleet," a fleet of small fishing boats that have been hauling in their catch here since the 1890s. Landlubbers can fish off the pier. The main street changes names to Balboa Boulevard near the pier, and continues down the peninsula to **Balboa Pier**, which extends over the ocean with a concrete boardwalk and landscaped parks. Ruby's Diner, a popular breakfast spot for locals, sits at the end of the pier. The **Balboa Pavilion** at 400 Main Street and Balboa Boulevard on the bay side of the peninsula is a fabulous Victorian structure built in 1905. The structure shelters passengers awaiting boats for harbor cruises and excursions to Catalina Island. Many visitors spend the day strolling along the boardwalk running from the pavilion along Newport Bay to Jetty View Park, where you can watch sailboats entering and leaving the protected harbor. The boardwalk includes a **Fun Zone** with an arcade housing old-fashioned pinball machines and newer video games. The boulevard is lined with shops and restaurants in this area, and is nearly impossible to drive along on sunny weekends. You're best off parking in a lot by one of the piers and walking around. For information about area hotels and attractions, contact the **Newport Beach Conference and Visitors Bureau** ((949) 722-1611 TOLL-FREE (800) 942-6278 FAX (949) 722-1612 WEB SITE www.regUCIedu/NEWPORT _BEACH_CVB.com, 3300 West Coast Highway.

Balboa Island is a small, upper-class neighborhood across the bay from Newport Beach. It's best to come over on the Balboa Island Ferry ((949) 673-5245 and walk around the small island, although cars also can be transported — a few at a time. The ferry has been in operation since the early 1900s, and runs daily from 6:30 AM to midnight (to 2 AM on weekend nights).

Corona del Mar State Beach, on the eastern bank of Newport Bay is a lovely beach which gets terribly crowded in the summertime. Come early to get one of the $6 parking spaces. Little Corona Beach, to the south, is a treat for both kids and adults when the tide is out and the tidepools are exposed.

South of Corona del Mar but before Laguna Beach is **Crystal Cove State Park** ((949) 494-3539 — just under 3,000 acres (1,200 hectares) of shoreline, tidepools and canyon lands designated as a nature preserve. Park hours are daily from 6 AM to sunset; the parking fee is $6 per car; there is no fee for walk-ins or bike riders. Park access is via the following streets off Pacific Coast Highway: El Moro Canyon, Reef Point, Los Trancos, and Pelican Point. Environmental campgrounds — which have picnic tables and chemical toilets — can be accessed from the El Moro Canyon parking lot; one must backpack four miles (slightly over six kilometers) in to the camp site. Camping fees are $7 to $11 per site (up to four people) depending

and hills rising straight up from the beaches has long made it a favorite spot of artists and writers. The beaches are just as popular with the more athletic surfers and swimmers. The mood here is festive year-round among the owners and visitors of the quaint antique shops and artists' galleries.

South Coast Highway (as State Highway 1 is called here) runs through the center of town and is lined with intriguing art galleries. Laguna Beach is known for its many artists, who began arriving in the early twentieth century to found the Plein Air School, determined to capture the fresh style and light revered by the French impressionists. The arts have been important to Laguna Beach

on the day of the week and time of year. Interpretive walks are led most weekends by volunteer docents — call ahead for the schedule. About a fairly rugged quarter-mile (400-m) hike from the Los Trancos parking lot is the **Crystal Cove historic district**, one-time home to ranch hands from the Company and now listed in the National Register of Historic Places. These beachfront bungalows should be available to the public for rent around the year 2000, when current leasees have relocated.

The park has many recreational opportunities, including birding, hiking, and mountain biking, horseback riding (BYOH — "bring your own horse"), sunbathing, and scuba diving and snorkeling in the offshore aquatic park.

Laguna Beach, about five miles (eight kilometers) south of Newport Beach, is a laid-back yet prosperous town. The setting of steep cliffs

ever since, and many visitors come to browse or buy in the many galleries located here in this charming seaside enclave. This section of the highway is also lined with casual (but expensive) restaurants and hotels, and is one of the most charming places to stay in Orange County.

Those who want to enjoy some of life's less expensive pleasures head for Laguna's beaches. **Main Beach** parallels the highway through downtown; here you'll find the impressive, glassed-in lifeguard tower and see rollerbladers dodging pedestrians on the wooden boardwalk. The beach continues uninterrupted toward the Aliso Pier and South Laguna, with lots of rocky coves. Access to

OPPOSITE: Victorian-style houses contrast with the laid-back ambiance at Huntington Beach. ABOVE: Police officers LEFT don chaps and spurs at the annual Huntington Beach Rodeo. RIGHT: Gondolas ferry romantics along the waters off Newport Beach.

the beach is somewhat limited south of town, due to the line-up of million-dollar homes claiming the view.

Laguna is home to several arts events. Staged in July and August, the **Sawdust Festival** ((714) 494-3030 WEB SITE www.sawdustartfestival.org is a major arts and crafts show. Art walks are led by docents during the festival, for a glimpse into the workshop of local artists. But the most famous of Laguna Beach's festivals is the **Festival of Arts and Pageant of the Masters** ((949) 494-1145 TOLL-FREE (800) 487-3378 WEB SITE www.foapom.com. The Festival of Arts showcases truly spectacular works by California artists; the Pageant includes a much-awaited stage show in which Laguna

Beach residents pose in *tableaux vivants* to recreate famous paintings. Both shows are held in the Irvine Bowl, at 650 Laguna Canyon Road, in July and August. The cost of the art festival is $3; ticket to the Pageant of the Masters vary from $10 to $35, and reservations are required.

Laguna Art Museum ((949) 494-6531, 307 Cliff Drive, is one of the few Southern California art museums to exhibit almost exclusively American art, especially Contemporary California Art. It is open Tuesday through Sunday from 11 AM to 5 PM. General admission is $5; $4 for students and seniors; children 12 and under free.

For more information contact the **Laguna Beach Visitor Bureau and Chamber of Commerce** ((949) 497-9229 TOLL-FREE (800) 877-1115 FAX (949) 376-0558, 252 Broadway, Laguna Beach, CA 92652.

Dana Point approximately eight miles (13 km) south of Laguna Beach on Coast Highway (State

Highway 1). It can also be reached on Interstate 5, taking the Pacific Coast Highway exit (if traveling south) and the Beach Cities exit if traveling north. The small community by one of the Orange County's biggest harbors was named for author Richard Henry Dana, whose *Two Years Before the Mast* records his sea journey from New England to California in the 1840s.

Once the only major harbor between San Diego and Santa Barbara, Dana Point's focus is still the **Dana Point Harbor** ((949) 493-8649, filled with yachts and sailboats. Pathways run along the harbor connecting parking lots, restaurants and park areas with picnic tables.

Surfers head to 62-acre (25-hectare) **Doheny State Beach**, donated to the state in the 1930s by Edward L. Doheny. Inside the visitor's center is a 3,000-gallon (11,350-liter) aquarium with fish native to the area; out along the rocky parts of the coast, people try to catch these natives with hook and line. Bike paths lead both south, to San Clemente, and north to San Juan Capistrano from here, making biking a pleasant day's activity.

For more information contact the **Dana Point Chamber of Commerce** ((949) 496-1555 FAX (949) 496-5321 WEBSITE www.danapoint-chamber-com, 24681 La Plaza, Suite 115, Dana Point, 92629.

Right on the southern border of Orange County is **San Clemente**, an upscale beach resort developed in the 1920s, that took the "pseudo-Spanish" style to the extreme. There are no streets or avenues here, only *avenidas* and *caminitas*.

The town's main claim to fame was the brief period when President Richard Nixon's beachfront house, Casa Pacifica, served as the "Western White House." When he resigned in disgrace in the wake of Watergate, Nixon chose to retire to New York and New Jersey, and Casa Pacifica was sold to the highest bidder, a local developer. The gardens are occasionally opened to the public, but the property is otherwise private and closed to the public.

SAN JUAN CAPISTRANO

San Juan Capistrano is one of California's most famous mission sites. The song *When the Swallows Come Back to Capistrano,* brought it fame and made it the most visited of the old missions. According to legend, the swallows returned to the mission every Saint Joseph's Day, March 19, and nested in the ruins. Despite the song, the crowds, and the fanfare, however, the swallows tend to show up when they darn well please, sometimes around the beginning of spring. Sadly, the crowds that come to wish the returning birds well seem to create the opposite effect, scaring the birds which then seek out more tranquil nesting sites.

Swallows swarm to San Juan Capistrano ABOVE in the spring while travelers arrive at the train depot OPPOSITE.

General Information

For information about hotels and attractions in San Juan Capistrano, contact the **San Juan Capistrano Chamber of Commerce (** (949) 493-4700 FAX (949) 489-2695 WEB SITE www .focusoc.com/cities/sanjuan/chamber, 26832 Ortega Highway.

What to See and Do

Founded in 1775, San Juan Capistrano was the seventh mission established in California and, for a time one of the most prosperous. It had a magnificent church that rose like a cathedral over the barren landscape, but this was destroyed by an earthquake in 1812. The story went that the service had just ended when the first quake hit; the people, who were outside the building ran back inside to pray and many were crushed when the walls and roof collapsed in the aftershocks. The mission site is just off Interstate 5; in fact, you can see what looks like a mission church from the highway. This church, though, is a fairly recent construction in the Spanish style, not a replica, and not part of the historic complex.

San Juan Capistrano's ruins are still quite impressive, and dominate the small town. Spreading out from the mission is a pleasant little town with several homely cafés right across the street from the historic complex. Directly south of town is Doheny State Beach, and below that, the city of San Clemente. San Diego County begins just to the south of San Clemente.

How to Get There

San Juan Capistrano is located at the intersection of Interstate 5 and State Highway 74, southeast of Laguna Beach. The charming train depot ((949) 240-2972 is located at 26701 Verdugo Street.

WHERE TO STAY

Orange County beach hotels are expensive, as a rule, but worth the cost for those who prefer the sound of the sea to freeway noise. Advance reservations are strongly advised for all hotels in the area.

Very Expensive

The swankest hotel in all of Orange County is the **Ritz-Carlton Laguna Niguel (** (949) 240-2000 TOLL-FREE (800) 241-3333 FAX (714) 240-1061, 33533 Ritz-Carlton Drive, Dana Point, 92629. Despite the name, the property is actually located in Dana Point overlooking the beach from its cliffside vantage point. The Ritz has top of the line amenities, including two heated pools (with Jacuzzi). There is a $15 per night resort fee for access to tennis, fitness center with steam and sauna, aerobics, yoga classes, beach equipment, four outdoor tennis courts. The lobby is awash in original art, especially nineteenth-century American art. Each room has its own small terrace; some have ocean views. This elegant hotel is not for the sweat-suit set: jacket and tie for men are required in the rather formal restaurant, **The Dining Room**, and in the **Club Grill**. Accommodations on the club floor provide access to complimentary Continental breakfast, light lunches, afternoon teas, and evening hors d'œurves and cocktails.

Though some rooms are less expensive, it's worth splurging on an ocean front suite with a private balcony over the sand at the **Surf & Sand Hotel (** (949) 497-4477 TOLL-FREE (800) 524-8621 FAX (949) 494-2897, 1555 South Coast Highway in Laguna Beach. A longtime favorite of artists and celebrities, the hotel has a heated outdoor pool overlooking beach, valet parking (a major plus on this crowded street), a Jacuzzi and fitness room,

as well as body salon for massages and facials. The restaurants are excellent. Classy and well-appointed describes the 285 rooms at the **Four Seasons Hotel Newport Beach** ((714) 759-0808 TOLL-FREE (800) 332-3442 FAX (714) 759-0568. In addition to the amenities you would expect from a luxury hotel are free loan of mountain bikes, a large fitness center, a business center, heated swimming pool and two restaurants. Golfers can reserve tee-times at one of the area's golf courses. The restaurants are among the best in Newport Beach.

Expensive

Huntington Beach's downtown hotel options include the rather luxurious **Waterfront Hilton Beach Resort** ((714) 960-7873 TOLL-FREE (800) 822-SURF FAX (714) 960-2542, 21100 Pacific Coast Highway, Huntington Beach. The pretty property

has rooms overlooking the beach and the pier; swimming pool, spa, and tennis courts. There is a restaurant and a jazz club.

Overlooking the Back Bay of Newport is the business-oriented **Marriott Suites Newport Beach** ((949) 854-4500 TOLL-FREE (800) 228-9290 FAX (714) 854-3937. Each of the 250 suites has a television and phone in both bedroom and living room, plus a refrigerator. Some of the 34 rooms and suites at the Spanish-style **Balboa Inn** ((949) 675-3412 FAX (949) 673-4587, 105 Main Street, Newport Beach, have fireplaces, others have whirlpool spas in the bathroom.

In Laguna Beach, each of the 66 rooms at the **Laguna Brisas Spa Hotel** ((949) 497-7272 TOLL-

Moonlit walks on the beach and afternoon tea enhance the feeling of luxury at the the Ritz-Carlton Laguna Niguel.

FREE (800) 624-4442 FAX (949) 497-8306, 1600 South Coast Highway, has a large Jacuzzi. It is just across the street from the beach, and there is a heated outdoor pool and spa as well.

In Dana Point, the **Blue Lantern Inn (** (949) 661-1304 TOLL-FREE (800) 950-1236 FAX (949) 496-1483, 34343 Street of the Blue Lantern, is a gorgeous bed and breakfast with New England architecture blending into hilltop scenery. The 29 rooms have gas fireplaces and whirlpool bathtub; some have an ocean or harbor view. Tower rooms have private decks and spectacular views of the harbor. In addition to a buffet breakfast, wine and appetizers are served each afternoon in the library.

from the terrace and Le Bar. In South Laguna, **Aliso Creek Inn (** (949) 499-2271 TOLL-FREE (800) 223-3309 FAX (949) 499-4601, 31106 South Coast Highway, is tucked at the base of the canyon not far from the beach on an 80-acre (32-hectare) compound. Rooms include apartments with full kitchens.

Doubletree Guest Suites Dana Point ((949) 661-1100 TOLL-FREE (800) 222-8733 FAX (949) 489-0628, 34402 Pacific Coast Highway, is located on a 10-mile (16-km) stretch of beach adjacent to the Dana Point Harbor. There are 196 suites, some with private patios. The restaurant specializes in Mediterranean cuisine; there is a gift shop, heated outdoor pool, spa, sauna and fitness center.

The **Marriott Laguna Cliffs Resort (** (949) 661-5000 TOLL-FREE (800) 533-9748 FAX (949) 661-5358, 25135 Park Lantern, Dana Point 92629, has 350 rooms and suites decorated in shades of white and aquamarine. Two lounges offer entertainment and dancing Thursdays and Saturdays; there are two lighted tennis courts, two heated pools, four spas, and a health club with indoor sauna and steamroom. You can also rent sports equipment from scuba gear to bicycles; there are some nice biking trails in the area.

Moderate

Built in the 1930s, the **Hotel Laguna (** (949) 494-1151 TOLL-FREE (in California) (800) 524-2927 FAX (949) 497-2163, 425 South Coast Highway in Laguna Beach, has no pool, but its own private beach in downtown Laguna. There is an ocean view from the very good restaurant as well as

Inexpensive

Colonial Inn Youth Hostel ((714) 536-3315 FAX (714) 536-9485, 421 Eighth Street, Huntington Beach, 92468, is a great place for budget travelers. The building is turn-of-the-century, the rooms are clean, and you can opt for either dormitory-style or private rooms at really reasonable prices. Near downtown, this hotel is also just three blocks from the beach. There are 48 beds in dormitory rooms, but if you're traveling with a partner, it's worth the $2 more to get one of the three private rooms, if available.

Sun 'n' Sands Motel ((714) 536-2543 FAX (714) 960-5779, 1102 Pacific Coast Highway, is located a few blocks from downtown and just across the highway from the beach; it has a heated pool as well.

In Newport Beach, **Newport Dunes (** (714) 729-3863 TOLL-FREE (800) 288-0770 or (in Canada) (800)

233-9515, 1131 Back Bay Drive, Newport Beach, is a non-membership recreational vehicle resort with 100 acres (40 hectares) of private beach along the bay. There are 405 double-wide sites with full hook-ups, as well as a private, 430-slip marina, playgrounds, swimming pool, spa, and grocery store. The Back Bay Café is open for breakfast and lunch. To keep you amused, bikes, canoes, kayaks, windsurfers, and other equipment is rented. Beachfront pavilions and cabañas are available for groups. The cost averages $47.

In Dana Point, **Doheny State Beach (** (949) 496-6171, 25300 Dana Point Harbor Drive at Pacific Coast Highway, is a beautiful site for day use or overnight camping (no hookups). Day use is $6, camping $17 to $23. There is a large grassy area with professional-level volleyball courts, and bike trails radiate north and south from the beach. Picnic sites and group campsites are also available and can be reserved ahead of time. For camping reservations call **Destinet** TOLL-FREE (800) 444-7275. The visitor center has a large aquarium displaying local marine species.

WHERE TO EAT

Some of the most exceptional (and expensive) restaurants in the beach towns are located in the hotels. Fine dining experiences are guaranteed at the Ritz-Carlton Laguna, the Four Seasons Newport Beach, and the Surf & Sand in Laguna Beach.

Inexpensive restaurants abound in Huntington Beach, where **The Sugar Shack (** (714) 536-0355, 213 ½ Main Street, has been serving locals and visitors for almost three decades. The popular breakfast menu is served all day long. Locals recommend breakfast and lunch at the **Park Bench Café (** (714) 842-0775, 17732 Goldenwest Street. **Mother's Market and Kitchen (** (714) 963-6667, 19770 Beach Boulevard, is both health food store and vegetarian restaurant. **Tosh's Mediterranean Cuisine and Bakery (** (714) 842-3315, 16871 Beach Boulevard, serves Turkish, Arabic and Greek food; it is open for lunch and dinner only and is closed on Monday. They have live entertainment Friday and Saturday nights.

The most famous restaurant in Newport Beach is **The Crab Cooker (** (949) 673-0100, 2200 Newport Boulevard. It's popular with locals as well as tourists, all of whom wait in line for a table in the busy, informal restaurant where Styrofoam cups hold the famous clam chowder and the namesake crab and grilled seafood are served on paper plates. The meals are moderately priced; no credit cards are accepted.

Ruby's ((714) 675-7829, on the Balboa Pier, is a 1950s-style diner famous for its inexpensive breakfasts, hamburgers, milkshakes and the ocean view from its rooftop patio. **Pascal (** (949) 752-0107,

1000 North Bristol Avenue, serves delicious, expensive French Provençal cuisine. Men must wear a jacket. It is closed all day Sunday and Monday evening. The adjacent delicatessen serves takeout food as well as meats, cheeses, and of course, baguettes. **The Pavilion (** (949) 760-4920, at the Four Seasons Hotel (see above), is a popular upscale dining venue near Fashion Island, which is open daily for breakfast, lunch and dinner and serves Continental food with a Mediterranean influence.

In Laguna Beach, the well-known **Beach House Inn (** (949) 494-9707, 619 Sleepy Hollow Lane, is especially popular with locals, who converge on the outdoor patio for breakfast. Also popular are lobster, steaks and seafood, all moderately priced.

In Dana Point, **The Regatta Grill (** (949) 661-5000 at the Marriott's Laguna Cliffs Resort, perched on a bluff overlooking the harbor, has a huge outdoor deck from which to enjoy the view. In the evenings live music is performed on the deck. The contemporary American cuisine, based mainly on Californian and Mediterranean cuisine, is prepared by Chef Jiff Littlefield, formerly of the Four Seasons Hotel in New York. The delicious "Sunday Blue Jean Brunch" is expensive but worth every penny.

The lifestyle may be casual but the price tags are astounding in trendy Laguna Beach.

Las Vegas

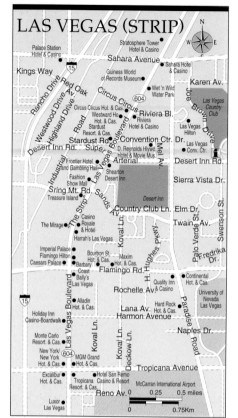

LAS VEGAS (STRIP)

IMAGINATIONS RUN AMUCK IN LAS VEGAS, where time hardly exists and money reigns supreme. Clever technoids play toward extremes as they create the latest visual sensations, transporting themselves (and their captive audiences) to hotels and casinos designed to resemble Rome, Venice, Paris, Italy and the twenty-fourth century. Marketers anticipate and create an insatiable demand for trendy logos and theme cafés. And tourists by the millions (29 million in 1997) respond, jetting in from Asia, Europe and the Americas. Driven by curiosity, amusement and/or greed, they buy into the Vegas scene with glee.

Exhilarating, overwhelming and downright dazzling, Las Vegas is the ultimate escape, except for those poor souls betting their futures on the big break. It's also the ultimate equalizer, guaranteeing opportunity and anonymity to millionaires and misfits alike. Its history is filled with glamour, danger and big-time crime; though much has been done to sanitize this image, Vegas still exudes a thrilling and edgy mystique.

Las Vegas is still glamorous, for sure; even T-shirted tourists arrive at the casinos in limousines. Wealthy high-rollers hide out in their penthouse suites at Caesars, the Hilton and Mirage and lay their big bucks on the line in gilded, heavily guarded baccarat rooms. But even the most exclusive, expensive casino hotels have slot machines, buffet meals and other enticements to lure less-endowed travelers.

The Las Vegas of the 1990s is sanitized, legitimized and family-friendly, yet still decadent in its own way. Kids in strollers, kids perched on grownups' shoulders, kids underfoot everywhere prove Las Vegas no longer caters just to the wealthy and to blue-hair bus tours. Change is the name of the game as established hotels race to compete with bigger, flashier, more outrageous newcomers.

BACKGROUND

Like much of the Southwest, Las Vegas was part of Mexico until the end of the Mexican-American War in 1848, when Nevada became a United States territory. In 1855 Mormon missionaries established a settlement in the Las Vegas area; in 1858, discouraged by disputes with the local indigenous groups, the Mormons dismantled their settlement and moved on. Less than a decade later gold miners discovered the remains of the Mormon settlement and restored the buildings. Miner Octavius Decatur Gass named his compound the Las Vegas Ranch and established business as a way station for desert travelers.

The ranch thrived through the late 1800s, and when the railroad connecting Utah and California was completed in 1905, settlers began moving to the Las Vegas region near the train tracks. The town began to boom and gain a Red Light District — an essential part of any railroad town. Brothels and bars were segregated into a certain area by law. By 1911 Las Vegas had a population of 15,000. Vegas prospered again in 1931 when construction began on the Boulder Dam (later renamed for Herbert Hoover), which coincided nicely with Nevada lawmakers' decisions to legalize gambling and quickie divorces. Vegas hosted its first convention in 1935, wooing some 5,000 Shriners to meet in Las Vegas. Hotels began rising on the Strip in the 1940s, fueled by mob money and influence that lasted for decades. Mobster Benjamin Siegel, forever immortalized in the Warren Beatty film *Bugsy*, opened the Flamingo Hotel on Las Vegas Boulevard in 1946; within a year the boulevard had become The Strip.

Las Vegas was already an established "Sin City" when developers with Mafia ties began constructing the Golden Nugget, Desert Inn, Stardust Inn, the Dunes and other Strip landmarks.

PREVIOUS PAGES: The dense array of beckoning neon and casinos RIGHT that draw people to Las Vegas. OPPOSITE TOP: Dazzling images compete for attention along the Las Vegas Strip. BOTTOM: Excess is the norm at the Luxor's Egyptian pyramid.

The emergence of the celebrity Rat Pack — a beloved nickname for singers Frank Sinatra, Dean Martin and their friends — brought a sense of glamour to the scene in the 1950s. Everyone knew Las Vegas had to be a crooked, illegal town where murder, extortion and money-laundering were common events. Every law enforcement agency imaginable cracked down on Las Vegas in the 1960s, and by the mid-1970s the Gaming Control Board and State Gaming Commission had licensing and regulation firmly entrenched.

Las Vegas as a family destination would have been impossible to imagine in the crime-ridden 1950s. But by the mid-1980s developers were building 3,000-room hotels with amusement parks. Several of the Strip's landmark hotels were razed by 1995 and replaced with mega-complexes housing hotels, theme casinos, shopping malls and thousand-seat showrooms.

At the cusp of the twenty-first century, Star Trek: The Experience was drawing crowds to the Las Vegas Hilton. People were talking about the next new Las Vegas, where luxury suites would run $300 a night and cater to guests who longed for glamour and relief from the swarming masses. The Four Seasons announced their partnership with Circus Circus enterprises to manage a hotel in their new Paradise complex. Ritz-Carlton was rumored to be moving in next to the MGM Grand. Once again, Las Vegas is reinventing itself, predicting the trends of the next century. Who knows where it will lead us?

GENERAL INFORMATION

Informational brochures and magazines are available through the **Las Vegas Convention and Visitors Authority** ((702) 892-0711 FAX (702) 892-2824 WEB SITE www.lasvegas24hours.com. The authority does not have a street address as it primarily distributes information through the mail. There is a **Visitors Information Center** ((702) 892-7575, 3150 Paradise Road, Las Vegas, NV 89109-9096. Vegas regulars are advised to subscribe to the monthly newsletter *Las Vegas Advisor* ((702) 252-0655 TOLL-FREE (800) 244-2224 FAX (7012) 252-0675, 3687 South Procyon Avenue, Las Vegas, NV 89103, for unbiased reviews of hotels, casinos, and restaurants.

WHAT TO SEE AND DO

The heart of Las Vegas is the Strip, a section of Las Vegas Boulevard from Tropicana Avenue north to Sahara Avenue. Most of the major casinos are located here, along with restaurants, shopping malls, and plenty of gaudy neon. The boulevard continues east to downtown and Fremont Street, site of many of the original casinos. It's nearly impossible to walk the length of the boulevard, and more efficient to stick with one area, explore it fully, then move on to the next.

THE CASINOS

Most visitors spend the majority of their time wandering from casino to casino, checking out the games, buffets and facilities. Most casinos feature slot machines, craps, keno, poker, race and sports books, baccarat, roulette and other games, with separate areas for the high rollers. Many also offer free classes for beginners—a good idea if you don't want to spend your wad on your first go. The Las Vegas Convention and Visitors Authority (see GENERAL INFORMATION, above) publishes a Las Vegas Gaming Guide with full descriptions on how to play the various games.

Most casinos also have casino clubs where you can sign up for free and earn points toward gifts,

free meals and hotel stays by spending your dough on the games. The best casinos to visit are:

Caesars Palace ((702) 731-7110 TOLL-FREE (800) 634-6661 FAX (702) 731-6636, 3570 Las Vegas Boulevard South, is one of the more elegant casinos, with gushing fountains, marble columns and gold-leaf chariots and horses at the entryway, along with the holographic The World of Caesar display and the Brahma Shrine designed to improve the feng shui (spirit) of the hotel. The interior is loaded with chandeliers, plush carpeting, marble arches and pillars and an anatomically correct reproduction of Michaelangelo's David. Boxing matches are staged in the indoor ring, and headliner acts showcased in the Circus Maximus showroom. The casino was once the haven of high rollers, and still coddles the big timers with private gaming areas (you can watch from outside the velvet ropes). Less endowed players head for the main casino's slots, video poker machines and gaming tables. The casino abuts Caesars Forum, where gaming continues beside elegant boutiques. Also elegant but more subdued is the **Desert Inn** ((702) 733-4444 TOLL-FREE (800) 634-6906 FAX (702) 733-4676, 3145 Las Vegas Boulevard South, which first opened in 1950. The inn is so private renowned recluse Howard Hughes lived there for a few years in the mid-1960s. Though the property is not quite that exclusive now, guests have the feeling of total pampering amid the facilities, thoroughly remodeled in 1997. Set amid 150 acres (61 acres) of palms and lawns with an 18-hole golf course, the Mediterranean-style buildings provide an eye-soothing break from the garish Strip. The casino is quieter than most, with attendants in suits and

---

Gambling thrives amid opulence at the venerable Golden Nugget.

ties catering to players. The inn's excellent spa and 18-hole golf course are open to non-hotel guests for a fee.

Homesick East Coasters needn't fly 3,000 miles (4,800 km) to go home, thanks to **New York New York** ((702) 740-6969 TOLL-FREE (800) 693-6763 FAX (702) 740-6920 WEB SITE www.nynyhotelcasino .com, 3790 Las Vegas Boulevard. A life-sized replica of the Statue of Liberty and a façade reminiscent of Manhattan scenes (complete with roller coaster) make the hotel and casino stand out on the Strip. Mock autumn leaves hang from fake trees over the slot machines inside, and various parts of the casino are meant to represent the Times Square, Greenwich Village and the Fulton Street fish market.

You can't miss **Treasure Island** ((702) 894-7111 TOLL-FREE (800) 944-7444 FAX (702) 894-7414 WEB SITE www.treasureislandlasvegas.com, 3300 Las Vegas Boulevard South in the heart of the Strip. Its sidewalk pirate show is only the beginning; inside is the stage for the incomparable **Cirque du Soleil** (see ENTERTAINMENT AND NIGHTLIFE, page 265). Next door, **The Mirage** ((702) 791-7111 TOLL-FREE (800) 627-6667 FAX (702) 791-7414 WEB SITE www.themirage.com, 3400 Las Vegas Boulevard South, is only slightly less frenetic. Volcanoes spurt fire at the entrance, and the entire property has the feel of a rather large tropical isle. Siegfried and Roy's famous white tigers (as well as white lions, Bengal tigers, not to mention a panther, an Asian elephant and a snow leopard) pose in the Secret Garden, enormous glass-fronted cages in one part of the hotel. Beyond the pool is the 2.5-million-gallon (9.5-million-liter) dolphin habitat. The gaming area is removed from the lobby, where huge aquariums of tropical fish mesmerize hotel guests at the front desk.

Other Strip casinos worth checking out include the **Luxor Las Vegas** ((702) 262-4000 TOLL-FREE (800) 288-1000 FAX (702) 262-4406, 3900 Las Vegas Boulevard South, which exudes Vegas excess from the Nefertiti statues near the entrance through the gaudy casino. The **MGM Grand** ((702) 891-7777 TOLL-FREE (800) 929-1111 FAX (702) 891-1000 WEB SITE www.mgmgrand.com, 3799 Las Vegas Boulevard South, is nearly intimidating in size, but showcases top-notch talent on its stages and has several good restaurants and shops. The **Flamingo Hilton** ((702) 733-3111 TOLL-FREE (800) 732-2111 FAX (702) 733-3499, 3555 Las Vegas Boulevard South, is one of the few original Strip hotels to still attract loyal fans and newcomers; its pool area is worth seeing and the gaming areas attract an interesting mix.

One of the great successes of the 1990s, the **Rio Suite Hotel and Casino** ((702) 252-7777 TOLL-FREE (800) 752-9746 FAX (702) 253-6090 WEB

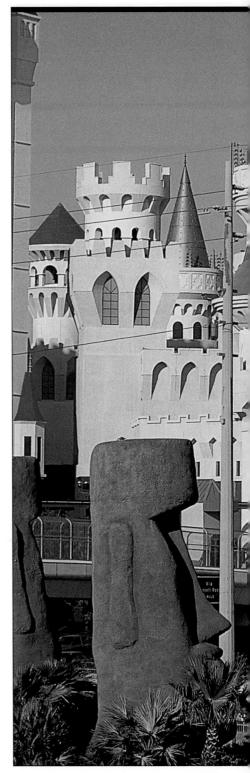

Children can't resist roaming the castles at Excalibur while their parents gamble.

SITE www.playrio.com, 3700 West Flamingo Road, is not on the Strip itself, but certainly worth a short cab ride. Its restaurants and buffets are legendary, the casino throbs with action, and the nightclubs and shows are among the hippest in town. The **Hard Rock Hotel & Casino** ((702) 693-5000 TOLL-FREE (800) 693-7625 FAX (702) 693-5010 WEB SITE www.hardrockhotel.com, 4475 Paradise Road, is also a bit away from the strip. Music fans occasionally spot the likes of Elton John strolling towards their suites, and the crowd is a combination of true hipsters and lookie-loos. The **Las Vegas Hilton** ((702) 732-5111 TOLL-FREE (800) 732-7111 FAX (702) 794-3611 WEB SITE www.lv-hilton.com, 3000 Paradise Road, is located beside the convention center. It boosted its image considerably in 1998 by opening Star Trek: The Experience (see RIDES AND AMUSEMENTS, below). The entire casino area has an outer space theme.

If you're traveling with children, try **Circus Circus** ((702) 734-0410 TOLL-FREE (800) 444-2472 FAX (702) 734-5897, 2880 Las Vegas Boulevard South. The decor is either cute or abominable, depending on your attitude. The casino is mildly amusing; most casual visitors head for the amusement area (see RIDES AND AMUSEMENTS, below). **Excalibur** ((702) 597-7777 TOLL-FREE (800) 937-7777 FAX (702) 597-7009, 3850 Las Vegas Boulevard South, attracts the kiddies with its castle-like edifice.

Downtown's casinos are fascinating for their touches of 1950s-style gambling and architecture. The **Golden Nugget** ((702) 385-7111 TOLL-FREE (800) 634-3454 FAX (702) 386-8362 WEB SITE www.goldennugget.com, at 129 East Fremont Street is one of the classiest hotels and casinos in town, and attracts a select crowd of high rollers as well as regular folk who enjoy sitting in cushy leather chairs while playing the slots. **Binion's Horseshoe Hotel and Casino** ((702) 382-1600 TOLL-FREE (800) 237-6537 FAX (702) 384-1574, 128 East Fremont Street, is a downtown classic with a Wild West feeling. The slots are in the older, darker part of the casino; poker tables attracting the best players in the world are located in a newer brass and glass wing. The casino hosts the annual World Series of Poker in May, with a million-dollar first prize.

RIDES AND AMUSEMENTS

The **Race For Atlantis** at Caesars Forum shops TOLL-FREE (888) 910-RACE exemplifies the family-style Las Vegas of the 1990s. It's a high-tech adventure ride designed to thrill all ages. The IMAX 3D motion-stimulator ride has an almost hallucinogenic effect on its subjects, who can't resist screaming as their chariots catapult into the next millennium. In terms of sheer visual beauty, Atlantis is a thrill. The ride is open daily Sunday

through Thursday from 10 AM to 11 PM, Friday and Saturday from 10 AM to midnight. Tickets are $9.50 for adults and $6.75 for children.

Star Trek: The Experience at the Las Vegas Hilton ((702) 732-5111 TOLL-FREE (800) 732-7117 FAX (702) 794-3611, 3000 Paradise Road, has brought crowds to the Convention Center neighborhood a few blocks east of the Strip. Space-age special effects flash about the casino's slot machines besides queues of eager and spaced-out fans of the television series depicted in The Experience. The average ticket holder spends at least 40 minutes studying displays of costumes, creatures and memorabilia before entering the Bridge for a four-minute jolting battle in space. After interacting

with Klingons and other strangers from the twenty-fourth century, you can chill at the restaurant or buy a souvenir at the gift shop, both of which are open to non-ticketholders. Tickets cost $15, and the ride runs daily from 10:30 AM to 11 PM.

Showcase ((702) 597-3134 FAX (702) 597-3117, 3769 Las Vegas Boulevard, is billed as the only non-gaming entertainment complex on the Strip. It includes a 12-screen movie theater complex, trademark museums and **GameWorks**, brainchild of the DreamWorks film team of Steven Spielberg, Jeffrey Katzenberg and David Geffen. A 75-ft (23-m)-high climbing wall literally anchors athletes as they ascend from the basement gaming room to the complex's top floor. The GameWorks adult video-game parlor is a playground for those entranced with virtual reality. Traditionalists are satisfied with pool tables, Foosball tables, pub-like bars and endless array of bicycles, Jet Skis, and snazzy cars facing video screens. Those looking for more of a rush play a "vertical reality shooting game." GameWorks is open Sunday to Thursday from 10 AM to 2 AM; Friday and Saturday from 10 AM to 4 AM.

Stratosphere ((702) 380-7777 TOLL-FREE (800) 998-6937 FAX (702) 383-4755, 2000 Las Vegas Boulevard South, has two rides atop the 100-story freestanding observation tower that are guaranteed to get your adrenaline pumping: the High Roller roller coaster, and the Big Shot, a free-fall ride. **New York New York** features a wrap-around roller-coaster that simulates the barrel roll of a fighter pilot. The **MGM Grand Adventures** (702) 891-3200, at the hotel of the same name, contains

dozens of rides and several theme and entertainment areas spread over several acres. The most popular attraction is the SkyScreamer, which drops riders in a free fall for 250 feet (76 m). The **Circus Circus Theme Park** is enclosed in an immense pink dome housing rollercoasters, water rides a carnival midway and a video arcade. Free circus acts are performed daily throughout the property.

MUSEUMS

The **Liberace Museum (** (702) 798-5595, 1775 East Tropicana Avenue, has long been the quirkiest museum in Vegas, with its dioramas on the life of the flashiest piano player to have made a fortune on the Vegas circuit. More 1990s is **Showcase** (see RIDES AND AMUSEMENTS, above), which houses **The World of Coca-Cola** (702) 270-5953 TOLL-FREE (800)

720-COKE, 3785 Las Vegas Boulevard, a three-story interactive museum and retail store. A three-story high Coke bottle marks the entrance to the museum, with real-life soda jerks dispensing Coke products, an intriguing display of Coke ads from around the world, and a film of classic Coke commercials. The retail shop is a marketers' dream run amuck, stuffed with Coca-Cola memorabilia.

Also encased in Showcase is **M&M's World**, where you can buy pounds of M&Ms by the color or a mini-dress, covered with beads and glitter in the shape of M&Ms and Snickers bars. **Ethel M. Chocolates** on the top floor of the chocolate side of the building features fresh candies, cakes and other sweets from the region's most famous chocolateer.

The car culture is celebrated at the **Antique and Classic Auto Collection** TOLL-FREE (800) 634-6441, 3535 Las Vegas Boulevard South at the Imperial Palace Hotel and Casino. Also of interest is **King Tutankhamun's Tomb and Museum** TOLL-FREE (800) 288-1000, 3900 Las Vegas Boulevard South.

SHOPPING

Logos reign supreme in Las Vegas, where it seems everyone is carrying a brand-name shopping bag. The best shopping center is the Forum Shops at Caesars (see CASINOS, page 258), with more than 100 shops and restaurants. The Forum's ceiling features a dawn to dusk light show with clouds floating overhead; the Festival Fountain features an hourly show where four robotic Roman gods move and speak amid dancing waters and laser lights. A second Atlantis display presents the story of Atlantis as told by sky-high moving statues; their tale is punctuated by raging fires and lightning bolts spurting from the fountain. A sky-high Trojan horse poses in front of the largest FAO Schwartz toy store outside New York's Fifth Avenue, and one restaurant serves vodka and caviar at $100 a plate. Designers including Armani, Versace, Versace, Gucci, Salvatore Ferragamo and DKNY all have boutiques here, along with less pricey brand names. The Thomas Charles Gallery features celebrity artists. There are dozens of restaurants as well.

The **Rio**'s shopping area (see WHERE TO STAY, page 267) includes designer Nicole Miller's largest United States store, several boutiques and VuDu, featuring good-luck charms and amulets and a fine collection of handcrafted masks from around the world. Magic shops featuring props and tricks are popular with shoppers and kids, and every hotel has logo T-shirts, polo shirts, baby baseball caps and ashtrays for sale.

OPPOSITE and ABOVE: High rollers steel their nerves at the gambling tables in the Golden Nugget and Four Queens casinos.

SPORTS

Golf is available at the Desert Inn (see CASINOS, page 258), host to many tournaments and celebrity guests since first opening in 1952. **Spas** appeared on the Vegas scene with typical excess in the 1990s; among the best that are open to non-hotel guests are those at the Caesars Palace and the Desert Inn. **Joggers** are pretty much out of luck along the Strip unless they hit the streets at dawn. Many hotels have exercise rooms or gyms; most charge an extra fee for use of the facilities.

EXCURSIONS

Las Vegas is strategically located amid unusual natural and man-made wonders, many accessible on day trips. **Hoover Dam** ((702) 293-8420, 34 miles (55 km) southeast of Las Vegas off US Highway 93 (or via US Highway 95 to the more scenic Lakeshore Scenic Drive), is a Depression-era wonder. Constructed in 1935 to harness the energy of the Colorado river, the dam is a permanent display of art-deco magnificence and natural beauty. The Visitor Center and tourist services at the dam were remodeled in 1995; the center mimics the original architecture of the dam's buildings and is a dazzling wonder of copper-tinged, faceted glass topped with an art-deco minaret. It includes exhibits and a film on the dam's construction. Guided 35-minute tours are available throughout the day, daily (except on Christmas Day). Many choose to book guided tours from Las Vegas, which include transportation to and from the dam.

Northeast of Las Vegas, **Valley of Fire State Park** ((702) 397-2088, off State Highway 169, is just 55 miles (88.5 km) away, yet seems like a landscape from another planet. The landscape of rust and russet colored sandstone formations is awesome, especially at dawn and dusk. Similar in topography and geology is **Red Rock Canyon National Conservation Area** ((702) 363-1921, off US Highway 95. Located 20 miles (32 km) west of Las Vegas, the park includes a one-way road that winds 13 miles (21 km) through dramatic rock formations. **Mount Charleston**, 45 minutes west of Vegas on State Highway 160, encompasses a small mountain town and the highest peak in the area, at over 11,000 feet (over 3350 m). Part of the Toiyabe National Forest, the mountain attracts burned-out desert rats and forest fans who crave the cool, moist air and scent of pines. Farther east, past the California border, is Death Valley (see page 282).

The following tour operators offer excursions to some or all of the areas mentioned above (most operate mainly by phone, so it is easiest to call for reservations): **Cactus Jack's Wild West Tours** ((702) 731-2425, 2217 Paradise Road, Suite A; **Las Vegas Discount Tours** ((702) 895-8996, 4699 Industrial Way, Suite 214; **Las Vegas Tour & Travel** ((702) 739-8975 (only operate by phone); **Gray Line Tours**, ((702) 384-1234 TOLL-FREE (800) 634-6579, 2040 East Lone Mountain Road. Helicopter tours of the Grand Canyon and a nighttime view of Las Vegas are offered by **Maverick Helicopter Tours** ((702) 261-0007, 105 East Reno.

ENTERTAINMENT AND NIGHTLIFE

Dinner shows, concerts, stage shows and circuses entrance visitors not glued to gaming, and are an essential part of the Vegas experience. The

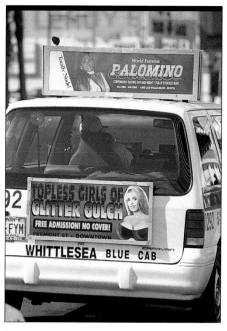

best by far is **Mystere** by Cirque du Soleil, the Montreal-based performance art troupe. The cirque's theater at Treasure Island ((702) 894-7790 (see CASINOS, page 258) was built specifically for the troupes' 72 performers including mimes, comedians, actors, singers, dancers, musicians and acrobats. Mystere combines a surrealistic blend of heart-pounding Japanese Taiko drummers, ethereal music, staggering trampoline and trapeze feats, lovable clowns and an obnoxiously funny mime. The troupe is having a second stage designed for it at the Bellagio Hotel.

OPPOSITE TOP: Live shows run the gamut from extravagant song-and-dance numbers at the Starlight Express to BELOW Country Western reviews. ABOVE: Taxis serve as roaming billboards for the city's seamier attractions.

Comedy

Upcoming and established comics run through their routines at **Bally's Celebrity Room** ((702) 739-4567 (see FLOORSHOWS, below); **The Improv** at Harrah's ((702) 369-5000 TOLL-FREE (800) 634-6765 FAX (702) 369-6014, 3475 Las Vegas Boulevard; and the **Hollywood Theater** at the MGM Grand ((702) 891-7777 (see CASINOS, page 258).

Concert Halls

Vegas has always been an essential stop for musicians on tour and a steady gig for certain performers. The *Los Angeles Times* and other California newspapers list upcoming Las Vegas concerts in their entertainment sections. If you spot something you'd really like to see, buy your tickets as soon as possible. The Rolling Stones finished their 1998 United States tour at **The Joint** in the Hard Rock Hotel ((702) 693-5000. The same weekend (Valentine's Day) Elton John rocked the crowd at the **Garden Arena** at the MGM Grand ((702) 891-7777. Top-name rock stars appear frequently at both venues. The **Circus Maximus Showroom** at Caesars Palace ((702) 731-7333 features country, jazz and blues performers, as does the **Crystal** showroom at the Desert Inn ((702) 733-4566.

Floorshows

Jubilee! at Bally's Casino ((702) 739-4661 TOLL-FREE (800) 237-SHOW, 3645 Las Vegas Boulevard South, opened in 1981 and has hardly been updated, which explains its cult following — it's so immune to modern trends. The **Follies Bergère** at Tropicana Resort and Casino ((702) 739-2411 has been running since 1959, and may well be the last and best dance revue show in the world. The **Radio City Music Hall Spectacular** at the Flamingo Hilton Las Vegas ((702) 733-3111 brings the famed Rockettes west from Manhattan to kick their heels up and dance. **EFX!** at MGM Grand Hotel and Casino ((702) 891-7777 TOLL-FREE (800) 929-1111 is a special-effects theatrical production featuring David Cassidy, presented in the 1,700-seat Grand Theatre.

Magic

Caesars Magical Empire in Caesars Palace is a themed, multi-chambered setting for dinner hosted by a magician in a rock-walled chamber, followed by visits to the Ramses Crypt and Sanctum Secorum lounges, both with light shows and magicians performing sleight-of-hand tricks. Don't miss Invisabella, the playerless piano that plays whatever tune you name. **Siegfried and Roy** at The Mirage ((702) 792-7777 have been Vegas' reigning illusionists for decades; their riveting show is often sold out in advance, so get tickets early. Magician **Lance Burton** performs in his custom-built theater at the Monte Carlo ((702) 730-7000.

Street Shows

A 100-ft (35-m)-high awning filled with light bulbs covers the downtown sidewalks at the **Fremont Street Experience**, located between Las Vegas Boulevard and Main Street. At dark, the awning explodes into a dazzling light show. The greats — Elvis, Frank Sinatra, Sammy Davis Jr. — croon their favorites over the sound system as light framed figures seem to dance in the sky. Gamblers in the Golden Nugget, the Four Queens and Binion's step out to the street top join a chorus of "Viva Las Vegas," then head back to the slots. The light and sound show has brought life back to the downtown area, and is well worth seeing. The crowd packs the sidewalk in front of Treasure Island each night at dark to watch pirate ships battle with blasts of fire and booming cannons in the street-side lagoon. Much of the crowd moves on to the Mirage, next door, where volcanoes explode into tropical waterfalls and pools.

Bellagio, the next spectacle hotel and casino from the owner of Treasure Island and Mirage, is scheduled to have an outdoor water theater for shows by the Cirque du Soleil in 1999.

WHERE TO STAY

It's hard to gauge room rates at Las Vegas hotels, which typically adjust their prices by as much as $100 depending on occupancy. Christmas, New Year's, and Valentine's Day are the most expensive times, though if there is a huge convention in town it may be hard to find reasonably priced rooms. The largest casinos have rooms in several price ranges; keep asking until you come up with something that suits your budget. Many of the hotels run specials, especially midweek, which are advertised in newspapers in most major California cities.

VERY EXPENSIVE

One of the latest trends among Vegas hoteliers is a return to the elegance and glamour of the 1950s, when Vegas attracted a monied set wearing furs (thanks to powerful air conditioning) and jewels. The Mediterranean-style **Desert Inn** ((702) 733-4444 TOLL-FREE (800) 634-6906 FAX (702) 733-4676, 3145 Las Vegas Boulevard South, was one of the first existing hotels to upgrade its faculties in such a manner. With only 715 rooms and suites it is almost a boutique hotel by Strip standards. An 18-hole golf course sprawls behind the hotel, giving it a secluded feeling despite its location. Elaborate floral displays, crystal chandeliers and beveled glass doors and windows provide a touch

The MGM Grand Hotel and Casino claims more guest rooms, restaurants, and live shows than most other venues in town.

of class to the public spaces. The rooms are spread about the grounds in five buildings; even the least expensive accommodations are elegant. Facilities include a golf course and spa, several excellent restaurants, and a fairly calm casino.

Bellagio ((702) 792-7111 TOLL-FREE (888) 987-6667 FAX (702) 792-7646, 3650 Las Vegas Boulevard South, is designed to resemble a Mediterranean village on a prime 122-acre (49-hectare) site at the crossroads of Flamingo and Las Vegas boulevards. The complex includes a nine-acre (three-and-a-half-hectare) lake with fountains and choreographed streetside water shows and 3,000 luxurious rooms. An art gallery featuring paintings by Manet, Matisse and Gauguin is certainly one of the more tasteful attractions on the Strip, as is the shopping arcade. Similarly upscale properties designed to resemble Paris and Venice are under construction on the Strip, as are hotels from Four Seasons and Ritz-Carlton.

EXPENSIVE

Caesars Palace ((702) 731-7110 TOLL-FREE (800) 634-6661 FAX (702) 731-6636, 3570 Las Vegas Boulevard South, has 2,471 rooms and suites, almost half of which are in the 29-story Palace Tower, which opened in 1998. All the rooms are posh and comfortable; the best are the 1,134 Palace Tower rooms and suites, all with whirlpool tubs. The tower also has a state-of-the-art gym and spa with a boxing ring, yoga studio and Zen meditation room. The Garden of the Gods' three inlaid marble swimming pools are set amid lavish gardens, fountains and Roman statues. The hotel has eight restaurants and several snack bars and lounges. The **Monte Carlo** ((702) 731-7110 TOLL-FREE (800) 311-8999 FAX (702) 730-7250, 3770 Las Vegas Boulevard South, is understated in design, though the pool area is like a small water park. Rooms at **The Mirage** ((702) 791-7111 TOLL-FREE (800) 627-6667 FAX (702) 791-7414 WEB SITE www.themirage .com, 3400 Las Vegas Boulevard South, were remodeled in 1997 and are quite pleasant and spacious.

Also in this price range is **Luxor Las Vegas** ((702) 262-4000 TOLL-FREE (800) 288-1000 FAX (702) 262-4406, 3900 Las Vegas Boulevard South. In the downtown, the **Golden Nugget** ((702) 385-7111 TOLL-FREE (800) 634-3454 FAX (702) 386-8362 WEB SITE www.goldennugget.com, 129 East Fremont Street, is the classiest choice, all marble, glass, and polished brass. Nearly 2,000 rooms cover two city blocks. The pool is in a central courtyard, and the casino spills out to the sidewalk and the Fremont Street Experience.

MODERATE

There are enough kinds of rooms and suites among the 5,007 units at the **MGM Grand** ((702) 891-7777 TOLL-FREE (800) 929-1111 FAX (702) 891-1000 WEB SITE www.mgmgrand.com, 3799 Las Vegas Boulevard South, to meet the demand in various price ranges. The hotel's size can be intimidating, but once you figure out the quickest route to your room it becomes manageable. The **Flamingo Hilton** ((702) 733-3111 TOLL-FREE (800) 732-2111 FAX (702) 733-3499, 3555 Las Vegas Boulevard South, has one of the best swimming pools on the Strip, with waters slides, waterfalls, and plenty of space for swimming. **New York New York** ((702) 740-6969 TOLL-FREE (800) 693-6763 FAX (702) 740-6920 WEB SITE www.nynyhotelcasino.com, 3790 Las Vegas Boulevard South, has a wide range of rooms with art deco decor; beware of the rollercoaster rattling around the building and choose your room accordingly.

Treasure Island ((702) 894-7111 TOLL-FREE (800) 944-7444 FAX (702)894-7414 WEBSITE www .treasureislandlasvegas.com, 3300 Las Vegas Boulevard South, is a good choice for families.

There's enough action at the **Rio Suite Hotel and Casino**, ((702) 252-7777 TOLL-FREE (800) 752-9746 FAX (702) 253-6090 WEB SITE www.playrio .com, 3700 West Flamingo Road, to keep guests content, though trips to the Strip involve taking a cab or car. The hotel has 2,563 suites, even the smallest of which are roomy and comfortable. The same is true for the **Hard Rock Hotel** ((702) 693-5000 TOLL-FREE (800) 693-7625 FAX (702) 693-5010 WEB SITE www.hardrockhotel.com, 4475 Paradise Road, but that doesn't deter rock fans hoping to spot celebrities.

Other hotels with rooms in this price range include **Las Vegas Hilton** ((702) 732-5111 TOLL-FREE (800) 732-7111 FAX (702) 794-3611 WEB SITE www.lv-hilton.com, 3000 Paradise Road; and **Stratosphere** ((702) 380-7777 TOLL-FREE (800) 998-6937 FAX (702) 383-4755, 2000 Las Vegas Boulevard South.

INEXPENSIVE

Vegas regulars rarely pay full price for their rooms, since the hotels keep track of return guests and mail out discount coupons. First timers are not as lucky, but can find bargains even at the major hotels if they visit during the week. As a rule, the downtown hotels are less expensive than those right on the Strip. The **El Cortez Hotel** ((702) 385-5200 TOLL-FREE (800) 634-6703 FAX (702) 385-1433, 600 East Fremont Street, is one of the best deals in town, with 200 mini suites with separate seating areas apart from the beds. Low price rooms can usually be booked at the **Binion's Horseshoe Hotel** ((702)

OPPOSITE: The Barbary Coast, a longtimer by theme.

382-1600 TOLL-FREE (800) 237-6537 FAX (702) 384-1574, 128 East Fremont Street, and the **Four Queens Hotel** ((702) 385-4011 TOLL-FREE (800) 634-6045 FAX (702) 383-0631, 202 East Fremont Street.

On the Strip, **Circus Circus** ((702) 734-0410 TOLL-FREE (800) 444-2472 FAX (702) 734-5897, 2880 Las Vegas Boulevard South, has 2,800 rooms and plenty of distractions for kids; there is also a recreational vehicle park with 384 spaces for motor homes. **Excalibur** ((702) 597-7777 TOLL-FREE (800) 937-7777 FAX (702) 597-7009, 3850 Las Vegas Boulevard South, is also designed for families. Kids will love the medieval castle façade, and there's something for nearly everyone in the more than 4,000 rooms.

WHERE TO EAT

Most of the restaurants in Las Vegas are in the casinos and hotels, though there are a few exceptional places with their own addresses. Buffets are immensely popular, and though all are good, some are truly outstanding, offering piles of fresh seafood and carved meats. Elegant dining rooms cater to the winners, who can't resist splurging some of their winnings on a gourmet meal.

VERY EXPENSIVE

Restaurant surveys among locals and visitors consistently cite **Monte Carlo** at the Desert Inn as a top spot for romantic gourmet dining. Tables are booked months in advance for Valentine's Day dinners and wedding nights. Set atop a curving stairway and replete with brass, glass and dark wood, the restaurant exudes class and privilege. The food is sublimely prepared and graciously served to guests, many of whom have been celebrating here for decades. **Andre's French Restaurant** ((702) 385-5016, 401 South Sixth Street, is located in a restored mansion in downtown and is consistently reported to have the best French chef in Vegas. **Spago** in the Forum Shops at Caesars ((702) 369-6300 is an offshoot of the famous Los Angeles restaurant featuring chef Wolfgang Puck. The gourmet pizzas, pastas, and Asian noodle dishes are composed of an eclectic blend of ingredients that excites jaded palates. Puck opened a second restaurant, **Chinois**, in the Forum as well. Also in the Forum is the **Palm** restaurant ((702) 732-7256, a branch of the famed New York power-lunch center. Prime rib, lobster, crab and other standards are served in a gracious setting. The **Brown Derby** at the MGM Grand ((702) 891-7318 has the rights to the name and menu of the old favorite Hollywood restaurant, and has a definite in-crowd feeling; starts from some of the Vegas shows have regular booths here. Also at the

MGM Grand is **Emeril's New Orleans Fish House** ((702) 891-7374, named after famed New Orleans chef Emeril Lagasse. The oyster bar and Cajun seafood dishes are terrific. The **Palace Court** (702) 731-7110 at Caesars Palace serves French Continental cuisine in an elegant dining room; the wine list is excellent.

Prime steaks with all the fixings are expertly prepared at **Ruth's Chris Steak House** ((702) 248-7011, 4561 West Flamingo Road, and 3900 Paradise Road (((702) 791-7011) and **Morton's of Chicago** ((702) 893-0703, at the Fashion Show Mall, 3200 Las Vegas Boulevard South. Both offer excellent side dishes (for an extra cost) along with the steaks and fresh seafood.

EXPENSIVE

Asian restaurants abound, thanks to the crowds of Asian gamblers who fly in by the charter load. **Hyakumi** ((702) 731-7110 Japanese restaurant at Caesars is one of the loveliest, with an excellent sushi bar and eclectic menu. **Ho Wan** in the Desert Inn is a Chinese classic specializing in Mandarin, Szechwan and Cantonese dishes served in three rotunda-shaped, ornately decorated dining rooms. Also popular are **Benihana Village** TOLL-FREE (800) 222-5361 at the Las Vegas Hilton, 3000 Paradise Road; and **P.F. Changs** ((702) 792-2207, 4165 South Paradise Road. The **Second Street Grill** ((702) 385-6277, in the Fremont Hotel at 200 East Fremont Street, has a tropical setting and a pacific Rim menu that attracts the crowds from Hawaii.

The best of the Italian offerings include Caesars' **Terrazza** with an indoor dining room and terrace by the pool, and **Il Fornaio** at New York New York. **Ristorante Italian** ((702) 794-9363, in the Riviera Hotel at 2901 Las Vegas Boulevard South, is a gracious Northern Italian spot.

The **Steak House** ((702) 734-0410 at Circus Circus is replete with leather, wood, and brass, and is a bit less expensive than those listed above.

MODERATE

Theme restaurants are all the rage in Vegas, and every chain worth its name has at least one branch on the Strip. The best of the lot focus on the food as much as the decor. At **Dive!** ((702) 369-DIVE, 3200 Las Vegas Boulevard South, mock submarines, real aquariums, and underwater videos provide the entertainment, and the salads, sandwiches, barbecued ribs and gargantuan deserts are all well prepared. **Harley Davidson** ((702) 740-4555, 3725 Las Vegas Boulevard South, has classic bikes hanging above the dining room, which is usually packed with motorcycle aficionados. The food is all-American and good. **The Official All Star Café** ((702) 795-TEAM, 3500 Las Vegas Boulevard South, is in the Showcase building and features loads of sports memorabilia and good burgers. **Planet Hollywood** ((702) 791-7827, at the Forum Shops at Caesers, 3500 Las Vegas Boulevard South, displays costumes and props from current movies along with a menu much like the other theme restaurants. **Puck's Café** ((702) 895-9653, at the MGM Grand, offers Los Angeles chef Wolfgang Puck's casual cuisine. The **Stage Deli** ((702) 893-4045, in the Forum Shops at Caesars, is the best New York-style deli in town with enormous corned beef and pastrami sandwiches, cold fish platters and slices of classic cheesecake. **Romano's Macaroni Grill** ((702) 248-9500, 2400 West Sahara Avenue, is a cavernous, noisy and immensely popular Italian eatery with good pastas, pizzas and bread.

INEXPENSIVE

You get the most food for the buck at the casino buffets, though some edge toward the moderate price range. Hotels and casinos often hand out coupons for these spreads; check the tourist brochures as well. Expect to wait in line (beside slot machines) for the most popular buffets. Rated the best in town for several years is the **Carnival World Buffet** ((702) 252-7577 at the Rio, where several stands offer everything from sushi to barbecued ribs; there is also a separate seafood buffet. **The Buffet** ((702) 385-7111, at the Golden Nugget downtown, is always rated one of the top by locals. The **Mirage Buffet** (702) 791-7355 is known for its shrimp, lox, and herring. Big, juicy hamburgers served 24 hours a day are the draw at **Fatburger** ((702) 736-4733, 3765 Las Vegas Boulevard.

La Salsa ((702) 369-1234, in the Forum Shops, has some of the best Mexican food in town.

HOW TO GET THERE

McCarran International Airport ((702) 261-5743, off Tropicana Avenue, about a mile (a little over one and a half kilometers) east of the Strip, is currently served by Continental Airlines, American Airlines, Alaska Airlines, Delta, Hawaiian Airlines, Northwest, Southwest Airlines, Reno Air, TWA and United Airlines.

The **Greyhound** bus station ((702) 384-9561 TOLL-FREE (800) 231-2222 is at 200 South Main Street.

Interstate 15 connects Las Vegas to Salt Lake City to the north and Los Angeles to the south. US Highway 95 connects Las Vegas to Reno and Death Valley to the north and to Laughlin in the south.

OPPOSITE: Amid the competition, Treasure Island garners rave reviews for its tropical gardens and pools. ABOVE: Hundreds of weddings are performed each week at the Little White Chapel on the Strip.

The Deserts: Palm Springs and Death Valley

PALM SPRINGS

Americans have created the best of several worlds in this opulent desert oasis. The climate is dry and warm in the daytime year-round, yet nearly always cool at night. All the creature comforts of modern American living, including air-conditioning and swimming pools, are taken to extremes that seem nearly untoward in the desert. At every turn, you see the lush green golf courses bordered by the rugged gray mountains or the burnt-brown desert sands. Overhead misters cool summer guests at pools set amid vacation resorts, where families set up housekeeping for a week or more.

The town of Palm Springs is actually just a small part of the overall Coachella Valley, which is lined with small towns and resort developments clustered under the name Palm Springs Desert Resorts. The region includes Desert Hot Springs, Cathedral City, Rancho Mirage, Palm Desert, La Quinta, Indian Wells and Indio, which all seem to blend into a sea of anonymous walls and lawns unless you cruise through the chain of downtowns on Interstate 10. The town of Palm Springs has a population of only 45,000, but every year millions of people visit this playground of the rich and famous. Although decidedly Republican and conservative in character, the mood here has always been unusually tolerant of different kinds of lifestyle. There is a large gay population in the area, and a surprising number of nudist resorts advertise in tourist brochures. Cosmetic surgery and substance-abuse rehabilitation facilities serve the local populace and frequent guests. There is a definite overlay of glamour and style in the area's social scene, and the list of celebrity-named streets goes on for miles.

Golf is one of the main attractions — there are more than 90 golf courses in the Coachella valley. There are also more than 600 tennis courts and 30,000 swimming pools. The Bob Hope Chrysler Classic and the Nabisco Dinah Shore LPGA championships are only two of the more than 100 golf tournaments staged here every year. It was golf that brought President Dwight Eisenhower to Palm Springs as a regular visitor and President Gerald Ford as a permanent resident. Bob Hope and many entertainment celebrities have long considered the desert city their home, and it was a personal getaway for the likes of Elvis and Liberace. In 1987, singer Sonny Bono was elected mayor of Palm Springs; he then went on to become a United States Congressman and died in a skiing accident in January, 1998.

Palm Springs was given the name *Agua Caliente*, or hot springs, by the Spaniards in 1774. It became known to Americans as a spa as early as the 1890s, but it was only in the late 1920s that it became a favorite weekend and winter retreat of Hollywood celebrities. The 1939 *W.P.A. Guide to California* speaks of it with light disdain as an extension of the (then) glamorous Hollywood Boulevard. But, as such things often develop, the "extension" in the desert has remained glamorous while the original boulevard has decayed.

The Agua Caliente Band of Cahuilla Indians still control 31,000 acres (12,500 hectares) in the heart of the valley, granted to them as a reservation in 1876. This includes 6,700 acres (2,700 hectares) inside Palm Springs' city limits and four incredibly beautiful canyons that are listed on the National Register of Historic Places. The 15 mile (24 km) long **Palm Canyon** is the most famous of these, in part because it served as the setting for

"Shangri-La" in the classic movie, *Lost Horizon*. A paved pathway leads down into the canyon where you'll find an abundance of the Washingtonia palm, the only one of 2,100 palms now growing in California that is indigenous to the place.

GENERAL INFORMATION

Palm Springs Tourism operates a **Visitor Information Center** ((760) 778-8418 TOLL-FREE (800) 347-7746 FAX (760) 323-3021 WEB SITE www.PalmSprings

PRECEDING PAGES: Sand dunes and stark mountains mesmerize hikers around Palm Springs, where residents favor flamboyant dress during celebrations. The Aerial Tramway OPPOSITE near Palm Springs is one of the area's major attractions and offers some spectacular views from the San Jacinto Mountains. ABOVE: Mules and horses can be rented by the hour for old-fashioned excursions into the canyons near Palm Springs.

.org, 2781 North Palm Canyon Drive, at the north entrance to the town of Palm Springs. There you will find helpful maps and brochures and notices of upcoming events. The center is open daily from 9 AM to 4 PM. The **Palm Spring Desert Resorts Convention and Visitors Bureau (** (760) 770-9000 TOLL-FREE (800) 417-3529 WEB SITE www.desert-resorts.com, 69-930 State Highway 111, Suite 201, Rancho Mirage 92270, covers the towns around Palm Springs. You can visit their web site to gather a myriad of information before your trip.

Visitors traveling from the United Kingdom can obtain information before they leave home from **Marketing Services (Travel & Tourism) Ltd**. **(** 44 171 4054746, Suite 433, High Holborn House, 52–54 High Holborn, London WC1V 6RB, attention Mr. John Sproul, Account Manager. German travelers may contact **MS-Marketing Service International**, Walter Stohrer und Partner **(** 49 69 6032023, Johanna-Melber-Weg 12, D-60599 Frankfurt, Germany, attention Mr. Martin Walter. Also of note is the **Yes Desk International Newsstand (** (760) 322-2100, which offers a large selections of newspapers and magazines from the United States and around the world. It is located at the Palm Spring Mall, 2377 Tahquitz Canyon Way.

WHAT TO SEE AND DO

The most popular single attraction in Palm Springs is the **Aerial Tramway (** (760) 325-1391 (recorded information) WEB SITE www.pstramway.com, at Tramway Road off State Highway 111, three and a half miles (slightly over five and a half kilometers)

off the highway. From the floor of Chino Canyon, the tramway takes you 6,000 ft (1,830 m) up to the top of 8,516-ft (2,600-m) Mount San Jacinto in approximately 14 minutes. You are warned to wear a jacket for the trip because the mountaintop is usually 40°F (22°C) colder than the desert floor. The trams operate Monday through Friday from 10 AM to 8 PM and from 8 AM to 8 PM on the weekends. The **Alpine Restaurant** serves tramway riders from its spectacular viewpoint and for a couple more dollars you can buy a tram ticket that will include your dinner. The tram ride takes you into the **Mount San Jacinto State Park (** (760) 659-2607, which adjoins the **San Jacinto Wilderness Area**. There are 54 miles (87 km) of hiking trails in the rugged 14,000-acre (5,700-hectare) park, offering a cool retreat in summer and a snowy wonderland in winter. The cross-country skiing is excellent and there is a complete ski shop at the **Nordic Ski Center (** (760) 327-6002, which offers instruction and equipment rentals.

The **Palm Springs Desert Museum (** (760) 325-0189, 101 Museum Drive, is a modern complex housing natural science exhibits, art collections and Native American artifacts. It is open year-round, Tuesday through Saturday from 10 AM to 5 PM, Sunday from noon to 5 PM, and is closed on Monday and major holidays. Admission is charged. It includes a performing arts center with a 450-seat auditorium,

the **Annenburg Theater**, where classical music, ballet, drama, and film retrospectives are staged throughout the year.

One of the most unusual events in the Coachella Valley is the annual **Date Festival** at **Indio**, held in February. The festival commemorates the successful transplanting of Middle Eastern date palms — still an important commercial crop — to the valley. Among the more exotic entertainment featured during the festival is camel racing.

Hiking trails are open in all of the canyons, with horseback riding available in some areas. As movie-goers two generations ago were stunned by the beauty of the enchanted scenes in *Lost Horizon*, the modern traveler will similarly be lost in an amazing array of flora and fauna along the creeks and waterfalls in these canyons. For more information on the canyons, write to **Tribal Council Office** ((760) 325-5673, 960 East Tahquitz Way #106, Palm Springs 92262.

A few miles east of Palm Springs, near Indian Wells, lies **The Living Desert** ((760) 346-5694, a 1,200-acre (486-hectare) park with desert animals and plant life left, for the most part, undisturbed in their

natural surroundings. Exhibits, shows, and guided tours are available. The park is open from September through May from 9 AM to 5 PM daily.

Golf

Many of the golf courses in Palm Springs are private clubs, but most have reciprocal arrangements with other clubs that enable members to use facilities elsewhere. Clubs are either open to the public or "semiprivate," meaning you don't have to be a member to play there. Expect to pay resort prices, especially at the more famous golf courses. Two truly outstanding world-class golf courses are located at La Quinta, southeast of downtown Palm Springs. These are the Dunes and Mountain courses at the **La Quinta Resort & Club** ((760) 564-7610, 49-499 Eisenhower Drive, both designed by Pete Dye and opened in 1980. The fee for Dunes course is $145; the Mountain course is $260.

Another famous Palm Springs course, designed by renowned golfer Jack Nicklaus, is the **PGA West Resort Course (Nicklaus)** ((760) 564-7170, 55-900 PGA Boulevard, opened in 1987. The fee for this course is $260. You'll pay considerably less at a public course. One option is the **Indio Municipal Golf Course** ((760) 347-9156, 83-040 Avenue 42. Fees are $10. Another choice

OPPOSITE: A Navajo Indian woman appears in native dress at the Indio Date Festival. RIGHT AND ABOVE: Elaborate costumes for beautiful women and their Arabian horses are the norm at the Indio Date Festival.

PALM SPRINGS

is **The Golf Center at Palm Desert** ((760) 779-1877, 74-945 Sheryl Drive, where course fees are $16.

Shopping

In and around downtown Palm Springs, there are many expensive specialty shops that you would expect to find in resort areas. The **Desert Fashion Plaza**, 123 North Palm Canyon Drive, brings them all together in one cool modern shopping center right in the heart of town with plenty of parking. There are more than 55 fashion boutiques, restaurants, galleries and specialty shops, including Saks Fifth Avenue. There is also the **Palm Desert Town Center**, 72-840 State Highway 111, a shopping, dining and entertainment complex with many specialty stores, and three major department stores. The bargain shopper might want to check out **Trader's Discount Place**, 67-555 East Palm Canyon Drive, with great values all under one roof.

Balloon Flights

An adventurous ways to sightsee in the desert is by hot air balloon. One of the companies offering this service is **Dream Flights** TOLL-FREE (800) 933-5628. You can sip champagne as you float over some of the most spectacular scenery in the country. **Fantasy Balloon Flights** TOLL-FREE (800) GO-ABOVE also offers sunrise or sunset champagne adventures in state-of-the-art balloons.

Horseback Riding

The desert area offers some extraordinary riding trails and guides. Organized rides can be arranged

easily through the following stables, both located in Palm Springs: **Smoke Tree Stables** ((760) 327-1372; and **Vandenburg Equestrian Center** ((760) 328-4560.

Jeep Tours

Desert Adventures ((760) 324-JEEP TOLL-FREE (888) 440-JEEP, 67-555 East Palm Canyon Drive, Suite A104, Cathedral City, will bounce you along in a red jeep on several different tours, some lasting two hours and some four. These include: "The Indian Canyons Adventure," which takes you into the ancient ancestral home of the Agua Caliente Band of the Cahuilla Indians, with cascading waterfalls and lovely palm groves, "The Santa Rosa High Mountain Adventure" is a climb into the rugged back country high above the Coachella Valley, past magnificent cliffs into the Santa Rosa Mountains National Scenic Area. The four-and-a-half-hour "Mystery Canyon Adventure" takes you through lush farmlands to the infamous San Andreas Fault.

WHERE TO STAY

Very Expensive

The Willows Historic Palm Springs Inn ((760) 320-0771 FAX (760) 320-0780 WEB SITE WWW .thewillowspalmsprings.com, 412 West Tahquitz Canyon Way, is one of the most gorgeous small hotels in California, the Willows has only eight rooms. The flawlessly restored historic mansion (built in 1927) is loaded with antique furniture, luxurious baths, and stone fireplaces. The gardens are spectacular with verbena, lupine, lavender and red salvia.

La Quinta Resort & Club ((760) 564-4111 TOLL-FREE (800) 598-3828, 49499 Eisenhower Drive, originally opened in 1926, is truly historic and seeped in Old World charm, with its Spanish hacienda design and desert decor. There are 25 sparkling pools, 38 hot spas, five different restaurants and a sports bar.

The Ritz-Carlton ((760) 321-8282 TOLL-FREE (800) 241-3333, 69-900 Frank Sinatra Drive, Rancho Mirage, offers a fitness center, swimming pools, tennis courts and a restaurant and coffee shop along with the chain's predictably elegant decor. The Givenchy Hotel and Spa ((760) 770-5000 TOLL-FREE (800) 276-5000 FAX (760) 324-6104, 4200 North Palm Canyon Drive, Palm Springs, was once the Gene Autry Hotel. Now the mansion, reminiscent of Tara, houses an opulent hotel and spa set amid 14 acres (slightly over five and a half hectares) of exquisite gardens. There are two swimming pools, two gyms, tennis courts, a beauty salon and boutique, as well as business and fitness center.

Expensive

The Korakia Pensione ((760) 864-6411, 257 South Patencio Road, Palm Springs, is a favorite of young celebrities who lounge about in a Moorish-style villa built in 1924. It's hard not to act like Marilyn Monroe or Clark Gable while sunning about the pool or simply relaxing in one of 19 private rooms.

Marriott's Desert Springs Resort & Spa ((760) 341-2211 TOLL-FREE (800) 331-3112, 74-855 Country Club Drive, Palm Desert, is the best of the large resorts. The hotel is a lavish affair, with caged macaws greeting guests beside an atrium lagoon that flows outside the hotel into a lake. Swan boats ferry guests via the water to several restaurants spread about the property; the Japanese knife-wielding hibachi chefs are a hit with kids, while grownups prefer the Italian restaurant at sunset, facing the Santa Rosa Mountains. Miramonte Resort ((760) 341-2200 TOLL-FREE (800) 237-2926 FAX (760) 568-0541 WEB SITE www.miramonte-resort.com, 76-477 State Highway 111, Indian Wells, is built on a smaller scale, reminiscent of a Mediterranean Italian village. With only 226 guest rooms and suites, the hotel is smaller than most in the area, yet sprawls over 11 acres (four and a half hectares) of lushly landscaped grounds amid olive groves, a citrus orchard and rose gardens. All the amenities that one would expect at a top-notch resort are available.

The DoubleTree Hotel & Golf Resort ((760) 322-7000 TOLL-FREE (800) 637-0577, 67-967 Vista Chino, Cathedral City, completed a $5 million renovation in 1998. There are 287 guest rooms, 12 deluxe suites and one presidential suite, 18,000 sq ft (1,600 sq m) of meeting space, racquet-

ball and tennis courts, two whirlpool spas and the new Sunflowers Café. The Hyatt Grand Champions Resort, ((760) 341-1000 TOLL-FREE (800) 233-1234, 44-600 Indian Wells Lane, Indian Wells, is located on 35 acres (14 hectares) at the foot of the San Jacinto Mountains. There are 336 rooms and all the amenities which you would expect at a first-rate resort, such as swimming pools, fitness center, and a golf course on site. Also recommended in this price range are Renaissance Esmeralda Resort ((760) 773-4444 TOLL-FREE (800) 552-4386, 44-400 Indian Wells Lane, Indian Wells, with 560 rooms; and the 62-room Estrella Inn ((760) 320-4117 TOLL-FREE (800) 237-3687 FAX (760) 323-3303, 415 South Belardo Road, Palm Springs.

Moderate

The Spa Hotel & Casino & Mineral Springs ((760) 325-1461 TOLL-FREE (800) 854-1279, 100 North Indian Canyon Drive, Palm Springs is located right in downtown and houses a gaming casino run by the Agua Caliente Band of Cahuilla Indians. Smoky, brash and a bit of a letdown, the casino is just part of the complex, which includes 230 large guest rooms and a spa featuring natural hot mineral water baths, a health club, sauna and massages. For a more intimate feel, try the 23-room Casa Cody B & B Country Inn ((760) 320-9346 TOLL-FREE (800) 231-2639, 175 South Cajuilla Road, in Palm Springs. Each comes with a fully equipped kitchen, wood-burning fireplace and a private patio. There are two pools and a secluded whirl-

Hikers are dwarfed by the Arches, just one of the many weird formations you'll find in Death Valley.

pool spa. **Agua Caliente Hotel & Mineral Spa** ((760) 329-4481 TOLL-FREE (800) 423-8109, 14-500 Palm Drive, Desert Hot Springs, with 117 units, is also recommended.

Inexpensive

Most of the inexpensive lodgings are located in downtown Palm Springs or on the highways into town. Recommended are the **Budget Host Inn** ((760) 325-5574 TOLL-FREE (800) 829-8099 FAX (760) 327-2020, 1277 South Palm Canyon Drive; **Bermuda Palms Hotel** ((760) 323-1839 FAX (760) 323-0969, 650 East Palm Canyon Drive; **Hampton Inn** ((760) 320-0555 TOLL-FREE (800) 732-7755, 2000 North Palm Canyon Drive; **Palm Court Inn**

Desert, and **Ruth's Chris Steakhouse** ((760) 779-1998, 74-040 State Highway 111, Palm Desert, cater to an upscale crowd who splurge on thick, aged steaks, plump shrimp, sautéed mushrooms and tasty spinach.

Moderate

Las Casuelas — The Original ((760) 325-3213, 368 North Palm Canyon Drive, Palm Springs, and **Las Casuelas Terraza** ((760) 325-2794, 222 South Palm Canyon Drive, Palm Springs, both serve good Mexican food without too many frills. The original restaurant is housed in a charming hacienda-style building with bubbling fountains and strolling mariachis. Of the myriad chain restau-

((760) 416-2333 TOLL-FREE (800) 667-7918 FAX (760) 416-5425, 1983 North Palm Canyon Drive; **Super 8 Lodge** ((760) 322-3757 TOLL-FREE (800) 800-8000 FAX (760) 323-5290, 1900 North Palm Canyon Drive.

WHERE TO EAT

Expensive

Despite all the trappings of healthy living — clean air, golf courses, and straight sidewalks that serve as walking and jogging tracks — Palm Springs is a beef and martini kind of place. One of the oldest and most beloved restaurants near downtown is **Melvyn's Restaurant** ((760) 325-2323, 200 West Ramon Road, Palm Springs, which caters to the green pants and plaid jacket crowd. The steaks, baked potatoes, and salads are served in hearty, well-prepared portions. **Morton's of Chicago** ((760) 340-6865, 74-880 Country Club Drive, Palm

rants in the resort areas, **Islands** ((760) 346-4007, 72-353 State Highway 111, Palm Desert, offers quality food and fast, reliable service in a lively tropical setting. Along the Paseo Drive shopping area in Palm Desert are several good restaurants including **Blue Coyote Grill** ((760) 776-8855, 72-760 El Paseo; **Café Des Beaux-Arts** ((760) 346-0669, 73-640 El Paseo; and **Caffe Valentino** ((760) 776-7535, 73-375 El Paseo. **Hamburger Hamlet** ((760) 325-2321 in the Desert Fashion Plaza (also in downtown Palm Springs) offers American and European dishes, with specialty hamburgers and great desserts.

Inexpensive

The side streets in downtown Palm Springs are lined with good coffee shops, Mexican restaurants and small cafés. Inexpensive eateries are harder to find in the resort areas. The breakfast crowd peruses the *Wall Street Journal* over eggs Benedict at **Le Peep Grill (** (760) 773-1004, 73-725 El Paseo, Palm Desert.

HOW TO GET THERE

The **Palm Springs Regional Airport** is located just three minutes from downtown Palm Springs and is serviced by many of the major airlines, including American Airlines, United, TWA, and some of the smaller commuter lines. For those arriving at the desert resorts by car, Interstate 10 runs east and west and would be the chosen route coming from Los Angeles, Orange County or San Diego from the west, and Phoenix from the east. If your prior stop was Las Vegas, you would come south on Interstate 15 and intersect with Interstate 10. Palm Springs is also accessible by rail, served by **Amtrak** TOLL-FREE (800) 872-7245. The train station is located on North Indian Avenue, south of Interstate 10. If the bus is your preferred mode of transportation, **Greyhound** buses are frequent and convenient. The station (** (760) 325-2053 is located at 311 North Indian Canyon Drive.

JOSHUA TREE NATIONAL PARK

This unique desert area was proclaimed a National Monument in 1936, a Biosphere Reserve in 1984, and a National Park in 1994. Its 792,000 acres (320,500 hectares) encompass the transition from the Mojave Desert to the Colorado Desert in Southern California. The changes in elevation create two distinct ecosystems within the park, with the lower elevation of the Colorado Desert featuring natural gardens of creosote bush, cholla cactus and ocotillo. Above 3,000 ft (900 m), the higher, moister and slightly cooler Mojave Desert is the habitat of the Joshua tree, forests of which occur in the western half of the park. This area also includes some fascinating geologic displays. You can hike through the park or camp; reservations can be made in advance. Make sure and bring plenty of water.

The park address is Joshua Tree National Park (** (760) 367-5500 FAX (760) 367-6392 WEB SITE www.nps.gov/jotr, 74485 National Park Drive, Twentynine Palms, 92277. If approaching from the west, take Interstate 10 and then State Highway 62. The north entrances are located at Joshua Tree Village and the city of Twentynine Palms. The south entrance is at Cottonwood Springs, 25 miles east of Indio, also accessible from via Interstate 10 from the east or west.

The park is always open, with the Visitor Centers open daily from 8 AM to 5 PM. Entrance to the park will cost you $10 per car and it is valid for seven days. For the international visitor, park information is available in Dutch, French, German, Italian, Japanese and Spanish.

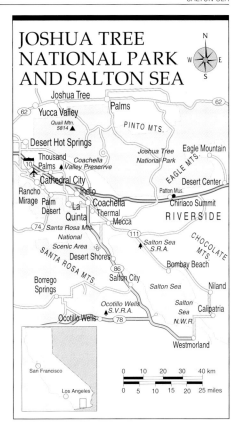

JOSHUA TREE NATIONAL PARK AND SALTON SEA

SALTON SEA

In 1905, the forces of nature and man combined to form the Salton Sea, a body of water 35 miles (48 km) long and 8 to 14 miles (13 to 22 km) wide that lies 235 ft (72 m) below sea level in the middle of the desert southeast of Palm Springs and northeast of San Diego. The lake was created by accident in 1905, when a dike broke during the building of the All-American Canal. With no outlets, the water gradually changed from fresh to salty. Faced with the challenge, the state's Department of Fish and Game decided to transfer ocean fish into the landlocked sea. The success of this effort has made Salton Sea what it is today — a favorite fishing ground for tourists and local enthusiasts. It is also a popular birdwatching spot.

The park's **visitor center (** (760) 393-3052 or (760) 393-3059 is located 25 miles southeast of Indio off State Highway 111. There are five campgrounds with a total of 1,600 campsites. Reservations for full hookup sites should be made in advance.

OPPOSITE: It took specially designed wagons to haul the borax across the treacherous deserts and some of them are on show at the Pacific Borax Museum.

IDYLLWILD

Idyllwild is a small mountain village tucked in the San Jacinto Mountains, within overnight hiking distance from the Palm Springs Tram. Drivers get there in about 90 minutes from Palm Springs if you take Interstate 10 toward Banning, then head south on Highway 243. Or if you prefer the scenic route across the desert forests and mountains, take the 130-mile Palms-to-Pines Highway. Take State Highway 74 at State Highway 111 in Palm Desert to a fork in the road branching right to Idyllwild and Mountain Center. Continue into the San Gorgonio Pass. The village is a popular weekend and country-home getaway for Southern Californians who appreciate the crisp air and scent of pines. There are several small inns around the town. The village center gets crowded on weekends when visitors pack the coffee shops, ice-cream parlors, real-estate offices and galleries.

DEATH VALLEY

Like the premature reports of Mark Twain's death, the reputation of Death Valley has always been an exaggeration of the facts. In truth, only one person died among the passengers of that first wagon train that gave the place its sinister name — and that was the only death recorded in Death Valley for the entire trek West during the gold rush.

Technically, Death Valley is not a valley, but a fault scarp, or graben, like many of the other California deserts. The spectacularly sharp and jagged mountains are the result of fairly recent — in geologic terms — uplifting and faulting in the earth's crust. The extraordinary fact about Death Valley is that the fault scarp is almost as deep as it is high — at the lowest point, 282 ft (86 m) below sea level, it is still 8,000 ft (2,440 m) down to bedrock.

It takes a firsthand view of Death Valley to begin to understand the awesome mystique that has grown up around the name. When you come across the rugged mountains on either side of the valley nowadays, you will want to stop at the frequent viewing points because of the overwhelming beauty of the place. But that beauty is best appreciated from the safety and comfort of an air-conditioned car or bus. To those first settlers, it must have seemed the very landscape of Hell — the hottest, driest, most barren place any of them had ever imagined outside the Bible's *Book of Revelations*. Their sentiment is clearly reflected in the names that had evolved for various points in the valley: Dante's View, Devil's Cornfield, Devil's Hole, Hell's Gate.

Death Valley extends for 140 miles (225 km) in Inyo County in eastern California, along the border of Nevada. In 1933, the federal government created the Death Valley National Monument.

The protected area now extends across the border into Nevada. The valley floor ranges from 4 to 16 miles (6 to 26 km) wide. Even in the hottest time of summer, there is a trickle of water in Salt Creek which oozes across the valley. The lowest point in the valley and in America is at **Badwater**, 282 ft (86 m) below sea level and only a 90-minute drive from **Mount Whitney** in the Sierra Nevadas, the highest point in the contiguous 48 states.

Few deaths were recorded in the early days of Death Valley because most settlers knew how to steer clear of it. However, as the mines began to peter out in California, prospectors began to spread out, looking for all kinds of minerals they could sell. There were some small strikes of silver and

gold in the valley, but what put the place on the map was the discovery of borax in 1880. Borax is used in the manufacture of glass and in glazes for ceramics and porcelain enamel. The boron minerals (or borates) come from hot springs and vapors of volcanic rocks. The seeping groundwater from the ancient lakebeds that covered much of Death Valley created rich veins of the minerals. When the lakes evaporated and formed the weird landscape of salt and sand, the borates became accessible.

The only problem was how to get the stuff 165 miles (265 km) to the nearest railroad once it had been mined. Enter the famous 20-mule teams. Using enormous, specially-designed wagons 16 ft (five meters) long with wheels seven feet (two meters) in diameter, the mules were able to get a load of 36 tons (including a 1,200-gallon, or 4,545-liter, water tank) across the desert. Twenty-Mule

Team Borax became a popular American trademark and stories from those days provided material for *Death Valley Days*, a weekly television series that ran from 1952 to 1972. As historian James D. Hart has noted, it was that series that "helped make Ronald Reagan widely admired and assisted him toward later political success."

GENERAL INFORMATION

The main tourist center of Death Valley is at **Furnace Creek (** (760) 786-2331, a natural oasis fed by fresh groundwater. This modern — and blessedly air-conditioned — visitors' center is maintained by the National Park Service and is open 8 AM to 6 PM, with hourly slide show programs available. Any tour of the valley should begin here.

Other ranger stations or sources of information are available at **Stovepipe Wells (** (760) 786-2342, open from 8 AM to 4 PM, **Scotty's Castle (**(760) 786-2392, open from 9 AM to 5 PM, **Beatty Ranger Station (** (760) 553-2200, open from 8 AM to 4 PM. You can also visit WEB SITE www.nps.gov/deva. A $10 vehicle entrance fee is valid for seven days. Campground fees range from $10 to $16 per night.

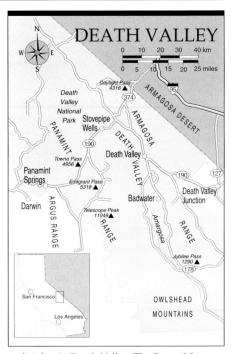

WHAT TO SEE AND DO

Among the most colorful and enduring prospectors of the area was **Death Valley Scotty**, whose elaborate castle is now a major tourist attraction at the north end of the valley. Walter Perry Scott was a flamboyant conman whose exploits intrigued a Chicago millionaire named Albert Johnson. In the 1920s, Johnson erected a fabulous retreat, replete with a 50-ft (15-m)-high living room, a guest house, a staff house, a bell-tower and stables, all designed in a neo-Moorish style — no small feat under the difficult conditions of Death Valley at the time. The Johnson family only lived at the house one month out of every year, and the enterprising Mr. Scott found himself a home, up until 1953. There are still dozens of fresh tales by and about him that you may hear on the guided tours of **Scotty's Castle (** (760) 786-2392. Now owned and operated by the National Park Service, the castle is open year-round and there are regular tours from 9 AM to 5 PM at a fee of $8 for adults and $4 for seniors and children. There is also a snack bar and gift shop at the castle. Of vital importance, one of three gas stations in Death Valley is located here.

Right behind the main visitors' center, you may be utterly amazed to come on a glistening emerald green 18-hole golf course, a startling contrast to the barren desert around it. The golf course is part of a private holding within Death Valley National Park which is the main commercial tourist complex originally built by Pacific Borax, the corporation which still owns nearly all min-

eral rights in Death Valley. The **Borax Museum (** (760) 786-2345 is also located in The Furnace Creek Ranch compound. Here you can see the huge wagons and stagecoaches that were all that once linked the valley with the outside world.

During the winter season, sightseeing tour buses leave at regular intervals from Furnace Creek. However, if you only have a day to see Death Valley, you can see much of it from your own car, driving through California State Highway 190 that takes from three to four hours. From Furnace Creek, the highway passes by **Zabriskie Point**, one of the most popular viewing points where you can look back on the broad sweep of the valley. From there, you cross over the Amargosa Range of mountains and take to US Highway 95 to Las Vegas or, at Death Valley Junction, you can take California State Highway 127 south to Interstate 15 to Los Angeles and San Diego.

Death Valley Junction has all the appearances of a ghost town, although officially it has a population of six. During the winter season, it also has the **Amargosa Opera House (** (760) 852-4441 FAX (760) 852-4138, a wonderful throwback to the days when performers would amble into town and put on a show. The interior of the tiny opera house is covered with elaborate murals. At center stage performs Marta Becket, a New York ballerina in her sixties who somehow landed here and

Calico is a picturesque ghost town now, all that's left of another dream of striking it rich in Death Valley gone bust.

created her own fantasy production starring herself. You can see Madame Marta's grand performances every Friday, Saturday, and Monday night during the winter season. Call ahead for reservations. Tickets are $8 for adults and $5 for children under 12.

Exploring Death Valley by Ruth Kirk, the wife of a Death Valley park ranger, is an excellent guide to the valley. It describes "both the harshness and the beauty" of the valley which, as a resident for three years, the author came to love "in spite of its desolation, or perhaps because of it." The book is available through the Death Valley Natural History Association, P.O. Box 188, Death Valley 92328. This association has an extensive list of more than 150 books and guides about the valley, including children's books, posters, maps, and photographs that can be ordered from the same address.

WHERE TO STAY AND EAT

The two best lodgings in Death Valley are part of **The Furnace Creek Inn** ((760) 786-2361 TOLL-FREE (800) 236-7916 WEB SITE www.amfac.com (numbers and WEB SITE for reservations at either the Inn and the Ranch), a luxury-class hotel was built by Pacific Borax in 1927 and completely renovated from 1996 to 1998. The hotel complex features a swimming pool, tennis courts, and an exotic "oasis garden." There dining room is a formal. Views of the desert sky at night from the hotel's rooftop terrace are indescribable. **The Furnace Creek Ranch** ((760) 786-2345 FAX (760) 786-2514 is the less expensive of the two places built by Pacific Borax, with rooms in the moderate range. In addition to its motel rooms, there is also a cafeteria, gift shop, gas station, post office, tennis courts, swimming pool, and the golf course. Lodging is also available at the **Stovepipe Wells Village** ((760) 786-2387.

Camping in Death Valley

Keep in mind that Death Valley is one of the driest and hottest places on earth, and that until very recent times it was virtually inaccessible by automobile. The warnings you see posted about travel into Death Valley should be taken very seriously. Be sure you have plenty of gas in the car and bottled water for yourself. If you should run out of gas or have car trouble of any sort, it could take hours for help to arrive and it will be expensive when it does arrive. Californians generally avoid desert travel in the summer months. Even the most experienced campers should check first with the **National Park Service** ((760) 786-2331, Death Valley National Par WEB SITE www.nps.gov/deva, PO Box 579, Death Valley 92328. The Park Service advises visitors to avoid the holiday weekends during the winter months when park facilities are filled to overflowing. Conditions vary at each of the campgrounds since they are located from 196 ft (60 m) below sea level to 8,200 ft (2,500 m) above. There is a fee of $10 or $16 at the campgrounds, depending on site and time of year. Most of the campgrounds operate on a first come first served basis, and not all camp areas are open all year round. Call the park service for this information.

HOW TO GET THERE

The valley lies parallel to the California–Nevada state line, between US Highway 395 in California and US Highway 95 in Nevada. US Highway 395 is an extraordinarily beautiful scenic route — through the Owens Valley, along the eastern wall of the high Sierras. At the intersection of US Highway 395 and California State Highway 136, is a **visitors' center** ((760) 876-6222 fully stocked with maps and guidebooks and staff people to answer any questions about a trip to Death Valley. Outside, on the center's patio, there is a viewing platform for Mount Whitney, located just across US Highway 395. State Highway 136 connects with California State Highway 190 which takes you on across the Panamint Valley and the rugged Panamint Mountains which form the western wall of Death Valley. The highways are well-maintained, but they are narrow and zigzag in places — with no guardrails and sheer drops of several thousand feet in parts.

US Highway 395 intersects with California State Highways 178 and 190, both of which enter the park from the west. Interstate 15 passes to the southeast of Death Valley, connecting with Route 127. Sixty miles (96 km) further north will bring you to State Highway 178, just past Shoshone, where you turn left into Death Valley National Park. US Highway 95 runs north and south to the east of the park, connecting with Nevada State Highways 267, 373 and 374, all of which will lead you into the park from the east. If you are traveling from Las Vegas, State Highway 160 takes you to Pahrump, turn left onto Nevada State Highway 132, which then becomes California State Highway 190. This will take you into the park and to the **Furnace Creek Visitor Center** ((760) 786-2331. There is no regular public transportation into the park.

Scotty's Castle at the north end of the Valley is the elaborate monument to a colorful conman.

The Deserts: Palm Springs and Death Valley

San Diego
and
Environs

IF CALIFORNIA'S THREE MAJOR CITIES are thought of as sisters, then San Diego is the shy one, overshadowed by its more famous siblings. Some maps of southern California ignore San Diego entirely, while pundits describe it with tired clichés — a Navy town full of retirees, a conservative outpost littered with aged hippies. San Diego's promoters work hard to dispel such images. But truth be known, San Diegans aren't all that interested in attracting attention to their piece of paradise.

Nature has blessed San Diego with the best of all of California's natural wonders in terms of beaches, mountains and deserts. Located in the extreme southwest corner of the United States, the city has the Pacific Ocean for its western boundary and its southern city limit is the international border with Mexico. San Diego Bay is protected at the north by a picturesque peninsula rising to a 1,000-ft (300-m) headland at Point Loma; a barrier of sand stretching from Imperial Beach and the Mexican border shelters the harbor at its entrance at Point Loma, providing a beautiful playground of beaches and training grounds for the omnipresent military forces. The San Diego Zoo and Wild Animal Park are world famous among animal lovers; Sea World is one of the country's most popular tourist attractions.

San Diego's natural beauty has been broadcast world-wide during political and sporting events including the 1997 Republican National Convention and the 1998 Super Bowl. Such attention has spurred an influx of tourists and new residents eager to sample the sunshine, mellow lifestyle and hidden opportunities in the nation's sixth-largest city.

Though San Diego's population was 1,183,102 in 1997, it seems much less crowded than most metropolitan areas. The city of San Diego is actually a series of well-defined neighborhoods adjoining other incorporated cities in San Diego County, which sprawls over 319.6 square miles (827.8 sq km) of coastline, canyons, mesas and mountains. The population of the entire county is 2.7 million, living in everything from urban condo towers to rambling cattle ranches. Much of the population is packed into the coastline west of Interstate 5, where a chain of beach towns attracts Navy and Marine personnel, wealthy retirees, young families, surfers and anyone lucky enough to live by the beach. The city and county's inland neighborhoods range from typical suburban enclaves to rural outposts, most with distinct characters.

San Diego's economy has traditionally depended on the military, aerospace, and defense industries, fishing and tourism. Of late, the attention has switched to high-tech research and redevelopment companies, and San Diego rivals the Silicon Valley in computer and electronics industries. The Scripps Institution of Oceanography, Salk Institute for

Biological Studies and other research headquarters attract the brightest minds from throughout the world; in fact, San Diego claims over a half-dozen Nobel laureates among its citizenry.

BACKGROUND

SAN DIEGO HISTORY

Beneath the palm trees, lawns and flowers that symbolize San Diego's modern image lies the brown, dusty land of the Kumeyaay and other Native American groups. The San Diegans of the sixteenth century, who are now known collectively as the San Digueños and Luiseños, lived by the sea and along the region's river valleys. They ate shellfish, wild game and native plants, dressed sparsely and kept to themselves — pretty much like the San Diegans of the twentieth century.

Climate and location have attracted outsiders since the first Spaniards arrived via the sea in 1542. San Diego was once part of Mexico, and became a United States territory in 1850. Like the Spaniards before them, the United States military quickly took up residence in the area, developing an integral tie that has remained critical to the city's character. Tourists and investors soon followed, moving the center of the emerging city from what is now known as Old Town to the current downtown. San Diego is now the sixth largest city in the nation, tucked at the far southwest corner of the mainland United States.

THE BEGINNING

The Spanish fleet, led by Portuguese explorer Juan Rodríguez Cabrillo, first landed at San Diego in 1542. Cabrillo and his men spent a few days in the

region they charted as San Miguel, then moved on to explore the northern coast. In 1602, Spanish explorer Sebastián Vizcaíno sailed into San Miguel and renamed the bay San Diego after the saint San Diego de Alcalá. The Spaniards, busy conquering other lands in the Pacific, ignored the region until 1769, when Spanish ships anchored in San Diego Bay and troops arrived by land from Baja California. The troops, led by Gaspar de Portolá, moved north toward San Francisco, leaving behind a small group of soldiers and settlers who set up their encampment on Presidio Hill.

Franciscan Padre Junípero Serra celebrated mass at the new settlement on July 16, 1769, be-

PREVIOUS PAGES: Architect Jon Jerde's fanciful Horton Plaza overflows with shops, theaters, restaurants, and diversions. ABOVE: The placid bay and the modern glass buildings of new San Diego reflect the setting sun.

ginning the first of 21 missions in Alta (or higher) California. On August 15, the Kumeyaay (who had been renamed the Digueños by the Spaniards) attacked the Presidio Hill settlement but were quickly overtaken. The padres and their Digueño followers moved from the military settlement in 1774, establishing the mission of San Diego de Alcalá in the San Diego River Valley. In 1798, the Franciscans started the Mission San Luis Rey, which would become the largest and most prosperous mission in California, in northern San Diego near what is now Oceanside.

The Spanish settlement at Presidio Hill continued to grow in the early 1800s, and a second fortress was built on Ballast Point at Point Loma. About 1600 Kumeyaay were baptized by the priests during this period; records show that about 9,000 of those Indians died from diseases brought by the Spaniards.

MEXICAN RULE

As the Spaniards continued to gain control in Alta California, Mexico began fighting the conquerors, gaining independence from Spain in 1821 and staking claim to Spain's northern territories in California. The Spanish flag was quickly replaced by the Mexican flag at San Diego's Presidio, and the settlers began moving away from the guarded fortress to the area now called Old Town. Mexico's Secularization Act of 1883 broke up the Catholic Church's land holding in the area, creating vast private ranches from mission lands. In 1835 San Diego became an official civil pueblo with some 400 Mexican residents. Juan Osuna was elected the first mayor and judge.

Mexico's reign in Alta California was short lived, however. The Mexican-American War, which began in 1846, quickly spread from Texas to California. On December 12, after fierce battles between the Californios and the Americans, the United States Army entered San Diego. On January 17, 1847, American Colonel John Charles Fremont garnered the surrender of the Californios in San Diego. The Mexican-American War ended with the signing of the Treaty of Guadalupe Hidalgo on February 2, 1848, and the United States paid Mexico $15 million for much of what is now the southwestern United States.

SAN DIEGO BECOMES A UNITED STATES CITY

California became the 31st state of the United States in 1850, with San Diego as its southernmost county and city. Development plans began almost immediately with the arrival of William Heath Davis, a wealthy financier. Davis and his part-

Surfboard and bikini are all a young woman needs for a fun day on the beaches near San Diego.

ners shunned the existing settlement at the base of Presidio Hill and purchased 160 acres (64.7 hectares) of land facing San Diego Bay for $2,304 to begin a "New Town." They laid streets, put up prefabricated houses and began building a wharf, but few buyers arrived. The San Diegans of Old Town called the new settlement "Davis's Folly" and stayed put in their neighborhood, which grew to include a courthouse, school, stage line stables and several handsome homes. Davis was forced to abandon his plan for New Town, and in 1851 the city of San Diego declared bankruptcy.

ALONSO HORTON CREATES A NEW CITY

Davis was quickly followed by another, more successful developer, Alonso Horton. Horton, who called the bayfront setting "the prettiest place for a city I ever saw," purchased 960 acres (388.5 hectares) in the downtown area at a land auction in 1867. He finished the wharf, built a hotel and plaza and began selling lots and prefabricated homes. By 1869, about 3,000 residents had moved into New Town. New settlers arrived when word of a gold rush in the mountains outside the city spread north, but the rush was short lived.

Horton's development received a substantial boost when a fire destroyed much of Old Town's business district in 1872, and the city progressed rapidly over the next 20 years. Railroad lines connecting San Diego with regions north, south and east were begun in 1885, and electric lights were installed in downtown in 1886. Trolley tracks and telephones lines soon followed, and by 1890 San Diego's population had reached 16,000.

THE TWENTIETH CENTURY

The United States Navy's battleship fleet sailed into San Diego Bay in 1908 while on a world tour, and the War Department began planning to dredge San Diego Bay to accommodate larger ships. In 1911, Aviator Glenn Curtiss landed his floating biplane beside the Navy cruiser U.S.S. *Pennsylvania* in the bay and convinced the Navy to allot $25,000 to the development of naval aviation. Curtis soon opened the first military aviation school in the country at North Island, and San Diego's status as a military center became firmly established.

At the same time, San Diego's leaders set aside 1,200 acres (485 hectares) of canyons and hilltops outside downtown for a community park and fair grounds. Commerce and tourism played a large part in this decision, since these San Diegans had decided to attract outside attention by staging the 1915–1916 Panama-California Exposition in Balboa Park. Many of the park's landmark Spanish-Colonial buildings were constructed for the exposition, which was a huge success. The Zoological Society of San Diego was formed under the direc-

tion of Dr. Harry Wegeforth in 1916, in part to protect the animals who had been brought in for the fair. The resulting San Diego Zoo has remained one of San Diego's leading and most endearing attractions.

The military continued building its presence in San Diego during the 1920s, establishing a Marine Corps recruit depot, a naval training station and a navy hospital. In 1923 San Diego became the headquarters of the Eleventh Naval District and the Pacific Fleet. Pioneer aviator T. Claude Ryan started Ryan Airlines, offering the first scheduled commuter flights from San Diego to Los Angeles. Ryan also began San Diego's defense manufacturing industry by opening Teledyne Ryan Aeronautical, a leading manufacturer of military and civilian aircraft and equipment. One of his first civilian clients was Charles Lindbergh, who hired the company to build a plane that could handle a solo flight across the Atlantic Ocean. Two months later, in 1927, the *Spirit of Saint Louis* was ready for flight. In 1928 San Diego's airport, Lindbergh Field, was dedicated as military planes roared in the sky.

Reuben H. Fleet brought his Consolidated Aircraft factory to San Diego in 1933, and later merged it with other companies to become Convair, and then General Dynamics. The company became one of the region's largest employers, along with the Ryan, Solar, and Rohr aircraft companies.

Banking on a rise in prosperity and the end of the depression, San Diegans decided to host a second exposition in Balboa Park, using many of the buildings from the 1915–1916 Panama-California Exposition. The 1935–1936 California-Pacific Exposition brought a new surge of tourists who decided to stay in San Diego. The advent of World War II brought even more new growth.

THE WAR BOOM

On December 7, 1941, loudspeakers at the San Diego Zoo broadcast a command for all military personnel to report for duty as news of the Japanese invasion at Pearl Harbor spread though local military bases. Local aircraft factories operated around the clock, and San Diego's population swelled with an influx of workers. Military units patrolled the beaches and large nets were strung into the bay to prevent submarines from entering the harbor. Much of Balboa Park was declared off-limits to civilians and was named Camp Kidd. The end of the war in 1945 brought a building boom to San Diego as entire new neighborhoods sprung up to house the thousands of military families who had no intention of moving away from the region.

City leaders began focusing once again on tourism in the 1950s and the 1960s. Voters passed a bond to create an aquatic center and tourist attraction at Mission Bay, and Sea World opened on 22 acres

at the edge of the bay in 1964. The San Diego Community Concourse, including the city's first convention center, also opened in 1964. By the 1980s, tourism was San Diego's third largest industry after manufacturing and military interests.

The region's burgeoning scientific and intellectual presence also received a boost in the 1960s with the establishment of the University of California at San Diego and the Salk Institute for Biological Studies, headed by Dr. Jonas Salk. The Scripps Institute of Oceanography, first established as the Marine Biological Association of San Diego in 1903, was already established as a world-class oceanographic institution. Researchers, scientists and academics found San Diego to be the perfect climate for their work, and the area since has become a leader in research, development, and high-tech industry.

San Diego's skyline began changing dramatically in 1969, when the arcing San Diego–Coronado Bay Bridge opened over San Diego Bay. City leaders began a major redevelopment effort in downtown in the 1970s. Much of Alonso Horton's New Town was slated for historic preservation in 1974, when the Gaslamp Quarter Association (now the Gaslamp Quarter Council and Foundation) was founded to oversee preservation and development in the historic district. The shopping, entertainment and dining center called Seaport Village, which opened in 1980, attracted tourists and locals to downtown's waterfront.

Horton Plaza shopping center, the centerpiece of downtown redevelopment, opened in 1985 and immediately created a flurry of activity in downtown. By the time the San Diego Convention Center opened on the edge of San Diego Bay in 1990, downtown was firmly reestablished as the cultural and economic hub of the San Diego region.

As San Diego enters the twenty-first century, the future looks promising. Despite cutbacks, the military maintains a strong presence in the area. The defense industry has dwindled, only to be replaced by high-tech, biotechnology and communications companies. Just as in the past, newcomers continue to be attracted to San Diego's climate and promises for new beginnings.

GENERAL INFORMATION

There are several tourist offices in the San Diego area. The **International Visitor Center** ((619) 236-1212, is located downtown at First Avenue and F Street at **Horton Plaza**. The excellent staff there is very helpful and conversant in Spanish, French, Italian and German. The center is open Monday through Saturday from 8:30 AM to 5 PM and on Sundays in June, July, and August from 11 AM to 5 PM. Another **visitor center** ((619) 276-8200 WEB SITE www.infosandiego.com, at 2688 East Mission Bay Drive, is open daily from 9 AM until

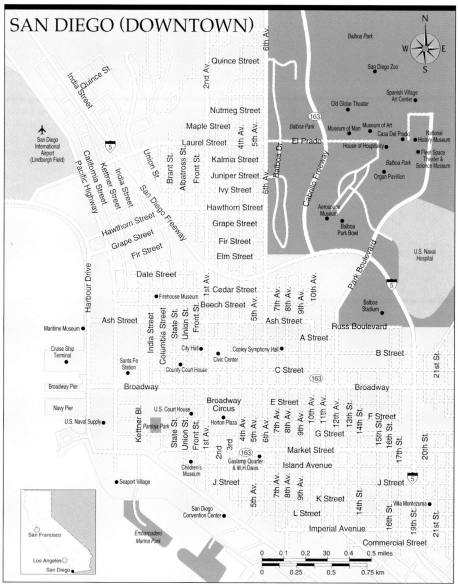

SAN DIEGO (DOWNTOWN)

dusk. The clerks there can provide you with brochures or help you make hotel reservations. If you would like to receive information before you leave home, the **San Diego North Convention and Visitors' Bureau** ((760) 745-4741 TOLL-FREE (800) 848-3336 FAX (760) 745-4796 WEB SITE www .sandiegonorth.com, 720 North Broadway, Escondido 92025, will send brochures or a good visitor's guide magazine.

WHAT TO SEE AND DO

Like many American cities, San Diego abandoned its downtown area for the suburbs in the 1960s.

Even the city's only daily newspaper moved out to a new building beside the new freeways and shopping malls. But unlike other cities, San Diego did not use its urban renewal money to destroy and rebuild the old buildings. Much of the downtown Gaslamp Quarter was saved because it just wasn't worth tearing down. Now, the Gaslamp and the rest of downtown are the center of an exciting renewal and many new businesses are replacing those that had fled the urban core. **Horton Plaza** (see SHOPPING, page 305) is at the center of downtown's revival. Completed in 1985, Horton Plaza shocked downtown San Diego back into life. The center contains 140 shops, four de-

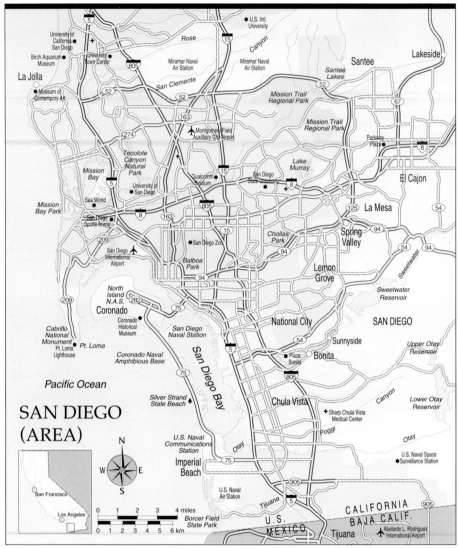

SAN DIEGO
(AREA)

Pacific Ocean

N
W + E
S

0 1 2 3 4 miles
0 1 2 3 4 5 6 km

San Francisco
Los Angeles

partment stores, restaurants, cinemas and the San Diego Repertory Theater. The shopping center had a most unlikely adviser involved in its design: science fiction writer Ray Bradbury. He said it's time developers thought of cities as theater and looked more to Disneyland for inspiration. He encouraged architect Jon Jerde to go ahead with his whimsical and unconventional design, to make it a "fun park," something that would "give us a reason to leave our homes."

The result is a mad blend of walkways and stairs, and clashing colors of banners and pennants and storefronts more like Coney Island than Fifth Avenue. Once lavishly praised by the architectural critic of the *New York Times*, **Horton Plaza** has been around long enough now to be ridiculed as "comic opera architecture." But whatever it is, Horton

Plaza works. It is a fun place to wander through, with jugglers or musicians usually performing in the various open spaces.

The more authentic side of San Diego frames the plaza in the streets of the **Gaslamp Quarter**, an intriguing collection of 1890s and early 1900s storefronts, bars, restaurants, and hotels. The **Gaslamp Quarter Association** ((619) 233-5227, 614 Fifth Avenue, offers walking tours of the district. Worth special attention in this area are **Fourth** and **Fifth Avenue**, between E and F Streets, where a number of particularly fine examples of Victorian architecture can be seen. Many of the streets in the quarter have recently been re-surfaced in brick, and more renovations are under way. Nearby (though not within walking distance) is **Villa Montezuma** ((619) 239-2211, at 1925 K Street, a beautiful Victorian built in 1887. The mansion now functions as a museum, focusing mostly on alternating exhibitions and period rooms, and has more than twenty impressive stained-glass windows. The museum is open from noon to 4:30 PM on Saturday and Sunday, with the last tour at 3:45 PM. The museum is only open on weekdays for groups of eight or more.

The focal point of San Diego's waterfront renovation is the **San Diego Convention Center** ((619) 525-5000, 111 West Harbor Drive. Teflon-coated sails top the sprawling structure, which opened to mixed reviews in 1990. Regardless of how you feel about the architecture, the Convention Center has spurned an amazing renaissance in a waterfront long devoted to commercial fishing, ship repair yards, and the United States Navy. South of the center, **Embarcadero Marina Park South** has become one of the busiest picnic and walking spots in downtown, and marks the beginning of a walkway running along San Diego Bay. The America's Cup Village was located here during the September 1988 race; it was the best place from which to view the boats going and coming to the race course out at sea. The park shelters the marina in front of the San Diego Marriott, where million-dollar yachts flying flags from around the world are berthed. **Harbor Drive**, which runs north along the waterfront from the park to the airport, connects all the landscaped pathways. Just across the drive from the convention center is the **Children's Museum San Diego/Museo de los Niños** ((619) 233-KIDS, 200 West Island Avenue, between Front and Union Streets. Admission is $5 for adults and children over two years of age. The museum is open Tuesday through Sunday, from 10 AM to 5 PM. This museum features many interactive and hands-on activities that will keep most children happy and busy for hours. One of the first organizations in the city to embrace the Mexican population in San Diego and Tijuana, the museum is deliberately bi-lingual and bi-cultural, offering interesting insights for kids and their chaperones.

Next in line is **Seaport Village** ((619) 235-4013, 849 West Harbor Drive, which is open daily from 10 AM to 10 PM. A 14-acre (a little over five-and-a-half hectare) dining, shopping, and amusement complex, the park opened in 1980 as one of the earliest harbingers of San Diego's revival. At first sight it seems like a New England fishing village plonked out of place and time set in San Diego. The lighthouse at the center of Seaport Village is a replica of a real lighthouse in Washington State; nearby is a fully restored Broadway Flying Horses Carousel, circa 1890. The village consists of a cluster of shops and restaurants right on the waterfront, among tropical flowers and foliage. There are four major restaurants, 13 fast-food places, and 75 shops that offer everything from handmade Christmas ornaments to fine art.

Harbor Drive continues on past the **Tuna Harbor** pier, center of the commercial fishing businesses that boomed here from the 1940s to the 1960s. The pier now houses the Fish Market, an enormous seafood restaurant. The walkway veers north at this point to San Diego's more traditional **Embarcadero** waterfront. Cruise ships dock at the **B Street Cruise Ship Terminal**, open when ships are in port. Ships departing for Alaska, the Panama Canal, Hawaii and Mexico are in port much of the year. For information on the different cruises available, call **Royal Caribbean International** TOLL-FREE (800) 327-6700, **Norwegian Cruise Line** TOLL-FREE (800) 327-7030 or **Celebrity Cruises** TOLL-FREE (800) 437-3111.

Walking north along the landscaped pathways around San Diego Bay you next encounter berthed United States Naval vessels and the **San Diego Bay Ferry** to Coronado. The *Silvergate* and the *Spirit of '76* take passengers from the San Diego Harbor Excursion dock at 1050 North Harbor Drive, downtown, across the bay to the Coronado Marketplace, on the harbor's east shore.

Nearby are two major harbor tour facilities. **Harbor Excursions** ((619) 234-4111, 1050 North Harbor Drive at the foot of Broadway, offers one-and two-hour tours of the bay in open tour boats throughout the day and dinner cruises at 7 PM and 9:30 PM on Fridays and Saturdays. **Invader Cruises** ((619) 686-8700, at 1066 North Harbor Drive, has two historic yachts (*High Spirits* and *Renown*, built in 1929 and 1940 respectively) used primarily for private cruises. Less impressive ships are used for one- and two-hour cruises of the bay. From December through March, the harbor tour boats all become "whale watchers" with daily schedules outside the harbor to watch the great gray whales swimming past. For a unique dining experience, cruise the harbor while enjoying dinner or Sunday brunch on one of the **Hornblower Dining Yachts** ((619) 234-8687. Call to get departure times and current rates. Reservations are recommended for dining cruises.

Next in line along the waterfront Embarcadero is The **San Diego Maritime Museum** ((619) 234-9153, at North Harbor Drive at West Ash Street, which is open daily 9 AM to 8 PM. The museum offers a floating display of several aspects of maritime history. The *Star of India* is a tall sailing ship first commissioned in 1867 and restored in 1961. It is currently the oldest iron merchant ship still sailing anywhere in the world. It was built on the Isle of Man, originally to shuttle British émigrés to New Zealand, and was later in service between the contiguous United States and Alaska. A ticket to tour this ship also entitles you to visit the exhibits on the old ferryboat *Berkeley* and the 1904 steam yacht *Medea*, which occasionally makes trips around the bay to this day. Across Harbor Drive from the ships is the graceful San Diego

County Administration Building designed by architect Sam Hamill and constructed during the Depression. Floodlights illuminate the Spanish Colonial/Beaux-Arts building at night.

CORONADO

Visible from along the waterfront is the graceful arch of the **San Diego–Coronado Bay Bridge** connecting downtown San Diego to Coronado. Though often referred to as an island, Coronado is actually a peninsula connected to the mainland by an isthmus of sand called the Silver Strand. One of the most gracious, gorgeous and serene incorporated cities within San Diego, Coronado

Coronado claims some of the best beaches near downtown, including a gorgeous stretch of sand along Ocean Boulevard to the **Hotel del Coronado**. The Del is a national architectural treasure and is said to be the oldest Pacific Coast resort in the United States. Constructed of Illinois oak, Honduran mahogany, redwood, fir, and pine, the hotel was the largest all-wood structure in the country when it opened in 1888. Ornate and grandiose, its façade consists of numerous peaks, towers, balconies, and turrets, all covered with red shingles. A stay at the Del inspires romance just like in the movies. The hotel has been featured in several films, including Marilyn Monroe's *Some Like It Hot* and Peter O'Toole's *The Stunt Man*. It is well worth

is home to several United States military installations, the historic Hotel del Coronado and neighborhoods of mansions and stately homes. The streets are wide and quiet — ideal for bicyclists. The easiest way to visit the island is to take **San Diego Bay Ferry** ((619) 234-4111 boats over from downtown to the **Ferry Landing Marketplace**. Ferries leave hourly from San Diego between 9 AM and 9 PM from Sunday to Thursday, and between 9 AM to 10 PM from Friday and Saturday. Ferries return from Coronado hourly on the half hour between 9:30 AM and 9:30 PM Sunday to Thursday and 9:30 AM to 10:30 PM Friday and Saturday. The fee is $2 per person.

There are restaurants and shops at the landing, and an excellent bicycle rental shop offering everything from beach cruisers to four-wheel, family-sized quadricycles. The Coronado Shuttle, runs from the ferry landing to most major sights.

a visit for its rich history and the beautiful woodwork of its exterior balconies, interior paneling, and enormous vaulted ceilings. Guests should take advantage of the long, tempting beach, the picture-perfect pool, and dinner in the Prince of Wales Grill.

The hotel sits on **Orange Avenue**, Coronado's main boulevard, landscaped with perfectly shaped cedar trees. Fascinating boutiques, galleries, bookstores and cafés line the avenue, which is the venue for huge Christmas and Fourth of July parades. The neighborhoods off the avenue are splendid, with restored Victorian mansions fronted by elaborate gardens—Coronado holds a highly competitive annual spring garden contest that encourages homeowners to fill their yards with hollyhocks, delphiniums, perfect roses, delicate poppies and gazebos covered with blossoming wisteria. There are small parks every few blocks, and enough churches to serve the faithful of every denomination. Orange Avenue leads southwest to the **Silver Strand**, one of California's most beautiful unspoiled beaches. The strand is a state beach staffed with parking lot attendants and lifeguards. It has picnic, restroom and camping facilities. If you fancy a walk along powdery sands for miles and miles without a hotel or any kind of development, then this is your spot. Whale-watching, fishing and swimming are popular ways of passing the time here. Across from the strand is the Coronado Cays development, a wealthy enclave of homes set on private canals.

BALBOA PARK

Of the great city parks in America, only New York's Central Park is older than San Diego's Balboa Park. In 1867, when 1,200 acres (485.6 hectares) was set aside for a park here, San Diego was a dusty little village of fewer than 3,000 residents. The town fathers reasoned that the barren hillsides and canyons weren't fit for development. San Diegans felt the land should be used cautiously.

The real turning point for the park was the 1915–1916 Panama–California Exposition. That's when "the park" became Balboa Park and the Spanish-Colonial style of architecture took hold here and spread throughout America. Several of the structures built for the exposition are still in place, and the park serves as an architectural museum for devotees of the work of architects Irving Gill, Carleton Winslow, Bertram Goodhue and William Templeton Johnson. The centerpiece of the exposition and an enduring local landmark is the 200-ft (61-m)-high tiled **California Tower**, where carillon bells chime the quarter hour. Most of the buildings constructed in this era have elaborate plateresque façades, Beaux-Arts balconies, baroque ornamentation and an abundance of arches, domes and courtyards.

When former president Theodore Roosevelt visited the ornate buildings at the exposition, he said he hoped the city would preserve them, for beauty was not only worthwhile for its own sake but could also be good for business. In 1935, when other cities were staging expositions to revive their economies after the Depression, San Diego spruced up the old buildings, added several new exhibits, and staged another successful exposition. Chicago's World's Fair had Sally Rand doing her exotic dances, but San Diego had a whole colony of male and female nudists on view in a "Utopian community" in the park. During both World Wars, the buildings were converted to military use. In recent years, they have become a unique cultural center, a vision of old Spain in the heart of the city.

Most of the original buildings now house an impressive collection of museums, including the **Museum of Man** ((619) 239-2001, **San Diego**

Natural History Museum ((619) 232-3821, **San Diego Museum of Art** ((619) 232-7931, the **Museum of Photographic Arts** ((619) 239-5262 and the **Botanical Building** ((619) 235-1100, a redwood lathe-domed structure filled with towering tree ferns, orchids, ponds, and seasonal flowers. The building is fronted by the Lily Pond, which was used as a therapy pool for wounded soldiers during World War II. Newer park buildings house the **San Diego Aerospace Museum** ((619) 234-8291 and the **Reuben H. Fleet Space Theater and Science Center** ((619) 238-1233, with an Omnimax theater and hands-on science exhibits. All the museums have admission fees, but you can purchase a "Passport to Balboa Park" at the **Visitors**

Information Center ((619) 239-0512, located in the House of Hospitality, 1549 El Prado, and open from 9 AM to 4 PM daily. This pass allows one visit to each of the park's museums (and includes entrance to one Omnimax show) during a one-week period.

Also within the park is the Simon Edison Center for the Performing Arts, better known as the **Old Globe** ((619) 239-2255, 1363 Old Globe Way. First constructed for the 1935 exposition, the old Globe Theatre was a faithful reproduction of Shakespeare's Theatre on the Thames where the Old Globe Players performed condensed plays. The theater complex was destroyed by an arson fire in 1978, causing considerable community heartbreak. Four years later the Simon Edison

OPPOSITE and ABOVE: Refined art and ornate architecture make the San Diego Museum of Art one of Balboa Park's greatest treasures.

Center opened with a new Old Globe Theatre and two other stages, one outdoors. The complex is one of the highlights in San Diego's robust theater scene; especially rewarding are the outdoor summer plays on warm summer nights.

Outdoor concerts and plays are staged throughout the year at two of the oldest exhibition sites. The magnificent **Organ Pavilion**, a gift of the sons of the multimillionaire German immigrant, Adolph Spreckels, was built at a cost of more than $100,000 in 1915. With 3,500 pipes, it is the largest open-air organ in the world. It was recently restored, and since its construction — except during World War II — concerts have been held every Sunday afternoon at 2:30 PM.

Built as part of the Ford exhibit for the 1935 exhibition, the **Starlight Theater** ((619) 544-7800, is an amphitheater offering a regular season of musicals and other performances.

The park grounds include a magnificent rose garden, a large desert garden, and the recently restored palm canyon. But the most famous attraction to grow out of the 1915 exposition is the San Diego Zoo, located behind the older buildings.

For many years, San Diego was known as "the place with the great zoo." The **San Diego Zoo** ((619) 234-3153 was perhaps the only thing in San Diego that was bigger and better than its counterparts in Los Angeles and San Francisco. First opened as part of the 1915 Exposition in Balboa Park, it was one of the first American zoos to take animals out of their cages and put them in their own environments. The zoo quickly became the pride of the city. While it has a world-wide reputation for its scientific work, the San Diego Zoo also loves to put on a good show. Its chief founder Dr. Harry Wegeforth was a lover of circus animals and his successors have carried on the tradition of animal performers. The zoo's goodwill ambassador, Joan Embrey, is a frequent guest on United States talk shows where she shows off the zoo's latest pets. More than three million people visit the zoo in Balboa Park every year. It covers 100 acres (40 hectares) of once barren hillsides that have been transformed into a tropical garden of 6,000 flowers and trees, every bit as rare and exotic as the 3,800 animals who live there. A ride on the Skyfari tram is a must for its view of the park's canyons and eucalyptus groves and the downtown skyline. Other attractions include the Children's Zoo, the Sun Bear Forest, Tiger River, Hippo Beach and a much-celebrated exhibit of Chinese pandas. The Zoological Society is renowned for its animal reproduction programs and work with endangered species. The San Diego Wild Animal Park (see WILD ANIMAL PARK, page 315) is also part of the overall San Diego Zoological Society; both are well-worth visiting. The San Diego Zoo is open daily from 9 AM to 4 PM. Admission is $16 for adults, $7 for children age 3 to 11; children age 2 and under are free, as is parking.

OLD TOWN AND MISSION VALLEY

The modern state of California began in an unpretentious settlement at the foot of Presidio Hill in what is now called **Old Town**. Located off Interstate 5 just north of downtown, the original San Diego (circa 1850) is now a state historic park. Traces of its Spanish-American origins have been incorporated into the present day shops, restaurants, and hotels, many housed in restored adobe and wood homes. Historic Old Town includes a full-sized working blacksmith shop, a nineteenth-century stable, La Casa de Machado y Silvas and the Mason Street School. All built around the mid-1800s, these historic buildings offer a good overview of San Diego in its Wild West days. The **Visitor's Center and Park Office** ((619) 220-5422 or (619) 293-0117 (recorded information line) are located in the **Robinson-Rose House** at 4002 Wallace Street, which is open daily from 10 AM to 5 PM. Admission is free. The center may move to new quarters in 1999, but the house will still be part of the park and you can get information there.

The biggest attraction in Old Town is the **Bazaar del Mundo** ((619) 296-3161, 2754 Calhoun Street, open daily from 10 AM to 9 PM, a colorful Mexican-style shopping, dining and entertainment complex within the state park. Shops featuring an ethnic, eclectic selection of kitchenware, jewelry, clothing, household adornments and books frame a central courtyard and gazebo where folkloric dancers perform during special celebrations. The Casa del Pico restaurant may well be the most popular spot for margaritas in all San Diego; locals know they'll be required to visit with out-of-towners amid the mariachis and costumed waitresses in this rambling outdoor patio and indoor restaurant. Fortunately, the drinks are excellent and the food usually up to par.

Just up the hill from the Old Town Historic Park is **Heritage Park**, where seven Victorian houses were moved after facing destruction in other parts of the city. As in the older park, the houses here have been put to commercial use as art galleries, gift shops, and restaurants.

Further up the hill is **Presidio Park**, at 2727 Presidio Drive, one of San Diego's most beautiful scenic spots. It marks the site of the original Spanish mission and fort. The mission was later moved six miles (10 km) up the valley. But in 1925, a mission-style museum was erected on the site. The **Serra Museum** ((619) 297-3258, designed by William Templeton Johnson is a picture-perfect Spanish-Colonial mission building from the early 1920s. It's often mistaken for the eighteenth-century mission in the valley. The hilltop park with the sweeping meadowlike lawns is a favorite picnic spot and backdrop for weddings. Maintained by the San Diego Historical Society, the museum provides an excellent introduction to San Diego's Mexican and Spanish past. The museum is open Tuesday through Saturday, 10 AM to 4 PM and on Sunday from noon to 4 PM. Adult admission is $3 and children under 13 are free.

For guided tours through Old Town, call the Old Town San Diego State Historic Park ((619) 220-5422. More information is available from the Chamber of Commerce ((619) 232-0124.

San Diego's **Mission Valley** was once fertile cattle-ranching land with large grazing spreads along the San Diego River. In the 1950s the river valley gave way to freeways and commerce; today Mission Valley is bisected lengthwise by Interstate 8 running east to Arizona. Several other major freeways interchange here, over and around two large shopping centers and a line-up of unexceptional hotels. East of the shopping centers is Qualcomm Stadium, site of the 1998 Super Bowl, and the eighteenth-century **Mission Basilica San Diego de Alcalá** ((619) 281-8449, 10818 San Diego Mission Road, open daily 9 AM to 5 PM, admission $2 for adults. Established in 1769 by Padre Junipero Serra, the mission was restored in 1931 and houses the **Father Luis Jayme Museum**, which includes original mission records, books and relics. Church services are held in the simple mission church. On-going archeological digs have uncovered many relics from the indigenous indian communities overtaken by the fervent padres.

POINT LOMA AND THE ISLANDS

Military installations cover much of **Point Loma**, a windblown peninsula sheltering the west side of San Diego Bay. On the crest of the ridgeline out to the point is **Fort Rosecrans National Cemetery**, with miles and miles of simple stones engraved with the name, rank, and military group of the dead. The memorial park overlooks the bay on one side, the ocean on the other. Just before you get to **Cabrillo National Historical Monument**, a road (marked "Tide Pools") veers off to the right down to the waterfront. This is a nature preserve, but you can walk out on to the rocks and observe the wide variety of sea life caught in the tidal pools. Closed to the public but clearly visible from the nature preserve are the picturesque old clapboard buildings of the Coast Guard Station. They stand beside the lighthouse, right on the waterfront, that currently marks the entrance to San Diego Harbor.

Back up on top of the point, a parking lot ($2 per car for a week-long pass) serves as the entrance to **Cabrillo National Historical Monument** ((619) 557-5450, open daily from 9 AM to 7:45 PM daily in the summer and from 9 AM to 5:15 PM the rest of the year. At 500 ft (152 m) above sea level, the hilltop park provides a wonderful overview of San Diego's topography and position in the Pacific

Ocean. Charts along the walkways describe the abundance of military vessels in the bay. Depending on military maneuvers, you could spot a nuclear submarine, aircraft carrier, or destroyer looming gray against a field of billowing sails. The monument's attractions include a small museum on the role of Juan Rodriguez Cabrillo, the Portuguese sea captain (of a Spanish ship) who was the first European to land here in 1542, and the landmark 1855 lighthouse. The book and gift shop has an excellent selection of books on San Diego and nature, and interesting scientific souvenirs.

Point Loma offers one of the most spectacular views of San Diego in all directions. On clear days you can locate the hills of Tijuana and the Coronado Islands to the south and the tip of La Jolla Cove to the north. From January through March you can often spot gray whales spouting off the point's western shores.

They seem a natural part of the landscape now, but **Shelter Island** and **Harbor Island**, which extend into San Diego Bay between Point Loma and downtown, are constructed from sand and sludge dredged from San Diego Bay. **Shelter Island**, built in the 1950s above a submerged shoal, is the center of Point Loma's boating and fishing community; the trail around the island is a perfect walking and jogging path passing by a boat ramp, marinas, long lawns with views of downtown, and several hotels. **Harbor Island** was constructed in the 1970s near the international airport, and holds several hotels and boat yards.

Locals claim that **Mission Bay Park**'s 4,600 acres (1,840 hectares) and 27 miles (44 km) of shoreline make it the country's largest public aquatic park. It is also one of the most pleasant places in the city to get away for a few minutes or a few hours. There are ample facilities available for recreation — boats and jet skis for rent and tennis at the nearby hotels. Walkers and joggers from throughout the city take to the miles of paved walkways. The lawns are available for picnics, kite-flying, and sunbathing. Mission Bay Park is the scene of many special events throughout the year. For information on events, call ((619) 276-8200.

Fiesta Island, another man-made isthmus composed of dredged-up sand, is located at the south end of the park. Although there's no development of any kind here, it has become so popular as a party place for the young set that the city had to clamp down with rigid rules against overnight visitors. Fiesta Island is also the favorite local place of jet skiers. You can pull your truck, van, or buggy right on to the beach, unload, and spend the day skiing and stretching out in the sun.

Located on 135 acres (55 hectares) on Mission Bay, **Sea World** ((619) 226-3901 is one of the city's major tourist attractions. First opened in March 1964 by four University of California at Los Angeles fraternity brothers, it was bought by the publishing and entertainment conglomerate Harcourt Brace Jovanovich in 1976, and is now owned by Anheuser Busch. The small aquatic park has become an enormous entertainment center.

Sea World has four aquariums, two rides, hydrofoil boat trips, cable railways, 30 educational exhibits, and seven extraordinary shows. The most popular of the shows involves Shamu and his orca friends performing in a six-million-gallon (22.7-million-liter) saltwater tank before a 5,000-seat stadium. In smaller stadiums, you can see dolphins and pilot whales in one show, sea lions and otters in another.

The largest of the aquariums is a 400,000-gallon (1.5-million-liter) tank that holds the largest live shark display in the world. You're not encouraged to go near the sharks, but there is a petting pool where visitors can feed and pet the whales and dolphins. One of the newer exhibits is the multimillion-dollar **Penguin Encounter**, the most extensive collection of penguins in captivity. Sea World is located on Sea World Drive in Mission Bay. If you are coming from the Los Angeles area, take Interstate 5 South to Sea World Drive, take a right off the freeway and follow the signs. If you are coming from the Riverside or San Bernardino area, go south on Interstate 15 to Interstate 8 west, then to Interstate 5 north. Take the first exit which is Sea World Drive, go left, then follow the signs. From the east, take Interstate 8 to Interstate 5 north and then follow above directions. Ticket prices are $34.95 for adults, $26.95 for children ages three to eleven, and children under two are free. Parking will cost you $5.

THE BEACHES

A series of small beach communities line the coast north of downtown. The first, at the west end of Interstate 8, is **Ocean Beach**. "OB" is a self-contained community with a distinct character, accommodating families who've lived here for decades and newcomers seeking their first taste of life at the beach. Though many outside OB consider it a somewhat seedy hangout for undesirable elements, the town has a thriving business community, a church on nearly every block of the main drag, and a strong sense of pride among its residents. Surfers are attracted to the especially powerful waves along OB's beaches, which have lifeguard stands, restrooms, fire rings, volleyball courts and large parking lots. The **Ocean Beach Pier** extends a half mile over the water at the north end of the beach; a bait and tackle shop at the far end of the pier supplies anglers who don't need a fishing permit to dangle their lines in hopes of catching mackerel, halibut or bass. A small café

Killer whale and human rider perform at San Diego's famed Sea World.

300   *San Diego and Environs*

tempts walkers with hot coffee and fresh fish lunches; public restrooms are available. The pier is occasionally closed during fierce storms. **Newport Avenue** runs through the center of downtown OB and is lined with coffee shops, beach bars, small stores and an overabundance of antique shops. **Sunset Cliffs Boulevard** runs south from the entrance to OB to the aptly named Sunset Cliffs, where locals and travelers walk, jog, sunbathe and congregate for the sun's show every evening. The sandstone cliffs here are somewhat unstable; sections are marked with barriers warning climbers to stay away. Experienced surfers congregate at the south end of the cliffs where the waves are particularly exciting. Beyond Sunset Cliffs is Point Loma, the long jut of headland that protects the entrance to San Diego Bay.

Mission Beach is the next town on the north side of Mission Bay, and is the quintessential Southern California beach town, with a three-mile (4.8-km)-long concrete boardwalk running along the sand. **South Mission Beach** is a quieter place favored by San Diego's young and upwardly mobile. The beach ends here with a long jetty of concrete boulders that protect the entrance to Mission Bay aquatic park. The true beach scene begins at **Belmont Park** ((619) 488-1549 at the intersection of Mission Boulevard and West Mission Bay Drive. The 18-acre (7.3-hectare) park was completely renovated in 1990, and the **Giant Dipper** rollercoaster, first constructed in 1925, was restored. The mint-green and pink coaster, illuminated with twinkling white lights, is a historic landmark; the coaster is in operation from 11 AM to 8 PM, Monday through Thursday and from 11 AM to 10 PM Friday through Sunday. Rides cost $3. Also within Belmont Park is **The Plunge** ((619) 488-3110, constructed in 1925 as the largest indoor saltwater swimming pool in the country. The pool (now filled with fresh water) was restored in 1990 and is open to the public. Amusement rides, restaurants, and souvenir shops fill out the park's offerings. Between the park and the beach is the **Boardwalk**, a must-see for any beach fan. Scantily clad beach bodies cruise about on rollerblades, bicycles, skateboards and foot, creating claustrophobia-inducing crowds on sunny weekends. Wall-to-wall private and rental homes, ragged beach bars, crowded restaurants and the occasional small park line the boardwalk for three miles.

The **Crystal Pier** bisects the boardwalk at the intersection of Garnet Avenue and Mission Boulevard in **Pacific Beach**. The pier was first constructed at the same time as Belmont park, in the 1920s, and was the site of the enchanting Crystal ballroom. Today it is home to the Crystal Pier Hotel, one of my favorite hostelries in San Diego. The hotel's blue and white cottages line the

400-foot-long pier, which ends in a T-shaped deck where anglers and sightseers lounge. Pacific Beach is a bit less frenetic than Mission Beach and more dweller-friendly. Grand and Garnet Avenues are filled with trendy coffeehouses, tattoo parlors, used clothing shops and ethnic eateries near the beach.

LA JOLLA

Although La Jolla (pronounced La Hoya) is within the city limits of San Diego, it has a separate zip code and a decidedly separate identity. Until fairly recent times, it was a secluded enclave inhabited by artists and writers living in little beach cottages and wealthier types in designer mansions. Luckily, it was also where the two eccentric sisters of newspaper tycoon E.W. Scripps made their home. The sisters watched over their private domain from the late nineteenth century far into the twentieth with a loving eye and a ready umbrella. Ellen Browning Scripps' many philanthropies include the **Museum of Contemporary Art** (expanded from her home), the Scripps Institute of Oceanography, the Scripps Clinic, and many others. But her most enduring gift was the waterfront itself which, along with Torrey Pines State Park, she bought and presented to the state and city as public preserves.

Some locals cling to the belief that La Jolla is a misspelling of the Spanish word for jewel, "La Hoya." Over the years, the relentless Pacific has hollowed out the sandstone cliffs below the center of town. Early this century, there was even a monumental natural arch out in the water, but that has long since crumbled into the waves.

The downtown area of La Jolla is centered around Prospect and Girard Streets atop a slight rise over **Ellen Browning Scripps Park** and the open Pacific. "The Village," as old-timers call it, is akin to an adult playground for the well-heeled. It's the best shopping area in San Diego (see SHOPPING, page 305) and is clogged with fine restaurants. A walk and meal here are essential to any San Diego vacation. The side streets in the village are filled with architectural wonders — public buildings and private homes all reflect a genteel style. All the main roads into La Jolla eventually lead to the coast and **La Jolla Cove**, an underwater preserve framed by sandstone cliffs and a small beach backed by century-old Washington palms. The **La Jolla Cave and Shell Shop (** (619) 454-6080, 1325 Coast Boulevard, has a stairway down to hollow caves etched by the sea at the north end of the cove. At the south end, divers, snorkelers and sunbathers don their gear on the lawns of Scripps Park before descending a stairway to the cove's small beach. A walkway parallels Coast Boulevard south from the cove to the **Children's Pool**, built inside a man-made cove. Picnics, soccer games, birthday parties and weddings take place on the lawns of Scripps Park most summer weekends, providing a friendly background for the vistas of waves spraying above the cliffs. The Children's Pool has long been a favorite swimming haunt for families and snorkelers, but is sometimes invaded by dozens of sea lions who lay claim on the sand for weeks.

Coast Boulevard travels south from La Jolla proper parallel to Prospect Street. Sandwiched between the two is the **Museum of Contemporary Art San Diego (** (619) 454-354, 700 Prospect Street, housed in the former estate of Ellen Browning Scripps. Designed by renowned architect Irving Gill in 1916, it is a beautiful setting for one of the premier collections of art in San Diego. The museum's permanent collection includes works by Andy Warhol, Frank Stella, and Kiki Smith, among others. The museum is open Tuesday through Saturday from 10 AM to 5 PM and Sunday from noon to 5 PM. Admission is $4 for adults, $2 for seniors and students, and children 12 and under are free.

Blue road signs depicting seagulls lead the way on a scenic drive south of La Jolla to several beach neighborhoods including **Windansea**, below the bluffs at Neptune Place. The beach was the setting of pop-journalist Tom Wolfe's *Pumphouse Gang*, named for the water pump atop a small rise overlooking the surf. Swimmers should avoid the treacherous waters here, which are legendary among surfers and informally reserved for only the best locals. Windansea's surfers remain an elite group that doesn't take kindly to new members, but there's no reason why you can't watch from the safety of the bluffs.

North of La Jolla Village and Scripps Park the land curves around La Jolla Bay along to **La Jolla Shores**, a fine, long beach with plenty of room for surfers, swimmers, sunbathers and strollers. Backed by the palatial homes in La Jolla's hillsides, the Shores is home to the private **La Jolla Beach and Tennis Club (** (619) 454-7126 and a an assorment of interesting shops and restaurants. On the beach itself are picnic facilities, lifeguards, a playground and restrooms. Torrey Pines Road travels above the shores to the Scripps Institute of Oceanography and its **Birch Aquarium (** (619) 534-3474, 2300 Expedition Way, which opened in 1992 and replaced the original 1950s-style Scripps Aquarium. This 49,000-sq-ft (4,552-sq-m) facility features 33 tanks of underwater sea creatures and an outdoor tide pool. Admission is $7.50 for adults, $4 for children ages 3 to 17, and those under

OPPOSITE: The best rooms at the genteel La Valencia Hotel overlook the palm-lined La Jolla Cove.

three are free. The aquarium is open daily from 9 AM to 5 PM.

For lovers of the great outdoors, La Jolla is a wonderful place. You'll find one of the most beautiful cliffside beaches in California at **Torrey Pines State Park** ((619) 755-2063. There are two large parking lots with an all-day fee of $3. Park either by the flat beaches at the base of the cliffs, or on top. This incredibly steep drive, part of the original coastal highway, is a favorite challenge for mountain bikers. At the top, a small museum explains the Torrey Pine that is found only here and on one of the channel islands, and the other flora and fauna (including rattlesnakes) that live in the nature preserve. Several nature trails wind

in and around the rugged bluffs. Two steep but nicely graded (with handrails) trails lead down to the beach.

Beneath Torrey Pines is San Diego's most notorious beach, **Black's Beach**, named for the family that once owned it. Sheer sandstone cliffs rise more than a 1000 ft (300 m) behind the beach. You'll often see the clifftops lined with people at the Torrey Pines Golf Course peering down through binoculars, ogling at the nudists that frequent the beach. For many years, the main access to the beach was over and down these cliffs. Just about every year, someone is seriously injured or killed by slipping off these trails. Rescue workers do respond to calls for help, but otherwise, visiting Black's Beach is strictly at your own risk; there are no lifeguards and no aid stations of any kind there. There are no signs directing you to Black's. You can get their either by walking south on Torrey Pines Beach or from the clifftop near the famed **Salk Institute** off Torrey Pines Road. There is a hang-glider station at the top of the cliffs; gliders come and go depending on the weather and insurance conditions; from time to time the port is closed because of safety concerns. There is a moderately safe path down the cliffs to Black's Beach just north of the glider station.

SPORTS

San Diego is an All-American sports-crazed town, at least when it comes to football and baseball. The San Diego Chargers were the western division football champions in 1994 and played the San Francisco Forty-Niners in the Super Bowl (San Diego lost). The San Diego Padres used to play on the waterfront Lane Field in downtown, and in 1998 were pushing for a new downtown stadium. Currently both teams play in Qualcomm Stadium ((619) 525-8282), which has a 24-hour recorded message on events scheduled at the stadium. The Stadium is located at 9449 Friars Road in Mission Valley. For information on the Padres, call ((619) 280-4636; on the Chargers, call ((619) 280-2121. The San Diego Gulls, an indoor hockey team, were champions in their league for three years (1995–1998). Tickets are available through the **San Diego Sports Arena** ((619) 224-4176 (events hotline), 3500 Sports Arena Boulevard, and **TicketMaster** ((619) 220-8497.

Naturally, much of San Diego's sporting life involves the ocean. Those interesting in **sport fishing** on either party or charter boats will want to check out the veteran sport fishing operations at **H&M Landing** ((619) 222-1144, 2803 Emerson Street, and **Fisherman's Landing** ((619) 221-8500, 2838 Garrison Street, in Point Loma. In Mission Bay, **Seaforth Sportfishing** ((619) 224-3383, 1717 Quivira Road, offers similar excursions. Anglers are allowed to fish off of most of San Diego's piers without a license and congregate at Shelter Island, Ocean Beach, Embarcadero and Crystal piers. For **boating** enthusiasts the **Mission Bay Sport Center** ((619) 488-1004, 1010 Santa Clara Point, is a one-stop water sports center with sailboat, catamaran, kayak, windsurfer, and water ski rentals. Boats can also be rented from several vendors in Mission Bay and some waterfront hotels.

Surfing is more than a sport — it's a lifestyle in San Diego. Some of the best surfing spots are: Ocean Beach Pier, Sunset Cliffs, Tourmaline Park Windandsea and La Jolla Shores. Boogie boarding and body-surfing are also popular at these beaches. **Scuba diving** and snorkeling are excellent at La Jolla Cove and La Jolla Shores and off Point Loma. Dive shops and gear rentals are listed in the phone book.

With nearly 80 **golf courses** in the immediate area, tourist officials say San Diego can easily claim to have more golfing opportunities per visitor than any other major tourist city in America. A complete list of the golf courses can be obtained from the San Diego Convention and Visitors Bureau (see GENERAL INFORMATION, page 292). Here are some of the more interesting courses. The 36-hole championship **Torrey Pines Municipal Golf Course** ((619) 570-1234, 11480 North Torrey Pines

Road, La Jolla, CA 92037, has been the site of the PGA Tour's Buick Invitational since 1968. This municipal course is difficult to get on but well worth the effort. Set on a sheer bluff 300 ft (91 m) above the ocean, many of the holes offer beautiful views of the gentle Pacific. The public **Mission Bay Golf Course Clubhouse and Sandtrap Restaurant and Lounge** ((619) 490-3370 are at 2702 North Mission Bay Drive in Pacific Beach. The only public golf course on Coronado is the **Coronado City Golf Course** ((619) 435-3121, 2000 Visalia Row, Coronado. **Pala Mesa Resort** ((760) 728-5881 TOLL-FREE (800) 722-4700 FAX (760) 723-8292, 2001 Old US Highway 395, Fallbrook, in North County, sometimes offers low-priced packages including accommodations and use of resort facilities, including use of the 18-hole, par 72 course as well as tennis and fitness facilities. The **Rancho Bernardo Inn Resort Course** ((619) 675-8470, 17550 Bernardo Oaks Drive in Rancho Bernardo, 25 miles (40 km) north of San Diego on Interstate 15, is open to guests of the resort, as are the courses in other north county hotels (see WHERE TO STAY, below).

SHOPPING

There are two huge California-style shopping malls off Friar's Road and Interstate 8 in Mission Valley. **Fashion Valley Shopping** ((619) 688-9113 Center, intersection of Highway 163 and Friars Road West, is a pleasant spot for walking and window shopping, and has a good selection of department and specialty shops. **Mission Valley Shopping Center** ((619) 296-6375, 1640 Camino del Rio Norte, is more trendy, with an appalling purple and yellow twenty-theater movie complex.

If you're looking for an exciting blend of all these, you'll find it at **Horton Plaza** ((619) 238-1596 at Broadway and Fourth Avenue in the heart of downtown. The complex includes 12 movie theaters and two innovative underground stages for the San Diego Repertory Theater. Four major department stores and over 100 specialty shops feature science gadgets, books, kites, adventure gear, food, and much more. Trade names run rampant here; you can check out the latest offerings from Warner Brothers, Disney, Planet Hollywood and Victoria's Secret if you must. There are several restaurants, and a food court with ethnic fast-food stands and outdoor shaded tables.

More tasteful shopping is available in La Jolla, where Armani, Banana Republic and the Gap rub shoulders. The shopping and sightseeing are excellent on Prospect and Girard Streets — check out the White Rabbit and Warwick's bookstores, Adelaide's Flowers, and the collection of galleries and clothing boutiques on Girard. The La Valencia Hotel is a must-see on Prospect, along with any shop or gallery that has a view of the cove. For arts and crafts, especially of Mexican origin, try the **Bazaar del Mundo**, 2754 Calhoun Street in Old Town.

WHERE TO STAY

Location is a critical factor when choosing a hotel in San Diego, since the city's various sights are spread far apart. Downtown is the most efficient option, since all modes of public transportation are easily accessed. But it's hard to stay away from the beach. The best hotels near the water are located in the beach towns and Coronado; at most places you'll pay dearly for a room with a view. Hotels fill up at unpredictable times, depending

on school vacations and major conventions being held in the city. Advance reservations are advisable at most times, especially if you want to stay by the beach. Try booking through **San Diego Hotel Reservations** TOLL-FREE (800) 728-3227 for an overview of choices and possible discounts.

VERY EXPENSIVE

Located off the tourist circuit on a private 15-acre (six-hectare) peninsula south of downtown Coronado, the **Loews Coronado Bay Resort** ((619) 424-4000 TOLL-FREE (800) 81-LOEWS FAX (619) 424-4400, 4000 Coronado Bay Road, is the ultimate self-contained resort for those seeking solitude, pampering, and relaxation. The compound, which lies adjacent to the private canals at the Coronado Cays, has 400 guest rooms and 37 suites, all with water views and balconies. An 80-slip private marina serves those arriving by boat, who mill about with hotel guests between the waterfront, four restaurants, three pools, tennis courts, health club and sports gear rentals. Biking paths lead to

OPPOSITE: The Museum of Contemporary Art serves as a venue for cutting-edge art, film, and music presentations. A true California girl rides a jet ski ABOVE as if it were a wind stallion, on Mission Bay off Fiesta Island, San Diego.

the long stretch of unbroken paths along the windy Silver Strand. Better yet is an evening champagne cruise for two in a gondola — one of the Loews' special touches that keeps regulars from Mexico, France and San Diego coming back. The Azzura Point restaurant features a view toward downtown Coronado and San Diego and excellent cuisine. The more informal RRR's café serves the best Sunday brunch (with plenty of seafood and Asian specialties) in San Diego.

The **San Diego Marriott Hotel & Marina** ((619) 234-1500 FAX (619) 234-8678, 333 West Harbor Drive, is located downtown between the Convention Center and Seaport Village. The two 25-story towers are angled away from the waterfront so

that nearly all 1,355 rooms and 56 suites have a view of the bay. Hotel facilities include six restaurants and bars and two nicely landscaped pools on the ground level. The hotel also operates the marina, with slips for 446 boats. There are tennis courts, a health club and sauna and a jogging trail. Several excursion boats also operate out of the marina. On the boardwalk, you can rent bicycles for your own excursion along the boardwalk and embarcadero.

The grande dame of all San Diego hotels is the **Hotel del Coronado** ((619) 435-6611 TOLL-FREE (800) HOTEL DEL FAX (619) 522-8491, located

OPPOSITE: A playful mural decorates the exterior of the Metropolitan Hotel, one of San Diego's award-winning new single-room occupancy hotels for lower-income people. ABOVE: Colorful stacks of pottery in all shapes and sizes are available along the roads in Baja California at very reasonable prices.

on the ocean at 1500 Orange Avenue. In 1988, "The Del" celebrated its 100th anniversary with a lavish multimillion-dollar party. On August 28, 1997 it was sold by the estate of M. Larry Lawrence, the United States Ambassador to Switzerland, to a large hotel conglomerate, ending decades of private ownership.

The Del is worth a visit for its rich history and the beautiful woodwork of its exterior balconies, the interior paneling, and enormous vaulted ceilings. Guests should take advantage of the long, tempting beach, the picture-perfect pool, and dinner in the Prince of Wales Grill.

Also included in this category is the modern, efficient **Coronado Island Marriott Resort** ((619) 435-3000 TOLL-FREE (800) 228-9290 FAX (619) 435-3032, 2000 Second Street at the edge of San Diego Bay. Elegant and serene, this waterfront hotel is within walking distance of the Bay Ferry and looks across the water to downtown's skyline. Its restaurants, especially Marius, are excellent.

In La Jolla, glamour and history enhance nature at **La Valencia Hotel** ((619) 454-0771 TOLL-FREE (800) 451-0772 FAX (619) 456-392, 1132 Prospect Street. With a settled unpretentious charm all its own, La Valencia offers 100 rooms and suites in Mediterranean-style buildings overlooking La Jolla Cove and Ellen Browning Scripps Park. The hotel has been an integral part of La Jolla's art, society and political scenes since its opening in 1926, and retains the sensibilities of an older, gracious resort with quirky-sized rooms and personalized service. The hotel's **Sky Room** has an incomparable view and an elegant ambiance.

In the hills north of San Diego, set amid the burgeoning research and development companies is the sleek **Sheraton Grande Torrey Pines** ((619) 558-1500 TOLL-FREE (800) 325-3589 FAX (619) 558-1131, 10950 North Torrey Pines Road in La Jolla.

EXPENSIVE

Thanks to the completion of the Convention Center in 1990, downtown has a glut of hotel rooms, which are booked solid during major events. Located in the center of commercial downtown, about 10 blocks from the waterfront, the **US Grant** ((619) 232-3121 TOLL-FREE (800) 237-5029 FAX (619) 232-3626, 326 Broadway in downtown San Diego, was beautifully restored and reopened in December 1985. A San Diego landmark since it first opened in 1910, there are 280 rooms and 60 suites, a fully equipped fitness center, meeting facilities and four restaurants. Classical chamber music is played in the lobby during happy hour. It's location is convenient to the Gaslamp Quarter, Horton Plaza and the Convention Center. A few blocks south

is the **Horton Grand Hotel** ((619) 544-TOLL-FREE (800) 542-1886 FAX (619) 544-0058, 311 Island Avenue. This hotel was reconstructed out of two turn-of-the-century hotels in 1986. It is richly decorated with Victorian furnishings and draperies, with each room being unique. The **Embassy Suites-San Diego Bay** ((619) 239-2400 TOLL-FREE (800) 362-2779 FAX (619) 239-1520, 601 Pacific Highway is one of the best choices for both business travelers and families. The rooms all have a separate living room good for meetings or bunking the kids, and amenities include complimentary continental breakfast in the atrium lobby. On the more elegant side, the **Westgate Hotel** ((619) 238-1818, 1055 Second Avenue,

Water-oriented travelers enjoy the **Kona Kai Plaza Resort** ((619) 221-1191 TOLL-FREE (800) 566-2524 FAX (619) 222-9738, located at 1551 Shelter Island Drive. The refurbished hotel, which had a south seas theme for many decades, is now designed in a Mexican style and sits beside Shelter Island's marina. The hotel has 211 units in rooms facing lawns, the marina or the bay; some have kitchens and living rooms. Amenities include tennis courts, pools, boat rentals, a health club and spa and a respectable dining room.

The **San Diego Princess** ((619) 274-4630 TOLL-FREE (800) 344-2626 FAX (619) 581-5977, 1404 West Vacation Road, a Princess Cruises Resort, is set in a large compound on Mission Bay near Mission

offers a subdued, chandelier-lit setting just off Broadway.

A good choice in Coronado is the **Glorietta Bay Inn** ((619) 435-3101 TOLL-FREE (800) 283-9383 FAX (619) 435-6182, 1630 Glorietta Boulevard. This historic landmark was formerly the mansion of sugar baron John Spreckels. It is located across the street from the Hotel del Coronado. There are 11 rooms in the original mansion, plus 17 family suites and a variety of modern rooms. Near the airport, the **Sheraton San Diego Hotel & Marina** ((619) 291-2900 FAX (619) 692-2338, 1380 Harbor Drive on Harbor Island and **Humphrey's Half Moon Inn & Suites** ((619) 224-3411 TOLL-FREE (800) 345-9995 FAX (619) 224-3478, 2303 Shelter Island Drive on Shelter Island both offer reliable rooms and service. Humphrey's presents a hugely popular series of outdoor concerts during the summer months.

Beach. All accommodations are single-level with either a garden, lagoon or bay view. There are 462 rooms and suites, four restaurants, five pools, a mile (over one and a half kilometers) of white sand beach, tennis courts and also an 18-hole architect-designed putting golf course.

Near Sea World and the sport fishing operations on Mission Bay is the **San Diego Hilton Beach and Tennis Resort** ((619) 276-4010 TOLL-FREE (800) 221-2424 FAX (619) 275-7991, 1775 East Mission Bay. Another sprawling compound with plenty of space to swim, rollerblade, jog and sail, the hotel has several good restaurants, a children's program, five tennis courts and a wide variety of rooms. More venerable and private is the **La Jolla Beach & Tennis Club** ((619) 454-7126, 2000 Spindrift Drive, La Jolla, with 15 hotel rooms and 76 apartments along a well-guarded beach. In downtown La Jolla the **Bed & Breakfast Inn** at La Jolla ((619) 456-2066, 7753 Draper Avenue, has 16 rooms in a historic home designed by architect Irving Gill. The **Prospect Park Inn** ((619) 454-0133 TOLL-FREE (800) 433-1609 FAX (619) 454-2056, 1110 Prospect Street, La Jolla, sits in the shadow of the La Valencia and has plenty of character and charm; smoking is not allowed in any of the rooms.

A great find just across the street from La Jolla Cove is the **La Jolla Cove Suites** ((619) 459-2621 TOLL-FREE (800) 537-8483 FAX (619) 454-3522, 1155 Coast Boulevard, La Jolla. Though far from luxurious, the ample suites come in a variety of styles, some with full sea views, kitchens and living rooms.

MODERATE

My favorite hometown escape is the **Crystal Pier Hotel** ((619) 483-6983 TOLL-FREE (800) 748-5894 FAX (619) 483-6811, 4500 Ocean Boulevard, Pacific Beach. Charming blue and white wood-frame cottages line a long wooden pier over the water. Guests drive their cars to the front door and set up housekeeping in a comfortable setting with a kitchenette, small living room, bedroom and back door deck over the surf. The water pounds under the pilings at night, making you feel as though you're sleeping on a boat. Pacific Beach's boardwalk and restaurants are right at your doorstep. Reservations are advised well in advance; a three-night minimum stay is required in summer.

Though most of San Diego's waterfront hotels are outrageously expensive, there are a few modest

finds in great neighborhoods. The **Dana Inn and Marina** ((619) 222-6440 TOLL-FREE (800) 445-3339 FAX (619) 222-5916, 1710 West Mission Bay Drive, is located on the Sea World side of Mission Bay Park with easy access to boat rentals, bike paths, swimming beaches, and picnic grounds. The 196 rooms are family-friendly, with few frills beyond small refrigerators and indestructible furnishings. The **Sea Lodge** ((619) 459-8271 TOLL-FREE (800) 237-5211 FAX (619) 456-9346, 8110 Camino del Oro in La Jolla, is another sure bet thanks to its location adjacent to the La Jolla Beach and Tennis Club. The 128 rooms face courtyards and the open ocean from Spanish-style buildings in a quiet residential neighborhood.

In Old Town, the **Heritage Park Inn** ((619) 299-6832 TOLL-FREE (800) 995-2470 FAX (619) 299-9465, 2470 Heritage Park Row, is a charming bed and breakfast in a Victorian home. Nearby, the **Hacienda Hotel-Old Town** ((619) 298-4707 TOLL-FREE (800) 888-1991 FAX (619) 298-4771 sprawls up a hillside in a series of Spanish-style buildings. There are 169 rooms spread out over several levels, with brick patios and gurgling fountains and lots of wood accents imported from Mexico.

INEXPENSIVE

Thanks to the ingenuity of architect Rob Wellington Quigley, downtown has several great budget hotels in modern buildings. The **J Street Inn** ((619) 696-6922 FAX (619) 696-1295, 222 J Street, is located near the Convention Center, as is the 198-room **Island Inn** ((619) 232-4138 FAX (619) 232-4183, 202 Island Avenue (at Second Avenue). **La Pensione Hotel** ((619) 236-8000 TOLL-FREE (800) 232-4683 FAX (619) 236-8088, 606 West Date Street, is a charmer located in the Old Italy section of town, near bus lines and great Italian restaurants. The **Inn at the YMCA** ((619) 234-5252/hostel ((619) 525-1531 FAX (619) 234-5272, 500 West Broadway (between Columbia and India Streets), sits right by the trolley stop and Amtrak station, within a few blocks of the waterfront. **La Pacifica** ((619) 236-9292 FAX (619) 236-9988, 1546 Second Avenue, with 106 units, all with kitchenettes, is also conveniently located.

The Youth Hostel system is well represented with the **Elliott Hostel** ((619) 223-4778 TOLL-FREE (800) 909-4776, Hostel Code 44, 3790 Udall Street, located in a residential neighborhood in Point Loma on the bus line to Ocean Beach. For information on other American Youth Hostel properties try the WEB SITE www.hiayh.org.

OPPOSITE and ABOVE: The Hotel Del Coronado on the beach across the bay from San Diego is the grande dame of all Southern California hotels.

Though not affiliated with the hosteling organization, the **Ocean Beach International Hostel** ((619) 223-7873 FAX (619) 223-7881, 4961 Newport Avenue, is similar in style. This older hotel on the main street of San Diego's most offbeat beach area has private and semi-private rooms with 60 beds in total.

WHERE TO EAT

San Diego's dining scene shouldn't be compared with that of San Francisco and Los Angeles. It's more a hybrid of local tastes than a contender for fame. There are many fine locals chefs who've moved about with opportunities within the county; check the dining listings in *San Diego Magazine* and the *San Diego Union Tribune* for the latest trends. Steak houses were doing booming business in the late 1990s, and seafood restaurants are always in vogue.

Mexican food is a factor in recipes nearly everywhere; tortillas and chilis are omnipresent. There's also a strong Asian flare, thanks to the Vietnamese, Hmong and Cambodian communities. Nouvelle California cuisine — a blend of organic greens, homegrown herbs, exotic grains and white meat or fish — affects menus even in the dozens of trendy Italian cafés downtown and in La Jolla.

There are cheap eats everywhere; all neighborhoods have inexpensive coffee shops, taco stands and pizza parlors.

VERY EXPENSIVE

Morton's of Chicago ((619) 696-3369, 285 J Street at the Harbor Club, opened near the Convention center in 1997 with a splash. It seems all the business travelers were seeking a dark, quiet spot to indulge in martinis and beef. Even the spinach is spectacular, and you can exhaust a hefty expense account easily on side dishes to accompany a prime, hefty, steak. Perched above the water between the cruise ships and the Maritime Museum is **Anthony's Star of Sea** ((619) 232-7408, 1360 North Harbor Drive, a long-time landmark. The restaurant has always been romantic in a linens and candlelight way, but the food has been spotty. A new chef and his reworked menu has brought the crowds back. Jackets are suggested here.

At Tuna Harbor, the **Top of the Market** ((619) 232-4TOP, 750 North Harbor, is quite possibly the best overall seafood restaurant in San Diego. Part of a two-story complex above The Fish Market (see below), this subdued and elegant dining room overlooks San Diego Bay. Seafood is imported from all over the world, and true connoisseurs can sample the world's best mussels, salmon, tuna and oysters.

In La Jolla, the **Top of the Cove** ((619) 454-7779, 1216 Prospect Street, wins rave reviews year after year; both the food and the view are sublime. **George's at the Cove** ((619) 454-4244, 1250 Prospect Street, is equally impressive. Both have a more formal dining room downstairs and an open-air upstairs terrace café.

EXPENSIVE

Italian restaurants predominate in the Gaslamp Quarter. **Fio's** ((619) 234-3467, 801 Fifth Avenue, and **Osteria Panivino** ((619) 595-7959, 722 Fifth Avenue, have survived and thrived among the competition. **Dobson's** ((619) 231-6771, 956 Broadway Circle by Horton Plaza, is a genteel hangout for the coat and tie set. **Celadon** ((619) 295-8800, 3628 Fifth Avenue, in the Hillcrest neighborhood above downtown, is the best Thai restaurant in the area.

The reigning Italian trattoria in Coronado is **Primavera Ristorante** ((619) 435-0454, 932 Orange Avenue. In Old Town, the **Café Pacifica** ((619) 291-6666, 2414 San Diego Avenue, has established itself as one of the city's premier seafood restaurants. The menu nearly always includes sublime seared ahi and imaginative presentations of the freshest fish. On the French side, **Thee Bungalow** ((619) 224-2884, 5007 West Point Loma Boulevard in Ocean Beach, is a cozy, unpretentious cottage where country cooking provides satisfying meals. Advance reservations are advised as the dining room is small.

La Jolla's ethnic offerings include the first branch of **Star of India** ((619) 459-3355, 1000 Prospect Street. Their northern indian curries and tandoori-style meats are usually well prepared. **Trattoria Acqua** ((619) 454-0709, 1298 Prospect Street in La Jolla, is pleasantly arranged in a below-street level complex between Prospect and the La Jolla Cove. The menu offers huge grilled vegetable and goat cheese sandwiches along with excellent pasta dishes; the best tables are in the brick courtyard and gazebo. The view is what's important at **The Marine Room** ((619) 459-7222, 2000 Spindrift Drive in La Jolla. The glass-walled dining room sits on the sand near the La Jolla Beach and Tennis Club; when the surf is high (usually in winter) the waves crash against the glass.

MODERATE

Downtown is filled with restaurants that serve hordes of office workers during weekday lunch hours. **Athens Market Tavern** ((619) 234-1955, 109 West F Street, is a favorite of lawyers, journalists and financiers and is the best Greek restaurant in the county. It's busy at dinner time as well, as is **Croce's Restaurant and Jazz Bar** ((619) 233-4355, 8022 Fifth Avenue.

Like its upstairs counterpart, **The Fish Market** ((619) 232-3474, 750 North Harbor Drive, has the best overview of imported seafood in a downtown restaurant. The dining room is gargantuan and noisy, but the selection and preparation of fish are excellent. There's also a sushi and oyster bar and a take-out counter. A second Fish Market ((619) 755-2277, 640 Via del la Valle in Del Mar, draws the racetrack crowds.

Crab sandwiches, shrimp salads and good fries and beer attract swarms to the outdoor tables at **Point Loma Seafoods** ((619) 223-1009, 2805 Emerson. Located beside Point Loma's sport fishing docks, this establishment is primarily a seafood market — the finest in town for fresh lobster in season (December through March), swordfish from Hawaii, and tuna, dorado (also called mahi-mahi), yellowtail and halibut from local waters. Sashimi-grade tuna sells here for caviar prices; the best sashimi plate is served at **Yoshino** ((619) 295-2232, 1790 West Washington Street between downtown and Old Town.

Old Town abounds in Mexican restaurants. Best of the lot are the **Casa de Bandini** ((619) 297-8211, 2754 Calhoun Street, located in a renovated hacienda beside the Bazaar del Mundo, and the **Old Town Mexican Café** ((619) 297-4330, 2489 San Diego Avenue, where perfect margaritas, fresh tortillas and bountiful platters of carnitas, fajitas, and enchiladas attract crowds.

Mission Valley is another haven for moderately priced restaurants. Among the best spots are **Adams Steak 'n' Eggs** ((619) 291-1103, 1201 Hotel Circle South, where bodacious breakfasts are served daily until 11 AM. Try the corn fritters, grits, and philly-style steak and eggs. Also in the valley is **Bully's** ((619) 291-2665, 2401 Camino del Rio South, one of three wood-and-leather restaurants specializing in prime rib and steaks. The others are at ((619) 459-2768, 5755 La Jolla Boulevard, and ((619) 755-1660, 1404 Camino del Mar in Del Mar. On the trendier side, the **Wolfgang Puck Café** ((619) 295-WOLF, 1640 Camino del Rio North at Mission Valley Center, is one of many offshoots from one of Los Angeles' most successful chefs.

Beach sunsets are awe inspiring from the tables at **Qwiig's Bar & Grill** ((619) 222-1101, 5083 Santa Monica Avenue in Ocean Beach. Fish, steaks, pastas and salads are on the menu here and at Cecil's Restaurant downstairs. In Pacific Beach, the fresh, innovative cooking at **Lamont Street Grill** ((619) 270-3060, 4445 Lamont Street at Hornblend Street, bring outsiders to a pleasant backstreet neighborhood.

INEXPENSIVE

The customers, decor and food are all intriguing at **Café 222** ((619) 236-9902, 222 Island Avenue, not far from the Convention Center in downtown.

Sushi Deli ((619) 231-9597, 828 Broadway, serves impeccably fresh sushi and sashimi at very reasonable prices.

Chilango's Mexico City Grill ((619) 294-8646, 142 University Avenue in Hillcrest above downtown, has the most varied Mexican take-out menu in the city. **El Indio** ((619) 299-0333, 3695 India Street, between downtown and Old Town is a San Diego institution. It's hefty burritos and quesadillas, bags of fresh tortilla chips and pints of salsa and guacamole are high-demand picnic fare. The **Vegetarian Zone** (298-7302, 2949 Fifth Avenue, also in Hillcrest, is (surprisingly enough) just about the only good health-food restaurant in town. Best bets at the beach include the family-run **Ortega's** ((619) 222-4205, 4888 Newport Avenue in Ocean Beach, and the classic beach bar **The Pennant** ((619) 488-1671, 2893 Mission Boulevard in Mission Beach. The **Kono Surf Club Café** ((619) 483-1669, 704 Garnet Avenue, on the boardwalk in Pacific Beach is the quintessential surfer café with healthy-sized breakfasts and burgers. Also in Pacific Beach is the original **Rubio's** ((619) 270-4800, 910 Grand Avenue. A local success story, Rubio's basically invented the United States version of the fish tacos sold in Baja. Fried or grilled fish is served in a crisp or soft tortillas with plenty of condiments — cabbage, special sauce, sour cream, and cilantro. Other Mexican items are good as well. There are several location in Carmel Mountain Ranch, Chula Vista, downtown, El Cajon, Kearny Mesa, La Jolla, La Mesa, Mission Bay, Mission Valley, Point Loma, Solana Beach and State College area.

ENTERTAINMENT AND NIGHTLIFE

San Diego has a wonderfully vital theater scene; many plays that gain notoriety on Broadway start out here. The **La Jolla Playhouse** ((619) 550-1010, formally known as the Mandell Weiss Center for the Performing Arts, on the campus of the University of California San Diego, has received international attention in the past decade. The **Old Globe Theater** ((619) 239-2255 in Balboa Park is equally impressive, staging an intriguing selection of new plays, older standards and the bard's own works at its three stages. The **San Diego Repertory Theater** ((619) 235-8025 has two stages in Horton Plaza.

The **San Diego Symphony** has been on an indefinite hiatus since going bankrupt in the early 1990s; community efforts to revive it have been unsuccessful thus far. The **San Diego Opera** ((619) 232-7636 is thriving, however, and performs from January until May at the Civic Theater. Concerts, dance performances and other live events are held at **Symphony Hall** ((619) 231-0938, 1245 Seventh Avenue; the **Spreckels Theater** ((619) 235-9500, 121 Broadway; the **Civic Theater** ((619) 570-1100,

Third and B Streets; the **Sports Arena** ((619) 224-4176, 3500 Sports Arena Boulevard, and other venues around town. Advance tickets are available through **TicketMaster** ((619) 220-8497. Reduced price same-day tickets for many events can be purchased at **ArtsTix** ((619) 497-5000 at Broadway Circle, Horton Plaza.

When San Diegans go for a night on the town, they usually go to the smaller bars that feature live music. The upscale set prefers **Croce's** ((619) 233-4355. Owned and operated by singer Jim Croce's widow, Croce's is located at the corner of Fifth Avenue and F Street, and offers a rare sophisticated experience in elegant dining and easy listening jazz. Around the corner is **Patrick's II** ((619) 233-3077, a tiny bar that has become an institution in downtown San Diego's nightlife. **Dick's Last Resort** ((619) 231-9100, 345 Fourth Avenue, downtown, is a raucous place with several rooms and a courtyards, good food, and a college-age crowd. Other popular downtown spots include **4th & B** ((619) 231-4343, 345 B Street; **The Bitter End** ((619) 338-9300, 770 Fifth Avenue; **Ole Madrid** ((619) 557-0146, 755 Fifth Avenue; and **Club E** ((619) 231-9201, 919 Fourth Avenue. **The Casbah** ((619) 232-4355, 2501 Kettner Boulevard north of downtown, is the best club for live alternative rock.

The Whaling Bar ((619) 454-0771, 1132 Prospect Street, at La Valencia Hotel in La Jolla, is a cozy piano bar. The **Belly-Up** ((619) 481-9022, 1435 South Cedros Avenue, Solana Beach, is up there at the top of everybody's list. A few miles south of Leucadia and Encinitas and 21 miles (38 km) north of San Diego, the Belly Up brings in world-class acts for a price, but its cover charge is nowhere near the price you'd pay to hear the same groups on the East Coast. The most popular venue for rock and pop music is the Humphrey's **Concerts by the Bay** ((619) 224-9438, 2241 Shelter Island Drive.

The best source for what's happening in San Diego's nightlife is the *San Diego Reader*, a weekly tabloid-sized newspaper published every Thursday and distributed free throughout the city. No other publication has such extensive and high-quality reviews of everything — restaurants, music, dance, comedy, and which wildflowers are presently in bloom. The *Reader* offers an especially good guide to the local music scene, which is constantly changing.

HOW TO GET THERE

San Diego International Airport ((619) 231-2100 (information line) at Lindbergh Field christened a beautiful and spacious new West Terminal in early 1998. Despite its name, San Diego offers only limited international service, but it is currently serviced by several major airlines. Most international flight connections are through Los Angeles.

There are two terminals — cleverly numbered Terminals 1 and 2. It's possible to walk between the two, but not to the Commuter Terminal which is a 5-minute drive away toward downtown. Always make sure you know which terminal your flight is departing from before heading to the airport. A red shuttle bus runs regularly between the terminals.

If you are driving to San Diego from the north, take Interstate 5 south or Highway 805 south; from the east take Interstate 8. If you are arriving from the south, Interstate 5 north or Highway 805 north will take you to most parts of the county. Travelers arriving from Riverside County or Las Vegas will take Interstate 15 west.

Amtrak TOLL-FREE (800) 872-7245 travels from the historic **Santa Fe Depot** in downtown San Diego to Los Angeles, making several stops along the way. The train station is located at 1050 Kettner Boulevard at Broadway, open daily from 4:15 AM until 9 PM, with nine departures on weekdays and eight on Saturday and Sunday.

The **Greyhound Lines** bus station ((619) 239-8082 TOLL-FREE (800) 231-2222 is also located downtown, just up the street from the train station at 120 West Broadway.

NORTH COUNTY COAST

Beach communities line the coast north from La Jolla to Oceanside and Camp Pendleton, a United States Marine base that serves as a greenbelt between San Diego and Orange counties. Interstate 5 parallels the coast all the way to Los Angeles, while State Highway 21 curves and dips through the small towns. The first enclave north of La Jolla and Torrey Pines State Beach is **Del Mar**, where the civic sensibilities are so rarefied that smoking is practically banned on the streets. The town has its own cable television channel and a politically-active populace. Buildings lining the main street in town are primarily Tudor-style; bookstores, boutiques and cafés are the prevalent businesses. At the intersection of Camino del Mar and 15th Street, the **Del Mar Plaza** ((619) 792-1555, 1555 Camino Del Mar, sits tastefully camouflaged by rock walls and plants atop a hill sloping down to the beach. The plaza has several excellent restaurants and shops.

Del Mar also has the beautiful **Del Mar Race Track** ((760) 755-1141, which looks like an idealized movie set. Bing Crosby, Jimmy Durante and their buddies invested in the track in the 1940s, establishing a sense of style and excitement that remains today. The track's Spanish and Mexican architecture emphasizing white stucco, red tile and lots of arches and niches prevailed during renovations in the 1990s; from atop the stands you can see the ocean and the track. Del Mar's racing season runs for 43 days starting in late July. In 1987, off-track betting for the other California tracks was installed at the Del Mar track.

The annual **Del Mar Fair** is staged at the racetrack for three weeks between late June and early July. It is a small-scale version of an old-time state fair, complete with bunnies, pigs and cows. Two huge exhibition buildings are packed with hucksters selling all the latest gadgets. Several buildings are devoted to photography, woodworking, painting and crafts exhibits. The garden section is superb, like a miniature tour through the best Southern California gardens and native plants. Ferris wheels and other amusement rides and

to migrating birds, herons, egrets and several aquacultural projects. Carlsbad is ideally located midway between downtown San Diego and Orange County's sprawling suburbs, and has become a bedroom community to both areas and even Los Angeles. Commuter flights to most Southern California airports depart regularly from Carlsbad's McClellan-Palomar Airport, and there is an Amtrak station near the sea.

Cedros Street in downtown Solana Beach has become devoted to interior design; the shops and galleries hold seasonal festivals that attract major crowds. The Carlsbad Ranch flower fields, just east of Interstate 5, blossom in acres of ranunculus blooms in April and May; hundreds of sight-

games line the Midway, and concerts are held on the racetrack.

The highway changes names with every new town it enters, starting with Solana Beach, where the road dips to sea level beside restaurants on the sand. Cardiff and San Elijo state beaches offer camping by the sea — unfortunately, the campgrounds are sandwiched between the surf and the road and railroad tracks. Encinitas is home to Moonlight State Beach, one of the best surf spots in North County, and a collection of funky record and art shops.

Carlsbad is the fastest growing town in California and one of the most prosperous. **South Carlsbad State Beach** offers a 10-mile (16-km) stretch of sand below high bluffs; recreational vehicle parking is available, as well as camp sites for pitching a tent. State Highway 21 runs between the sand and several major lagoons that are home

seers stop by to admire the flowers and pose for snapshots. The town sprawls east of Interstate 5 into entirely modern communities, many centered around courses. La Costa (see WHERE TO STAY AND EAT, below) is an established venue on the professional golf and tennis circuit. The Four Seasons Resort Aviara opened another spectacular course in east Carlsbad as well. Legoland is attempting to repeat the success of its Danish theme park in Carlsbad; its village of plastic creations opens in 1999. Upscale restaurants and shops thrive in this area, and Carlsbad's evolution is setting the pace for the rest of North County.

Oceanside, the last beach town in San Diego County, abuts Camp Pendleton Marine Base; the military has had an overwhelming presence

Brilliant red, yellow, and orange ranunculus cover the hillsides of Carlsbad in early Spring.

here for decades. Its waterfront includes a long fishing pier and a sizable harbor. Inland from the town is **San Luis Rey de Francia** ((760) 757-3651, 4050 Mission Avenue, the largest of all the mission churches in California. Completed in 1815, it proved to be the most successful, with more Indian converts and more cattle and sheep than any of the other missions. The buildings here were also saved from ruin when the mission was reopened as a seminary in 1893. Located in the town of San Luis Rey, just off State Highway 76, the mission is five miles (eight kilometers) inland from Oceanside. San Luis Rey de Francia is open daily. Sightseeing is not allowed during services.

WHERE TO STAY AND EAT

North County is dotted with excellent hotels, most quite expensive. Del Mar, Carlsbad and Oceanside have a good selection of mid-range chain hotels near the highway and interstate. Budget travelers have the beach campgrounds to consider, but advance reservations are essential. See TRAVELER'S TIPS, page 341, for state park information.

Very Expensive

The most exciting resort property in North County is the **Four Seasons Resort Aviara** ((760) 603-6800 TOLL-FREE (800) 332-3442 FAX (760) 603-6801, 7100 Four Seasons Point in Carlsbad. Set on an inland bluff overlooking the ocean and the wildlife sanctuary at the Batquitos Lagoon, the hotel is part of a 1,000-acre (405-hectare) planned community. Its superb restaurants are the social headquarters for North County's elite: Vivace, the Italian dining room, serves innovative dishes with superb flavors — even the low-calorie spa dishes are worth trying; the seafood buffet and Sunday brunch in the California Bistro attract crowds. The 331 spacious rooms have balconies with ocean and lagoon views and are blissfully comfortable. There is an 18-hole golf course adjacent to the hotel; facilities include a full gym, spa, tennis courts and a children's program.

Also highly recommended by reclusive tennis buffs is **Rancho La Valencia** ((619) 756-1123 FAX (619) 756-0165, PO Box 9126, Rancho Santa Fe, CA 92067.

La Costa Resort and Spa ((760) 438-9111 TOLL-FREE (800) 854-5000 FAX (760) 438-3758, 2100 Costa del Mar Road in Carlsbad, is a posh 400-acre (162-hectare) resort and spa with two 18-hole golf courses.

Expensive

Race fans pack the lavish suites at the **L'Auberge Del Mar** ((619) 239-1515 TOLL-FREE (800) 553-1336 FAX (619) 755-4940, 1540 Camino del Mar. The hotel's low-rise buildings descend down a landscaped hill toward the railroad tracks and the

beach. The lobby and public areas are decorated with racetrack photos and memorabilia; the spa and restaurant are both very good. Del Mar Plaza is right across the street, offering plenty of dining and shopping options. Also memorable in this price range is **The Inn at Rancho Santa Fe** ((619) 756-1131 TOLL-FREE (800) 654-2928 FAX (619) 759-1604, 5951 Linea del Cielo. Located east of Solana Beach, Rancho Santa Fe is home to horse farms, mansions and millionaires. It also has one of the finest restaurants in Southern California, **Mille Fleurs** ((619) 756-3085, 6009 Paseo Delicias.

Moderate

North County has several immensely popular, reasonably-priced hotels that book up months ahead. For a listing contact the **San Diego North Convention and Visitors Bureau** ((760) 745-4741 TOLL-FREE (800) 848-3336 FAX (760) 745-4796

WILD ANIMAL PARK

San Diego County sprawls over an ever higher and drier landscape inland from Interstate 5 — thus the bumper stickers favored by beach dwellers reading "There is No Life East of I-5." But the East County is a fascinating area, especially away from the multiple mini-cities that have sprouted up along major roadways. The biggest attractions is the **San Diego Wild Animal Park** ℂ (619) 234-6541, where 2,400 animals native to Africa and Asia have more than 1,800 acres (720 hectares) in which to wander. The main feature of the park is the Wgasa Bush Line Monorail, a 50-minute train ride through the park. For the more daring, there is the **Kilimanjaro**

hiking trail. By special arrangement, ℂ (619) 747-8702, you can also book places on **photo caravans** in open trucks that drive right up to the animals. As with the original zoo, there are open stages here for animal performances. (The trainer for the bird shows once worked with Alfred Hitchcock in the movie, *The Birds*.) Admission to the Wild Animal Park is $18.95 for adults, $11.95 for children from 3 to 11 years old, seniors $17.05, and children under the age of three are admitted free. Parking is $3. The park is open every day of the year, including holidays, from 9 AM to 4 PM. Located in the beautiful San Pasqual Valley, the park is 30 miles (50 km) north of downtown San Diego. It can be reached by way of Highway 163 and Interstate 15, turning at Via Rancho Parkway

Just one of the 2,400 non-human residents of San Diego's spacious Wild Animal Park.

at Escondido. From Los Angeles, take Interstate 5 to Oceanside, then State Highway 78 east to Interstate 15, and then south to Via Rancho Parkway where signs lead the way. For information on towns and accommodations in the East County contact the **San Diego East Visitors Bureau** ((619) 463-1166 FAX (619) 463-6466, 4695 Nebo Drive, La Mesa, CA 91941.

THE MOUNTAINS AND DESERTS

Interstate 8 and State Highways 78 and 76 lead east from the coast to the county's back country mountains and deserts. At the north end of the county, State Highway 76 leads to the edge of the **Cleveland National Forest** and **Mount Palomar**. County Road S6 climbs a mile up the mountains to the **Mount Palomar Observatory** ((760) 742-2119, built in 1928. The building enclosing the 200-inch (508-cm) Hale telescope is sometimes open to the public; the grounds around the observatory are great for hikes and picnics in the pines. South of Palomar State Highway 76 intersects with State Highway 79 to **Julian**, a short-lived gold mining town in the late 1800s and now a pleasant mountain community. Known for its spring mountain flowers and fall apple crop, Julian attracts hordes of tours on some weekends, especially during the fall Apple Days festivities and Harvest Festival. Contact the **Julian Chamber of Commerce** ((760) 765-1857, 2129 Main Street, Julian 92036. South of Julian is **Cuyamaca Rancho State Park** ((760) 765-0755 FAX (760) 765-3021, 12551 State Highway 79, Descanso 91916, with 25,000 acres (10,000 hectares) of mountains peaks, deciduous forest (a rarity in San Diego), streams, and plenty of hiking trails. Campgrounds are available. The Cleveland National Forest and Mount Laguna are south of Cuyamaca; many San Diegans make a day of driving a long circuitous route through these various mountain parks. It gets especially crowded in the winter when there is snow on the peaks.

Once across the mountains, east on State Highway 78, you will head straight into **Anza-Borrego Desert State Park** and some of the most beautiful desert scenery in California. Covering 600,000 acres (240,000 hectares), it is California's largest state park. It was named for Juan Bautista de Anza, the Spanish priest who first traversed it in 1774, and for the bighorn sheep (borrego). At first glance, the landscape may seem barren, but in fact there are more than 600 species of plants and 350 kinds of vertebrate animals found here. Spring in the desert is extraordinary. Willowy ocotillos burst into bloom with feathery red flowers, and the ground is covered with flowering cacti, Californian poppies and desert lupine. Traffic reaches bumper-to-bumper congestion on spring weekends — visit during the week if you can. In general, locals avoid the deserts in June, July, and

August when the daily temperatures rise well above 100°F (38°C). In the winter months the desert temperatures can change 30°F (16°C) degrees in 24 hours, and nights are downright cold.

The biggest town in the Anza borrego desert is **Borrego Springs**. Even though its developers had envisioned it as a Palm Springs south, Borrego Springs has remained a small town on the Borrego Valley floor surrounded by steep mountain ranges. The **Borrego Springs Chamber of Commerce** ((619) 767-5555, PO Box 420, Borrego Springs 92004, can provide you with information. The best lodgings are at **La Casa del Zorro** ((619) 767-5323 TOLL-FREE (800) 824-1884, 3845 Yaqui Pass Road, with cottage-like buildings spread about cactus gardens, lawns and pools. Borrego Springs has several motels, apartments, and condominiums available for short-term rental. Nearby are trailer parks and campgrounds. There are tennis courts and three public golf courses open to the public.

Camping facilities in the park include the modern facilities of the **Resort Palm Canyon**. You can also camp in **Coyote Canyon, Pegleg Smith Monument**, or **Borrego Sink** where it's just you and nature. The **Agua Caliente Campground** has an enclosed thermal pool fed from a natural hot spring. For camping information contact the state park numbers in TRAVELER'S TIPS, page 341. A volunteer organization, the Anza-Borrego Desert Natural History Association, operates a Visitors' Center ((760) 767-4205 and short desert flower trail built right into a hillside so as not to disturb the landscape. It's located near the Park Headquarters on Palm Canyon Drive. Staffed by true desert lovers, it offers an excellent slide program on desert geology and plant and animal life. The center is open from 9 AM to 5 PM daily from October through May, and from 10 AM to 3 PM on Saturdays and Sundays only in June, July, August, and September.

Ocotillo Wells, a state park, is located right on State Highway 78. It has a store selling picnic supplies, and an adjoining trailer park. Most appealing are its wide open spaces and the freedom to drive right on if you have a vehicle that can do it. This is one of the state parks open to off-road or all-terrain vehicles, but if you stray out of bounds into one of the nature preserves, a park ranger or private citizen will warn you back to the approved area. It is a strange, mysterious landscape, with sandy flats along wide dry riverbeds, and trails leading across the dunes up on to the mesas. When you stand on the edge of one of nature's own tabletops and watch the sun cast its shadow over the battered landscape, you begin to understand the planet we humans inhabit.

The heat doesn't seem so bad when you stumble upon natural pools and springs hidden amid cacti in the Anza-Borrego Desert.

South
of the
Border

THE BAJA CALIFORNIA PENINSULA is a mysterious and challenging place, where stark deserts and forested mountains are bounded by the Pacific Ocean and the Sea of Cortez. Baja (lower) California was once the capital of all the Californias spreading from the southern tip of the peninsula north beyond present-day San Francisco. It wasn't until 1848 that the border between the United States and Mexico was etched across the northern peninsula to Texas; since then, Baja California has been an outpost of both countries, straddling the first and third worlds. Far removed from the capitals of both countries, Baja and San Diego have grown simultaneously, sharing common heritages and political, environmental, financial and social concerns. Tijuana, which sprawls over rugged hillsides just 18 miles (29 km) south of downtown San Diego, is Mexico's fourth-largest city. San Diego is the seventh largest city in the United States. Combined, the two create a metropolitan area with about four million residents.

The region closest to the border is Baja's most populous; south of Tijuana, Rosarito Beach and Ensenada the 775-mile (1,250-km)-long peninsula is dotted with agricultural valleys, fishing villages, isolated mountain parks and long stretches of empty beach and sand.

With more than 3,000 km (1,860 miles) of coastline, Baja has become a popular getaway for Californians. Naturally, the majority head to the northern area for quick breaks. San Diegans are accustomed to hopping down to Tijuana, Rosarito or Ensenada for day trips or weekend breaks, and there are entire neighborhoods of Americans living on the Mexican coast and commuting to jobs in the United States each day. Travelers unaccustomed to border life may initially be straddled at the foreignness of northern Baja, but quickly find plenty of distractions to enhance their trips.

BACKGROUND

Baja has been inhabited since around 7500 BC, when cave dwellers left petroglyphs looking much like those in France. Little is known about these earliest inhabitants; the first written information about the area comes from Hernán Cortés. In 1535, while searching for the legendary kingdom of the Amazons ruled by the black queen, Calafia, Cortés landed a party at Baja's southern tip, near the present-day city of La Paz. Although the Spanish did not find the fierce women warriors here, they did give the land the queen's name — California.

Hearing rumors of an abundance of pearls in the bays along the peninsula, Cortés organized several later expeditions which met with open hostility from the Indians. It was not until the late seventeenth century that any permanent European

settlement began here. In 1697, three Jesuit missionaries arrived to begin proselytizing and converting native tribes. When more priests followed in 1720, they brought the additional spiritual benefit of smallpox, which destroyed the native populations.

The missionaries persevered, believing it better to die as a Christian than live as an Indian. By 1750, there were few Indians left, and their populations have never rebuilt. Today the Indian population of Baja is less than 1,500. In spite of their expiring clientele, the missionaries continued to work up and down the length of Baja, planting vineyards and olive and date groves. When the Jesuits were expelled from Mexico in 1767, these

missions were prosperous enough to be coveted and taken over by the Franciscans, and then by the Dominicans in 1772.

The missions spread from Loreto northward into Alta (or higher) California, where they grew and prospered. The lower peninsula remained part of Mexico after California became a United States state in 1804. The peninsula was appropriated briefly by the United States during the Mexican-American War. After the Mexican War of Independence, it was incorporated into the Republic as a territory, but the actual border between the two countries was not officially delineated until

OPPOSITE: Statue of a jai alai player stands in front of Tijuana's grand Jai-Alai Palace. ABOVE: One of the army of Border Patrol agents assigned to the frontier between Mexico and the United States rides a three-wheeler all-terrain vehicle, now outlawed for sale in the United States.

South of the Border

1948. Baja California became a Mexican state in 1952, and Baja California Sur in 1974.

TIJUANA

Tijuana is Mexico's fourth-largest city, with an official population of one-and-a-half million, and a real population probably much larger. Dingy, crowded, and poor at first sight, Tijuana is one of Mexico's fastest-growing cities and one of its most prosperous. To the casual visitor, Tijuana seems uniquely foreign yet familiar. English is commonly spoken — in fact, most city residents and visitors speak a hybrid language called "Spanglish," with a mix of both languages that allows complete comprehension. The situation is different in the poorer hillside settlements, where transplants from throughout Mexico and Latin America live in intolerable deprivation while seeking the promise of riches on both sides of the border. The dollar is as mighty (if not mightier) than the peso in Tijuana, since the city thrives on the thousands of tourists who cross the border from the United States daily. Most travelers stay but a day, shopping, drinking, and dining in designated tourists traps. It's worth spending a night or two, however, if you wish to sample the city's thriving dining and nightlife scene.

BACKGROUND

Tijuana may well be "the most visited city in the world," as its city fathers claim. The San Diego-Tijuana border crossing is said to be the busiest in the world, used daily by commuters crossing to and from work on both sides of the border, by families visiting relatives, and by tourists who typically cross the border both ways in a day. The city's name is said to be a derivation of the Indian word, *ti-wan*, meaning "nearby water." But popular lore has the name coming from *Tia Juana*, or Aunt Jane, the name of a ranch near the border. Either way, Americans insist on calling the city Tia-wana instead of its proper name, Ti-wana.

Tijuana has been a popular getaway for Californians ever since the United States Prohibition in the 1920s, when the border offered easy access to liquor for "dry" Americans. Even after the repeal of prohibition, Tijuana retained its reputation as a desirable destination providing types of fun frowned upon by many across the border — raucous nightlife, drugs, cheap liquor, bullfights, and gambling on horses, greyhounds, and jai alai. All such vices are still available (live horse racing has ended, but you can still bet on races transmitted via satellite from the United States). But Tijuana has many other attractions. Its Cultural Center introduces thousands of visitors to the history, archeology and cultures of mainland Mexico. Its restaurants and markets offer a wonderful entree to the cuisines of Mexico, and its shops display the best of the folk art the mainland has to offer. Residents from throughout the country populate Tijuana's neighborhoods, offering a microscopic view of Mexico's many cultures. The experienced eye can spot descendants of Aztec, Maya, Mixtec and Zapotec forbears in the faces of Tijuana, and those conversant in Spanish quickly find that cab drivers, waiters and store clerks often hail from Oaxaca, Mexico City, Veracruz and other far-flung areas.

GENERAL INFORMATION

The **Tourist Information Office** ((66) 831405 just inside the border crossing is open daily from 9 AM to 7 PM; the staff go out of their way to attract visitors and dispense information. There is another **Tourist Information Office** ((66) 840537, Paseo de los Héroes 9365, in front of the Centro Cultural in the Zona Rio. It is open Monday through Friday from 9 AM to 5 PM.

Baja Information ((619) 298-4105 TOLL-FREE (800) 522-1516 (from California, Nevada, and Arizona) or TOLL-FREE (800) 225-2786 (from the rest of the United States and Canada) FAX (619) 294-7366 E-MAIL impamexicoinfo@worldnet.att.net, arranges hotel reservations throughout the peninsula; for written information contact them at 7860 Mission Center Court #202, San Diego, CA 92108.

WHAT TO SEE AND DO

Tijuana's civic boosters are constantly dealing with their city's negative image and finding new ways to attract tourists. Though most visitors just spend the day, there are several good hotels catering to the business travelers and those moving on through Baja and Mexico. Most of Tijuana lies to the south of the usually dry riverbed of the Tia Juana River. The shopping, bartering and beseeching begin the moment you cross the border and walk along **Calle 2** toward downtown. A large complex of pottery yards and souvenir stands lines Calle 2 between Ocampo and Nigrete; if you're walking, this is a good place to begin examining possible purchases and prices. Refrain from buying that terracotta pig, Ninja turtle *piñata*, or beaded velvet sombrero that seems so irresistible. You may find something better later on; if not, you can pick it up on your way back through the border instead of hauling it around all day.

The city's main tourist zone, **Avenida Revolución**, once held a tawdry assortment of bars and brothels. It now caters to tourists seeking a good time and shoppers determined to find bargains. Stores, restaurants and bars seem to undergo constant renovation in an attempt to appear more hip, trendy and attractive to jaded visitors seeking something new. Burros painted like zebras still pose at street corners so tourists can don velvet sombreros and be photographed in the standard Tijuana cliché. But an element of class has managed to creep into the Avenida Revolución scene, and there are several fine stores and restaurants to compete with the tacky souvenir stands and rowdy bars.

The most significant building on the strip is the Moorish-styled **El Palacio Frontón** ((66) 384308 TOLL-FREE (800) PIK-BAJA, a jai alai palace at Avenida Revolución and Calle 8. Jai alai games begin at 8 PM every night except Thursdays. The games are fast-moving and interesting, and the betting adds to the fun. The palace serves as the loading and unloading zone for tour buses, and is

on Paseo de los Héroes at Avenida Independencia (free admission; open daily from 9 AM to 8:30 PM), have become Tijuana's most precious landmarks. Designed by architect Pedro Ramírez Vásquez, the Centro houses an excellent permanent exhibit of Mexican history and has rotating shows of contemporary Mexican artists. The center's bookstore carries an extensive collection of books on Mexico in both English and Spanish. **Mexitlán** ((66) 384165, Avenida Ocampo between Calles 2 and 3 (admission fee; open Wednesday through Sunday from 9 AM to 5 PM), is a fascinating outdoor museum with miniature replicas of Mexico's most famous archaeological sites, colonial buildings, churches and parks. Designed to resemble a

a good place to reconnoiter with your friends after dividing up for shopping and partying. The **Bazar de Mexico** ((66) 865280, Avenida Revolución at Calle 7, and the **Mexicoach Terminal** ((66) 851470, Avenida Revolución between Calles 6 and 7, both offer a more soothing shopping experience than in the older arcades and have refreshments for sale. One of the newer attractions near Revolución is the **L.A. Cetto Winery** ((66) 851644, on Cañon Johnson at Avenida Constitución. Tours of the winery (a branch of one of Mexico's most famous) are available along with wine tasting and sales.

The more dignified shopping centers, hotels, restaurants and nightclubs are located a few blocks east in the **Zona Río**, a 10-minute walk on Calle 8A across Avenida General Rodolfo Taboada. The globe-shaped Omnimax theater and boxy museum at the **Centro Cultural Tijuana** ((66) 841125,

colorful colonial plaza, **Pueblo Amigo**, on Paseo Tijuana between Puente Mexico and Avenida Independencia, is a nightlife and dining center within walking distance of the border; though businesses change here, there's always a good party-style restaurant and a popular nightclub.

Avenida Revolución becomes Boulevard Agua Caliente southeast of downtown; some of the city's wealthiest neighborhoods are located above the boulevard in the Lomas de Chapultepec (Chapultepec Hills). The smaller of the city's two bullrings, **El Toreo de Tijuana** is on Boulevard Agua Caliente. Bullfights are held here on Sunday afternoons from May to September. But the top matadors usually take on *el toro* at the bull-

Mariachi bands roam the streets of Tijuana, charging $2 to $3 for a song, the quickest and most enjoyable way of making money in this impoverished country.

ring by the sea, **Plaza de Toros Monumental (bull-fighting)** ((66) 842126 or (66) 878519 in Playas de Tijuana south of town. The Tourist Information Offices have the prices and schedules. Admission varies according the fame of the matador. Golf is available at the **Tijuana Country Club** ((66) 817855 on Boulevard Agua Caliente east of downtown.

Beyond El Toreo de Tijuana is the racetrack, **Hippódromo de Agua Caliente** ((66) 862002 TOLL-FREE (800) 745-2252 (from the United States), on Boulevard Agua Caliente at Salinas. Horses no longer race at the track, but there are (somewhat) live greyhound races on the weekends. The racetrack is now connected via satellite to racetracks in California, giving gamblers the chance to loose money in two countries at once.

Shopping is the number-one tourist activity in Tijuana. Visitors who have never been to mainland Mexico are fascinated by the abundance of silver jewelry, leather boots and jackets, wool *serapes*, cotton blankets, velvet sombreros, cartoon-character *piñatas* and every imaginable type of tacky souvenir. The shopping experience hits its height in the block-deep arcades along Avenida Revolución, where buskers can't resist pleading, pushing, jostling and otherwise snatching your attention. All the classic border scenes come smack in your face. Wide-eyed boys and girls entreat passers by to purchase Chiclets, woven bracelets and Styrofoam balls covered with bits of mirror. Locals call the Indian-looking women from Chiapas and Oaxaca who wrap themselves and their babies in blankets and beg on the street, the *Marias*. Their heart-wrenching displays of poverty dismay those unfamiliar with third-world conditions.

The most rewarding shopping experience is the instant Mexican immersion course one receives at the **Mercado Hidalgo** on Avenida Independencia at Avenida Sanchez Taboada, about six blocks east of Avenida Revolución. All household necessities from beans to rice to plastic mops can be found in the market stalls, interspersed with religious medallions, herbal potions and piles of produce. The setting is far classier at **Tolan** ((66) 883637 on Avenida Revolución between Calles 7 and 8. Folk-art collectors never miss a stop here to survey the latest collection of antique carved wood doors, stained glass panels, religious statues, pottery and crafts from throughout Mexico. **Sanborn's** ((66) 841462, on Avenida Revolución at Calle 8, is part of a national chain of restaurants and shops displaying high-quality folk art, books and jewelry.

The beaches just south of the city, **Las Playas de Tijuana**, are popular among Mexicans. So far

A sombrero salesman plies his trade on the Avenida Revolución, in front of the fittingly Basque restaurant, Chiki Jai.

they have no major hotels and only a few small restaurants.

WHERE TO STAY

Tijuana's hostelries once consisted of cheap flop houses and few tourist hotels. The advent of the *maquiladora* (assembly plant) industry in the 1980s brought business travelers from mainland Mexico, Asia, Europe and the United States, and Tijuana's hotel scene changed immensely. Today there are several upscale hotels catering to a mixed clientele of business travelers and tourists. You can usually get better value for your money on the Tijuana side of the border; those

planning on sampling the city's night scene can rest comfortably close to the action. Inexpensive hotels are abundant and usually unpleasant (unless you enjoy constant noise and shabby conditions). Always check out a few rooms before choosing where to stay and keep close watch on your possessions.

Expensive

You know a Mexican city has hit the big time when prestigious national chains invest in hotels. The **Camino Real** ((66) 334000 TOLL-FREE (800) 722-6466 (for reservations in the United States) FAX (66) 334001, on Paseo de los Héroes, is a clear sign of Tijuana's prosperity. The modernistic hotel sits at a prominent intersection in the Zona Río and offers 235 rooms and 15 suites with all the amenities upscale travelers expect. Back in the 1980s, when Tijuana began to boom, local entrepreneurs

built twin mirrored towers on Boulevard Agua Caliente as a symbol of prosperity. One tower houses a hotel that has gone through several changes in management. It's now called the **Gran Hotel** ((66) 817000 TOLL-FREE (800) 472-6385 (for reservations from the United States) FAX (66) 817016, Boulevard Agua Caliente 4558. The atrium lobby is one of the most popular see-and-be-seen spots in the city, and the restaurant and bar are always buzzing with activity. The 422 rooms vary in upkeep and amenities; those on the highest floors command astounding views of Tijuana's sprawling tentacles.

Moderate

A favorite with those desiring traditional Mexican architecture and style, the **Lucerna** ((66) 647000 TOLL-FREE (800) 582-3762 (for reservations from the United States) FAX (66) 342400, Paseo de los Héroes and Avenida Rodríguez, is one of the Zona Río's anchors. Gardens about the pools are well established, and the 147 rooms and 28 suites are dark and comfortable, with colonial-style furnishings. The **Holiday Inn Vita Spa Agua Caliente** ((66) 346901 TOLL-FREE (800) 465-4329 (for reservations from the United States) FAX (66) 346912, Paseo de los Héroes 18818 in the Zona Río, has become one of my favorite Tijuana hotels, thanks to its wonderful spa. The hotel sits beside the underground spring that fed the pools at the Prohibition-era Agua Caliente resort; the steaming mineral waters are now piped to the hotel's giant outdoor hot tub and private baths in the spa. Mud and oil wraps, massages, facials, and other treatments fill out the spa menu. The hotel's 122 rooms and five suites are less luxurious than one might expect, but fit the bill comfortably.

Inexpensive

I'm most comfortable suggesting **La Villa de Zaragoza** ((66) 851832 FAX (66) 851837, Avenida Madero 1120, for budget travelers. It's located right off Avenida Revolución, a major plus for those traveling by foot. The 66 rooms are serviceable and well maintained. This place books up quickly.

WHERE TO EAT

As with hotels, Tijuana's restaurant options have become more expansive, offering everything from gourmet dining rooms to bustling homestyle cafés. Most upscale and tourist-oriented restaurants are meticulous about health considerations, cleaning their produce with purified water.

Ensenada OPPOSITE offers a change of pace from Tijuana; the bars, such as the one ABOVE are not raucous, and there is the nearby stretch of placid beachfront at Estero Beach.

South of the Border

Expensive

Cien Años ((66) 343039, on Avenida José María in the Zona Río, is the hit of the 1990s, offering an elegant ambiance and excellent nouvelle Mexican cuisine. Many of the favorite regional dishes from throughout Mexico are prepared and presented beautifully in a tasteful setting.

Moderate

The traditional favorite for regional Mexican dishes is **La Fonda de Roberto (** (66) 861601, in the La Siesta Motel on the old Ensenada Highway, also called Calle 16 de Septiembre, near **(** (66) 847562, at Plaza Fiesta and Paseo de los Héroes, is the best of many ethnic eateries in this plaza, which fills up with hip young students on weekend nights. **Tia Juana Tilly's (** (66) 856024, on Avenida Revolución at Calle 7, has three locations on Revolución; this is the largest and is fronted by an outdoor café, great for people watching while munching on nachos. **Señor Frog's (** (66) 824964 in the Pueblo Amigo Center, Paseo Tijuana, is rowdy, raucous and fun, and serves good barbecued ribs and Mexican combo plates.

Inexpensive

My favorite spot for a taste of real Mexico is **La Especial (** (66) 856654, on Avenida Revolución 718. The huge, busy restaurant is located at the foot of a stairway leading down from street level; *enchiladas, carne asada* and tacos are prepared home-style, with a bit of spice. Baby goat is the draw at **Birrieria Guanajuato** (no phone), Avenida Abraham González 102, while roasted pork pulls in the crowds to **Carnitas Uruapan (** (66) 856181, Boulevard Díaz Ordáz 550. Both are informal places where you order the main course by the kilo along with beans, rice, salsas and tortillas and prepare your feast at long wooden tables.

NIGHTLIFE

Border dwellers are heavily into Tijuana's nightlife scene, which offers everything from sleazy bars (clustered on the side streets off Avenida Revolución) to swank dance clubs. The **Hard Rock Café (** (66) 850206, on Avenida Revolución 520, between Calles 1 and 2, is the standby for cautious travelers; while **Rodeo la Media Noche (** (66) 824967, on Avenida Paseo Tijuana at Pueblo Amigo in the Zona Río, is a wild place where indoor rodeos are presented at midnight (hence the name). The club also has several dance floors. **Como Que No (** (66) 842791, Avenida Sanchez Taboada 95, and **Dime Que Si (** (66)

842791, next door, are popular with fashionable young professionals from both sides of the border. **Baby Rock (** (66) 342404, on Calle Diego Rivera 1482, in the Zona Río, is the best place for the all-round disco scene.

HOW TO GET THERE

Tijuana's Aeropuerto Alberado Rodriguez international airport is located five miles (eight kilometers) from the United States border, but no United States or European airlines fly to or out of Tijuana. Aeroméxico, Mexicana, AeroCalifornia, Taesa, and a few regional airlines fly throughout Mexico and Latin America (and Cuba). Travelers touring Southern California sometimes choose to move on to Mexico through Tijuana, where airline fares are cheaper than those from San Diego or Los Angeles.

Drivers heading south from San Diego on Interstate 5 have two options when they reach the border at San Ysidro. The easiest is to park in one of the many huge lots on the United States side of the border. Most charge about $5 a day. Be sure to lock your car — for added security park in a guarded lot. If you wish to take your car into Mexico you must purchase Mexican auto insurance at one of the booths just before the border. You must present the auto registration and your license and can buy insurance by the day. The cost depends on the age and make of the car and whether you choose liability or full coverage. Drivers enter the border at San Ysidro, where they are either waved on or signaled to pull to the right into the secondary inspection area where cars are searched for guns and drugs (illegal in Mexico). Moving on, you can choose to head toward the Zona Rio, Centro (downtown), or the highway south. Once you've reached your destination park in a guarded lot.

Travelers can also use the **San Diego Trolley** to reach the border by boarding any trolley stop in San Diego and transferring to the San Ysidro line. The trip takes about 30 minutes from downtown San Diego. Once at the border you can walk across to the Mexico side on a pedestrian overpass. Buses await the trolley as well and will drive you through the border to Avenida Revolución. **Greyhound/Trailways** offers frequent service from their San Diego station to the Tijuana terminal near Avenida Revolución.

Baja California Tours ((619) 454-7166 FAX (619) 454-2703, 7734 Herschel Avenue, Suite O, La Jolla, CA 92037, offers informative trips from San Diego to Tijuana's museums and neighborhoods. **Contact Mini Tours (** (619) 477-8687 TOLL-FREE (800) 235-5393 FAX (619) 477-0705, 1726 Wilson Avenue, San Diego, CA 91950, picks up passengers at several San Diego hotels and drops them at a depot on Avenida Revolución.

In the markets of Tijuana, you'll find a colorful clutter of *piñatas* for sale.

ROSARITO BEACH

Heading south from Tijuana along the Pacific coast, the first major town is Rosarito Beach. An enormously popular weekend getaway for Southern Californians, Rosarito has rapidly expanded from a small fishing village to a town of some 110,000 full-time residents. Tasteful and garish hotels, bars and restaurants line Boulevard Benito Juárez through the main part of town; bumper-to-bumper traffic is not uncommon. In 1996, director James Cameron chose Rosarito for the filming of *Titanic* and built a huge movie production studio south of town. The resulting attention added to the area's

huge picnic spreads, and the beach always has a festive feel. Swimming is safe here but only when the water is clear; if it's been raining recently chances are the water is polluted and you should stay on the sand. The beach runs parallel to **Boulevard Benito Juárez**, though the water isn't visible from the main street. Instead, what you see is a shoulder-to-shoulder collage of shopping plazas, bars and hotels. Hard to miss is the roller-coaster façade of **Festival Plaza**, a hotel and restaurant complex that has become the town's party center. The **Rosarito Beach Hotel** (see WHERE TO STAY, below) a block south was the town's first attraction, built during Prohibition. The hotel, with its abundance of handcrafted tile, carved wood beams, murals

crowds and fame, and attracted hundreds of part-time residents with plenty of discretionary cash. Other films are expected to be made here, keeping Rosarito's fortunes rising.

GENERAL INFORMATION

The **Tourist Information Office** ((661) 20396 or (661) 23078 is on Boulevard Juárez on the second floor of the Quinta Plaza shopping center.

WHAT TO SEE AND DO

Rosarito's main attraction is its wide beach stretching the length of town, vendors stroll the beach selling straw hats, fake silver jewelry, T-shirts and toys; others push carts holding cold drinks, cotton candy and snacks. Tourists play impromptu volleyball and football games, local families set out

and ballroom, is a must-see, though it's hardly as glamorous as photos of the 1920s indicate. **Misión el Descanso**, the original settlement from which Rosarito grew, is 12 miles (19 km) south on the Old Ensenada Highway just past Cantamar (turn left under the toll road). A dirt road leads two-thirds of a mile (one kilometer) to the ruins of the mission, built in the late 1700s by the Dominicans.

The proliferation of vacation home developments along the coast has made Rosarito a profitable center for interior design shops, and most travelers spend at least a few hours browsing the strip. At the north entrance to town the road is lined with furniture and pottery stands; several good shops are located in the Quinta del Mar Plaza, the first major complex after you enter town. I never fail to stop at **Interios del Río Casa del Arte y La Madera** ((661) 21300, Quinta del Mar Plaza, for its selection of brightly-painted chairs and tables and unusual handicrafts from mainland Mexico. **Taxco Curios (** (661) 21877, Quinta del Mar Plaza, has a good selection of glassware. In the Rosarito Beach Hotel shopping center **Casa Torres (** (661) 21008, sells imported perfumes and cosmetics; **Margarita's** (no phone) has a good selection of handicrafts shops. Pottery yards lined the street south of town leading to **Casa la Carreta (** (661) 20502, at km 29 on the Old Ensenada Highway, and you'll also find the best wood craftsmen in the area.

Golf is available north of Rosarito at **Real del Mar Golf Club (** (661) 31340, on the Ensenada toll road. **Horseback riding** on the beach is a favorite activity; horses can be rented at the north and south ends of Juárez and on the beach south of Rosarito Beach Hotel. **Surfing** is not exceptional in Rosarito proper, but the waves are good at Popotla, km 33; at Calafía, km 33.5; at Costa Baja, km 36; and at km 38 on the Old Ensenada Highway.

WHERE TO STAY

Developers are racing to keep up with the demand for rooms in Rosarito; the result is an unattractive mix of architectural styles and plenty of construction sites. Rooms are scarce on summer and holiday weekends and should be reserved in advance. Several hotels are represented by **Baja Information (** (619) 298-4105 FAX (619) 294-7366 E-MAIL impamexicoinfo@worldnet.att.net, Mission Center Court, Suite 202, San Diego, CA 92108.

Moderate

The **Rosarito Beach Hotel (** (661) 20144 TOLL-FREE (800) 343-8582 (from the United States) FAX (661) 21125 (or write to PO Box 430145, San Diego, CA 92143), Boulevard Juárez, at the south end of town, would be the most desirable hotel in town if the rooms were better maintained. Unfortunately, the 186 rooms, 61 suites and 28 two-bedroom suites vary considerably in repair and comfort levels; those in the unsightly tower beside the main hotel are in the best shape. The hotel has a nice spa and good restaurant.

Festival Plaza ((661) 20842 TOLL-FREE (800) 453-8606 (for reservations from the United States) FAX (661) 20124, Boulevard Juárez 11, offers several types of rooms, from ocean-facing *casitas* to motel-type boxes; you're sure to find one to meet your comfort needs and price range among the 108 rooms, five penthouse suites, seven *casitas* and 13 villas. Noise is a concern here; the main courtyard area includes a working rollercoaster and a concert stage.

Los Pelicanos Hotel ((661) 20445 FAX (661) 21757, Calle Cedros 115 at Calle Ebano (or write to PO Box 433871, San Ysidro, CA 92143), is a favorite of those seeking serenity close to the beach. The 39 rooms are well maintained; some have balconies facing the beach. There is no swimming

pool, but the second-story restaurant and bar are perfect for sunset watching over drinks.

Inexpensive

Though it's located right on the main thoroughfare, **Brisas del Mar (** (661) 22547 TOLL-FREE (888) 871-3605 (for reservations from the United States) FAX (661) 22547 (or write to PO Box 18903, Coronado, CA 92178-9003), Boulevard Juárez 22, seems quiet and secluded once you're within the complex. The 69 rooms and two junior suites are in good repair. Also recommended in this price category are the **Motel Colonial (** (661) 21575 on Calle Primero de Mayo with 13 rooms and **Motel Don Luís (** (661) 21166, on Boulevard Benito Juárez, with 31 rooms, some of which have kitchen facilities.

WHERE TO EAT

Gourmet restaurants are not Rosarito's style. Instead, the town is filled with places where drinking is as important as dining. Tacos and seafood are the main fare, along with plenty of tequila and beer.

Moderate

If steaks, lobster and conversation are your preferences, try **El Nido (** (661) 21430, Boulevard Juárez 67. **La Leña (** (661) 20826, in the La Quinta Plaza, is a bit removed from the action and serves tasty and unusual beef dishes and Mexican food. **El Patio (** (661) 22950, on Boulevard Juárez in the Festival Plaza, is the most reserved of this complex's restaurants and serves authentic regional cuisine including *mole* and chicken with *poblano* sauce. **La Taberna Española (** (661) 21982, on Boulevard Juárez across from Festival Plaza, is a branch of the popular Tijuana *tapas* bar.

Inexpensive

La Flor de Michoacán ((661) 21858, Boulevard Juárez 291, is the place to try *carnitas*, succulent chunks of pork with guacamole and homemade tortillas.

HOW TO GET THERE

Rosarito is 18 miles (29 km) south of Tijuana and is most easily accessed by the toll road out of Tijuana. The Rosarito exit leads to Boulevard Juárez and the Old Ensenada Highway, which travels south of town past several small hotels and residential areas. There is frequent bus service from Tijuana

PUERTO NUEVO

Once a simple collection of a few rustic fishermen's homes, Puerto Nuevo has become a major attraction. Why? Because it's known for having the best

A lone horseback rider and sailboat share the open space at the Estero Beach Resort just south of Ensenada.

lobster on the coast: grilled or deep fried and served with lime wedges, melted butter, tortillas, beans and rice. The original collection of small restaurants has expanded to at least three dozen set on a dusty cliff top. There's hardly enough lobster in local waters to meet the demand; much of what's served is imported. Prices and selection are basically the same at all the restaurants; few have phones or take reservations. I've always been fond of the family that runs **Ponderosa**, one of the older, smaller restaurants. **Ortegas** may well be the most popular, and has four restaurants here and two in Rosarito. Puerto Nuevo is 7.5 miles (12 km) south of Rosarito; you can tell you're getting close when you see an abundance of pottery yards on the sides of the road.

WHERE TO STAY

There are several popular hotels in this area, some within easy walking distance of the lobster restaurants. Most book up quickly on summer and holiday weekends.

Moderate

The prettiest option is **Las Rocas** (/FAX (661) 22140 at km 37 on the Old Ensenada Highway. The best of the 74 rooms and suites have fireplaces and microwave ovens. **Hotel New Port Baja** ((661) 41166 FAX (661) 41174, at km 45 on the Old Ensenada Highway, has 147 rooms framing a large swimming pool. Excellent musicians play in the lobby bar. **La Fonda** (no phone) at km 59 on the Old Ensenada Highway, is as popular for its restaurant as it is for the 26 rustic rooms perched on various levels on a cliff over the sea.

ENSENADA

Although very much a tourist town, **Ensenada**, 67 miles (108 km) south of the border on the Bahía de Todos Santos, is also an important seaport and Baja's largest commercial fishing port. The Portuguese captain Juan Rodríguez Cabrillo was the first to chart this protected bay, in 1542; the Spanish explorer, Sebastián Vizcaíno, gave it its name Ensenada-Bahía de Todos Santos. Missionaries and ranchers arrived in the late eighteenth century, discovered gold and Ensenada became a boom town. But the mines were soon depleted and Ensenada became a sedate agricultural and fishing community. It had a moment of glory as capital of Baja California Norte from 1888 to 1910, and another during Prohibition when thirsty Americans came in search of liquid gold. Its popularity waned when liquor could be found at home, but it has remained a weekend party town.

GENERAL INFORMATION

The **Tourist Information Office** ((61) 782411 or (61) 788588, on Boulevard Costero 1477, is open on weekdays from 9 AM to 5 PM, closed from 1 PM to 2 PM for lunch.

WHAT TO SEE AND DO

The toll highway from Tijuana ends at Ensenada's northern entrance at Boulevard Costero. The first attraction, and one of the most popular, is the **Fish Market**, at the northernmost point of Boulevard Costero and Plaza de Marina. The market itself is a giant warehouse filled with stands displaying fresh shrimp, tuna, marlin, yellowtail and whatever happens to be in season, all spread out on heaps of ice. Outside the market dozens of taco stands proffer the same treat — the classic Baja fish taco. Strips of flaky white rock cod or other fresh fish are dipped in batter and deep fried, then wrapped in a corn tortilla. Condiments including shredded cabbage, cilantro, onions, and radishes, mayonnaise and several salsas sit in small bowls on the counter; diners stuff their tacos and settle on stools at the taco stands to devour this treat. The massive **Plaza Marina** now blocks the view of the market from the street, and is one of many partially inhabited structures marring Ensenada's scenery. South of the market is the **Plaza Cívica** at Boulevard Costero and Avenida Riveroll, where large busts of several Mexican leaders dominate a small park. The **Centro Artesanal de Ensenada** on Boulevard Costero was constructed to attract cruise ship passengers disembarking at the nearby pier. Unfortunately, the few ships that still come to town anchor in the bay and passengers are tendered to the boat docks north of town. The Centro still has a few good shops. Most notable is the excellent **Galería de Pérez Meillón** ((61) 740399, displaying museum-quality pottery from Casas Grande. Ensenada's most cherished landmark is the Prohibition-era gambling palace called the **Riviera del Pacifico** ((61) 764310, at Boulevard Costero and Avenida Riviera (admission fee; open daily from 9 AM to 5 PM). The hacienda-style white building once housed a hotel, ballrooms, gambling halls and restaurants; it's now a civic center housing a small museum on Ensenada's history. Take time to wander through the ballrooms and gorgeous gardens.

Ensenada's main tourist area is one block inland along **Avenida López Mateos** Shopping plazas, restaurants and hotels line the busy street; you can easily spend a few hours browsing through folk-art shops and department stores, taking time to stop for a drink or meal. Among

A crusty old Mexican stands ready to sell a bunch of the bright-colored paper flowers you see throughout Tijuana.

the best shops for good quality Mexican folk art and jewelry are **Artes Don QuijoteArtesanías Castillo** and **Girasoles**. The vineyards and wineries in the valleys around Ensenada produce some of Mexico's best wine. You can tour the in-town winery of **Las Bodegas de Santo Tomás (** (61) 783333, Avenida Miramar 666 (call ahead for tour hours). Across Miramar from the winery is **La Esquina de Bodegas**. This and other wineries in the surrounding valleys are open for tours. Most hotels and the tourist information office have details on exact openings. **Lady of Guadalupe**, on Avenida Floresta at Avenida Juárez is Ensenada's largest cathedral.

Ensenada's beaches are not particularly attractive; the best are south of town at **Estero Beach**. The ocean puts on a grand show at **La Bufadora**, 20 miles (31 km) southwest of Ensenada. Waves explode in a blast of thunder and spraying water at this large blowhole in the coastal cliffs. Legends tell that the spray comes from a whale trapped in the rocks. La Bufadora was spiffed up in the mid-1990s and has become a bona fide attraction with artisan's stands, seafood restaurants and parking fees.

One of Ensenada's main attractions is **sport fishing**. From May to October, sportsmen come for yellowtail. Also abundant are barracuda, tuna, marlin, mackerel and bonita. Fishing excursions can be arranged at the **Ensenada Sport Fishing Pier** at Boulevard Costera and Avenida Macheros and should cost approximately $50 per person per day on a group boat. **Whale-watching** boats depart from the Ensenada Sport Fishing Pier from December through April, when gray whales are migrating from the Bering Straits to southern Baja's lagoon. **Golf** is available at the **Baja Country Club (** (61) 730303, on Highway 1 south of Ensenada at Maneadero. Ocean **Kayaking** off Punta Banda is available through **Southwest Kayaks (** (619) 222-3616 in San Diego.

WHERE TO STAY

Regulars have their favorite hangouts and many of Ensenada's best hotels fill up quickly, even when you might not expect them to. Advance reservations are a good idea at most of the places listed below.

Expensive

The **Hotel Coral & Marina (** (61) 750000 TOLL-FREE (800) 862-9020 (for reservations from the United States) FAX (61) 750005 on Mexico Highway 1 north of town, opened in the mid-1990s, offering a new level of luxury accommodation for the city. The 600-slip marina attracts boaters from southern California, and many of the hotel's 140 rooms and suites have a view of the

water. Facilities include a large swimming pool and whirlpool, tennis courts, a gym, and decent restaurants. Similarly modern, **Las Rosas (** (61) 744320 FAX (61) 744595 on Highway 1 north of Ensenada is the prettiest hotel on the coast. Its atrium lobby glows against the night sky, and the pool seems to disappear off into the horizon. Some of the 32 suites have fireplaces and whirlpool bathtubs. The restaurant under the atrium has a beautiful view of the sea and serves good international cuisine.

Moderate

Favored by the relaxed beach crowd, **Estero Beach Resort (** (61) 766235 FAX (61) 766925 (or write to

482 San Ysidro Boulevard, Suite 1186, San Ysidro, CA 92173), on Highway 1 between Ensenada and Maneadero, is the best hotel on the water in the area. Families pack the 110 rooms during the summer months; the most desirable suites (in the very expensive range) are the two-story ones right at the sand. The least expensive rooms face parking lots. The hotel's large complex includes several shops, a recreational vehicle park, a pool, a large children's playground and a good restaurant with indoor and outdoor seating. In town, the **San Nicolas (** (61) 761901 FAX (61) 764930, on Avenida López Mateos and Guadalupe, is an older hotel with lots of character. The plain-looking two-story building houses 148 guestrooms and frames a long courtyard pool and gardens. The pool extends inside — a plus in the winter months — and the rooms are refurbished regularly. The restaurant serves good Mexican food.

Inexpensive

Though it faces the water near downtown, the **Corona Hotel (** (61) 760901 FAX (61) 764023 (or write to 482 San Ysidro Boulevard, Suite 303, San Ysidro, CA 92173), Boulevard Costero 1442, doesn't have a beach. The 90 rooms aren't always well maintained. If you're passing through town on route south, try the **Joker Hotel (** (61) 767201 FAX (61) 767201, on Highway 1 at km 12.5 between Ensenada and Maneadero. The design is rather bizarre, emphasizing clown faces and such, but the parking lot is guarded and the 40 rooms are satisfactory.

WHERE TO EAT

Seafood is Ensenada's forté, from the humble fish taco to succulent fresh lobster and shrimp. The abundance of wineries in the region also encourages restaurateurs to experiment with Mexican and international cuisine, with the result that there are a few exceptional restaurants. Most are casual, and nothing beats the simple taste of grilled fresh fish served at one of the city's landmark restaurants.

Expensive

El Rey Sol ((61) 781733, Avenida López Mateos 1000, which has been owned and operated by the same family for decades. The owners operate their own vegetable gardens, are well acquainted with the wines of the region, and buy their fish and game from the best purveyors. French, Mexican and American recipes bring out the best in the fresh ingredients used here; all the breads and pastries are baked in house. Although newer (it opened in the early 1990s), **La Embotelladora Vieja (** (61) 740807, Avenida Miramar 666, has acquired a cross-border reputation as an excellent restaurant in the quarters of the Santo Tomás winery. Teetotalers might have a bit of a problem here, since the beef, poultry and fish dishes are typically prepared with wine sauces, but the chefs do all they can to accommodate individual tastes. The dark wine cellar setting is perfect for intimate dinners amid candlelight and chandeliers.

Moderate

I've always been fond of **Casamar (** (61) 740417, Boulevard Lázaro Cárdenas 987, for standard seafood dinners made from the freshest fish. Order your fillet of dorado, tuna or shark prepared *mojo de ajo,* with oil and garlic. Not fond of fish? Try **Bronco's Steak House (** (61) 761901, Avenida López Mateos 1525. The western cowboy decor, complete with branding irons, saddles and wagon wheel lamps, sets the mood for meals of *carne asada* (marinated beef strips) and robust steaks with charred green onions and chilis.

Inexpensive

Mariscos de Bahía de Ensenada ((61) 781015, Avenida Riveroll 109, is a down-home, formica-table-type spot good for sampling seafood among locals. **El Charro (** (61) 783881, Avenida López Mateos 475, is the best place in the tourist zone for chicken roasted on a rotisserie and served with excellent tortillas, beans and rice.

NIGHTLIFE

Ensenada's nightlife scene can be rowdy during spring break and holiday weekends, when people of all ages escape nearby cities on both sides of the border.

     Hussong's Cantina ((61) 740145, on Avenida Ruíz at López Mateos, is the most legendary bar in all of Baja; few can resist strolling past the guard at the door to view the huge, semi-dark room packed with revelers, mariachi bands, lottery-ticket sellers and photographers. **Papas and Beer**, across the street from Hussong's, has a second-story terrace where beer drinkers can yell down to their friends on the street. Nearly any excuse is sufficient for staging a *fiesta.* Yacht, car and bicycle races attract crowds from Southern California, and all national Mexican holidays are celebrated with fervor.

HOW TO GET THERE

Ensenada does not have a commercial airport; transportation is available from the Tijuana airport to the bus station, where you can catch a bus to Ensenada.

At Hussong's Cantina the beer and cheer are both served in abundance and next door there's a busy boutique where you can buy souvenirs of the famous old bar.

Travelers' Tips

GETTING TO CALIFORNIA

Nearly all major domestic and international airlines offer service to the huge airports in San Francisco and Los Angeles. See HOW TO GET THERE in these chapters, respectively page 116 and page 231, for further information.

MAJOR AIRLINES SERVING CALIFORNIA

The following is a list of the major airlines serving Los Angeles (LAX), San Francisco (SFO) and San Diego (SAN), plus their toll-free telephone numbers:

Aer Lingus (LAX) TOLL-FREE (800) 474-7424.
Aerolineas Argentinas (LAX) TOLL-FREE (800) 333-0276.
Aeromexico (SFO) (LAX) (SAN) TOLL-FREE (800) 237-6639 WEB SITE www.aeromexico.com.
Aeroperu (LAX) TOLL-FREE (800) 777-7717.
Air Canada (SFO) (LAX) TOLL-FREE (800) 776-3000 WEB SITE www.aircanada.ca.
Air France (SFO) (LAX) TOLL-FREE (800) 237-2747 WEB SITE www.airfrance.com.
Air New Zealand (SFO) (LAX) TOLL-FREE (800) 262-1234.
Alaska Airlines (SFO) (LAX) (SAN) TOLL-FREE (800) 426-0333 WEB SITE www.alaskaair.com.
Alitalia (SFO) (LAX) TOLL-FREE (800) 223-5730 WEB SITE www.alitalia.it.
All Nippon Airways (ANA) (SFO) (LAX) TOLL-FREE (800) 235-9262 (English) and (800) 262-2230 (Japanese).
America West Airlines (SFO) (LAX) (SAN) TOLL-FREE (800) 235-9292 WEB SITE americawest.com.
American Airlines (SFO) (LAX) (SAN) TOLL-FREE (800) 433-7300 WEB SITE www.americanair.com.
Austrian Airlines (LAX) TOLL-FREE (800) 843-0002.
British Airways (SFO) (LAX) (SAN) TOLL-FREE (800) 247-9297 WEB SITE british-airways.com.
Canadian Airlines (SFO) (LAX) TOLL-FREE (800) 426-7000 WEB SITE www.cdair.ca.
Cathay Pacific Airways (SFO) (LAX) TOLL-FREE (800) 233-2742.
China Airlines (SFO) (LAX) TOLL-FREE (800) 227-5118.
Continental (SFO) (LAX) (SAN) TOLL-FREE (800) 523-3273 WEB SITE flycontinental.com.
Delta (SFO) (LAX) (SAN) TOLL-FREE (800) 221-1212 WEB SITE delta-air.com.
Finnair (SFO) (LAX) TOLL-FREE (800) 950-5000
Hawaiian Airlines (LAX) (SAN) TOLL-FREE (800) 367-5320.
Iberia (SFO) (LAX) TOLL-FREE (800) 772-4642.
Japan Airlines (SFO) (LAX) TOLL-FREE (800) 525-3663.

PRECEDING PAGES: Volleyball tournaments and kite-flying contests draw crowds to Southern California's sunny beaches.

KLM (SFO) (LAX) TOLL-FREE (800) 374-7747 WEB SITE www.klm.nl.
Korean Airlines (SFO) (LAX) TOLL-FREE (800) 438-5000.
LACSA (SFO) (LAX) TOLL-FREE (800) 225-2272.
LOT Polish Airlines (LAX) TOLL-FREE (800) 249-0739.
Lufthansa (SFO) (LAX) TOLL-FREE (800) 645-3880 WEB SITE www.lufthansa.com.
Mexicana Airlines (SFO) (LAX) TOLL-FREE (800) 531-7921 WEB SITE www.mexicana.com.
Northwest Airlines (SFO) (LAX) (SAN) TOLL-FREE (800) 225-2525 WEB SITE www.nwa.com.
Philippine Airlines (SFO) (LAX) TOLL-FREE (800) 435-9725.
Qantas (SFO) (LAX) TOLL-FREE (800) 227-4500.
Reno Air (SFO) (LAX) (SAN) TOLL-FREE (800) 736-6247.
Scandinavian Airlines (SAS) (SFO) (LAX) TOLL-FREE (800) 221-2350 WEB SITE www.flysas.com.
Singapore Airlines (SFO) (LAX) TOLL-FREE (800) 742-3333.
Southwest Airlines (SFO) (LAX) (SAN) TOLL-FREE (800) 435-9297 WEB SITE iflyswa.com.
Swissair (LAX) TOLL-FREE (800) 221-4750 WEB SITE www.swissair.com.
TACA International Airlines (SFO) (LAX) TOLL-FREE (800) 535-8780.
TWA (SFO) (LAX) (SAN) TOLL-FREE (800) 221-2000 WEB SITE www2.twa.com.
US Air (SFO) (LAX) (SAN) TOLL-FREE (800) 428-4322 WEB SITE www.usair.com.
United Airlines (SFO) (LAX) (SAN) TOLL-FREE (800) 241-6522 WEB SITE www.ual.com.
Varig (SFO) (LAX) TOLL-FREE (800) 468-2744.
Virgin Atlantic Airways (LAX) TOLL-FREE (800) 862-8621 WEB SITE www.flyvirgin.com.

OTHER WAYS TO REACH CALIFORNIA

The great age of American **rail travel** has long since passed, but **Amtrak** TOLL-FREE (800) 872-7245 still serves more than 550 destinations in the United States and Canada. Cross-country rail service to California is available from several major cities in the Midwest and Eastern states. The *Coast Starlight* connects Seattle and Los Angeles with stops in Portland, Sacramento, the Bay Area and the Central California coast. The *California Zephyr* connects Chicago and San Francisco with stops in Omaha, Denver, Salt Lake City, Reno and Sacramento. The *Southwest Chief* connects Chicago and Los Angeles with stops at Kansas City, Albuquerque and Flagstaff (Grand Canyon). The *Sunset Limited* connects Florida and Los Angeles with stops in Orlando (Disney World), Jacksonville, Mobile, New Orleans, Houston, San Antonio, El Paso and Tucson. Rail fares are comparable to and sometimes exceed air travel.

A high-speed rail line between Los Angeles and Las Vegas is under construction but won't be finished until well into the twenty-first century.

Another fading transportation form is cross-country **bus service**, although generally it's still the cheapest way (other than hitchhiking) to get from one place to another. **Greyhound Bus Lines** TOLL-FREE (800) 231-2222 (English) or (800) 531-5332 (Spanish) faithfully serves hundreds of American cities, including all major Californian destinations. Regular coach service is also available from terminals in downtown Los Angeles and San Diego to border cities like Tijuana and Mexicali.

Cruise ships also call on California with Los Angeles/Long Beach, San Francisco and San Diego as the major ports. However, there is no regular steamship or ferry service to foreign destinations or other American ports.

By far the most popular way to reach California from other states is **driving**. Interstate highways make the cross-country journey a breeze, although it still takes three days to drive all the way from New York or Florida and two days to reach the West Coast from Chicago. The following are major interstate routes:

Interstate 5: Vancouver, Seattle, Portland, Sacramento, Los Angeles, San Diego.

Interstate 80: New York, Cleveland, Chicago, Omaha, Wyoming, Salt Lake City, Reno, San Francisco.

Interstate 15: Montana, Idaho, Utah, Las Vegas, Los Angeles, San Diego.

Interstate 40: North Carolina, Nashville, Memphis, Little Rock, Oklahoma City, Albuquerque, Flagstaff (Grand Canyon), Los Angeles (via Interstate 15).

Interstate 10: Florida, New Orleans, Houston, San Antonio, El Paso, Tucson, Phoenix, Los Angeles.

Interstate 8: Phoenix/Tucson to San Diego.

VISAS

Most citizens of Britain, Canada, France, Germany, Italy, Japan, New Zealand and most other Western European nations qualify for a visa exemption. They may enter the United States without a visa if they are traveling for holiday or business and staying less than 90 days. A valid passport and return ticket are also required.

Citizens of all other countries require a valid passport (which won't expire until six months after the termination of their United States visit) and a tourist visa from a United States embassy or consulate overseas. Tourists visas can vary from single entry to multiple entry; length of stay also varies.

CONSULATES

(SF) = San Francisco; (LA) = Los Angeles; (S) = Sacramento; (SD) = San Diego.

Travelers' Tips

Argentina (LA) 5055 Wilshire Boulevard ((213) 954-9155.

Australia (SF) 1 Bush Street ((415) 362-6160; (LA) 2049 Century Park East ((310) 229-4800 611.

Austria (LA) 11859 Wilshire Boulevard ((310) 444-9310.

Belgium (LA) 6100 Wilshire Boulevard ((213) 857-1244.

Bolivia (SF) 870 Market Street ((415) 495-5173.

Brazil (SF) 300 Montgomery Street ((415) 981-8170.

Canada (SF) 50 Fremont Street ((415) 495-6021; (LA) 300 South Grand Avenue ((213) 687-7432; (SD) 4370 La Jolla Village Drive ((619) 597-7050.

Chile (SF) 870 Market Street ((415) 982-7662; (LA) 1900 Avenue of the Stars ((310) 785-0113.

China (SF) 1450 Laguna Street ((415) 674-2900; (LA) 443 Shatto Place ((213) 807-8088.

Colombia (SF) 595 Market Street ((415) 495-7195; (LA) 8383 Wilshire Boulevard ((213) 653-4299.

Costa Rica (SF) 870 Market Street ((415) 392-8488; (LA) 3540 Wilshire Boulevard ((213) 380-7915.

Denmark (SF) 601 Montgomery Suite 440 ((415) 391-0100; (LA) 10877 Wilshire Boulevard ((310) 443-2090; (SD) 1405 Savoy Circle ((619) 224-7640.

Dominica (SF) 870 Market Street ((415) 982-5144.

Egypt (SF) 3001 Pacific Avenue ((415) 346-9700.

Finland (LA) 1900 Avenue of the Stars ((310) 203-9903.

France (SF) 540 Bush Street ((415) 397-4330; (LA) 10990 Wilshire Boulevard ((310) 235-3200; (S) 1831 Rockwood Drive ((916) 488-7659.

Germany (SF) 1960 Jackson Street ((415) 775-1061; (LA) 6222 Wilshire Boulevard ((213) 930-2703.

Great Britain (SF) 1 Sansome Street ((415) 981-3030; (LA) 11766 Wilshire Boulevard ((310) 477-3322.

Greece (LA) 12424 Wilshire Boulevard ((310) 826-5555.

Iceland (SF) 222 Front Street ((415) 433-0444; (LA) 1551 Westwood Boulevard ((310) 474-8485.

India (SF) 540 Arguello Boulevard ((415) 668-0683.

Indonesia (LA) 3457 Wilshire Boulevard ((213) 383-5126.

Israel (SF) 456 Montgomery Street ((415) 398-8885; (LA) 6380 Wilshire Boulevard ((213) 852-5524.

Italy (SF) 425 Bush Street ((415) 788-7142; (S) 5347 Folsom Boulevard ((916) 456-1950.

Korea (SF) 350 Clay Street ((415) 921-2251; (LA) 3243 Wilshire Boulevard ((213) 385-9300.

Lebanon (LA) 7060 Hollywood Boulevard ((213) 467-1253.

Mexico (SD) 1549 India Street ((619) 231-8414; (S) 1010 8th Street ((916) 441-2987.

Netherlands (LA) 11766 Wilshire Boulevard ((310) 268-1598.

Norway (SF) 20 California Street ((415) 986-0766; (SD) 6240 Brynwood Court ((619) 582-5586.

Paraguay (LA) 18377 Beach Boulevard (Huntington) ((714) 848-3168.

Poland (LA) 12400 Wilshire Boulevard ((310) 442-8500.

Russia (SF) 2790 Green Street ((415) 202-9800.

South Africa (LA) 50 North La Cienega Boulevard ((310) 657-9200.

Switzerland (SF) 465 Montgomery Street ((415) 788-2272.

Thailand (LA) 611 North Larchmont Boulevard ((213) 962-9574.

Uruguay (LA) 429 Santa Monica Boulevard ((310) 394-5777.

Venezuela (SF) 455 Market Street ((415) 512-7694.

CUSTOMS

Visitors to the United States should keep in mind that the country is involved in a massive drug war, posting literally thousands of law enforcement officers at major points of entry with the sole purpose of checking for illegal drugs. If you enter the United States from one of the major drug producing countries — Mexico, Colombia, Thailand, Burma — you may be subjected to a thorough search for no other reason than the stamps in your passport. If you are caught trying to bring in any kind of illegal drug, you will be dealt with severely.

Aside from the extraordinary security precautions regarding illegal drugs, the United States Customs are not that different from the major countries of Europe. With certain exemptions — the major ones are clothes, jewelry, toilet articles, hunting and fishing equipment and any other personal effects — articles bought outside the United States are subject to a customs duty and internal revenue tax. Such articles valued at more than $300 cannot be sold within three years unless a duty is paid to the District Director of Customs.

Non-residents are also allowed to bring in a quantity of alcoholic beverages and tobacco without paying duty. The United States Customs allows up to one liter of beer, wine or liquor to be brought in for personal use; anything over that will be taxed. United States Postal laws do not allow the shipping by mail of alcoholic beverages. As for tobacco, non-residents can bring in duty free up to 200 cigarettes (a carton), 50 cigars or four and a half pounds (two kilograms) of smoking tobacco.

The laws regarding importation of motor vehicles are quite complex and you should consult with a United States Embassy or Consulate before attempting to bring in an automobile, airplane, motorcycle or any kind of vehicle even for personal use. In general, a vehicle may be imported for personal use for up to one year. However, you must own the vehicle at the time and its arrival must coincide with your own; and all vehicles must meet United States air pollution, cost saving and safety standards. If you sell your vehicle within one year of your arrival, duty must be paid to the United States Customs.

Household effects and professional equipment are exempt for persons emigrating to the United States, but again, the rules here vary and are quite complicated. For example, theatrical scenery and wearing apparel are not considered professional equipment.

In addition to the exemptions already named, a gift exemption is allowed non-resident visitors to the United States. A gift valued up to $100 may be brought in duty free provided you plan to stay in the United States 72 hours and the article remains with you. An additional 100 cigars may be included under the gift exemptions, but no alcoholic beverages are allowed as gifts. Non-residents are allowed higher exemptions ($200 and four liters alcoholic beverages) if they are in transit through the United States and the articles will be continuing on to a place outside United States Customs jurisdiction.

Anything above the exemption rate up to $1,000 will have a flat duty rate of 10% charged, based on the article's retail value in the country of purchase. Articles purchased in "duty free" shops in foreign countries are also subject to customs duty in the United States.

Many fruits and vegetables, plants and seeds are prohibited from entering the United States. For more information on agricultural products, write to Quarantines, USDA-ATHIS-TTQ, Federal Building, Hyattsville, MD 20782.

Firearms and ammunition may be brought in as sporting equipment, provided it is personal equipment that leaves with you when you leave the United States. For detailed information on firearms, write to the Bureau of Alcohol, Tobacco and Firearms, Department of the Treasury, Washington, DC 20226.

The United States prohibits the entry of any merchandise from the following countries: Cuba, Iraq, Iran, Libya and North Korea.

The only restriction regarding money is that you must file a report (Customs form 4790) if you bring in or take out more than $10,000. Failure to file this report can result in civil and criminal penalties.

A leaflet on bringing pets into the United States and a more general pamphlet called *United States Customs Hints For Visitors (Non-Residents)* can be ordered from the United States Customs Service ((202) 927-6724, PO Box 7407, Washington, DC 20044.

TOURIST INFORMATION

The state's primary government tourist and travel information bureau is the **Californian Division of Tourism** ((916) 322-2881 TOLL-FREE (800) 862-2543 (from United States or Canada) FAX (916) 322-3402 WEB SITE gocalif.ca.gov, 801 K Street, Suite 1600, Sacramento, CA 95814.

URBAN TOURIST INFORMATION

Los Angeles Convention & Visitors Bureau ((213) 624-7300 or (213) 689-8822 FAX (213) 624-9746 or (213) 624-1992, 633 West Fifth Street, Suite 6000, Los Angeles, CA 90071.

Palm Springs Desert Resorts Convention & Visitors Bureau ((619) 770-9000, The Atrium, 69-930 State Highway 111, Suite 201, Rancho Mirage, CA 92270.

Sacramento Convention & Visitors Bureau ((916) 264-7777 FAX (916) 264-7788 WEB SITE www .sacto.org/cvb/, 1303 J Street, Suite 600, Sacramento, CA 95814.

San Diego Convention & Visitors Bureau ((619) 232-3101 or (619) 236-1212 or (619) 276-8200, 401 B Street, San Diego, CA.

San Francisco Convention & Visitors Bureau ((415) 391-2000 WEB SITE www.sfvisitor.org, 201 Third Street, Suite 900, San Francisco, CA 94103. 24-hour recorded events information: ((415) 391-2001 (English), (415) 391-2003 (French), ((415) 391-2004 (German), (415) 391-2122 (Spanish), ((415) 391-2101 (Chinese).

Santa Barbara Conference & Visitors Bureau ((805) 966-9222, 12 East Carrillo Street, Santa Barbara, CA 93101.

REGIONAL TOURIST INFORMATION

Eureka and Humboldt County Convention & Visitors Bureau ((707) 443-5097 FAX (707) 443-5115 WEB SITE www.redwoodvisitor.org, 1034 Second Street, Eureka, CA 95501.

Mount Shasta Chamber of Commerce & Visitors Bureau ((530) 926-4865 TOLL-FREE (800) 926-4865 FAX (530) 926-0976 WEB SITE www .mtshasta.com, 300 Pine Street, Mount Shasta, CA 96067.

Napa Valley Conference & Visitors Bureau ((707) 226-7459 FAX (707) 255-2066 WEB SITE www.napavalley.com, 1310 Napa Town Center, Napa, CA 94559.

Shasta Cascade Wonderland Association ((530) 365-7500 FAX (530) 365-1258, 1619 State Highway 273, Andersen, CA 96007.

Sonoma County Convention & Visitors Bureau ((707) 586-8100 TOLL-FREE (800) 326-7666 FAX (707) 586-8111 WEB SITE visitsonoma.com, 5000 Roberts Lake Road, Rohnert Park, CA 94928.

Trinity County Chamber of Commerce ((800) 487-4648 WEB SITE www.trinitycounty.com, 210 Main Street, PO Box 517, Weaverville, CA 96093.

OUTDOOR RECREATION INFORMATION

California Department of Parks and Recreation ((916) 653-6995 WEB SITE ceres.ca.gov/ceres/ calweb/state-parks.html, PO Box 942896, Sacramento, CA 94296. State park campground reservations TOLL-FREE (800) 444-PARK. Sno-Park Hotline ((916) 324-1222.

California Department of Transportation TOLL-FREE (800) 427-7623 (automated road condition information).

California Ski Industry Association ((415) 543-7036.

Outdoor Recreation for Travelers with Disabilities ((415) 474-7662; Accessible California ((619) 279-07097 WEB SITE www.electriciti.com/ accessed (operates the Environmental Traveling Companions program).

United States Forest Service ((415) 705-2874 or (415) 556-1787, 630 Sansome Street, San Francisco,

CA 94111 (manages more than 20 national forests and 129 wilderness areas in California).

NATIONAL PARKS

More than 20 wilderness, recreation and historic areas in California are maintained by the federal National Park Service. Most of these are covered under individual headings. For more information on the parks in California, write to the Park Service's **Western Region Headquarters** 450 Golden Gate Avenue, Box 36063, San Francisco, CA 94102. General inquiries can be directed to the **National Park Service** ((415) 556-0560 WEB SITE www.nps.gov/parklists/ca.html.

Casually dressed Californians watch a fourth of July (Independence Day) parade in Sausalito.

A camping guide to the national parks is available free of charge from the Superintendent of Documents, United States Government Printing Office, Washington, DC 20402. Another booklet on visitor facilities in the parks can be obtained by writing to the Garner B. Hanson Conference of National Park Concessions, Mammoth Cave, Kentucky 42259.

Camping **reservations** for the more popular California national park sites can be made up to three months in advance by calling the following numbers. Yosemite: TOLL-FREE (800) 436-7275. Sequoia, Kings Canyon, Death Valley, Joshua Tree, Whiskeytown-Shasta-Trinity: TOLL-FREE (800) 365-2267.

The following is a list of the National Parks in California and the addresses where information can be obtained about them:

Cabrillo National Monument, PO Box 6670, San Diego, CA 92106.

Channel Islands National Park, 1901 Spinnaker Drive, Ventura, CA 93001.

Death Valley National Park, Death Valley, CA 92328.

Devils Postpile National Monument, c/o Sequoia and Kings Canyon National Parks, Three Rivers, CA 93271.

Eugene O'Neill National Historic Site, c/o John Muir National Historic Site, 4202 Alhambra Avenue, Martinez, CA 94553.

Fort Point National Historic Site, PO Box 29333, Presidio of San Francisco, CA 94129.

Golden Gate National Recreation Area, Fort Mason, Building 201, San Francisco, CA 9412.

John Muir National Historic Site, 4202 Alhambra Avenue, Martinez, CA 94553.

Joshua Tree National Park, 74485 National Monument Drive, Twentynine Palms, CA 92277.

Kings Canyon National Park, Three Rivers, CA 93271.

Lassen Volcanic National Park, Mineral, CA 96063.

Lava Beds National Monument, PO Box 867, Tulelake, CA 96134.

Manzanar National Historic Site, PO Box 426, Independence, CA 93526.

Mojave National Preserve, 222 East Main Street, Suite 202, Barstow, CA 92311.

Muir Woods National Monument, Mill Valley, CA 94941.

Pinnacles National Monument, Paicines, CA 95043.

Point Reyes National Seashore, Point Reyes, CA 94956.

Redwood National Park, 1111 Second Street, Crescent City, CA 95531.

Santa Monica Mountains National Recreation Area, 22900 Ventura Boulevard, Suite 140, Woodland Hills, CA 91364.

Sequoia National Park, Three Rivers, CA 93271.

Whiskeytown-Shasta-Trinity National Recreation Area, PO Box 188, Whiskeytown, CA 96095. **Yosemite National Park**, PO Box 577, Yosemite National Park, CA 95389.

TRAVELING IN CALIFORNIA

AIR TRAVEL

The best deals on air travel are flights between major airports in Southern California (Los Angeles, San Diego, Burbank, Orange County) and major airports in Northern California (San Francisco, Oakland, San Jose, Sacramento). Otherwise, flying is the most expensive way to move from one city to another. Top discount airlines are **Southwest** TOLL-FREE (800) 435-9297 and **Reno Air** TOLL-FREE (800) 736-6247 which publish special intercity fares in local newspapers.

BUSES

Greyhound Bus Lines TOLL-FREE (800) 231-2222 (English) or (800) 531-5332 (Spanish) serves dozens of Californian cities, including San Francisco, Los Angeles and San Diego. **Amtrak** TOLL-FREE (800) 872-7245 offers "thruway" bus service along popular tourist routes like Merced to Yosemite Valley, Bakersfield to Las Vegas and Napa Valley to Eureka. Amtrak buses depart from train stations along the company's railroad routes.

RAIL SERVICE

The poor or non-existent passenger rail service in California is a fitting memorial to the robber barons who made their fortunes off the American railroads. Never mind that the rails were laid on government property and that much of the construction was carried out through government subsidies, the private railroad owners by the 1950s realized that there was far more money to be made transporting freight than could ever be realized moving people, their original purpose. Amtrak, the government's own passenger service was established after the private rail companies either stopped passenger service altogether or made that service so poor and unpredictable nobody would ride the trains. The "Eastern Corridor" between Washington and Boston was always profitable and service there never faltered. However, in the American West, passenger train service all but disappeared for a time and even now the trains are few and far between.

The most successful route in California is the line between Los Angeles and San Diego which is plied by three different rail services: **Amtrak** TOLL-FREE (800) 872-7245, **Metrolink** ((213) 347-2800 TOLL-FREE (800) 371-LINK out of Los Angeles, and **Coaster** ((760) 722-6283 TOLL-FREE (800)

COA-STER out of San Diego. It's a very pictur-esque route, passing right along the beach for several miles south of San Clemente. There are also two of the country's grand old train stations at either end. Union Station in downtown Los Angeles is located just below the historic Pueblo de Los Angeles district and is a wonderful art deco gem that has survived largely because of all the movies that have been shot there. The old Santa Fe Depot in San Diego was built in time for the Panama Exposition there in 1915 and is a classic example of Spanish mission style. There are ten trains daily between Los Angeles and San Diego. Otherwise, it's best forget train travel in California. There is only one train daily between Los

In San Diego, you'll find a new rail transit system that overnight became a southern counterpart of the cable cars in San Francisco. In establishing the **San Diego Trolley** ((619) 231-8549 the city had two major advantages: there was existing track no longer used by the railroads already in place where the trolley should run. The bright red trolley cars chug right down to the Mexican border, stopping beside the United States Customs building. The line also connects other major points of interest in the San Diego area including Old Town, Seaport Village, Qualcomm Stadium, Mission Valley and Fashion Valley shopping malls, the Convention Center and the downtown Santa Fe train depot (connections to Amtrak and the

Angeles and San Francisco, leaving at 9:55 AM and arriving at 9:05 PM.

URBAN METRO AND RAIL

A number of California cities have developed urban mass transit rail systems over the last 20 years including San Francisco, San Diego, Sacramento, and San Jose/Santa Clara.

The slick underground and underwater subway system that links San Francisco with cities in the East Bay is called **BART** (Bay Area Rapid Transit) ((415) 992-BART or (510) 465-BART. The city also operates **Caltrain** TOLL-FREE (800) 660-4287, a commuter rail service that runs down the peninsula to Milbrae (San Francisco Airport), San Mateo, Redwood City, Menlo Park, Palo Alto, Mountain View, Sunnyvale, Santa Clara and San Jose.

Coaster). Tickets for the trolley line can be purchased at the various stops.

The new **Santa Clara County Light Rail** ((408) 321-2300 connects points of interest in the San Jose area including Paramount's Great America amusement park, the Children's Discovery Museum, the San Jose Civic Center, San Jose Airport and the Amtrak train stations in both San Jose and Santa Clara. **Sacramento Light Rail** ((916) 321-BUSS operates service from downtown and the State Capitol area to suburbs in the northeast and eastern parts of the metropolitan area.

Decades late, the city of Los Angeles has finally begun development of a commuter rail and subway system which will not be fully operable until early in the twenty-first century. **Metrolink**

The striking, clean lines of Union Station Los Angeles' only railway station. The most frequent service is to San Diego.

Travelers' Tips

((213) 347-2800 TOLL-FREE (800) 371-LINK operates regional rail service on six routes in the Los Angeles metropolitan area including service from downtown Los Angeles to Burbank Airport and other points in the San Fernando Valley; Lancaster near Magic Mountain theme park; Oxnard (Channel Islands Harbor) in Ventura County; the San Gabriel Valley, San Bernardino and Riverside in the east; Fullerton, Anaheim (Disneyland), Santa Ana and San Juan Capistrano in Orange County.

Metro Rail ((213) 626-4455 or (310) 639-6800 operates three controversial and very expensive transit lines in Los Angeles' central area. The ambitious project was originally supposed to include 79 miles (127 km) of rail with 71 stations, but by mid-1998 only 47 miles (75 km) and 49 stations had been completed at a staggering cost of $5.5 billion. So far only about one percent of Los Angeles County's population uses Metro Rail during peak hours, not a great drain away from the crowded freeways. The network's **Blue Line** connects downtown Los Angeles with downtown Los Angeles; along the way are the giant Del Amo shopping mall and the various ghetto areas that comprise South Central Los Angeles. The **Green Line** cuts across the heart of the Los Angeles basin from Norwalk in the east to El Segundo (Los Angeles Airport) and Redondo Beach in the west. The largely unfinished **Red Line** subway will eventually connect downtown Los Angeles with MacArthur Park, the Wilshire Corridor, Hollywood and the San Fernando Valley.

CAR RENTAL

Car rental offices are located convenient to the baggage check out or customs offices in all major airports in the State. However, most travelers will want to make reservations for a car rental at the same time reservations are made for air travel; this is the only way to insure that the particular car you want to rent will be ready and waiting when you arrive. Travelers to sunny southern California may want to take advantage of the convertible cars that can be rented from Budget rental cars.

The services offered by rental car agencies throughout California vary from place to place, even within the same agency. If you plan on traveling into Mexico, check with the agency first. Some do not allow their cars to travel into Mexico; others will provide the Mexican insurance necessary for such travel.

The following is a list of the toll-free numbers of the major agencies found in every part of the state. If you're looking for budget prices, the best deals can usually be made through the small local agencies. For long-term leases, the best bets are the major auto dealers such as Ford or Chevrolet.

Alamo TOLL-FREE (800) 327-9633
Avis TOLL-FREE (800) 331-1212
Budget TOLL-FREE (800) 527-0700
Dollar TOLL-FREE (800) 421-6878
Hertz TOLL-FREE (800) 654-3131
National TOLL-FREE (800) 328-4567

A few low-cost rental companies that will normally rent to people under 25 years include **Stopless Rent-A-Car** ((310) 673-9899 and **Fox Rent-A-Car** ((310) 641-3838 in Los Angeles and **Bargain Auto Rentals** in San Diego ((619) 299-0009. Fox offers free drop-off to any of their locations in Los Angeles, while Stopless will take a cash deposit from those who don't have credit cards. Bargain also rents four-wheel drive and other vehicles that can be taken into Baja California.

MOTORCYCLE RENTALS

If your dream is to cruise California on a Harley-Davidson, then contact **Eaglerider** TOLL-FREE (800) 501-TOUR. Rental offices in San Francisco at 1555 Burke Street and Los Angeles at 20917 Western Avenue offer a wide range of Fatboys and Low Riders.

MOTOR HOME RENTALS

Motor homes that sleep from two to six people are available from **El Monte RV Center** TOLL-FREE (800) 478-5040. Several rental offices in California including 12818 Firestone Boulevard, Santa Fe Springs (Los Angeles area); 6301 Scarlett Court, Dublin (San Francisco area); 1321 North Harbor Boulevard, Santa Ana (Orange County). In Buena Park, near Disneyland, is **Cruise America** ((714) 772-9030 FAX (714) 670-7596, 7015 Knott Avenue, Buena Park, CA 90620.

FREEWAYS

For many years, the freeways in Los Angeles seemed decades ahead of their time. They were a quick and efficient way of getting from one part of the sprawling city to another. But those days are long gone. The freeways, be they in Los Angeles, San Francisco or San Diego, are now desperately inadequate to handle the millions of cars that use them. In general, avoid the freeways during rush-hours between 7 AM and 9 AM and between 4 PM and 6 PM. A small amount of planning can save you from getting caught in one of those massive traffic jams that can leave you sitting still for up to an hour.

ACCOMMODATION

A full range of accommodation is available in California, from major luxury hotels and quaint bed and breakfast inns to national park camp-grounds and the ubiquitous motels that border many highways. Major international chains like Hilton, Sheraton and Hyatt are well represented, as are America's top budget motel chains like Days Inn, Travelodge and Motel 6. The choice is almost endless, especially in major tourist destinations like Los Angeles, San Francisco, and San Diego.

Advance reservations are absolutely necessary during the summer months (June, July, August) and peak holiday periods during the remainder of the year (Christmas, Thanksgiving, Easter, Memorial Day, Labor Day). The best way to make reservations is calling the toll free number of the hotel/motel chain or individual property where you want to stay. Ask plenty of questions before confirming your room: Find out the exact location of the hotel or motel, its distance from the places you want to see, and the facilities it has to offer.

LUXURY AND UPMARKET HOTEL CHAINS

Hilton TOLL-FREE (800) 445-8667
Holiday Inn TOLL-FREE (800) 465-4329
Howard Johnson TOLL-FREE (800) 654-2000
Hyatt TOLL-FREE (800) 233-1234
Marriott TOLL-FREE (800) 228-9290
Ramada Inn TOLL-FREE (800) 228-2828
Sheraton TOLL-FREE (800) 325-3535

INEXPENSIVE HOTELS AND MOTELS

Comfort Inns TOLL-FREE (800) 228-5150
Days Inn TOLL-FREE (800) DAYS INN
Motel 6 TOLL-FREE (800) 4-MOTEL-6
Quality Inns TOLL-FREE (800) 228-5151
Super 8 TOLL-FREE (800) 843-1991
Travelodge TOLL-FREE (800) 255-3050

HOTEL PRICES

The categories of hotel, motel and bed and break-fast prices listed in this guide are calculated on the cost of a standard double room:

Very Expensive over $250
Expensive $151 to $250
Medium $75 to $150
Inexpensive under $75

RESTAURANTS

California offers even more choice in food than it does in accommodation: thousands of gourmet restaurants and tens of thousands of fast-food outlets. Edibles run a gamut from traditional American burgers and steaks to cuisine from must about every country in the world. For more information on California cuisine, see GALLOPING GOURMETS, page 59. For recommendations on the state's top restaurants, see LIVING IT UP, page 40.

RESTAURANT PRICES

Price categories used in this book are based on the average cost of a meal per person, not including drinks:

Very Expensive over $50
Expensive $21 to $50
Moderate $10 to $20
Inexpensive under $10

TIPPING

Gratuities are well-ingrained in the American lifestyle. Restaurants usually do not apply a man-

datory service charge unless your group has more than eight people. Otherwise, you should tip about 15% of the total charge. A little trick of the trade: 15% is double the tax listed at the bottom of the bill. You are not expected to leave a tip in fast-food outlets or anywhere else with counter or deli-style service. Bartenders and cab driver also expect about 15%, although this depends on the level of service. Your other big interface with tipping is porter service. Budget accommodation normally doesn't provide bellhops so there's no need to worry about tipping. However, bellhops at mid-range and luxury properties, as well as

The Los Angeles freeway system is not quite so complex as it might appear in this picture of the major interchanges; however it is still best to avoid the freeways during morning and late afternoon rush hours.

airport and train station porters, will expect $1 to $2 per bag.

BANKING AND MONEY EXCHANGE

Although most of California's cities are major international tourist stops, you will not find services such as currency exchanges as common here as in major world capitals. It's better either to arrive with traveler's checks in United States dollars or, to exchange money at the air terminal or border crossing when entering the country. Once inside the state, there are only a small number of exchange offices in the major cities. Bank of America and Wells Fargo offer exchange services at their major downtown offices and many branches, but few local or suburban banks will handle foreign currency.

Banks are generally open from 9 AM to 3 PM Monday through Friday. Some offer late hours on Friday (5 PM or 6 PM) and an increasing number are open from 9 AM to noon on Saturday morning. Automated teller machines (ATMs) can be found nearly everywhere that people need money. Wells Fargo, for instance, offers ATMs inside every Vons supermarket. Credit card use is also pervasive. Visa and Mastercard (and their overseas equivalents) are accepted nearly everywhere, American Express, Diners Club and other cards to a lesser extent.

THOMAS COOK FOREIGN EXCHANGE LOCATIONS

San Francisco Bay Area: 75 Geary Street, San Francisco; Building M Level 2, Pier 39, Space M-10, San Francisco; 86 Stanford Shopping Center, Palo Alto; San Jose International Airport, Terminal C.

Los Angeles Area: Seventh Marketplace, 735 South Figueroa Street, downtown Los Angeles; 452 North Bedford Drive, Beverly Hills; Bank of Los Angeles, 8901 Santa Monica Boulevard, West Hollywood.

San Diego: 177 Horton Plaza, downtown San Diego; University Towne Center, 4525 La Jolla Village Drive, Suite D1B, La Jolla.

Orange County: Newport Fashion Island, 1113 Newport Center Drive, Newport Beach.

Sacramento: 300 Capital Mall.

BASICS

TIME

California is eight hours behind Greenwich Mean Time (GMT). Between the last Sunday in April and the last Sunday in October, the state observes Daylight Savings Time, which makes it seven hours behind GMT.

ELECTRICITY

America powers up on 110–120 volts at 60 cycles. Anyone visiting from outside North America should bring a 110-volt converter and an adapter plug if they want to use their travel appliances (hairdryer, etc.) or laptop computer in California.

WATER

The water that comes out of California's faucets may not be the world's tastiest, but it's generally safe to drink unless labeled otherwise.

WEIGHTS AND MEASURES

America still clings to its old weights and measure system, spurning the metric world. Temperatures are expressed in Fahrenheit rather than in Celsius. Clothing and shoe sizes also vary from Europe.

1 inch	2.54 cm
1 foot	30.48 cm
1 yard	91.44 cm
1 mile	1.6 km
1 ounce	28.35 grams
1 pound	453.5 grams
1 ton	907 kg
1 fluid ounce	29.5 ml
1 pint	473 ml
1 quart	0.94 liter
1 gallon	3.79 liters

CLIMATE

In San Francisco, they say, more than one clothier has made a fortune from unwary first-time visitors who come unprepared for the city. They come expecting the dry warmth of Southern California, only to find a damp fog setting in; they come expecting a laid-back casual place, when many restaurants require more formal dress.

One British actor said he had to leave Los Angeles because he "kept looking out the window, waiting for the rain that never come." What you should be prepared for, in the deserts in particular and Southern California in general, is a sharp drop in the temperature when the sun goes down. It is a desert climate and the low humidity is, perhaps, its most attractive feature; but that means the thermometer will fall to 30°F or 40°F (17°C or 20°C) and sometimes more at sundown.

As for the beaches, one nasty little secret about Northern California is that the beaches are often fogged in; so often, in fact, many people in San Francisco prefer the inland "beaches" or banks along the Russian River where the sunshine is more predictable. In Southern California you'll find people on the beaches no matter what the weather — in fact, the rougher the weather, the better it is for the truly dedicated surfers seeking the good waves bad weather brings. In general, the way to tell a tourist in Southern California is somebody who goes in the water. The water is so cold most of the year, locals avoid it (in favor of volleyball, jogging or simply sun-bathing) like the rare un-sunny day.

EARTHQUAKES

Don't be misled by all the jokes. Earthquakes are a very serious matter in California. There's not much you can do about the initial jolt, but you can take cover before the aftershocks hit. On those rare occasions when people are killed in earthquakes, they are hit by falling plaster or beams, so get under a table, a doorway, or anything that offers protection. Keep a flashlight with good batteries on hand at all times, have a supply of bottled water and canned food, and know where to shut off the gas lines. Advisories are broadcast every day on California radio and television stations by the state Earthquake Preparedness Commission.

SWIMMING

Visitors are advised to be cautious about swimming at any of the California beaches. As picturesque as they may seem from a distance, the waters can be rough and the undertows in many places are very dangerous. Don't swim if there are no lifeguards around. Don't be fooled by the ease with which the young surfers handle the rough waters; these people are expert swimmers who know what they are dealing with.

COMMUNICATIONS AND MEDIA

TELEPHONES

California has one of the most modern telephone systems in the world, although the choice of different phone companies and services can sometimes seem overwhelming for foreign visitors. Most pay phones accept coins or calling card numbers and there is an increased number that accept credit cards. A growing number accept credit cards directly but the concept of a pre-paid plastic phone card with computer chip, common in Europe, really hasn't caught on in America. The flat fee for most local calls is 35 cents.

For local calls in your same area code, dial the phone number without any prefix. For direct dial calls outside of your area code, dial one (1) plus the area code and local phone number. For direct dial international calls, dial the United States overseas access number (011) plus the country code, city code and local number of the place you are trying to ring. To make an operator-assisted call (such as collect, person-to-person, third party)

dial zero (0) followed by the area code and phone number, and then follow the recorded instructions. If you don't know the area code or country code of city of the place you're trying to call, dial double zero (00).

NOTE: All toll-free numbers given in this book are available to subscribers in the United States and some are available from Canada. These numbers are either not obtainable or not toll-free when dialed from other countries.

PHONE SERVICE NUMBERS

Directory assistance (information): (411; for different area code, dial 1 + area code + 555-1212; for toll free numbers, dial ((800) 555-1212.
Repair service: (611
Emergency Phone Numbers:
Police, Fire, Paramedic (911;
Poison Control Center TOLL-FREE (800) 876-4766;
Crises Team Hotline (suicide counseling) TOLL-FREE (800) 479-3339.

MAIL

Post offices are generally open 8:30 AM to 5 PM Monday to Friday, but hours can vary greatly from one branch to another. Some are open 9:30 AM to noon on Saturday. A growing number of commercial communications centers provide similar services — stamps, registered mail, air courier, PO boxes and packaging, plus notary services, photocopies and stationery supplies — including the Mailbox USA and Postal Annex chains. For the location and opening hours of United States Post Offices, as well as ZIP code information, call TOLL-FREE (800) 275-8777.

MASS MEDIA

Media is not hard to come by in California. Every major city has its own television stations, most of them affiliated with the nationwide networks (ABC, CBS, NBC, Fox, UPN and WB). Satellite and cable provide another 60 or so channels including all news (CNN, MSNBC), all sports (ESPN) and children's (Disney, Cartoon, Nickelodeon) formats. Programs are listed in daily newspapers and the weekly magazine *TV Guide* available at newsstands and supermarkets.

Radio stations are also abundant, with formats that range from rock and jazz to country western and talk. There are two bands: FM, which tends to be more music oriented; and AM, which leans toward all-news and talk show formats. All-news radio is your best bet for traffic reports, stations like KNX (AM 1070) and KFWB (AM 980) in Los Angeles.

Major **newspapers** in California include the *Los Angeles Times, San Francisco Examiner, San Diego*

Union-Tribune, Sacramento Bee, Orange County Register and San Jose Mercury News. National papers like the ultra-conservative Wall Street Journal and cartoonish USA Today are available on most newsstands, as is the highly respected New York Times. Overseas papers can be found at larger newsstands and book stores in Los Angeles, San Francisco and San Diego.

California doesn't have a state **magazine** per se, but Sunset with its monthly features on West Coast travel, cuisine, architecture and lifestyles might as well take the title. Los Angeles magazine offers a monthly middle-of-the-road view of life in the City of the Angeles, while Buzz presents a much younger, hipper slant. San Diego magazine is the nation's oldest city magazine. California's alternative press is quiet lively, publications like the Bay Guardian in San Francisco and the L.A. Weekly in Los Angeles.

HEALTH

Visitors should keep in mind that the United States and South Africa are the only countries that do not have any kind of national health insurance coverage. If you are injured in an accident, there are emergency rooms in the county hospitals that are required to treat you; however, no hospital will admit a patient without proof of insurance or some other proof of your ability to pay for treatment.

The Los Angeles County Medical Association operates a physician referral service from 9 AM to 4:45 PM Monday to Friday. Los Angeles' 24-hour emergency rooms include **Saint John's Health Center (** (310) 829-5511, 1328 22nd Street in Santa Monica; **UCLA Medical Center (** (310) 825-9111, 10833 Le Conte Avenue in Westwood; and **Cedars-Sinai Medical Center (** (310) 855-5000, 8700 Beverly Boulevard, near Beverly Hills and Hollywood.

In San Francisco, there are several clinics that offer outpatient services: **Physician Access (** (415) 397-2881 at 26 California Street; and **San Francisco General Hospital (** (415) 206-8812 at 1001 Potrero Avenue.

San Diego's 24-hour emergency facilities include **Scripps Memorial Hospital (** (619) 457-4123, 9888 Genesee Avenue in La Jolla; **Mercy Hospital (** (619) 294-8111, 4077 Fifth Avenue in the Hillcrest area; **Sharp Medical Center (** (619) 482-5800 in Chula Vista; and **Grossmont Hospital (** (619) 465-0711, 5555 Grossmont Center Drive in La Mesa.

You can find a **first aid and survival guide** (in English and Spanish) in the front of the Pacific Bell telephone directory white pages with helpful hints on what to do in case of bleeding, drowning, broken bones, burns, earthquakes, electric shock, heart attacks, poisoning and drug overdose.

WHAT TO TAKE

In San Francisco, to be sure, you should come prepared, with rain gear, a coat and tie, or a fancy dress for evening wear. In the rest of California, the casual mode prevails and only the most exclusive places have any kind of dress code. Except in Northern California you can forget about the rain gear. It's not true, as the song says, that "It never rains in Southern California," but rain is so rare you don't really have to plan for it or worry about it spoiling your picnic. Southern California can be chilly at night, even in the summer if you happen to be lingering along the coast. Likewise, when you travel from the low deserts to the higher mountains, you'll need a sweater or a jacket.

MEXICO

Mexico sets virtually no restrictions on visitors to the border areas. No papers of any kind are required for visits up to 72 hours to the border towns, including Ensenada. See below for restrictions about reentering the United States.

VISAS

Tourist cards are required for any visit 30 miles (50 km) beyond the borders, excluding Ensenada which is 65 miles (105 km) south. Cards are good for up to 180 days. They can be obtained from travel agents, airlines, or Mexican consulates. Tourists of all ages are required to carry these cards at all times. In addition, minors (under 18 years of age) must have notarized letters from both parents; those traveling with only one parent must carry a letter from the absent parent.

The **Mexican Consulate (** (619) 231-8414 in San Diego is located at 1549 India Street, San Diego, CA 92101. The consulate offers assistance with tourist visas, fishing permits, vehicle permits, and other concerns.

TOURIST INFORMATION

The best source of specific information on Baja is **Baja Information (** (619) 298-4105 TOLL-FREE (800) 522-1516 (from California, Nevada, and Arizona) or TOLL-FREE (800) 225-2786 (elsewhere in the United States and Canada) FAX (619) 294-7366 E-MAIL impamexicoinfo@worldnet.att.net, 7860 Mission Center Court, Suite 202, San Diego, CA 92108. For tourist information in the individual towns see GENERAL INFORMATION in each section.

HEALTH

The most common complaint of visitors to Mexico is "Montezuma's Revenge," a severe form of diarrhea caused by the body's adjustment to a different set of bacteria. Avoid tap water, uncooked vegetables, fruits without peels, and street food such as the tacos sold at sidewalk stands. Some hotels have water purification systems or provide bottled water; if neither is available buy bottled water at any market, liquor store or pharmacy.

CURRENCY

The currency of Mexico is the new peso. The rate of exchange alters somewhat daily with fluctuations in the economy. At press time, the exchange rate is 8.4 new pesos to the dollar. In the border areas, you will find a fair exchange in most shops, restaurants, and hotels — and there is really no need to change money since dollars are accepted everywhere.

RETURNING TO CALIFORNIA

If it seemed easy going south of the border, be prepared for all manner of inconveniences coming back into the United States. This crossing is not only the busiest border crossing in the world, but also a major artery for illegal drugs entering the United States.

If you appear the least bit suspicious in dress or behavior, it is likely that you will be waved over to the "secondary" inspection area, where a more detailed questioning and thorough search of your vehicle will take place. In general, United States citizens with nothing to declare at customs are waved on through. However, foreign travelers whose passports have stamps from any of the major drug-producing countries may find themselves subject to searches.

A number of pocket guides about United States Customs can be obtained through the United States Customs Service ((202) 927-6724, PO Box 7407, Washington, DC 20044.

United States citizens may bring back up to $400 worth of goods purchased in a foreign country if they are for personal use. This can include 100 cigars (Cuban cigars are forbidden), 200 cigarettes, and a liter of wine, beer, or liquor. Remember to keep all receipts as United States Customs may ask for proof of purchase. Severe restrictions are imposed on agricultural and meat products coming from Mexico. A list of permitted items is available from the United States Customs service (see CUSTOMS, page 340).

The main border crossing at Tijuana can become extremely congested, and waits over a half-hour are not uncommon. A second crossing at Otay Mesa, northeast of the city, is used primarily by business travelers and truckers dealing with the factories on both sides of this border area. To reach this crossing, follow signs to the "Aeropuerto," go past the airport toward Mexicali, and then follow signs (left or north) that say "Garita de Otay." The Otay crossing is closed from 10 PM to 6 AM. Both border crossings are best avoided at morning and evening rush-hours. The worst time of all is Sunday afternoon and early Sunday evening.

CAR RENTAL SOUTH OF THE BORDER

In general, United States rental cars cannot be taken into Mexico. Many agencies in San Diego, however, provide Mexican insurance and allow their cars to be taken into Mexico as far as Ensenada. Always confirm this with the agency before crossing the border.

DRIVING AND AUTO INSURANCE

The most important warnings about travel in Mexico relate to automobiles. United States or any other foreign insurance is not valid in Mexico. Moreover, an automobile accident is considered a felony and everyone involved will be detained until financial responsibility is determined. You will either have to pay cash on the spot or provide proof of Mexican insurance. Mexican insurance can be obtained from travel agencies or offices located under huge billboards on the United States side of the border. The largest and most convenient of these is called **Instant Mexico Auto Insurance Services**. There is a drive-in window and all that you need to do is prove that you own the vehicle. You can also obtain hunting and fishing licenses here. The agency publishes a very good road guide to Baja California. And if you want to learn Spanish as you ride along, you can buy cassette tapes with lessons here. For travel on the mainland of Mexico, all cars are required to have permits. Contact the Mexican Consulate in San Diego for details (see VISAS, page 339).

Recommended Reading

BOYLE, T. CORAGHESSAN. *The Tortilla Curtain*. New York: Viking, 1995. A poignant look at turbulent Anglo-Mexican relations in modern Los Angeles as seen through the eyes of two couples whose lives intersect in more ways than one.

CHANDLER, RAYMOND. No one writes about the underbelly of Los Angeles as well as Chandler, who produced a string of Southland classics including *The Long Goodbye* (London: H. Hamilton, 1953) and *The Big Sleep* (New York: New Avon Library, 1943).

CLARK, THURSTON. *California Fault*. New York: Ballantine Books, 1996. A fascinating journey along the San Andreas Fault by one of America's most noted travel writers.

DANA, RICHARD HENRY. *Two Years Before the Mast*. 1840; New York: West Vaco, 1992. An excellent account of clipper ships and whaling off the California coast in the early 1800s.

DUNNE, JOHN GREGORY. *Monster*. New York: Random House, 1997. A fascinating study of how the film industry really works and how nearly everyone must corrupt their dreams to get a movie made today.

ELLROY, JAMES. The master of retro noir has produced half a dozen novels that reflect volatile 1950s Los Angeles including *Black Dahlia* (New York: Mysterious Press, 1987) and the highly acclaimed *L.A. Confidential* (New York: Mysterious Press, 1990).

FITZGERALD, F. SCOTT. *The Last Tycoon*. 1941; New York: Collier Books, 1988. A reflection of the author's own disenchantment with the Hollywood dream machine; unfinished at the time of his death.

GRAFTON, SUE. The doyen of California's female crime writers has produced a spirited series of novels based on Santa Barbara gumshoe Kinsey Millhone. *"A" Is For Alibi* (New York: Holt, Rinehart, and Winston, 1982), *"B" Is For Burglar* (New York: Holt, Rinehart, and Winston, 1985), *"C" Is For Corpse* (New York: H. Holt, 1986), and so on.

HAMMETT, DASHIELL. *The Maltese Falcon*. 1929; New York: Vintage, 1992). The story of San Francisco private eye Sam Spade set the style for an entire generation of American literary noir.

HARTE, BRET. *Outcroppings*. San Francisco: A. Roman and Company, 1866. Acute observations and terse opinions on the gold rush era and the early days of statehood from the doyen of California journalists.

HUNTER, MARY. *The Flock*. 1906; Santa Fe, New Mexico: W. Gamon, 1973. A largely forgotten classic about turn-of-the-century sheepherders in the Central Valley.

HUXLEY, ALDOUS. *After Many a Summer Dies the Swan*. 1939; Chicago: I.R. Dee, 1993. Huxley takes aim at three California icons: Los Angeles, Forest Lawn and William Randolph Heart.

JACKSON, HELEN HUNT. *Ramona*. Boston: Robert Brothers, 1884. The plight of the California Indians brought to life in a best-selling romantic novel from Wild West times.

LONDON, JACK. He was California born and bred, but most of his great books were set outside the Golden State. *Martin Eden* (1909; New York: Penguin Books, 1984) is a semi-autobiographical account of his school days in the San Francisco Bay Area.

MOSLEY, WALTER. *White Butterfly*. New York: Norton, 1992. A Black perspective on 1950s Los Angeles, seen through the eyes of lead character Easy Rawlings.

NORRIS, FRANK. California's leading resident writer during the Guilded Age produced a series of hard-hitting classics like *McTeague* (1899; New York: Modern Library, 1996) and *The Octopus* (1901; Boston: Houghton Mifflin, 1958), the latter a harsh critique of the railroad barons.

SAROYAN, WILLIAM. *The Daring Young Man on the Flying Trapeze*. 1934; New York: New Directions Publishing, 1997. A collection of short stories based on characters the author knew growing up in Fresno and San Francisco.

STAHL, JERRY. *Permanent Midnight*. New York: Warner Books, 1995. The memories of a self-destructive screenwriter who hit the top Hollywood heap and then crashed to rock bottom.

STEINBECK, JOHN. The state's greatest homegrown talent wrote half a dozen classics about California life in the 1920s and 1930s including *The Grapes of Wrath* (1939; New York: Penguin Books, 1992), *Of Mice and Men* (1937; New York: Penguin Books, 1986), *Tortilla Flat* (1935; New York: Viking, 1986) and *In Dubious Battle* (1936; New York: Penguin Books, 1992).

STEWART, GEORGE. *Ordeal by Hunger*. 1936; Boston: Houghton Mifflin, 1992. The nitty gritty details of the Donner Party tragedy in the High Sierra.

TWAIN, MARK. *Roughing It*. 1872; New York: Literary Classics, Viking Press, 1984. Just one of many adventure stories that Twain penned during his gold rush sojourn.

WAMBAUGH, JOSEPH. *The Onion Field*. New York: Delacorte Press, 1973. A rivetting true account of the murder of a Los Angeles police detective by two young hoods in the 1960s.

WEST, NATHANAEL. *Day of the Locust*. 1939; Alexandria, VA: Time-Life Books, 1984. An all-time California classic that portrays the seedy side of Hollywood life in the 1930s.

Quick Reference A–Z Guide to Places and Topics of Interest with Listed Accommodation, Restaurants and Useful Telephone Numbers

attractions
  Dumont Dunes   35
general information
  Information Center ((760) 733-4040   35
Mojave National Preserve   28, 33
accommodation
  campgrounds at Mid Hills and
    Hole-in-the-Wall   35
attractions
  Kelso Dunes   33
  Mitchell Caverns   35
money   346
Monterey   18, 29, 48, 50, 59, 176
access   178
accommodation   178
  Inn at Spanish Bay ((831) 647-7500
    TOLL-FREE (800) 654-9300   179
  Lodge at Pebble Beach ((831) 624-3811
    TOLL-FREE (800) 654-9300   179
  Monterey Hotel ((831) 375-3184   178
  Spindrift Inn ((831) 646-8900
    TOLL-FREE (800) 841-1879   178
attractions
  17-Mile Drive   34, 178
  Allen Knight Maritime Museum
    ((831) 375-2553   178
  Cannery Row   34, 177–178
  Colton Hall   178
  Fisherman's Wharf ((831) 373-0600   177
  Monterey Bay Aquarium
    ((831) 648-4888   34, 48, 178
  Monterey State Historic Park   51
  National Steinbeck Center ((831) 735-6411
    FAX (831) 753-0574   178
  sea lions   177
festivals and special events
  Pebble Beach Concours d'Elegance
    ((831) 659-0663 FAX (831) 659-1822   179
general information
  Monterey Peninsula Visitor and
    Convention Bureau ((831) 649-1770   177
history   84, 176
restaurants
  Cibo Ristorante Italiano ((831) 649-8151   178
  Rappa's ((831) 372-7562   177
sports
  golf and kayaking   30, 57
Monterey Peninsula   34
Morro Bay   32, 56, 183
attractions
  Morro Rock   32
Moss Landing   34
attractions
  beaches   34
shopping
  antique and crafts shops   34
Mother Lode   156
Mount Laguna   316
Mount Lassen   77, 148
Mount Palomar   316
attractions
  Mount Palomar Observatory
    ((760) 742-2119   316
sports
  hiking   316
Mount Saint Helens   77
Mount Shasta   25, 28, 31, 38, 65, 77, 143, 341
golf
  Mount Shasta Resort   28

sports
  skiing   31
Mount Shasta (region)   143
access   146
accommodation   145
  Abrams Lake RV Park ((916) 926-2312   145
  Alpenrose Cottage Hostel
    ((916) 926-6724   146
  Alpine Lodge ((916) 926-3145
    TOLL-FREE (800) 500-3145
    FAX (916) 926-5897   146
  Joanie's Bed & Breakfast ((916) 964-3106   146
  McCloud Hotel ((916) 964-2822   146
  Mount Shasta Cabins and Cottages
    ((916) 926-5396   146
  Mount Shasta Ranch Bed & Breakfast
    ((916) 926-3870   146
  Mount Shasta Resort ((916) 926-3030   145
  Railroad Park Resort ((916) 235-4440   146
  Shasta Lodge Motel ((916) 926-2815
    TOLL-FREE (800) SHASTA 1   146
  Stewart Mineral Springs ((530) 938-2222   146
  Stoney Brook Inn Bed & Breakfast
    ((916) 964-2300
    TOLL-FREE (800) 369-6118   146
  Tiffany House Bed & Breakfast
    ((530) 244-3225   145
attractions
  Mount Shasta mountain and town   143
  Shasta Trinity National Forest   143
  Trinity Alps Wilderness   145
  Whiskeytown-Shasta-Trinity National
    Recreation Area   145
general information
  Mount ShastaVisitors Bureau ((530) 926-4865
    TOLL-FREE (800) 926-4865   145
golf
  Lake Shastina Golf Resort ((530) 938-3201 145
restaurants   146
  Café Maddalena ((916) 235-2725   146
  Jack's Grill ((530) 241-9705   146
  Lalo's ((916) 926-5123   146
  Lily's ((916) 926-3372   146
  Michael's ((916) 926-5288   146
  Mike & Tony's Restaurant
    ((916) 926-4792   146
  Serge's ((916) 926-1276   146
sports
  hiking, fishing, skiing,
    snowmobiling, snowshoeing   145
Mount Shasta (town)   143
access   146
accommodation   145
restaurants   146
Mount Tamalpais   92
sports   ·
  hiking   92
Mount Whitney   25, 77, 169, 282, 284
Muir Beach   136
restaurants
  Pelican Inn ((415) 383-6000
    FAX (415) 383-3424   136
Muir Woods   14, 90, 92
attractions
  Muir Woods National Monument   14
Murphys   21, 158
accommodation
  Dunbar House ((209) 728-2897
    TOLL-FREE (800) 692-6006   158